Economic and Social Development into the XXI Century

Edited by
Louis Emmerij

Published by the Inter-American Development Bank
Distributed by The Johns Hopkins University Press

Washington, D.C.

1997

**Cataloging-in-Publication data provided by the
Inter-American Development Bank
Felipe Herrera Library**

Conference Development Thinking and Practice (1996 : Washington, DC)
    Economic and social development into the XXI century / edited by Louis Emmerij.
       p. cm.
    Includes bibliographical references.
    ISBN: 1886938210
    1. Economic development—Congresses. 2. Economic development—
Social aspects—Congresses. 3. Economic policy—Congresses. I. Emmerij, Louis.
II. Inter-American Development Bank. III. Title.
338.9 C37—dc 20   97-74185

CONTENTS

Foreword

Enrique V. Iglesias[1]

The central aim of the present volume is to ask what we have learned about economic and social development from years gone by and where we are headed now. The answer to the first question is that we have learned a great deal, on every front. But we could perhaps signal three areas in which we have gained special insight.

The first is in acknowledging the sheer complexity of the issue of development, far more complex than is commonly thought. The second is in understanding that only a comprehensive approach to development will do: monistic approaches simply will not work. We have had ample opportunity to confirm the truth of this assertion in the course of time. But perhaps the most salient area of insight gained is in understanding that development is decidedly possible. The last thirty or forty years have afforded many confirmations of this fact, though the numbers of countries and people reaping the fruits of development are still few. We have learned about examples of avenues of solution, some of them now being pursued in Latin America.

The other central question is whether we are now advancing toward a new development paradigm. I am inclined to say we are not—and indeed, to wonder if a new paradigm is needed at all. What *is* needed is the right assortment of concepts and tools to manage the economic development process in all its complexity. The scholars who are eager for a paradigm have every right to be concerned; we could concede to them that any such paradigm would need to be flexible and incremental, one that builds on experience. An incremental model is needed because each step follows from a previous one and itself leaves behind a corpus of lessons learned that will inform the next stage.

One might arrange the deliberations and discussions here into three broad categories of principles: those that appear to elicit general agreement, the controversial ones, and the philosophical ones (the latter being every bit as controversial but more difficult to pin down). To mention briefly the issues on which a consensus exists, experience has shown us that standard building blocks in the enterprise of development include orderly macroeconomic management; stable prices, financial systems, and domestic saving and investment policies; skilled human resources; the removal of financial and trade constraints to ease economies into the global marketplace; and export expansion and diversification. We could even talk of certain "codes of growth," which are far better defined than was the case 25 years ago, in Latin America particularly.

[1] President of the Inter-American Development Bank and Chairman of the Board of Executive Directors of the Inter-American Investment Corporation.

The more controversial issues call for concrete, individualized responses on the part of countries or regions. With more experience, it may become possible to draw valid generalizations on these issues as well, but this clarity will be some time in coming.

One such issue is the policy mix question. Comments have been offered on various facets of the issue: how to achieve stability; the role of exchange and interest rates; the role of external funding; volatility; and the pace at which economies and financial systems open up. Considerable strides have been made on these crucial fronts, but so far, no across-the-board approach has held; in Latin America as elsewhere, countries are having to wrestle with different alternatives.

Yet another focus of lively discussion is the role of the state, another front on which countries are moving firmly forward. The issue is not the existence of the state *per se*; the question rather is what form this state should take. It is understood that the state has a place in basic functions such as education, health care, environmental protection, the fostering of savings, and the instituting of legal and judicial systems. There also exists a measure of consensus as to how these needs should be satisfied, not least by looking to the private sector as well. This aspect is in fact one of the pivotal themes of the crossover into the twenty-first century: how the public and private sectors can and should work in concert to seek answers to many of these issues.

Another of the more contentious topics is the approach to microeconomic issues, microeconomic reform, and what part the state ought to play in this. Some examples might be possible, such as state support for industry and the export sector or the state's stepping in to remedy market imperfections. These questions will no doubt continue to spark debate in the years ahead.

The question of social policy has also come in for comment and discussion here, underlined in Edgardo Boeninger's admirably precise contribution. Here again, no obvious solutions are as yet on the horizon. It is not at all clear how income distribution and the employment situation can be improved. We know what the ingredients are, but we have yet to learn what the ideal mix would be.

The third and final broad category of principles discussed in the present volume is the one we referred to earlier as philosophical; these are questions that go to values. Amartya Sen's thoughts take the development debate onto a far loftier plane, as befits a reflection on values. Lourdes Arizpe correctly points out, these considerations are cultural in nature. The question is how countries should address themselves to such considerations as they choose among development options.

Two other important subjects also fall into the realm of political philosophy. One is the matter of governance and political systems, of which Alain Touraine writes: how a country manages these processes, which takes us into the art of politics. Development is ultimately the making of choices in a society that is alive, that makes known its views, that reacts, and that knows how to assess and evaluate.

A further issue coming under the sphere of political philosophy is globalization. Aldo Ferrer and others are giving us much food for thought here. Globalization is a reality: we have no choice but to operate in the world marketplace. There are disadvantages to this and not a few risks; but there is also a great deal to be gained. Exactly how we shall join in this process, what sort of challenges it poses for public policy, and how the region's people will operate in that world of the future are questions that are clearly waiting to be tackled in the years ahead.

A few words are in order now concerning Latin America, which naturally is the central concern of the Inter-American Development Bank as a Latin American institution. The mood as to the region's situation appears to be split. The pessimistic mood is the one portrayed by the statistics; but depending on the analytical context, statistics can be read with an optimistic or a pessimistic bent. Something that often gets forgotten is that, as Angus Maddison reminds us, for the first three-fourths of this century Latin America led the world in economic growth. Here, clearly, was an opportunity that the region did not forgo.

But one can also choose to look at the state of affairs with responsible optimism, as Gert Rosenthal has done. We both stand among those who see Latin America and Latin American society as undergoing truly far-reaching changes. How much longer will this process take, and how can the undeniable risks be countered? There exist growing signs in Latin America of an increasingly active society, with a possibility that serious disruptions could be triggered in some quarters—risks that even we responsible optimists must agree would be a mistake to ignore or downplay.

Another topic discussed here is the so-called Washington consensus. This is something with which I have had some measure of personal experience, dating back to my time with ECLAC and, some years later, with the government of Uruguay. The consensus was an effort to reinstate rational economic management in Latin America. It would be incorrect to term it as in some way a violation of national sovereignty in the region. It is in essence a set of policies reflecting what could be a form of Latin American consensus on a series of problems bequeathed from the past, a consensus that was in turn meant to be a starting point for a progression toward renewed sound economic management in the region. This process is being strengthened and extended as more experience is gained and new frontiers are incorporated. The region must continue to build on experience.

ECLAC has been doing just that in recent years, producing studies that embody the serious thought being given to these issues. Much economic criticism of Latin America has been leveled in hindsight and is therefore extremely unreliable, not least because, as Aníbal Pinto phrased it, anyone can be a general after the battle. The real intellectual challenge is to assess policy options in their true context, whether the subject at issue is import-substitution or external-debt policy or any other. Every approach to every such issue was framed and pursued at a specific juncture; to criticize it without a full understanding and acknowledgment of its original context can be a seriously misguided act. During the era leading up to the Cartagena consensus, for instance, every possible avenue of solution to the external-debt problem was put on the table for discussion, including opting out of the international club altogether. Right or wrong, the governments elected to stay in (and in my view, they did well). So all of this cannot be viewed as some willful imposition: it was a reasonable choice made from among the menu of options open at the time, and we look upon it now as a sort of starting point. We of course cannot confine Latin America's future responses within the narrow limits of that first stage of what we call the Washington consensus.

What then are we to conclude from all this? At the heart of Latin America's quest is a determination to strike a balance among the three ideas in which we all believe and to which we all aspire: development, equity, and democracy. And that is democracy without modifiers: democracy, plain and simple. We are driven by this belief and sustained by these values.

The present volume also points toward an especially intriguing idea that has been at the back of my mind for some time: the possibility of finding a harmonious balance among development, equity, and democracy by tapping the creative force of democracy itself. It would be sad indeed for Latin America were we not to trust that the move toward democracy is a powerful source of inspiration that can help create virtuous circles in which democracy nurtures the other two aims: development and equity. Democracy's creative power as an instrument for striking such a balance definitely merits continued examination.

With the return of orthodoxy—a major turn in the course of events—the prestige and credibility of development theories were called into question. I well remember on trips to Washington in the 1960s and 1970s, visiting specialty bookstores with their shelves full of texts on development. All of that now seemingly belongs to the past, somewhat shunted aside when orthodoxy returned to the scene. The novel solutions being advanced looked simple and appeared to be technically viable. Today, however, we seem to be coming back to much of that earlier view of the complexity of the development phenomenon, though now with the benefit of so many enlightening foundational experiences.

The present book gives us a remarkable opportunity to weigh currents in development thinking and practice, to remind ourselves of how vital it is to hold on to essential elements from the past yet to look decidedly toward the future with due regard for all the many facets of the development enterprise. This was indeed the guiding principle behind the IDB's Eighth Replenishment, which handed us a mandate to move into these areas.

I would like to express my gratitude to the government of Japan for its generous support and to Louis Emmerij for organizing the conference on which the present publication is based and for bringing the results together in this volume.

Washington, D.C.
March 1997

PART I

Development Thinking and Practice: Introductory Essay and Policy Conclusions

Development Thinking and Practice: Introductory Essay and Policy Conclusions

Louis Emmerij[1]

The dawn of the new millennium appears to be stimulating an increasingly imaginative search for hard answers to real and specific problems, contrasting with the approach that prevailed during the "quiet and consensual 1980s" and early 1990s. This change from consensual to innovative, from monochromatic to variegated, from classical to baroque, is apparent in the field of economic and social policies and in many other areas as well.

Illustrative of this shift is Europe's present renewed cultural interest in creative and controversial works (such as those of German playwright and film director Rainer Werner Fassbinder, who died at age 37 during the early 1980s, when the flat years began). Why this renewed interest in such works? At least two reasons come to mind. The first is that the European artistic scene aspires once again to be innovative and polemical—and by definition, controversial—in contrast to the quieter years of the 1980s. The second reason—and this seems to be true more for some countries (France, for instance) than for others—is that the post-1968 mentality in general seems to be coming back with a vengeance and the search for alternatives seems to be resuming, within an ever-evolving view of human culture and development.

Today's search for alternative approaches is not limited to Europe. One can feel a rising tide everywhere and across all sectors. This deep shift responds in part to the fact that on all fronts there exist huge and mounting problems that the current economic orthodoxy has been unable to address effectively—problems that it has in many cases actually aggravated. For instance, the employment problem in Europe is now 20 years old, and yet no sign exists that this illness can be cured with the current medicine; on the contrary, structural unemployment is expanding and deepening. Poverty in the bulk of the developing countries shows no sign of diminishing and every sign of increasing. The economic and financial policies of the 1980s have created more millionaires but also have witnessed an increase in the number of people living in poverty, often absolute poverty. In the United States, the employment problem has been tackled at a price—namely, low productivity and diminishing income of the middle classes (broadly defined). More than one person per household must now work outside the home to support the family. Median income has declined during the period from the early 1970s to the early 1990s.

---

[1] Special Adviser to the President of IDB and responsible for the IDB's Social Agenda Policy Group.

Often one problem has been solved only to create another, as in the U.S. example just mentioned. Another illustration comes from East Asia, where high rates of economic growth and employment creation have exacerbated the region's environmental difficulties.

But hope remains, because even during those consensual years, and particularly since the early 1990s, innovative thinking has been going on. The World Bank and the regional development banks have put poverty alleviation once again at the center of their development strategies and lending programs, although there still can exist quite a gap between their words (research and other reports) and their deeds (where the money they lend actually goes). The Inter-American Development Bank has developed an ambitious program on social reform as a necessary complement to economic and financial reform, even though that program is only slowly being integrated into and absorbed by IDB's operational departments. And the United Nations Development Program (UNDP), through its series of annual *Human Development Reports* initiated in 1990, has rediscovered the obvious—namely, that "people are both the means and the end of economic development." UNDP has set out, through its reports, to integrate people into the development process, even if the implications for the daily work of the organization are not yet clear and although the associated analyses have stirred controversy.[2]

In our introductory essay we shall be looking at the past, present, and future of development thinking by considering several key issues explored in the articles contained in the present volume. The articles were presented at IDB's "Conference on Development Thinking and Practice" (September 1996) and constitute the unifying concept and structure of our essay, although we shall frequently be going beyond that structure. The key issues that we shall be discussing here are the following:

- evolving development policies and practice at the national and international levels over the past 35 years or so
- the optimal balance that now must be sought in regard to globalization, technology, governance, competition, and the urban question
- a forward look and the effectiveness of present policy in regard to industrial-country employment problems and developing-country social-reform needs
- globalization and the effectiveness of current policies and institutions
- the present state of development policy and the evolving nature of development thinking and practice
- implications for the future development of Latin America and the Caribbean.

Evolving Development Policies and Practices
At the National Level
A circular movement took place in national development thinking and practice between 1960 and 1980. During the 1960s, many believed that economic growth was the most important element in a country's development equation and that growth was both nec-

---

[2] Mahbub ul Haq, *Reflections on Human Development* (OUP, 1995).

essary and sufficient to settle a host of other problems, including such social questions as employment and poverty. During the 1960s, variations on the labor surplus model guided both development thinking and development practice (a very interesting illustration of the impact of theory on practice). This labor surplus model made the now-famous distinction between modern and traditional sectors in a country's economy and maintained that all "eggs"—investment eggs, technology eggs, and so forth—must be put in the basket of the modern sector. To mix our metaphors, that same model assumed that after an *acceptable transition period*, the "locomotive" function of the modern sector would move the entire convoy, consisting mainly of wagons from the traditional sector, to an end station that was envisioned as a sort of economic and social nirvana.

It took until the end of the 1960s to discover that we could have high rates of economic growth with deteriorating employment and poverty situations. This was the beginning of a search for increasingly employment-intensive economic- and social-development strategies. Could a set of policies be designed that would be economically effective and efficient and that would also create more opportunities for productive employment?

This search for more employment-intensive development policies was undertaken in order to tackle poverty and to improve income distribution. The first breakthrough concerned the actual definition of the employment problem. Three distinct components were identified: first, open unemployment, in which income equals zero; second, employment that gives only a poverty return in terms of income; and third, employment that does not live up to the expectations of the individual. The first component consists of the definition of unemployment in industrialized countries; this component is relatively small in most developing countries simply because people cannot afford to be unemployed in the sense of this definition in the absence of social-security protection and unemployment benefits. The main problem lies within the realm of the second component; here we find people who are (according to any criterion) employed, sometimes overemployed (like many women), but who get only a poverty return from their labor because of low productivity or other reasons. The third employment problem component, although small in quantitative terms, is important politically; here we find the educated unemployed, who (given their level of educational attainment) expect a certain level of job and remuneration and who, if the latter are not forthcoming, prefer to remain voluntarily unemployed (to queue, so to speak) until the "right" job comes up.

A second breakthrough in the search for increasingly employment-intensive development policies was the rise of the "informal" sector. Many people moved from the countryside to the formal, modern, urban sector during the 1960s and beyond, attracted by the lights of the city and the hope of a higher income. Little did they know that they were being caught up in a sort of employment lottery in which only a few could draw the winning tickets. The bulk of these rural-urban migrants thus found themselves expelled to the periphery, geographically as well as economically. Instead of returning to the rural sector, however, they simply stayed where they were between the urban modern sector and the rural traditional sector, in what came to be labeled an "urban informal sector," very often situated at the margin of the city. This informal sector was and is characterized by ease of access, low skill levels, small-scale activities, and (very often) self-employment. But in line with the logic of the labor surplus model, anything that was not part of the modern sector, and therefore not part of the "locomotive," tended to be neglected by officialdom. Through their actions, norms, and standards, governments discriminated against the informal sector, in favor of the formal, modern sector. Little did governments see the real wonders of innovation and invention taking place in the informal sector, and hence they tended not to notice the formidable development potential embodied in that sector. The breakthrough came when government attention was drawn to this development potential and thus, to the importance of discriminating *in favor* of the informal sector rather than against it. The key was the establishment of operational relationships between the modern sector and the informal sector.

A third breakthrough came in the field of technology. It became clear that simply identifying appropriate or intermediate technologies was one thing, but that implementing such technologies in actual fact was quite another. The existing macroeconomic and fiscal incentives had largely favored (again, in a manner quite consistent with the labor surplus model) the utilization of highly capital-intensive techniques and the adoption of exchange rates and fiscal policies that would stimulate the introduction of such techniques; in other words, all the signals in developing countries were pointing against labor and in favor of capital. It took a while until it was understood that the mere identification of more-appropriate technologies was not sufficient in itself and that the incentives structure needed modification.

A fourth breakthrough was related to the interpretation of the complex relationship between income distribution and employment. At one time, many economists and policymakers believed that unequal income distribution contributed to maximization of economic growth because of the implied existence of a strong and wealthy upper class with high savings levels that could support the investment necessary for high sustained economic expansion. The low-income groups were viewed as unable or unwilling to save and as very likely to dissave or worse. But empirical research eventually revealed that the rich in developing countries do indeed tend to save a good deal—although not necessarily in the country of origin, but rather abroad; moreover, the rich in developing countries tend to have a consumption pattern characterized by high import levels and high capital intensity of the items purchased. The poor, on the other hand, have a consumption pattern in which there exists a high proportion of locally produced goods and of products made in a labor-intensive fashion. Moreover, the poor do save, but in their case, saving and investment are often one and the same thing. For instance, each time they build a feeder road, a school, or a house, the poor are actually combining both saving and investment. They do not first go to the bank to deposit money and then let the bank look after the investments; instead, the poor often manage to telescope the two operations. Therefore, the adoption of a policy to reduce the inequalities in income distribution would create a virtuous instead of a vicious circle: through the promoted consumption patterns and the ensuing product mix, more employment would be created in the lower-income circles, thereby further improving income distribution, increasing employment, and producing other positive effects.

Many more such breakthroughs occurred, but suffice it to present one last illustration, this one from the field of education. The level-to-level sequencing of education in many countries has a certain "cannibalistic" aspect: students go from primary education to secondary education to university education with the focus more on preparation for the next educational level than for immediate success in the world outside. In countries in which only a few students actually reach the top of the educational pyramid, the majority will end up unprepared for the world of work—a situation that can be addressed only by seeking to bring the world of the school and the world of work closer together (through programs of recurrent education, for instance).

In view of such breakthroughs, much progress had been made by the mid-1970s in designing more employment-intensive socioeconomic policies. Soon enough another important issue emerged: because employment creation was increasingly viewed not as an end in itself but rather as an intermediate tool for reaching a set of human-oriented goals, work started on the design of what came to be called "basic-needs development strategies" and on strategies founded on the concept of redistribution with growth.[3] And so, toward the end of the 1970s, many believed that we had identified and achieved an excellent level of integration between the pursuit of economic growth on the one hand and on the other hand, the distribution of the fruits of this economic growth through creation of productive employment, in order to meet a given set of basic human needs. And then, the world economic depression set in; with it came a drastic change in the policy approach to development problems, placing heavy emphasis once again on economic growth itself rather than on the pattern of this growth. In less than two decades, policy had gone full circle and was back at its mid-1960s point of departure. The question that historians will eventually have to answer is whether the 1980s were a decade of ideology or a decade of a healthy reaction to the allegedly extreme policies of the 1970s that called for a reequilibrating force.

In any case, the 1980s were definitely the decade of the international debt problem. During that decade we saw yet another cycle run its full course. During the early 1980s, heavy emphasis was put on "adjustment" programs, which turned out to cut heavily into public investments, both physical and human, and which brought economic growth to a grinding halt. This was the period of "adjustment without growth." It was also the period in which Latin America transferred US$100 billion (between 1982 and 1984) to Northern Hemisphere banks. The savings and adjustments that were made did not result in additional investments to stimulate economic development but instead went straight into the bottomless pit of the debt problem. The burden of adjustment was put on one actor only (namely, the debtor nations), leaving the other two actors (namely, the commercial banks and the creditor countries responsible for the enormous jump in the real

---

[3] See, among many other publications, ILO, *Employment, Growth and Basic Needs: A One-World Problem* (Geneva 1976) and Hollis Chenery *et al., Redistribution with Growth* (published for the World Bank by OUP, 1974).

rate of interest) to go free. And thus the per capita income in Latin America on average regressed to levels that had prevailed at the beginning of the decade. In Africa the situation was worse; per capita income went back to levels of some 15 years earlier.

During the mid-1980s there began a second phase that could be called "adjustment with growth." For instance, in one of the Mexican "deals" (the one of December 1986), it was explicitly agreed that if economic growth fell below a certain level, then more capital inflows had to be secured.

And then (thanks to such factors as the exceptional efforts made by UNICEF) we entered into a phase of "adjustment with growth and equity."[4] During this phase it was posited that adjustment policies must safeguard economic growth and also education and health; they should improve the productivity of existing resources and ensure the satisfaction of the basic needs of the poorest groups in society. This approach was based not only on concepts of social security but also on an important economic rationale emphasizing the importance of human resources and the human factor in economic development and going back to the concepts of basic needs and redistribution with growth.

The 1980s saw the concomitant consolidation of what came to be called the "Washington consensus," further elaborated and updated in Part II of this volume. This approach called for development of a market economy that would create confidence among private entrepreneurs and enterprises, leading them to increase their productivity and exports. Liberalization of imports, deregulation, privatization of most state-owned enterprises, and radical reform of the government sector would stabilize and improve macroeconomic conditions, strengthen market forces, and bring about achievement-oriented competition and (primarily through a heavy commitment by foreign investors) the specialization of the economies through pursuit of optimal participation in the global marketplace.

Nevertheless, the pursuit of such policies has not been an easy task. A Chilean bishop has stated the following:

> The macroeconomic reforms have been good. Almost all of the indicators are positive: the external debt has been reduced, inflation is down, and there is less unemployment; reserves have been built up, we are experiencing sustained economic growth, and markets and exports have been diversified. A more modern, enterprising business mentality has emerged. No longer do we need to look to the state to provide for everything or wait for foreign handouts. Finally, there is a glimmer of hope: now there exists the possibility of eliminating the poverty around us.
>
> It is not possible, however, to hide the negative side of this experiment—the high price that has been paid for this success:
>
> 1. The transformation of the productive apparatus has been an extremely difficult process that is hardly compatible with the democratic system of governance.

---

[4] UNICEF, *Adjustment with a Human Face* (Oxford: Clarendon Press, 1987).

2. The heaviest burden has been borne by the poor. The deregulation of the labor market produced massive unemployment. Wages fell to very low levels, and labor was overworked.

3. The unions were broken up. All progress they had achieved was lost, and they were rendered powerless by draconian legislation.

4. The proposed system has produced social disparity so great that a deeply divided society has been created in terms of living standards and even cultural differences. This situation is explosive. The growing inequities in the distribution of income have been alarming.

5. The need to reduce the size of government resulted not only in the privatization of state-owned companies but also in the reduction in social spending for health services, education, and social security. Those most affected by this retrenchment have been the poor, and in many cases the damage has been irreparable.

6. The resulting inequities are flaunted in advertising, which encourages the consumer to spend by creating fictitious and unattainable needs that give rise to deep-rooted frustration and the search for easy money through violence, prostitution, and theft.

7. Finally, the market economy has undoubtedly become an end in itself for which everything is sacrificed. Of serious concern in particular is the loss of any sense of community. The great social nequalities that exist in our countries have left many sectors of society on the margin.[5]

And so we have seen two circular movements: one that took less than two decades (1960s and 1970s) and another that took less than one (1980s). But would it be true to say that we have only been running around in circles and that one cannot speak of an evolution? This would be a very pessimistic view. Perhaps we are now moving toward a more balanced approach in economic- and social-development policies. One thing we clearly have been forced to notice thus far is that we have moved from one extreme to the other: from planning to individual initiative; from the role of the state to adjustment and privatization; and from the emphasis on growth, redistribution, and full employment to a renewed emphasis on economic growth alone. Since 1990, however, the pendulum is swinging toward the center, as we shall point out later.

At the International Level

At the international level also there have occurred swings from one extreme to another in public opinion and in policy related to development. In the 1960s and early 1970s, it was customary to put heavy emphasis on international or "exogenous" factors to explain economic events in individual developing countries. But in the 1980s, we moved to the other extreme, and the emphasis was on national responsibility or "endogenous" factors.

---

[5] Quoted in Enrique Iglesias, "Economic Reform: A View from Latin America." In John Williamson, ed., *The Political Economy of Policy Reform* (Washington, D.C., 1994), 496–7.

These swings in opinion are very tiresome and to a large extent a waste of time: the truth is rarely to be found at the extremes of the spectrum but rather somewhere in the middle. It is as naive to put the bulk of the responsibility on national factors as it is to put it on international factors. Both are important as illustrated below.

With respect to exogenous or international factors, the prices of raw materials are not set by the developing countries and therefore cannot be considered to fall within the realm of domestically controllable factors; the same is true with respect to the prices of industrial products. With respect to access to OECD markets, the developing countries have only a very limited amount of bargaining power. And then we have the determination of the level of the rate of interest that, for example, governs the international debt situation: between 1981 and 1982, the real rate of interest increased to nearly 10 percent, a level the world had not known before and an increase that had nothing to do with the wishes of the developing countries but everything to do with the internal situation of the industrialized countries in general and of the United States of America in particular.

But, of course, national or endogenous factors also play a crucial role. An illustration here can be found in the contrast between the speed and effectiveness with which certain Asian countries have restructured and diversified their economies and the relative stagnation of many African economies. One cannot continue to hide behind the maxim that 25 years ago one had to pay many fewer bags of raw materials in order to import a tractor than today. The point here is that the tractor has probably changed and improved while the raw materials are still the same. If an economy does not restructure, if it does not keep up with what is going on elsewhere in the world economy, obviously it will be left behind.

A multifaceted example of the amount of control that national governments have and do not have over vital parts of their economies is given by the agricultural policies of the OECD countries. The world has been moving gradually from a global deficit into a global surplus situation with respect to foodstuffs. The OECD policies are finally going to shift because of the incredibly high level of subsidies, because of the big expense involved in stockpiling; because of the shrinking export markets in Asia and in Eastern Europe, and because of the outcome of the Uruguay Round. Through these traditional OECD policies and the ensuing dumping of agricultural products on the world market, the world prices of most agricultural products have been kept artificially low. From the moment OECD policies begin to behave in a more market-conforming manner, world food prices will tend to increase. Developing countries that are net food exporters will stand to gain. But the overwhelming majority of net food importers stand to lose, and the consequences for the hunger problem may be more negative than commonly anticipated.

In general, the important thing is for developing countries to identify the right mixture of national changes needed in order to minimize the impact they feel from negative international factors over which they have little or no control. Asia has been more successful than Latin America in the economic-development race. This result certainly has something to do with the former's good policy balance. Let us consider some of the reasons that Asia has been so much more successful than was anticipated 35 to 40 years ago. First, Asian countries have significantly raised their share of productive accumulation as a percentage of GNP. Second, the Asian countries have placed considerable emphasis on domestic-resource mobilization, and hence they have a relatively small proportionate dependence on external financial flows. Third, the legitimacy of state intervention in economic affairs has never been put in doubt in the Asian countries. Fourth, Asian governments have consistently paid attention to land productivity and to the importance of land reform. Fifth, Asian countries have made a constant effort to diversify their export patterns as much as possible and in line with changes taking place in the world economy. This successful Asian policy balance is set out in much more detail in the article by Eisuke Sakakibara and in Part III.

While these swings in the emphasis of development policy went on—from the belief in the importance of exogenous factors to the belief in the importance of endogenous factors—the world economic scene and the actors in it were undergoing drastic changes. From national actors the trend has shifted again toward multinational actors, and we have witnessed a renewed spurt in the globalization of markets and of enterprises.

**Finding the Optimal Balance: Globalization,
Technology, Governance, Competition and the Urban Question**
Summing up what has been said thus far, the past 40 years have seen considerable developmental-policy changes. The emphasis is again very much on growth itself rather than on the redistribution of the income from that growth; on free trade, whatever the robustness of the national economy; on the market approach whatever the ensuing distortions in the economy and in the society; on global markets, whatever the societal implications; and on privatization, whatever the importance of the firm or the enterprise in question for the strength of the nation. It can be objected that in the 1970s too much emphasis was given to redistribution, protectionism, the state, nationalized enterprises, and parastatals. Although this matter does invite debate, no one would deny that an effective approach does not consist of swinging from one extreme to the other. It follows that a proper *balance* is of the essence. In every developmental undertaking, a judicious mixture must be found of the best of the "old" and the best of the "new" policy ideas; of "hard" and "soft" issues of international and national policies; of public and private sectors; and so forth.

In the world economic and social scene of the mid-1990s, the following five major policy issues stand out, each of which we shall discuss in turn:

- globalization and its effects on the nation-state, with particular reference to the social sectors: moving beyond the dichotomy of free market and the (welfare) state
- employment creation and productivity increases: going beyond the dichotomy of growth and redistribution
- global markets and global governance: moving beyond the dichotomy of private versus public power

- the paradox of competition: going beyond the dichotomy of black lamb and grey falcon[6]
- the urban paradox: moving beyond the dichotomy of the best of times and the worst of times.

The Paradox of Globalization: Global Wealth and National Poverty

Globalization is a phenomenon driven by the private sector. Global enterprises undertake their multifarious activities in those geographical locations in which it is most cost-effective for them to do so; this truism applies also to the payment of taxes. Globalization sharpens competitiveness, and therefore, ever-greater efficiency and cost-effectiveness are required on the part of individual enterprises. Companies' ability to produce bits and pieces of their final product nearly anywhere in the world, their successful attempts to minimize payment of taxes, and the increasing footlooseness of their production units are some of the reasons that many national governments are becoming relatively impoverished, both in terms of decision-making power as well as financial income.

Other problems related to globalization are also mounting and intensifying, such as unemployment and underemployment, drug trafficking and drug use, crime, and political and economic refugeeism. Such problems themselves, are taking on global characteristics: the employment problem has become worldwide, drug trafficking has itself become a global enterprise, and refugees are covering ever-larger distances. Questions that arise in this context and that need urgent further examination are the following:

- What are the exact relationships between the rise of globalization and the rise and intensification of other phenomena such as unemployment, drug use, and crime? Clearly, these relationships are real; there in fact exists a growing body of literature spelling this fact out.[7]
- What are the costs and benefits of globalization in the economic and financial spheres? How can the benefits be maximized and the costs minimized? Given the relationship between globalization (economic and financial) and increased social problems, should one not think of imposing special taxes on global economic and financial activities in order for the nation-state to be better armed to tackle the social issues? An example here is the so-called Tobin tax, named after economist James Tobin, Nobel prize winner.[8]
- Considerations such as the foregoing raise all the important issues of today—namely the relationship between state and market; the relationship between free trade and protection; the relative emphasis to be given to economic versus social consid-

---

[6] Rebecca West, *Black Lamb and Grey Falcon—A Journey through Yugoslavia* (Penguin Books, 1994, 907–15). Basically the title refers to an old Serbian poem about the conqueror and the vanquished.

[7] For an excellent summary, see UNRISD, *States of Disarray: The Social Effects of Globalization* (Geneva, 1995).

[8] See the UNDP *Human Development Report 1995* (Oxford University Press), and for more details Haq, Kaul, Grunberg, eds., *The Tobin Tax: Coping with Financial Volatility* (OUP, 1996).

erations; and the relationship among international, regional, and national activities and policies.

The paradox of globalization illustrates the degree to which an active world level private sector has placed passive and impoverished nation-states on the defensive.

The Paradox of Technological Progress: A Curse and a Blessing

It is under the topic of technological progress that the issues of employment and unemployment arise. The blessing of technological progress is, of course, that it enables people to produce more with less effort. But it is amazing to observe how this blessing has been turned into a curse through lack of insight and organizational skills on the part of human beings.

In the case of industrial countries, the core problem is that economic and technological changes have not been accompanied by the needed societal changes. Labor markets, educational systems, pension schemes, and the like continue to be organized and structured in the same way as they were decades ago. They have not kept pace with the new economy that has emerged during the present period.

This lag in societal change has given rise to the curse of high levels of open and hidden unemployment in industrial countries in general and in Europe in particular. The blessing has indeed been turned into a curse. We do now produce more with less effort and fewer hours, but these advantages are distributed in a terribly misguided fashion. We are faced with a new distribution problem—namely, how to distribute the "less work" and "fewer hours" in a more rational fashion that avoids pushing 25 percent to 30 percent of the population into the margins of the economy and of society.

Old-style full employment most probably is no longer attainable and is not even desirable. We have to move toward a new-style full employment, based on a different societal structure in which people can move in and out of school, job, and (creative) leave in a recurrent fashion rather than a sequential one. This approach will lead to qualitative changes in the economy and in society and to a different form of full employment that can be combined with a more creative life.[9]

As long as the employment problem in industrial countries remains unresolved, the latter will remain on the defensive with respect to East and South. The solution of the employment problem in the West is therefore of crucial importance for developing countries and for countries in transition.

The problem in developing countries is not different in essence but needs a different policy treatment because of the degree to which the difficulty presents itself. The emphasis in these countries must be much more on identifying the right mixture between high-tech production in the export sectors and equally high-tech but more labor-

---

[9] The author has written extensively on the necessity of changing the concept of full employment. There are indications that finally European thinking and practice are coming around to such a concept, which brings the societal structure in line with the economic and technological changes that have taken place in recent years.

intensive production in the domestic sectors. The main issue here is not to redistribute the available work in a smarter and more creative fashion but instead to create additional employment opportunities and also to increase the productivity of those presently employed at low levels of productivity and income.[10]

Global Markets and Global Governance

As mentioned earlier, globalization is basically a phenomenon driven by the private sector. Today's regionalization, on the other hand, is a state-driven phenomenon. As usual, the public sector is running one lap behind the private sector.

At the national level and regional level alike, we can observe a growing imbalance between the private sector and the public sector. At the global level, this public-private imbalance becomes a chasm.

Just as there should be a balance between the state and the private sector at both the national level and the regional level, so should there be a public-private balance at the global level. At present there exists at the global level no equivalent to the state. Even worse, at the very moment such an equivalent is most needed, the weak institutions we do have (such as the United Nations and the Bretton Woods Institutions) are coming under increasingly severe attack, as might well be expected in the political and ideological situation that has emerged during the past 15 years.

What is needed now is a very sensitive and subtle approach, because it is easy to go overboard and to come up with utterly unrealistic proposals. Basically, we are concerned here with revitalizing the institutions currently existing at the global and regional levels, in order to make them relevant and effective in addressing the new situation of global markets and global enterprises—in short, in addressing today's global private power.

The Paradox of Competition

Globalization tends to push competition to an extreme intensity worldwide. Nobody would deny that a degree of competition is positive. Healthy competition—at school, at work, in research, as well as in the economy—helps a society or an individual to progress and to remain innovative. The Latin root of the verb compete is *competere,* which means "to seek together."

But the intense competition in today's global era is a far cry from this old ideal. Competition has become a weapon to wipe out the adversary. It has become an ideology and an imperative, and some even speak of the "gospel" of competition.[11]

Competition in short has come to be seen as an answer to almost all economic ills. Is there a worsening unemployment problem? Then what is needed is to become more competitive. Is there a growing poverty problem in certain countries? Then what is needed is for them to become more competitive. Education and training must be geared more and more to the panacea of competition. The discussion is reminiscent of the proposals

---

[10] See UNDP, *Human Development Report 1996* (OUP 1996)—in particular, Chapter 4.
[11] See the Group of Lisbon, *Limits to Competition* (MIT Press, 1995).

concerning a "flat tax" in the United States during the presidential campaign of 1996. In both cases a single proposed remedy is supposed to cure every ill in society.

Competition is in the process of becoming viewed as the only solution to the problem of globalization. The result is that the world's societies are increasingly engaged in a ruthless economic battle. Reports abound with such titles as "Winning in a World Economy," and the cult of competition even has its own "scientific" instrument—namely the World Competitiveness Index, published every year by the World Economic Forum, which ranks countries' competiveness in much the same way that the ATP classifies professional tennis players.

Competitiveness taken to such an extreme has undesirable effects, such as distortions in national economies. It also has negative social repercussions, such as growing unemployment and downward pressure on salaries and income—and hence, growing inequality.

Such an extreme system is bound to flounder. Indeed, extreme competition diminishes the degree of diversity existing in a society and contributes to social exclusion: individuals, enterprises, cities, and nations that are not competitive are being marginalized and eliminated from the contest. This approach is unacceptable morally and inefficient economically. The more a system loses its variety, the more it will lose its capacity to renew itself. But above all, the ideology of competition devalues cooperation and seeking together. It wipes out solidarity, and therefore we are not surprised that this era is also witnessing heavy attacks on the welfare state.

The question could reasonably be asked, What will the declared "winner" of this competition rat race actually *do* after leaving everybody else in the world so far behind? But the most important weakness of this "competition fundamentalism" is that it is incapable of integrating social justice, economic efficiency, environmental sustainability, political democracy, and cultural diversity.

The Urban Paradox Today

The facts are well known: one-half of the world's population lives in urban conglomerates; 75 percent of the population of industrial countries and of Latin America lives in cities; the increase in the urban population since 1965 has been 1.5 billion; over the next 10 years, there will be another 1 billion more people living in the city, most of them in the developing countries; and 17 out of 21 megacities are to be found in the Southern Hemisphere.

Behind these cold figures are increasing problems common to industrial and developing countries alike, problems that have given rise to the "urban question." The growing inequality observed between and within nations over the past 15 to 20 years is most starkly reflected in the city. There exist growing urban dualism and growing informalization, which have given rise to the specter of cities divided against themselves.[12]

---

[12] "Every city or house divided against itself will not stand" (Matthew 12:25).

The essence of the urban problem is social in character: the poverty and the marginalization have become structural. Simultaneously with the globalization of the economy and of the financial system, we observe a global social problem: old-age pensioners, one-parent families, the unemployed, the disabled, and certain ethnic varieties are becoming increasingly marginalized by the to-them impenetrable new economy that is appearing before our eyes. On top of that, we observe in many urban centers more and more street children, child prostitution, child labor, and drug addiction.

In consequence, we see an increasing lack of social cohesion, leading to the phenomenon of divided cities. Most cities are losing the battle against poverty, and different urban groups are growing rapidly apart.

The urban explosion of course also has a sunny side, which is well captured in the words of Lewis Mumford: "The city is the most precious collective invention of civilization…second only to language itself in the transmission of culture." Indeed, the city offers better quality and more choice in education, material comforts, medical care, employment opportunities, and self-expression. It provides a wide variety of skills, services, culture, delivery systems, and the like. People are not fools when they let themselves be attracted by the bright city lights. They will eventually find their universe within this mass of steel and glass.

Or at least so they hope. But many of them run straight into their cities' dark side. The megacities of the South, and increasingly those of the North, are "Romes without empires." They have been boosted artificially; they are too expensive (for example, in terms of infrastructure investments); they tend to foster open unemployment and squatterism; they breed crime; and they waste resources (for instance, in terms of workers' daily commute to and from work and of the necessity to pump city dwellers' drinking water from farther and farther away).

The urban question clearly has many dimensions, including poverty, housing shortages, unemployment and underemployment, slum areas, crime, drugs, and the plight of street children. But one of the urban question's more baffling aspects is that it amounts to more than the sum total of these different specific problem areas. It is difficult to express just what this synergistic negative "value added" is, but it certainly has a lot to do with the quality of life—or more precisely with the lack of quality of life—in many urban settings. This phenomenon harms not only the poor; the rich also are negatively affected by the deterioration of the urban situation, and they have to move farther and farther away from the city center and to live in increasingly bunkerlike bungalows.

In the industrial countries, cities have started to grow again. A cycle—from the center to the suburbs to even more-distant "developments" and then back again to the city center—is now coming full circle. But one of the paradoxes here is that in many instances the downtown areas have indeed started growing again, as have the suburbs, but the slums have continued to deteriorate.

In industrial and developing economies alike, we can observe issues common to urban conglomerates worldwide. These include the following:

- growing inequality, dualism, and informalization, leading to the phenomenon of "cities divided against themselves"
- the *social* character of the urban problem, with poverty and marginalization now being structural in nature.

These problems are reflected not only in the growing numbers of people who have no entry into today's globalizing and liberalized economies but also in the magnitude of the street children issue, child prostitution, child labor, and drug addition. Bangkok, with its rate of economic growth of 10 percent, is a spectacular illustration of global wealth harboring individual misery at the urban level. Within many of the world's cities, we observe a spreading social divisiveness, a losing fight against urban poverty, and a rapid drifting apart of the different urban groups, with a "new apartheid" looming on the horizon.

In general terms, current trends in globalization and competitiveness are intensifying the world's social problems (such as unemployment, downward pressure on income levels of parts of the population, and skewed income distributions). These problems are becoming themselves globalized, as are the related ills of drug trafficking, crime, and the whole range of urban difficulties.

These intensified social problems (intensified by the global financial and goods markets) are left on the doorstep of nation-states that are themselves already facing problems of public finance and that hence are cutting back their welfare systems at the very moment these systems are needed most. There exists now a growing imbalance between the power of the free market and the influence and weight of the state. Nowhere is this public-private imbalance more visible than in the social arena and in the lack of the equivalent of the state at the global level.

The world economic and social scene is evolving very quickly, and change is in the air with respect to socioeconomic policies and institutions, in the light of huge and mounting social problems that have remained unsolved and that are becoming increasingly serious. It is indeed time to take stock of these problems and to examine the new policy ideas that are now emerging as ways of effectively addressing them. The issue of globalization is examined in more detail in Part II of this volume.

A Forward Look and the Effectiveness of Current Policies

There is indeed change in the air in a whole range of areas, from the arts to philosophy through economic and social policies. In general, it would appear that these changes are caused by the following: the policies of the 1980s, which are now being seen as a reaction to previous policies rather than as a well-thought-out, balanced, and comprehensive policy approach for tackling the huge problems facing the world today; the lack of discussion of these consensual policies of the 1980s; the lack of success of these policies in solving many of the big problems of our age; and the new global economic and social phenomena that are becoming ever more evident.

At the worldwide *"Conference on Development Thinking and Practice,"* organized at the Inter-American Development Bank in September 1996, many of the "changes in the air" were identified, "quantified," and (during a final session) interpreted with a focus on Latin America and the Caribbean. The present volume is the written reflection of that conference as well as of the social-reform research carried out within the framework of IDB's Social Agenda Policy Group (SAPG). Standing now on the shoulders of these articles and of the discussion at the conference, let us seek to draw major policy conclusions for economic and social policy into the twenty-first century.

It is obvious—and has been shown empirically—that in most countries that have undertaken market-friendly economic reforms during the past 15 years or so, the distribution of income has worsened more or less significantly, poverty has tended to increase, and employment trends have been very uneven, with increases in unemployment or in the intensity of the employment problem. The causal linkages have not yet been well understood, but the association between the adoption of market-friendly economic reforms and the accentuation of problems of inequality and poverty is cause for serious concern. What is more, neither theory nor practice provides much evidence on how intransigent these recorded negative effects will prove to be. This huge issue will be considered here in two parts—namely, the employment problem in industrial countries and the issue of social reform in developing countries.

The Employment-Productivity-Income Nexus in the Industrial Countries

It is apparent that current policies can tackle either the employment problem or the income problem, but not both. Europe has kept a decent floor in the income structure but cannot come back to full employment as we have known it. The United States is running at close to full employment but has had difficulty in maintaining income levels, which for more than half of the economically active U.S. population declined between the early 1970s and the early 1990s. What are the changes necessary in economic, financial, and social policies in order to arrive at new-style full employment in an economy that is becoming increasingly globalized?

In general, the dialogue on employment and unemployment in the OECD countries is uninspired, counterproductive, and lacking in imagination.[13] Technology is seen as a danger instead of as an opportunity. Competition is viewed as a way of wiping out the others instead of as *competere* ("seeking together"). In international trade, Europe is told to lower the cost of its labor so that it can underbid China or Albania instead of restructuring the European economies and identifying niches in the global market in line with the European countries' own competitive advantages instead of those of China and Albania.

During the days after World War II, technology was seen as a means to produce more with less effort, to earn more with less work because of increased productivity. Now the day has arrived that we do in fact produce more with less labor, but the dream has turned into a nightmare because the "less labor" has been arrived at by allowing only 70 to 80 per-

---

[13] See the "Jobs Study" of the OECD, published in 1994 after more than three years of intensive research.

cent of the employable work force to work and pushing 20 to 30 percent to the margin. We are faced with a **new distribution problem:** a problem of time rather than of income.

European countries should have an offensive approach rather than a defensive one. They should stimulate high-tech improvements and the concomitant productivity increases; they should resist the temptation of the "Albanization" of their economies and not try to compete in product lines in which developing countries and countries in transition are more cost-effective. If the worst that would result from such an innovative and individualized approach would be the impossibility for Europe to return to full employment as we have known it, so be it. Let us then move on to a new concept of full employment more in line with the economic and social situation at the end of the twentieth century and the beginning of the twenty-first century. The new concept of full employment must be based on a better, more equitable, and more productive distribution of available work over the population than is the case today. But it must take account of at least two key constraints.

First, there is the possibility that we are wrong about the impossibility of reaching old-style full employment, just as many were wrong 60 or 70 years ago. In other words, measures that will lead to a new concept of full employment must in themselves be good social and economic investments and must be **reversible** or at least flexible enough to adjust to changing circumstances. This constraint would rule out most of the traditional measures—such as fewer hours of work per day, fewer workdays per week, longer holidays—which quickly become "acquired social rights," hence inflexible and certainly very difficult to reverse.

A second constraint is that any measures leading to the new concept of full employment must make people more robust and better equipped to enter the labor market at a later stage. Unskilled labor, instead of accepting lower wages, must become skilled so that it can be put to work in economic sectors in which Europe has a competitive advantage.

In other words, the policy measures leading up to the new distribution of available work must be productive for the society, the economy, and the individual. In order for this to be the case, the policy measures must be tied to educational and other creative activities.

How might such a work redistribution shape up, given the aforementioned constraints? The starting point cannot and must not be to take as the relevant unit of time the workday or the workweek, but rather the time an individual spends in different activities over his or her lifetime.

The life of an individual is divided into the following three parts, separated in most countries by impermeable partitions: the period spent at school (and for the more fortunate, at a university); active life, whether spent in the labor market or not and whether remunerated or not; and the retirement period. These periods follow one another sequentially. We go to school at an early age and remain there until age 16 or 18 (depending on the country) or in the case of university students, very often to the age of 25 or even older. Then we enter the period of so-called active life until the age of 60 to 65, when we are kindly but firmly asked to take retirement.

It is very difficult, particularly in most European countries, to reverse or otherwise alter the sequence of these three events. But it is the essence of a creative system of recurrent education to transform this rigid sequential system into a more flexible regimen in which people will be able to combine or alternate periods of education, work, and retirement throughout their adult lives.

The idea of recurrent education that spans the first two periods of life (education and active life) has been discussed for more than 25 years. The complementary idea of retirement *à la carte* (freely selected by each individual) has been discussed less frequently, but it is the logical extension and the mirror image of recurrent education because it encompasses the second and third periods. Individuals could even be given the opportunity to combine all three periods by, for example, taking at age 30 a period of six months of anticipated retirement in order to receive further education or training. Although this approach sounds extremely straightforward and simple, in reality it amounts to a social and cultural change of the first order. But the potential advantages of such an almost revolutionary approach for the various actors and partners, social and individual, in OECD countries are significant.

In the first place, this much more flexible approach would enable an equally flexible *labor market policy* to be introduced that would have advantages both for employers and for workers. The employers would obtain a labor force that could be more easily and more quickly retrained in response to technological changes; the workers would have more easily available and more frequent chances to reorient or retrain themselves. The educational system as it exists at present is extremely rigid and is characterized by a long lag between a given policy change and the outcome of that policy change. In the 1950s and 1960s, forecasts of the occupational and educational structure of the labor force were fashionable. These long-term forecasts reflected the long gestation periods inherent in the educational production process. Indeed, it takes approximately six years to complete each of the main levels of the educational system; hence, the school will react very slowly to changes in technology, and this slowness in turn has implications for the required skill structure of the labor force. But experience has shown that it is in reality almost impossible to make reliable long-term forecasts of the occupational and educational structure of the labor force. It is therefore much more realistic and desirable to shorten the schools' response time to technological change, because by so doing, the educational system will become more adaptable, and the relationship between school and work will become closer, more effective, and more beneficial to all parties.

In the second place, the recurrent-education approach would be a positive change for the *individual*, in terms of self-fulfillment and of being able to realize his or her full potential. We know that motivation occurs at very different moments in each person's life and not necessarily at those junctures established by the sequential educational system. Educational opportunities and achievements will definitely be enhanced if individuals can go back to school when they are motivated to do so, instead of being pushed by parents or by other persons in authority to remain in school. In the present setup, it is difficult to return to school after having dropped out. What is true for the individual's educational opportunities is equally true for occupational and income opportunities. In the global, societal approach favored here, one has more than one occasion to orient (or reorient) oneself in the labor market. Furthermore, individuals can be offered anticipatory retirement earlier in life during which they do not necessarily have to return to school but can do other things that they are strongly motivated to do at that particular time.

In the third place, its flexibility also makes the suggested recurrent-education approach an effective *anticyclical weapon*. At times when a particularly strong but temporary economic storm flails our countries, more people could be encouraged to withdraw for a while from the labor force in order to benefit from recurrent education or from a sabbatical period.

In the fourth place (and this is a related but structural weapon), fewer people will be in the labor market at any given moment than is presently the case. This is because people will on average opt to spend more of their time in the first and third blocks of their lives *vis-à-vis* the second. In this way there will occur a reduction in the total basic labor supply.

Thus the approach advocated here represents a generalization of traditional trade union demands for shorter working hours, more holidays, and earlier retirements, and it also supports the more recent proposals with respect to part-time work, the sharing of jobs, and rationing of the labor supply in general. Our proposed reformulation of work distribution therefore gets several birds with one stone. Official economic parameters will at last mesh with the sociocultural objectives of the individual. Instead of a diminishing majority that works harder and harder and an increasing minority that is expelled shamefully from the labor market, it is proposed here that available work be rationed more intelligently, more comprehensively, and more productively than it has been thus far.

This proposal is global and comprehensive in that it implies a deep restructuring of our societal structures in the domains of education and training, the labor market, personnel policy at shop floor level, pension schemes, and the like.

But what about the financial implications of such a sweeping change? It is clear that the financial obligations involved must be borne in tripartite fashion by employers, employees, and government. For the government it is "merely" a question of turning money already spent for "negative" purposes to positive use; instead of spending billions on unemployment benefits to push people to the margins, this amount (probably less, given the other two financial sources) can in the proposed scheme be used to make people more robust and ready to keep up with the changes of the time.

Employers have a natural interest in investing in their personnel, to keep them motivated and on their toes. The same applies to individual employees who invest in themselves, who get a second or third educational chance in life, and who come back to the labor market better prepared.

It is easy to find myriad complicating factors, but the proposed societal change can be introduced without additional financial burdens to be shouldered by the state. The financial sacrifices asked of employers and employees are investments with a rate of return infinitely higher than those from any alternative investment available.

This proposal must be viewed as complementary to the discussion in Part III concerning the European performance.

The Issue of Social Reform in Developing Countries

Social reform in one way or another has become the battle cry of widely divergent groups in our societies. In industrial countries it has become entangled in the debate about the welfare state. In developing countries it is related to adjustment policies' negative impact on the social budgets.

What must be examined here for developing countries—with special reference to Latin America—is social reform's definition, social reform's relationship to economic and financial policies, and the way in which we might arrive at an integrated set of economic, financial, and social policies within a robust and sustainable macro framework.

There exists a clear difference between carrying out social reform and simply putting increased emphasis on the social sectors: the latter approach normally amounts merely to doing more of the same things that have already been tried.

This difference has been made apparent by the empirical evidence gathered by the Social Agenda Policy Group (SAPG) of the IDB through its eight Pilot Studies on Socioeconomic Reform.[14] They are discussed more thoroughly in Martin Paldam's article (Part IV). What are the social-reform priorities that emerge from this body of empirical evidence?

Employment and Productivity: It is fair to say that the first two priorities are the creation of productive employment opportunities, and the enhancement of the productivity of people presently employed in low-productivity and hence low-income sectors. These findings stand to reason, if poverty reduction is truly one of the main aims of national development policies. Governments talk a lot about poverty alleviation and poverty reduction; they spend time and money to measure poverty; but when it comes to doing something about it, their record consists more of words than deeds.

There exist basically three policy approaches when it comes to tackling the poverty problem. The first one is employment creation; the second, productivity increases; and the third is a redistribution of income through fiscal or other measures. Without excluding the third policy measure in general, it becomes clear from the SAPG work that

---

[14] The eight studies are the following:
- Social Agenda Policy Group, *Building National Consensus on Social Policy: Trinidad and Tobago* (IDB, 1993)
- SAPG, *Hacia una Política Social Efectiva en Venezuela* (IDB, 1993) (also available in English as *Toward Effective Social Policy in Venezuela*)
- SAPG, *Modernizar con Todos: Hacia la Integración de lo Social y lo Económico en Chile* (IDB, 1994)
- SAPG, *A la Búsqueda del Siglo XXI: Nuevos Caminos de Desarrollo en Costa Rica* (IDB, 1994)
- SAPG, *Bolivia: Desarrollo Diferente para un País de Cambios* (IDB, 1995)
- SAPG, *Challenges for Peace: Towards Sustainable Social Development in Peru* (IDB, 1995) (also available in Spanish as *Desafíos para Alcanzar la Paz: Hacia un Desarrollo Social Sostenible en el Perú* (IDB, 1995)
- SAPG, *Cooperative Republic of Guyana, Building Consensus for Social and Economic Reconstruction* (IDB, 1995)
- SAPG, *Cities Divided against Themselves: The Case of Fortaleza—Social Reform in a Brazilian Metropolis* (IDB, 1996)
A first and as yet incomplete synthesis study of these eight cases is available. See Louis Emmerij, *Social Tensions and Social Reform: A Progress Report* (Washington, D.C.: IDB, January 1995).

on the whole the first two measures are viewed with more sympathy in today's context. Moreover, they combine economic growth with the attainment of important social objectives. They provide, therefore, an illustration of the intimate relationship between economic and social objectives.

Why is there so little action on the employment creation front? One of the reasons is that governments believe that the creation of employment opportunities is something that should be left to the private sector and that governments should not meddle in it. The findings from the Pilot Mission Reports undertaken by the SAPG show this attitude to be misguided. The evidence points to the obvious fact that governments can stimulate the private sector to undertake or not to undertake activities in given sectors and in certain areas of the country, whether through fiscal incentives, infrastructure projects, credit facilities, or some other mechanism. The Trinidad and Tobago report, for instance, lists a whole range of activities, both on the demand and supply side, that can boost the creation of employment and help achieve a more employment-intensive pattern of economic development. These would work on many fronts at once by making the economy more diversified and robust, making it less dependent on oil exports, creating more productive employment, and hence reducing the amount and intensity of poverty in the country.

The report on Chile illustrates quite clearly how important it is, at the present stage of that country's economic and social development, to focus on productivity increases in all economic branches. Again, government incentives are crucial here, as exemplified by measures such as fiscal incentives to introduce new technologies (including productive intermediate technologies) in low-productivity sectors such as certain micro-enterprises and small and medium-size industries.

The East Asian Development model has shown that a judicious cooperation effort between the state and the private sector can do a lot to boost technological changes and productivity increases throughout the economy; that point is extensively demonstrated in Part III of the present volume. There is no reason that the same policy cannot be used successfully in Latin America and the Caribbean. Productivity increases are instrumental to increasing individual incomes and hence to combating poverty, and thus they constitute a policy measure that targets economic as well as social objectives. Both Albert Fishlow and Victor Tokman have more to say on this in Part IV.

Urban Policy: If the first two priorities for social reform in the region are employment creation and productivity increases, the third priority should undoubtedly be an all-out effort to improve the quality of life in the region's urban conglomerates. There have been many studies in Latin America on poverty and other social questions at the national and regional levels. But the urban situation, which is the most urgent and explosive, paradoxically has received relatively less attention. This oversight is all the more surprising in view of the fact that the region is already 75 percent urbanized and contains many of the world's largest cities.

As illustrated by the SAPG study on Fortaleza, Brazil, the fundamental problem is to define a comprehensive policy approach to tackle the multifaceted and increasingly serious urban predicament. Priority in this effort must be given to the aforementioned effort to create productive employment. Low-cost, labor-intensive activities in services, commerce, and small and medium-sized industries (including micro-enterprises in the urban informal sector) must be generated. An overall strategy is needed for the entire urban informal sector, which at present is plagued by chaotic official efforts to regulate it.

Clearly, it is important to change the established urban educational system, which is often dysfunctional with respect to job preparation. But in the short run, nonformal and on-the-job training must be given a massive boost in the urban areas.

With respect to urban infrastructure, mass transportation has been neglected. The result, besides a lot of human misery, is diseconomies in the location of employment sources vis-à-vis the location of dense urban populations.

A strategy for encouraging a redirection of employment opportunities toward the countries' small and medium-sized cities is also required. An urban strategy cannot neglect the millions of landless families and others living in rural poverty, all of whom constitute a pool of potential unskilled urban poor.

And then there is the increasingly explosive situation in the *favelas* and other *ciudades de miseria*—the web of shantytowns encircling the traditional city centers of the region. It is here that we encounter the new plagues: crime, drug abuse, and drug trafficking.

From the Pilot Studies undertaken by the SAPG, it is striking to note that none of the countries studied had a comprehensive urban policy. Plenty of piecemeal policy approaches could be found, but no policy that tries to look at the situation as a whole and attempts to identify the optimal priorities in urban policies.

Implementation and Decision-Making Structures: The fourth social-reform priority coming out of the SAPG work—and some would consider this the top priority—relates to the whole question of social-policy implementation, and in general to the structure of the related political decision making. If it is already difficult to identify clearly *what* must be done in socioeconomic reform, it is even more daunting to try to get a clear understanding and a good grasp of *how* these priorities might be translated into *implementable* policies.

One is confronted here with the twofold reality of what might be called the horizontal implementation structure and the vertical implementation structure. The horizontal structure refers to the different actors that influence the decision-making process. It is a serious mistake to believe that once the government or a ministry settles on a certain policy that the adopted policy will come out of the final implementation process in the same pure form as when it was originally introduced. Many different actors besides the government (such as the Church, trade unions, employers, nongovernmental organizations, individual enterprises, and other pressure groups) intervene. Proposing policies without taking this fact of life into account is rather naive.

The vertical implementation structure refers in the main to governmental decision-making at the national, provincial, municipal, and local levels. We have observed of late a strong tendency in the region toward municipalism and localism. This trend does look like a move in the right direction, in that many decisions can and must be undertaken at lower levels of the decision-making process. But very often such attempts at decentralization have been empty gestures, because although responsibilities (for example, in education and health) may have been decentralized, the related finances have not been. The result has often been even more disarray in the provision and quality of the affected social services.[15]

Another crucial element in the implementation structure relates to the delivery systems for social services and to the question of the optimal mix of publicly provided versus privately provided social services. Privatization of service delivery is fashionable even in education and health. But simplistic thinking is rampant in this whole area. The real questions are, of course, What has gone wrong (if anything) in the public provision of the targeted social service? and Can we remedy the problem by a shift to private provision of that same social service? If the second answer is "yes," the next questions are, what proportion of the service must remain in the public domain? And what proportion could be privatized?[16]

Although questions of implementation are being discussed in the region, there is not much evidence as yet that these issues are being taken into account in practice. The result may very well be that although policymakers believe they are creating a given program, when all is said and done a totally different program could be what ultimately emerges.

Interestingly, the priorities mentioned thus far all relate to cross-sector issues—that is, to issues not specific to a given economic or social sector but instead that cut across all of those sectors. This nonspecificity may be yet another reason that governments are not yet tackling these problems head on: it is much easier to work within given sectors (such as education, health, sanitation, and so forth) for which specific government agencies exist than to work in economy-wide and society-wide policies that demand the involvement of a multiplicity of ministries and other decision-making centers.

Quality of Human Resources: The fifth priority concerns the quality of human resources in the region—a well-known and widely accepted priority and one that is in many ways sector specific (education and health). It has been conventional wisdom for the last 40 years that education and health are not only consumer goods that one can afford after having attained a given level of income and development, but that they are also very much investments in human capital that are as necessary for reaching given levels of income and development as are investments in physical capital. In other words, education and health are prerequisites for economic growth.

It has, therefore, been disturbing to observe how grievously the education and health sectors have suffered during the economic and financial reforms of the 1980s. Indeed, adjustment policies have hurt education and health disproportionately; implic-

[15] Antonia Silva, ed., *Implementing Policy Innovations in Latin America* (SAPG-IDB, 1996).
[16] E. de Kadt and E. Zuckerman, eds., *The Public-Private Mix in Social Services,* (SAPG-IDB, 1997).

itly these sectors were once again considered to be "soft" sectors rather than sectors essential for economic growth. Expenditures on education and health were considered dispensable, at least for a while. Apparently, in regard to finance priorities, lessons from the past are easily forgotten and must be learned all over again by each new generation.

Today, the conventional wisdom puts heavy emphasis on *basic* education. International financial institutions have practically ceased to lend for anything within education that goes beyond the first cycle of the secondary level. In particular, university education now seems to be on the blacklist.

The necessity for this heavy and nearly exclusive emphasis on basic education is not confirmed by the Pilot Studies. What the empirical evidence indicates, of course, is that basic education, particularly the quality of it, is important. How could it not be? But in a relatively sophisticated region like Latin America and the Caribbean, technical and vocational education, high-quality secondary education, and also university education (including graduate studies and research) are equally important. In other words, the real challenge is for each country to determine what the optimal structure of its educational system must be, which qualitative changes must be introduced into the different levels and types of education, and which delivery systems (public, private, or a combination of both) must be employed.

The main reason that the international financial institutions have practically ceased to lend for higher education has less to do with priorities and more to do with how the universities are financed. It is a well documented fact that heavy state subsidization of university systems is regressive, in terms of income distribution, because the social class structure of the university student body is still heavily biased toward the better-off social classes. In such circumstances, subsidizing higher education means a transfer of income from the poorer segments of the population to the richer. The debate, therefore, should be about the equitable financing of higher education and not about sacrificing higher education in favor of basic education.

The SAPG studies show that there exists relatively less controversy in the region regarding health policy priorities. The international financial institutions' current stress on preventive health care (as compared with the much more expensive curative health care) is correct. But once again, such an assertion is not totally sufficient. The challenge is to determine the right expenditure balance between preventive care and curative care (much of the latter possibly to be provided by new larger hospitals).

In general terms, the whole area of social reform is as important as economic and financial reform. Again, a balanced policy is of the essence. Ideally, economic, financial, and social reforms should be introduced simultaneously. This has not been done. Thus, there now exists no alternative but to introduce them sequentially. What we have shown here is that social reform must not be restricted to education, health, social security, and social safety nets. It must also include vital employment creation policies that go beyond labor market considerations; productivity and income policies; a comprehensive plan of attack on urban problems; and a thorough look at matters of policy implementation and social-service delivery systems.

Ideally, economic and social objectives and policies should be viewed as one, but this approach has not prevailed in Latin America or anywhere else. Worse still, economic-adjustment policies have actually had negative effects on social policies by squeezing them financially, as explained by the Martin Paldam article in Part IV. Employment policies have been sorely neglected because the current orthodoxy has concentrated on the battle against inflation, leaving employment to be created by market forces. This approach has proven inadequate and has pointed up the need once again for an integrated approach to economic and social policy.

Globalization and the Effectiveness of Current Policies and Institutions[17]

Many countries' decision makers are increasingly linking globalization with the negative aspects of world competition and with the employment problem; this perception has given rise to defensive pleas to concentrate on economic regionalization rather than on economic globalization. It is becoming obvious as well that global enterprise and globalization in general are giving rise to an intensification of social problems at both the national and world level.

We have already discussed the issues of competition, governance, and employment as related to globalization. We shall therefore be dealing here mainly with social and institutional issues in the globalization context.

A notable acceleration has occurred in the tempo of globalization in recent years. Globalization's effective scope has also widened beyond the realm of the economy to embrace the domains of social, cultural, and political norms and practices. This ever-intensifying globalization has been accompanied by major changes in the roles and responsibilities of a wide range of human institutions: families, communities, civil-society institutions, business corporations, states, and supranational organizations. One of the most obvious consequences of these changes has been a rise in insecurity at the level of the individual and of the family. This greater personal insecurity not only affects individual welfare but also has broader economic, social, and political impact.

Globalization, as we have said, is often equated primarily with the growing integration of national economies. But it should also be understood to include the rapid spread worldwide of several dominant social, cultural, and political norms and practices. In the economic sphere, globalization is reflected in the increasing acceptance of free markets and private enterprise as the principal mechanisms for promoting economic activities. The social dimension of globalization comprises social relations and customs (family relations, social organizations, etiquettes of social behavior) and consumption patterns and lifestyles (consumer goods and services such as consumer durables, fashion and design articles, and foods and beverages). The cultural dimension includes the important domain of values, religion, and identity; it also embraces such leisure pastimes as television,

---

[17] This section owes much to Dharam Ghai, "Economic Globalization, Institutional Change and Human Security" paper presented at the VIII General Conference on "Globalization, Competitiveness and Human Security," of the European Association of Development Institutes (EADI) (Vienna, September 1996).

videos, popular music, dance, sports and foreign travel. At the political level, globalization is reflected in the spread of plural systems, multiparty democracy, free elections, the independent judiciary, and human rights.

Within the economic domain, the world's financial markets have come the closest to achieving the supposed ideal of global integration. But world trade—despite impressive postwar progress in removing trade impediments—continues to be subject to a range of tariff and nontariff barriers (although the results of the Uruguay Round may reverse this trend and speed up trade liberalization in hitherto highly regulated markets such as textiles, leather products, and certain agricultural commodities). Another major exception to global economic liberalization is provided by the world's labor markets: although the growing volume of migration flows is often cited as another aspect of increasing globalization, the fact is that the general trend in the past decade in most parts of the world has been toward increasing restrictions on migration from poorer regions. The pattern of global economic integration displays other sharp biases as well. Whether in the area of trade, capital flows, foreign investment, technology transfers, or the activities of transnational enterprises, most "global" transactions take place among the world's richer and more developed countries. In other words, a handful of countries accounts for the great bulk of international flows. Although this "handful of countries" does also include some of the large Asian and Latin American economies, most of the poorest and least developed countries are still largely bypassed by the intensifying circuits of world trade, capital, and investment flows.

Globalization in the social and cultural spheres has also been marked by discontinuities and contradictions. The consumption patterns and lifestyles of the middle classes in rich countries have penetrated only a thin layer (consisting largely of the affluent minorities) in poor countries. In most manifestations of cultural and social life, the vast majority of populations in the non-Western world continues to adhere largely to inherited traditions.

In the domain of politics as well, the ideals of liberal democracy have not been uniformly embraced worldwide. The conceptions and contents of democracy and human rights show wide variations even among countries generally accepted as falling into the camp of liberal democracy.

In terms of its roots, the overall process of globalization has been driven by a number of forces. Worldwide expansion of capitalism and the achievement of rapid technological progress are at the core of the dynamics of globalization. These forces have actually been in operation to some degree for centuries but have increased in scale and intensity in recent decades.

Many nations have indeed reduced state economic intervention, privatized public enterprises, deregulated the economy, and liberalized foreign trade and capital flows. The collapse of communism in Europe is only the most dramatic manifestation of this global trend. The economic reforms in China and other communist countries in Asia and elsewhere are additional striking evidence of the global appeal of free markets and private enterprise.

In addition, the great speed of technological change—especially in transport, communications, and information processing—has been a decisive element in the acceleration of globalization. Likewise, the rapid expansion of the media—the press, radio, television, and videos—has made a great contribution to globalization in the social, cultural, and political domains. Enormous growth in communications, travel, and tourism has been critical in advancing globalization along all fronts.

Unfortunately, the coincidence of globalization with economic crises and stagnation has meant that the efficiency gains from globalization's improved resource allocation appear also to have accentuated the existing problems of poverty, unemployment, and inequality. It can be argued that these globalizing efforts have laid the basis for faster and more efficient growth in the medium to long term, but this result remains to be seen.

With regard to growth, there may again be conflict between short-term and medium-term considerations. The short-run impact of globalization has clearly been a mixed blessing. Increased competition nationally and internationally has resulted in relentless pressures to reduce costs and enhance productivity through such ploys as reductions in employment and wages. This tactic has contributed to increased human-level uncertainty about job prospects.

The longer-term effects are even more uncertain. There is little doubt that individual countries or groups of countries will be able to forge ahead rapidly, as has been the case with many Asian countries. But it remains to be seen whether—in the absence of effective mechanisms for coordinating policy at the world level—the global market forces and a new environment can counteract the aforementioned contractionary influences and provide a stimulus for sustained and well-balanced expansion of the world economy.

In the short run at least, most of the changes associated with globalization are likely to deepen inequalities. A greater role of market forces in the labor and capital markets can be expected in most countries to lower wages, especially of "no-longer-needed" workers. The overall impact of these changes is likely to be negative on the working class in most countries. In the industrialized countries, employment and wages are under pressure from three sources: increased competition internally and from abroad, technological progress, and the internationalization of production; the fate of the working class in the industrialized countries would be even worse if there were no restrictions on labor immigration. Economic policies pursued at the national level will obviously be critical in determining the distributional implications of globalization.

Furthermore, cultural and social globalization has aroused widespread opposition and resistance. This backlash has occurred both in industrialized and developing countries, and has taken many forms. Governments have tried in various ways to restrict the exposure of their populations to imported products and programs, in an attempt both to minimize the latter alleged negative effects and to preserve and promote national cultural and social practices and values. These governmental actions have been prompted or supported by other important domestic bodies such as political parties, cultural associations, and religious organizations. The inflexible opposition by fundamentalist and xenophobic movements is only an extreme example of widespread concern about foreign influences on local society and culture.

A basic aspect of social and cultural globalization is that vast multitudes of people in poor countries, and increasingly also in the rich countries, are left outside the privileged circles of leisure activities and continuous conspicuous consumption. The excluded sectors' resultant sense of frustration and deprivation is fueled by their relentless media exposure to the temptations and seductions of the good life enjoyed by the fortunate few. It is hardly surprising that this situation leads them into the get-rich-quick activities typically associated with illegal acts such as crime and arms trade, prostitution, pornography, and the production and sale of drugs.

At the institutional level, the world's trade unions, cooperatives, and peasant associations have seen an erosion of their political power and effectiveness. Political parties representing the interests of organized workers and of the working poor have either become marginalized or have adapted their policies and campaign platforms to the dominant neoliberal ideologies. Everywhere, the power and scope of government have been diminished. In the area of economic policy, the ability of government to regulate the economy through official monetary, fiscal, trade and exchange rate policy has been restricted in varying degrees.

The touchstone of the success of public policy has become its impact on efficiency and competitiveness. Any redistributive policies and programs for social expenditure are routinely denounced for supposedly having adverse effects on incentives and for undermining individual initiative and responsibility. The reduced effectiveness of popular institutions and progressive parties has further weakened the countervailing power against neoliberal policies. Government—with its reduced autonomy, mounting debts, and growing reliance on capital markets—often has little choice but to follow the dictates of the dominant domestic and foreign interests. The articles in this volume indicate a change for the better in this respect, however.

One of the main consequences of accelerated globalization and of its associated changes has been to intensify economic and human insecurity. Increased economic insecurity is at the center of the rising spiral of human insecurity. Economic security cannot be enhanced by simply reverting to the conditions and policies of earlier years. The forces of globalization cannot be rolled back. Technology alone has forever changed the world in which we live. Nor does it make sense to try to reverse the reliance on free markets and private enterprise as the primary mechanisms for promoting economic progress. The great challenge is instead to devise policies and institutions to ensure greater security *within* the new situation created by accelerated globalization and technological advance. It must be admitted that this task is a daunting one and that little progress has been made thus far in this respect, either at the level of thought or action.

The problems of human security differ among the world's industrialized, transitional and developing countries, and therefore so must the policies to deal with these problems. A case in point concerns the blanket prescription of higher growth rates to combat unemployment and poverty.

Most developed countries were able to achieve nearly full employment in the first three decades of the postwar period in large part because of their historically unprecedented high rates of economic growth, but it is unrealistic to assume that this experience can be repeated in those countries in the future. It is much more probable that their growth rates of the past two decades, more in line with the historical experience, are likely to prevail. Our earlier described policy on employment might then be beneficially pursued.

In contrast, for most developing countries, rapid economic growth is indeed indispensable for employment generation and poverty reduction. In the past, the growth rate in poor countries was tied largely to economic conditions in the industrialized nations. Increased integration of the world economy might be expected to intensify this dependent relationship. But for many countries, this link appears to have been attenuated, if not totally severed. They have succeeded in attaining high growth rates even in years of stagnation or low growth in the rich countries. This independence is especially true of the Asian region. The emergence of similar trends in other developing regions could create the possibility that poor countries will be able to attain high growth rates independently of the economic performance by the rich countries. In fact, the world may even be moving in a direction in which growth in the industrialized countries comes to depend increasingly on expansion in the erstwhile transitional and developing countries.

But rapid growth alone cannot suffice to make a significant dent in the developing and transitional countries' unemployment and poverty problems. This much has become clear in earlier sections of the present essay. To ensure broad diffusion of the benefits of economic expansion, the pattern of growth must be an employment-intensive one. This effort to increase employment will require appropriate policies regarding macroeconomic factors, trade, technology, asset distribution, and human-resource investment. Several countries in Southeast Asia and elsewhere have succeeded in combining high rates of economic growth with rapid labor absorption. In many other countries, rapid growth has made only a limited contribution to the relief of unemployment and destitution, primarily because of highly unequal patterns of asset distribution (especially of land) and emphasis on capital-intensive technology.

In conclusion, the globalization of the economy and of economic policies must be matched by a globalization of social policy. Industrial countries must solve their internal employment and income problems lest an increasingly defensive attitude continue to prevail in their relations with the South and the East—an attitude that could result in regionalization being turned into an obstacle rather than a stepping-stone to globalization. Nor should we forget the other important social and cultural dimensions that are also being affected by globalization. These interrelationships merit much more policy priority than they are presently receiving.

State of Development Policy and the Evolving Nature of Development Thinking and Practice

As briefly mentioned earlier, during the 1970s there existed an important school of thought—espoused by scholars from the World Bank (Hollis Chenery), from the United

Kingdom (Dudley Seers and Hans Singer), and elsewhere—that set out to design a development strategy sometimes called "redistribution with growth," at other times "redistribution from growth," and at yet other times a "basic (human) needs" approach. Whatever the label, the idea was the same—namely, to design a set of economic and social policies that would improve income distribution at the margin—and hence, in the end, *in toto*—by pushing income growth harder in the low-productivity and low-income sectors. All of this was done because of the conviction that the actual pattern of economic growth was as important as economic growth itself, if poverty reduction and employment creation were priority objectives.

All such orientation virtually disappeared (as Enrique Iglesias mentions in his foreword) from the scene during the 1980s. There reappeared instead, whether implicitly or explicitly, the earlier idea that economic growth alone could solve social issues. But today we are once again confronted with the same old difficult problems of distribution and poverty—problems that are now explicitly recognized by the economic profession and by international and national decision makers, as reflected in the articles in this volume.

It is true that the strategies of "redistribution with growth" had assumed that government could effectively tackle a certain number of politically sensitive key issues such as land reform and the effective collection of taxes. This assumption practically vanished in the 1980s, during which decade not only was the role of the state minimized but also such crucial issues as land reform were seen as too politically sensitive to be addressed. The search for alternative and less-sensitive policies followed. This shift of focus resulted in an extremely heavy weight given to the role of basic education, which came to be seen as a major policy instrument for influencing future income distribution.

What must be done now is not to go back to the 1970s and resuscitate lock, stock, and barrel the ideas and strategies of "redistribution with growth" that were advanced at that time, but instead to update those ideas in the light of the new national and international situation of the 1990s. This updating has been done in the articles by Irma Adelman, Nancy Birdsall, and Amartya Sen, as well as in various other articles contained in the present volume.

Angus Maddison in his paper quotes a 1968 publication by Erik Lundberg to the effect that the "establishment view" in the 1960s was to focus on the achievement of full employment and rapid economic growth. Lundberg contrasted these priorities with those of the old interwar period, which consisted of the annual balancing of the budget, the stability of the price level, and the preservation of specific exchange rates—goals that Lundberg concluded "today (1968) would largely be considered as either intermediate, secondary, irrelevant or irrational targets."[18] Maddison in turn concludes that "the establishment wisdom has now reverted completely to the old-fashioned (interwar) reli-

---

[18] Erik Lundberg, *Instability and Economic Growth* (Yale University Press, 1968), 37.

gion: full employment and rapid economic growth have been jettisoned, and ancient goals have been embraced with crusading zeal."[19]

Although one can make a case for this reversal to "ancient goals" in the 1970s and early 1980s, it is a matter of puzzlement that this course was continued in the face of very uncertain (to put it euphemistically) results in economic growth, employment creation, and income distribution. Not only was it continued but, implicitly or explicitly, it was also given universal validity. And so whether it was Latin America, Africa, or the countries in transition, basically the same policy prescriptions were tendered. Even the East Asian development experience was by and large incorporated into the new orthodoxy.[20]

But Irma Adelman concludes in her contribution here that based on both European and East Asian development history, had the neoliberal Washington consensus been enforced on the East Asian miracle countries during the 1950s, 1960s, and early 1970s, there would not have *been* any East Asian miracle at all. The process of successful economic development in the long run apparently implies a changing dynamic interaction among institutional change, technological progress, international trade, and accumulation—an interaction in which government policies play a key role.

It can be (and has been) shown that the process of economic development in the world has in fact been nonlinear and multifaceted.[21] Historically, one can distinguish distinct development paths, such as the following: the autonomous, export-led industrialization path (Great Britain and France as early industrializers); the government-led, inward-oriented industrialization path (Germany, Italy, Japan, and Russia as large latecomers to the industrial revolution); the balanced-growth, open-economy, limited-government-intervention path (Denmark, the Netherlands, Sweden, as small European countries); and the agricultural, primary-export-oriented, dualistic path pursued both by land-abundant (Argentina, Australia, Canada) and densely populated countries (China, Egypt, and India).

Historical development experience, therefore suggests that different initial economic and institutional conditions matter. We must also conclude that one single theoretical framework is not likely to offer a good explanation of the development process over the entire range of development experience and that a given single-factor development theory ("trade is enough" or "human capital is enough") is likely to apply (moderately) well to only a small range of countries. In sum, policy prescriptions based on generalizing across countries that are at very different levels of socio-institutional and economic development are likely to be seriously misleading.

For instance, as becomes clear in many contributions throughout this volume, the contemporary East Asian development pattern has entailed the following: a process of

---

[19] Present volume.

[20] World Bank, *The East Asian Miracle* (Washington, D.C., 1993).

[21] The following pages are inspired by an enlightening paper: Irma Adelman and Cynthia Taft Morris, "Development History and Its Implications for Development Theory: An Editorial," *World Development*, Vol. 25, no. 6 (June 1997).

government-led capitalist development with high government investment in and own-ership of industry; initially substantial foreign aid; little foreign direct investment; high private and public investment in human resources and almost no reliance on foreigners; and a short period of generalized infant industry protection followed by export-led growth combined with selective import-substitution and government promotion of those industries that would become the core export industries in the next phase of dy-namic comparative advantage. This approach has resulted in very fast, widely shared, eq-uitable development in East Asia.

By contrast, the rather less successful (at least after 1950) Latin American pattern has involved the following: a process of government intervention that has been less develop-mental in nature and more responsive to pressures from tradition-oriented economic elites; a lengthy period of import substitution; moderate investment rates; moderate lev-els of human-capital development; substantial reliance on foreign investment and foreign entrepreneurship in both agriculture and industry; and extensive agriculture, character-ized by the predominance of large owner-absentee commercial farms. All of this has led to dualistic and rather inequitable development in the Latin American region, as further elaborated by Albert Fishlow and Martin Paldam in this volume.

Historically, Great Britain has been the only country that industrialized without tar-iffs, during its industrial revolution. The nineteenth-century colonies' inability to adopt import substitution policies (because of domestic and international constraints) has re-sulted in their remaining underdeveloped until today. No contemporary developing country (other than the crown colony of Hong Kong) has been able to start industrial-ization without an initial period of infant industry protection.

The inevitable conclusion must be that development theories today tend to suffer from misplaced universality. They must be changed to take full cognizance of historical and situational relativism and of the multifaceted nature of the development process.

Irma Adelman and Cynthia Taft Morris conclude that the most appropriate theo-retical description of the economic-development process for the least-developed 40 per-cent of countries is offered by the Lewis model. But that model must be restated so that it becomes an open-economy model with trade in primary goods.

The subsequent, early phase of increasing development in the next-more-developed one-third of developing countries is best described by models like the Rosenstein-Rodan and Nurkse big-push models. These models center on raising investment rates and di-recting them to infrastructure creation and to the coordination of investments in exter-nality-generating industries. The important actors in this process are governments, the functions of which are to build up economic and institutional infrastructural capital, to raise incentives for private savings and investment, to develop human resources and en-trepreneurship, and to maintain checks upon the divisive sociopolitical processes that du-alistic development engenders. Infant industry protection is required.

Once economic, institutional, and social development have proceeded to the point at which countries are ready to enter the semi-industrial stage, continued development requires a big push on the buildup of institutional and human capital and on the expansion of technological modernization within the industrial sector. This phase entails a shift in trade policies away from import substitution toward export promotion. Developmental governments are essential at this stage both to promote institutional and social development and to engineer the requisite shifts in trade policy and in the balance between the state and the private sector.

No development theory (whether focused on government or on open-economy growth or on the building of human capital) is irrelevant in this last phase, nor is any single theory completely applicable without serious amendment. The purely neoclassical Washington consensus fully applies primarily to the handful of developing countries currently engaged in the final process of transition to OECD status.

Judging from the articles in the present volume, it would appear that this move away from "universality of theory and policy" has been understood once again. Nancy Birdsall stresses the big-push requirement ("high levels of capital accumulation") and the role of government ("explicit strategic intervention"), but her most interesting and novel point is that "a low level of income inequality is good for growth because growth must be generated from below." Indeed, the understanding of the relationship between economic growth and equitable income distribution has come around full circle: from a negative correlation some 30 years ago, via a spurious correlation, to a positive correlation now. In other words, the present contention is that the less unequal the distribution of income in a country is, the higher is that country's rate of economic growth. The point made here is not so much one of redistribution from above but rather from below through a participatory pattern of development. There is a need "of the poor becoming cooks too, and of more cooks preparing a bigger pie."[22] We are thus moving toward a comprehensive (economic, social, cultural, and political) development theory linking economic growth, social development, and political and economic democracy.

In his contribution to this volume, Amartya Sen says, "The fact that social development may not work on its own to generate economic growth is fully consistent with the possibility (for which there now exists a great deal of evidence) that social development does strongly facilitate fast and participatory economic growth if combined with market-friendly policies that encourage economic expansion."[23] The renewed emphasis on "human capital" (education, health) in development theory and practice cannot and should not be restricted to the investment aspect implied by the very term "human capital." Such a focus would not do justice to the importance of human beings in the process of development. After all, the glorification of human beings as "instruments" of economic growth cannot be the whole story of development.

Our focus then must not be limited to economic growth but should center as well on the **expansion of human freedom** to live the kind of lives that people have reason to value and that they feel will enhance their quality of experience. It is very much up to the people themselves to define the quality of life they value and the societal process that

---

[22] Present volume.
[23] Present volume.

would lead up to it. Thus, the link between democratic choice and the development process should be clear. Democratic political and social choice is essential for moving toward a view of development that celebrates the expansion of human freedom and capabilities. Democratic economic choice is essential in order to introduce development from below, to get more cooks into the kitchen, and thus to produce a bigger pie together. Economic growth will be maximized, equitably distributed, and brought within the critical scrutiny of people themselves.

Development thinking and practice, therefore, have their work cut out for them as we move into the twenty-first century. A framework must be developed that links political democracy, social and cultural development, and economic efficiency; it must give real choices to people in order to let them define the ultimate values they want to achieve through economic growth. Elaborating such a framework requires integrating economic and other policy areas and hence a truly interdisciplinary approach.[24]

If this sounds overly ambitious and even utopian, the articles that follow will show that we are already well on our way to a better understanding of the nature of development and to the elaboration of precisely the kind of framework alluded to here.

Implications for Latin America and the Caribbean

What can Latin America and the Caribbean learn from the changes in the air elsewhere? What policy changes are emerging in the region itself? What changes would be desirable in the light of unsolved major problems present and emerging? How do globalization and regionalization affect the region?

Latin America on the whole has entered the third (semi-industrial) stage described earlier. It is therefore ready for the elaboration and implementation of a comprehensive development framework as described in our previous section. A big push is required on the buildup of institutional and human capital, with continued emphasis on broadening access for more economic actors and of course with continued emphasis on high savings and investment rates. Development-oriented governments are essential at this stage in order to steer policies toward deepening political democracy; toward economic democracy, in order to promote greater participation of the people in the development process; and toward social progress, in order to achieve greater and more equitable development. Latin America understands the need for a deeper and more comprehensive development framework bringing civil society much more explicitly into the picture, as is brought out in Edgardo Boeninger's article. He clearly underlines the need for and the interrelation of "political stability, economic progress, and social peace."[25] For him, democracy is the only path that can lead to political stability in Latin America, and social peace implies that the people perceive that the development process increases equity.

Latin America thus stands on the threshold of a new conception of development along the lines set out in the present essay. But as Albert Fishlow, Victor Tokman,

---

[24] See Emanuel de Kadt's article in the present volume.
[25] Present volume.

Martin Paldam, and Gert Rosenthal (among others) remind us, there are matters that require urgent attention in the region.

These urgent matters include first of all the region's present low domestic savings capacity linked to the low levels of tax collection. A savings rate below 20 percent is clearly not sufficient to get the growth engine in higher gear and to create enough income-earning opportunities for the present unemployed and underemployed as well as for the future generations presenting themselves on the labor markets. As Fishlow points out, the only place where a substantial increase in savings can occur in the short term is in the public sector. Now that inflation in the region is being brought under control, there is no reason that less than 10 percent of GDP continues to be collected in taxes (against 20 percent to 30 percent in OECD countries). This is a tough nut to crack, but it must be done; it will require government that is strong but also perceived as standing for fair and equitable development. Excessive reliance on external savings is not a sustainable policy.

Obviously, bringing more cooks into the kitchen and going for a more participatory development approach will help in this context. When people are being stimulated to participate in the decisions that shape their own (economic and wider) future, they will tend to invest more of their time and resources in building up their environment. Savings and investment may in such cases be one and the same thing.

This leads us to the second urgent point for attention—namely, the question of the highly unequal income distribution in the region. The inequitable development pattern of Latin America is well known, and the stabilization policies of the 1980s and the region's increased integration into global markets have made this matter worse rather than better. There exists today a strong belief that education—and particularly, basic education—is key to a positive change here, but there must also be a more equitable pattern of ownership of the region's physical assets.

On education and the need for rapid accumulation of human capital, enough has already been said, and general agreement prevails; but this is not the case with the necessity of the redistribution of wealth. In Latin America the latter basically means land reform, on which not very much has been said during the last 15 years. As the experience of East Asia—particularly of Japan, Korea, and Taiwan—shows, an initial commitment to equalization (and particularly land reform) can play a major role in the realization of a high and equitable growth path.

Again, an interrelationship exists between income distribution and the components of our proposed development framework. Giving people in the rural traditional and in the urban informal sectors greater access to credit, training, land, education, and higher-productivity and higher-income work opportunities through increased political and economic democracy not only will improve income distribution but also will lead to higher overall growth and a better quality of life in general.

Creation of productive employment for those who are unemployed and the achievement of increases in productivity for those who are employed in low-productivity and hence low-income sectors constitute the third urgency. Enough has been said about these crucial aspects earlier in this essay, and no further elaboration is required.

Latin America—as Enrique Iglesias has earlier noted—is undergoing far-reaching changes within a globalizing world economy and society. Globalization must take place not only among nations but within countries as well; perhaps we should call this latter aspect a "deepening and broadening" of the development framework. The resultant increases in democracy, equity, and development can each then indeed generate virtuous circles of their own as long as the fundamentals on which to build are kept in place.

PART II

Globalization and the Current Orthodoxy

Globalization amid Diversity
Elsuke Sakaklbara

The Washington Consensus Revisited
John Williamson

COMMENTS BY
Frances Stewart
Bishnodat Persaud
Toru Yanagihara

Successes and Failures of Development Experience since the 1980s
Gustav Ranis

COMMENTS BY
Lawrence Klein
Richard Jolly

Globalization and Competitiveness: Implications for Development Thinking and Practice?
Paul Streeten

Globalization and Competitiveness in the XXI Century: A Japanese Perspective
Ryokichi Hirono

COMMENTS BY
Dharam Ghai
Lourdes Arizpe

Development and Underdevelopment in a Globalized World: Latin American Dilemmas
Aldo Ferrer

Globalization amid Diversity

Eisuke Sakakibara[1]

John Williamson[2] in the late 1980s defined what he called the "Washington consensus" in relation to the policy conditionality attached to Latin American countries at the time of the debt crisis. The consensus essentially boiled down to "free markets and sound money." Developing countries in Asia and Central and Latin America and post-socialism countries in transition opened their economies following this consensus. According to David Hale, "During the 1990s, more than 50 developing countries have established domestic capital markets in order to encourage the privatization of public enterprises and to attract greater foreign investment. Their combined stock market capitalization is now $2.1 trillion, compared with less than $400 billion in the late 1980s."[3]

These moves had a great impact upon developing countries and were an accurate reflection of the political consensus formed within the developed world in the 1980s following the Reagan and Thatcher neoconservative revolution.

During that same decade, a series of dramatic domestic deregulations allowed the United States, the United Kingdom, Japan, and other developed countries to enjoy a period of continuous high growth—ending, however, in the creation of unstable asset "bubbles." These bubbles burst in the late 1980s and early 1990s, and the resultant asset deflation quickly induced recessions in these countries. In fact, Japan, the latecomer, is still struggling to neutralize the effects of bursting these asset bubbles, which seriously damaged the financial sector. The relatively stagnant condition prevailing in the economies of certain developed economies with low interest rates soon encouraged investors to look again at opportunities in the third world, resulting in the exportation of large volumes of developed-country financial resources to the developing economies. Seen from this angle, the Washington consensus has been crucial to the acceleration of globalization, through its role in increasing world financial flows, mostly private, to developing countries.

Globalization and Localization

The key concept to be analyzed here is "globalization." Today, Latin America—like other parts of the world—is being engulfed in the globalization process. So first of all, we need

[1] Vice-minister for International Affairs, Ministry of Finance, Japan. Views expressed here are purely personal and do not necessarily represent those of the Japanese Government.
[2] John Williamson, ed., *Latin American Adjustment: How Much Has Happened?* (Washington, D.C. Institute for International Economics, April 1990).
[3] David Hale, "Global Economic Integration after the Cold War, or How Will the Economic Order Created at Bretton Woods Adjust to Three Billion New Members?" (Mimeo, September 1994).

to define exactly what globalization is. Does globalization imply, for instance, that a universal model or uniform set of rules as envisaged in the Washington consensus will eventually spread to all parts of the world and that the world will become homogeneous, both economically and culturally? Definitely not. We have to recognize that what can be called "localization," or an identification with local cultural values, is proceeding along with globalization. In this context, the rather monolithic view held by many governments in the developed world and international organizations that there is only one universal model to which all countries in the world should adhere is actually quite problematic. The monolithic universal model consists of pluralistic congressional or parliamentary democracy, on the political side, and of the neoclassical market economy, on the economic side.

This universalism originated in Europe, with the United States providing the finishing ideological touches after World War II. At the center of this universalism lies neoclassical economics. The basic message of this doctrine is very simple. If you loosen the "market" from the yoke of government regulation and if macroeconomic policies are property conducted by the authorities, the economy will grow steadily, reflecting the universal power of the market. The market, here, is the supposedly magic word. In the abstract model of Walrasian general equilibrium, the market is defined as the place where numerous economic agents gather and carry out transactions with each other under the centralized command of the auctioneer. The auctioneer here represents, in the abstract, all of the public infrastructure necessary for realizing numerous economic transactions in the market in a smooth and legitimate manner. The problems of asymmetric information, monopoly, deception, or fraud do not exist, because the auctioneer is assumed to be omnipotent in managing the "market." In reality, of course, such a perfect market does not exist. Markets can be defined, in general, only as networks for transactions among economic agents, mediated by traders, dealers, and financiers and supported by the legal and administrative infrastructure of the authorities. In other words, markets are networks within which economic agents, mediator merchants, and authorities interact, the patterns of interaction differing depending upon the particular historical and institutional environment in which they happen to occur. One key element in the structure of these markets is the particular pattern of interaction between mediator-merchants and authorities; differences in these patterns, among other elements, lead to the formation of different types of market economies.

Another caveat needs to be given concerning the Walrasian notion of the auctioneer-dominated universal market. Here, what is being implicitly assumed is that the objects of the transactions among economic agents are physical goods. Transactions of stock such as land and human capital do not seem to fit very smoothly into this framework. Regarding such stock, it seems only natural that the roles of the "market" and of the auctioneer are somewhat limited relative to the prevailing political or legal infrastructure. Despite these problems with the Walrasian market model, most neoclassical economists tend to apply this universal model unilaterally to all countries, neglecting the historical and cultural backgrounds of the countries in question. In particular, many international organizations seem to adhere to some version of neoclassical economics and tend to impose one market model on all developing countries or countries in transition. The Walrasian market, in concrete terms, is often interpreted as what might be called the Anglo-American model, where the only primary role of the public sector is the management of macroeconomic policies. Two specific policies recommended on the basis of this doctrine have been deregulation and privatization. The earliest possible deregulation of price controls and of controls on financial transactions, including foreign exchange, has been urged and made one of the primary conditions for the provision of assistance. State and public corporations have also been urged to privatize, and stock market capitalization stemming from such privatization has increased dramatically in the 1990s. These policy recommendations have probably been a reflection of the financial deregulation and globalization that took place in the developed countries during the late 1970s and the 1980s. In view of the increasing amount of funds available for global investment by mutual funds and pension funds at a time that developed economies were still relatively stagnant, such a need certainly existed from the suppliers' side. But in fact, these are the very funds that move across national borders seeking primarily high short-term returns, and they can be quite volatile, not necessarily meeting the long-term needs of developing countries.

Indeed, deregulation and privatization have accelerated the flow of private funds to Latin America and Asia during the 1990s and have helped fuel dynamic growth in the newly privatized sectors of these economies. The question, however, is the sustainability of such dynamic growth supported by foreign portfolio investments, including some hot money, which cannot normally be expected to tolerate long incubation periods. A sudden large-scale capital flight is always possible if adverse developments in certain areas are perceived by the market as crucial. In the case of Mexico, in the 1994–95 period, for example, political instability was the trigger that suddenly highlighted that country's prolonged current-account deficits and the real appreciation of the currency despite those deficits. In actual fact, the macroeconomic performance of the Mexican economy had long been unsatisfactory, and experts were well aware of those developments. But, fund managers and traders in the market had not perceived those indicators as crucial and thus kept on investing until the trigger was pulled.

The situation has improved since then, and countries and the market are again becoming euphoric about the future of Latin economies. Nevertheless, caution needs to be taken, since the basic structure of the region seems unchanged: low savings ratios supplemented by inflows of foreign capital, including hot money. This time, approximately 90 percent of the inflow is private, mostly in the form of bonds and securitized instruments, with some derivatives such as options.

Diversity and Interaction

An increasing number of economists have began to doubt the universal validity of the Walrasian general equilibrium model, or the neoclassical paradigm, in view of economies of scale, bounded rationality, asymmetric information, and other types of market imperfections. Among the doubters is a group of economists at Stanford University who have engaged in what they term comparative institutional analysis.

There is no timeless and universal economic system with normative values. The mechanical application of implications of the Walrasian general market equilibrium model, which is nothing but the product of metaphysical thinking, is not effective in analyzing the U.S.–Japanese economic relationship or the institutional reforms of economies in transition from socialism to a market economy. Rather, we should honestly recognize the existence of plural economic systems and analyze their origin, evolution (historical development), comparative merits and demerits, and the possibility of economic gains from diversity. The analysis should not only be focused on the market systems in question but extended to the interdependence of a complicated network of various systems.[4]

This view of comparative institutional analysis parallels that of Toynbee-Huntington in that both recognize the plurality of economic systems or civilizations and emphasize interaction among them. The key concept here is not universality, but diversity and interaction.

In comparative analyses of economic systems, comparison of the Japanese model with the Anglo-American and continental European models is particularly interesting. Japan is unique in that it has modernized or industrialized its system while at the same time retaining, to some extent at least, its own traditions and culture. Other developing countries have not quite modernized their systems, either because of long periods of colonization or the rule of socialism. In other words, Japan is perhaps the only non-Western country that has succeeded in modernizing its system. Countries like the United States, Australia, and New Zealand have modernized and become complete members of Western civilization, although their lack of historical evolution along European lines makes those countries somewhat unusual in that they have been able to experiment with various abstract ideas of capitalism or democracy more or less from scratch. In this sense, the United States has become the country where the neoclassical paradigm has been implemented in its purest possible form. In contrast, many European countries—particularly continental European countries such as Germany and France, where what Macpherson called possessive individualism[5] has not been so solidly established—have developed institutions somewhat different from the more neoclassical ones prevailing in the United States or the United Kingdom. Michel Albert classifies Western capitalism into two categories: the Anglo-Saxon model and the Rhine-Alpen model.[6] Although Albert considers Japan as belonging to the Rhine-Alpen group, it is perhaps more appropriate to create a third category: a Japanese or, potentially, an East Asian category. The present author is not prepared to engage in a wholesale comparative institutional analysis of Anglo-Saxon,

---

[4] Masahiko Aoki, Keizai Shisutemu no Shinka to Tagensei, *Evolution and Plurality of Economic Systems* (Toyo Keizai, April 1995).

[5] C.B. Macpherson, *The Political Theory of Possessive Individualism, Hobbes to Locke* (Oxford University Press, 1962).

[6] Michel Albert, *Capitalisme contre Capitalisme* (Paris: Editions du Seuil, 1991).

Rhine-Alpen, and Japanese capitalism here. Nevertheless, let me illustrate my point by considering an alternative approach to deregulation and privatization.

It has been argued by many neoclassical economists that deregulation must be implemented as intensively as possible, simultaneously and quickly on many fronts so that distortions stemming from partial deregulation can be avoided. This approach implicitly assumes that Anglo-American institutions and social environments complementary to these institutions are already in place or can be very quickly established by enlightened reformers with the help of consultants and international organizations. This neglect of the validity of different cultures and evolutionary processes of history is typical of neoclassical prescriptions and has often led to confusion and the collapse of the existing order rather than to reform. The alternative would be strategic deregulation of some selected sectors while retaining most regulations, at least at the outset. Most importantly, foreign exchange controls, particularly on capital transactions, should be retained. Under the old GATT-Bretton Woods regime up to 1971, early deregulation of foreign-exchange controls on current transactions was encouraged, but not on capital transactions. Now, however, with the advent of the floating-rate regime, early deregulation of foreign-exchange controls on all transactions has somehow become the norm. For developed economies—where financial infrastructure, including a solid central-bank system, is well established—deregulation of capital controls is not inappropriate, provided that the coordination of macroeconomic policies and of foreign-exchange market interventions is conducted smoothly. The situation is completely different, however, for countries where the domestic banking system and the monetary policy mechanisms have not yet been fully developed. If deregulation is forced on those countries, they simply lose sovereignty in the area of policy controls on their own economies and are subjected to volatile movements of international money without having effective policy instruments to deal with them. Neoclassical economists have often argued that if proper macroeconomic policies are implemented, confusion would not arise, even in a regime of deregulated foreign exchange. But how can proper macroeconomic policies be conducted if the necessary infrastructure such as a central banking system and an effectively governed enterprise system do not exist?

My second point is related to privatization. What is the ultimate purpose of privatization for the countries in question? The establishment of private ownership a la Macpherson that is, Anglo-American possessive individualism—seems to occupy center stage in the discussion of privatization. But the issue should be dealt with less ideologically and more pragmatically—that is to say, the important thing for countries, at least in the short run, is not ownership privatization but management privatization. Management of state-owned enterprises or of public corporations is often dominated by insiders (namely, managers, workers, and government officials), and there is a lack of effective outside control. What is necessary for restructuring those enterprises is the establishment of management that is sensitive to market competition and can be effectively governed by an appropriate combination of stakeholders. The Anglo-American response to such a need is to establish shareholders' sovereignty coupled with ownership privatization. Various investment fund schemes in Russia, Poland, and other East European countries are cases in point.[7] Such an approach has not necessarily been successful, however, and has even resulted, in some instances, in the strengthening of insider control by the ancient regime rather than in restructuring.

An alternative approach would be to use banks, rather than investment funds and the stock exchange, to strengthen corporate governance and to channel the necessary funds toward restructuring enterprises. Under this approach, ownership privatization does not have to be implemented so quickly. What is important is "management privatization." To achieve this objective, reform of the central-bank system and of the general banking system should be a priority. Central banks and public as well as private banks have to gain independence from the planning authorities that directly control enterprises. Policies should be implemented to channel a major portion of domestic savings through the banking system. The encouragement of savings by ensuring attractive interest rates on bank deposits through a noninflationary monetary policy is absolutely essential. Second, corporate governance should be organized around banks and insiders rather than around shareholders and managers. This is the German or Japanese style of corporate governance as opposed to its Anglo-American counterpart. In particular, Japan has developed the so-called main-bank system, in which an enterprise has one key bank, called the main bank, to monitor management as well as cash and capital requirements continuously and to take over management in case of contingencies. Aoki called this type of corporate governance "contingency governance," which retains corporate control by managers and employees under normal circumstances but yields it to main banks during contingencies.[8] Third, in order to nurture domestic banks in the medium to long run, the activities of foreign banks and security houses should be closely monitored and should be regulated to the extent necessary. The flows of foreign short-term funds, in particular, should not be freely allowed, and foreign participation should be directed more toward long-term joint ventures and direct investments.

If such an approach is followed, ownership privatization need not be implemented immediately, but rather, authorities could concentrate their initial efforts on structuring a credible banking system that provides the necessary public and semipublic infrastructure for moving smoothly toward a market economy.

Toward Systemic Diversity

With the demise of socialism, its counter ideology—namely the Walrasian or neoclassical paradigm—seems to have lost its luster as well. Economic policies in developed countries from the United States and Europe to Japan, which are based to an extensive degree on neoclassical economic theory, have led to some chronic or structural problems,

---

[7] For the analysis of investment funds in transitional economies, see Masahiko Aoki and H. Kim, eds., *Corporate Governance in Transitional Economies: Insider Control and the Role of Banks,* EDI Developmental Studies (Washington, D.C.: World Bank, 1995).

[8] For the analysis of main banks, see Masahiko Aiko and Hugh Patrick, eds., *The Japanese Main Bank System* (Oxford: Clarendon Press, 1994).

while volatile movements in capital and money have regularly caused foreign-exchange or monetary crises. Developing countries in Latin America, Asia, Eastern Europe, and elsewhere have become new frontiers and testing grounds for developed countries to continue their economic policies based on the neoclassical paradigm. The success of such experiments so far has been limited, however, and adhering further to this same path may endanger the economic future of these developing countries, as well as that of the world at large. It seems that we are at a vital crossroads now, where we must start pursuing alternative approaches and choosing diversity rather than uniformity. Japanese or continental European models may serve as interesting references. But the point here is that each country would be well advised to establish its own model of capitalism and democracy. The world as a whole should gain from systemic diversity rather than suffer from the confusion and catastrophe caused by the forceful application of a universal model.

Even so, one needs to be cautious and not indulge in too extreme a form of cultural relativism. Extreme relativism can degenerate into barren nihilism or a dangerous anarchism. What is important here is to capture the totality of the system with diverse elements. This is what I call the paradoxical coexistence of globalization with localization. Looking back on the history of the premodern world, this coexistence of diverse civilizations under globalization does seem possible. What connected the diverse civilizations back then was the networking of Eastern and Western merchants. In this sense, globalization amid diversity is nothing new.

Thus, what we need to aspire to in the twenty-first century is an interconnecting global system linking all regions or countries of the world while respecting their diverse cultures and their own special socioeconomic systems. I am no expert on Latin American countries, but I think I can at least say that the Latin American countries' systems should differ quite significantly from the Anglo-American model, just as the French, Italian and Spanish systems differ from the German model.

The Washington Consensus Revisited

John Williamson[1]

When in 1989 I listed ten policy reforms that I believed "Washington" would agree were needed in Latin America, I hardly anticipated being asked to revisit the topic seven years later at such an august conference as this. My "Washington consensus" (see appendix) became vastly more renowned—and more controversial, than I could have conceived at that time, in part because it was interpreted by some as a "neoliberal" policy manifesto. Even the name "Washington consensus" aroused resentment in readers and others who construed it as implying a claim that Washington had designed and imposed the reform programs that Latin American countries were implementing.

I propose to try to disarm at least some of my critics by offering some brief comments on my objectives in framing that Washington consensus, on my choice of terminology, and on my ideological attitude toward "neoliberalism." But the present opportunity seems far too precious to be squandered upon merely defending what I wrote seven years ago. I therefore propose to do now what many of my critics seem to have believed I was doing in 1989—that is, to outline a policy manifesto of the leading reforms that Latin America ought in my view to be implementing. This new offering will differ from the Washington consensus for two reasons: first, because I shall be presenting what I personally believe to be of primary importance to Latin America itself rather than presenting the lowest common denominator of what I once judged could command a consensus in Washington and second, because Latin America has changed since 1989. I shall of course endeavor to identify which of these two reasons is responsible for the differences between the Washington consensus and the present Williamson wish list agenda.

Why the "Washington Consensus"?

My reason for compiling the Washington consensus was simply to document or report on the change in policy attitudes that I sensed was occurring in Latin America but of which Washington seemed largely unaware at the time. To this end, the Institute for International Economics convened a conference on the topic "Latin American Adjustment: How Much Has Happened?" in November 1989, at which authors from Latin American countries commented on national attitudes toward a series of policy reforms, including the extent to which such reforms had been implemented. My Washington consensus consisted of the list of policy reforms that each author was asked

---

[1] Senior Fellow, Institute for International Economics. The author acknowledges helpful comments by Louis Emmerij and by participants in the conference.

to examine. The results (published in Williamson 1990) confirmed that there had indeed occurred a sea change in attitudes since our institute's 1986 publication of a policy manifesto called *Toward Renewed Economic Growth in Latin America* (Balassa et al. 1986), which had not been met with a very friendly reception in the region.

If we had actually been trying to make propaganda in favor of policy reform by Latin America, it is difficult to think of a less diplomatic label than "Washington consensus." And in any case, insofar as the object of the exercise could have been interpreted as that of making propaganda rather than that of simply reporting on what was happening, the target of any such propaganda would clearly have been Washington rather than Latin America.

In presenting the conclusions of the conference, I did doubtlessly find it difficult to conceal my view that it was a thoroughly good thing that Latin America was making the changes that I was arguing were already happening. Whatever my personal responsibility for the perception of the Washington consensus not as a simple reporting job but instead as a policy manifesto, there is no question that it did become interpreted that way.[2] This outcome was in one sense odd: the consensus was actually quite successful as a report on the lowest common denominator of the policy reforms that Washington could agree Latin America needed to be making,[3] but it strikes me as quite inadequate as a policy manifesto.

In the main section of the present paper I shall elaborate on my own perceptions of the inadequacies of the consensus as a policy manifesto. My personal intellectual standpoint is that of a classical liberal who likes to think of himself as in the tradition of John Locke, Adam Smith, and John Stuart Mill. Furthermore, once I had understood what a "neoliberal" is—a concept that was not immediately obvious to me (and I have still not found any dictionary definition of the current meaning of the term) but that everyone else seemed to understand instinctively—I also concluded that the consensus was quite inadequate even from a neoliberal standpoint. Let me explain why.

When I eventually tracked down something close to a considered definition of the term "neoliberal," it was in a book by Mario Simonsen (1994, p. 280), who wrote "*...o movimento [do neoliberalismo] for liderado por Ronald Reagan ...e Margaret Thatcher... Entre os economistas, Friedrich von Hayek e Milton Friedman foram los principais inspiradores do movimento.*" Having thus discovered that neoliberalism consisted of the economic doctrines espoused by Ronald Reagan and Margaret Thatcher (and having repressed the thought that these two would certainly have repudiated being described as any kind of "liberals"), I could at last understand what it was that so many people were denouncing. But I then begun to puzzle over why they thought the Washington consensus was a neoliberal manifesto. True, it did espouse developing and using the market rather than denouncing, repressing, and distorting markets (a point on which liberals

---

[2] For an entertaining discussion of alternative interpretations of the nature of the Washington consensus, see Toye (1994, p. 39).

[3] Its biggest failing in that respect concerned exchange rate policy, as I note subsequently.

and neoliberals are in agreement), and did incorporate privatization, which was Margaret Thatcher's personal contribution to sensible economic policy. But it nevertheless omitted many other articles of neoliberal faith: it did not declare that the only legitimate way to restore fiscal discipline was to slash government expenditure; it did not identify fiscal discipline with a balanced budget; it did not call for overall tax cuts; it did not treat as plunder the taxes raised in order to redistribute income; it did not say that exchange rates had to be either firmly fixed or freely floating; it did not call for the proscription of capital controls; it did not advocate competitive moneys or argue that the money supply should grow at a fixed rate. As a statement of the neoliberal creed, the consensus was quite deficient. And that was because it was in fact intended to summarize the common ground between neoliberals and the rest of Washington, not to present the viewpoint of the former. The fact that there did exist a lot of common ground, like the fact that this consensus had made so much progress in Latin America, was of enormous interest, but it did not imply that all of Washington or all of Latin America had endorsed or should endorse every quixotic doctrine of Hayek and Friedman or their political disciples.

An Agenda for 1996

How similar to the Washington consensus would a true policy manifesto appropriate for the conditions of the present time be? In a couple of previous papers (Williamson 1993, 1994) I have tried to ask whether and how the policies that could command a consensus in Washington have changed since 1989, but I am not sure this is a very interesting question or even that I got the answer right. Perhaps an alternative question, that of what I believe an ideal policy agenda should look like in 1996, will prove to be of more interest.

In order to facilitate comparison between the Williamson wish list and the 1989 Washington consensus, I shall now describe the major reforms in economic policy, broadly interpreted, that I judge that Latin America most needs currently, treating these reforms in an order similar to that of the 1989 presentation. I compare each wish list entry with what was said on the topic in the Washington consensus and discuss whether the differences stem from the changed circumstances in Latin America or from the fact that I am free here to present my own convictions rather than a lowest common denominator. The Washington consensus leads me straight to eight current topics; two further wish list topics relate to what I regard as additional reforms urgently needed in the region. (A summary version of the Washington consensus is presented in the appendix for the convenience of those who wish to consult it.)

High Savings

The first entry in the "Washington consensus" referred to the need to restore fiscal discipline. Latin America has made a remarkable transformation in this regard in the last decade, cutting the average budget deficit (including that of the Caribbean) by two-thirds, from 5.5 percent of GDP in 1988 to 1.8 percent of GDP in 1995.[4] But it is important for governments to avoid becoming complacent about their success in having transformed the fiscal situation; just as eternal vigilance is the price of liberty, so is perpetual Gladstonian housekeeping the cost of maintaining fiscal discipline.

At the same time, the 1994–95 Mexican crisis has shown us again (as the Chilean crisis did in 1982) that fiscal virtue is not enough: inadequate private savings can also (at best) throttle growth and (at worst) lead to economic collapse.[5] Hence, I choose to generalize the first heading of the Washington consensus to state the need for a high level of savings, which includes but is not limited to the need for fiscal discipline.

In fact, this topic reflects what is perhaps the most consistent theme in development economics: the need to mobilize savings in order to finance the investment that is required in order to modernize an economy. Saving is much lower in Latin America (some 19 percent of GDP in 1993) than in East Asia (around 34 percent of GDP). A recent ECLAC/CEPAL report estimates that achieving a 6 percent growth rate in the medium term would require a 28 percent investment ratio while generating savings of only 23 percent, leaving a 5.5 percent-of-GDP shortfall to be filled by some combination of foreign borrowing and increased savings rates (United Nations Economic Commission for Latin America and the Caribbean 1996, p. 51). The report argues, and I concur, that sustained foreign borrowing on that scale would risk a recurrence of financial crises such as the one that hit Mexico at the end of 1994. It follows that increased savings are imperative.

Continued fiscal virtue is important to achieving high savings, even though stronger budget positions do not translate one for one into higher savings. The stylized fact seems to be that some 50 percent to 60 percent of an increase in public saving is offset by a reduction in private saving (IMF 1995). But that still leaves the fiscal consolidation as having generated a useful 1.5 percent increase in the saving ratio—a gain that cannot be thrown away. At the same time, it would not be wise to rely on higher public-sector saving to generate the entire needed increase in saving; high taxes do have disincentive effects. The most promising way to raise private saving would seem to be to follow the Chilean model of switching from pay-as-you-go to funded pensions,[6] although it should be noted that for this approach to have a large impact on saving in the short run, it is necessary also to follow the Chilean model in financing the transition through taxes rather than through borrowing. A number of countries are in fact already following the Chilean

[4] Brazil's budget deficit also declined by two-thirds, but it remains a dangerous 4.5 percent of GDP.

[5] Like Nigel Lawson in Britain in 1988, the Mexican authorities appealed to their fiscal virtue to argue that the current-account deficit posed no policy problem, because its counterpart was private-sector investment that exceeded savings. But unfortunately, a large part of the deficit corresponded to lower savings rather than to higher investment, and that proved unsustainable. Had Mexican savings been higher, then one would have expected lower interest rates in Mexico and hence a more competitive exchange rate, with some combination of higher investment and lower current-account deficit, reflecting in turn some combination of higher exports and lower imports, and leading to less foreign debt.

[6] Chile did this in the context of privatizing pensions, but it can also be done through the public sector, as in Singapore.

example in privatizing their pension systems, although whether they are being equally tough on the financing of the transition is another matter.

Is the broadening in emphasis that I here recommend, from fiscal discipline to higher saving, a consequence of interim changes in Latin America or instead a result of my freedom to prescribe unfettered by the need to articulate a consensus view? The former. Fiscal discipline was an urgent necessity in 1989 in order to bring inflation under control, and the task of achieving it was daunting. The task of maintaining the newly established discipline is still crucial, but subsequent events have shown that fiscal discipline needs to be supplemented by an increase in private-sector saving.

Public-Expenditure Priorities

This heading is the same one that I used in the Washington consensus, and I see little need to modify what I wrote before, which was the following: "Expenditure should be redirected from politically sensitive areas—which typically receive more resources than their economic return can justify, such as administration, defense, indiscriminate subsidies, and white elephants—toward neglected fields with high economic returns and the potential to improve income distribution, such as primary health care and primary education, and infrastructure." In Williamson (1990) I concluded that less reform had been accomplished in this respect than in almost any of the other areas; although I cannot claim to be a specialist in this field, it is my impression that the same is true today.

Now that I am not constrained to reporting a consensus view, I would expand the areas of public expenditure that merit increased support to include effectively targeted social expenditures. It is surely no accident that one of the few Latin American countries to have been reporting an improved income distribution (admittedly starting from a poor base) is Colombia, which has greatly expanded its social spending in recent years.

Tax Reform

The Washington consensus urged cutting marginal tax rates so as to sharpen incentives, and it advocated compensating for the revenue loss this tax rate cut would entail by broadening the tax base and improving tax administration, which, I argued, could prevent any erosion of progressivity. I particularly recommended subjecting to taxation the interest income on assets held abroad ("flight capital"), an approach that would require both a major shift in tax principles in many countries (from the source principle to the destination principle) and the negotiation of a set of agreements for sharing tax information with the major destination countries for flight capital.

Tax reform, particularly in the form of the spread of the value-added tax, appears to have continued to progress in Latin America. In contrast, my pet proposal, for making an effort to tax the interest income on flight capital, is still in limbo, except that Mexico did sign a (rudimentary) agreement with the United States on the sharing of tax information.

Given that my new set of proposals is not constrained by the need to represent a consensus view, I would like to extend the specification of desirable tax reforms to include an effort to begin the process of building a tax system that would internalize environmental externalities. By now we are familiar with the idea that the reason that environmental considerations get short shrift in a market economy is that many of the environmental consequences of economic actions are spillovers that accrue to agents other than the primary actors. For instance, if I use my car rather than public transport, then congestion and pollution costs are imposed on third parties. Or, for instance, when a stretch of forest is clear-cut, then the consequential flooding and silting occur to those whose property lies downstream, the loss of scenic beauty affects anyone who visits the area, and the diminution of biodiversity is a global cost.

The standard antidote to externalities has long been a Pigovian tax. This approach is widely agreed to provide a justification for heavy taxes on gasoline. But in fact, congestion taxes, imposed by metering the use of road space and charging for it at higher rates when the roads are congested, would actually be more appropriate and are on the verge of being technically feasible. Imposing taxes that would internalize the spillover effects of land use is an even more challenging undertaking, but one for which the potential rewards are so substantial that it deserves to be tackled without delay. What seems to me to be needed is a variable-rate land tax, by which the tax rate would depend upon the environmental impact of the way the land was used. Pristine wilderness and land that harbors endangered species would be zero tax rated; land that was developed responsibly would carry a moderate tax rate; but abusive land use would be taxed at a penal rate. The benefits could be immense, in terms of allowing development to proceed in a way that will preserve the unique environments with which Latin America is so richly endowed.

So far as I am aware, no such variable-rate land use tax has yet been developed anywhere in the world. But until Curitiba showed the way, no city in the world had developed an urban transportation system that was at once people-friendly, environment-friendly, and affordable. Curitiba is now winning worldwide attention and admiration for its innovation. I see no reason why some Latin American country should not win similar plaudits for pioneering an eco-sensitive land tax.

Banking Supervision

The next item on the agenda of the Washington consensus was financial deregulation. Although the process is doubtless still incomplete, it has come a long way since 1989. But the priority in this area has changed. As we learned during the IDB's excellent October 1995 conference on banking crises, financial deregulation has not been accompanied by the development of adequate banking supervision, as a result of which the region has been afflicted by a series of banking crises, most notably in Argentina, Mexico, and Venezuela.

The financial sector provides the perfect context to illustrate the governmental role change that needs to accompany economic liberalization. Financial liberalization involves getting the state out of the business of deciding who should receive credit, but it does not mean that the state can wash its hands of responsibility for the financial sector. On the contrary, as is now widely recognized, financial liberalization demands a strengthening of prudential supervision if the risk of financial crises is to be contained: a state too weak to supervise the financial system properly will jeopardize the functioning of the market. Unfortunately, this reality was not adequately recognized in Latin America, with the result that the region suffered a series of crises. Remedying that weakness needs to be the next priority.

A Competitive Exchange Rate

The fifth heading in the Washington consensus referred to the need for an exchange rate sufficiently competitive to nurture a rapid growth in nontraditional exports. As I have already confessed (footnote 3), I have decided that this is the one topic on which I gave a seriously misleading summary of Washington opinion as of 1989, for there certainly existed no real unanimity on the need to manage the exchange rate to achieve an adequate level of competitiveness as opposed to either fixing it so that it could provide a nominal anchor or floating it so as to let the market determine the outcome. I fear that I allowed myself to be carried away by wishful thinking. Since I am no longer under an obligation to try to report a consensus view, however, I can reinstate my original formulation with a clear conscience.

Latin American countries have pursued widely differing exchange rate policies in the past few years. Chile and Colombia provide a model in having used a wide crawling band in order to maintain a competitive exchange rate despite strong pressures from capital inflows (Williamson 1996). Brazil has de facto done something fairly similar, although less formalized and with a narrower band. Venezuela, after an unfortunate period in which it attempted to revert to the adjustable peg and got itself back into the worst practices of foreign-exchange rationing and multiple exchange rates, decided to liberalize and float its exchange rate and has recently moved on to a crawling band. In contrast, Peru has a floating exchange rate, and at the other extreme, Argentina has a rigidly fixed rate backed up by a currency board. Mexico was also closer to this latter model prior to its crisis, despite having a slowly widening band, because it was attempting to use the exchange rate as a nominal anchor in order to reduce inflation rapidly. My recommendation is to follow the example set by Chile and Colombia.

Trade Liberalization

The Washington consensus recommended rapid elimination of quantitative restrictions on imports, followed by the progressive reduction of tariffs until tariff levels reached a uniform low rate in the range of 10 percent to 20 percent. I noted that there existed differences of opinion about the speed with which the tariff reduction should take place and about whether the pace of trade liberalization should be independent of macroeconomic conditions or whether an adverse macroeconomic environment (low growth combined with large payments deficits) could justify delay. Although it was not stated explicitly, the discussion clearly referred to unilateral liberalization.

Latin America has progressed a long way since 1989 in terms of import liberalization, and there have even been occasions (for example, in Mexico) in which I personally would have welcomed some slowdown in trade liberalization's pace, because of adverse macroeconomic conditions. By and large, it may well be that—apart from spikes for things like automobiles—the region has now reached the tariff range of 10 percent to 20 percent. That achievement does not mean that the process of trade liberalization should stop. But those last few percentage points of remaining tariffs do not create major distortions, and their eventual strategic removal can be a useful bargaining counter in reducing other countries' tariffs and thus in improving market access for one's own exports (which is also important to national welfare, however reluctant some trade economists are to concede the point). It is thus a perfectly sensible strategy to have shifted in recent years from unilateral tariff reduction to the construction of regional free-trade arrangements like Mercosur, NAFTA, and the various bilateral agreements. The long-term dream of a Western Hemisphere Free-Trade Area, in the context of continuing liberalization in world trade arrangements, is the logical culmination of this process.

The next heading of the Washington consensus referred to the desirability of an analogous liberalization of the rules restricting foreign direct investment. This reform seems to have been accomplished everywhere, and accordingly, I drop that 1989 heading from my revised agenda.

A Competitive Economy

The Washington consensus went on to urge privatization and deregulation, both of which (especially privatization) have made substantial (if uneven) progress in Latin America in the last few years. Unfortunately, these reforms have not always been implemented in a manner designed to promote competition. It is not clear how much welfare gain can be expected from replacing a state monopoly with a private monopoly: incentives to efficiency may be strengthened, but so is the incentive to exploit monopoly power.

I have now merged privatization and deregulation into one new heading—namely, a competitive economy—chosen in order to emphasize what is, or at least ought to be, the main logic underlying both of them, which is to subject all enterprises to the disciplines of competition in the context of hard budget constraints. Privatization is not primarily about improving the fiscal situation, but about changing the incentives that firms face so as to improve their efficiency. And the deregulation that is needed is that of rules that impede entry of new firms and that restrict competition, not (as Dan Quayle seemed to think) the gutting of regulations that had been designed to ensure safety, to preserve the environment, or to safeguard the financial system. The new heading also draws attention to the need to ensure that an adequate official (anti-trust) policy on competition is in place.

The deregulation that has been undertaken so far has in most cases bypassed the labor market. This trend may be politically understandable, because the beneficiaries of labor market regulations tend to be the most politically active element of those who think of themselves as underprivileged, but the trend is also unfortunate, since the beneficiaries are far from being the most underprivileged element of society and their gains come primarily at the expense of those even worse off. For instance, restrictions on firing generally cost more jobs than they save, but the jobs saved are those of people who have jobs that they know are worth saving, whereas those who do not get the jobs that are not created because of the restrictions are the politically impotent unemployed. Although there may exist a case for a modest minimum wage, since a higher wage for those on low pay may be worth the risking of a limited number of jobs, most other labor restrictions should probably go.

Property Rights

The last element in the Washington consensus (somewhat ignored as yet) referred to the need to make secure and well-defined property rights available to all, including the informal sector, at reasonable cost. It was inspired by the writing of Hernando de Soto (1989) but reflected also the impact of the Chicago law and economics school. Apart from Peru since 1990 and one or two of the Central American countries, I am not aware that property rights constitute a cause that has made much progress. Meanwhile, the research on the economics of transition has identified this as an issue of fundamental importance. In the most basic terms, it is pointless to expect people to invest effort in working hard, in saving and investing, and in building up their skills unless they have a reasonable assurance of being able to benefit from the bulk of the fruits of their efforts.

One specific aspect of property rights, aiming at a less uneven distribution of rural property, has come back on the policy agenda in Brazil, at least in a modest way. Land reform seems to me entirely consistent with an agenda that emphasizes the importance of property rights, and it can be expected to contribute to greater equity.

Institution Building

My self-imposed rules now give me two degrees of freedom with respect to additional topics to include in the new agenda. I start by endorsing the thesis advanced by Moisés Naím (1995), that the next generation of Latin American reforms is going to demand a major effort at building, or in some cases rebuilding, institutions. Examples cited by Naím were the building of equivalents to the U.S. Securities and Exchange Commission, the organizing of well targeted social programs to compensate the poor, and the providing of adequate supervision of the banking system. I have already endorsed the latter and have also indicated my sympathy for greater social spending, which certainly needs to be well focused and therefore may well demand institutional innovation.

The general point is that the focus of policy needs to shift from cutting back a state that had become bloated to strengthening a number of key state institutions the efficient functioning of which is important for rapid and/or equitable growth. The bodies to be strengthened are typically small, elite institutions—not large bureaucracies, many of which may still merit drastic pruning. My own list of the institutions that need to be nurtured would start off with an independent central bank, which, following the examples set by Chile and Colombia, might advantageously be given responsibility for exchange rate policy as well as monetary policy. Fiscal policy is no less deserving of an adequate institutional underpinning, so a budget office should be added to the list (Hausmann and Eichengreen 1996); an issue currently salient in several Latin American countries is decentralization, the fiscal implications of which have proved particularly troublesome. Then the courts surely need attention, inter alia to strengthen the protection of property rights as discussed earlier, which again is likely to include a need for greater independence from the executive power.

I would not choose to include any sort of planning ministry or industry ministry on the list. The debate is still unresolved on whether East Asian countries have grown so impressively because of or despite their industrial policies, but one thing that does seem clear is that in order to benefit from an industrial policy, a country must have an unusually competent, dedicated, and uncorrupt civil service. I doubt that many, and perhaps any, Latin American countries would currently qualify on that count. A much better idea for activist policies in the industrial field has recently been promoted by Joseph Ramos (1996), who commends the Chilean creation of productivity missions modeled on those that European countries sent to North America as part of the Marshall Plan. His account suggests that these missions, which are composed of a cross section of industry representatives and which visit firms employing best-practice technology in a range of countries, are proving highly cost-effective in raising industrial productivity. The modest cost of creating an agency to sponsor such missions makes an approach like this eminently worthwhile.

Improved Education

The consensus section on reordering public-expenditure priorities mentioned education as being an area in which expenditure cuts should be avoided, but such a brief mention hardly reflects education's centrality to the future of Latin America. I take this as my second additional topic to include on the new agenda.

It can be argued that an educated labor force is the most fundamental prerequisite for a country's rapid development—more important even than savings, foreign exchange, and infrastructure, which are to an important extent endogenous. If there already exists an educated labor force capable of producing goods for the world market once any needed capital or infrastructure is in place, then the country benefits, because capital or infrastructure can be supplied far more quickly in a country than an uneducated labor force could have been trained. This is the conventional explanation for why Europe recovered after World War II far more quickly than poor countries were able to develop, and it is surely correct.

Nor are the benefits of a well-educated labor force restricted to boosting the economy's growth prospects. Poor education tends to mean that a large part of each age cohort receives very little education, rather than that almost no one gets a first-rate university education. The consequence is to deprive a large part of the population of all age groups of the ability to do any jobs other than the most menial, and thus to earn any wage more than the minimal. Poor education tends also to impact disproportionately on girls, resulting inter alia in continued high birth rates and consequential pressures on the environment. Better education would be good for growth, for income distribution, and for the environment. Indeed, it would directly promote overall human development quite aside from the economic benefits that one can expect.

Education has not been a strong point of Latin America's performance in recent years. The quality of public education has declined, and spending in a number of countries is strongly biased toward providing free university education for those who get far enough to benefit from it (which tends to be those whose parents can afford private schooling). There is a need both to spend more and to refocus expenditure on primary and secondary schooling. Those lucky enough to get to university could perfectly well be expected to finance themselves through student loans. This would be a strongly egalitarian reform, even though it would do no more than eliminate privileges that perpetuate inequality.

Summary

The new agenda that I have suggested may be summarized as follows:

- increase saving by (inter alia) maintaining fiscal discipline
- reorient public expenditure toward (inter alia) well-directed social expenditure
- reform the tax system by (inter alia) introducing an eco-sensitive land tax
- strengthen banking supervision
- maintain a competitive exchange rate, abandoning both floating and the use of the exchange rate as a nominal anchor
- pursue intraregional trade liberalization
- build a competitive market economy by (inter alia) privatizing and deregulating (including the labor market)
- make well-defined property rights available to all
- build key institutions such as independent central banks, strong budget offices, independent and incorruptible judiciaries, and agencies to sponsor productivity missions
- increase educational spending and redirect it toward primary and secondary levels

In his article in the present volume, Gert Rosenthal identifies the unresolved problems facing Latin America as the following: restoring growth, increasing employment, and reducing inequality. Would the Williamson wish list agenda suffice to achieve those objectives? I believe so. Underlying this new agenda is a conviction that enterprise will flourish when society has organized itself to provide both macroeconomic stability and the social and physical infrastructure of a market economy and when society gives equitably educated people a chance to insert themselves into the world economy (with no need for governments or conferences to debate exactly how they should be inserted). That outcome requires the sobriety for consistently pursuing best-practice and well-tested[7]

---

[7] With the exception of the innovative eco-sensitive land tax.

ideas such as those just presented. The flourishing of enterprise will then restore growth; in turn, without major distortions like import substitution, one can expect this growth to expand employment; and this expanding employment, allied with replacement of the education system's inegalitarian bias with a more level playing field and with a pro-egalitarian bias in social policy, will ultimately help Latin America shed its unwholesome reputation as home to the most uneven income distributions in the world.

The new agenda is not inspired by one single big idea, like capital formation, or import substitution, or *dependencia*, or even neoliberalism, such as those that intellectuals like to see at the core of policy agendas.[8] But a point worth reflecting on is that East Asia had no collective world view that inspired its own stunning success in modernization in recent decades. That region's freedom from ideological baggage allowed it to implement selected common sense bits of the Washington consensus (like maintaining fiscal discipline and competitive exchange rates), while on a few of the items (notably financial liberalization, import liberalization, and deregulation) the region's policy was in places pretty illiberal but still pragmatic. East Asia is now busy trying to invent a formal worldview to schematize what it accomplished, but the fact is that, on all the traditional ideological issues like planning and the role of the state and the welcoming of multinationals, there exists no single monolithic East Asian model. So if my revised agenda strikes some as eclectic rather than ideological, I hope that this quality will commend it rather than stigmatize it.

---

[8] Any Latin American who is inclined to feel embarrassed at the region's past embrace of such slogans might feel reassured to reflect that none of them, except perhaps *dependencia,* was as demonstrably wrong as the doctrine that flourishes to their north under the name of supply side economics, which claims that tax cuts are a panacea for achieving growth.

REFERENCES

Balassa, Bela, Gerardo M. Bueno, Pedro-Pablo Kuczynski, and Mario Henrique Simonsen. *Toward Renewed Economic Growth in Latin America.* Mexico City: El Colegio de México; Washington: Institute for International Economics; and Rio de Janeiro: Fundação Getúlio Vargas, 1986.

de Soto, Hernando. *The Other Path: The Invisible Revolution in the Third World.* New York: Harper and Row, 1989.

Hausmann, Ricardo, and Barry Eichengreen. "Reforming Budgetary Institutions in Latin America" (mimeo). 1996.

International Monetary Fund. *World Economic Outlook.* Washington, D.C.: IMF. May 1995.

Naím, Moisés. "Latin America the Morning After." *Foreign Affairs* (July/August 1995).

Ramos, Joseph. "Política Industrial y Competitividad en Economías Abiertas." Paper presented to an IDB Conference. June 6, 1996.

Simonsen, Mario Henrique. *Ensaios Analíticos.* Rio de Janeiro: Editora da Fundação Getúlio Vargas, 1994.

Toye, John. Comment on paper by John Williamson in J. Williamson, ed. *The Political Economy of Policy Reform.* Washington, D.C.: Institute for International Economics, 1994.

United Nations Economic Commission for Latin America and the Caribbean. *Strengthening Development: The Interplay of Macro- and Microeconomics.* Santiago: CEPAL/ECLAC, 1996.

Williamson, John. *Latin American Adjustment: How Much Has Happened?* Washington, D.C.: Institute for International Economics, 1990.

_____ "The Emergent Development Policy Consensus: The Market-Oriented Model." Paper presented to a conference on "Sustainable Development with Equity in the 1990s" at the University of Wisconsin at Madison. 1993.

_____ "Latin American Reform and the Washington Consensus." Paper presented to a conference on "Brazil and the New World Order" at UERJ in Rio de Janeiro. 1994.

_____ *The Crawling Band as an Exchange Rate Regime: Lessons from Chile, Colombia, and Israel.* Washington, D.C.: Institute for International Economics, 1996.

APPENDIX
A Summary of the 1989 Washington Consensus

• **Fiscal Discipline.** Budget deficits—properly measured to include provincial governments, state enterprises, and the central bank—should be small enough to be financed without recourse to the inflation tax. This size typically implies a primary surplus (that is, before adding debt service to expenditure) of several percent of GDP, as well as an operational deficit (that is, the deficit disregarding that part of the interest bill that simply compensates for inflation) of no more than about 2 percent of GDP.

- **Public-Expenditure Priorities.** Expenditure should be redirected from politically sensitive areas—which typically receive more resources than their economic return can justify, such as administration, defense, indiscriminate subsidies, and white elephants—toward neglected fields with high economic returns and the potential to improve income distribution, such as primary healthcare, primary education, and infrastructure.
- **Tax Reform.** Tax reform involves broadening the tax base and cutting marginal tax rates. The aim is to sharpen incentives and improve horizontal equity without lowering realized progressivity. Improved tax administration (including subjecting interest income on assets held abroad— "flight capital"—to taxation) is an important aspect of broadening the base in the Latin context.
- **Financial Liberalization.** The ultimate objective of financial liberalization is market-determined interest rates, but experience has shown that, under conditions of a chronic lack of confidence, market-determined rates can be so high as to threaten the financial solvency of productive enterprises and government. Under that circumstance, a sensible interim objective is the abolition of preferential interest rates for privileged borrowers and achievement of a moderately positive real interest rate.
- **Exchange Rates.** Countries need a unified (at least for trade transactions) exchange rate set at a level sufficiently competitive to induce a rapid growth in nontraditional exports and managed so as to ensure exporters that this competitiveness will be maintained in the future.
- **Trade Liberalization.** Quantitative trade restrictions should be rapidly replaced by tariffs, and these should be progressively reduced until a uniform low tariff in the range of 10 percent (or at most around 20 percent) is achieved. There exists, however, some disagreement about the speed with which tariffs should be reduced (with recommendations falling in a band between 3 and 10 years) and about whether it is advisable to slow down the process of trade liberalization when macroeconomic conditions are adverse (recession and payments deficit).
- **Foreign Direct Investment.** Barriers impeding the entry of foreign firms should be abolished; foreign and domestic firms should be allowed to compete on equal terms.
- **Privatization.** State enterprises should be privatized.
- **Deregulation.** Governments should abolish regulations that impede the entry of new firms or that restrict competition, and then should ensure that all regulations are justified by such criteria as safety, environmental protection, or prudential supervision of financial institutions.
- **Property Rights.** The legal system should provide secure property rights without excessive costs and should make such rights available to the informal sector.

Frances Stewart[1] on
John Williamson and the Washington Consensus Revisited

The debate about the Washington consensus (WC) is a debate about process—who makes policy, the legitimacy of the process and the right to freedom of thought. It is also a debate about content—whether the contents of the WC are right in themselves ever, for all countries, for all times, sufficient or necessary conditions of development, and so on. There exist, of course, some overlap between the two debates: if the content of the policies were right for all time and as well established as the rotundity of the earth, then the debate about process would have less legitimacy, even though process would still be a matter of concern, since democratic principles and human rights justify people's making wrong as well as right decisions. In the present commentary I shall differentiate between the two, discussing first process, then content.

Process

When John Williamson introduced the term "Washington consensus" in the late 1980s, and used it to describe what he suggested were Latin American governments' agreed economic policies, he delighted critics and confounded supporters, not so much for the content of the WC package, as for its name. It seemed to critics that in using this name, Williamson was coming clean about who made policy in the late twentieth century—not governments, but Washington. "Washington" was a very good term, as it embraced not only the IMF and World Bank but also these institutions' less-than-shadowy master—the U.S. Government—and behind it, that governments own shadowy masters, namely, the American economics profession and Western business interests.

In his current presentation, Williamson tries to "disarm his critics" in this respect by acknowledging this charge. Yet he does not try to refute it: he did use the term Washington consensus and not the more natural one, Latin American consensus, to describe the agreed set of policies, and he included only policies that he "judged could command a consensus in Washington." Indeed, his acknowledged aim was to convince Washington that Latin American governments had come to accept Washington-approved policies.

The 1980s can be seen as a prolonged battle about policymaking in Latin America. From the 1950s to the end of the 1970s, as is well known, most governments followed

---

[1] University of Oxford. I am grateful for helpful comments from Rosemary Thorp on an earlier draft.

protectionist and state-centered policies, often combined with fiscal deficits, low interest rates, and the like. The intellectual justification of these policies came partly from Keynesian economics, but that justification was also in part home grown under the strong influence of Prebisch, ECLAC and *dependencia* thinking. In the 1980s, Washington made a concerted effort to shift policies toward monetarist, market-oriented, open, noninterventionist policies—that is, toward WC policies. The debt situation and Latin America's desperate need for finance gave Washington huge leverage. There's no question that Williamson was right: there was a revolution in policymaking in Latin America in the 1980s, and the WC package was broadly accepted, although the pace and completeness of the acceptance varied from country to country.

The process was basically that of Washington institutions determining what they considered the right policies were and then imposing their views on Latin America, and also on other countries, through policy conditionality, which was pervasive in the 1980s.[2] Intellectual support for the new policies did also come from within Latin America, as cohorts of newly trained PhDs from U.S. economics departments returned to high positions in their countries' civil services. But these, too, were in a sense the product (if via a more subtle route) of Washington. The students had generally received generous scholarships from the United States to learn and internalize the consensus—just as in the colonial era, promising young Indians, Moroccans, and others were given scholarships in Oxford, Cambridge, and Paris.

The force of the conditionality of the IMF and World Bank was reinforced by bilateral donors and private-sector financial realities; Paris Club rescheduling depended on IMF and World Bank approval, and private sector debt agreements similarly required the IFI stamp of approval. More recently, as countries have become dependent on financial markets, WC policies of the most orthodox kind are becoming essential to keeping the markets happy.

The process raises serious questions about who determines policies in Latin America. Democratically elected governments are free to adopt WC policies: they may also choose how far and fast they go in certain directions, and then may add on policies not included in the consensus. But are they really free to adopt alternative packages? To be Keynesian? Protectionist? Populist? To nationalize rather than privatize? The answer is yes, if they don't mind becoming international pariahs; no, if they want to borrow from the IMF/World Bank, reschedule their debt, or participate in financial markets. Washington rules, OK. In the 1980s, the direct origin of this orthodoxy was the institutions on 18th and 19th streets. Now, even if the IMF and the World Bank disappeared, the world's financial markets would still probably require a very similar set of policies on the part of participating countries. The success of the World Bank in opening up economies to global financial markets has let out of the bottle a genie that is stronger than Washington and

---

[2] Seventeen Latin American and Caribbean countries had IMF programs in the 1980s for more than two years (of which five countries had programs for more than five years); 12 countries had World Bank structural adjustment programs for more than two years.

to which Washington itself must now bow. Moreover, this genie is more sinister than Washington. When Washington was responsible, it lay down an explicit policy package (WC), clearly defined and open to debate (even if only one side was permitted to win that debate). Occasionally, at least verbally, Washington even made concessions to its critics— for instance, by focusing on poverty alleviation as well as on adjustment. But the requirements of financial markets are less clear and are not open to rational debate, as there is no one to debate with, only financial analysts who claim to know what "the market" thinks and how it will react. The World Bank has been replaced by market consensus (MC), which is less liberal and less reasonable than Williamson's WC, and much less so than the amended version of the WC that he presents in this volume.

There exists only one way for countries to avoid both WC and MC (and even here the gate is narrowing). That is by being basically independent of Washington and of international markets. This is what the successful East Asian countries achieved, and it gave them leeway to adopt a set of policies that in important respects differed from the WC/MC and that were, of course, spectacularly successful. This brings me to the content of the WC.

Content

We should start with objectives: Gert Rosenthal in the present volume has suggested that the three basic economic-policy objectives for Latin America should be the restoration of growth, the expansion of employment, and the reduction of inequality. I broadly agree, although I would prefer to see sustained human development as the central objective, for which economic growth, higher employment, and reduced inequality are means, as is the environmental sustainability of policies. Nevertheless, the Rosenthal objectives have the great merits of transparency and measurability, so I'm happy to go along with the Rosenthal Consensus (RC).

In general, the WC policies have not been successful in bringing about the RC objectives. Growth has been restored in some countries, but on a rather fragile basis, heavily dependent on financial inflows. Meanwhile, inequality of primary income has in fact worsened (see table 2.1). The region's tax reforms have reduced the redistributive potential of the state, so that actually and potentially, secondary distribution has also worsened. Formal-sector employment has tended to be sluggish, increasing much less than proportionately with growth. Hence, it seems that the WC is not the perfect solution to the economic problems of the region (although some might claim that this is because that consensus has not been fully adopted). East Asia (and now Southeast Asia) seems to have done much better on all three objectives—growth, employment, and equality. Yet in important respects East Asia did not follow WC. Most of my disagreements with the WC policy package consist of policies that were adopted by these successful economies. The following eight points are among the major differences.

First, domestic, not foreign, savings have led in East Asia, and total savings and investment have been very high. The initial WC included governmental financial discipline (that is, the reduction of government dissavings) but had nothing to say about private

TABLE 2.1. Income Distribution in Latin America over the 1980s

Country	Gini around 1980	Gini around 1989
Argentina (metro)	0.408	0.486
Bolivia (urban)	0.516 (86)	0.525
Brazil	0.594	0.633
Chile (urban)	0.585	0.532
Costa Rica	0.475	0.460
Guatemala	0.579 (86/7)	0.595
Honduras	0.549 (86)	0.591
Mexico	0.506 (84)	0.550
Panama	0.488	0.565
Paraguay (metro)	0.450 (83)	0.398
Uruguay	0.436	0.424
Venezuela	0.428	0.441

Source: Psacharopoulos et al., 1993; Graham, 1994

savings beyond the raising of interest rates. It is now well established that this approach does not increase total savings. Moreover, private investment tended to be depressed by the cutbacks in government investment through the resulting loss of the crowding-in effect. Investment may also have been discouraged by the high interest rates. The need for high domestic savings is included by Williamson in his new consensus (NC). His policy proposal, a new way of funding pensions, may achieve the objective, but this tactic is not how the Asian countries raised savings. More research is needed on how they achieved such high voluntary household savings.

Moreover, what is needed in addition to savings is very high levels of investment, an area regarding which the old WC had nothing to suggest. The NC implies that investment would automatically increase with savings, but many believe that things are more likely to be the other way around and that it is therefore necessary to find an active way of raising investment.

Second, land reform played a key role early on in Taiwan and Korea, leading to low inequality at the outset and reducing the burden of luxury consumption, in strong contrast to the situation in Latin America. Land reform is also accepted in the NC but was not part of the WC. In any case, even if accepted and put into practice, land reform would not now solve the problem of inequality in Latin America because land ownership patterns are no longer the dominant source of this inequality. Progressive taxation, ruled out by WC and even more firmly by MC, is essential.

Third, high levels and high quality of education were an essential part of the Asian experience. This area was almost entirely omitted from WC, which indeed led to worsening human resources through the public-expenditure cuts of the 1980s. The need for good education forms part of Williamson's NC.

Fourth, the Asian success was based largely on growth of labor-intensive manufactures. One key was low exchange rates. Williamson now says that although he included this in the 1989 WC, it was wrongly included as not all countries adopted it and Washington, if not Williamson, was ambiguous about it. It is now part of his NC.

Fifth, another important element in East Asia that facilitated labor-intensive exports was that region's very low wage costs initially, based on low opportunity costs of labor, arising from the relatively weak natural-resource base. This situation cannot be duplicated in Latin America, where the basic factor endowment is different. Hence, pursuing comparative advantage in Latin America is likely to lead to a different, more resource-based set of exports, which may be less labor absorbing, thus posing problems for the employment objective of RC. If export success is to be achieved in Latin American manufacturing, it will need to be in higher-skill, high-wage activities—again underlining the need for education to be given first priority. It also points to the need for industrial policies to promote this type of high-skill, high-wage industry. This difference in patterns of comparative advantage is likely to make employment of the unskilled more of a chronic problem in Latin America than in Asia.

Sixth, the East Asian countries did not follow the noninterventionist, import-liberalizing package embodied in WC and NC. It has now been well established by Pack and Westphal, Amsden, Wade, Lall, and others that the East Asian governments adopted active policies to promote particular industries. These interventions involved the use of much-hated-by-WC subsidized credit, the similarly despised import protection, and even the beyond-the-pale public ownership. Many of the industries successfully promoted were ones that went against the existing comparative advantage of the countries (for instance, steel, shipbuilding, cars) and that had heavy learning economies. These governments did not pick winners, which any betting person will tell you is very difficult anyway; rather, they actually created winners, by choosing industries to promote that made sense from the point of view of international markets, skill requirements, and the like. They also used government policy to support the necessary physical, scientific, and technical infrastructure. The Asian policies differed from the import substitution policies that Latin America and other regions had adopted less successfully in the 1960s and 1970s in that the former were much more selective and were designed not to bring about import substitution but eventually (once the learning period was over) export substitution; they were intended to be temporary and to be abandoned after a certain period, whether this meant letting the successfully nurtured industry fly on its own or aborting failures.

This particular set of Asian policies is the one that is most dramatically different from those of WC. Far from being associated with the low across-the-board levels of protection that form part of WC and NC, they involved high levels of protection/promotion for a few selected industries. It is not clear how easy these policies are to replicate. There's a lot of talk that only certain governments are, for some reason, capable of carrying them out, but there is no convincing analysis of why this should be so. Clearly, selective protection/promotion policies cannot be ruled out dogmatically as "wrong" as in the WC and also NC. For Latin America, given the resource endowment noted earlier, it is of greater importance to break into moderately high-skill/high-scale global industries, where an initial learning period may be essential. Hence, the policies may be even more relevant to Latin America, than to Asian countries, where factor costs in many cases permit successful expansion of labor-intensive exports that have a relatively short learning period.

Seventh, in his NC, Williamson points to the need for institutional development, a factor not included in the WC. I totally agree with him. (This, too, was part of the East Asian story). The buildup of a high-quality, prestigious civil service motivated by trust is a very difficult, but important, requirement of successful development. As Williamson points out, the area of official regulation—not just financial but also to avoid abuses of private monopolies, to protect the environment, and to promote safety—has become of much greater importance in the more market-oriented and privatized economies. Other institutions that need to be developed and improved are those of local government and those related to research and development, technology transfer, and credit for the low-income sector of the population. The development of all these institutions will work well only if the people involved are motivated not just by market incentives (or put crudely, money) but also by public interest, a pride in their work, the desire for respect, and other ideals. Yet the philosophy of WC, and even more MC, is against this type of motivation.

Eight, I come finally to the other NC add-on, but one that is also shared by the Washington institutions: targeted social expenditures. Williamson rehearses the well-known arguments, that "targeting" avoids wasting money on the well-off and thereby increases resources for the target population. But targeting of this kind in fact does not work: it is almost always as much a mirage as the television pictures of Patriot missiles in the Gulf War bringing down Scud missiles without causing any human suffering. When put into practice, such targeting has a number of flaws: (a) it misses many of the population in poverty because they do not come forward or do not fit the targeting criterion (for instance, in Jamaica, often cited as a successful example of targeting, half the poor population was omitted[3]); (b) the "undeserving" still manage to get around their intended exclusion (in Sri Lanka, one third of the beneficiaries of the targeted subsidies were above the poverty line); c) the poor do not benefit from greater resources per person, as suggested by advocates, because invariably, schemes that replace general with targeted subsidies reduce total expenditures, and benefits per recipient typically fall; and (d) the targeted schemes have little political support, as they benefit only a minority, and as a result they are normally reduced in value or withdrawn after a short period. Well-designed general subsidies are usually preferable to targeted ones, from the point of view of getting resources to those in need on a sustained basis. Even when some significant proportion of the benefits of general subsidies goes to those above the poverty line, such subsidies are invariably more progressive than the original income distribution, and they confer genuine benefits on the poor. Moreover, the benefits received by the undeserving can readily be reclaimed by additional progressive taxation.[4]

---

[3] See Grosh 1992.
[4] See Cornia and Stewart 1993, where these arguments are elaborated.

My strong objection to the advocacy of targeted social expenditures is that such advocacy tends to be an excuse for avoiding the real issue, which is that the WC package frequently fails to create adequate employment or to incorporate the poor. This failure needs to be centrally acknowledged and a solution sought. Such a solution is likely to involve public-employment schemes, low-income credit, land reform, the support of nonagricultural employment opportunities, and a push toward industrialization. Some progressive taxation (indirect and direct) will be needed to finance this solution and also to provide the universal education and health services essential for human development, inequality reductions, and economic success.

Conclusion

The use of the term "consensus" implies general agreement; it carries the further implication that the agreement derives from the fact that the correct solution has been identified. The word is often used by those who would like their own views to be accepted. When Williamson first used the term WC, he implied that everyone agreed with Washington, and further that this agreement indicated that Washington was right. The Latin American governments did, by 1989, largely accept the WC policies, often because of the strong conditionalities imposed by public and private financiers. But this acceptance does not imply that the WC was right. Williamson himself has amended the package in a number of ways in his present paper, with most of which I agree. There are other amendments I would make that are not in the NC.

But my views—or even Williamson's—are not important. What is important is to consider what the appropriate policies are in the light of the countries' own objectives and how policies work in practice. In this light, WC has not done well. The package may have done better than the policies it replaced, in the circumstances of the 1980s. But complacency about having found the solution is not justified. Other policies, as exemplified by those adopted by East Asian countries, have a better record, although some might not work in the different circumstances of Latin America and the 1990s. Hence, the search needs to go on. The idea that a consensus has been reached is objectionable because it suggests that we know and agree on what is the best path. We neither know nor agree.

REFERENCES

Amsden, A. *Asia's Next Giant.* Oxford: OUP, 1989.

Cornia, G.A., and F. Stewart. "Two Errors of Targeting." *Journal of International Development* 5,4 (1993): 459-96.

Graham, C. *Safety Nets, Politics and the Poor: Transitions to Market Economies.* Washington, D.C.: Brookings Institution, 1994.

Grosh, M.E. "The Jamaican Food Stamps Program: A Case Study In Targeting." *Food Policy* 17, 1 (1992): 23-40.

Lall, S. "Industrial Policy: The Role of Government in Promoting Industrial and Technological Development." *UNCTAD Review* (1994): 65-89.

Pack, H., and L. Westphal. "Industrial Strategy and Technological Change: Theory vs. Reality." *Journal of Development Economics*, 22 (1986): 87-128.

Psacharopoulos, G., et al. *Poverty and Income Distribution in Latin America: The Story of the 1980s.* Washington, D.C.: World Bank, 1993.

Wade, R. *Governing the Market.* Princeton: Princeton University Press, 1990.

Bishnodat Persaud[1] on

The Washington
Consensus Revisited

General Observations

I am very much in the mold of John Williamson in the orientation of my thinking. As a commentator on his paper, I find this similarity to be not a bad thing, since there is perhaps more consensus and convergence in development thinking today than ever before, which provides a better chance for constructive engagement and advance in our economic discourse. Like John Williamson, I am eclectic in my approach, although the strong underlying emphasis I give to markets and to the private sector might suggest to many that my approach borders on the ideological.

Let us begin with the view that the thinking on development issues is not where it was even ten years ago. And I doubt that the trend has run its course. Many of us now accept a smaller role for the state in general and almost no role for it in running business enterprises. Thinking has perhaps contributed less to this evolution than have certain crisis-induced imperatives. Yet, I still detect a strong ideological influence when I see the emphasis given in some of the literature to market failures, in defense of a continuing substantial role for intervention, when equally obvious, if not more so, is evidence of failures in state management, especially in conditions of underdevelopment.

There is truth in the simple proposition that in the pursuit of economic efficiency, the discipline imposed by competitive markets cannot be matched in the public sector; even where democratic controls function well, strong disciplines are difficult to impose in the public sector and are easily subverted, especially in conditions of underdevelopment. This proposition leads to the conclusion, probably controversial, that a strong market orientation is even more relevant to the circumstances of developing countries, notwithstanding the fact that markets operate better in the improved framework that good public-sector management could provide.

John Williamson's 1989 Washington consensus made an important contribution in documenting the change that had taken place in Latin American economic thinking and the extent to which there existed support for market-friendly reform policies. These policies do not have to coincide with those coming from the Washington-based institutions. The World Bank may have development as its objective, but Latin American and Caribbean institutions themselves and their staff and management tend to have their own

---

[1] University of the West Indies.

interests, which could intervene. I suspect that this basic trend of change in development thinking in Latin America has continued and that if John Williamson were to repeat his survey, he would find even wider support.

It is an insult to these reform economists that this change in thinking should be seen as a kind of brainwashing from Washington and from the U.S. universities at which they had their training. These economists have learned on their own from government intervention's massive failures when states tried to force the pace of industrialization, to undertake industrial programming, to promote import substitution, to supply services in ways totally unrelated to demand, to own basic industries, to finance institutions, to limit foreign investment and ownership, and to expand public employment. These policies have encouraged capital flight, the migration of skills, food shortages, corruption, tax evasion, repression of financial-sector development, and the existence of illegal activities.

As we examine the success of intervention policies beyond those that would be accepted as market friendly, let us not lose sight of the whole history of the efforts in developing countries to establish mixed economies and the heavy costs such efforts have imposed.

We need to take into account the fact that only a small number of countries have made a success of some of these intervention policies. Import substitution policies have failed in most other countries. They tend not to foster export orientation but actually to be adverse to it. In my part of the world—the Caribbean with small economies—the limitations of strong import substitution policies are now widely recognized and a return to them is most unlikely. Even if East Asian experience indicates the possibility of valuable use of these policies in a limited and targeted way, managing them in such a way will not be easy for many other countries. But the greater constraint is the changed world circumstances and the difficulty of gaining tolerance to such policies and avoiding retaliation in the context of trade liberalization, in which developing countries have a strong interest and are now deliberately more directly involved through the World Trade Organization (WTO). Any significant resort to import controls by major developing countries could endanger the whole international trading system.

Other policies also raise questions of their wider relevance. Countries sensitive to issues of income and wealth distribution may not find Japanese encouragement to cartelization or Korean assistance for the enlargement of family businesses to be attractive.

Most likely, the recent shift to reform policies in developing countries does not represent just one more policy shift in an endless cycle of policy changes. Economic performance in developing countries relates strongly to the availability of proven policies or conversely, to the political failure to adopt and implement such policies because of the particular political circumstances of individual countries. I suspect that the good results coming from countries that adopt them and persist with them might well lead to increasingly wider adoption and might give the model even greater credibility. My optimism arises from the limited scope for alternative models, from the widespread failure of active intervention, and from the fact that economic failure often results from a country's policy implementation difficulties. In other words, what is often required when success in not being achieved is an attitude of persistence, adaptation, and refinement rather than abandonment.

I have in mind here the good results that are coming from the market-friendly policies being adopted in Southeastern and Southern Asia (for instance, India) and in other parts of the world like Botswana, Chile, Guyana, Mauritius, and Uganda. In my own part of the world—the Caribbean—for the independent members of the Caribbean Community, growth in 1995 averaged 3.6 percent. While not substantial, this growth represents a continuation of recovery. Five countries—Barbados, the Dominican Republic, Grenada, Guyana, and Trinidad and Tobago—have undertaken varying degrees of structural reform in the late 1980s and 1990s and have begun to enjoy favorable results. In the case of Guyana, growth exceeded 6 percent for the period 1991-95. In the case of Suriname and Haiti, where reform is very recent, the economies rebounded in 1995, and growth of more than 4 percent was achieved in both cases.

Some Caribbean countries, especially the smaller islands, have largely escaped the need for structural reform, and good growth rates have continued. When countries have experienced stagnation or declining growth, it is largely because adjustment programs are not complete—Belize and Jamaica—or need to be initiated, as in Antigua.

Jamaica is the only Caribbean country experiencing persistent difficulties despite a long period of reform. In its case, stabilization has not yet been achieved, and there exist difficult social problems that make the issue a complex one. Inflation rates are below double-digit levels in most countries, and despite their small size, many of them have been able to attract substantial FDI flows. On the whole, the Caribbean region is expecting further strengthening of its recovery. It remains hopeful, and there is as yet no significant disenchantment with orthodox reform policies.

The policy stance represented by the Washington consensus is a general framework that is recent, that is continuing to evolve, and that will continue to need refinements and adaptation to the circumstances of individual countries. It should be noted that even where mistakes have been made that have led to serious problems (such as in Mexico), there has been persistence with the general policy stance.

It was once fashionable not only to recommend statist policies but also to see most of the problems faced by developing countries as arising from their debilitating international trading and financial policies, which tended to bias attention away from those countries' domestic-policy failures. Clearly, distortions in the international system do remain, as in the case of highly protective policies by developed countries in agriculture, textiles, and garments. And powerful countries are likely to continue to use their position to influence policies on trade, global environmental problems, intellectual property rights, and so forth, in the direction of their own interests, regardless of the consequences for developing countries.

Furthermore, we have all learned enough from economics to recognize some of the important development requirements, and there is no doubt that well-administered selective governmental actions for favorably influencing some of these crucial variables (like savings, investment, and exports) could be helpful, as they have been shown to be in East

Asia. And since I do not believe that the results from impersonal market forces and from the invisible hand could coincide exactly with human requirements and society's purposes, I am happy to examine the case for selective intervention. But I doubt that any of this would point to the need for any significant shift from market-friendly policies. The model over time has come to recognize not only the importance of safety nets but also the crucial significance of investing in people and of ensuring that the poor have access to assets through land reform and credit, as well as access to training. The model may, however, need to be more sensitive to the fact that development is intended for actual human beings, who should not be seen mainly as a factor of production.

In addition, it behooves us to err on the side of caution, especially since economic processes are complex and what may seem benign may have very adverse secondary effects. Even when a policy instrument seems to have succeeded in other countries, account must be taken of the capacity of a particular government to make a success of it. The mix in the Washington consensus as revisited follows policies that are already generally accepted for industrial countries. These countries differ in terms of levels of development (in fact, some countries still regarded as developing have actually advanced beyond some industrial countries); nevertheless, there is no major questioning of the basic relevance of these policies for the less developed industrial countries.

The evidence is not showing that poor countries have less capacity for growth nor that they require a different set of policies to stimulate it. Much intervention was based on the view that people were not capable on their own of making use of economic opportunities. The experience now is that where the framework was right, people have surprised governments with their capacity to respond to economic opportunities. Even today, the fast expansion of the informal sector in many countries and its contribution to economic activity and employment are emerging as a favorable development, and that sector is seen as in particular need of support.

The emphasis must therefore be on creating a competitive economy. This focus does not rule out the need to pay particular attention to people on the margins who must be helped with access to land, credit, and training to assist them in positioning themselves to contribute and benefit from a freer economy. Poverty and unemployment need attention in most countries of the world, and they need particular attention in developing countries, where they tend to be on a larger scale and more deep seated. Equity is a related priority, especially in plural societies, which many Latin American and other developing countries are.

It is difficult to make recommendations about policy priorities, as countries are at different stages of the reform process. But in general, the priority has to be to get the basic policy framework right. There remains much to be done in this regard in many countries in basic areas (like property rights, the justice system, incentive prices for agriculture, institutional rehabilitation and reform, improvement of public administration, labor market reform, supervision and deregulation of the financial sector, land reform, capital market development, and so forth) before other areas calling for cautious policy intervention (like selective protection and subsidized credit) can be given attention.

Areas like prudent financial regulation and land reform are not market intervention policies. They are part of the enabling framework and are greatly needed in Latin America. There are strong institutional as well as economic dimensions to land ownership and the structure of holdings, with important implications for cropping patterns, the intensity of cropping, and the widening of economic opportunities. If land reform is seen as market intervention, then it is the kind of intervention that has proven its worth. And even here, the precise policy depends on local circumstances: where land is abundant, as it is in many Latin American countries, redistribution is still compatible with retaining large holdings for extensive agriculture.

My own position then is one of general support for the Washington consensus of 1989 and for that consensus as revisited in the present volume. My differences with it are minor. I would say that on the issue of development, the ideological debate should come to an end and that our discussion must now be on building consensus and convergence. And in examining relative economic performance, more attention needs to be given to the political constraints that prevent countries from establishing the policies and institutions that have met with success in other countries.

The foregoing is meant to serve as a background to my comment on the tone of the paper. One caveat is that I may be pointing to some omissions and emphases that the author actually supports but could not deal with in a short paper. Although the paper is not arguing for a larger role for state intervention, I believe that in some places, in the light of experience, the suggested policies could be more aggressively market oriented (for instance, privatization, tariff reduction, property rights, and scope for private finance and cost recovery in some social services, infrastructure provision, and public research and development activities). In other places, the paper overestimates the capacity of weak states to take on complex public-management tasks (such as implementing a variable land tax according to the environmental impact of use).

Let me end by saying something about the choice of items. I would have found a place in my list for the promotion of sustainable development, meaning by that not the traditional usage in terms of sustained development, but the notion of integrating environmental and economic policies.

Sustainable Development

John Williamson does mention the importance of dealing with environmental externalities in his section on tax reform, but in development thinking generally, the environment does not get the attention that it deserves. This fact is somewhat surprising in that the issue of environmental externalities, and dealing with them through a Pigovian tax, is part of the prewar economic literature.

There exists some justification for the charge that economists have some responsibility for the public environmental squalor that is accompanying private development. I suspect that in the profession there is not sufficient awareness of the widespread nature of the phenomenon of social damage arising from production processes and from products and their packaging. Generally, the absence of early recognition of the extent of damage caused through ignorance, policy mistakes, and mismanagement has led to widespread use of technologies that are inappropriate from the standpoint of sustainable development. In the distant past, our planet had the capacity to absorb the waste and pollution generated by humanity's production and consumption activities. But increasingly, this is not the case. Population density and its spread, together with the accompanying production intensity, are exhausting absorptive capacity for waste materials, especially in urban areas and in intensive agriculture. Externalities now cannot be neglected.

But externalities are not the only major cause of environmental problems. Another phenomenon, also not new to economic literature, is the problem of dealing with open-access resources (such as forests, parks, water sources, and fisheries), which are commonly owned, as well as the damage to these resources that results from excessive use arising from divergences between private and public interests in their exploitation and conservation.

Environmental degradation has become so widespread and obvious that inattention to it by economists and others has become less excusable. For economists, the issue goes beyond the extent of damage. There is also the fact that economists have a crucial role in dealing with these problems in a targeted and efficient way, bringing interesting variety in recommendations on protective measures, by adding economic instruments to the more widely used and sometimes blunter instruments of command and control measures. Command and control measures such as standards and regulations are appropriate in some circumstances, but they urgently need complementation by economic instruments such as taxes, incentives, tradable pollution permits, user fees, property rights, and deposit refund schemes. Such instruments (guided largely by the "polluter pays" principle and ensuring right-price signals for the use of public resources) could transform fiscal policy—hence their importance not only to economic policy generally but also to the reform process.

I would also have given a greater priority to decentralization of administrative and economic management. Beyond local government that deepens democracy, makes greater use of local knowledge, and responds better to local interests, people must also be given greater scope to develop community-based management and to provide an improved enabling environment for their private economic activities, by people-driven institutional development at local and other levels, which represents a good addition to social capital and good scope for improving environmental management. And I wonder also, if labor market reforms might have deserved a separate heading. There exists a great need to make labor markets less restrictive and more amenable to relating pay and promotion more closely to merit and productivity while recognizing the importance of trade unions in providing balance between the rights of workers and those of employers.

Toru Yanagihara[1] on
The Washington Consensus Revisited

John Williamson has rendered a valuable service once again in compiling a policy manifesto for Latin America, deliberately meant as such this time. The "Williamson wish list" will no doubt become as renowned as the original "Washington consensus" and possibly more so on the merit of its message and thanks to the improved image conveyed by the new label.

In the present essay I shall comment on his wish list from an eclectic East Asian perspective. The discussion will be mostly conceptual and schematic but will reflect my understanding and interpretation of East Asian development experiences, especially in terms of economic-system evolution.

Both the Washington consensus and the Williamson wish list present a listing of government actions for policy and institutional reforms needed to achieve ultimate goals of socioeconomic development. The wish list is more tilted toward long-term issues and social development compared with the Washington consensus, reflecting the lapse of half a dozen years and, presumably, also the difference in ideological positions between Washington and John Williamson. In the main, however, the two listings stand on the same methodological premise in that they both subscribe to what I call the "framework approach."

The wish list is meant to be "a policy manifesto of the leading reforms that Latin America ought to be implementing or the major reforms in economic policy, broadly interpreted, that I judge that Latin America most needs currently," including "two extra reforms most urgently needed in the region."

The key term here is "reform." Reforms are purposive actions geared toward the attainment of certain goals. The author's goals are sometimes explicit and sometimes not. He refers to stability, efficiency, equity, and the environment in discussing some of his ten wishes. The time horizon for the reforms is not always explicitly stated. What is common to the ten items in the new list is that, according to the author, all of them are immediately needed.

First, let me summarize the new list according to my classification scheme.

---

[1] Hosei University and United Nations University.

Getting the Framework Right with the Wish List
Market Signals
Items 6 and 7 in the list are key elements defining the incentive framework for resource allocation and utilization. Here two concepts of efficiency are involved. First is allocative efficiency, which relates to the question of distortions in the incentive framework. Second is unit efficiency, which relates to the question of discipline imposed by a competitive environment. The author moderates the primacy of efficiency considerations by supporting negotiated import liberalization in pursuit of improved market access and by accepting a modest minimum wage.

Item 5 is more explicitly growth oriented, emphasizing as it does the need "to nurture rapid growth in nontraditional exports." The term "competitive" here refers to the capacity to offer lower prices against competitors from abroad. This strikes a sharp contrast with item 7 where the same term "competitive" is taken to mean the principle of market-mediated economic transactions.

Public Institutions
Item 8 represents a fundamental institutional environment for effective operation of the market economy. The author's espousal of extending property rights to the informal sector and of land reform will prove to be controversial.

Similarly, items 4 and 9 relate to "key state institutions the efficient functioning of which is important for rapid and/or equitable growth." The author describes them as "typically small, elite institutions." He is not inclined to advocate capacity building for economic planning or for industrial policy.

Item 3 addresses an inevitable interface between state and society. Here politics large and small is fought out in pursuit of lower tax burdens. Broadening the tax base and improving tax administration will most probably mean infringing on many de jure and de facto loopholes. This will presumably include throwing a tax net over the informal sector.

Getting the Ingredients Right with the Wish List
Items 2 and 10 relate to the ingredients of an economy that are essential for development—namely, a healthy and educated labor force and good infrastructure.

Specific Questions and Comments
I do not know where I should place Williamson's item 1 with its new emphasis on increasing private savings. Chile is mentioned as a success case on this score, and that country's reform in its pension system is alluded to as an important factor. In the case of Chile, however, the steady rise of private savings in the 1980s was realized largely through the increase in corporate savings. The latter, it might be argued, was a result of higher profits generated in the wake of policy changes. There seems to be no apparent link between the reform in the pension system and the increase in corporate savings. If that is the case, one is left with the recognition of the need for heightened private savings but with no obvious means to address it. I would see private savings as an endogenous variable deter-

mined by investment and export (as well as import substitution) performances. Savings follow, rather than lead, investment and export, and the key for private savings might be continued generation and realization of export-oriented investment opportunities, as in the case of Chile.

One question on the exchange rate regime: the author states that "Chile and Colombia provide a model in having used a wide, crawling band." According to the IMF classification of exchange rate arrangements, however, Chile is one of the two countries in the world whose currencies are "adjusted according to a set of indicators" (the other is Nicaragua), while Colombia is among the countries adopting "other managed floating" together with other Latin American countries like Brazil, Costa Rica, Ecuador, and Uruguay. It would be helpful if the author could elaborate on his classification scheme in relation to that used by the IMF.

Another question relates to financial volatility of external origins. The author approvingly cites Chilean and Colombian attempts "to maintain a competitive exchange rate despite strong pressures from capital inflows." I am keen to learn what the author might have to say about the feasibility and effectiveness of proposed measures to throw sand into the international financial machinery—that is, a Tobin tax—as a means of reducing the pressures of international capital flows.

On property rights, it would help if the author could clarify what he considers as the most problematic situations at present and what aspect of change in Peru since 1990 he cites as notable progress. Possibly related, it might be questioned whether there is urgent need to formalize property rights in the informal sector.

More General and Possibly Fundamental Issues

The central question is whether this episode of policy reform represents a once-and-for-all change or another phase of a long swing in economic policy making. The answer will ultimately hinge on how richly and how soon the new model will deliver the promised returns. And on this the author seems to present an optimistic outlook.

According to Williamson, "Underlying this new agenda is a conviction that enterprise will flourish when society has organized itself to provide both macroeconomic stability and the social and physical infrastructure of a market economy and when society gives equitably educated people a chance to insert themselves into the world economy.... The flourishing of enterprise will then restore growth; in turn, without major distortions like import substitution, one can expect this growth to expand employment; and this expanding employment, allied with replacement of the education system's inegalitarian bias with a more level playing field and with a pro-egalitarian bias in social policy, will ultimately help Latin America shed its unwholesome reputation as home to the most uneven income distributions in the world." The logical structure here is clear: the adoption of reforms designed to provide stability, infrastructure, education, and freedom leads to enterprise, which in turn generates growth and, cooperating with some of the reforms, employment and better income distribution. And this is a powerful restatement of the trust in the invisible hand.

In arguing the inadvisability of industrial policy, the author points to the necessity "to have an unusually competent, dedicated, and uncorrupt civil service" Latin American countries seem to lack. There are two questions related to this issue. First, in what way and to what extent do the bureaucratic institutions required for successful industrial policy differ from those in other fields? Second, is there any rationale for trying to build up a supply of highly competent and disciplined civil servants in elite institutions, if the problem lies in the scarcity of such a commodity? Or is this a case of system being corrupt beyond repair? More fundamentally, and judging from the foregoing quotation, the author seems to be of the opinion that a nation does not need a national or industrial development policy defined in terms of a future vision (of ingredients) of the economy as practiced in some of East Asian economies. This represents a forceful restatement of the distrust of the visible hand.

The wish list focuses on the framework of the market economy. True, it is concerned with the ingredients of economic development in its own way (that is, an educated labor force and good infrastructure), but they are viewed as stocks of available resources. The invisible hand will take care of their proper allocation. In my view, the central question of development is how investment opportunities are generated and realized in a sustainable manner. I believe that it will take more-purposive actions on the part of government to counter coordination failures that will otherwise stifle the realization of investment opportunities. It is a question of institutional arrangements rather than institutional environments, and formal property rights will not resolve this problem. What matters is the kind of enterprise, the kind of market, and the kind of competition. From this perspective, the essence of industrial policy lies in facilitating the formation of desirable industrial organization, desirable from the perspective of sustained capacity to generate and realize investment opportunities. The informal sector may be filled with enterprising individuals, but that will not immediately translate into sustained development.

This leads us to the question of social capital. Social capital may be defined as private agents' collective capacity to arrange mutually beneficial transactions without recourse to state power. The informal sector is an expression of social capital thus defined. Unlike physical and human capital, social capital is an essentially relational concept. It is intangible, but it nonetheless empowers people in the same way physical and human capital do. Social capital facilitates coordination among economic agents and thus helps realize more investment opportunities. It also facilitates group learning and capacity enhancement, thereby contributing to the generation of new investment opportunities.

Under certain conditions and for some purposes, social capital and state-mediated regulation, whether of property rights or industrial policy, stand in substitutive relations; rapid growth of investment in China and Vietnam under grossly imperfect systems of (formal) property rights is a case in point. In other cases, they might instead be characterized as complementary to each other. East Asian economic systems and relations between government and the private sector have both been formed largely on the basis of existing social relations. In considering the role of social capital, one particularly important area will be primary education, since the role of government there will need to be embedded in the total process of the socialization of children.

I believe that development needs to be viewed as an interactive process of mutually supporting enhancements in productive capacity of economic agents, on the one hand, and as the organizational and institutional arrangements within and between them, or the economic system, on the other. Furthermore, economic relations might need to be viewed in relation to, or in the context of, social relations or systems.

In sum, I find both the Washington consensus and the Williamson wish list wanting in system-evolution perspective. The wish list is presented as a reduced-form solution to the problem of development and as such does not fully specify underlying structural relationships. Probably that is a strength rather than a drawback in that it allows the list to be viewed as of universal applicability. The author claims that they are "best-practice and well-tested ideas." Maybe so. But as the author himself states in the aforementioned quotation, the case for his agenda is ultimately based on a conviction. We might want to try to be better prepared for a structural shock or two, just in case!

Successes and Failures of Development Experience since the 1980s

Gustav Ranis[1]

The 1980s were generally a forgettable decade for the developing world, beginning with the debt crisis and ending with a crisis of confidence in important components of the "Washington consensus" package. That decade witnessed the overall failure of growth in Sub-Saharan Africa; meanwhile in 1990, even Latin America found itself with a per capita income 7 percent below 1980 levels, and for its part "miraculous" East Asia did continue on its growth path, but generally at somewhat reduced speed. Unemployment and underemployment rates appear to be worsening virtually everywhere—as a consequence of macroeconomic restraint combined with microeconomic restructuring and privatization efforts—and governments now find their willingness or ability to address worsening income distributions and large holes in the social safety net clearly diminished.

Furthermore, the international community—although demonstrating its ability to respond with alacrity to the clear and present danger (to others and to itself) arising from the debt crisis—has equally clearly absconded domestically with any of the hoped-for post-Cold War peace dividends and has moved the development problem increasingly to the back burner. Debt relief for Sub-Saharan Africa, not subject to the usual moral-hazard arguments, is in danger of getting stuck, and even the stalwarts of development cooperation—the multilateral development banks, able to resist the unfavorable tide in the past—are coming under increasing budgetary pressure and are being asked to yield the field to private capital, even in regions not yet ready to attract such flows.

Despite all of this, the development glass may yet be more than half full. Distributional equity may have worsened overall, but wherever growth has in fact occurred, the percentage of people in absolute poverty seems to be on the wane. Thus, the developing world has experienced continuous improvements in the basic quality of life of its citizens, despite the uneven growth performance of the past. For instance, in Sub-Saharan Africa taken as a whole, life expectancy advanced from 46 years to 51 years during the 1980s, and infant mortality declined by one-fifth. Although this result clearly does not give cause for complacency, since these levels are still abysmally low and with reasonable growth, much more could and should have been accomplished in the past; it does, however, show that it would take very little to make a big difference in the future.

---

[1] Yale University.

The primary reason for remaining optimistic is the fact that we have learned a good deal during the difficult past decade concerning the trade-offs and complementarities among societal objectives and concerning the dos and don'ts of getting to some societal preferred policy combination—knowledge that can be put to good use in the years ahead. Some of the adverse exogenous shocks of the past decade may have actually materially contributed to creating the kind of new political-economy setting needed for parlaying an improved understanding into a more successful development performance by more countries at the turn of the century. Although no one has all the answers, the problem has become less technical in character and more one of determining the extent to which countries really have poverty reduction and economic development as their fundamental objectives.

The following is a review of some of these lessons as they have emerged from the successes and failures of recent development practice, as well as a brief summary of the reasons for a degree of optimism with respect to future economic development.

The 1980s and Early 1990s:
Successes and Failures of Thought and of Action

The debt crisis of the early 1980s undoubtedly led to a consensus regarding those fiscal and monetary "fundamentals" that absolutely need to be in place to allow anything else to work, whatever a country's mixture of markets and government. Despite continuing disagreement on whether the annual inflation rate needs to be brought down to 20 percent or to 5 percent —and at what sacrifice (see current Argentine rates of unemployment)—hardly anyone still questions the basic need for proximate macroeconomic stability. Hidden deficits (such as those in the form of subsidies to state enterprises) are being made more transparent and are being reduced, and governmental borrowing from the non-bank public at high rates of interest is increasingly being recognized as only postponing the day of reckoning—and not by very long at that.

Clearly there has occurred a major change in the views of policymakers of the less developed nations, particularly those of Latin America, regarding the importance of macroeconomic balance and the need to diminish the inflationary threat. Fiscal-policy constraints and monetary-policy constraints have become part of the accepted catechism, with the old explanations based on structuralism and cost/push inflation generally having been relegated to the sidelines. And if there does still exist major unfinished macro business today, it is much more likely to reside in arguments about the maintenance of exchange rate credibility (that is, about viewing the exchange rate as a steadying anti-inflationary anchor versus viewing it along with other prices simply as a flexibly adjusting absorber of exogenous shocks).

Even so, not all of the general lessons from the earlier Southern Cone's adjustment process have yet been fully digested in Latin America. For instance, until crisis struck, Mexico adhered to a stabilization package based on a fixed exchange rate—a package that admittedly was helpful for a time, but only as long as there existed confidence that rising current-account deficits, accompanied by modest relative inflation and overvaluation, would be covered by (mostly portfolio) foreign-capital inflows. Once it became clear that 8 percent current-account deficits, even in the presence of minimal (1 percent) public-sector fiscal deficits, were being used for a private-consumption binge, the bloom quickly came off the rose, and probably only Mexico's membership in NAFTA and in GATT prevented a return to "temporary" import controls and other assorted "stop" measures. As the East Asian experience of the late 1980s has made abundantly clear, continuation along a path of adjustment by monetary restraint and by export expansion rather than by additional borrowing is a much safer, if initially more painful, route. Once the all-important credibility of macroeconomic policy is lost, a country's cumulative gains of almost a decade of policy change can indeed be dissipated virtually overnight.

Much less agreement, however, has emerged on the microeconomic or structural changes needed in order for an economy to take advantage of that often painfully obtained macroeconomic balance. Increasingly, the IMF/World Bank "set pieces" in this arena are being questioned, and there has arisen increasing insistence on more-nuanced packages and sequences. In this context, reinterpreting the clearly successful East Asian experience's possible relevance to other parts of the third world has become a popular parlor game. What had previously been summarily dismissed as entirely irrelevant to, say, the Latin American, the South Asian, or even the African cases is now being seriously scrutinized. Questions based on the varying interpretations of what really happened in East Asia—including (1) the role of government relative to markets, (2) the role of trade, and (3) the role of foreign capital—are now being critically examined, often for the first time. The chances for improved outcomes in the future are clearly tied to our ability to look with new eyes at these three issues as related to the successes and failures of the past. Let us examine each of the three in turn.

Turning first to the role of government, a debate has been raging of late on the importance of industrial policy in East Asia, including postwar Japan. The World Bank, in its 1991 *World Development Report*, did acknowledge that "market-friendly" interventions undoubtedly played a positive role, but the report did not go so far as to define that concept. Then in the context of the *East Asian Miracle* study, initiated and substantially financed by Japan, the World Bank acknowledged that directed credit, an important instrument of industrial policy, may have made a contribution to successful industrialization efforts in East Asia; the bank waffled, however, on just what this directed credit meant in terms of the desired liberalization of various markets (including credit markets), a policy stance that the bank has clearly maintained. The controversy continues to simmer, especially in Japan, which finds itself generally dissatisfied with the conclusions of the *Miracle* study and is supporting a number of follow-up seminars and critiques, as well as further studies.

Undoubtedly, a mistake was made in asking the World Bank to play a central role in examining the historical validity of its own doctrines as applied to East Asia's experience. Moreover, the role of East Asian governments, even after they emerged from their common early import substitution phase, clearly went substantially beyond pure neoclassical prescriptions of "law and order plus infrastructure." But it is equally true that the current murky reevaluation of the merits of industrial policy is giving unwarranted aid and comfort to vested-interest groups eager to reject liberalization entirely and to start on a second round of import-substituting industrialization. Although certainly not intended to have this effect, selected elements of Krugman's "new trade theory" and Stiglitz's reference to nonmarket "contests" have both been eagerly seized upon and often misapplied in this context. One hears frequent references to South Korea's Pohang Steel Mill, which was originally condemned by World Bank experts and later presumably became an internationally competitive producer. Simultaneously, Robert Wade's views of government interventions as "governing" markets and Alice Amsden's advice to "get prices wrong" (supposedly based on Taiwanese and South Korean experience, respectively) are gaining currency and adherents. As is so often the case in the development arena, there exist some danger that the policy pendulum, having undoubtedly swung too far in a religious *laissez-faire* direction in the heyday of the "Washington consensus," is now in danger of swinging too far in an antiorthodox or revisionist direction.

The present author freely admits to not being in possession of an integrated, defensible model but nonetheless wishes to express an opinion as to where this particular pendulum ought to come to rest—namely, at a point denoting balance, not inertia. Any controversy is not about fundamentals but about the extent and nature of strategic market-friendly or supportive governmental interventions. What I caution about in regard to the East Asian experience is that although comparative advantage can indeed be usefully "stretched," the following four specific conditions must be carefully adhered to: (a) interventions ought not to ignore price signals and certainly should not follow Amsden's advice to move purposely against such signals; (b) interventions on behalf of a particular industry that are designed to extend beyond rectifying other distortions should be highly selective (the main method of selection in East Asia was for a country to look down the road at what Japan had moved to earlier on, as well as to look over its own shoulder at the other East Asian NICs; the tellers of the Pohang story neglect to mention that other portions of that heavy-industry and chemical-industry push in South Korea did not fare as well in terms of predicting the path of dynamic comparative advantage); (c) interventions should be transparent, time-constrained, and reversible, in order to ensure that their costs are visible and able to be debated along with their possible benefits and that these rents are clearly viewed as temporary by both the civil servants who give them out and by the private recipients; and (d) avoidance of mistakes and of the encrustation of such mistakes, all too common in recent development experience, may be assisted by the creation of deliberation councils or similar devices permitting governments to engage the private sector in some form of indicative planning.

The experience of Japan's MITI is often cited in this connection (incidentally, given the Honda story, it is cited by both adherents and critics of industrial policy). But the main problem with the World Bank's *Miracle* study, as well as with much of the commentary that followed, is that it focused almost entirely on the Japanese postwar experience, which was indeed one of substantial interventionism yielding only gradually to liberalization efforts. In truth, the relevant period for comparative purposes is prewar

Japan, which was indeed a developing country moving through various sub-phases of transition; postwar Japan should be viewed as a developed economy recovering from the interventionism of the 1930s and the destruction of World War II. If one wants to compare the Korean, Taiwanese, and Singaporean transition from their earlier, heavily interventionist, import substitution sub-phases into their generally more market-oriented export substitution phase by the late 1960s, with a comparable transition period in Japan, the appropriate Japanese period would be the era surrounding the turn of the century. An examination of Japan's industrial policy between 1880 and 1930 would provide much better guidance as to what worked and what did not work once the system opened up more fully to the rest of the world. Those who have studied the period prior to the takeover by the Japanese military describe that period as increasingly noninterventionist in character, in particular as far as the credit markets were concerned. In contemporary Taiwan in recent years, two organized credit market interest rates, both positive, were in effect: a lower rate for public enterprises and a higher rate for private enterprises. Exporters, large or small, public or private, obtained access at the same lower rates.

The proper conclusion to be drawn from all this is that although a degree of correction to World Bank orthodoxy on industrial policy was certainly in order, current statements are considerably wide of the mark when they describe Latin America's economies as less intervened in than those of East Asia. Latin American industrial policy has in the past been much more across the board, much more deeply ingrained, and much more resistant to change than the East Asian. It would indeed be a tragedy, just when Latin America is beginning to emerge from its inward orientation of long standing, to have the aforementioned misinterpretation of the East Asian experience provide the rationale for yet another fluctuation in policy.

Indeed, if there is one dimension of governance that seems to stand out above all others, it is the need to achieve stability and credibility and to avoid such traditional stop-and-go patterns, alternating between more-liberal and more-interventionist policy spells, consequently probably achieving the worst of both worlds.

This need for policy credibility also extends to adherence to property rights and regulatory evenhandedness, to reducing the overwhelming power of the central government's executive branch vis-à-vis that of parliament and the judiciary (the rule of law), and to the devolution of more fiscal and resource allocation powers to local governments. In fact, there has been a lot of discussion and evidence concerning the merits of decentralization, especially of the vertical type, in today's developing world, but practice generally still lags considerably behind. One can detect an increasing tendency toward deconcentration or delegation of power but real devolution is generally not yet encountered—certainly not in unitary states and not even in many federal states. More than many other regions of the developing world, Latin America remains fairly centralized: the decision-making process as to what to do, and where and how to do it, in terms of both infrastructural and social-sector allocations, is generally still heavily dominated by administrations working through central-government finance ministries and other line ministries. One does not have to be an adherent of a romantic view, ignoring the presence of power elites at the local level, to maintain nonetheless that local officials are likely to be more knowledge-able about where the proverbial "shoe" pinches and also more capable of translating such knowledge into effective implementation than are distant central-government officials managing large "black-box" projects. Although there clearly exist nonfeasance and malfeasance at all levels, the "goldfish bowl" effect or relative-transparency effect sets some limits at the local level. The usual counterargument—that local governments are not yet "ready" because of deficient technical or administrative capacities—is painfully reminis-cent of arguments of the past concerning the ignorant peasantry. In both instances, the response yielded by exposure to a more pressured environment in which economic actors are forced to produce and are given a chance to learn by doing (and by sometimes fail-ing) was and is likely to surprise in a positive way, but central authorities' unwillingness to relinquish additional fiscal power to local bodies undoubtedly constitutes the main obstacle.

Similarly, the executive branches of LDC governments generally retain their relatively predominant interbranch position as inherited from the early postcolonial days, with only scattered evidence of any growth of countervailing power in the form of a strengthened legislative branch and generally even less in the form of a truly independent judiciary. One might even assert that in most cases it is the finance ministries that continue to play an inordinately dominant role relative to that played by the central banks and the social ministries. There can, of course, be legitimate room for doubt as to whether certain forms of enhanced participation and democratization are intrinsically stabilizing or destabiliz-ing in the short run but there can be little doubt about their positive impact over the longer term. This whole issue undoubtedly represents an area of much unfinished busi-ness, but also one in which change—although it will surely come—will undoubtedly have to proceed in ways sensitive to the individualized institutional and political cir-cumstances of each country. The whole debate on the respective roles of governments ver-sus market failure can be rescued from becoming quite sterile if a much greater effort is made to disaggregate not only markets but also the government.

Turning now from our discussion of the role of government relative to markets, there is a second area in which recent development experience has been adversely affected by conceptual misunderstandings—namely, in regard to the role of international trade. There can be little doubt of trade's important facilitating or "handmaiden" role, as Kravis put it, for successful economic development, but the drumbeat for "openness" or-chestrated by the Bretton Woods institutions has led to the view that exports constitute the main "engine of growth" and that export promotion, in particular of nontraditional goods, represents "the" solution in virtually all circumstances.

The intrinsic difficulty with this position is that it seems to put aside the valid no-tion that development success or failure continues to be determined largely "at home," with the open-economy aspects, including trade and the associated international move-ments of capital and technology, admittedly of potentially great help but only in a com-plementary sense—that is, as an assist to the basic domestic effort. One should not accept the notion that exports somehow "explain" success, even in the case of relatively small countries. One important causal chain does indeed run from exports to growth via the contribution of enhanced competitiveness as well as via the direct impact of imported technology embodied in machines, patents, and human capital often associated with direct foreign investment. But there is also another important casual chain that runs from the particular type of domestic growth that has been generated to trade; this chain comprises not only obvious elements such as investments that reduce transport costs but also the all-important contribution by domestic human-capital formation and R&D, which, together with domestic macro-level and micro-level policy, critically affect the responsiveness of an economy to existing international trade opportunities.

In a large number of countries, not yet of NIC or near NIC status, this idea can perhaps be conveyed most convincingly with respect to the agricultural sector. Even in a place like Taiwan, now associated in most people's minds with rapid growth led by industrial exports, 70 percent of the initial 1954–1967 export boom was actually composed of processed agricultural goods—including pineapples, mushrooms, and asparagus—all heavily promoted by agricultural research under the structure formed by the Joint Commission on Rural Reconstruction and the farmers association. Assisted by land reform, agriculture thus played a critical role at the early stages of Taiwanese development.

A bit later, East Asia's ability to become a major competitive industrial exporter in a relatively short time was directly related to that region's domestic educational and R&D strategies. With respect to education, the flexibility demonstrated in shifting from compulsory primary to secondary vocational education to science-oriented and technology-oriented university training at just the right time enabled the system continuously to follow a growth and export path dominated by dynamic comparative advantage. This effort was complemented by a whole array of government-sponsored specialized research institutes, science parks, and the like, which were increasingly obliged to meet their budgets by selling their research services to private entrepreneurs.

The large role of public-sector research, especially in cash crop agricultural exports, such as sugar, has long been recognized. But that role is much smaller in the case of nontraditional agricultural exports and nonagricultural exports. Especially in the case of countries that need to rely on the rapid expansion of medium-scale and small-scale firms, which often cannot afford to do their own R&D (such as in the case of China's Township and Village enterprises and Taiwan's small-scale and medium-scale enterprises), this need for public sector research is only gradually coming to the fore. Admittedly, many horror stories could be told concerning the "white-elephant" aspect of a number of LDC science and technology institutes that seem to set their own agendas quite independently of the actual needs of the economy. But these stories do not obviate the point that when increasingly "hard" budgets can be made credible, R&D as a public good can have an important role to play in permitting the continuous realization of an export drive powered by dynamic comparative advantage.

Achieving balanced growth between the domestically oriented agricultural sector and the nonagricultural sector thus remains at the heart of the development problem in many countries, certainly at the relatively early stages of their development. The notion that

food-producing agriculture can somehow be carelessly neglected and the action that industrial exports can somehow by themselves pull an economic system into modern economic growth are dangerously misleading and just plain wrong. The recent relative
neglect of the domestic economy, and especially of the rural domestic economy, can perhaps be better understood as a consequence of the debt crisis, which (superficially at least)
seemed to represent an "external" problem rather than the visible tip of a deep-seated do-
mestic-development problem.

No one, of course, is suggesting that the rural dynamism of East Asia can somehow
be duplicated in Latin America or Africa, given the great differences among the three in
terms of population densities and of institutional, human capital, and physical infrastructure, as well as in other dimensions of the famous "initial conditions." Nevertheless,
if we analyze not only the total allocation of physical overhead capital but also the allocation of scarce organizational and institutional energies in Latin America, both factors
do continue to be heavily biased toward traditional cash crop exports or toward large-
scale urban industry. Within agriculture proper, the present suboptimal allocation of
R&D and extension expenditures remains a particularly serious problem. Good examples
abound: for instance, large irrigation projects continue to have priority over the unsilt-
ing of local waterways, and superhighways crowd out feeder roads. And in nonagricul-
ture, basic research-oriented private R&D and "big-science"-focused institutes continue
to take oxygen away from the innovative activities centered around adaptive research and
learning by doing.

The same holds true for the impact of most price support programs affecting staples. Overall budget constraints do create a tendency to curtail the urban consumer subsidies that so often burden LDC treasuries, but the differential impact of other
interventions in commodity markets often remains to be addressed. Intersectorial commodity markets in all too many cases continue to be biased against domestic food-producing agriculture (except in some cases the cash crop subsector). Since we are dealing
here only with a possible reallocation of given public goods and energies, and are not
asking for additional dispensations from budgets that are already overburdened and constrained, it should not be impossible to act but powerful vested-interest groups usually
must first be overcome.

A closely related issue worthy of attention is that of possible reforms of the patent
system and of R&D incentives in general. One need only point to the substantial discrepancy among developing countries in terms of total factor productivity or (as some observers such as Krugman seem to prefer) of the efficiency of investment allocation in
order to be convinced that an increased emphasis on indigenous applied science and technology is bound to pay off. Tax codes can be modified to encourage greater risk taking,
and increased flexibility in the legal and implementational dimensions of intellectual
property rights can be ensured as a country moves up the development ladder. The possibility of instituting an additional patent option (such as the utility model, with its shorter periods of protection and its lower threshold for discovery) is an option worthy of
much additional attention. Latin America still relies too heavily on imported patents and

imported technology and has not yet sufficiently mobilized its own adaptive or "blue col-lar" technological-change capacity.

The third major question that warrants our attention in terms of diagnosing the rea-sons for some of the development successes and failures of the past relates to the role of public capital inflows—in particular, inflows of the fast-disbursing policy-based loans or structural-adjustment loans (SALs) provided primarily by the multilateral development banks (MDBs). This loan instrument has become the subject of lively debate, ranging from the cost-effectiveness of the resources spent in support of developing-country pol-icy reforms all the way to the implications of the international financial institutions' con-ditionality lists affecting recipients' most sensitive internal affairs. Given the admittedly mixed record of past SALs (see the World Bank's own internal evaluations), the argument is now being made by some that the time may be right to abandon the instrument alto-gether and to return to project lending.

Structural adjustment lending or program lending can, in theory, support devel-oping countries, to help them achieve any agreed objective, such as growth accompanied by improvements in the level of human development. Nevertheless, one must of course admit that—just as in any other multi-cook, multi-instrument context—it is extreme-ly difficult to judge precisely the ultimate contribution of fast-disbursing loans coupled with conditionality. Any fair assessment would have to compare outcomes in very sim-ilarly situated countries that have been exposed to the same exogenous shocks and that have and have not submitted to such a program. But such laboratory situations rarely exist in the real world, and the counterfactual is typically unknowable. Moreover, there is the time element—meaning that the effects of program lending may be very differ-ent down the road from what they are in the near term—which makes it difficult to de-termine the appropriate moment for rendering either a negative or a congratulatory assessment.

Therefore, probably the most that one can do, in all candor, is to present some rea-sonably informed judgements on how the SAL instrument has been deployed in the re-cent past and on how this may have affected the instrument's mixed record of success and failure. It may be helpful to begin by briefly contrasting recent SAL experience and the parameters of earlier (1960s) USAID (Agency for International Development) program loan initiatives: for instance, in negotiations with Pakistan in the early 1960s, the United States offered to provide substantial additional balance-of-payments support as import controls in Pakistan were shifted to an import bonus auction system and as that country's domestic agricultural price controls were lifted. A similar, if more comprehensive, pattern could be observed in the case of Taiwan, when substantial U.S. aid ballooning between 1959 and 1963 was associated with Taiwan's adoption of the famous "Nineteen Points" of negotiated reforms. According to one widely cited evaluation of U.S. assistance to Taiwan, "aid probably doubled the annual growth rate of GNP" (Jacoby 1967). It also helped improve income distribution and the level of human development. One element of the program was a comprehensive dialogue (in part through the Joint Commission on Rural Reconstruction), so that the Taiwanese Government felt real ownership. The

United States, for its part, not only offered significant additional flows but also made the salutary announcement that economic assistance would cease by 1965.

More recent experience revolving primarily around the World Bank's structural adjustment loans has produced relatively few success cases (such as Chile, Ghana, and Poland). Given the fact that we probably now know more than ever before about the necessary technical ingredients, macro and micro, for successful transition growth and given also the large volume of resources expended and the formidable array of human intelligence invested, it is of more than passing interest that the MDBs have not done better with their fast-disbursing loan programs.

One of the reasons for this is that the World Bank—unlike AID and of course, unlike the regional MDBs—sports an unduly centralized structure. Only in a few borrower countries does that bank have full-fledged resident missions, and even in such cases, the substantive decision-making locus for new commitments and policy advice is found principally in Washington. The World Bank generally operates through a large number of relatively brief visiting missions, some focused on the macro picture, others on specific sectors, and still others on preparing program or project appraisals. The Volcker Commission found that typical World Bank staff members spend less than 10 percent of their time on recipient country contacts. Under such circumstances, not only is it difficult to be sure about the quality of the data and of the micro analysis but also it is virtually impossible to guarantee full local understanding, jointness, and agreement in the determination of resource requirements and reasonable "conditions precedent." The bank itself, given the substantial turnover in the composition of its mission personnel, is not always in a position to move beyond a relatively narrow, technocratic assessment of a country's macro, and especially of its micro or structural, situation. Its advice consequently often lacks realism and nuanced depth with respect to the institutional and political-economy dimensions of the situation.

Undoubtedly, the most telling criticism of past MDB policy-based lending is that both parties are in too much of a hurry; there is all too frequently a rush to judgment, to put together a package that can be signed off on so that the money can flow. Bank staff and loan recipients are similarly motivated; the former see their rewards and promotions in terms of the number of agreements signed and the volume of resources committed; the latter see their rewards in terms of the relief expected from fast-disbursing funds. All the rhetoric about the importance of quality notwithstanding neither side necessarily wants to take the time needed or to risk the possible criticism to be incurred in carefully assessing what precisely should and can be done in a broader sociopolitical and institutional context and in seeking to ensure that the package is more than superficially "owned" by the recipient. The banks, in other words, too often do not act like banks, and the borrowers too often have a strong incentive simply to go through the motions in order to obtain quick relief.

Thus, the desire to lend is overwhelmingly strong, and the attached list of conditions is often too long but insufficiently differentiated—realities well recognized by borrowers. Frequently, too little effort is made to set sensible priorities and to sequence a gradual reform program for borrower societies, which in most cases cannot reasonably be expected to do very much at any one time. Indeed, it is no overstatement to say that both parties, having gone through this particular procedure many times in the past—with or without the benefit of a consultative group—already know full well that ultimately the need to lend will overcome the need to ensure that the conditions precedent are indeed met.

As a consequence, although the additional resources are supposed to ease the pain of adjustment, they may instead serve to take the pressure off and permit the recipient to avoid adjustment. Therefore, what usually occurs, at the risk of some exaggeration, is a rather time-consuming and expensive ritual dance. Not many SAL tranche releases get canceled: usually they are only delayed. Few countries, certainly not many large ones, have ever had prolonged breakdowns in their relations with the World Bank, despite the fact, reported by Tony Killick, that between 1990 and 1994, for example, only a quarter of the bank's SALs have proceeded according to their intended schedule.

If both lender and borrower know that the MDB must commit to a fast-disbursing loan in order to meet its own lending target, it clearly is difficult to maintain a credible threat of cutting off loans in case of noncompliance. Aware of this dynamic, both parties have an incentive to fashion a superficial agreement. The MDB achieves the desired commitment of resources, and the LDC has the pressure for painful change actually relieved by the fast-disbursing flow. Moreover, both parties can claim that reform and loan disbursement targets have been met and can, in the absence of externally verifiable measures of program effectiveness, declare the package a success.

One of the inherent difficulties that need to be addressed is that, as Tinbergen tried to teach us generations ago, it is difficult to maximize the achievement of two different objectives with one instrument. If, in the wake of the Brady Plan, the MDBs are asked to pump out the money on behalf of debt relief, we should not expect the attendant pronouncements concerning policy change to be taken very seriously by either party. The same goes for the U.S. effort over several decades to use nonproject lending to the Philippines both to secure continued military-base rights and to assist with policy reform in that country.

Other impediments internal to the culture of the MDBs also need to be addressed. Concentrating a large number of unquestionably highly talented professionals in powerful institutions that are defending somewhat standard and relatively insular views is bound to create problems associated with the stifling of policy dissent and diversity. New approaches are too often dismissed or taken lightly, especially those suggested by the non-Anglo-Saxon academic and policymaking communities, which are advancing subtle, area-specific modifications to relatively monolithic interpretations of the current paradigm. For instance, it took considerable pressure before Japan, while not even challenging the "basics" of fiscal and monetary-policy restraint, could finally get the World Bank to revisit the bank's views on the role of government in East Asia's success story.

The World Bank has a position of predominance in gross public lending, applied research, and the generation and diffusion of new developmental emphases and ideas;

therefore, it often functions as a powerful (some would say unassailable) authority on development policy. Even though the so-called "Washington consensus" elsewhere discussed in this volume is undoubtedly less monolithic and more subtle and differentiated today than many critics have asserted (the acceptance of "market-friendly" government interventions and the acknowledgment that governments may do well by organizing "contests" and by rewarding [or punishing] performance constitute a case in point), the kernel of truth nevertheless remains: the World Bank is populated by large numbers of highly talented professionals who have shown relatively little willingness to deviate from the in-house conventional wisdom by considering important differences in initial conditions and in the historical stage of development reached by a recipient.

Moreover, in all too many cases, inadequate attention has been given to the changing relationship between the MDBs and the private-capital flows that are increasingly dwarfing MDB and bilateral ODA (official development assistance) flows to the developing world, especially in Latin America. Quite aside from the issue of what the MDBs can and cannot do directly in supporting domestic private-sector activities (given the charter restrictions relevant to most MDBs), their most important function remains one of signaling economic agents (that is, of providing information and "seals of approvals") regarding potential recipient countries' economic conditions. Private developed-country investors depend heavily on both published and unpublished country analyses provided by the MDBs, especially by the World Bank. In this regard, the MDBs' "yellow" versions of country reports may contain more candid assessments of actual country conditions, but unfortunately, by the time the yellow version reach their "grey" and published stages, differences of opinion between the borrower country and the MDB in regard to the recipient's economic conditions have often been so papered over that their discriminatory value is lost. The basic difficulty is that there is insufficient capillary action between the two circulatory systems within the World Bank: on the one hand, the analytical network capable of providing high-quality assessments of a country's status, prospects, and additional reform requirements; on the other, the lender network interested primarily in getting on with it and in maintaining good relations with recipients. Thus, in the end, the grey books have been sanitized, the ritual dance continues, and even the independent information flow to private capital markets is adversely affected.

There is still another set of MDB interactions with private-capital flows that warrants our attention. Aside from the still small, if expanding, IFC (International Finance Corporation) and IFC-equivalent activities in the regional banks and the growing opportunities for joint financing with private capital, there is the issue of how MDB lending can be directly supportive of private-capital flows to the third world. A traditional channel for this support has been government development banks, which relend to the private sector. These two-step loans have received a bad reputation not so much, as is claimed, because such banks are intrinsically inefficient but because government credit policies regarding the level of second-step interest rates and collateral requirements have typically remained seriously deficient.

Reasons for Cautious Optimism near the Turn of the Century

The picture that has just been sketched is not one of unrelieved gloom, but it does point to a number of critical areas in which shortfalls in development thinking have caused inadequate performance in practice in many parts of the developing world. Why then, in the face of decreases in public resources and in the attention paid to the problems by the industrial countries, can we still be optimistic (although cautiously so) about LDC development at the turn of the century?

For starters, there can be little doubt that post-debt-crisis policy mixes in Latin America as well as in South Asia and elsewhere have recently tended to move in the general direction of what might be more appropriately called a global consensus rather than a Washington consensus. This trend applies largely to the macro stabilization arena, but to some extent, it also has been seen in the agenda on microeconomic structural change. Growth is gradually resuming, and concern with distributional equity and with building safety nets for the poor generally constitutes at least part of the dialogue. Such exchanges may not necessarily be irreversible, but a more realistic view of the need for government intervention is nevertheless clearly required at this point. Official interventions should accommodate rather than obstruct the evolution of the system, and there should be a secularly increasing role for markets as the number and the complexity of decisions that need to be made rise geometrically alongside development. Given Latin America's past pattern of across-the-board and long-term rather than selective and temporary interventions, the temptation to revert in the face of some exogenous shock seems to be on the wane. Failed heterodox stabilization programs (such as, the Cruzado plan in Brazil and the Austral plan in Argentina) have undoubtedly had an impact, as have NAFTA and MERCOSUR, toward placing limits on national stop-go reactions. As importantly, the more balanced view afforded by the lessons to be drawn from East Asia concerning the relative roles of government and markets has had a very salutary effect. All the returns obviously are not yet in, but recent Mexican experience seems to indicate that—although admittedly "the region has a history of reform and relapse" (*The Economist*, Nov. 26, 1994)—stop-go in response to some external shock seems to be giving way to soft, if socially painful, landings. Enhanced international commitments, regional and global, are undoubtedly making a contribution to the return to access to the international financial market, but the current adherence to and deepening of Mexican reforms have essentially been "made in Mexico," not in Washington.

Progress on the issue of trade and of export-led growth, as opposed to export-assisted growth, is clearly less universal or clear cut. But here also one can observe more attention being paid more than before to agriculture and rural development—witness the politically daring *ejido* reforms in Mexico and the recent decentralization efforts in India, to cite but two prominent examples. This particular East Asian lesson—namely that balanced growth on the domestic front may well have to precede nontraditional export expansion—may have particular relevance to Central America, South Asia, and Sub-Saharan Africa.

Finally, turning to the role of foreign capital inflows, and especially those inflows from the multilateral development banks, it is, of course, increasingly clear that although public-flow totals are mounting, private flows are dwarfing public flows in the aggregate. Yet it also remains true that access to private inflows of foreign direct investment (FDI) or of portfolio investments is still highly concentrated in the more advanced developing countries, and that substantial portions of the third world, preponderant certainly in terms of population, will still require concessional assistance of the IDA (International Development Association) type or, at a minimum, loans emanating from the harder-term windows of the MDBs. Admittedly, the past performance of the MDBs—using as the chosen instrument their fast-disbursing loans with conditionality—has been far from optimal. But that fact should not lead us to conclude that the instrument is itself inherently flawed. In fact, quite the contrary is true: when deployed appropriately, such loans may represent a very good, if not optimal, way, of promoting development/graduation objectives among the developing countries. To return to a "projects only" approach, on the grounds that the structural-adjustment concept has been found wanting, would be a large mistake. Of course, one should never be doctrinaire about the precise composition of any individual country program, but structural-adjustment lending or program lending, if combined with fully "owned" self-conditionality, probably remains the best device to help interested borrowers achieve graduation. This result will not, however, be achieved easily or painlessly; if it is to work, present practice as described earlier will have to give way to a substantially altered way of doing business.

Most importantly, donors must recognize that in the absence of full joint conceptualization and prior agreement as to what needs to be done in the way of reform and as to what additional resources are required in order to get there, no amount of conditionality will really work. Recognition of this critical, if obvious, point implies something else perhaps less obvious—namely, the abandonment of at least the implicit annual country and regional or global lending targets. Of course, it would be institutionally and politically unrealistic to expect MDBs to be in a position to abandon completely the practice of defining some sort of routine minimum annual country loan levels, but major "humps" or ballooning in lending, associated with major changes in policy, should be negotiated on a "when-and-if" basis, with the MDBs taking a more passive attitude and with the initiative shifted to the borrower.

Such a posture would require a nontrivial change in the underlying *modus operandi* of most MDBs. Although some level of "business-as-usual" lending would, realistically, continue, a new window would need to be opened for major policy-based program lending activities. The MDBs would need to become more banklike—that is, to become able to sit back, while encouraging would-be borrowers to approach them whenever ready, at borrower initiative, with plans for longer-term reform packages. The MDBs, possibly working through consultative groups, could, of course, if requested, provide technical assistance to help fashion such plans, although it might be preferable to finance more extensive use of arm's-length independent consultants, while drawing also upon the substantial expertise and experience that has accumulated within the MDBs and in the developing world.

The major component of such a lending window would be the abandonment of the annual ritual dance (with or without consultative-group music) that claims to focus on conditionality and quality but is mutually recognized to focus really on quantity in the end. What gives cause for optimism is that all parties now increasingly recognize the need to abandon the current dysfunctional and routinized procedures, even if no one is quite sure what to do next. The *sine qua non* of any credible change would clearly have to be the fullest possible prior agreement and commitment by both borrowing country and donor to a policy-and-resources package over a longer (say five-year) period. Such a procedure would acknowledge the growing professional competence of LDC policymakers and would emphasize the fact that a program should be *ab initio* fully "owned" and "self-conditioned" by the borrower; it would also lend much-needed freshness and credibility to a process that has become increasingly fatigued and stale. The fashioning of realistic programs of reform—supported over a period long enough for the borrower's economic and political risks to be matched by external-resource commitments—would not of course be easy; nor would it typically occur more than once in a decade in most country cases. But this approach is what may well be required in order to achieve genuine change, along with the additional resources needed to hold off vested-interest groups, ease the pain of adjustment, and provide the required psychological reassurance.

Any such serious effort to enhance the quality of the fast-disbursing policy loan process must include donors' willingness to enhance that effort's credibility by occasionally refusing to lend and by more than occasionally curtailing their lending in midstream. The suggested infrequent ballooning of resource flows would take place in only a handful of countries at any given time, while some level of "business-as-usual" lending, as previously defined, continues everywhere. Presumably, the anticipated success of a selective approach such as this would itself serve to reverse the present malaise and would lead to a greater willingness by the industrial countries to support the MDB role, in concert with bilateral donors, in order to bring more developing countries to graduation. The application of additional catalytic pressure to induce (usually reluctant) borrowers to accept graduation from soft-loan windows to hard-loan windows and eventually to reliance exclusively on private-capital inflows would, of course, become part of the overall negotiating process, permitting the MDBs to turn their attention increasingly to the poorer countries and at the same time demonstrating the chances for success, one or two countries at a time.

In addition, a more imaginative division of labor among the MDBs is warranted. By way of illustration, if "growth with poverty reduction" or, preferably, "growth with improvements in human development" is the objective, then, the needed country-specific measurements of income, poverty, and human-development indicators remain inadequate, especially with respect to their distributional dimensions. There exists an urgent need for more nuanced country-specific analysis here, focusing on how the links between the nature of the growth path and the basic societal objectives are affected by such factors as the extent of decentralization, the character of the fiscal system, the strength and direction of technology change, the labor force participation level of women, and the role of NGOs. Such analysis, truly essential for fashioning effective reform-with-lending programs, requires a detailed understanding of local institutions and human-resource availabilities—a domain in which the regional development banks, working with indigenous institutions, would seem to have a comparative advantage, with the World Bank possibly contributing at the level of macro analysis of growth, environmental implications, and the like. The present system—having everyone "in on the act," drawing poverty lines, measuring human-development levels, commissioning parallel data collection and analytical efforts, and with each MDB gearing up its own technical-assistance and lending programs—goes well beyond the limits of healthy competition.

At a minimum, in cases in which both the World Bank and a regional development bank or a bilateral donor are active, the latter's contribution can be brought more fully "into the loop" early on, and not viewed as a World Bank subcontract or piggyback operation. Of course, borrowers would rightly be concerned about anything approaching a monolithic stance by the international lending community, but improved efficiency could be expected to result from enhanced interplay between the World Bank (which will undoubtedly continue to be more centralized) and other relevant donors, concentrating on activities that require more local orientation and expertise. This is not to suggest that any precise, therefore rigid and confining, blueprint for an improved division of labor on a country or sectorial basis is in the offing, but only that a more cooperative and less dismissive or paternalistic attitude by the World Bank seems to be in the wind under its current leadership.

James Wolfensohn recently expressed his frustration at the difficulty of getting the World Bank staff to "go along" with his ideas. He apparently recognizes the need to change the signals governing personnel evaluations and promotions, away from today's inputs (that is, MDB lending), and toward the outputs of the day after tomorrow (that is, recipient performance). Such outputs are likely to be diffuse and difficult to attribute to any one actor, so the task of changing the internal MDB rewards system is not going to be an easy one and will require careful thought and a good deal of subtlety. But there does exist recent evidence of greater sensitivity to differences in country conditions, of more openness to recipient as well as third-party expertise, and of a greater willingness to decentralize the decision-making process.

Memories of the debt crisis notwithstanding, private-capital flows to developing countries have quadrupled since 1990 and now constitute approximately 70 percent of the total. These private-capital inflows are heavily concentrated into the upper-income or middle-income LDCs of Asia and Latin America, and so MDB policy-based lending (of the soft loan, mixed, and hard loan varieties) does continue to have an important role to play, especially in Central America, South Asia, and Africa. But the mission of this lending is that of gradually working itself out of a job, as more and more countries graduate. In places where foreign private capital is still largely absent, MDB attention is likely to be focused on mobilizing complementary domestic private capital; later on, joint financing with foreign equity or loan capital becomes possible. This outcome is best approached through carefully negotiated sequential policy changes associated with program lending. Public-sector lending that enhances private-sector activity in this fashion is far superior to private-sector lending that leaves the suboptimal domestic-policy environment untouched or that actually helps to entrench suboptimal policy by taking the pressure off.

If policies have indeed been undergoing dramatic change in some developing countries in recent years, it is mainly because learning is going on, because the East Asian experience has had an impact, and because the debt crisis has concentrated borrowers' minds. It seems clear from such cases as Chile, India, Mexico, and Poland that the lending-with-conditionality process works better when local polities themselves have decided to address their reform needs, to effect certain policy changes sequentially, and to approach the international community for financial help in getting there.

The Brady Plan, focusing on the most indebted middle income developing countries, claimed to have two objectives: to rescue countries through a quick infusion of foreign exchange and to achieve structural change. We learned the hard way that it is difficult to achieve two objectives with one instrument. In the 1970s and early 1980s, petrodollars in the form of commercial-bank lending circumvented most high-quality policy discussion and took the pressure off LDC reform efforts. In the 1990s, bilateral and MDB donors have been tempted to do the same with the help of concessional capital, plus complementary private funds responding to these lender's "signals." But now there exists reason to hope—although admittedly no assurance as yet—that these lessons have not been lost on borrowers and lenders alike as we approach the turn of the century.

REFERENCES

A.H. Amsden. "Why Isn't the Whole World Experimenting with the East Asian Model to Develop?: Review of the East Asian Miracle." *World Development,* 22 (April 1994): 627.

Bretton Woods Commission, convened by Paul Volcker. "Bretton Woods: Looking to the Future" (commission report). July 1995.

Helpman, E., and P. Krugman. *Trade Policy and Market Structure.* Cambridge, MA: MIT Press, 1989.

Jacoby, N.H. *U.S. Aid to Taiwan: A Study of Foreign Aid, Self-Help, and Development.* New York, NY: F.A. Praeger, 1967.

Killick, T. *IMF Programmes in Developing Countries: Design and Impact.* New York, NY: Routledge, 1995.

Kravis, I.B. "Trade as a Handmaiden of Growth: Similarities between the Nineteenth and Twentieth Centuries." *Economic Journal* (December 1970).

Stiglitz, J. E. "Technological Change, Sunk Costs, and Competition." *Brookings Papers on Economic Activity* (Winter 1987): 883.

Tinbergen, J. *On the Theory of Economic Policy.* Amsterdam: North Holland. 1952.

Wade, R. *Governing the Market: Economic Theory and the Role of Government in East Asian Industrialization.* Princeton, NJ: Princeton University Press, 1990.

World Bank. *The East Asian Miracle: Economic Growth and Public Policy.* New York, NY: Oxford University Press, 1993.

Lawrence Klein[1] on

Successes and Failures of Development Experience since the 1980s

Gustav Ranis has prepared a stimulating essay that covers the major development events of the last 15 years or so, the actors involved, and the major participating institutions, especially the multilateral development bodies that have responsibilities similar to those of our host institution, the Inter-American Development Bank. I find the paper to be admirable and comprehensive, but I tried to look at the issues involved through different eyes.

At the outset, Professor Ranis looks back at the 1980s and brings things up to date with a very brilliant, sharp, and compact two-paragraph statement about where the developing parts of the world stand after emerging from the LDC debt crisis and the ending of the Cold War. Then he states that he believes that the "...thumbnail picture..." was overdrawn.

It is undoubtedly true, as he says, that life expectancy and infant mortality have improved—even in Sub-Saharan Africa. But does he account for the slaughter in Angola, Rwanda, Somalia, and other African states? Is the quality of life getting better when per capita GDP is falling and when inequality measures are extremely high or worsening?

In commenting on the debt crisis of the 1980s, Ranis speaks of the consensus that evolved in terms of what the developing countries should do about macroeconomic objectives for stability. This observation is, of course, appropriate, but it is only part of the story. Culpability was present on both sides, not only in the developing countries (debtors) but also in the banks and other financial institutions of the developed countries (creditors), and he has nothing to say about good banking behavior, covering such elementary steps as proper collateralization of loans.

Did the institutions, private and public, in the developed world learn from the experience of the 1980s? They learned how to renegotiate ill-considered loans by stretching maturities, swapping debt for equity, and other financial strategies, but they did not learn much about building better early-warning systems or creating analytical-information flows—certainly not enough to head off another kind of crisis in December 1994 in Mexico, which posed the threat of possibly spreading into a much larger crisis.

Professor Ranis quite properly devotes a great deal of attention to East Asian economic development with a question ever present: Can the spectacular development in the

---

[1] University of Pennsylvania.

Far East be duplicated to some extent in Latin America or other areas that want to grow faster in a noninflationary environment? In this respect, he considers such strategies as industrial policy, export-led growth, and agricultural development.

Professor Ranis associates industrial policy with import substitution and special features in financial markets—say, dual or multiple exchange rates. That association is correct as far as it goes, but there are additional facets of industrial policy that I find more significant: these are **real** actions to promote the buildup of specific industries. In my opinion, Japan led the process in the 1950s and 1960s by picking the winners in steel, electronics, cars, Western-style hotels, and many other fields. Tax concessions were used, as well as the international pricing policies of trading companies. Dualism, between the modern and the traditional sectors enabled the former to keep a highly dedicated work force through the use of "lifetime" employment systems.

Although Professor Ranis concentrates on the 1980's and early 1990s, these earlier Japanese industrial policies have been deemed very successful and were adopted throughout East Asia, first in the "New Japans" (or "Tigers") and by the 1980s throughout a wider area of Asia-Pacific. For Japan in the 1980s, the problem has been that industrial policy was less astute and missed picking the winners.

In my opinion it is not that industrial policy is improper but that the quantitative analysis can be faulty, leading to mistakes in such things as HDTV and supercomputer choices. The industrial policies that are now being implemented in the Asia-Pacific region are doing much better in selecting winners instead of losers.

As for import substitution, that may not be the most appropriate lens for examining the international-trade side of development. Much successful development of the 1980s and 1990s in Latin America and in East Asia is associated with the encouragement of imports, subject to careful application of industrial policy in order to gain access to higher-quality, world class goods and technical know-how.

The growth process is often characterized as export led, especially in East Asia during the 1980s and continuing at present. I prefer to emphasize the strategic importance of imports for growth, and a principal role for exports is to help pay for these imports so that the external deficit will not become too much of a burden, as it did for many developing countries in the 1980s and for Mexico again in 1994.

In general, I do not like simplified one-way bivariate relationships in economics; they almost always break down. But if I had to choose between the catch phrases "export-led growth" or "import-led growth," I would prefer the latter.

With respect to international trade, there is one feature that does not enter significantly or constructively into Professor Ranis's discussion. I call that feature, broadly speaking, South-South trade. This term refers to trade among developing countries. A remarkable aspect of the way East Asian economies are interacting with one another is the strong growth in trade within the region. This trade increase is of great importance because for years the naysayers repeated over and over again that these economies were too heterogeneous to support a formal system of regional economic cooperation. But in fact, very strong complementarities have been present all along. Now they are coming to highly visible fruition.

This reality is not simply a fact to be pointed out. It has analytical importance for assessing the staying power of Asian economic expansion. Not only are there large domestic internal markets in China, Indonesia, and other populous countries but also there is a huge regional market in which there takes place a great deal of trade interaction.

A defining characteristic of the East Asian expansion is its longevity. It became noticed on a regional basis in the 1980s, but the underpinnings in lead countries—Japan and the "New Japans"—have been in place for a few decades. This fact is one of the very important features that Latin American countries must contemplate. If they are to draw some lessons from the Asian experience, they too must show that they can achieve impressive economic performance for decades before they can feel that they have really made the "big league". On many occasions in the past three or four decades, some Latin American nations have shown some spurts of economic-growth activity, but these spurts were not sustained, because they had no solid South-South trade to rely upon when they were battered by Northern business cycles, the debt crisis, and most recently the Mexican crisis. There are, however, rays of sunshine in the sense that MERCOSUR may blossom and NAFTA may spread in ways that previous attempts at Latin American regional integration were never able to achieve for long periods of time.

There is an interesting discussion in Professor Ranis's paper about "achieving balanced growth between the domestically oriented agricultural sector and the nonagricultural sector." He analyzes the existing emphasis on trade and manufacturing or industrial activity; this emphasis can lead to neglect of the constructive role that agriculture can play. This idea has merit, but no country is going to graduate through primary reliance on agriculture. Agriculture and food sufficiency are very important, but they are only part of the development process.

When China opened to economic reform in 1978, agriculture played a trigger role. Liberalization and land reform, in the Chinese style, were of extreme importance, and it can be said that the early years after 1978 were, in a fundamental way, characterized by agriculture-led growth—certainly not by export-led growth. There had to be follow-on developments such as liberalization of small enterprises, creation of TVEs, creation of SEZs, importation of financial capital, and development of significant export activities. There is more to come in this step-by-step process of gradualism. It is not the only way to develop, but it is a way that other developing or transition nations should study carefully.

This discussion of agriculture leads me into another aspect of development that is not explicitly treated by Professor Ranis but which is one I believe to be very important— namely, land reform. Before the land reform in China, there was land reform in Taiwan and in South Korea—and much earlier in Japan. Land reform is closely related to issues of the distribution of income and wealth. A characteristic of Asian economic progress is serious land reform—not everywhere, but in several stunning cases. Most recently it could have been possible in the Philippines, but Mrs. Aquino failed to carry through the program of providing rural families with seven hectares. When I asked very knowledge-able observers of the political and economic scene in the Philippines if seven hectares would have been adequate for individual-family subsistence, the reply was that double cropping (beans and palm trees) would do the trick. When I posed the same question to a substantial landowner in the Dominican Republic, he expressed doubt that such a dis-tribution would work, but when the issue was posed to the landowner's agronomist, the latter replied that seven hectares would indeed be adequate.

Land reform still has much potential, but the deeper issue is to achieve more eco-nomic equality (or to lessen the degree of inequality). Throughout much of the Asia-Pacific area, enhancement of economic equality has been another factor contributing to the longevity of the expansion. This is a lesson that has not yet been learned in Latin America or in other areas where there is a yearning for the material fruits of powerful eco-nomic growth.

In the postmortems on the Mexican crisis of 1994, great attention is paid to ex-change rate movements and policies, interest rates, inflation rates, foreign-exchange re-serves, and composition of the financial-capital inflow. These are all very important matters, but they are not decisive. Inequality, a tendency toward its "worsening," and po-litical instability are at least as important in explaining the onset of the crisis as are the macroeconomic indicators.

It is an incomplete approach simply to look for lessons from East Asia for the rest of the developing world. The reverse issue is also important—namely: Can a Mexican-type crisis occur in East Asia? The answer is not that such an event is impossible but that it is improbable, because in East Asia there exist the following:

- less economic inequality
- more political stability
- higher standards of education and stronger human capital
- a more expansive regional market
- better macroeconomic conditions
- a better flow of economic, financial, and general-business information.

Whether or not there is less corruption is hard to say.

Finally, I want to comment on Jan Tinbergen's ideas about targets (objectives) and in-struments. Professor Ranis writes as follows:

"…as Tinbergen tried to teach us generations ago, it is impossible to achieve two ob-jectives with one instrument."…and

"We learned the hard way that one instrument and one objective should be the rule."

With some mathematical assumptions about nonsingularity, we can say that Tinbergen showed that equality between the number of instruments and the number of targets made it possible to choose instruments in nonstochastic systems such that targets can be precisely determined. If the number of instruments exceeds the number of targets, there exists an infinity of solutions for achieving the latter. If the number of instruments is less than the number of targets, we have a setup for a problem in which an objective (loss or gain) function can be optimized with respect to variations of instruments, giving us an efficient frontier of relationships among targets.

This quibble may seem to be pedantic, but to me Tinbergen's analysis does not mean necessarily that one instrument and only one objective should be the rule. The making of economic policy should be a highly multivariate, dynamic, and flexible process in both developed and developing countries. Policymakers must pursue multiple targets and use all the instruments at their disposal in order to achieve good outcomes in this stochastic and dynamic world. Even step-by-step gradualism, which I admire, does not restrict policymakers to one objective per instrument.

Richard Jolly[1] on

Successes and Failures of Development Experience since the 1980s

Before turning to specific comments on Gus Ranis's paper, I would like to make one or two general comments on the record of Latin American development over the last two or three decades. In looking to the future, Ranis describes himself as a cautious optimist. In looking back at the record of Latin America, I would describe my position also as one of qualified optimism.

In terms of human development, the record of Latin America is impressive. The 1996 *Human Development Report* (p. 15) shows that in 1960, the index of human development for Latin America was the highest among all the world's developing-country regions. Over the subsequent three decades, the index nearly doubled, from .465 to .824, maintaining Latin America's position ahead of all other developing-country regions. Latin America had also moved marginally ahead of the CIS countries (which, with the difficulties of transition, had slipped during the late 1980s and early 1990s). Latin America's positive performance in terms of human development is no figment of the statistical imagination. Life expectancy, child mortality rates, access to water and sanitation, levels of malnutrition, improvements in primary education (including increases in completion rates), declines in fertility—all of these indicators register independent evidence of significant improvement in most Latin American countries and of clear improvement also in the regional averages. This progress is impressive by historical standards and impressive also when contrasted with what was expected or even thought possible in the 1950s and early 1960s. Problems galore remain. But we should not ignore or undervalue this important evidence of success—especially in matters of human development, which are increasingly accepted as central to the proper assessment of overall development.

Nevertheless, optimism over this human-development record must be severely qualified by noting the weakness of the record in economic growth and its implications for living standards. The indicators of economic-growth performance over the same 1960-to-1993 period are much worse than most people appear to realize. Almost two-thirds of the 34 countries of Latin America and the Caribbean for which we have time-series data show real per capita income in 1994 lower than that of many years earlier. For three countries—Haiti, Nicaragua, and Venezuela—real income per capita is less today than in 1960 or before. For three more countries—Bolivia, Guyana, and Peru—today's per

---
[1] Special Advisor to the Administrator, UNDP.

capita income is less than at some time in the 1960s. For seven more, including Argentina, Jamaica, and Mexico, it is less than at some date in the 1970s. And for seven others, including Brazil, it is less than at some time in the 1980s. Only for Chile, Colombia, Costa Rica, and seven of the smaller (mostly island) economies was peak income reached in the 1990s. In terms of sustained economic growth, the record has been a disaster.

Much of this record relates of course to the lost decade of the 1980s. It is a mistake to imagine that this lost decade is now totally behind us. The decline in many cases was so deep that it will take years to recover the lost ground. Full recovery is delayed further because the growth rates achieved by many countries in the last few years are still below the growth rates of the 1960s and 1970s.

One must beware of averages. Of the 28 countries for which we can compare rates of economic growth in the late 1980s and 1990s with pre-peak growth in the 1960s and 1970s, 20 showed higher growth in the earlier period than in the later one. The very successful performance of Chile pulls up the recent averages. One needs to look at the country-by-country record to get the real picture.

The data tend to reinforce comparisons with the Great Depression. In fact, the declines in Latin America in the lost decade of the 1980s were in most cases more sustained and in many cases deeper than those of the Great Depression in the industrial countries in the 1930s. The Great Depression in Latin America in the 1930s was an altogether milder and briefer set of interruptions to growth and economic performance. The declines of the 1980s indeed warrant much more serious analysis and comparison with earlier periods than they have received.[2]

My second set of comments relates to the main body of the Ranis article—the successes and failures of thought and action in the 1980s and early 1990s. Here Ranis uses a lot of strong language about the inadequacies and extremes of the Bretton Woods organizations: the Bretton Woods "drumbeat for openness," the World Bank's "waffling" on just what the *East Asian Miracle* study meant in terms of the needed liberalization of markets, the "ritual dance" of structural adjustment. He recognizes the need for new approaches by the World Bank and for stronger roles by other parts of the international system, including the United Nations.

But I confess that I found something a bit overcautious about the listing of issues and differences with the Washington consensus. Ranis uses strong words, but when all is said and done, he ends up by adopting much of the criticized agenda. Ranis himself seems to admit as much: "There is some danger that the policy pendulum, having undoubtedly swung too far in a religious *laissez-faire* direction in the heyday of the Washington consensus, is now in danger of swinging too far in an antiorthodox or revisionist direction."

---

[2] Indeed, I have been able to identify only two comparative studies of the Latin American situation and the Great Depression: the study edited by Rosemary Thorpe and the OECD study by Angus Maddison. Both were undertaken in the early 1980s, before the main effects and sustained experience of the lost decade had taken place. Thorpe, Rosemary, ed., Latin America in the 1930s: *The Role of the Periphery in World Crisis* (New York, St. Martin's Press, 1984)344; Maddison, Angus, *Two Crises, Latin America and Asia 1929–38 and 1973–83,* (Paris, OECD 1985), 105.

Ranis then gives his views of where "this particular pendulum ought to come to rest." I do not much care for the metaphor at this point: a pendulum comes to rest when the clock stops, at least with an old-fashioned clock. But Ranis goes on to identify the elements of a "market-oriented" strategic approach, sticking pretty closely to a pure market situation to guide decisions related to comparative advantage.

Ranis identifies a list of possible reforms relatively neglected so far. Again, his list is like that of a cautious politician campaigning today—a list of microspecifics within an otherwise unchallenged macroconservative frame. Ranis suggests reform of the patent system, some strengthening of research and development expenditures, modification of tax codes to encourage greater risk taking, and some adaptations of agricultural policy.

In contrast, I believe there is a great need for action to be much bolder in looking forward to the twenty-first century. At the top of the list should be such basic issues as equity and income redistribution, land reform, environmental protection, debt relief (at least in some countries), and disarmament. The whole question of employment policy must also be central, and here the record is not encouraging. As regards disarmament, neither the Ranis paper or any of the others refers to the recent abolition of the armies in Haiti or Panama—both important beginnings, if still far from a completed process.

Costa Rica remains a shining example of sanity and military restraint. But why should it be the only such example? In 1994 in Latin America, $18 billion was spent on the military, a sum virtually unchanged from ten years earlier, with more soldiers on active duty than in 1985 and with more imports of armaments than in 1990. President Arias has recently pointed out that international support will be needed if countries are to demobilize soldiers, in order to finance the former soldiers' retraining and to help set them up in other jobs.

As regards the future, more than a stance of cautious optimism is required. Clear goals are also needed, with a much greater emphasis on human-development parameters as the guidelines for the whole process. The crucial questions to be raised now concern where Latin America is likely to be by the 2010-to-2025 period—questions about human development, the eradication of poverty, and the establishment of a stronger global position for Latin America in the world economy. Many Asian countries have had the courage to develop such a vision for the future. For instance, Malaysia has clear goals for 2020, and Korea has set up a commission for "Korea-2050." The experience of the Asian countries shows that long-run goals can be effective guidelines for the whole process of development. These goals need not be heavy handed nor need they constitute a starting point for old-style Soviet planning or for the somewhat academic exercises of much earlier Latin America planning.

Goals for the long run are needed if the process of Latin American development is to tackle long-seated issues and problems in a way that will make the twenty-first century more positive and successful.

Globalization and Competitiveness: Implications for Development Thinking and Practice

Paul Streeten

> *If present trends continue,*
> *economic disparities between*
> *industrial and developing nations*
> *will move from inequitable*
> *to inhuman.*
>
> —James Gustave Speth
> Foreword to *Human Development Report* 1996.

Integration and Interdependence[1]

We read everywhere that international integration is proceeding rapidly as the result of the increased flow of trade, capital, money, technology, people, information, and ideas across national boundaries. International integration implies the adoption of policies by separate countries as if these countries formed a single political unit. The degree of integration is often tested by the extent to which interest rates or share prices or the prices of goods are the same in different countries' markets.

But in fact, if we take integration simply to mean the creation of equal economic opportunities whatever the degree of inequality among the initial endowments of the various members of the integrated area, the world was actually more integrated at the end of the nineteenth century than it is today. Admittedly, tariff barriers (in countries other than those of the United Kingdom) were higher back then (20 percent to 40 percent compared with 5 percent in 1990), but nontariff barriers were much lower, capital and money movements were freer under the gold standard (that is, without the deterrent of variable exchange rates), and the movement of people was also much freer in the sense that passports were rarely needed and citizenship was easily granted. Today, international migration is strictly controlled. During the 1880s, the average annual rate of immigration into the United States was 9.2 per 1000, reaching upward of 10 in the first decade of the present century; in contrast, during the 1980s, the average annual rate of immigration was only 3.1 per 1000 of the U.S. population.[2]

Furthermore, today's world has experienced the fragmentation of the four functions that are coordinated in an integrated international system that aims at economic devel-

[1] I am grateful to Louis Emmerij and Hans Singer for helpful comments on earlier drafts.
[2] *Statistical Abstract of the United States,* (Washington, D.C.: U.S. Government Printing Office, 1991), 9, 54.

opment.[3] These functions are the following: (1) the generation of current-account surpluses by the center; (2) the operation of financial institutions that convert these surpluses into loans or investments; (3) the production and sale of producer goods; and (4) the maintenance of military power to keep peace and enforce contracts. Before 1914, all four functions were exercised by the dominant power, Great Britain; between the wars, there existed no international order, Britain no longer being able and the United States not yet willing to assume the functions; for a quarter of a century after the last war, the functions were exercised and coordinated by the United States. Today, however, we live in a disjointed and fragmented world, one without coordination. Nontariff trade barriers imposed by the OECD countries and restrictions on international migration have prevented fuller global integration. The result has been deflation, unemployment, and slow or negative growth in many countries of the South.

Between 1870 and 1914, the world was integrated unaware. Today, national economic policies are constrained by the activities of multinational companies and banks. Before 1914 the world had been more integrated than it is today. Integration, however, was no guarantee of peace: it did not prevent the World War I.

Later, many objectives of government policy were added to the night watchman state's duty to maintain law and order; the additional objectives included full employment, economic growth, price stability, wage maintenance, reduced inequality in income distribution, regional balance, protection of the natural environment, and the creation of increased opportunities for women and minorities. Strong and wide-ranging national postwar monetary and fiscal policies led to greater integration of national economies by promoting employment and the welfare state; but at the same time, they led to international disintegration. Such disintegration is, however, entirely consistent with a high degree of international **interdependence**.

Interdependence is measured by the costs of severing the relationship. The higher the costs to one country, the greater is the degree of **dependence** of that country. If a small country benefits more from the international division of labor than a large country, then the small country's dependence is greater. If high costs from severing economic links were to be incurred by both partners to a transaction, there would be **interdependence**.

International interdependence is often said to be strong and to have increased. International trade is taken to be an indicator of this interdependence, and trade's high and (with some interruptions) rapidly growing values are accepted as evidence. Between 1820 and 1992, the world population increased by a factor of 5, per capita income by a factor of 8, world income by a factor of 40 and world trade by a factor of 540.[4] Three im-

---

[3] See Paul Streeten, "International Cooperation," in Hollis Chenery and T.N. Srinivasan, eds., *Handbook of Development Economics,* 2 (Amsterdam: North Holland, 1989).

[4] Angus Maddison, *Monitoring the World Economy* (Paris: OECD, 1995).

[5] See Paul Streeten, "International Cooperation," in Hollis Chenery and T. N. Srinivasan, eds., *Handbook of Development Economics* 2 (Amsterdam: North Holland, 1989), 1153–86. For a more recent skeptical treatment of the claim of globalization, see Robert Wade, "Globalization and Its Limits: Reports of the Death of the National Economy Are Greatly Exaggerated," in Suzanne Berger and Ronald Dore, eds., *Convergence or Diversity? National Models of Production and Distribution in a Global Economy* (Ithaca: Cornell University Press, 1997).

portant points are now in order.[5] First, if we were to consider not the absolute trade increase but instead the ratio of international trade to national income, then the rapid total trade growth during the postwar decades might be taken by some to be simply a return to pre-1914 trade-to-GNP ratio values after the interruptions of two world wars, the Great Depression, and high protection. The share of world exports in world GDP rose from 6 percent in 1950 to 16 percent in 1992; for the industrial countries, it increased from 12 percent in 1973 to 17 percent in 1992. By comparison, for 16 major industrial countries, the share of exports in GDP was 18.2 percent in 1900 and 21.2 percent in 1913.[6] The comparisons in the ratios are very similar for particular countries.[7] But these trade-to-GDP ratios are somewhat misleading. Over the postwar decades, the share of services (including government services) in GDP increased enormously; many of these services are not tradable. If we were to take the ratio of international trade to the production of **goods only**, the trade ratio would indeed show a substantial increase not only compared with the interwar period, but also compared with the time before 1913.

The second point is that, as for the notion that unprecedented globalization is now taking place, in reality developing countries (and groups within these countries) that have participated in the benefits from growing trade (and also from foreign investment, which is highly concentrated on East Asia, Brazil, Mexico, and now China) have in fact been few, not more than a dozen, although their number is rising. The large, poor masses of the Indian subcontinent and of Sub-Saharan Africa have thus far not participated substantially in the benefits from the growth of international trade and investment. In fact, the bulk of the international flow of goods, services, direct investment, and finance occurs among America, Europe, and Japan. The group of least developed countries accounted for only 0.1 percent of total global investment inflows and for 0.7 percent of inflows to all developing countries. Africa in particular has been almost completely bypassed.[8]

The third point takes us back to the earlier-mentioned fact that in any case, it is not the volume or value or growth rate of trade that should be accepted as the true or only indicator of economic interdependence, but rather the damage that would be done by the relationship's elimination—that is, consumers' and producers' surpluses. These surpluses are difficult to measure. Much trade is conducted in only slightly differentiated goods, which could readily be replaced by similar domestic products without great loss to buy-

[6] Deepak Nayyar, *Globalization: The Past in Our Present*, Presidential Address to the Seventy-Eighth Annual Conference of the Indian Economic Association (Chandigarh: December 28-30, 1995), 3–4; A. Maizels, *Industrial Growth and World Trade*, (Cambridge: Cambridge University Press, 1963); A. Maddison, *The World Economy in the Twentieth Century* (Paris: OECD Development Center, 1989); P. Bairoch, "International Industrialization Levels from 1750 to 1980," *Journal of European Economic History (1993)* (Brighton: Wheatsheaf, 1993).

[7] This increase in the trade/GDP ratios occurred despite a general increase in tariff protection between 1870 and 1913. It was therefore not the result of trade liberalization. In the pre-1913 period of globalization, the role of the state increased, not decreased. See Paul Bairoch and Richard Kozul-Wright, *Globalization Myths: Some Historical Reflections on Integration, Industrialization and Growth in the World Economy*, (UNCTAD/OSG/DP), 113.

[8] TEP: The Technology/Economy Program, *Technology and the Economy: The Key Relationships*, (Paris: OECD, 1992), 233.

ers and without great increases in costs. But on the other hand, a small and slowly growing volume of trade could be of great importance, and its curtailment could lead to substantial losses; like a link in a bicycle chain, it could, though small, make a big difference to the working of the whole system. For instance, the United States depends strongly on quite small imports of manganese, tin, and chromium.

Trade is, as noted, only one, and not the most important, among many manifestations of economic interdependence. Another is the flow of capital, technology, enterprise, and various types of labor across frontiers; there are also the exchange of assets and the trans-border acquisition of legal rights, information, and knowledge. The global flow of foreign exchange has reached the incredible figure of $1 trillion per day.

After about 1895, the losers from the international integration process began to revolt, and the claims for trade protection and for restrictions on immigration became louder. Between the two world wars, the international order broke down. Today's low-skilled workers in America and in other advanced countries may similarly claim that the economic rise in the South is a threat to them. But in the developing countries as well, corresponding visions are now calling for a reversal of the trend toward globalization.

In addition to economic interdependence, there are educational, technological, ideological, cultural, ecological, military, strategic, and political impulses that are also rapidly propagated throughout the world. Money and goods, images and people, guns and drugs, diseases and pollution can now be moved quickly across national frontiers. When the global satellite communications system was established, instantaneous communication from any part of the world to any other became a reality. Not only was it the creation of a 24-hour money market that had become possible, but the flashing of pictures of national leaders and film stars across the globe, making these faces more familiar than those of our next-door neighbors.[9]

We hear much of the creation of a borderless world and the end of the nation-state. It is true that satellites and the Internet have greatly increased the speed at which the communication of cultural and informational impulses occurs propagated throughout the globe. But here again, as in trade and investment, vast areas in the poor South either are left out (subsistence farmers are not affected by global forces) or suffer the backwash effects of globalization, and the rise of particularism and of religious fundamentalism is a sign that many people are in protest.

It has become a cliché to say that international interdependence is great, has increased, and will continue to grow. This concept is often intended to refer to trade, foreign investment, the flow of money and capital, and the migration of people. Technology advances such as jet airplanes, telex, satellite TV, container ships, supertankers, and super ore carriers, as well as technical progress in transport, communication, travel, and information, have indeed shrunken the world. History may not have ended, but geography, if not coming to an end, certainly seems to matter less each day.

---

[9] Anthony Giddens, "Affluence, Poverty, and the Idea of a Post-Scarcity Soviet," United Nations Research Institute for Social Development, Discussion Paper 63 (May 1995).

Meanwhile, the international spread of ideological and cultural impulses is at least as important as the diffusion of economic impulses. Observe the young in the capitals of the world; from Ladakh to Lisbon, from China to Peru, in the East, West, North, and South, people's attitudes and dress styles have become global—jeans, hairdos, T-shirts, jogging, eating habits, musical tastes, and attitudes toward homosexuality, divorce, and abortion. Even the acts of criminals—such as those relating to drugs, the abuse and rape of women, embezzlement, and corruption—have become similar worldwide.

But this impression of global cultural uniformity can be deceptive. Just as trade, foreign investment, and the flow of money have affected only a few regions of the world and have left the rest comparatively untouched (except for some negative effects), so this parallel globalization of culture is only partial. It is indeed evident in the towns and suburbs and in the more advanced countryside. But the poor in the rural hinterlands, despite of the spread of transistor radio and television, have been largely bypassed. And in many lands there has occurred a reversion toward tradition and tribalism. Global integration has then fueled national disintegration. Ethnic or cultural passions are fracturing societies and regions. We witness Islamic fundamentalism in the Muslim world. Evangelical fundamentalism is spreading not only in the United States, but also in East Asia, Africa, and Latin America, often linked to a Calvinistic, entrepreneurial ethic of saving and hard work. Hindu fundamentalism is evident in India and Judaic fundamentalism in Israel. Nations have broken up into smaller, ethnic groups. All this movement is a reaction against westernization, the alienating effects of large-scale, modern technology, and the unequal distribution of the benefits from industrialization. In the former Soviet countries, the assertion of ethnic identities is the result of the weakening powers of the state in the face of globalization. The complaint is that development has meant the loss of identity, of a sense of community, and of personal meaning.

People in many countries are asserting their indigenous cultural values. Indigenous values are often the only thing that poor people can assert. Traditional values bring identity, continuity, and meaning to their lives. Between the two opposite forces—globalization on the one hand and the assertion of peoples' identities on the other or between what Benjamin Barber calls Jihad and McWorld,[10]—states have found their traditional bases undermined.

The difficult task is to build modernity on tradition. Japan has suceeded in this. Traditional consumption habits and community loyalties have contributed to the fantastic economic growth of the country. Neither all tradition nor all modernity is to be welcomed. The repressive nature of both some traditional values and structures and of some modern ones is evident. Tradition can spell stagnation, oppression, inertia, privilege; modernization can amount to alienation and a loss of identity and of sense of community.

This discussion thus far suggests that the perception is of a greater degree of globalization and integration than has in fact occurred. Direct foreign investment constitutes

---

[10] Benjamin Barber, *Jihad vs. McWorld* (New York: Times Books/Random House, 1995).

only a small portion of total investment in most countries. Domestic savings and domestic investment are more closely correlated now than they were before 1914, implying that even finance capital is not very mobile. This result is explained in part by the fact that government savings play a greater role today than in the past and in part by the existence of exchange rates, which can raise uncertainties and constitute a barrier to long-term commitments. The same point is made by noting that current-account deficits and surpluses are now a much smaller proportion of countries' GDP than they were between 1870 and 1913. Britain ran a current-account surplus that averaged 8 percent of GNP and invested it overseas, compared with 2 percent to 4 percent for the West German and Japanese surpluses (and the American deficit) in the 1980s. These modest levels are surprising in view of the talk of the globalization of capital markets. The bulk of foreign investment has been the capital import by the United States and the outflow from Japan.

Transnational corporations are more domesticated than some of the literature would suggest. Most of them hold most of their assets and have most of their employees in their home country and conduct most of their R&D there. This assertion is confirmed by the fact that 89 percent of U.S. patents taken out by 600 of the world's largest firms in the second half of the 1980s listed the inventor as a resident of the home base.[11] Hence, strategic decisions and innovations come from the home country. This situation may, however, be modified by a wider global spread of R&D as a result of telematics, the convergence of computer, communication, and control technology.

The movement of people in today's world is severely restricted, much more so than in the nineteenth century. Therefore—despite the fact that states are more pressured than they used to be, on the one hand by current global economic forces and on the other by peoples (minorities', tribes', ethnic groups') asking for rights, participation, or independence)—the recent reports on "Sovereignty at Bay" (Raymond Vernon), "The Twilight of Sovereignty" (Walter Wriston), and "The End of the Nation-State" (Kenichi Ohmae and others) are still somewhat premature. The illusion of rapidly increasing globalization arises from a limited historical perspective that looks only at the last 30 or 40 years, at the beginning of which the countries of the world were exceptionally closed as a result of the Great Depression and World War II.

Views differ regarding the benefits and costs of the mobility of the different items, such as trade, finance, technology, and ideas. Keynes wrote, "Ideas, knowledge, art, hospitality, travel—these are things which should of their nature be international. But let goods be homespun whenever it is reasonably and conveniently possible; and, above all, let finance be primarily national."[12] Today it has become rather fashionable to deplore the "cultural imperialism" of television and of the other mass media, to bewail the global spread of mass culture, and to attempt to confine culture to local knowledge, activities

---

[11] Robert Wade, "Globalization and its Limits: Reports of the Death of the National Economy Are Greatly Exaggerated," in Suzanne Berger and Ronald Dore, eds., *Convergence or Diversity? National Models of Production and Distribution in a Global Economy* (Ithaca: Cornell University Press, 1997).

[12] J. M. Keynes, "National Self-Sufficiency," *Yale Review* (Summer 1933). From *Collected Writings of John Maynard Keynes,* XXI (Activities 1931–39) (1982) 237.

and products while advocating free trade in goods and services. Neoliberals advocate lais-sez-faire but not free movement of people, or laissez-passer—perhaps because they fear that the latter would accelerate population growth in the low-income countries of emi-gration and therefore would not contribute to raising those countries' welfare, or that it would interfere with economic objectives (especially the level and distribution of in-come), cultural values, social stability, or security in the receiving country.

Uneven Benefits and Costs of Globalization

Globalization has created undreamed-of opportunities for some people, groups, and countries. Human indicators such as literacy and school enrollment levels, infant mor-tality rates, and life expectancy have enormously improved in the last few decades. The Cold War has ended, and the prospects for peaceful settlement of old disputes have grown brighter from West Asia to South Africa and Northern Ireland. Democracy has spread throughout the world and has replaced autocratic regimes. Globalization has been particularly good for Asia, for the global growth of production, for profits, and for those possessing capital or sophisticated skills (see balance sheet).

At the same time, the liberalization, economic restructuring, democratization, tech-nological change, and fierce competition that accompanied globalization have con-tributed to increases in impoverishment, inequalities, and work insecurity, to the weakening of institutions and social-support systems, and to the erosion of established identities and values. The liberalization and reduced protection of agriculture have raised the price of food, and as a result, the world food-importing countries have suffered. Globalization has been bad for Africa and bad (in many other parts of the world) for those without assets or for those without high-level skills and abilities or with rigidly fixed and unadaptable skills. International competition for markets and jobs has forced gov-ernments to reduce taxation (and therefore, the tax-dependent social services that had protected the poor) and to cut public services and regulations that had protected the en-vironment; it has forced governments and firms to "downsize," "restructure," and "re-en-gineer" and has made necessary all kinds of steps to ensure that the cost of labor is low. At the height of the welfare state, it was thought that government can steer an economy to full employment, and in the quarter century after World War II, the resultant national integration led to international disintegration. In similar fashion, after the early 1970s (a degree of) international integration led to (partial) national disintegration; Beveridge and Keynes had to be dismissed in the face of the pressures of globalization, which weakened the pursuit of national monetary, fiscal and social policies, and the position of organized labor.

As Tables 1 and 2 in the annex show, during the 1960–1994 period, the developing countries' share in the global distribution of wealth has shrunk. Even the rich countries have experienced rises in unemployment, homelessness, crime, and drug abuse. New con-flicts have replaced old ones, terrorism is widespread, and people's lives have become more insecure. New technologies, new types of organization, and competition from low-cost imports have rendered redundant large numbers of semiskilled workers.

Balance Sheet of Globalization

Good for:	Bad for:
Japan, Europe, North America	Many developing countries
East and Southeast Asia	Africa and Latin America
Output	Employment
People with assets	People without assets
Profits	Wages
People with high skills	People with few skills
The educated	The uneducated
Professional, managerial and technical people	Workers
Flexible adjusters	Rigid adjusters
Creditors	Debtors
Those independent of public services	Those dependent on public services
Large firms	Small firms
Men	Women, children
The strong	The weak
Risk takers	Human security
Global markets	Local communities
Sellers of technically sophisticated products	Sellers of primary and standard manufactured products
Global culture	Local cultures
Global peace	Local troubles (Russia, Mexico, Turkey, Cyprus)

In the poor countries, poverty, malnutrition, and disease have grown side by side with improvements in living conditions. Nearly one-third of the population of developing countries and more than one-half of that of Africa live in absolute poverty. The dissolution of the old system of the extended family, together with the increasing reliance on market forces and the dismantling of state institutions, has left many victims of the competitive struggle stranded and helpless.

Income disparities between the rich and the poor nations have doubled during the past thirty years. At the end of the nineteenth century, the main agents on the international scene were states, dominated by Britain until 1913 and by the United States for a quarter of a century after World War II. But today, transnational corporations and international banks have joined the power ranks of the states and to some extent have even gained ascendancy. The world's 37,000 parent transnational corporations and their corporations' 200,000 affiliates control 75 percent of world trade. One-third of this trade is intrafirm.[13] The principle guiding their actions is profit. At the same time, very few of these firms are genuinely transnational or even international (Shell and Unilever are the exceptions in being at least genuinely duonational: British and Dutch). Most companies

---

[13] *States of Disarray: The Social Effects of Globalization* (UNRISD, 1995) 27.

that operate in various countries are stamped by the country of their headquarters. As we have seen, the prediction that national sovereignty was at bay and that the nation-state, confronted with ever-larger and more-powerful transnationals, would wither away was (like the premature reports of Mark Twain's death) somewhat exaggerated. Many countries have successfully dealt with, regulated, and taxed these firms.

In addition to the influence of states and private companies and banks, there has been a growth of international nongovernmental, nonprofit organizations and voluntary agencies that form the international civil society; there are also the multilateral institutions such as the United Nations and its agencies, the World Bank, the International Monetary Fund, the regional development banks, and the like. The beneficiaries from the activities of these nongovernmental organizations and of the multilateral institutions have often been not the poorest but the better-off among the small entrepreneurs; there has been polarization in this regard even within the informal sector. Finally, there are the international labor unions, which are weak compared with national unions; globalization that relies solely on market forces further weakens the power of national and international labor unions alike.

It does not follow that developing countries would have been better off had they closed themselves off from the process of globalization and tried to become autarkic. Joan Robinson once said that there is only one thing that is worse than being exploited by capitalists, and that is not being exploited by them. The same goes for participation in globalization. Those with skills and assets take advantage of the opening up to globalization; those without them get left behind. But there do exist better options than to allow the latter people to become the victims of the blind forces of globalization. Measures such as social safety nets, guaranteed employment programs and training provisions—all designed to cushion poor people in low-income countries against being battered by these forces—should be built into the system of international relations. This effort is necessary not only for political stability but also for reasons of our common humanity.

Unemployment

Globalization has led to the need of firms to compete internationally, and international competition has reinforced globalization. Cost reductions, greater efficiency, and higher incomes have been achieved at the cost of uncertainty, unemployment, and inequality. Globalization has reduced the ability of national governments both to maintain full employment and to look after the victims of the competitive struggle.

Persistent high unemployment in most OECD countries has been a leading policy issue in the last two decades. Some of this unemployment has been attributed to globalization and to the new information and communication technologies. Kurt Vonnegut, in his novel *Player Piano,* describes a future nightmare society in which the divine right of machines, efficiency, and organization has triumphed and in which the large underclass of unemployed is handed out plenty of goodies, by a small group of affluent managers but lacks what John Rawls regards as "perhaps the most important primary good," which is self-respect. Vonnegut's unemployed eventually revolt.

The concern in the advanced countries has become jobless economic growth (although, some of those countries have suffered from jobless economic nongrowth). Growth in the output of goods without the need for additional unpleasant work is of course to be welcomed, not condemned; it is the very essence of productivity growth. Some authors today regard employment as a basic need, but Sidney Webb, the cofounder of the Fabian Society and the London School of Economics, more properly regarded leisure as a basic need. Many forms of monotonous, dirty, hard, or dangerous work are a burden, not a blessing. The foundation for the salvation of humanity lies in the growth of productivity. Increases in output per worker are to be welcomed—but only so long as output itself grows rapidly enough to absorb all those seeking work or the reduced work load can be spread evenly, with corresponding equal distribution of worker incomes. These conditions prevailed during the Keynesian golden age after World War II. But if, as has been the case in the OECD countries in the last decade, total output grows insufficiently fast to generate employment for the whole work force and if the work is unevenly distributed, then we find ourselves in a society in which John Kenneth Galbraith's private affluence amid public squalor is joined by private affluence amid private squalor. Anyone walking through the streets of New York or London has witnessed the homeless sleeping in mid-winter on benches in the open.

Whether the cause of growing unemployment is the globalization of economic relations, inadequate growth of demand (because of inflation fears and balance-of-payments crises), technological change that calls for new skills that are and perhaps will remain scarce, or low-cost imports from developing countries, the unemployed underclass does not even benefit from Vonnegutian managerial handouts. The underclass lacks both recognition and necessities. Doing "more with less" (as a popular classic on re-engineering puts it) is good for economic growth and for the economy, while people become superfluous. The market does not nurture the dignity of those who lose their jobs or live under the threat of losing them. A recent headline in the *Wall Street Journal* ran: "No Need to Fear Lower Unemployment."[14]

Jobless economic growth is not confined to the advanced countries. China has been enjoying spectacularly high growth rates, but unemployment, particularly urban unemployment, has become a major problem.[15] The result of globalization has been the need to cut unit labor costs. Formerly the state and collective firms in China practiced a concealed system of unemployment insurance, a kind of indoor unemployment relief. All members of the labor force had been guaranteed employment, which meant gross overmanning of factories. When China began to be integrated into the global economy, it had to reduce labor costs in order to become competitive and to attract direct foreign investment. In 1986, a new regulation decreed that employment in state enterprises had to be based on fixed-term contracts for three to five years, and enterprises were granted the

---

[14] James Annable (chief economist at the First Chicago Bank), "No Need to Fear Lower Unemployment" *The Wall Street Journal* (August 21, 1996).

[15] See A. R. Khan, "Globalization and Urban Employment: Some Issues in an Asian Perspective," Paper for the UNDP/Habitat Round Table in Marmaris, Turkey (1996).

power to dismiss workers. In 1988, a State Bankruptcy Law was introduced that made it possible to liquidate or restructure state enterprises, which led to reductions in employment. This decline in employment was sharpest in collective enterprises: 15.5 percent between 1991 and 1994.

Similar growth in unemployment has occurred in those formerly socialist countries that have experienced economic growth. Although official unemployment figures for Russia are low, there have in reality occurred substantial withdrawal from the labor force and significant nonregistration of many of those thrown out of employment.

Among the basic human needs are not only food, water, health care, sanitation, shelter, transport, and education but also job security. Job security is as important as food security, both in itself and as a means for securing food security. If job security is to be achieved in a progressive economy, it cannot mean tenure in given jobs (for these will change with technical progress and changing demand) but instead the option for a worker, if dismissed from one job, to enter a new job.

The current justification for the existence and tolerance of widespread unemployment is different in the industrial, the formerly socialist, and the developing countries. In industrial countries it is the fear of inflation and of balance-of-payments difficulties that prevents the achievement of full employment. And inflation may hit hard the same groups of people that are hit by unemployment. The difficult and as yet largely unsolved problem is that of designing a strategy that combines (1) full or overfull employment with (2) absence of inflation and with (3) free wage bargaining and democratic government. Creation of this happy triangle has so far been an elusive goal. It seems that a reserve army of unemployed or a less metaphorical army of police and soldiers have been the only options available thus far for avoiding inflation.[16]

The efficiency wage literature has added to the macroeconomic objective of avoiding inflation various reasons for claiming that the quality of labor and the efforts of those employed are improved by the existence (and therefore the threat) of unemployment. Higher-than-equilibrium real wages combined with unemployment are justified in this literature on the ground that they improve both the ability and the willingness of workers to work harder and more effectively. An important precursor to this literature, Karl Marx, long ago wrote of the need for a reserve army of unemployed to make capitalism work. The recent literature has put new clothes on Marx's analysis and discusses it in terms of the principal-and-agent relationship and of the inability to monitor properly the effort every worker puts into the work: unless workers fear unemployment, they will slacken and reduce their efforts.

Quite apart from its reduction of workers' opportunity to exercise free choice, unemployment reduces the incentive for those with jobs to accept labor-saving innovations if workers are liable to lose their jobs as a result of those innovations. This effect seems to

---

[16] Hans Singer has pointed out that the golden age of the Keynesian consensus of the 1950s and 1960s proved that this happy triangle is in fact possible if the necessary mild controls of inflationary pressures are accepted. The critics would reply that it took two decades for the workers to see through the money illusion.

have been ignored by the efficiency wage literature. On the other hand, as the evidence from Eastern Europe shows, overfull employment can have detrimental effects on product quality and variety, product and process innovation, and workers' and managers' discipline.

Another approach, suggested by Robert Solow,[17] is to analyze the labor market as a social institution and to attach the notion of fairness to the provisions of a higher wage than that which would simply equate total demand for and supply of labor. In their own self-interest, the unemployed then do not underbid this wage, because at some later date they expect to benefit from it. Were they to offer themselves at lower wages now, all workers would be thereafter worse off. It might be in the immediate interest of any one single worker to underbid whether others do the same or not, but this stance would lead to a prisoners' dilemma outcome, everyone ultimately being worse off than had individuals refrained from underbidding. Repeated "games," or instances, however, lead to eventual adherence to the norm that prevents such self-destructive outcomes.

The answer to the employment problems created by globalization lies in the right combination or package of government policies. Simple Keynesian remedies, such as expansion of effective demand, no longer work. Many unemployed are long-term unemployed. Expansion of demand would therefore rapidly produce an excess demand for labor, in that employers would reject the long-term unemployed as unsuitable for hiring. There would then occur a rise in money wages and in prices and no reduction in unemployment. Among the additional measures mentioned are usually education and training programs for workers in order to achieve higher productivity and reduce unemployment, income support for low-paid workers, tax policies to create jobs and prevent environmental degradation, population controls, and social safety nets.

On the other hand, there are those who say there is no need to fear inflation, that inflation is dead. Global competition and corporate restructuring will supposedly keep prices down while productivity gains will let growth flourish.

But what about those unemployed whose disabilities in the light of globalization and of the information and communication revolution—namely, lack of learning ability or self-confidence or self-discipline—render them unemployed and perhaps unemployable? This group raises the set of problems that used to be discussed under the heading of structural unemployment, and later (mainly in Latin America) marginalization, and now social exclusion.[18]

The standard answer to the combination of skill shortages with surplus unskilled labor has been education, vocational training, adjustment assistance, and flexibility (as well as, of course, raising the total level of demand). Experience has shown that these have indeed worked for the bright and well motivated; but for those not so bright and not committed to the work ethic, these approaches have only reinforced a sense of failure.

---

[17] Robert M. Solow, *The Labor Market as a Social Institution* (Cambridge, Mass.: Basil Blackwell, 1990).
[18] Ronald Dore has written illuminatingly about these problems. See for example his comments on Lord Dahrendorf's lecture, mimeographed.

Ronald Dore has said, "Vocational training is an area where Say's law does not operate; supply emphatically does not create its own demand."[19] The new information and communication technologies and their global spread have brought with them inequality related to learning ability. The new underclass should be our concern both from the standpoint of sympathy and social solidarity and of the threat their continued unemployment poses for society in terms of the rise in crime and drug use, and the like.

There is also unemployment caused by low-cost imports from the low-income countries. Even though the percentage of these imports is small, they occur in the labor-intensive sectors, and firms often displace labor by capital in order to remain competitive.

To sum up, the causes of unemployment in the OECD countries are global competition, lack of skills in an age of high and rapidly advancing technology, slow growth, and imports from low wage countries.

Few would maintain today that inducing a higher level of effective demand (for instance, through public investment), even if buttressing with an incomes policy to keep inflation under control, is the whole answer to "structural unemployment." But such an approach would surely make a contribution to reducing unemployment if implemented as part of a package. And it is not at all clear that society cannot use plenty of health workers, child care workers, gardeners, plumbers, sweepers, protectors and restorers of the environment, and other service workers who do not need the advanced and scarce skills demanded by modern technology and whose services cannot be replaced by either computers or imported low-cost goods from low-income countries (though imported low-cost labor from poor countries should be welcomed). Many of these service jobs are, however, in the currently despised or neglected public sector and may call for even more highly despised tax increases. They are also often ill paid and not recognized as valuable. We need to change our valuation of such work and should guarantee minimum standards of reward for them.

In the former socialist countries the reason for unemployment is the need to close down inefficient, overmanned public enterprises and those that produced for the military and to relocate labor into more-efficient activities in order to produce goods in demand. The breakdown of institutions is the primary cause of the large amount of unemployment, often not registered as such.

In developing countries the causes of unemployment are multiple. Above all, the following factors account for it: (1) the absence, scarcity or inadequacy of cooperating factors such as capital, materials, management, infrastructure; (2) the absence of institutions such as labor exchanges, training programs and systems of widespread land ownership; (3) inhibitions and aspirations in attitudes to work that prevent some workers from accepting certain jobs, so that unemployment is accompanied by labor shortages; (4) barriers to work resulting from inadequacies in workers' nutritional, health, and education levels; (5) the low level of demand in the industrial countries for the exports of the developing countries, as a result of slow growth, technical progress, and trade barri-

---

[19] Comments on Dahrendorf [see preceding note].

ers; and (6) the policies of the developing countries that often overprice labor, underprice capital, and overvalue local currency and thus hamper the full and efficient utilization of labor.[20]

Another set of circumstances prevalent in many low-income countries relates to the fact that higher wages can often actually increase worker productivity by enabling workers to become better nourished. Absence of malnutrition increases workers' alertness and their physical strength and reduces illness-related absenteeism. But the individual firm is not usually in a position to decide to pay these higher wages, in part because it might not be able to hold on to its increasingly productive labor force and might thus only be financing the eventual profits of others and in part because it may not recognize the profit opportunities and the ultimate economy of higher wages. When factory legislation was introduced in England in the nineteenth century, English industrialists predicted that the higher costs would ruin British industry. In fact, industry flourished.

Globalization and Income Distribution

Globalization goes with the opening up of national economies, the adoption of outward-looking policies, and the expansion of international trade and finance. How does globalization affect income distribution within poor and rich countries? Theoretical arguments and empirical evidence both suggest that the expansion of trade in services and manufactured goods between the South and the North reduces inequality in the South between skilled and semi-skilled workers (with primary and some secondary education) who can find jobs, while increasing such inequality in the North.[21] In the South, increases in exports raise the demand for and the wages of workers with only basic education relative to those with higher skills (the exception is when international competition precipitates the abandonment of minimum-wage legislation and the weakening of trade unions, thereby lowering the wages of factory workers and public employees). In the North, with increasing North-South trade, skill differentials in wages can be expected to widen and semiskilled workers to suffer a relative reduction in wages (or under sticky wages, unemployment among the semiskilled can be expected to grow).

Overall, however, the rise in the demand for skilled labor in the North is only to a small extent the result of actual or anticipated increases in imports of manufactures produced in developing countries. Instead, the main reason has been technical progress that saves semiskilled labor. Cheap energy and the first wave of automation eliminated most of the North's manual jobs. Electronics is now eliminating routine white-collar jobs. But technical progress also saves some types of skilled, even highly skilled, labor, as "Deep Blue," IBM's chess-playing supercomputer, demonstrates. It proved itself a fair match to Garry Kasparov. Activities that can be reduced to simple rules, even if these rules may give rise to apparently infinite possibilities, are targets for automation.

---

[20] David Card and Alan Krueger have recently found that for some fast-food restaurants in New Jersey and neighboring Pennsylvania (as a control group), higher minimum wages have led to higher employment.

[21] Adrian Wood, *North-South Trade, Employment, and Inequality: Changing Fortunes in a Skill-Driven World* (Oxford: Clarendon Press, 1994).

On the other end of the spectrum, the income differential between unskilled and semi-skilled workers is expected to widen in the South; unskilled workers are to be found mainly in small-scale agriculture, not in manufacturing, and in cases in which unskilled workers are plentiful, that country is not usually a large exporter of manufactures. The situation in those countries that export primary goods (often some of the poorest nations) is interesting.[22] Mineral exports tend to increase inequality: they require little unskilled labor, the ownership of minerals is usually highly concentrated, and reductions in wage inequality in that sector depend on the government's capturing a large share of the rent of the mining companies and spending it on the poor. In turn, the effect of agricultural exports on internal distribution depends on the specific pattern of land ownership: when exports are produced on plantations or privately owned large farms, their expansion will tend to increase inequality (unless the workers are organized into powerful trade unions), but if the increased exports are produced on small farms worked by the owners and their families, then wages inequality will tend to be reduced.

The foregoing analysis has several limitations. One is that it is concerned only with wage inequality rather than with poverty, which some would regard as a greater evil. In any expanding economy, it would not be surprising to find that some groups move ahead of others; such a situation would not matter as long as there were no increase in absolute poverty and as long as those initially left behind would eventually catch up with or overtake those ahead.

Another limitation is that the analysis is concerned only with different kinds of wages and not with other incomes, such as profits and rents (except for the brief discussion of exporters of primary goods). There exist much evidence that globalization has led to growing inequality between incomes from labor and those from capital.

This far we have considered globalization impact on domestic income distribution. One can approach international income distribution among countries by examining the impact of multinational corporations, whose role in the globalization process has enormously increased. Capital, know-how, enterprise, management, and marketing are highly mobile internationally and are combined with the plentiful but internationally much less mobile domestic semiskilled labor. The first factor mentioned (enterprise, management, knowledge, and capital) are in relatively **inelastic** supply in **total**, but if not dependent on local natural capital such as mines or plantations, these factors are easily moved around the world in response to small differential rewards; they are therefore in highly **elastic** supply to **any particular country**. The other factor, labor, is in **highly elastic supply** domestically but is relatively **immobile** across frontiers. The situation is equivalent to one in which plentiful semiskilled labor itself (rather than the physical product of such labor) is what is exported by the host country: the surplus of labor's efficiency over wage as a result of cooperation by other factors that are in less elastic supply accrues to foreigners. The differential international and internal elasticities of supply in response to dif-

---

[22] See Adrian Wood (1994: 244) (previous note) and Bourguignon and Morrison (1989: 273–81) as quoted in Adrian Wood (1994).

ferential rewards, and the monopoly rents entering the reward of these factors, have important implications for the international distribution of gains from investment.

Now let us assume that the package can be unbundled and that some components of the package, such as high skills, can be transferred to the developing country. Let us consider a model (such as air transport) in which two types of service have to be combined—one highly skilled and the other less skilled. The providers of the skilled service, say pilots, are in relatively scarce total supply but are highly mobile between countries in response to financial incentives. On a clear day, an airline pilot can see the world, while the scruffy people who clear the ashtrays of the airplanes on the ground are wholly earthbound. The semiskilled factor, ground personnel, is in highly elastic local supply but is immobile between countries. (Other parallel examples are transnational advertising, hotel chains, and tourist enclaves.) The result will be that pilots will earn large rents, while ground personnel will get the bare minimum wage. Any country—even a very poor one—wishing to have an airline will have to pay its pilots the high international salaries or it will lose them. An egalitarian domestic policy on incomes will be impossible, not so much because of the brain drain (the loss to foreign countries of trained professional manpower) but more in order to counteract that brain drain and to prevent that loss. In such a case, international and domestic inequalities will both have to be large. Once again, partial international integration (that of the skilled and professional) leads to national disintegration. An egalitarian incomes policy is made impossible.

Because the firms operate in oligopolistic and oligopsonistic markets, cost advantages are not necessarily passed on to consumers through lower prices or to workers through higher wages, and the profits then accrue to the parent firms. The operation of this type of international specialization depends upon the following: (1) continuation of substantial intercountry wage differentials (hence, trade unions must be weak in the host country so that low company costs are maintained in regard to wages); (2) continuation of access to the markets of the parent companies (hence stronger political pressure by the importing interests than by the domestic producers that are being displaced by the low-cost components and processes, including trade unions in the rich importing countries); and (3) continuation of permission by host countries to operate with a minimum of taxes, tariffs, and bureaucratic regulation.

The packaged or complete nature of the contribution of the transnational enterprise, usually claimed as its characteristic blessing, is then the cause of the unequal international division of gains. If the package broke or leaked, some of the rents and monopoly rewards would spill over into the host country. But if the package remains tightly secured, only the least scarce and weakest factor in the host country derives any income (and even this is limited) from the operations of the transnational firm.

In some cases, these tendencies can be and have been offset. For instance, the developing country could use its bargaining power to extract a share of these rents (although taxation of footloose MNCs suffers from the aforenoted prisoners' dilemma) and could apply the resultant income to social services or to public works for the poor. Or for instance, investment in human capital could create domestically some of the scarce factors and could thereby skim off some of the company's rents, as has occurred in the more successful developing countries. This is, indeed, what development is all about: as the developing country increases the domestic value added in its exports, that country's growth rate rises. This process is in fact one of the very forces making for globalization. It also shows the limits of the conventional distinction between import substitution and export orientation: the increased domestic value added is actually a form of import substitution, while the increase in exports represents at the same time export orientation.

Technology and Institutions

The world is suffering from the fact that its existing institutions lag behind technology. The revolutions in the technologies of transport, travel, communications, and information have unified and shrunk the globe,[23] but the world's organization into nation-states dates back to the Peace of Westphalia in 1648, to the American constitution and the French revolution in 1789, and to the nineteenth century when Germany and Italy were unified. And even as technology marches on to organize the world into a single unit, nations are becoming more numerous and more acutely identity conscious—or, to put it in Marxian terms, a contradiction exists between the forces of production, which have been globalized, and the relations of production (which reflect the nation-states).

Biotechnology and materials technology do offer considerable promise, but it is the microelectronic revolution in information and communication technology that has been the most relevant to globalization. Few manufacturing and service industries have remained untouched by the application of the microprocessor to new products and new processes.[24] Communication, information, and the media have been utterly transformed by it, and these advances in telecommunications and information technology are expanding the boundaries of tradeability in services, which constitutes the fastest-growing component of trade and foreign direct investment.

When the nation-states were founded, the city-states and the feudalism that preceded them had become too small for the scale of operations required by the Industrial Revolution. The political institution therefore was adapted to the new industrial technology, to the roads, railways, and canals. The nation-state was then a progressive institution. This development does not mean that some form of technological determinism was at work; the adaptation of institutions to technology is not an inevitable process. (For instance, the Middle Ages almost totally lost the Roman technology about roads, baths, aqueducts, and amphitheatres, and these constructions were allowed to fall into disrepair.) But in today's world, the nation-state, with its insistence on full sovereignty, has clearly become, at least in certain respects, an obstacle to further progress. It has landed us in several "prisoners' dilemma" situations: each nation acts in its own perceived rational self-interest, and frequently the result is that all countries end up worse off. The

---

[23] This does not mean that people have necessarily benefited from this technological globalization. At the global level, economic and technical progress translates automatically into human well-being even less than at the national level.

[24] Charles Oman, "The Policy Challenges of Globalization and Regionalization" OECD Development Center, Policy Brief 11.

current arrangement initially rewards each nation to pursue this short-sighted seemingly self-interested course, whether the overall world situation worsens or not as a result. To overcome such ultimately mutually destructive outcome calls for a high degree of trust, moral motivation (even if, as in the case of the prisoners' dilemma, it is honor among thieves), cooperation or compulsion.

We shall not discuss here the feasibility or even the desirability of a world government. If such a government ever were to come about, it would probably be the result of a trend we are already beginning to observe. What we do want to discuss is the creation of technically clearly defined areas of international cooperation or the delegation of covered functions upward to a global body. The Universal Postal Union, established in 1875, may serve as a model.

Common interests and conflicts are running nowadays across national boundaries. For instance, European farmers as a whole are in conflict with European industrialists, with the European public, and with outside competitive producers, all of whom have to pay for the Common Agricultural Policy. And the advanced countries' textile manufacturers are aligned (under the Multifibre Arrangement) against third-world textile exporters and consumers in their own countries. The nation-state has shown itself to be an inappropriate level at which such issues can be resolved.

Clearly, prisoners' dilemma outcomes move the world economy away from more-efficient to less-efficient allocations of resources. There exist, therefore, potential gains, to be had from moving back to more-efficient allocations. According to Coase's theorem, in the absence of transaction costs and in the presence of full information, of a legal framework, and of well-defined property rights, it pays each state to reach agreements with other states to avoid, by compensation payments, this damage and make all better off than they would have been in the outcome of the prisoners' dilemma.[25] For instance, the United States emits pollutants that cause acid rain in Canada. If the damage is greater than the benefits to the United States, then Canada could offer compensation to that country for relinquishing the emission of sulfur dioxide, the chief component in acid rain, and still be better off than it would be in accepting the acid rain; or if the benefits to the United States are greater than the damage to Canada, then the United States can offer compensation to Canada for accepting the acid rain and still be better off than it would have been had it been prevented from inflicting the damage. But as we all know to our regret, we are far away from outcomes according to Coase's theorem, although we are not always at the other end of the spectrum, the prisoners' dilemma. Coase's theorem remains useful, despite its unrealistic assumptions, because it draws our attention to the fact that unexploited mutual-profit opportunities exist when prisoners' dilemma situa-

---

[25] I am indebted to Michael Lipton's analysis of the relation between the prisoners' dilemma and Coase's theorem in a different context in "The Prisoners' Dilemma and Coase's Theorem: A Case for Democracy in Less-Developed Countries?" in R.C.O. Matthews, eds., *Economy and Democracy,* (New York: St. Martin's Press, 1985), 49–109. Farrell has shown that the Coase theorem, according to which individuals could resolve problems of externalities and public goods as well as governments can, provided that property rights are assigned, is not correct. See M.J. Farrell, "Information and the Coase Theorem," *Journal of Economic Perspectives* 1, 113–29.

tions arise. Obviously, this does not mean that compensation always, or even often, ought to be paid. The losers, such as the English landlords after the repeal of the Corn Laws in 1846, may not deserve to be compensated; or even if they do deserve it, the administrative costs and the losses from imposing taxes to finance that compensation may be so large as to make the compensation uneconomic. But the fact that compensation **could** be paid draws our attention to potential unexploited gains.

Under the present system, there exist apparent gains to uncoordinated action. It pays any one country to establish protectionist barriers whether others do so or not; building-up arms brings a promise of security to any one country whether others do so or not; any one country can to its advantage pollute the common air and the oceans whether others do so or not; it pays any one country to attract capital from abroad by tax incentives whether others do so or not, thereby eroding the tax basis. These ultimately self-damaging (and possibly even self-destructive) actions can be avoided, in the absence of self-restraint, only by having a dominant world power impose the needed restraints, or by cooperation, or (best of all) by delegation of some decisions to a transnational authority with the power to enforce restraint or contributions.

It has been shown that iterative games of the prisoners' dilemma type eventually lead to nondestructive outcomes.[26] The partners finally learn and adopt mutually beneficial strategies. As noted earlier, countries find themselves in between the two extremes of prisoners' dilemmas and Coase's theorem outcomes. For several reasons it is harder to reach cooperative agreements in international transactions than in others, in which mutual trust and a sense of duty play stronger parts. There now exist many nation-states, nearly 200, and the large number makes agreements more difficult and defection more likely. We do not have a world government or a global police force that could enforce agreements. Change is rapid, which undermines the basis of stability on which agreements are founded. The absence of a hegemonic power also removes the possibility of sanctions against breaking the agreement. And all these factors prevent the creation of the mutual trust that is a prerequisite for international agreements.

Coordination and enforcement of policies are clearly needed. But coordination means that each country has to do things it does not want to do. The United States has to balance its budget in order to lower the world interest rates; Germany has to grow faster, but it does not want to draw in guest workers from Turkey and Yugoslavia; many say Japan should import more, but it does not want to hurt its domestic industries. And so on.

Even Margaret Thatcher—that archpriestess of free markets and state minimalism—showed in a speech to the United Nations in New York November 8, 1989, that she had come to recognize that in order to avoid global warming and coastal flooding, the countries that emit carbon dioxide and other gases that trap heat in the atmosphere would have to act together, that restrictions would have to be obligatory, and that the application of these restrictions would have to be monitored carefully. Any one country

---

[26] R. Axelrod, *The Evolution of Cooperation* (New York: Basic Books, 1984).

acting by itself in a pro-environmental fashion would be at a competitive disadvantage by incurring the higher costs of protecting the environment.[27]

The challenge is to replace the past international order based on dominance and dependence—or the past disorder that showed fragmentation and lack of coordination—with a new pluralistic global order built on equality and fairness.

Technology and the International Location of Industry

A question that has preoccupied scholars and policymakers is the impact of the new technologies on the location of industries. More specifically, the question has been raised whether the revolution in electronics and the accompanying move to flexible production and the declining trend in low-wage labor costs will not deprive the developing countries of their comparative advantage in labor-intensive activities and relocate plants back to the advanced countries. There are at least five points to be made that make prospects for the developing countries more hopeful.

First of all, the new technologies economize not only in labor but also in some technical, supervisory, and managerial skills (particularly those that can be encapsulated in rules). These skills are scarce in many developing countries, and these countries' comparative advantage in those particular economic activities may therefore be restored.

Second, based not only on the experience of the newly industrializing countries but also on eighteenth and nineteenth century economic history, both unemployment and the inability to compete with the most advanced country in an open market have been predicted repeatedly and often mistakenly. The Luddites opposed the introduction of machinery, and Friedrich List thought that Britain's advanced technology would not give Germany an opportunity to develop. The steam engine also replaced much labor, but that labor was absorbed in new activities. The lessons of history thus far are that there always exist some products and processes in which countries at an earlier stage of development have a comparative advantage. The product cycle is becoming shorter, but it does continue to exist—despite the possible implications of the story of the Oxford College that received a large private bequest. In the senior common room, the fellows were discussing how the money should best be invested. The bursar finally said, "Well, let's invest it in property. After all, property has served us well for the last thousand years." Then the senior fellow chirped up and said, "Yes, but you know the last thousand years have been exceptional." Similarly, perhaps the experience of the developing countries will turn out to be like that of the man who fell out of the 32nd floor who, when he reached the fourth floor, shouted out, "So far, so good!" There may eventually turn out to exist discontinuities in history that make the electronics revolution now under way different from anything that has ever happened before. But the weight of the evidence is on the other side.

Third, electronics offers hope for latecomers because the field depends on classroom-learned science—instead of on the production engineering favored by the relatively old-

---

[27] *The New York Times* (November 9, 1989), A–17.

fashioned processes—combined with more on-the-job training. Such classroom learning is much less expensive than learning that has to be accompanied by working on expensive equipment. It is true that the science to be learned is more advanced than earlier science, but the ability to master it is not confined to any one group. A careful analysis of the most appropriate methods of training should therefore be high on the research agenda.

Fourth, flexible specialization, which in many firms is replacing Fordist and Taylorist methods of mass production, is suited for developing countries. The method is intensive neither in capital nor in foreign exchange, nor is it dependent on economies of large-scale production.

Fifth, the new technology, even if developed and applied in the advanced countries, will provide cheaper and better or new imports of goods and services for the developing countries. Of course, the developing countries must be able to earn the foreign exchange to pay for these imports, but there exist pointers as to how to do so. There also exist other activities, such as certain services in information technology, in which the developing countries will maintain or attain a comparative advantage.

The main conclusion to be drawn from the foregoing brief discussion is that the threat may not come so much from the nature of technical progress in the advanced countries as from its pace. The greatly accelerated rate of technical change calls for a high degree of flexibility and adaptability in the developing countries. Those countries that cannot achieve these qualities will lose.

International Institutions

From the point of view of human development, there exists no justification for "one state, one vote" in the United Nations General Assembly (even though its resolutions have only recommendatory power): respect for persons applies to equality of status enjoyed by individuals within a nation but not to corporate entities such as states. Nevertheless, in the United Nations context, it could be said that the voting rights in the Assembly compensate for the gross economic inequality manifested in international trade and for the military inequality recognized in the great powers' permanent membership and veto power on the Security Council, which can reach decisions with binding force. It should also be remembered that the large and growing majority of the world's people does live in the developing countries. A further justification for voting by states lies in the overriding importance of avoiding war. And the state is the institution with a monopoly of force. Yet, considerations of law and order in international relations have to be tempered by those of social justice. In civilized relations, including international relations, bargaining and negotiation do not occur in a space of pure power politics but always instead appeal openly or tacitly to mutually accepted or acceptable values and norms.

The United Nations and its many agencies have not yet adjusted to the demise of the Cold War. They have been subjected to many criticisms, and numerous proposals have been made for their reform. Many have put the blame on institutional inadequacies. It is true that badly designed institutions can be formidable obstacles to needed reform. But even the best institutions cannot work if they are not supported by political power. In the final analysis; the past defects of the United Nations agencies were not the result of institutional inadequacies, of overlaps here and gaps there, of low-level representation at important meetings, of lack of coordination, or of managerial flaws, but of lack of commitment by member governments. There were successes: the crises in Africa, in Cambodia, and in El Salvador called forth the best in the UN. In the prevention of natural disasters, in the eradication of contagious diseases, and in limiting damage to the environment, the UN agencies have been quite successful. Some argue that the United Nations has been more successful in the social and economic fields than in peacekeeping; others see it the other way around.

State sovereignty, which still dominates the world order, has become inadequate and indeed dangerous. In the area of peacekeeping, the unrealistic distinction between external aggression and internal oppression should be abandoned. The predominant threat to stability is conflict within countries and not between them. There is an urgent need to strengthen international human rights. Many of the most destabilizing troubles come from within states—either because of ethnic strife or repressive measures by governments. Conditions that lead to tyranny at home sooner or later are likely to spill over into search for enemies abroad. Consider the Soviets' invasion of Hungary and Czechoslovakia, the old South African regime in Angola and Mozambique, and Iraq in Kuwait. An ounce of prevention is better than a ton of punishment. And prevention of aggression is an important task for the UN.

There already exist many additional international institutions that work well, even though they never hit the headlines. They carry out their allotted tasks in a quietly effective manner. The already-mentioned Universal Postal Union, founded in 1875, whose task it is to perfect postal services and to promote international collaboration, the International Telecommunication Union, the World Meteorological Association, the International Civil Aviation Organization, and the World Intellectual Property Organization—all of these have clearly and narrowly defined technical mandates, are nonpoliticized, and implement their tasks competently. The advantages from them are great and manifest. Their success is largely the result of their covering technical, non-politicized, important issues.

International coordination has worked well in areas in which the advantages are great and visible: the wide, although not universal, adoption of the metric system; the 1884 adoption of Greenwich Mean Time, on which the world's time system is based; and the establishment of an international regime for containing contagious diseases.

International coordination or cooperation can take different forms.[28] There can be full harmonization of policies, such as the adoption of common standards—for exam-

---

[28] See Richard N. Cooper, "Panel Discussion: The Prospects for International Policy Coordination," in William H. Buiter and Richard C. Marston, eds., *International Economic Policy Coordination* (Cambridge: Cambridge University Press, 1985), 369–370.

ple, the metric system. Or it can mean joint expenditures for a common purpose, such as international air traffic control. Or it may involve submitting to agreed-upon rules. Or it can amount to the continual exchange of information, such as that on illegal flight of capital or on matters of public health. Or, as in the case of macroeconomic coordination, it can involve joint decision making on monetary, fiscal, trade, and exchange rate policy.

The kind of institutional innovations at the global or transnational level that would avoid prisoners' dilemma outcomes would be those that would realign modern technology and political institutions, would coordinate the four functions (mentioned earlier) that a global system concerned with development should fulfill, and would avoid the negative-sum games to which prisoners' dilemma situations typically give rise.[29]

Institutional innovation does not imply the funding of legions of international bureaucrats or gleaming, glass-plated headquarters buildings and pools of high-paid consultants requiring additional support staff. The emphasis here is instead on procedures, processes, rules, norms, and incentives implying changes in behavior and forums for negotiation or exploration. The existing market, for example, is an institution. Many of the needed functions can be adopted by existing organizations. Nor is more coordination of functions necessarily involved. Some of these innovations can take a regional form, and others should be global.

The Role of Micro-Enterprises and the Informal Sector

Globalization refers not just to liberalization and expansion of trade in goods and services but also to international movements of capital, technology, marketing, and management. These in turn call for an understanding of the firm. Globalization, with its intensification of competition and its expansion of the operations of multinational firms, has sometimes hurt firms in the informal sector and micro-enterprises. It has put a premium on skills and large scale and has penalized the low skilled, small, and weak. Many of the latter have disappeared because they were incapable of facing the competition, the size, and the power of the large firms. On the other hand, globalization has also had some positive effects, both direct and indirect on the informal sector. Exports have been encouraged both directly (when there were institutions providing marketing, design, and credit) and indirectly (when the domestic formal sector subcontracted to informal enterprises).

Some aspects of adjustment policies, liberalization, privatization, decentralization, and deregulation, normally regarded as hostile to the poor, were actually favorable to the informal sector. Austerity programs made some leaders more receptive to the needs of the poor. Greater emphasis was given to jobs, incomes, and the productivity of the poor. Even the act of getting prices right can be used for the benefit of the informal sector. Kenya introduced a tariff rebate for small firms fifteen years after it was recommended in

[29] See Paul Streeten, *Thinking about Development,* (Second Lecture) (Cambridge: Cambridge University Press, 1995).

the ILO Employment Mission report. Balance-of-payments and debt problems, by restraining imports, can also favor the informal sector. The fashion for decentralization can mean empowerment of poor groups, with a switch to NGOs and away from large state bureaucracies.

The recent emphasis on the role of private enterprise and free markets has been useful. It has been in part a healthy reaction against excessive early faith in the power of governments to direct the economy, to manage businesses, and to correct market failures. But unregulated markets can be both inefficient and cruel. Joan Robinson said that the "invisible hand" can work by strangulation. We know that both markets and governments may fail and that the failure of one does not automatically constitute a case for the other. It is now widely accepted that market failure is not necessarily a case for government intervention. It is less generally realized that government failure does not necessarily constitute a case for private enterprise. There is no *a priori* presumption as to which is preferable in any given situation.

The fact of government failure and bureaucratic failure suggests that it is important to concentrate the activities of the government even more on areas in which private efforts fail. Government activity often is complementary to private enterprise and efficient markets. The aim should be to avoid crowding out and to achieve "crowding in." Government intervention should provide the conditions in which markets and enterprise can flourish. Market orientation and state minimalism, far from going together, are incompatible. A well-designed policy calls for interventions to maintain competition and avoid restrictive practices, monopolies, and cartels, and to provide physical and social infrastructure, and some research efforts. It may require new types of institutions as well. Governments should also take care of the victims of the competitive struggle, both for humanitarian and for efficiency-related reasons. The informal sector can play an important part in providing a safety net. But the policy of looking after the victims of the competitive struggle by encouraging the informal sector to provide a safety net (it should not be a safety hammock) can be carried out beyond this point and can make a substantial contribution to production and productivity growth.

There are four reasons for paying attention to the informal sector. They arise from the triple need to increase production, employment (a source of recognition and self-respect), and incomes and the need also to avoid rebellion.

First, the informal sector represents a potentially large reserve of productivity and earning power. Although not all informal-sector activities contribute actually or potentially to productivity and earnings, some do.

Secondly, the labor force in the low-income countries is likely to grow rapidly in the next fifteen years, and neither agriculture nor the industrial formal sector is capable of absorbing even a fraction of these additions, to say nothing of the large number of already unemployed or underemployed. Workers seeking remunerative employment are likely to grow at a rate of 2 percent to 3 percent per year in Africa. The labor surplus economies of Java and Bangladesh represent the future for Africa. The situation is aggravated by the low world economic growth rates. The combination of globalization, population growth, urbanization, and recession has swelled the informal sector, which presents the only hope for jobs.[30]

A third reason is that, although the informal sector should not be equated with the poor (some members of the informal sector earn more than some in the formal sector, and many poor are outside the informal sector), it is in the informal sector that many poor people are to be found. By harnessing the sector's potential for generating incomes (and self-respect), not only is efficient growth promoted but also poverty is reduced. If informal-sector productivity and remunerativeness can be raised without depriving the high-productivity formal sector of needed resources (and hence of more production and the opportunity of future employment) then no conflict exists between efficiency and equity.

A fourth reason is that prolonged unemployment leads to alienation and a sense of worthlessness and can be a source of rebellious instead of productive activity. Governments in power have a particular interest in stability, in not upsetting the existing order, and in using the informal sector as a vote bank.

In general terms, one would wish the informal sector neither to be subsidized at the expense of the high-productivity formal-sector firms nor to be squeezed out by any privileged treatment given to such formal-sector firms.

Utilization of informal-sector enterprises would require changes in government policies. The first step would be to stop repressive regulation, harassment, and discrimination against the informal sector: to stop, for example, demolishing informal-sector houses (subject, of course, to some urban planning for open spaces). In Peru, a Union of Formals and Informals has been formed to reduce government regulations and bureaucratic meddling.[31] It is an interesting example of a reformist alliance, in which

---

[30] This approach has been criticized as excessively Eurocentric. The critics say that the notion of a "labor force" comprising all able-bodied men and women between, say, fifteen and sixty is not applicable to many developing countries. The problem is not to find jobs, but to redefine "work." The "idleness" of the women in purdah, the gossips in the cafés, the begging priests and monks, the small-scale rentiers, the useless peddlers, and the idle bureaucrats should, according to Clifford Geertz, not be suppressed, and these people should not be encouraged to "work," but the notions of "idleness" and "work" should be redefined, so that these "underemployed" are kept "outside the work force but inside society" (Clifford Geertz, "Myrdal's Mythology," in *Encounter* (July 1969), 34.) The evidence does not seem to have confirmed that this is the preference of the workless, whenever opportunities to earn arise. It would, however, be worth exploring whether activities in the informal sector that do not show high economic returns may not be valuable by some other standards.

[31] See Alan Riding, "Peruvians Combating Red Tape," *The New York Times* (July 24, 1988), 3. This article cites Hernando de Soto, head of the Institute for Liberty and Democracy in Lima, that 60 percent of Peru's work force operates outside the formal economy and accounts for 38 percent of that country's gross domestic product. Some 95 percent of public transport in Lima is in the hands of informal operators; some 98 percent of new homes, most of them in shantytowns, are built without permits; and 80 percent of clothing and 60 percent of furniture are produced by the informal sector. According to the same source, it takes 289 days to register a new company, so most people do not bother. Since this article appeared, Hernando de Soto's book *The Other Path* (New York: Harper & Row; London: I. B. Tauris) has been published. It contains an impassioned introduction by Mario Vargas Llosa. There de Soto estimates that in Peru the informal sector makes up 48 percent of the total labor force. Its members work 61 percent of all man-hours and create 38 percent of the GDP. They have set up 274 markets in Lima; they run 93 percent of the buses; and they have built 42 percent of the houses. See also "An Interview with Hernando de Soto, *Health and Development* 1,1 (March/April 1989). There are, however, critics of de Soto's enthusiasm. My friend Jaime Mezzera, with the International Labor Organization (PREALC) in Santiago, estimates the informal sector's contribution in any Latin American country at no more than 15 percent.

formal-sector enterprises make common cause with informal ones, sharing with them their experience and uniting in exercising political pressure. The next step would be to adopt policies and to create institutions with respect to the provision of credit, training, information, and imported inputs (for instance, tariff remission for the informal sector). As to credit, innovative steps are needed for small loans and the acceptance of new types of collateral such as inventories, an unlicensed bus, or plots of land in shantytowns. Another option is the mobilization of peer pressure, as in the Grameen Bank in Bangladesh. A third step would be to remove legislation that gives the formal sector special advantages in buying from or selling to the informal sector.

The policy implications of this proposal are quite radical. For instance, the common prescription is to lower real wages in order to raise employment. But in the suggested model, a rise in real wages may increase employment and incomes in the informal sector. Spare-part production, repairs, and ancillary activities such as cleaning, transport, and packaging are carried out inside the firms in the organized sector while wages are low, but when wages are raised, such activities become worth contracting out to small informal-sector firms not subject to minimum-wage legislation. The informal-sector firms carry out these activities in a more labor-intensive way and benefit from the new contracts. Even if the workers previously engaged in these activities inside the formal-sector firms were to be dismissed (rather than redeployed) and were to add pressure on incomes in the informal sector, the formal firms' savings in capital and profits may be enough to produce higher incomes as well as more jobs for the subcontractors. This would be the case, for example, if the self-employed small entrepreneur works harder than the same man as paid foreman or manager. A similar effect is produced by legislating for a shorter workweek, to which the informal-sector firms are not bound. Higher taxes, avoided or evaded by these enterprises, work in the same direction.[32]

Additional measures are needed in order to implement a positive policy for the informal sector. Let us briefly examine seven such measures.

First, a more favorable overall economic environment for the informal sector should be created. At present, macropolicies tend to discriminate against it. For instance, investment incentives confine tax concessions to formal sector-firms. Exchange rate overvaluation, import restrictions, and interest rate undervaluation handicap informal firms' access to inputs and credit.

Second, it is necessary to design new institutions to help improve poor peoples' access to assets. In agriculture this policy has worked. It is more difficult to apply it in urban industry. Steps are being taken to provide these small entrepreneurs with credit. The Grameen Bank in Bangladesh has found many imitators in other countries. The Inter-American Development Bank wants to establish itself as the bank for Latin America's informal sector. The International Fund for Agricultural Development has

---

[32] Ronald Dore has suggested that the same effect can be achieved by the Japanese practice of high average wages with lifetime employment and a retirement age at 50. The worker then sets himself up in a small subcontracting business and makes use of his connection with the large firm, which regards him as loyal and reliable.

successfully lent to businesses without collateral. Pressures for repayment can be exercised by peer groups and by making small loans for short periods. Loans should be primarily for working capital. Judgment of the borrower's reliability can replace conventional collateral requirements.

Third, returns to these enterprises must be raised. It is not enough to raise their productivity: productivity gains can be passed on in the form of lower prices to frequently better-off formal-sector buyers or can be offset by the charging of higher prices for inputs. It is the earning power, the remunerativeness of the enterprise, that matters.

Fourth, employment opportunities must be improved. Even though the informal sector is often defined as labor supply driven, there exist obstacles to entry and to employment that should be reduced.

Fifth, the demand for the informal sector's production should be raised. Poor people tend to buy the goods produced by the poor people in the informal sector, and thus, policies that generate incomes to poor people will also raise the demand for their products.[33]

Sixth, access to education, training, and health services must be improved, both as an end in itself and in order to raise the productivity of the poor. Both technical training and instruction in simple managerial techniques such as cost accounting, bookkeeping, and marketing are important. The identification and provision of missing components (such as market information, infrastructure, or technical know-how) can yield great benefits at little cost.

Seventh, certain transfer payments out of public funds are also required in order to provide a safety net, not only to aid the unemployables, the disabled, the sick, and the old but also to tide people over during temporary periods of no earnings, of failure of their enterprises, or of temporary inability to work.

In the manner just described, the informal sector can be made complementary to the formal sector and can be linked with the global economy with respect to access to markets, inputs, information, and technology and with respect to linkages of the small-scale firms to large-scale firms, domestic to foreign firms, public to private firms, and nongovernmental organizations to governments. The production system of foreign retailers or importing houses is an example of the symbiosis between foreign large and domestic small enterprises. Similarly, private voluntary organizations engaged in helping informal-sector projects should find ways of cooperating with government departments and multinational corporations, which are often in a better position to finance and replicate successful projects.

It has already been emphasized that this encouragement of complementarities should not be carried out at the expense of the growth of the high-productivity modern sector. On the contrary, the small units should contribute to raising the productivity of the large ones. Nor should there be any form of exploitation such as child labor, inhuman working conditions, sweatshop labor, or monopsonistic depression of the prices at which

---

[33] Liedholm and Mead have referred to this. See also Radha Sinha, Peter Pearson, Gopal Kadekodi, and Mary Gregory, *Income Distribution, Growth, and Basic Needs in India,* (London: Croom Helm,1979).

outputs are bought. Fears have been expressed that the informal-sector enterprises have been reduced to a state of "peonage" by their formal-sector principals.[34]

Encouragement that the informal sector, or at any rate the sector containing small-scale firms, can be the dynamic sector of the future comes from an unexpected source: the literature on flexible specialization, mainly applied to trends in the advanced, industrial countries.[35] The move from standardized, large-scale mass production to small-scale, flexible firms is the result of changes in demand and in supply. On the demand side, the mass consumer has been replaced by a more sophisticated type with higher purchasing power and more-differentiated tastes. On the side of supply, the technology for energy and information has encouraged decentralization of production and smaller size of firms. "Mass production is the manufacture of standard products with specialized resources...; flexible specialization is the production of specialized products with general resources..."[36] In Mexico, innumerable small, decentralized workshops (maquilas) and household units are subcontractors for large firms. The uncertainties of the 1980s encouraged the rise of these small units, which produce specialized products with a broadly skilled and weakly specialized labor force.

The division of labor resembles the Japanese kanban, in which many small suppliers and subcontractors are clustered around a large firm. Similar patterns are to be found in Northern Italy (the so-called "Third Italy") and other parts of Europe, with their regional clusters of small, cooperating, flexible firms.[37] As demand and technology change, skills and products can be easily switched and adapted to the new situation. The shoe industries around Novo Hamburgo in Brazil and León in Mexico are organized on this basis and have encouraged the growth of rural industries.

As Judith Tendler has pointed out, there has occurred a role reversal: in this literature, the formal-sector firms—interpreted as the traditional, large-scale, fixed-cost, mass-production firms—are seen as "sick," whereas the flexible, small firms are capable of responding dynamically to changing demand and technology. Not only have the small firms taken over the function of leadership but also they are more humane and responsible in their work relations. There is a new form of cooperation among the small firms. Furthermore, the old confrontation between labor and capital is replaced by one between

---

[34] Sanjaya Lall, "A Study of Multinational and Local Firm Linkages in India" in Sanjaya Lall, *Multinationals, Technology, and Exports,* (London: Macmillan, 1985). 270. Lall, however, concludes from his case study that "on the whole, their benefits from being linked outweigh their costs" (p. 288).

[35] See Judith Tendler, "The Remarkable Convergence of Fashion on Small Enterprise and the Informal Sector: What Are the Implications for Policy?" (1987), mimeo; and Charles F. Sabel, "Changing Models of Economic Efficiency and Their Implications for Industrialization in the Third World" (Cambridge: MIT Department of City and Regional Planning 1987) and in Alejandro Foxley, Michael S. McPherson, and Guillermo O'Donnell, eds., *Development, Democracy, and the Art of Trespassing: Essays in Honor of Albert O. Hirschman,* (Notre Dame, Indiana: University of Notre Dame Press, 1986), 27–55.

[36] See Charles F. Sabel, p. 40. The *marxisant* terms are "Fordism" and "post-Fordism"—not, of course, named after the Ford Foundation but after Henry Ford and his famous remark that the American public could have their model T any color they liked as long as it was black.

[37] Recent evidence shows, however, that some of these firms in the Third Italy have gone bankrupt, and that others have been taken over by large firms. It seems that they have a tendency to merge either into the First or Second Italy.

(on the one hand) the managers, owners, and workers in the small, subcontracting firms and (on the other hand) the large buyers of the small firms' output. In addition, supportive local institutions evolve that provide information, technical know-how, and training. One does not have to accept the view of the disappearance of the large firm to accept the growing role of these small enterprises. Indeed, the thesis propounded here is that the two should become complementary. All this holds out great productive and social promise for the informal sector, especially if supported by the right social policies.

Global Financial Flows

Global financial flows have increased tremendously and now on an average day are on the order of $1 trillion. This level represents a ratio of foreign-exchange dealings to world trade of nearly 70 to 1 and equals the world's total official gold and foreign-exchange reserves. The enormous growth of these flows is the result of the collapse of the Bretton Woods system in 1973 combined with the deregulation and liberalization of capital flows and with the opportunities this change has provided for speculation on variable exchange rates.

The 24-hour international capital market has given rise to the fear that the international financial system is unstable. But the recent difficulties point to the strength, rather than the weakness, of the international system. The effects of the different crises—the Latin American debt crisis, the American savings-and-loan fiasco, the BCCI scandal, Mexico, Barings, Daiwa—did not spread internationally. Many individuals were hurt, including taxpayers, but these were mainly residents of the immediate areas, and the rest of the world was sheltered. The system did not break down. Obviously, this does not mean that it cannot do so in the future.

Globalization of financial flows, as of trade, has been partial: there are hardly any flows to low-income developing countries, and although private flows to middle-income developing countries have enormously increased, official development assistance has stagnated. The bulk of the flows occurs among OECD countries, and there is some foreign investment in a selected group of developing countries, mostly China and countries in Latin America and East Asia. This situation contradicts neoclassical theory, according to which capital should flow from the capital-abundant to the capital-scarce countries. In fact, the United States, one of the countries richest in capital, has attracted the most capital. And among developing countries it is those with substantial human capital and with good government policies that have attracted financial capital.

Some pessimists worry about two contradictory things: first, that a massive outflow of capital from rich to poor countries will export jobs and second, that cheap imports from the South will lead to a current-account deficit of the North (which must mean a capital flow from the South to the North) and therefore again to job losses. Neither should be a cause for worry. A current-account deficit of the South is more likely, and the resulting expanding markets in the South will create jobs in the North.

In the light of this large increase in financial flows, it is a puzzle to find that domestic savings and domestic investment are closer together for most countries than they were before 1914. This means that net flows are much smaller than gross flows. Many explanations have been offered for this paradox, among them the possible obstacle posed by fluctuating exchange rates to long-term real investment. Deregulation and liberalization have accelerated neither investment nor growth, nor have they resulted in high levels of employment nor in a better income distribution, nor in lower borrowing costs. They have also increased the volatility of asset prices.

Global financial deregulation and liberalization have brought some benefits but also greater risks for investors and for the financial system. In the 1980s, the tasks of stabilizing high inflation, dealing with the debt crisis, and carrying out structural adjustment had preoccupied many governments. In the 1990s, problems of coping with rapid swings in capital flows became more pressing, highlighted by Mexico's financial crisis in 1995. This situation raised the question of whether a return to control of capital markets was indicated.

There does exist a need for re-regulation and harmonization of legislation. The more oriented a country is toward free enterprise, the greater is the need for official supervision. Deregulation has resulted in higher and less-stable interest rates, less-stable exchange rates, boom and slump in property prices, and gambling on asset values and interest and exchange rates. The danger of business failure is high. If we do not wish to have to bail out financial institutions, deregulation has to be supported by close and well-coordinated supervision.

The Bretton Woods system was based on the premise that currency convertibility, multilateral trade, and stable exchange rates require constraints on international capital mobility. Financial liberalization, carried too far, can damage the more important trade liberalization. For instance, when a country should devalue the currency because its domestic prices have risen by more than have foreign prices, it may be unable to do so because of speculative short-term capital inflows. Or conversely, changes in capital flows can produce large exchange rate swings, which are detrimental to trade. One way to slow down short-term capital movements would be the Tobin tax—a small, uniform tax imposed on all international capital flows. There has been a good deal of recent discussion on the matter, and a book has been published that discusses the desirability and feasibility of the tax, from both sides of the aisle.[38]

Competitiveness

The notion of competitiveness among countries has recently taken a few hard knocks. Paul Krugman has shown that competitiveness does not really apply to any relationship between countries, as opposed to firms. In the competitive struggle, as in competitive sports, the gains for one are at the expense of another.[39] Not so between countries, where

---

[38] Mahbub ul Haq, Inge Kaul, and Isabelle Grunberg, eds., *The Tobin Tax: Coping with Financial Volatility*, (Oxford: Oxford University Press, 1996).

[39] This is not quite true. In conditions of oligopoly, firms work with suppliers, build alliances, and thrive on trust and loyalty. Business is no longer a branch of warfare, and cooperation can pay off (sometimes at the expense of buyers or workers or the environment). In theory, the assumption of perfect competition has been replaced by game theory. Although globalization can increase competition, oligopoly obviously applies even more in the global than in the national arena.

the gains of one can be shown to lead to gains for others. If missapplied, or abused, the notion of competitiveness can in fact lead to calls for protection, which hurts everyone.

Countries do of course have different rates of economic growth, different rates of productivity growth, and different rates of improvement in living standards. It is widely agreed that the rule of law, clearly defined property rights, high savings and investment in physical and human capital, good education, flexible labor markets, good macroeconomic policies aiming at labor-intensive growth, and high levels of technology, management, and infrastructure, all have important roles to play. Some would add the need for the redistribution of productive assets (particularly land) in countries where they are very unequally distributed. In brief, certain legal and political institutions and certain policies are more conducive to growth than others. Whether the openness of an economy to trade and investment is a cause of high growth and good export performance, or a consequence, or both, is controversial, but all of these elements are clearly linked. Most economists say that openness is an important cause of growth.

The process of globalization, according to some definitions, means liberalization, or opening up to trade and international finance. In the last decade, such liberalization was pursued primarily by the formerly socialist countries, which turned away from central planning in order to link up with the world economy, and by the developing countries, which changed from import-substituting industrialization processes to export-oriented ones. Some OECD countries, on the other hand, have implemented additional nontariff barriers such as the so-called voluntary export restraints, procedural protection (most notably in the form of antidumping actions), and specific subsidies to exports and to goods and services competing with imports. The Multifibre Arrangement and the Common Agricultural Policy of the European Union are blatantly protectionist devices. Other barriers have been raised against imports of steel, electronics, and footwear.

Growing international competition is not solely the result of the existence of fewer barriers to trade. Another important cause is the accelerated pace of invention and innovation. As the ratio of GNP spent by high-income countries on R&D rises from 2 to percent to 3 percent and higher, social and technological change has accelerated in the last few decades. Today, the time lag between innovative idea, invention, engineering application, and commercial exploitation is much shorter than in the past. The time lag between the invention of the steam engine and the onset of the railway age or the time lag between the invention of the internal-combustion engine and the advent of the economic, social, and cultural (not to mention sexual) revolution and difussion wrought by the motor car was measured in generations. But the time lag between the invention of television, the microchip, the jet engine, or even the zip fastener, their subsequent engineering and commercial applications, and the intellectual and cultural transformations in their train is measured in years; the application of the discovery of the structure of DNA to bioengineering took only ten years. Faraday's law of electromagnetic induction was announced in the late nineteenth century, but did not give birth to the first electric motor until about forty years later. In contrast, Bardeen and Brittain announced the laws governing semiconduction in the late 1940s, and transistor application followed only five years later. The lag in the application of laser technology was even shorter. Gore Vidal rightly wrote, "Thanks to modern technology…history now comes equipped with a fast-forward button."[40]

If most economists are right, liberalization should in theory lead to higher growth rates and to faster improvements in living standards. Yet the empirical evidence for this expected result is slender, if not altogether absent. Annual growth rates of GDP per head in East and Southeast Asia were 6 percent to 8 percent per year between 1986 and 1993, but in Latin America and Sub-Saharan Africa in the same period they were only 0.36 percent to 0.37 percent per year. Growth in these latter areas remained elusive; the exceptionally high performers have been Chile and Costa Rica in Latin America and Mauritius and Botswana in Africa. Comparing the annual growth rates of GNP per head in the two periods 1965–1980 and 1980–1993, we get for all developing countries 4.6 percent and 4 percent, and for the OECD countries 3.9 percent and 1.6 percent.[41] Table 4 shows the position of country group growth rates in the periods 1972–1981 and 1982–1991 as compared with the 1960–1971 average.

Even if it were true that liberalization leads to higher growth, one would have to examine the policies in the preceding period that laid the basis for the subsequent success. All successful liberalizers had pursued selective trade and industrial policies, laying the foundations for their good performance.

Regional Blocs: Building Blocs or Stumbling Blocs to Globalization?

Let us turn now to a discussion of the possible future formation of regional blocs that would manage their members' external trade and other economic relations. This tactic would, of course, represent at least an actual retreat from wider globalization. The forces that could lead to it are the reactions by Europe and the United States to the dynamic expansion of exports by Japan and the East Asian economies (including China), a slowing down or reversal of economic growth, a revulsion against some of the undesirable manifestations of globalization, and a reversion to indigenous cultural values. These forces may take the form of protectionist pressures under the pretext of the need for universal standards on labor, employment, and environmental protection.

The most recent historical precedent of such bloc formation is that of the interwar period after the long pre-1913 period of globalization. There were the Ottawa Agreement of 1932 and the Sterling Area, or (as it was then called) the Sterling Block. There were the French Union and the United States with its Monroe Doctrine. The fragmentation of the world into blocs gave scope to the ruthless rather than to the strong. Trade among blocs had been minimized. The exclusion of the Japanese from South and Southeast Asia by the British, French, and Dutch was a major cause of Japanese aggression. The exclusion of Germany from the Western blocs contributed to World War II.

---

[40] Gore Vidal, *Screening History* (Cambridge, Mass.: Harvard University Press, 1992). Ronald Dore has argued that technological change has been more important than globalization in promoting competition and changing the character of our societies. Ronald Dore, "Ralf Dahrendorf, Quadrare il Cerchio: Comment" (typescript).

[41] *Human Development Report* 1995 and *World Development Report* 1995.

The formation of the Group of Five and then of the Group of Seven and the calling of the Summits were not in the spirit of the multilateral system built in the quarter century after World War II. What some observers see emerging is something that resembles Orwell's picture in his novel *1984*: Oceania, Eurasia, and Eastasia. Lester Thurow has pronounced in Davos, which is located in a Swiss valley next to the valley in which Nietzsche pronounced God as dead, that "GATT is dead" and that multilateralism will be replaced by blocs. But it is well known that GATT (or its successor) has nine lives. The creation of the World Trade Organization bears witness to the continued relevance of the multilateral approach. We may echo the British imperial cry, "The king is dead; long live the king!"

At the same time, the liberal world order that the United States had advocated after the war had never been accepted by Europe and Japan. Germany yielded to demands to open its market in return for American troops and defense against the Soviet Union. In the 1980s, the United States itself retreated from liberal trade. And the United States, Japan, Germany, France, and Britain retreated from multilateral institutions.

If this trend continues, we may someday see the formation of three blocs. Europe with her former colonies in Africa would become "Fortress Europe." The United States, Canada, Mexico, the Caribbean Basin, and parts of Central and South America would form a second bloc. Japan and the Pacific Rim—together with the four Asian tigers, possibly with ASEAN (Indonesia, Philippines, Malaysia, Singapore, and Thailand), and with Australia and New Zealand under the Closer Economic Relations Agreement—would form an East Asian-Pacific bloc.

But it must be remembered that although Japan's trade with Asia is larger than its trade with North America, Japan's largest single market is now the United States, taking 39 percent of total Japanese exports. Furthermore, South Korea and Taiwan are more integrated with the United States than with Japan, and as yet there exist no formal agreements between Japan and any of her neighbors to reduce trade barriers. Members of the blocs will continue to reach out to outsiders, such as some Caribbean countries to Britain, former French colonies to France, the European Union to Central and East Europe, and so forth, and these tentacles will weaken the bloc formation.

Not much support now exists for bloc formation. Singapore and Malaysia, for example, are keen to preserve a multilateral, open trading system and to maintain a strong American presence, and they are suspicious of a yen bloc. Japan's attempt at regional bloc formation could be the reaction to fears that there may be a retreat from GATT-led free trade and that it may be excluded from its two main export markets, the United States and Europe.

Much would depend on what form these blocs would take—on whether Europe would continue to be on the whole an open, outward-looking community, part of a global order, or if it would become a highly regulated bureaucratic bloc and on whether the United States, possibly with Canada and Mexico, would yield to protectionist pressures or resist them. It is well known that a global system cannot be achieved all at once, and so regionalism may well point the way to globalization and be a step toward it. Trade creation would prevail over trade diversion, and the competitive power of firms would be strengthened. In such a case, the regional blocs, instead of being stumbling blocks, would be building blocks for a multilateral system. On the other hand, the political interests appeased and created by trade diversion may gather power, oppose trade liberalization, and create inward-looking blocs that manage trade with outsiders. Since trade diversion creates sales and jobs inside the bloc while trade creation destroys them in the short run, the political pressures of particular interests will be toward trade diversion.

Furthermore, the inward-looking-bloc solution need not be as horrifying a prospect as Orwell painted it to be. It is a second-best approach when compared with the multilateral, global solution, but it can nevertheless produce a very functional global system. We have succeeded in avoiding major wars for more than half a century, during at least part of which a considerable amount of trade had been managed, while the global integration before 1913 did not prevent the World War I. The bloc system would permit styles of living to be maintained within each bloc. The Europeans would not have to give up their long holidays, generous social-welfare system, workers' participation in management, and minimum wages, nor would they have to accept the low rates of return on investment by the Japanese, who are more interested in long-term presence and in maximizing market shares than in short-term profits. There would of course be problems of origin, in that excluding Japanese producers may mean excluding American products if such products were made by Japanese interests in America. The trade among the blocs would be managed through market-sharing and cartel agreements.

A faster rate of growth within each bloc—fostered by homogeneous attitudes, policies, and institutions, by greater political stability, and by policies that weaken or defeat growth-impeding, vested special-interest groups, although at the expense of some gains from global specialization—could lead to **more** trade among the blocs, even though the ratio of trade to GNP is lower for any given level of income than in a more open (but more slowly growing) global economy. Regional blocs are also likely to attract more private foreign investment, which would compensate for some of the losses from trade diversion.

But there are drawbacks to such a system. For instance, exclusivity, like that in the interwar period, may encourage aggression. Furthermore, some areas may be left out of all blocs; this is matter of concern, even if it were not to lead to aggression. It is not clear what South Asia's role would be. And India is a potentially important large country in the global economy, but there is no clear role for India in this scenario. What would be the role of Russia and the other former Soviet countries? Could there be an alignment of Europe with them? And where would all this leave China, which in a few decades will be the largest economy in the world?

Interesting normative questions arise from the bloc scenario. Apart from the question of the nature of the blocs and their policies, there is the question of the optimum number and optimum size of the blocs. Are three blocs, *ceteris paribus*, better than two? The literature on optimum currency areas is only part of this subject.

Whatever the future fate of regional blocs or of budding region-states such as the

European Union, for purposes of analysis and policy we have to look at regions both below and beyond the boundaries of the state. We should analyze events and policies in terms of these regions, both within and beyond countries, rather than countries only or only the whole globe. The San Francisco Bay area, Silicon Valley, the North Carolina Research Triangle, the Singapore-Johor-Batam-Riau Islands region of Singapore, Malaysia and Indonesia, Hong Kong and Shenzen, and the region around Bangalore are all significant growth poles. Policies and events cannot be understood unless we look beyond and below national frontiers: Japan's influences in East Asia, India's links with West Asia, and relations among countries in the Southern Cone of Latin America, beginning with MERCOSUR.

Eleven Implications for Development Thinking and Practice

First, a need exists both for transnational (or global or regional, not just international) institutions and for local ones. We have argued here that technology has moved ahead of institutions. Revolutions in transport, travel, communication, and information have (partially) unified the world. But institutionally, we are still stuck with the nation-state. The nation-state has usurped too many functions, which it can no longer carry out efficiently. Some of these should be delegated upward, others downward. Upward delegation is necessary because technology and private enterprise have become global while their supervision and regulation have remained national. A few examples are global control of the arms trade, a global competition policy, a global investment trust that recycles current-account surpluses to capital-starved developing countries, steps toward a global central bank and toward progressive global taxation, a global energy policy, a global debt facility, a global environmental protection agency, a global investment board, commodity price stabilization, a global technology agency, a global migration policy, and a global health policy. A global antimonopoly, anticartel, and antirestrictive-practices policy, for example, would bring international policies in line with national ones. As things are, U.S. companies are prohibited from colluding and forming cartels in the home market but are encouraged by the Webb Pomerene Act to do so against foreign countries. Japanese companies' distribution networks are barriers to trade, and many Japanese firms rely on exclusive local suppliers of components; the World Trade Organization should in principle be able to take on this issue. In theory, price discrimination in international trade is countered by permitting antidumping duties to be imposed, but in reality, such duties are actually used by most governments as protectionist devices, not to promote competition but to thwart it. Clearly, a competition policy is a task for a supranational institution, because national governments would be tempted to tailor such a policy to the advantage of their own national firms.

Second, it is a challenge to design ways of achieving these goals without too many global bureaucrats and to show how to concentrate on processes, rules, norms and incentives to achieve the objectives.

Third, both existing international and future global institutions should be made more participatory, so that the voice of the people is heard. Reform of the UN system in this direction is necessary. One possibility would be the creation of a second chamber in which participatory NGOs would be represented. At the same time, these NGOs themselves should be made participatory.

Fourth, where power distribution in the global arena is very unequal, there should exist counterbalancing power centers: for instance, a Group of Non-Seven to balance the Group of Seven, and a Monopolies and Restrictive-Practices Commission to balance the power of multinational monopolies and cartels.

Fifth, there exists an obligation to look after the victims of the competitive struggle. When globalization has caused unemployment, the state should provide a safety net, including public-works programs, education and retraining facilities, a program for changing attitudes and motivation, and the like.

Sixth, problems of liberalizing international migration in line with the liberalization of trade and finance should be given a higher priority on the international agenda and should be examined from the point of view of their impact on the receiving country, as well as from the viewpoint of the migrants themselves and of their countries of origin.

Seventh, strategies should aim at selecting the positive impulses of globalization and encouraging them, while minimizing the impact of the negative impulses and cushioning the losers against them.

Eighth, for thinkers the task is to explore the ways in which different regions, countries, sectors, and groups are affected by globalization, to determine who gains and who loses (absolutely and relatively) and ways in which the forces of globalization can be supplemented by provisions that protect the weak and the poor and that help to integrate them into the process.

Ninth, thinkers may also wish to explore the interaction between globalization forces and the forces of reaction against globalization, in order to discover how beneficial aspects of globalization can be combined with the desirable components of local tradition and cultural diversity.

Tenth, thought should be given to ways in which to reduce the heightened insecurity in people's lives that has resulted from a combination of unemployment, precarious job conditions, poverty, inequality, and reduced social services with reduced public expenditure on social services: how to match economic globalization with social globalization.

Eleventh, the interaction of policies and institutions at five levels should be explored: the micro-micro-level (what goes on inside the firm, farm, household); the micro-level; the meso-level (the impact of policies and institutions on different groups and regions); the macro-level; and the macro-macro-level or global level. The division of duties at each of these levels among private, public (national, international, and global), and voluntary agencies should also be explored, as well as the impact of globalization (and of localization) on the power of the state.

ANNEX 1

TABLE 1. Global Distribution of Wealth, 1960–94

	Industrial Countries (%)	Developing Countries (%)	Former USSR & Eastern Europe (%)
1960	67.3	19.8	12.9
1970	72.2	17.1	10.7
1980	70.7	20.6	8.7
1989	76.3	20.6	3.1
1994	78.7	18.0	3.3

TABLE 2. Global Distribution of Wealth, 1960–94
(Excluding the former USSR and Eastern Europe)

	Industrial Countries (%)	Developing Countries (%)
1960	77.3	22.7
1970	80.9	19.1
1980	77.4	22.6
1989	78.8	21.2
1994	81.4	18.6

TABLE 3. Long-Term Private and Official Financial Flows to Developing Countries
(US $ billions)

	1987	1994
Long-term net resource flows, total	68.5	227.3
Private flows	25.1	172.9
Net private loans	9.8	55.6
Foreign direct investment	14.6	77.9
Portfolio equity investment	0.8	39.5
Official development assistance	43.4	54.4
Official grants	16.9	30.5
Net official loans	26.4	23.9

Source: World Bank *Annual Report* 1995, 214.

TABLE 4. Growth Rate of GDP per capita, as compared with the 1960–71 Average

	1972–81	1982–91
All countries (57)		
Decade ratio higher than 1960-71	18	10
Decade ratio lower than 1960-71	39	47
All non-oil-exporting countries (48)		
Decade ratio higher	11	7
Decade ratio lower	37	41
OECD countries (20)		
Decade ratio higher	1	2
Decade ratio lower	19	18
Latin America (10)		
Decade ratio higher	4	1
Decade ratio lower	6	9
East and South East Asia (7)		
Decade ratio higher	5	3
Decade ratio lower	2	4

Source: John Eatwell, "International Capital Liberalization: An Evaluation" a Report to UNDP (SSA 96-049, (April 1996); David Felix, "Financial Globalization versus Free Trade: The Case for the Tobin Tax," UNCTAD Discussion Paper, 108; World Bank, *World Tables.*

ANNEX 2

Definitions of Globalization

"[Economic] integration is synonymous with [economic] globalization: the tendency for the economic significance of political boundaries to diminish." (David Henderson)

(Globalization involves) "the growing interpenetration of markets." (Manuel R. Agosin and Diana Tussie)

"It is true that the immense cheapening of international transport and communication—the ability to communicate instantaneously by voice, by fax-transmitted paper, or by electronic bits at very low costs—together with the lowering of tariffs and the (very partial) dismantling of trade barriers under the aegis of the GATT, has been one crucial factor intensifying competitive pressures on manufacturers and bankers alike, and it is a factor aptly named 'globalization.'" (Ronald Dore)

(Globalization involves) "the increasing internationalization of the production, distribution, and marketing of goods and services." (R. G. Harris, "Globalization, Trade and Income," *Canadian Journal of Economics,* November 1993)

"When it comes to acid rain or oil spills or depleted fisheries or tainted groundwater or fluorocarbon propellants or radiation leaks or toxic wastes or sexually transmitted diseases, national frontiers are simply irrelevant." (Benjamin Barber, *Jihad vs. McWorld,* 12.)

"'Globalization is the growth—or, more precisely, the accelerated growth—of economic activity across national and regional political boundaries. It finds expression in the increased movement of tangible and intangible goods and services, including ownership rights, via trade and investment, and often of people, via migration." (Charles Oman, "The Policy Challenges of Globalization and Regionalization")

"Globalization is, briefly, the intensification of economic, political, social, and cultural relations across borders." (Hans-Henrik Holm and George Sørensen, "Whose World Order?")

"Techno-globalism" is defined to encompass the growing degree to which "multinational firms are exploiting their technology globally and, to a lesser though increasing degree, are gaining access to new technology globally through the worldwide diffusion of R&D and through collaboration." (Sylvia Ostry and Richard R. Nelson, *Techno-Nationalism and Techno-Globalism: Conflict and Cooperation*)

Globalization as increased internationalization of economic intercourse vs. globalization in the broad sense includes "every aspect of social activity—be it communication, ecological matters, commerce, regulation, ideology, or whatever." (Jan Aart Scholte, quoted in Holt and Sørensen)

"Globalization…is driven by a widespread push toward the liberalization of trade and capital markets, increasing internationalization of corporate production and distribution strategies, and technological change that is rapidly dismantling barriers to the international tradability of goods and services and the mobility of capital." (Zia Qureshi, *Finance and Development,* March 1996)

"The manifestations of globalization include the spatial reorganization of production, the interpenetration of industries across borders, the spread of financial markets, the diffusion of identical consumer goods to distant countries, massive transfers of population within the South as well as from the South and the East to the West, resultant conflicts between immigrant and established communities in formerly tight-knit neighborhoods, and an emerging worldwide preference for democracy." (James H Mittelman, *Third World Quarterly,* September 1994)

"Globalization is the process whereby the world's people are becoming increasingly interconnected in all facets of their lives—cultural, economic, political, technological, and environmental." (George C. Lodge, "Managing Globalization in the Age of Interdependence")

"In common parlance, globalization is often equated with growing integration of national economies. But as employed here, the concept also refers to the rapid spread worldwide of some dominant social, cultural, and political norms and practices." (*Social Movements in Development,* Staffan Lindberg and Arni Sverrison, eds.)

"Globalization…refers to a set of emerging conditions in which value and wealth are increasingly being produced and distributed within worldwide corporate networks." "Globalization refers to the stage now reached and the forms taken today by what is known as 'international production,'"—namely, value-adding activities owned or controlled and organized by a firm (or group of firms) outside its (or their) national boundaries." (TEP: The Technology/Economy Program, *Technology and The Economy: The Key Relationships,* OECD Paris 1992)

"According to the various points of view, we could take globalization to mean the establishment of a global market for goods and capital, the universal character of competing technologies, the progression toward a global system of production, the political weight that the global system carries in the competition for global or regional hegemonies, the cultural aspect of universalization, etc.… In its broadest sense, globalization refers to the existence of relations between the different regions of the world and, as a corollary, the reciprocal influence that societies exert upon one another." (Samir Amin, "The Challenge of Globalization," *Review of International Political Economy,* Routledge, Summer 1996.)

"Globalization identifies both a process in which the production and financial structures of countries are becoming interlinked by an increasing number of cross-border transactions to create an international division of labor in which national wealth creation comes, increasingly, to depend on economic agents in other countries, and the ultimate stage of economic integration where such dependence has reached its spatial limit." (Paul Bairoch and Richard Kozul-Wright, "Globalization Myths: Some Historical Reflections on Integration, Industrialization, and Growth in the World Economy," UNCTAD/OSG/DP/113, March 1996.)

Globalization and Competitiveness in the XXI Century: A Japanese Perspective[1]

Ryokichi Hirono[2]

As we stand at the vantage point of the last five years of the twentieth century, we cannot but be aware of the many political, economic, and social developments of this century and ponder which of them might accompany us into the next century. On the political side, beginning with the tearing down of the Berlin Wall, the radical political democratization of the COMECON countries, and the eventual collapse of the Soviet Union at the turn of this decade, we have witnessed the end of the 45-year Cold War regime. In the wake of this collapse, there has been cause for joy and fear, with many people around the world talking about the supposed "peace dividend." Today many industrial countries—led by the United States and Russia, the two military superpowers—are in fact taking significant steps forward in conventional and nuclear disarmament, while many developing countries are seeking to expand their military capabilities. People speak of a power vacuum in the post-Cold War era, in which groups and countries vie for power and independence against one another in a sea of confused alliances and unclear ideologies.

On the economic side, the postwar trend toward increasing economic interdependence among nations has been accelerated with the conclusion of each of the multilateral trade negotiations beginning with the Kennedy Round of the 1960s through the Tokyo Round of the 1970s and the Uruguay round of the 1980s through 1993, as well as with further deregulation of national economic regimes and further liberalization in finance, investment, and technology flows among nations. With further economic globalization the international cooperation and collaboration among nations, particularly among the major industrial countries, have become ever more crucial, as the national economic-policy changes in one of the major powers would have deep repercussions on the others and, for that matter, on the rest of the world.

[1] The present essay is a revised version of my paper, "International Development Cooperation in the Twenty-First Century: Facilitating Trade and Investment Expansion through a Differentiated Approach," submitted to the Ministry of Foreign Affairs, the Government of Japan (GOJ), in August 1995. It draws heavily on my recent undertaking with the UNU/WIDER research project on "Reorienting International Development Cooperation in the Twenty-First Century for Sustained Growth, Equity, the Environment, and Human Development." The author also wishes to express his appreciation for all the constructive comments made by participants in the IDB Conference on Development Thinking and Practice.
[2] Seikei University, Tokyo.

With the global energy crisis of 1973 and 1974, the need for international cooperation to exchange views and experiences and, if at all possible, to coordinate national economic policies (both to minimize the adverse impact of any major policy changes and to sustain the momentum of global economic growth) has become an acute necessity, giving birth to the establishment of the Group of Seven (the Summit meetings of the heads of state of seven major industrial countries) and the Group of Five (the meeting of the finance ministers of five major industrial countries). The end of the Cold War regime in 1990 has precipitated economic globalization onto the former socialist countries, now transition economies moving from centrally planned to market-oriented economies, thus placing the entire world economy under increasingly intense global market competition and simultaneously under a growing need for global policy cooperation and coordination.

Today, through the concerted efforts of the international community, we seem to be eking out a peaceful solution to the bloody Bosnian conflict and the protracted Arab-Israeli conflict, evidencing the continued necessity of such international organizations as the United Nations. The Social Summit in Copenhagen and the International Women's Congress in Beijing, showed us that much remains to be done to raise the social overhead and participation of all groups of people in development and the status of women and set an aggressive agenda for both developed and developing countries to strive for into the twenty-first century.

We must reflect seriously on these international cooperative efforts to deal with such critical global issues as rapidly rising population, slow reduction in arms spending and broadening illicit arms trade, increasing numbers of refugees, global environmental degradation, widening use of narcotics, and an AIDS epidemic. The fiftieth anniversary last year of the United Nations and the Bretton Woods Institutions reminded and encouraged us all to band together to seek multilateral, participatory solutions to global problems in all sectors—economic, political, environmental, military, health, and social welfare. Not only do there exist many opportunities for international cooperation but many fronts on which we must cooperate merely to stay afloat. This is indeed a challenging time and an exciting era.

Increasing Globalization: Challenges to Nation-States
Political Independence and Economic Globalization
Since the inauguration of the United Nations and the Bretton Woods Institutions in 1945, the world has observed the birth of more than one hundred new nations and the successes and failures of national development led by both old established and new fragile nation-states. Such national development efforts and international development cooperation have produced profound changes in the economic, political, and social scenes both within industrial and developing countries and at the international level.

Political independence has brought political equality among nation-states in terms of "One Vote for One Nation" in the decision-making forums of the United Nations, but economic interdependence has become increasingly important among the old industrial countries and among the new developing countries and between the two groups—although with the old trying to retain their traditional economic and political influences and even military might globally and the new challenging the old. These newly independent developing countries as a group have during the last three decades experienced higher economic growth rates than those attained by the old industrial countries either concurrently or in their comparable stages of national development, but at the same time, great economic differentiation has been seen among the developing countries themselves. Global development and cooperation have thus been complex and challenging and offer simultaneous reasons for encouragement and despair

Most of the colonies in Asia and Africa as well as in the Middle East gained political independence in the period covering the mid-1940s through the 1960s, and they began to embark on a gigantic task of nation building, with high expectations for rapid economic and social development and quick attainment of higher standards of living for their own people. Some developing countries have succeeded, while others have failed at bringing about political stability, maintaining domestic peace and security, restructuring their national economies, raising their per capita GDP, and improving the living standards and the level of human development.

As a result, an increasing dichotomy and widening gap have appeared in the developing world, for example, between the dynamic economies of East Asia, the stop-and-go economies of Latin America, and the stagnating economies of Sub-Saharan Africa. Most countries of South Asia, the Middle East, and North Africa (with the exception of some oil-rich countries) seem to be situated between these two extremes. We must hasten to add, however, that in recent years some South Asian countries such as India have come closer to East Asian countries by having achieved sustained economic growth through economic liberalization.

Many developing countries (particularly in East Asia) having been successful in national economic and social development, have now come closer to the lower end of the old industrial countries in terms of per capita GDP, patterns of consumption, and human development, while others in Sub-Saharan Africa have deteriorated badly and are even worse off than during their pre-independence days, with deepening poverty and ethnic conflicts at home. Those succeeding in development have been able to integrate their national economies with the rest of the expanding world economy, while those failing seem to have been increasingly delinked from the rest (Hirono 1981).

With the collapse of the USSR, most of the former Soviet republics (such as the Central Asian republics) have joined the ranks of the developing countries. Also, all the former COMECON countries of Central and Eastern Europe (including the Russian Federation) that now are undergoing a transition to market-oriented economies have become recipients of foreign aid rather than donors (Simonia 1996, Szentes 1996).

There have also occurred enormous changes in the international monetary, trade, investment, and aid regimes during the last fifty years. The fixed-exchange-rate regime under the supervision of the International Monetary Fund (IMF) gave way to the floating-exchange-rate regime officially agreed upon in February 1973, although effective in

August 1971 following the unilateral announcement by President Nixon of his New Economic Policy which delinked the U.S. dollar from gold.

The international trading regime has gone through enormous changes in the direction of further liberalization, beginning with the Kennedy Round of multilateral trade negotiations of the 1960s, followed by the Tokyo Round of the 1970s, and finally the Uruguay Round of the 1980s. All of these negotiations have successfully reduced tariff and nontariff barriers (NTBs) to trade in goods, although not to the complete satisfaction of those countries promoting free trade. Trade barriers in services have also increasingly become a target for multilateral negotiations in recent years and under the World Trade Organization (WTO) regime that started in 1995.

In addition, the international investment regime has become extremely liberalized in industrial countries under the guidance and monitoring of the Organization for Economic Cooperation and Development (OECD). In many developing countries, major changes in economic policies were initiated by their own governments in the 1960s and 1970s, as seen in East Asia in the mid-1960s shifting from an anti- to a pro-foreign-direct-investment stance. This major policy turnaround was echoed by most other governments later in the 1970s (Hirono 1981).

Liberalization of national economic policies and accelerated administrative deregulation began more forcefully with the inauguration of President Reagan in 1981 with his Reaganomics, endorsed strongly by Mrs. Thatcher, the prime minister of the United Kingdom. International pressures for economic and administrative deregulation and privatization, like the Christian Crusade, swiftly spread the world over, engulfing the centrally planned economies of Central and Eastern Europe. This worldwide trend of economic liberalization and deregulation set the stage for a historically unprecedented, rapid expansion in trade and investment among both industrial and developing countries and between them.

The process has been facilitated by the rapid development of transport and telecommunications technologies, thus furthering the globalization of production, finance, and distribution in every sector of the national economies. Furthermore, the bilateral and multilateral aid regime, although undergoing enormous changes in the postwar world, has certainly facilitated such trade and investment expansion through the expansion and improvement of economic and social infrastructures in developing countries (Hirono 1996, Sherk 1996).

Despite these national and international efforts, many developing countries (particularly in Sub-Saharan Africa) have not been able to attain sustained economic growth and human development and instead have remained low income and stagnant. Furthermore, they have suffered from population explosions and increasing social tensions, as reflected in the growing internal ethnic and religious conflicts, and from increasing environmental degradation as reflected in rapidly spreading desertification and deforestation (Swantz/ Massawe 1996). Furthermore, many transition economies (particularly in central Asia, together with most other former Soviet republics), have not been able since 1990, to recover the past growth trend seen in earlier periods (Simonia 1996, Szentes 1996).

Even in the high-performing East Asian economies, the very process of rapid economic growth and restructuring—although steadily improving the general level of education, health, and sanitation and reducing the size of the population living in absolute poverty—has exacerbated the shortage of adequately trained professional and managerial manpower, and led to infrastructure bottlenecks, income and wealth disparities, regional imbalances, and environmental deterioration (including deforestation, acid rain, water pollution, urban slums, crime, and traffic congestion).

The issues of political freedom and human-rights protection, including the rights of women and children, have also become more pronounced and crucial to sustained political stability in these societies as the latter have become more affluent in both household income and national wealth. The enormous economic and social gains in these societies during the last thirty years, therefore, will have to be discounted by the growing problems of social inequity, regional disparities, and environmental deterioration (Hirono 1996, Ng 1996).

Thus—although it has contributed to trade, investment, and income expansion not only in industrial but also in developing countries to an extent hitherto unheard of in the world—the economic globalization process (facilitated by economic liberalization policies and technological innovations in transport and communications) has weakened the capacity of each individual nation to manage its own economic affairs (including foreign-exchange volatility in the short run and misalignment in the longer run) and has produced growing differentiation (particularly among developing countries), growing disparities between the "haves" and the "have-nots" within both industrial and developing countries, and so-called jobless growth in mature industrial countries. It has also intensified the global issues of population, refugees, environment, drugs, AIDS, and terrorism adversely affecting nations and people all over the world, although in varying degrees.

Those responsible for formulating and implementing national and international development policies and bilateral and multilateral development cooperation programs must address the aforementioned issues squarely, by asking the following:

- why many developing countries (including those in Sub-Saharan Africa) have failed—despite the increasing economic globalization during the last three decades—in terms of both national economic development and sustainable human development and what these countries must do to turn this situation around, in terms of alternative policies and actual implementation of such policies
- why the international community has been unable for so long to help the aforementioned countries to overcome these increasing and pressing hardships and what it could do to reverse this trend
- what the international community could do to help the high-growth developing countries to eradicate poverty and inequities in the latter's economic and social spheres, to assist them in protecting their environment, and to join them in assisting the lower-growth developing countries in a more effective manner than hitherto observed.

Globalization and Major Factors Determining Growth of Developing Countries

Those developing countries that, despite today's increasing globalization, have not succeeded in national development, whether in Sub-Saharan Africa or elsewhere, often exhibit the following characteristics (Hirono 1996):

- political instability and domestic conflicts and insecurity
- shortage of well-educated, well-trained, and well-disciplined labor force
- underdevelopment of economic infrastructures such as power, transport, and telecommunications networks
- absence of active entrepreneurship
- low level of domestic savings
- lack of political commitment at the highest level to national economic, social, and human development
- absence of macroeconomic stabilization and appropriate (coherent, consistent, stable, flexible, and open-door) growth policies
- prevalence of corruption and inefficiency at the national and local levels.

In contrast, all the East Asian countries that have achieved sustained national development during much of the postwar period have been blessed with a broad range of development management capacity related to the maintenance of political stability, the development of human resources (such as skilled, technical, and professional manpower), the availability of good economic infrastructures, the mobilization of domestic savings, the installation of an efficient bureaucracy, and the sustenance of a strong political commitment to high growth and to appropriate macroeconomic and structural reform policies (Hirono 1992 and 1995, Ng, 1996).

In addition, the economic-growth successes of East Asian countries have been facilitated by the postwar international globalization-promoting economic regimes in terms of the following: freer trade in goods, services, and technology; more liberal flows of foreign investment, direct and indirect; and increased flows of bilateral and multilateral aid. As a result, there has occurred increasing penetration by each of these industrializing and high-growth developing economies (taking advantage of their respective comparative advantages), into the markets of both industrial and other developing countries. These developments have increased the successful East Asian economies' dependence upon external trade, technology, and finance and have subjected them to global economic fluctuations and disturbances. They have also forced them to make counterbalancing macroeconomic policy adjustments to maximize the benefits to them of world economic growth and to minimize the cost to them of external shocks, as well as to adopt those microeconomic and restructuring policies essential to staying competitive on the world market (Hirono 1995, Ng 1996).

It must be noted emphatically, however, that the postwar forces for globalization in trade, investment, and aid regimes surrounding the successful East Asian countries have largely been the same as, if not worse than, those globalization forces confronting the

Sub-Saharan African and other stagnant developing countries and that the latter developing countries have not been able to take advantage of the favorable international economic regimes of globalization as much as have the East Asian, largely because of those domestic constraints mentioned earlier (Sood 1996, Swantz/ Massawe 1996).

This contrast implies without any doubt that internal rather than external factors have been chiefly responsible for the successes of many developing countries and the failures of many more in terms of sustained national development during the postwar period. As emphasized in the 1974 *Economic and Social Survey of Asia and the Pacific* published by the U.N. Economic and Social Commission for Asia and the Pacific (ESCAP), what was really needed was not so much a program of action for the establishment of a new international economic order but rather a program of action for the establishment of a new internal economic order.

It is important to note in this regard that in these high-performing developing East Asian countries, the internal capacities to absorb the external shocks and disequilibria and to adjust to the changing external world had been developed over a relatively long period through their heavy investment in human resources and institution building. This fact points clearly to what the Sub-Saharan and other stagnant developing countries must do internally to realize the successes of those East Asian countries—and therefore what the international community ought to do in assisting those developing countries that have not yet achieved the same successes as the East Asian.

Obviously (as discussed later), because of radical changes in the international development scene and in national development priorities, the same medicine and approaches that were effective in the 1960s and the 1970s can no longer be considered effective in the 1990s and beyond without appropriate modification.

Globalization, Competition, Trade, and Economic Friction

Economic globalization has accelerated world economic growth in the postwar period and has brought about gains in the economic well-being both of industrial countries and of developing countries capable of coping with the challenges of globalization. It has, however, also produced an intensification of interfirm and interindustry competition at home and abroad, which has been accompanied by a variety of domestic and external economic issues that have required government intervention in the market. These government interventions have included (on the one hand) national efforts in promoting regional/subregional economic cooperation to reduce the incidence of bilateral trade disputes and economic disputes and prevent them from developing into bilateral political strains and (on the other) positive adjustment measures to reduce the adverse impact of global competition upon corporate behavior, employment, and income distribution.

Economic globalization has been accompanied by political and social globalization in recent years. Along with it there has emerged increasing irritation among many developing countries (of different social values and political orientations) concerning the inroads made by the present process of political and social globalization, which has tended to impose the values and priorities of one civilization (usually that prevailing among old industrial countries) over those of other civilization claiming the former to be not only universal but also superior to the latter. Let us now examine five of the aforementioned issues in some detail.

Intense Competition at Home, Leading to Corporate Failures, Restructuring, and Malprac-
tice and to the Incidence of Rising Unemployment and Economic Inequity

Advances in economic liberalization and administrative deregulation in both industrial and developing countries, together with economic globalization, have increasingly led to nearly cutthroat competition among industrial, financial, and service companies, forcing them to re-engineer and restructure their corporate activities constantly in order to stay competitive on the domestic and world markets. These competitive pressures have had positive and negative consequences. On the positive side, they have generated an enormous corporate investment in creating labor-saving and resource-saving technologies and production processes and in furthering research and development (R&D) to introduce new technologies, new machinery and equipment, new industrial raw materials, and new products and services, thus contributing to higher productivity and income levels.

On the negative side, however, competitive pressures have driven a large number of corporate employees—young and old, men and women, skilled and unskilled—off the payroll. If lucky, they were able to rely for some time on unemployment insurance, and if unlucky, they were sent to open-sky streets as the homeless and/or the destitute. Thus, the distinction between the "haves" and the "have-nots" has become glaring and alarming in most industrial countries, deepening a sense of social uneasiness and bearing the unwelcome fruits of social crimes, including drug addiction (and the often-attendant spread of HIV/AIDS) and the physical attack on the homeless in city parks.

The number and size of corporate failures and bankruptcies have increased in all industrial countries, producing a growing and staggering amount of nonperforming assets and financial crises in one country after another, including Japan. The competitive pressures, intensified to some degree by market deregulation, have also been behind the regrouping of corporate affiliations through mergers and takeovers, not only within but also across industries and not only at home but on a worldwide scale. As a result, the already enormously powerful multinational corporations in every sector have come to be seen as threatening the survival of national and international competition policy and competitive forces in the market. Actions would be required at both national and international levels, calling for more rigorous antitrust legislation and more stringent enforcement thereof.

Globalization of economic activities and fierce global competition through liberalization of trade, deregulation, and privatization have not solved all existing domestic economic problems either. Ineffective allocation of economic resources, be they financial or real, not only remains but worsens when increasing rigidities emerge at micro-and macroeconomic levels, as shown in the inability of workers in the short run to adjust their skills, occupations, and expectations to the changing competitive situations facing their corporations or industries.

In the meantime, trade unions and agricultural cooperatives, once at the vanguard of social progress, have now turned their backs on the public interests of the consumers by protecting their members' vested interests, and through unholy alliances with less-productive employers, they have posed a barrier to economic restructuring and productivity improvement. Budgetary and current-account deficits have now become structural issues in nearly all industrial countries, despite ongoing financial liberalization and economic globalization.

Intense Global Competition, Leading to Increasing Trade Disputes and Economic Disputes among Trading Nations

On the international front, good progress has been made since the early 1960s because of multilateral trade negotiations under the General Agreement on Tariffs and Trade (GATT), economic-policy advice by The Bretton Woods Institutions and regional development banks, and various international Summit conferences (both within and outside the United Nations) for building international consensus on the need for more-active and coordinated policies for sustaining and expanding open, market-oriented economies. There have emerged, however, some disturbing signs in international development in recent years that reflect negatively on globalization.

A slowdown has been observed in world economic growth since 1990 and is expected to continue for the rest of the present century. In the beginning of the twenty-first century there may occur an upturn in world economic growth, propelled largely by the spread of East Asia's rapid economic growth to most countries of South Asia and possibly to several more Latin American and Caribbean countries, but industrial countries do not seem to be able to revive and accelerate their growth and will probably continue, at least during the rest of the present century, to suffer from either a standstill or from slow economic growth (JERC/*STEF* 6/1996, UNCTAD/*TDR* 1996).

More intense competition within a slow-growth environment among major industrial and newly industrializing economies has thus far led to, and will continue to bring about, more-frequent and more-overt bilateral trade friction, macroeconomic-policy conflicts, and a variety of protectionist measures (including antidumping measures, involuntary "voluntary export restraints" [VERs], domestic selling price adjustments, and health, safety, environmental, and other nontariff barriers) (see Table 2.1).

More than a dozen cases have already been brought to the dispute panel in the WTO since its January 1995 installation. The United States, a major WTO member, had dropped out of the final process of negotiation of a multilateral agreement on services concluded in July 1995 on the grounds that the degree of liberalization of trade in financial services as agreed upon in the final WTO text was insufficient. Although averting at the last minute a trade dispute on auto parts, the United States has in an increasingly bitter manner forced Japan to negotiate other bilateral trade disputes (such as the political maneuvering for an increased share by U.S. computer chips in the do-

TABLE 2.1. Antidumping Actions by the European Union, Japan, and the United States, 1990–1995

(Number of actions)

Asian Exporter	European Union		Japan		United States	
	Initiated	In force	Initiated	In force	Initiated	In force
Bangladesh	—	—	—	—	—	—
China	30	28	1	1	38	34
Hong Kong	2	2	—	—	1	—
India	10	2	—	—	8	5
Indonesia	10	2	—	—	—	—
Malaysia	7	1	—	—	2	1
Pakistan	3	—	1	—	—	—
Philippines	1	—	—	—	—	—
Republic of Korea	15	12	—	—	19	16
Sri Lanka	—	—	—	—	—	—
Taiwan	—	—	—	—	—	—
Province of China	6	6	—	—	15	17
Thailand	15	12	1	—	6	4

Source: Semi-annual reports to the GATT/WTO Committee on Antidumping Practices, various issues.

mestic market of Japan)—a stance that is completely contrary to the spirit of WTO as the arbiter of free and fair trade (Hirono 1996).

Such increasing trade disputes and economic friction between the United States and Japan are a good example of the intensification of global competition. They have emerged essentially for two reasons.

First, the U.S. perception of Japan's trade policy has long been negative, based on the belief that Japan has been erecting a variety of protectionist tariff and nontariff barriers against imports from abroad and that it has been subsidizing its exports, particularly of those high-technology products and financial and other services in which U.S. firms have a comparative advantage vis-à-vis their Japanese counterparts. Japan's own perception of U. S. trade policy in recent years has also become increasingly negative, claimingthat contrary to the "free and fair" trade policy repeatedly professed by the U.S. Government, the United States has taken a number of protectionist measures including those mentioned earlier (Hirono 1995). Sadly, retaining the old image of Japan as not following the fair rule of the international trading regime, the U.S. Government has not adjusted its perception of Japan's present trade policy even after the latter has been drastically liberalized through multilateral trade negotiations during the past thirty-three years (see Table 2.2).

Second, although the United States is essentially responsible for having maintained its age-old perception of Japanese import policy, Japan itself is also partially to blame, because Japan's trade liberalization measures have come rather slowly in the 1960s and 1970s, much more slowly than those of the United States and of many other OECD

TABLE 2.2. Trade-Weighted Pre- and Post-Uruguay Round Average MFN Tariffs and GSP Tariffs in Major Markets by Product Group
(Percentage)

Product Group	European Union MFN Pre-UR (1992)	European Union MFN Post-UR	European Union GSP (1992)	United States MFN Pre-UR (1992)	United States MFN Post-UR	United States GSP (1992)	Japan MFN Pre-UR (1992)	Japan MFN Post-UR	Japan GSP (1992)
Electronics	6.8	2.9	0.0	2.5	0.9	0.0	4.7	0.1	0.0
Textiles and apparel	12.4	10.6	0.0	16.6	14.8	0.0	12.7	8.5	5.0
Misc. manufactures	6.6	2.8	0.0	6.4	1.9	0.0	4.8	1.0	0.0
Metals	6.5	3.3	0.0	5.0	2.8	0.0	4.8	0.6	0.0
Rawhide and leather products	9.5	7.7	0.0	11.4	10.8	0.0	12.7	12.6	6.9
Machinery and equipment	5.7	3.2	0.0	4.5	2.9	0.0	5.1	0.5	0.0
Prepared foodstuffs	15.1	11.6	8.9	6.8	5.6	0.0	19.4	15.2	7.3
Rubber and plastic products	7.9	5.4	0.0	4.4	3.1	0.0	5.9	3.2	0.0
Chemicals	7.7	4.6	0.0	6.4	3.5	0.0	6.1	3.0	0.2
Transport equipment	11.0	9.6	0.0	4.6	4.2	0.0	3.7	0.0	0.0
Wood and paper products	7.3	2.5	0.0	6.0	3.8	0.0	13.6	6.7	0.3
Mineral products	8.6	6.5	0.0	9.5	6.4	0.0	4.4	0.3	0.0

Source: UNCTAD Trade Control Measures Information System.
Note: The average (MFN or GSP) rate for each product group relates only to those tariff lines for which the pre-Uruguay Round MFN tariffs actually applied were above zero. The weights used are the corresponding (MFN or GSP) imports in 1992 of the products concerned.

countries, despite the Japanese Government's intention announced in 1961. Japan does still maintain a high tariff wall and a number of quantitative import restrictions on rice and other agricultural and sensitive products, but it also has lower average tariff rates on manufactured imports than do the United States and the European Union (EU).

The increasing economic and trade-related friction between the United States and Japan reflects the inability of the two "democratic" governments to go ahead with, and stick to, the principle of free trade consistent with government intervention through industrial-restructuring policies at home. Japan is still saddled with inefficient agriculture, finance, and service sectors, while the United States, having no forward-looking interventionist domestic policy, has simply resorted to many of the aforementioned protectionist nontariff barriers. In other words, competitive weaknesses in both the United States and Japan have been externalized by these countries' respective governments through protectionist measures brought about by strong political pressures from the less competitive but strategic segments of the national economy—agriculture in Japan and selected manufacturing sectors in the United States (automobiles, iron and steel, semiconductors, and other industries).

Economic Regionalism: A Step toward Globalization?

Rising regionalism has been observed—in this age of globalization—among major economic powers, as in the formation of the North American Free-Trade Agreement (NAFTA) and the European Union (EU), with the risk that these blocs may turn inward and protectionist. These regional trends in the European and American continents—although claimed by their respective member countries as a step forward toward accelerating the tempo of global liberalization in trade, finance, and investment—have in fact generated increasing concern among many developing countries in Asia, Africa, the Middle East, and Latin America and a greater interest in enhancing subregional economic cooperation among other neighboring and like-minded countries through special trade and financial arrangements (Hirono 1996).

Confining our illustration to East and Southeast Asia, the six member countries of the Association of Southeast Asian Nations (ASEAN) (set up in 1967 as an anticommunist political grouping declaring the Zone of Peace, Freedom, and Neutrality), have expanded intra-ASEAN economic cooperation over the last two and one-half decades and concluded in 1992 an ASEAN Free-Trade Area (AFTA) to promote trade, technology, and investment cooperation among themselves on the basis of a common effective preferential tariff (CEPT) system. There has arisen growing interest among them to enlarge ASEAN membership, resulting in the accession of Vietnam as the seventh member in July 1995, with Cambodia and Laos scheduled to become members in 1997 and with Myanmar (Burma), now an observer, expected to become the tenth ASEAN member in 1998 (Hirono 1996, Ng 1996).

In continental Southeast Asia, increasing efforts are being made to promote subregional trade and economic cooperation among the three Indochinese countries Myanmar, Thailand, and Yunnan Province of the People's Republic of China, as recently evidenced by the Forum for the Comprehensive Development of Indochina initiated by the Government of Japan in 1993 in association with the Asian Development Bank (AsDB) and the United Nations Development Program (UNDP).

There also exists increased interest in forming some kind of East Asian/Western Pacific economic grouping to prevent the EU and NAFTA from becoming inward-looking. An attempt in 1990 by Malaysia to organize an East Asian Economic Group (EAEG), however, has been resisted by industrial-country partners of the Asian and Pacific Economic Cooperation (APEC) group on the grounds that the proposed EAEG, in excluding all the industrial APEC members except for Japan, contradicts the spirit of broader economic cooperation under APEC established by most of the Pacific Rim countries in 1989. To avoid any misgiving, another form of expanded regional economic cooperation has been proposed under the name of East Asian Economic Cooperation (EAEC), which includes in its membership Australia, New Zealand, and the South Pacific island countries (Hirono 1996, Ng 1996).

Without any formal free-trade agreement, APEC—with member countries embracing the Pacific on both the eastern and western shores—has seen its intraregional trade expand as fast as that in NAFTA and in the EU. APEC has made remarkable progress in recent years toward a free-trade area. The Bogor Declaration in 1994 set the trade liberalization target date as the year 2010 for APEC's industrial member countries and the year 2020 for its developing member countries. The Osaka Declaration in 1995 expanded beyond trade liberalization to promote the liberalization of trade in services and investment. The Manila Declaration in 1996 is intended to call for the submission by its member states of all concrete schedules of trade liberalization up to the year 2000, welcoming the acceleration of the liberalization that is to occur beyond the year 2000.

In turn, South Asian countries have long formed a subregional cooperation forum entitled the South Asian Association for Regional Cooperation (SAARC), but SAARC's progress has been rather slow, particularly in economic and trade-related areas. Here the globalization of economic activities has been long resisted both by strong groups of vested interests existing in all the member countries and by smaller member states lest they be swallowed up by big neighbors like India. Having become impatient with the slow progress of SAARC, some South Asian countries such as India and Sri Lanka have shown an interest in joining either ASEAN or APEC, to enhance their trade and growth potential during the rest of the 1990s and the early part of the twenty-first century. India, like China, has already joined Australia, Canada, the EU, Japan, New Zealand, and the United States as a dialogue partner with ASEAN (Sood 1996).

Emerging Domestic Issues of High-Performing East Asia and Economic Globalization
Despite continued success in economic and social development and despite the efforts by regional and subregional economic cooperation to promote sustained economic growth, the fast-growing East Asian and Latin American countries have not yet been able to overcome all of the development constraints facing them. With a successful development phase now behind them, they are confronted with difficult issues, including the following: a growing bottleneck in the area of economic infrastructure, such as power, transport, and telecommunications; an increasing scarcity of skilled, technical, professional, and managerial manpower; adverse environmental impact and health hazards caused primarily by rapid industrialization, urbanization, and population pressures in certain high-growth regions; glaring urban-rural disparities; greater inequity in income and wealth distribution; and large pockets of poverty still remaining both in urban and rural areas. The governments of these high-growth developing countries are under increasing pressure at home to address these critical domestic issues (Hirono 1995, Ng 1996).

Meanwhile external pressures from industrial and developing countries have continued bilaterally and multilaterally (through GATT/WTO and through regional cooperation forums such as NAFTA, APEC, and the Lomé Convention) on these same more-advanced developing countries in East Asia and Latin America to implement further liberalization of their national trade and investment regimes and further deregulation of their economic activities, including the privatization of all the remaining state-owned enterprises. These upper-income or high-income developing countries have had little quarrel, as the economic packages of globalization have thus far fit comfortably (with minor exceptions), their long-term national economic well-being.

Nevertheless, as expressed so often by developing countries at the APEC meetings, a differentiated and step-by-step approach rather than a universal and standardized approach is needed for developing countries at different levels of economic and social development and economic, social, and political integration. Because of the contrast between its unfortunate prewar and very successful postwar experiences of integration into the rest of the world economy, Japan has been at the vanguard in promoting the gradualist approach rather than the big-bang approach or shock therapy. The shock therapy approach by the then-imperialists and then-colonialists of the Western world to force Japan to open up to the rest of the world in part through imposing on Japan the infamous "unequal treaty of navigation and commerce" led to Japanese involvement in imperialistic wars and "social dumping" in the prewar days. In contrast, Japan in the postwar period was able, with U.S. support, to integrate itself smoothly and steadily into the rest of the world economy.

Although the international economic and political environment facing developing countries in the 1990s is different from the one facing Japan during the prewar period, a gradualist approach would still make it easier for these governments to attempt to solve their critical domestic issues mentioned above by granting sufficient time and resources for carrying out such a difficult task.

Rising Pressures in the Framework of Political and Social Globalization
As can be observed in the IMF/World Bank structural-adjustment programs introduced in most countries of Asia, Latin America, and Sub-Saharan Africa during the past decade, external pressures have increasingly been directed at the reduction of the role of the state, the protection of human rights, further democratization, and the enhancement of participatory development and good governance. Developing countries have not shown any fundamental objection to these goals as such. But what has aroused dissatisfaction and objection among the political leadership in the developing world is the way in which these goals have been "pushed onto" developing countries as "political conditionality" in bilateral and multilateral aid programs. Japan is perceived in this regard to stand in the middle between the hard-nosed Western countries and the struggling developing countries.

Many developing countries argue that societies differ in their particular stage of economic development; that each society has its own political and social structures and cultural values; that the role of the state and the substance of national policies vary according to the needs and requirements of each society's political and social structure and cultural values; and therefore that what is appropriate to one society in terms of national policies and the role of the state may not be appropriate to another society at a different level of economic development and with different political and social structures and cultural values.

The need for a differentiated approach had long been obvious, in view of the remarkable successes of the East Asian development experience. Also, not only Sub-Saharan African countries and transition economies but also high-performing East Asian and Latin American countries have been increasingly confronted with critical issues of growing income and wealth disparities among different segments of the population and worsening environment both in urban and rural areas.

A differentiated approach is clearly needed for international development cooperation (a facet of economic globalization), but support given by developing countries to globalization does not go beyond the economic arena. Political globalization is firmly resisted as interference in their national sovereignty, and social and informational globalization is often interpreted as an outright intrusion into their social norms and values and as symbolic of cultural imperalism (Hirono 1996) .

Tailoring National and International Development Strategies to the Changing Needs of the XXI Century

In view of the growing diversity of the developing world—coupled with rising domestic constraints, both economic and political, in industrial countries—national and international development strategies in the future will have to differ among countries. Development strategies must now, in fact, begin to respond effectively and without further delay to the new and emerging domestic issues in industrial countries, to the dynamic and emerging countries of East and South Asia, to the stop-and-go economies of Latin America, to the moderately growing economies of the Middle East and the Mediterranean, and to the stagnating economies of Sub-Saharan Africa—as well as to those serious global issues increasingly threatening human security.

Industrial and developing countries alike have already begun as of the early 1990s to reorient their national and international development strategies in response to these new and emerging issues, in addition to addressing the older domestic issues already confronting them (Cox/Healey 1996, Hirono 1996, Laporte/Bossuyt 1996).

Macroeconomic Support through Trade, Investment, and Aid

On the macroeconomic side, industrial countries have agreed at various ministerial meetings of OECD and at the Summit meetings of the G-7 on the following objectives (Hirono 1994, 1995):

- sustain economic growth and stability at home, thus providing an even larger global market for every country, whether industrial or developing
- continue national efforts toward greater market access and toward a steady reduction and/or elimination of tariffs and nontariff barriers in accordance with the Uruguay round agreements under the WTO
- intensify efforts to reduce the growing budget deficits at home through tax reforms and public-expenditure cuts, thus providing the private sector and individual households with opportunities to enhance savings and to expand investment and employment
- facilitate a steady process of reduction and/or elimination of institutional and policy barriers (particularly in financial markets), in order to allow multinational cor-

porations to expand investment and employment overseas, transferring technology and management know-how, and thus contributing to increases in export earnings to and sustained economic growth

- increase and improve ODA and OOF to developing countries, in order to meet the growing bottlenecks and critical issues in developing regions and countries more effectively
- continue assistance to transition economies, with a view to smoothly transforming centrally planned economies into market-oriented ones
- reinforce efforts in the regional and international forums to reform the international monetary regime under the IMF, to maintain the open international trading and trade-related investment regime under the new WTO, and to improve the international development finance and assistance regime under the World Bank and the United Nations in favor of sustainable human development
- enhance regional and subregional efforts to increase trade and economic cooperation among neighboring and like-minded countries, consistent with the new WTO regime
- respond positively to calls of the international community for effective handling of urgent issues at the global level, including the protection of the environment.

Promoting Economic Restructuring to Counteract Bilateral Trade Disputes
To avoid allowing the atmosphere of bilateral trade disputes and economic friction between the United States and Japan mentioned earlier to generalize to other countries, the following three lines of argument may be appropriate.

First, to the extent that the world is composed of sovereign states, the government of every country must give priority to the peace, security, and prosperity of its own people, while simultaneously realizing that these desirable conditions depend upon the efforts of the rest of the world as well. Free trade is in the long-run interest of all peoples of the trading world, but it does bring about various short-run social costs in varying degrees to different segments of the population, and so every country must install appropriate domestic economic restructuring policies while keeping its door open to the rest of the world.

Second, the globalization of national economies leading to global industrial restructuring, which would in turn result in higher productivity and economic benefits the world over, will require both a liberal import regime and positive government intervention to lessen the adverse and abrupt impact of global competition upon the less competitive industries. The adverse and abrupt impact of global competition upon the weaker segments of the population must also be lessened to ease their pains, granting a reasonable period of time for retraining and reemployment in growth sectors.

Third, positive adjustment measures stimulated by the state constitute the only way to ensure the international community's commitment to steady progress in trade and investment liberalization and to the eventual achievement of global free trade. Otherwise, economic globalization and global competition will (beyond a certain point) inevitably produce protectionism whether in the form of safeguards or temporary import restrictions.

Economic Regionalism Open to the Rest of the World

Industrial and developing countries alike will increasingly be attracted to regional and subregion cooperation mechanisms (such as EU, NAFTA, APEC, MERCOSUR, and the Southern African Development Cooperation [SADEC]). Through such regional and subregional cooperation, member countries hope to be better able to absorb the shocks and cost of enhanced economic globalization and to gain the benefits of closer relations in trade, investment, and aid.

Thus, in order to maximize the benefits of economic globalization and minimize its adverse impact, globalization may have to be contained at first within homogeneous regions or subregions before proceeding further. In the meantime, however, it is vital that regional and subregional economic cooperation remain open to the rest of the world. Otherwise, each area will become an economic bloc, protecting its own market and resources against other similar blocs, eventually leading not to one globalized free-trade area but instead destroying all the achievements made thus far by the international community in favor of an international trading regime under the GATT/WTO.

It is vital in this connection that—as highlighted already by the United Nations Meeting of Experts on South-South Cooperation in New York in August 1995—national and international development strategies in the twenty-first century recognize the growing importance of South-South cooperation involving developing countries on both sides, either as trading and investment partners or as donors and recipients.

Democracy and the Market under Economic Globalization

Democratic societies would not tolerate governments that, leaving everything to the market, do nothing to help lessen the pains of those adversely affected by the economic restructuring that must inevitably result from the onslaught of economic globalization and global competition. The benefits to society of economic globalization should be large enough to underwrite measures to reduce the social cost of those adversely affected by such globalization.

Democracy and the market, therefore, do not seem to be able to coexist without some adjustment. If democracy is considered more essential, then the market will have to be adjusted, and the forces of a developmental market economy for developing countries and of a social market economy for industrial countries will have to replace those of a liberal market economy. If instead market is considered essential and is given top priority, then democracy will have to be adjusted, and guided democracy for developing countries and social democracy for industrial countries will have to replace liberal democracy.

It is likely that the poorer developing countries, faced with economic globalization, will place priority on development. Here the market takes precedence over democracy, with the forces of a developmental market economy operating under guided democracy. On the other hand, in richer industrial countries with liberal traditions of democracy and market, social democracy and social market economy seem to be the only options consistent with economic globalization. In other words, democracy and the market can coexist only with necessary adjustments for minimizing the social cost associated with economic globalization.

Toward Broad-Based Development

In conclusion, in an increasingly globalized and liberalized world economy, expansion of trade and investment by the private sector, being the engine of economic growth, must be sustained by governments through appropriate macroeconomic and microeconomic policies, human-resource development, and infrastructural and institutional capacity building. The needed ODA, which will become increasingly scarce in the rest of the 1990s and in the early twenty-first century, will and must be provided by the international community to assist developing countries to lay down the basic foundations for the production of goods and services (including economic infrastructures), to enhance domestic human-resource and institutional capacity, and to install appropriate macroeconomic policies conducive to growth with equitable distribution. In this sense, ODA will be (as it has been in the past), a supplement to private-sector financial, technical, and managerial resources in the recipient developing countries (Hirono 1995).

The international development strategy of the twenty-first century will have to give priority to assisting developing countries to integrate their economies further with the rest of the world economy, to promoting trade and investment expansion, and to channeling ODA to those sectors that contribute most effectively to trade and investment expansion, while simultaneously addressing other priority programs for sustainable human development (such as poverty reduction, health, education, and environmental improvement). In so doing, however, the extent, depth, and combinations of such ODA packages—which are now determined either unilaterally or through donor-recipient dialogues—will in the future have to be in line with some form of multilateral agreements or guidelines, so that the impact will be more coordinated.

REFERENCES

Asian Development Bank. *Annual Report* 1993. Manila: AsDB, 1994.

Cox, Adrian, and John Healey. "Aid in the European Union: Management Effectiveness and New Directions." In Ryokichi Hirono, ed, *Reorienting International Development Cooperation in the 21st Century for Sustained Growth, Equity, Environment and Human Development.* Helsinki: UNU/WIDER, 1996.

Hirono, Ryokichi. "More Interdependence, More Diversity: Trends and Issues in Trilateral Relations with Centrally Planned and Third World Countries." In *The Trilateral Countries in the International Economy of the 1980s.* New York: Trilateral Commission, 1981.

_____. "Economic Development of Singapore and Its Social Values." *Seikei Journal of Economics and Business (SJEB)* (March 1992). Tokyo: Seikei University, 1992.

_____. "Japan's Environmental Policies and Assistance for Sustainable Development: Comparative Perspectives." *SJEB* (March 1994).

_____. *International Development Cooperation in the 21st Century: Facilitating Trade and Investment Expansion through a Differentiated Approach.* Tokyo: Ministry of Foreign Affairs (GOJ). August 1995.

_____. "Reorienting International Development Cooperation for the 21st Century: Summary and Conclusions" and "Reorienting International Development Cooperation: A Japanese Perspective." In R. Hirono, ed. *Reorienting International...* Helsinki: UNU/WIDER, 1996.

Japan Economic Research Center (JERC). *Shihanki Keizai Yosoku (Quarterly Economic Forecasts).* (June 1996). Tokyo: JERC, 1996.

Laporte, Geert, and Jean Bossuyt. "Realistic Implementation Strategies: The Missing Link in International Cooperation." In R. Hirono, ed. *Reorienting International...* Helsinki: UNU/WIDER, 1996.

Ng, Chee Yuen. "Reorienting International Development Cooperation in Southeast Asia." In R. Hirono, ed. *Reorienting International...* Helsinki: UNU/WIDER, 1996.

Organization for Economic Cooperation and Development (OECD). *Shaping the 21st Century: The Concept of Development Cooperation.* Paris: OECD, May 1996.

OECD/Development Assistance Committee (DAC). *Development Cooperation 1996.* Paris: OECD, 1996.

Sherk, Donald. "Foreign Aid: A United States Perspective." In R. Hirono, ed. *Reorienting International...* Helsinki: UNU/WIDER, 1996.

Simonia, Nodari A. "Reorienting International Development Cooperation: A Russian Perspective vis-à-vis Central Asian Republics." In R. Hirono, ed. *Reorienting International...* Helsinki: UNU/WIDER, 1996.

Sood, Krishnalekha. "Reorienting International Development Cooperation in South Asia." In R. Hirono, ed. *Reorienting International...* Helsinki: UNU/WIDER, 1996.

Swantz, Marja Liisa, and Peter A.L. Massawe. "Reorienting International Development Cooperation in Sub-Saharan Africa." In R. Hirono, ed. *Reorienting International...* Helsinki: UNU/WIDER, 1996.

Szentes, Tamas. "Reorienting International Development Cooperation: An East European Perspective." In R. Hirono, ed. *Reorienting International...* Helsinki: UNU/WIDER, 1996.

United Nations. *World Economic and Social Survey 1996.* New York: UN, 1996.

United Nations Conference on Trade and Development (UNCTAD). *Trade and Development Report 1996.* Geneva: UNCTAD, 1996.

United Nations Economic and Social Commission for Asia and the Pacific (ESCAP). *Economic and Social Survey of Asia and the Pacific 1974.* Bangkok: ESCAP, 1974.

World Bank. *Wapenhans Report.* Washington, D.C.: World Bank, 1992.

_____. *Learning from the Past, Embracing the Future.* Washington, D.C.: World Bank, 1994.

Dharam Ghai[1] on Papers by Hirono and Streeten:
Globalization and Competitiveness: Implications for Human Security and Development Thinking

Globalization is a broad concept embracing technological, political, economic, social, and cultural dimensions. Many different factors have contributed to its acceleration in recent decades. Globalization's consequences are likely to be manifold and far reaching; at present, these consequences are visible in only partial and attenuated form, but they are likely to manifest themselves with increasing force in the coming years and decades. The growing appreciation of their importance has already unleashed a flood of publications and conferences on the subject. Given the complexity and the extensive scope of globalization, it is not surprising that publications on the subject tend to cover a vast terrain. The Hirono and Streeten papers are no exception. It is therefore possible here to comment on only a few of the many themes developed in those two studies.

Hirono's paper provides a broad survey of the highlights of the development process of third-world countries since the end of World War II, drawing useful and sensible lessons from those countries' successes and failures and applying these lessons to future developmental and foreign-aid policy. His differentiation among countries with different experiences and at varying stages of development is a useful antidote to the more-usual sweeping generalizations on developing countries. Likewise, his distinction between the traditional and the more recent aid donor countries is helpful in seeking to understand the emerging patterns of world development assistance. His skepticism will be shared by many regarding the efficacy (or the lack thereof) of the increasingly inconsistent imposition of political conditionalities on aid recipients.

Given the broad sweep of the paper, it is inevitable perhaps that it should contain at least some oversimplified generalizations and distorted interpretations. Hirono has a tendency, for instance, to lump the Latin American countries with the East Asian ones as examples of successful development experiences; but similarities in current per capita income figures do not really imply similar growth experiences. The literature in fact is full of illustrations of striking differences between these two groups of countries in regard to social and economic inequalities, the structure of their resource endowments, and the nature and results of their development strategies.

---

[1] Director, United Nations Research Institute for Social Development (UNRISD), Geneva.

The reader also gets the impression that the economic performance of African countries throughout the past three to four decades has been one unmitigated disaster. The true picture is of course very different. In the 1960s and early 1970s, economic growth in Africa was comparable to that in other developing regions. It has been only since the mid- to late 1970s that there has occurred a marked decline in economic performance in most African countries. The author is also perhaps too hasty in attributing poor African performance entirely to domestic economic mismanagement. No doubt wrong economic policies and incompetent management have been important factors in several countries. But to ignore totally the impact of the secular decline in the countries' terms of trade and the mounting burden of debt stemming from high interest rates in the 1980s is to give a very misleading analysis of the African crisis. Similarly, the paper glosses over the African economies' structural conditions that greatly impede the possibilities of rapid sustainable growth—namely, poor infrastructure (roads, transport, power, and communications), the low level of education and skills, and the difficulty of forging political stability and social cohesion in ethnically fragmented societies that (in most cases) do not have an experience of precolonial nationhood encompassing the current boundaries.

Paul Streeten's paper is extraordinarily ambitious and wide ranging. Like his other writings, this paper is distinguished by Streeten's ability to recognize complexity, to question conventional wisdom, to discern unexpected and unusual consequences, and to make original and insightful proposals for policy and institutional reform. This capacity makes the paper one of the more enlightening and thoughtful among the flood of publications on the subject.

In most respects, his analysis and conclusions are right on the mark. He does contend, as some others have done, that despite the great excitement created by the recent upsurge of globalization, in many respects the extent of current world economic integration is not as great as that achieved over the period 1870-1914. This may be so, of course, but we must remember that contemporary globalization is in many respects **qualitatively** quite different from that of the earlier period. In particular, the shrinking of space and time brought about by astounding progress in travel, communications, and media has no counterpart in earlier periods. The recent phase of globalization is further distinguished by its all-encompassing nature, comprising as it does the domains of culture, technology, social relations, and politics.

Streeten's discussion on new technologies and microenterprises is insightful. He shows that new technologies are a many-edged sword and contain several features advantageous to the competitive position of developing countries. His analysis of microenterprises not only rightly stresses the heterogeneous character of the informal sector but also imaginatively explores the range of new possibilities offered by the dominance of multinational enterprises.

The paper does not contain a serious discussion of the efficiency and growth consequences of the processes associated with globalization; the enthusiasts of globalization pin much of their faith on its alleged contribution to improvements in resource allocation and in growth to be forthcoming at least in the medium to long run, and so therefore a critical discussion of that belief would have been useful. Globalization is also associated with faster economic and technological change and with greater uncertainty; it would have been useful to explore the full policy and well-being implications of this aspect of the process.

Globalization and Human Security

One of the main consequences of accelerated globalization and its associated changes has been the intensification of human insecurity. This phenomenon appears to have occurred across a wide spectrum of countries varying in socioeconomic systems and levels of development. This insecurity can be traced to changes in the areas of economy, society, politics, and culture. Any dynamic system generates human insecurity, but when changes occur with startling rapidity, the cumulative impact can be quite frightening. And when the institutions and mechanisms in place to cushion insecurity begin to crumble under the impact of the same forces, the effect is intensified.

Increased economic insecurity is at the center of the rising spiral of human insecurity. The key contributory factors to economic insecurity are intensified competition, internationalization of production, changes in methods of production, surges of financial speculation, and rapidity of technological innovations. These dynamic forces have generated unprecedented pressures on livelihood security that are expressed in different ways for different groups in different countries. In most countries, a central element in economic insecurity is intensification of the unemployment problem. This characteristic is common to many OECD countries, the formerly centrally planned economies of Europe, and most countries in Africa, Latin America, and the Middle East. Even people with jobs have experienced a deterioration in conditions of employment, as reflected in the decline in employment security, the increase in casual and part-time work, the increase in work pressure from employers, and the need for constant adjustment to rapidly changing circumstances. More and more these pressures are being felt not just by unskilled workers but also by personnel in higher grades such as technical, professional, and managerial cadres. Owners of enterprises also experience the anxiety and uncertainty generated by intensified competition and innovation. Globalization forces have contributed to pressure on wages in low-skilled jobs; in many countries, such wages have declined, stayed constant, or risen more slowly than the earnings of persons with higher skills, thereby widening income inequalities.

These sources of economic insecurity have been reinforced by changes in government policies in the field of income redistribution and social security. Influenced by new ideologies and buffeted by the aforementioned factors, the governments in most countries have been cutting down on subsidies on items of mass consumption, increasing charges for social services, and reducing the level and range of benefits under social-security and welfare programs. Thus, unemployment benefits, health coverage, and old-age pensions are being adversely affected for most citizens. Family and community structures are also undergoing important shifts under the influence of globalization and associated changes and are thus less effective in cushioning the impact of adverse economic changes. Some existing and new institutions such as religious bodies and citizens' organizations are trying to fill the void, but their efforts have at best had limited impact.

The sources of insecurity are also to be found in other domains of human activities. In the sphere of politics, the close bonds between political parties and their supporters have become loosened in recent years; workers, the unemployed, and other categories of low-income groups lack confidence in the traditional parties to defend their interests, and so it is not surprising to find a growing disenchantment and lack of interest in the political process. In the social domain, the weakening of community and family structures has exacerbated a sense of personal insecurity; changes in the established patterns of relations between generations, sexes, and peer groups have added a potent new source of anxiety for many. In the sphere of culture, the clash between traditional values and those propagated by the media and the consumer society has contributed to conflicts and uncertainty.

When confronted with the malaise induced by insecurity, people tend to turn for support to institutions such as the state, work organizations, communities, and families. But, as noted earlier, the ability of such institutions to offer material and psychological support is much reduced. The void so created is filled increasingly by ethnic and religious bodies. At moments of deep anxiety for their people, such organizations supply material needs, cultural identity, and secure values. Unfortunately, in many circumstances these organizations also espouse extremist visions characterized by intolerance, exclusion, hatred, and violence. Material deprivation and cultural crisis provide a fertile ground for the operation of ethnic and religious entrepreneurs with their own power-seeking and ideological agenda. All too often these initiatives end up in religious and ethnic violence and wars of secession with their inevitable accompaniment of mass killings, physical destruction, and forced displacement of people as external and internal refugees.

People turn in many directions in their search for security of livelihood. The processes of globalization do create new and enlarged opportunities, but not all of them are legal and benign. Nor are all the beneficiaries indigent and helpless. Growing numbers of people turn to illegal and clandestine ways to earn vast fortunes or to augment their meager means. This expanding complex of activities ranges in space from the transnational to the village level and in numbers from teams of thousands to operations of individuals. Trade in armaments and illegal drugs runs into scores of billions of dollars and involves a complicated chain of industrialists, growers, merchants, banks, retailers, and consumers. Robberies and thefts also come in many shapes and sizes. Commerce in sex and pornography has taken new and perverse forms. Entrepreneurs have even found ways of profiteering from moving people around illegally and dealing in human parts!

Globalization and Development Theory

In exploring the issue of globalization and development theory, it is useful to posit the extreme position of complete economic globalization. A state of complete globalization presumably implies that there exist no barriers to flows of capital, technology, enterprise, skills, goods, or services. (We do retain the assumption of continuing barriers to free movement of unskilled workers) These conditions are equivalent to the assumption of a unified economic space in which political boundaries have no economic significance except for their input on the movement of labor.

In such a world, a good deal of development theory as it has evolved over the past five decades becomes irrelevant. This irrelevance derives principally from the modification and curtailment of the role of the state in promoting economic development. For instance, trade policy—which has occupied much space in development theory—becomes redundant if there are no barriers to the movement of goods, services, capital, or enterprise. The same applies to exchange rate policy, which is determined by supply and demand for foreign exchange. Likewise, the scope for monetary and fiscal policy is much reduced. The ability of a government to engage in deficit financing and the freedom to determine taxes and expenditure are curtailed by the need to retain the confidence of foreign and domestic savers and investors. In such a world, the distinction between foreign and domestic savings and investment loses all significance. The size of the domestic market also becomes an increasingly insignificant factor in determining growth prospects.

Development policy becomes synonymous with enhancement of the attractiveness of the country for financiers, investors, and enterprises. Thus, political stability, social harmony, and a sound macroeconomic framework assume cardinal importance. Other key factors in determining competitiveness are a well developed physical infrastructure (especially in regard to transport, power, and communications) and an educated labor force, together with an abundance of managerial, technical, and entrepreneurial skills. Low tax rates and a stable currency are additional elements of a package designed to enhance the international attractiveness of a place. In short, development economics becomes supply side economics. A country that succeeds in developing these conditions can expect miraculous rates of economic growth for the global market, and the world's pool of savings, investment, technology, skills, and enterprise can break all supply and demand constraints to growth. On the other hand, countries lacking many of these conditions will see their economic situation greatly worsened by the globalization forces' facilitation of the outflow of capital, skills, and enterprises.

This scenario is of course an extreme one. The world is not yet in such a situation, but it has moved rapidly in this direction in recent years, and if present trends continue, the reality will increasingly approximate the scenario sketched out here, with its drastic implications for development thinking and practice as evolved during postwar decades.

Lourdes Arizpe[1] on the Papers by Hirono and Streeten

Culture as the Context of Development

At this watershed point in human history, telecommunications and the global market have brought all the cultures of the world into permanent contact. Although this is indeed an astounding historical achievement, it is bringing with it liabilities as well as benefits. Increased trade, if conducted in a just and equitable manner, may provide more people with access to commodities and services; yet it may also wipe out livelihoods and leave people destitute if they are unable to have access to the new markets. Expanded communication among cultures may foster either greater understanding or more-bitter confrontations. More sophisticated technology increases our ability to manage the physical world and our own genetic processes; yet it may also lead to the devaluation of many of the world's cultures and the loss of local knowledge accumulated over centuries.

For this reason, culture needs to be brought to the fore as the context in which development takes place. Development thinking and policies must now incorporate the concepts of cooperation, trust, ethnicity, identity, community, and kinship, since these make up the social fabric on which the polity and the economy are based. In many places, the narrow emphasis on competition and gain within the market place is altering these sensitive equilibrium factors and thus exacerbating cultural tensions and feelings of uncertainty.

Unless the values of cooperation are emphasized as much as those of competitiveness, conflicts rather than peace will intensify in the coming decades. People all over the world have learned, through television and newspapers, that they are entitled to share in the opportunities of the globally accumulated wealth. Yet conditions are making it difficult or even impossible for this sharing to occur, especially if inequality in access to jobs and incomes continues to grow. Skills may not be upgraded as quickly as is necessary (especially between different generations), and the world's natural-resource base may become more and more depleted, while demographic and morbidity trends will create new realities of their own. Even so, history has shown the enormous resilience of cultures—that is, the capacity of people to adapt and to develop responses to urgent social and environmental challenges.

The report of the World Commission on Culture and Development—entitled *Our Creative Diversity*—states that development is embedded in culture and not the other way

---

[1] Assistant Director-General for Culture, UNESCO, Paris.

around. In his introduction to the report, Javier Pérez de Cuéllar, president of the commission, clearly states that "building cultural insights into the broader development strategies, as well as a more effective practical agenda, has to be the next step in rethinking development." The report was able to bring together the views of many people from many regions of the world and on that basis to build a general cultural perspective on the development—one based on satisfying not only the fundamental economic requirements for a decent standard of living but also the social, psychological, and philosophical requirements that will allow people to share and to cooperate for a fulfilling life.

Culture and Globalization

An important consideration is that for the first time in history, the effects of global geo-atmospheric and biological changes will affect all the inhabitants of the world. This new environmental interdependence, coupled with economic interdependence, will call for a level of global coordination that—as Paul Streeten notes in his chapter—is absent in international relations at present. This new reality of global change is being driven by processes of scale, interaction, and complexity, but the old models on which policy decisions are being made are still linear and are restricted in the number of factors they take into account.

Globalization is usually referred to as a single process, yet its diverse components are expanding at different rates and are creating diverse effects on societies around the world. Paul Streeten argues that "the perception is of a greater degree of globalization and integration than has in fact occurred." This perceived difference is perhaps the result of the greater pervasiveness of the cultural components of globalization than of the economic components.

As a microcosm, the recent Zapatista uprising in southern Mexico illustrates this complexity of the globalization process. The driving force of the uprising was not simply the poverty and marginalization that have been there for five centuries. The precipitating factor was instead the widely held perception that now that Mexico was so near the First World, higher standards of living were at hand's length.[2] This perception was strongly fostered by the mass media, by the government's emphasis on the opportunities that a liberalized market would offer, and by the demonstration effect of the wealth that was rapidly amassed by a few heavily subsidized cattle ranchers in Tabasco and Chiapas who had political connections. When the benefits of economic development continued to concentrate in the hands of the state oligarchy and when the price of coffee, as well as of other agricultural products, fell to historic lows in the international market, local farmers felt not only marginalized but cheated out of this proclaimed historical opportunity.

---

[2] Although the book deals with deforestation, the research we carried out before the Zapatista army appeared sheds a great deal of light on the causes of the rebellion: Lourdes Arizpe, Fernanda Paz, and Margarita Velázquez, *Culture and Global Change: Social Perceptions of Deforestation in the Lacandon Rainforest* (Ann Arbor: Michigan University Press, 1996).

External versus Internal Factors

The Zapatista example shows that economic liberalization implemented through old political systems based on authoritarianism and clientelism will increase income gaps, thereby leading to the possibility of social uprisings at the local level. Such an analysis supports Ryokichi Hirono's observation in contrasting the world's economically successful and unsuccessful developing countries. He argues that political instability, domestic conflicts, and the prevalence of corruption and inefficient bureaucracy at the national and local levels are some of today's major roadblocks to national development. Hirono concludes that "this contrast implies without any doubt that the internal rather than the external factors have been chiefly responsible for the successes of many developing countries and for the failures of many more in terms of sustained national development during the postwar period."

It must be said, however, that at least in Latin America, the distinction between these internal and external factors is sometimes blurred. In some cases, corrupt centralized regimes were supported externally at a time that Cold War considerations overrode all others. In some cases, governmental and private-sector corruption continues to be fostered by the obsolete management systems still in place (although we should not discount the role still being played by external agents). Moreover, corruption has been amplified by the erosion of the values of political morality—not least, it must be said, by the monothematic insistence on getting rich as the only desirable goal in life.

The issue of corruption has been mentioned several times at the Conference on Development Thinking and Practice, and the eradication of corruption should continue to be strongly emphasized. This problem is not a simple one and must be understood in the framework of complex cultural interactions and of its input within the system of checks and balances in the political as well as in the judiciary systems. For instance, in the Mexican case, the inefficiency and multiple cover-ups in the investigation of the two highly publicized cases of recent political assassinations have all but destroyed the credibility of the judiciary in its efforts to provide justice. A further complication, which will make it even more difficult to clean up corrupt practices in the years to come, is the advancing infiltration of drug traffickers' money at all levels of government.

Culture as the Context of Development Policies

Interestingly, most of the internal barriers to successful national development listed by Ryokichi Hirono are related to culture. He refers to the work ethic and patterns of consumption, to principles and honesty in public service, to civic behavior and to ethnic, language, and religious intolerance. At the conference, many speakers have mentioned that social and cultural factors are becoming increasingly visible as key variables for the development process. Already, trust, confidence, and cooperation are emphasized as social capital. The perception that a given economic policy will have different results in different cultural settings is now gaining ground, even though we as yet lack the analytical tools to examine, measure, and understand precisely the relationship between culture and development.

Culture is indeed the next frontier of the international economic development effort, now that policies have been put in place on the environment, population, gender, social development, and other related areas. Some cultural themes are in fact already being included in development analysis through the concepts of human development, capacity building, institutional innovation, and social capital. But the overall cultural perspective itself is still missing.

In this sense, the publication of the aforementioned report of the World Commission on Culture and Development is quite timely and should foster more-rigorous and much-needed debate in the field, leading ultimately to the formulation of more-appropriate development policy. The report asserts that a global ethics must be developed, based on the principles of human rights, democracy, and science and committed to fostering the respect for cultural and social diversity necessary for holding together our multipolar world. The report advocates the strengthening of civic cultures on which to rebuild national and international governance institutions, based on increased local-community participation and gender quality. It furthermore proposes actions to preserve the world's cultural heritage, as well as to manage rationally the life support systems that we need in order to continue to live on this planet.

One of the recommendations of the report is that UNESCO sponsor an independent team that will produce and publish a world report on culture, in order to survey recent trends in this field, to monitor events affecting the situation of different cultures worldwide (highlighting selected cultural practices and policies at local, national, and international levels), and to construct and publish quantitative cultural indicators.

Another of the commission's recommendations concerns the fact that the nature of conflicts is changing. Of the 82 substantial conflicts that have occurred in the world during the last three years, some 79 have occurred within individual nations. The underlying cause of many such conflicts is the lack of development, which results in a rising tide of human despair and anger. The commission strongly recommends, therefore, that professional analysis be undertaken of the new dimensions of human security (including economic, political, cultural, and environmental security) and that UNDP and UNESCO, along with other agencies, take the lead in assisting countries in formulating new human-development strategies that preserve and enrich people's cultural values and ethnic heritage rather than destroying them.

At the two Royaumont Abbey workshops for exploring the methodological issues for the world culture report that will be focused on development, we first asked, "What are we going to measure? Cultural development? Cultural vitality? Cultural well-being?" And we came to the conclusion that what must be measured is **the cultural components of human well-being**. This understanding is relevant to the whole notion of development thinking and practice.

In much the same way—and in support of Amartya Sen's argument that economics is a means and not an end in itself—we should ask, "Is there such a thing as economic well-being as an isolated state, detached from the total state of human well-being?" Indeed, there cannot be, as is clearly shown by data from around the world showing economic success coupled with political instability, social uprisings, and cultural anomie.

The Globalization of the "Imaginaire"

Eisuke Sakakibara and Alain Touraine have raised the issue that globalization can be perceived by some as an ideological process to impose a given "global culture" on the rest of the world. This perception is echoed around the world as people express their concern over the risk of cultural homogenization implied in the image of the "global village."

An entirely new cultural field now expanding at the speed of thought is the emerging culture of cyberspace. It is changing the notion of world distances, cultural communication, community, and individual responsibility, as we grapple with the challenging notion of "virtual self" and "virtual community." Already we were watching traditional "culture" become delocalized, dematerialized, dehistoricized, and delegalized to transmuted forms of cultures in plural; unbounded cultures in a borderless world were already producing unimagined shifts in human fantasy. It is quite riveting at this point to find—now that the technology exists, through the Internet—ways to crystallize a "virtual" sphere of reality, which parallels people's current attempts to rematerialize identities, heritage, and traditions. New boundaries are being drawn, and we must by all means oppose exclusions in ways that we are only just now beginning to imagine possible.

The new planetary reach of telecommunications—through optic fiber, satellites, parabolic antennas, and now the integration of the informatics and telephone systems—carries images to the ends of the world. Not only do these images have greater planetary reach every day but also the amount of time that people spend watching them is increasing. In the United States, people spend an average of seven hours per day watching television, which almost matches the amount of time they spend at work (on average eight hours per day for most people). Moreover, images have a way of occupying mental space and of becoming cultural referents that makes them even more persuasive and pervasive.

Interestingly, the reactions to "cultural globalization" (for want of a better term) differ greatly across cultural settings. One reaction has been retrenchment into different degrees of ethnic, national, or religious chauvinism, which, significantly, can be found in both the North and the South. In the North, cultural conservatism is leading toward xenophobia and religious fundamentalism, which could become new forms of cultural protectionism that may create new nontariff barriers to international trade and to the flow of people and cultures across borders. Other spin-offs in the North are the creative explorations of New Age lifestyles and of other antimaterialist ideologies.

In the South, cultural conservatism has given rise to ethnic conflicts, religious fundamentalism, and even fragmentation of nation-states. One tragic result has been the disappearance, irreversible and absolute, of languages and knowledge cultivated, sifted, and refined during centuries. A parallel exists between the loss of biodiversity and the loss of cultural diversity, in which humanity loses the creativity accumulated by many generations and, importantly, painstakingly adapted to different geobiological settings.

We still do not know what the overall consequences of this loss of cultural diversity and differentiation will be, just as we do not yet know what the consequences will be of the loss of biodiversity. In terms of the impact on economic development, the question has not yet been adequately explored. Is economic development helped or hindered by cultural diversity? The empirical examples are not monolithic. The United States as a diversified cultural melting pot contrasts with Japan and France as monocultural states, yet all are economically successful. Cultural diversity in India, Thailand, and Mexico, among many others, has produced some of the world's richest artisanal traditions, which are now important export sectors of their economies. But at another level, cultural ties and solidity have provided the cohesion and coordination necessary for some individual groups to benefit from the opportunities being offered by the international market; a case in point is that of the Otavalo Indians of Ecuador, who have been very successful in expanding the commercialization of their traditional crafts to European and North American markets. So it is hard to give a simple answer. One thing is clear, however: cultural diversity that becomes confrontational is hindering development in all regions of the world, including Europe.

Toward a Multicultural Capitalism

In 1992, of the ten largest economies in the world, only three were in the third world. In contrast, by the year 2020, of the world's ten largest economies, only three will be Western, and the other seven will be Asian. Does this shift mean that globalization is creating multicultural capitalism? Eisuke Sakakibara has made a distinction among Japanese, American, and trans-Alpine forms of capitalism. Yet capitalism has in essence always been multicultural, because cultural differences were already there during the past century in the North Atlantic, although all within the Western cultural matrix.

To answer the question of the emergence of multicultural capitalism, we need much more research. In order to perform this research, we especially (and this is where economists can collaborate fruitfully with sociologists and anthropologists) need to develop innovative and effective methodological tools for the areas of culture and of economic development, in order to create measurements and models that will answer this and the other questions formulated earlier.

The greatest asset human beings have for navigating the civilizational transition we are now experiencing is our human creativity. A huge amount of investment is being made today in manufacturing, in services, and in filling the mass media spaces with entertainment. We need to ask ourselves how much investment is being made in thinking about new governance institutions, new pluralistic national legislation and institutions, new global arrangements, new philosophies, and new images that better represent this new, competitive-but-cooperative, localized-but-globalized world. Without such investment in creative thinking, we cannot successfully meet the challenge of attaining sustainable human development in the twenty-first century.

Development and Underdevelopment in a Globalized World: Latin American Dilemmas

Aldo Ferrer[1]

The fundamentalist view of globalization exerts considerable influence on the design of structural-adjustment strategies and stabilization strategies in Latin America. According to that view, the world economy is currently driven by forces beyond the control of political systems and nation-states. We are supposedly in the presence of a new **natural order,** the laws of which must be obeyed as the very underpinnings of rationality itself. The external-debt crisis, compounded by the imbalances and social inequity of earlier development models, helped to establish this fundamentalist view of globalization and the policies that prevail today.

The globalization issue is a crucial one, because, external ties constitute determining factors in the development or lack of development of countries. External ties influence capital formation and technological change, the structure of national production and external trade, income distribution, the long-term job creation rate, and short-term macroeconomic balances.

This paper refers to the present-day dilemmas that stem from the nature of involvement of our countries in today's world economy. We shall present a brief description of the fundamentalist view of globalization, followed by a point-by-point criticism of that view, and we then shall attempt to identify the options for Ibero-America with regard to alternative ways in which the region can respond to the problems of development in a globalized context.

The Fundamentalist View: Seven Myths of Globalization

From the fundamentalist vantage point of globalization, the international system presents seven main features. Let us briefly examine each one on its own terms.

First, globalization of the current world order has no historical precedent. Supposedly, the modern technological revolution marks a watershed in the history of humanity. The processes of the internationalization of production, markets, and finances respond to deep forces that have created an order of relations among countries and social agents that has absolutely no precedent in human experience. In the past there were no technological changes or economic and social processes that led to such diverse and deep

[1] Director, MERCOSUR Masters Degree Program, University of Buenos Aires.

links among countries and social actors. In other words, never before in the world order have countries faced situations that would so radically transform their internal realities and their international linkage.

Second, national spaces have been dissolved in the global order. The accumulation of capital and the production and distribution of goods and services take place today chiefly on the world market. Nation-states have ceased to be the stage on which the main decisions regarding resource allocation, capital accumulation, technological change, and income distribution take place. Those decisions are now made on a transnational level by corporations and financial markets, which command most of the resources in the world economy. Therefore, in a world without borders, the national dimension has been dissolved in the global order.

Third, economic development and competition have changed in nature. In the global order, increases in productivity occur in the context of a world market, as a result of the decisions of transnational corporations and financial markets. Competition no longer takes place among domestic economies but among production units that operate on the global market. Competitiveness is therefore a microeconomic dimension on the company level and not a dimension of the national system in each country. Macroeconomic policy is subordinated to the need to maximize the competitiveness of individual businesses.

Fourth, national policies should dovetail with market expectations. Since decisions are made by markets and companies, public policies that contradict the expectations of private operators generate negative reactions that abort the objectives pursued. The system is thus rightly ruled by the expectations and decisions of private operators and not by politicians. In democratic systems, voters elect their leaders from time to time, but the markets vote every day; they are, in a nutshell, the decision makers. Thus, the only viable policies are market-friendly policies.

Fifth, full deregulation of markets is the only possible system. Given the heavy weight of transnational agents in the decision-making process and given the fact that the world order is currently rooted in forces beyond the control of nation-states and even of international organizations, the only possible organization of the world system lies in *nonorganization* and in total freedom for the operations of transnational agents. There exist no alternative policy options. The system is simply imposed by reality.

Sixth, the problem of development in a globalized world is nonexistent today. In the past, countries retained considerable freedom to decide on their styles of development and of involvement with the international context. For instance, protectionist policies could stimulate industrialization and transform the comparative advantages of national economies. This orientation is impossible today. Any move contrary to private expectations will depress investment and economic activity. The only possible response to globalization is to set the stage for private operators to view a country as a good prospect for investment and productive development. A systemic national approach to development is now irrelevant, and governments are powerless to put such an approach into practice. The enrichment of a country's social tissues (through solidarity, income redistribution, and cultural development), the creation of linkages among national science and technology systems, and the production of goods and services are all, at best, merely good intentions. In any event, education and culture should be directed today to enriching, as inexpensively as possible, the supply of skilled human resources for companies competing in the global economy.

Seventh, an invisible hand will make interests compatible and will spread well-being. In short, the market will take charge of efficiently allocating resources on a world scale and of equitably distributing the fruits of technological progress and development. The classical invisible hand will make private interests compatible with social interests in the global order.

Globalization, History and the Real World

The aforementioned propositions of the fundamentalist view of globalization are not rooted in reality or in history. Let us turn briefly to the same seven main issues, as seen from a more realistic and historical standpoint.

In the first place, globalization actually began five centuries ago. European expansion overseas in the fifteenth century culminated in the discovery and conquest of the New World and also in the arrival of Portugal's Vasco da Gama in Calicut, India. During that epoch, a system of relations among peoples and countries on a planetary scale was built for the first time (Ferrer 1996a). Since then, events have taken place that have transformed the development conditions of all the countries in the world order.

In the sixteenth century, for instance, as a consequence of the incorporation of America into the world order built by the Europeans, about 80 percent of the native American population was exterminated. The greatest demographic catastrophe in history was one of the results of the formation of the first world economic order. In turn, sugar production and the establishment of an international market for that commodity led to the first large-scale transfer of African slaves to American plantations. These two extraordinary events marked the ethnic profile of the New World forever and continue to be decisive factors in the social stratification and development of the countries of the Americas.

Then in the nineteenth century, the spread of the Industrial Revolution radically transformed the development process and international relations. The railway and the steamship, the telegraph and the underwater cable, led to a headlong expansion in international economic and financial relations. In turn, the partition of Africa and the European and North American penetration of the Orient led to extraordinary changes that were far reaching for the world order.

In fact, on the eve of the World War I, the indicators of the relative weight of international trade and the investments of transnational corporations with respect to the total product and capital formation in the world economy were similar in scope or larger than they are today (UNCTAD 1994).

Thus, although modern globalization does have a decisive influence on the behavior of the world order and on the development of countries in our time, similar or even more momentous events have also occurred in the past. The railway, for instance, has probably been more important for the development and establishment of the world order than the modern information revolution has been.

In the second place, nations do continue to be the basic venue for economic transactions. Despite the development of world trade, of transnational corporations, and of international financial marketplaces, the balance of resources points to the following: domestic markets absorb 80 percent of world production, and more than 90 percent of fixed-capital accumulation is financed with domestic savings, while world exports account for only about 20 percent of global GDP, and the investments of the subsidiaries of transnational corporations account for less than 5 percent of fixed world investment. With respect to this last point, the consolidated balances of the current accounts of all countries show similar international transfers of savings out of total fixed-capital accumulation. As for jobs, around 9 out of every 10 workers in the world is employed in serving domestic markets.

Admittedly, in the most globalized activities (such as the automotive and electronics industries and different services), the world market is the main destination of production. These are also the activities exhibiting the most rapid growth. In them, transnational corporations and external credit finance most investments. Nevertheless, it is not even remotely certain that command of most of the resources in the world economy is in the hands of transnational agents; furthermore, it is unlikely that such a scenario will become reality in the foreseeable future.

By the same token, small and medium-sized producers of goods and services and small and medium-sized domestic-market suppliers will probably continue to be the agents who use most of the resources employed in the world economy. The slowdown in growth and the aggravation of social problems apparent in the industrialized countries, in Latin America, and elsewhere, probably reflect the irrationality implicit in managing most resources (which are generated and used outside of the global order) in accordance with the views and interests of transnationalized segments.

In the third place, the competitiveness of companies depends to a great extent upon the level of development of their country of origin. Efficiency in a company's use of resources depends basically on factors that are beyond the company's control, such as the supply of skilled labor, the quality of the national science and technology system, the level of stability in the rules of the game, the efficiency of public services, the development of capital markets, the cost of money, the transportation system, access to information, the rate of growth in demand, and income distribution. Competitiveness depends above all on the country of origin's macroeconomic picture and on its social tissue. It is in this context that companies can be less or more competitive on the world scale. It is difficult to develop effective policies to promote microeconomic competitiveness in unfavorable macroeconomic contexts.

In the fourth place, national policies are decisive for economic development. The decisions taken within nations continue to be essential for the economic and social development of countries and their international integration. The technology revolution and the increasingly complex and systematic linkage between production units and their domestic and international contexts make national decisions the keys to sustainable development.

In the fifth place, the dilemma of development in a globalized world is as relevant today as in the past, or even more so. The style in which each country is integrated into the international market depends chiefly on the options it adopts based on its own objectives and domestic power structure, history, and the available resources. There do exist more models than one for guiding a country's insertion into the world economy. Therefore, the dilemmas posed by the globalized world order and by alternative responses to development problems continue to exist. The latter may or may not be consistent with the development and preservation of a reasonable margin for national economic independence within the international scenario. To illustrate the existence of such alternatives, it is sufficient to compare the avenues of development and external linkage followed by Latin America with those followed by the countries of East and Southeast Asia.

In the sixth place, regulatory frameworks are essential for the operation of the world order, and such frameworks depend on political decisions. The political decisions of the centers of world power establish the rules of the game. The globalization of financial markets has been expedited through the deregulation of exchange markets and of capital movements. Changes in the regulatory framework would discipline international market behavior, as illustrated by the application of the exchange transactions tax designed to discourage movements of speculative capital, as suggested by Professor James Tobin.

But, it should be remembered that on the eve of the crisis of the 1930s, the gold standard and the multilateral system of trade and payments seemed, like today's givens, to respond to absolute situations imposed by reality itself. Nevertheless, that crisis radically changed the regulatory frameworks and the operation of the system. Today, the so-called evidence of the sovereignty of markets constitutes merely a self-fulfilling prophecy.

In the seventh place, distribution of the benefits of development is becoming more equal and widens social gaps within countries and in the world order. Far from reflecting the existence of an invisible hand that equitably balances the interests of transnational agents with those of society as a whole, there has actually occurred an increase in income distribution inequality and in the social imbalances in the main centers, in Latin America, and in other countries. In the last 30 years, the difference in average income between the wealthiest 20 percent of the population and the poorest 20 percent rose from 30 to 60 times. In the same period, the second group's share of world income has fallen from 2.3 percent to 1.4 percent and that of the first has risen from 70 percent to 85 percent (UNDP 1992 and 1996).

This situation stems in part from the fact that the modern technology revolution contributes to market fragmentation and to the exclusion of traditional-sector producers and of less-skilled workers. The increase in productivity focuses on activities that incorporate technological change and that operate in the fastest-growing segments of demand. Left to its own devices, globalization reproduces existing patterns of growth or backwardness; in any case, it does not help rectify preexisting imbalances in the international system.

Latin America's Dilemmas

The solution to the current problems in the larger international scenario depends basically on the decisions of a small group of advanced countries. Latin America is a secondary actor, and its ability to influence prevailing world trends is close to zero.

The challenge for the region is to find its own responses to enable it to develop in the international system as that system exists today. The region can and does call for a new world order based on solidarity and the solution of social and environmental problems. Official Latin American positions at the large international conferences on development, on the environment, and on population in recent years do converge with those of other countries in the South and with those of some in the North. These positions advocate a new world order to promote growth, eradicate poverty, ensure governability, and consolidate international peace and security.

But as Helio Jaguaribe suggests, elsewhere in this volume, Latin America does not have an infinite amount of time in which to solve its problems, and it cannot wait for changes in the world context that might someday act from the outside to promote growth and eliminate poverty in the region.

In sum, solving development problems in a globalized world depends first and foremost upon domestic decisions—or as suggested by Osvaldo Sunkel and others, upon growth from the inside and inclusion in the world order through domestic hubs of accumulation, technological change, and social transformation. Historical evidence is conclusive: from the establishment of the first world economic order (Ferrer 1996a) to the present—that is, in the last five centuries—there has existed no other effective avenue for national economic development.

The historical course of Latin American underdevelopment can be explained in function of the region's inability to find valid responses to the problems of national development within a globalized world. Today as in the past, there exist no possibility of introducing a development process that will be sustainable over the long term without the prior consolidation of the internal factors of capital accumulation, technological change, and social transformation, which are in fact the building blocks for broader and deeper relations with the rest of the world.

In contrast, the application of policies based on the fundamentalist view of globalization points to paths leading in exactly the opposite direction. Resource allocation, income distribution, capital formation, and the incorporation of technology will tend increasingly to revolve around transnational hubs ever more distanced from local realities. This situation will lead to ever-widening gaps in the social system, to the destruction of a large part of the productive capacity built up in the past, to increases in poverty, and to social inequalities. National systems in such a scenario will tend to center on modern enclaves surrounded by underdevelopment and poverty, and stability will become increasingly dependent on the expectations of the financial markets. The external debt and the dependency of public finances on short-term capital will tend to subordinate economic policy to market decisions: the success or failure of economic policy will come to be measured by policy's influence on access to financial markets rather than by its impact on production, exports, or jobs.

Financial globalization in turn introduces severe restrictions elsewhere, although (as demonstrated, for example, by the exchange turmoil in recent years in the European monetary system) many of those problems have thus far been solved with moderate adjustments in exchange rates, with increases in the floating range, or with temporary withdrawals from the system—in other words, without major disruptions. Nevertheless, in various Latin American countries, external financial vulnerability has led to blaring changes in exchange rates, prices, economic activity, and employment.

Latin America is therefore facing urgent challenges. The ideas of Raúl Prebisch, Celso Furtado, and other prominent Latin American economists are again coming to be viewed as valid avenues for finding answers to the difficulties encountered today in developing in a globalized world (Ferrer 1996b). It is necessary to get back to the spirit of these economists' work: to observe reality with a critical eye and from our own vantage points—in other words, not to be a slave to conventional wisdom, which today consists of the fundamentalist view of globalization. It is imperative that the region engage in a broad and deep debate on the behavior of the modern world system and that it identify and address the problems of how to develop in a globalized world.

Some issues are clear enough. The first issue is that each Latin American country's own house needs to be put in order as a necessary condition for sustainable development. Judicious resource utilization, macroeconomic balance, effective fiscal and monetary policy, and balance-of-payments adjustments consistent with stability are all requisites for carving out more room for self-determination in a globalized world and for catalyzing sustainable development.

The second issue is that the sphere of social and public action in Latin America needs to be rebuilt. The objective should not be to dismantle or shrink government but to strengthen the official instruments for promoting development and equity. The market does not spontaneously solve problems; left to its own devices, it actually worsens social imbalances and tensions. Reconstruction of the public sphere includes revival of the nation-state as the arbitrator of sector struggles, as the buttress for the development of private initiative, and as the chief agent in the redistribution of income and in the design of social policies. The social and public area includes the lower levels of government (provinces, municipalities) and the organizations that promote solidarity and behavior based on the **common** interest. The future of democracy in Latin America depends essentially on reconstruction of the social and public area in this broad sense.

The third issue is that regional integration processes have now become crucial in reinforcing the capacity for self-centered development in a globalized world. Regional and subregional spaces are venues for solidarity, for self-focused development policies, and for opening up to the rest of the world from the inside out. The fortunes of MERCOSUR will reveal the extent to which this potential can be realized (Ferrer 1995).

President Fernando Henrique Cardoso asserts that Brazil is not an underdeveloped country, but an unjust one. This interpretation also holds true for other Latin American nations. The removal of injustices is a moral imperative, a key condition for national and outward development, and a primary responsibility of all our countries. No one will do for Latin America what it must do for itself. In turn, injustice and poverty cannot be effectively addressed as long as our countries fail to affirm their own identity and responsibility and to seek their own developmental paths in a globalized world. The latter approach, unfortunately, is not the route being following today under the dominance of the fundamentalist view of globalization.

REFERENCES

Ferrer, Aldo. "MERCOSUR: Trayectoria, situación actual, y perspectivas." Mexico: *Revista Comercio Exterior* (noviembre 1995).

_____. *Historia de la globalización: orígenes del orden económico mundial.* Buenos Aires: Fondo de Cultura Económica, 1996a.

_____. "Raúl Prebisch y los problemas actuales de América Latina." Buenos Aires: *Revista Ciclos* 10 (1996b).

UNCTAD. *World Investment Report* (Chapter III). New York and Geneva, 1994.

UNDP. *Human Development Report.* New York, 1992 and 1996

Development Thinking and Policies in Latin America and the Caribbean: Past and Future

Gert Rosenthal[1]

The present essay will attempt to address several topics: how development thinking and policies have evolved over time in Latin America and the Caribbean; what the effects of those policies have been in recent times; what lessons can be learned; and what predictions can be made regarding the course of development thinking and policies for the future. This is, to say the least, quite a tall order—in the first place, because there seems to exist something of a Manichaean tendency in the way development economics is approached in Latin America: the debate alternates between inward-led growth versus export-led strategies; *dirigisme* versus *laissez-faire; estructuralismo* versus *monetarismo.* But in fact, reality defies such neat characterizations; rather than consisting of one single paradigm, the real story usually includes a whole spectrum of policies and strategies that make up the overall menu. These are difficult to characterize in a brief article.

The same can be said of trying to establish cause-and-effect relationships. By some observers, economic performance is perceived in terms of factors originating exclusively in the international economy; conversely, other commentators narrow their analysis down to the results of domestic policymaking. The real world, of course, is more complicated, and the characteristics of policymaking as well as cause-and-effect relationships must inevitably be presented in different shades of gray, rather than in black or white.

Furthermore, the usual *caveat* applies: Latin America is made up of many and widely differing countries. Neither the modalities of the 1950s nor those of the 1980s were applied uniformly: some countries embraced each model earlier—or more fervently—than did others, and marked differences in policymaking appear in terms of the pacing, sequencing, and mixing of different practices. In addition, similar policies in different countries have led to disparate results, precisely because each context is different. It is always risky, therefore, to try to draw universal conclusions from the enormous variety of experiences that the region has to offer.

Despite these reservations, we offer the following comments with the aim of highlighting some issues and introducing some parameters that will help clarify the debate regarding differences in economic and social policymaking over time both within Latin America itself and in contrast to policymaking in other developing regions. The presen-

---

[1] Executive Secretary, Economic Commission for Latin America and the Caribbean (ECLAC/CEPAL).

tation is divided into five necessarily brief sections: the *first* section examines the shifts in policymaking over time; the *second* concentrates on economic reforms put in place since the 1980s (a topic that John Williamson covers at greater length in his article revisiting the "Washington consensus"); the *third* seeks to garner some lessons from economic and social performance insofar as such performance is linked to the aforementioned reforms; the *fourth* presents some brief remarks contrasting the East Asian experience and the Latin American experience; and the *fifth* probes the future.

Trends and Shifts in Policymaking

Economic thinking is apparently subject to a phenomenon akin to the cycles that affect economic performance. The equivalent of the Kondratieff waves—the long cycles—is shaped by current fashions and attitudes in thought, usually regarding the related issues of the economic role of government (from Smith's *The Wealth of Nations* to Keynes' *The End of Laissez-Faire*) and the degree of "openness" to international trade. The shorter cycles are presumably shaped by excesses in the application of the policy actions that arise from the world of ideas. In other words, ideas shape action, and action then retroshapes ideas.

The Latin American region certainly has experienced such cycles over the past 80 years or so, both in the realm of economic thinking and in the domain of economic action. At least two abrupt shifts have occurred: the first shift took place between the interwar period and the post-World War II period in response to the Great Depression and the effects of World War II; the second shift occurred in the 1980s in response to the debt crisis and globalization. (Some authors would identify a third or intermediate shift in the mid-1970s, at least in the Southern Cone, but more on that later.) Within these seemingly abrupt shifts, continuous modifications were taking place both conceptually and in practice.

This continuous change—which some like to view as a pendular movement and others describe as "stages" (Birdsall and Lozada 1996)—reflected a combination of universal trends and more-parochial responses both to external shocks and to domestic events. Further, when examining these dynamics, it is hard to discern whether economic thinking and policy actions shaped economic performance or whether economic thinking was instead shaped by economic realities; in fact, of course, both phenomena were going on simultaneously.

The first major shift in question occurred during the 1930s and 1940s, a period in which the majority of the countries of the region abandoned *Laissez-Faire* orthodoxy and embraced industrialization based on import substitution, with its attendant interventionist policies. The economic realities that drove this change stemmed from the foreign-exchange crunch and the profound Depression of the 1930s, as countries started to cope by restricting imports and promoting domestic alternatives. Even when the foreign-exchange shortage was alleviated (reserves had accumulated during World War II), the difficulty of gaining access to manufactured goods on international markets kept import substitution in place, especially in the larger countries of the region.

As is well known, the conceptual framework for this trend came in part from the Economic Commission for Latin America, under the inspired leadership of Raúl Prebisch. ECLA (now ECLAC) developed a persuasive argument in favor of both industrialization and a strong state presence, based on the asymmetrical relations between the "center" (or more-developed economies) and the "periphery" (ECLAC 1951). The accent was placed on removing the structural impediments to development—almost the antithesis of recourse to the "magic of the market." The time frame of the approach was the medium and the long term; little importance was attached to short-term economic policymaking, especially in the sphere of monetary, exchange rate, and fiscal policy.

Prebisch did warn of the dangers of excessive protection, but over the years the ECLA/ECLAC "message" was stereotyped into being strongly inwardly oriented and *dirigiste*. Indeed, important pressure groups developed (exemplified by the countries' chambers of industry and unions of blue-collar workers) in favor of keeping protection in place and even of strengthening it, thereby generating a self-perpetuating dynamic that other pressure groups (as exemplified by the chambers of commerce and agriculture) were unable to moderate. It is thus fair to argue that the import substitution strategy was maintained in Latin America much longer than circumstances warranted. Furthermore, the region's economic performance in the 1950s and 1960s, at least in terms of growth, was more than respectable: average real per capita GDP nearly doubled between 1950 and 1970.

Not surprisingly, therefore, the voices of opposition to ECLA/ECLAC's approach during the 1950s—in Latin America, in academia (for notable examples, see Viner 1953 and Corden 1966) and also in the Bretton Woods Institutions—were at first muted. But opposition began to gather momentum in the 1960s, giving rise to serious questions from both ends of the ideological spectrum. The *dependentistas* implicitly called for more state intervention and less dependence on trade and capital flows; the more orthodox liberal approach called for less state intervention and for more traditional *laissez-faire* economics. Further, import substitution industrialization ran into trouble in the real world, given its anti-export, antirural biases and the fact that it was found that the model actually increased external vulnerability rather than mitigating it.

At the same time, in the world surrounding Latin America a shift in thinking was taking place that influenced the debate within the region. Although the question of "openness" to international trade was not at the center of the ferment, mainstream post-Keynesian economics was being attacked from the conservative flank (the Chicago School libertarianism) and from the progressive flank (the so-called radical economists). Still, for the next decade or so, the "inward-looking" model stayed alive in Latin America through doing the following: by expanding domestic markets through formal economic integration arrangements; by mitigating the anti-export bias of policymaking through selective policies (especially fiscal incentives) meant to promote nontraditional exports; and by dealing with foreign-exchange restrictions through having greater access to international financing, especially from public sources in the 1960s and private ones in the 1970s.

The more brusque counterrevolution began, as is well known, in the mid-1970s and was limited at first to the Southern Cone countries. All three of those countries (Argentina, Chile, and Uruguay) suffered severe macroeconomic disequilibriums and price distortions; all were ruled by authoritarian military regimes; and all returned to what one author calls "neoconservative economics" (Ramos 1986) and another labels "international monetarism" (Fishlow 1985). Fishlow points out that "the objective of the initial application was to reduce domestic inflation. The way to do so was by a pre-specified, decreasing adjustment of the exchange rate, using the law of one price. The way to keep inflation down, once it had fallen, was by a fixed exchange rate. Free trade and capital movements would both facilitate stabilization and guarantee development" (p. 135). Certain other features of the Southern Cone approach were actually harbingers of things to come in the 1980s (Corbo 1988): trade liberalization, the liberalization of domestic financial markets, opening up to international capital flows, deregulation, the reduction of fiscal deficits (less so in Argentina than in the other countries), and restrictive monetary policies. In general, free prices were restored as the central mechanism for the efficient allocation of resources.

But as Albert Fishlow correctly points out, the Southern Cone's "international monetarism did not work as advertised," owing to three important limitations: "an application to the short term of long-run equilibrium conditions; inadequate attention to the components of the balance of payments and concern only for a bottom-line total; and a focus on macroeconomic equilibrium rather than on economic development" (pp. 136–7). In effect, overvalued exchange rates and excessive short-term capital inflows, as well as insufficient attention to the supply side of the equation, led to a profound recession and to banking system insolvency.

Despite the lack of total success, there had clearly occurred a crucial break with the past strategy in all three countries; correcting the more obvious flaws of the new approach (as described by Fishlow) meant building on some of the new foundations rather than returning to the old ones, although a certain tension did exist between proponents of each of these options.[2] The debt crisis of 1982 finally ushered in a major shift in economic thinking and policymaking throughout Latin America, not only through the force of circumstances but also because the new and acute balance-of-payments crisis highlighted the weaknesses of the previous strategy (its vulnerability to international shocks, its price distortions, and its shortcomings in regard to international competitiveness); these flaws had been gradually accumulating over the years.

At first, the region's adjustment and stabilization were approached in a disorderly manner and at an extremely high social cost. A curious mixture of controls and liberalization, of heterodox and orthodox approaches, can be found in the first half of the 1980s. Much was made of the "heterodox" adjustment programs of Argentina, Brazil, and Peru, which sought to control inflation without falling into recession, by means of

---

[2] This tension was reproduced within the ECLAC Secretariat at the time, with proponents of both strategies engaged in a lively debate.

guiding expectations through price and income controls in the short run and liberalizing markets in the medium term. Contrary to the Israeli experience during the same period, all of these programs ultimately failed, each for somewhat different reasons (Bruno et al. 1988).[3] But there was also a learning process going on, and a gradual convergence on the main parameters of a new approach, which undoubtedly represents a return in the direction of greater orthodoxy.

Recent Reforms

The aforementioned convergence on the main parameters of a new approach can be found in several key areas of policymaking, which prominently include a conspicuous trend toward trade liberalization, a greater confidence in market forces as the prime allocator of resources, decreased public-policy intervention, and greater coherence of macroeconomic policymaking. In other words, just as the crisis of the 1930s gave rise to import substitution and to greater public-sector intervention, the crisis of the 1980s ushered in a move toward more-open, market-oriented economies.

There has been an effort to characterize this shift in economic thinking as the emergence of a new paradigm; the Latin American media often call it "neoliberal." More modestly, some years ago John Williamson referred to the common denominator of the framework of policymaking as "the Washington consensus" (although it was not conceived in Washington and does not reveal a consensus and although John Williamson himself tells us he has come to regret the term). This approach is reflected in some key reforms affecting policies and markets, and it pursues the common and twin objectives of macroeconomic stabilization and the development of international competitiveness. More specifically, despite differences of degree and emphasis, the elements common to the approach include the following:

- explicit trade liberalization measures (characterized by the elimination of quantitative restrictions and the establishment of moderate tariffs, narrow spreads, or even better, a uniform low tariff)
- fiscal discipline (deficit reduction or even surplus of the total public sector through redirecting and prioritizing public expenditures)
- tax reform (broadening of the taxpayer base, improvement of administrative procedures, and abolition of special exemptions)
- monetary discipline (including moderate but positive real interest rates)
- financial liberalization (with gradual abolishment of preferential interest rates for privileged borrowers)
- privatization of most state enterprises and deregulation to eliminate rules restricting competition (except in the case of natural monopolies or other exceptional situations)

---

[3] Bolivia is also considered by some to be a story of heterodox stabilization, and a successful one at that. But at the levels of inflation being experienced by Bolivia at the time (1985), orthodoxy and heterodoxy tend to merge in terms of policy responses (Morales and Sachs 1988). A more contemporary effort of such a heterodox approach, but with greater fiscal control than in the described programs, can be found in Brazil's *Plan Real.*

- deregulation of financial and labor markets
- elimination of barriers to the entry of direct foreign investment
- creation of a legal and institutional framework that strengthens property rights (Williamson 1990 and elsewhere in the present volume).

More recently, some observers mention a "second generation" of reforms that includes the following: creation of independent central banks; imposition of budgetary constraints on state, provincial, and local governments; creation of a modern and effective national civil service; improvement of citizen's security; and (as an adjunct to strengthening the rule of law) reformation of the judiciary (Edwards 1996).

Equally important to the foregoing characterization is an element that was not included—namely, the overwhelming importance that came to be attached to market signals as practically the sole basis for resource allocation, resulting in the virtual disappearance of selective incentives, of investment promotion schemes, and above all, of industrial-policy measures. Indeed, some would argue that the approach is a formula for stabilization but that it is not really a development strategy. Thus, not only did policymakers dwell on short-term policymaking but also they implicitly accepted the notion that firms would somehow adapt on their own to the new regulatory framework and to macroeconomic incentives, eventually acquiring international competitiveness simply through the "magic of the market."

The characterization given is not an exact paradigm. There existed marked inter-country differences in the manner in which each economy approached the practical application of the different elements, in regard to specific content, to the pace, scope, and sequence of the elements' implementation, and to the overall mix (the "menu") of policies.

Three eloquent examples can be cited. The first is in the realm of exchange rate policies. All of the countries share the goals of unifying their exchange rates and of maintaining stable and competitive rates, but they have adopted differing approaches, which vary from a relatively free-floating exchange rate (within limits), a "dirty" float, and a pre-fixed and controlled float, to a fixed exchange rate.[4] The second example is in the various features of the region's anti-inflation programs, varying mainly with regard to the pace of implementation and to whether the conventional monetary and fiscal restrictions are or are not accompanied by price and income policies designed to influence the expectations of economic agents; thus, one finds gradual programs (accompanied by price indexing) and also radical-shock programs. A third example is found in the liberalization of the capital account, a process that in some countries is applied simultaneously with the liberalization of the current account, while in others it is applied sequentially (Ffrench-Davis et al. 1995).

---

[4] But it is worth pointing out that in no country has the market been allowed to set the exchange rate freely, without selective interventions on the part of the Central Bank—even where future markets for the corresponding currency exist.

Other areas of differentiation to be found in policymaking include the following: the actions designed to counteract the regressive effects of economic policies (targeting of public expenditure, transfers); the actions aimed at promoting specific productive activities; the political will to privatize public enterprises, especially those engaged in the exploitation of mineral resources for export (oil in Mexico, copper in Chile); the means of regulating monopolies of privatized public services; the adaptation of the legal and institutional framework governing the right of ownership; the adoption of legal norms consistent with the goal of fiscal and monetary discipline; the incorporation of the goals of vertical equity and allocative efficiency into tax reform processes; the content and scope of social-security, welfare, and labor law reforms; and the relative contribution of the public sector to the gross domestic product (which varies from 10 percent to 30 percent among the different countries).

These distinguishing characteristics—combined with the differing political outlooks of the governing teams, the varying traits of the political systems, and the differing degrees of economic and technological maturity of the productive systems in the various countries—explain not only the varying pace and content of the reforms but also the unevenness of the results achieved.

Nevertheless, whatever the intercountry differences, the more significant institutional reforms carried out by most countries of the region beginning in the early 1980s did imply a genuine shift in policymaking and in the level and scope of state intervention in the economy. This change accelerated and shaped the development pattern transformation that had already been on the horizon prior to the debt crisis. The shift included a move away from import substitution and public investment more toward exports and private investment as the main engines of growth. Clearly, the manner in which this general thrust has been implemented has varied greatly from one country to another.

One final comment regarding policymaking in the 1980s concerns formal economic-integration arrangements. As is well known, several free-trade or common-market agreements were signed in the 1950s and 1960s. These were all highly functional to import substitution industrialization, and as the latter strategy came under attack so too did those integration agreements. During the first half of the 1980s, their implementation virtually disappeared from the regional landscape, only to be reborn in a new form: a second generation of agreements spawned in the last decade and more compatible with export-oriented strategies. This form of "open regionalism" (ECLAC 1994) gained momentum in the 1990s and even came to embrace the possibility of hemispheric integration with the signing of the North American Free-Trade Agreement among Canada, Mexico, and the United States and the subsequent commitment assumed by heads of state and government to create a "Free-Trade Area of the Americas" beginning in the year 2005.

Some Lessons from Recent Reforms

Which major socioeconomic problems have been successfully tackled by the policies of the 1980s, and what lessons have we learned? Despite the difficulty of establishing causal relationships between ideas and action, between policies and performance, there indeed exist salient characteristics of the 1990s and lessons to be learned (ECLAC 1996a, 1996b).

As to performance, the shift to a more market-oriented approach and the greater coherence and stability shown in macroeconomic management—especially in the fiscal and monetary spheres—have undoubtedly had a major impact in bringing inflation under control. During the second half of the 1980s, several countries (Argentina, Bolivia, Brazil, Peru, Nicaragua) were afflicted with hyperinflation; the weighted average yearly inflation for the region was in the order of 1,000 percent in 1988, 1989, and 1990. By 1995, the weighted average yearly inflation was 25 percent, and about half of the countries had either reached single-digit inflation or were close to achieving it. This progress clearly is the result of stabilization policies that affected aggregate demand and the expectations of economic agents.

Moreover, early in the 1990s, most Latin American countries had simultaneously recovered the capacity to grow, albeit at moderate sustainable rates. (Some countries grew rapidly for one or two years but then faced the need to adjust; Chile is virtually the only country that has been able to sustain high growth rates for an extended period). The fact that growth was not more dynamic reflects, in part, the trade-offs between policies designed to maintain stability and those designed to promote growth—an issue that continues to elicit lively debate (Dornbusch and Werner 1994).

Another expression of potential trade-offs between growth and stability is found in the external sector. As the region began to move from current-account surpluses to growing deficits, the pattern of moderate growth with increasing price stability was aided, beginning in 1991, by a heavy influx of international capital attracted by high interest rates combined with the confidence inspired by improved macroeconomic management, progress in structural reforms, and the consolidation of democratic political regimes. (This is a rather remarkable achievement in view of the extended period of net financial outflows that characterized the region only some years back). But the magnitude of these capital inflows in the period 1993-1994 was such that in many countries, such inflows contributed to exchange rate appreciation and obliged monetary authorities to push interest rates even higher. This syndrome, combined with faulty domestic policies, was part of the underlying cause of the Mexican financial crisis of December 1994 (Sachs et al. 1995), reminding policymakers that the maintenance of macroeconomic equilibriums will be a permanent challenge. In other words, the conditions under which their economies are evolving leave the countries vulnerable. In many cases, macroeconomic stability has been achieved at the cost of large balance-of-payments current-account deficits, financed at times with volatile capital likely to withdraw at the appearance of any circumstance that dampens investor confidence.

To make matters worse, the considerable level of external savings was not being channeled toward increasing investment; rather, a significant proportion was fueling the consumption of imported goods. The ratio of national savings to GDP had been growing very sluggishly, and the ratio of total investment to GDP is far below the levels before the debt crisis. In the specific case of Mexico, for example, external savings increased from 3.6 percent of GDP to 7.0 percent of GDP between the 1990-91 period and the 1993-94 period, but national savings decreased from 18.5 percent of GDP to 15.6 percent of GDP during the same period (ECLAC 1996b, p. 53).

Another manifestation of continued vulnerability despite the progress achieved can be found in two structural dimensions. One dimension is the weakness of the financial systems in some countries, frequently compounded by failures on the part of regulatory agencies; the spread of financial crises affecting some of the large banking institutions has required rescue operations at a high fiscal cost. The second dimension of vulnerability refers to fiscal stability, since the progress achieved so far has proved to rest on somewhat fragile foundations; in both Argentina and Mexico, the economic contraction of 1995 was accompanied by a disproportionate fall in fiscal revenues, forcing both governments to raise tax rates.

But perhaps the most glaring insufficiency of economic performance in the past few years—related, to be sure, to modest growth rates—has been in the realm of equity. Although the incidence of poverty has gradually fallen in most countries, the levels are still considerably higher than those observed in 1980, while income distribution appears to have worsened in virtually all cases (Uruguay seems to be the main exception),[5] except in those economies in which rapid disinflation has taken place (Brazil in 1994–95). The relatively poor results on the equity front (ECLAC 1995) can be traced to three different phenomena.

In the first place, the type of productive restructuring that resulted from the adjustments, the shifts in relative prices, and the liberalization of trade have thus far failed to generate enough job opportunities to absorb the entrants to the labor force. In the current phase of moderate growth, the number of productive job opportunities has increased very slowly, and the wage differential between jobs requiring different levels of training has tended to widen.

Second, public policies designed to alleviate the most serious manifestations of deprivation and marginalization have thus far suffered from insufficient capacity and limited efficacy. Social spending has been constrained by efforts at budgetary discipline, and social-policy management has not progressed with the desired agility and effectiveness.

Third—although the present verdict is far from definitive and although considerable debate exists regarding the matter (Scobie 1990, Taylor 1988)—except for the cases in which rapid disinflation has occurrred, evidence exists that policymaking has actually had a regressive bias, given the initial effects of adjustment on real wages, real interest rates, employment levels, and public expenditures.

Worsening patterns of equity have been reinforced at the microeconomic level, where the processes of adjustment, macroeconomic stabilization, and structural reform

---

[5] It is tantalizing to surmise that the exception in Uruguay is in part the result of the generous social-security system available to an aging population, which is a leftover of the "welfare state" era, in direct contradiction to the trends of past decades.

have acted as powerful selective mechanisms, forcing each firm to try to adapt to the new scenarios governed by price signals and the new patterns of regulation of productive activities. It is not surprising that different firms have had very varied reactions to these phenomena depending on the activity, the area of the country, and the type of production involved. In general, the segments most hurt by the changes in the rules of the game and in the regulatory framework have been the industries that produce for the domestic market, the engineering-intensive activities, the small and medium-sized firms, and the state enterprises as a group. In contrast, export sectors, productive activities based on natural resources, large domestically owned conglomerates, and many transnational corporations have been able to adapt more successfully to the evolving circumstances.

Restructuring has forced the region's productive systems to revert to their traditional areas of comparative advantage (basic and industrial commodities), although in a number of cases they have been able to incorporate new technologies that have expanded the access to available natural resources and that have modernized the methods of their exploitation. The structural heterogeneity characteristic of the region's productive systems has been accentuated, as productivity differences have tended to widen between the large world-class firms in the forefront of the modernization process and the many and varied activities that are lagging behind. This trend has been reinforced by the segmentation of credit, which has largely excluded small and medium-sized firms from access to the main flows of capital. These trends are apparent even in domestic commerce, where large American-inspired shopping malls managed by domestic or international conglomerates are rapidly eliminating the traditional *tiendas*. The net result has been that although both total factor productivity and labor productivity have improved rapidly in the "modern" sectors, there has also occurred a degradation of productivity at the other end of the scale, partially neutralizing the improvements for the economies as a whole.

In short, the shift in policymaking in the 1980s has been accompanied by a less-than-satisfactory record in terms of economic performance. To be sure, in contrast to the disastrous previous decade, important improvement has taken place. Further, the reform process presumably places the countries in a much stronger position to face the future challenges of globalization. Still, said improvement has proved to be insufficient and fragile in terms of achieving sustained growth, financial stability, and improved equity. The lessons being learned are contributing to new adaptations of economic thinking and policymaking. Among those lessons, two overarching ideas are emerging.

In the first place, a stable macroeconomic environment seems to be an essential precondition for stimulating savings and investment and for achieving higher rates of growth. In order to match effective demand with the production frontier and to cushion the effects of external shocks, what countries require (allowing for differences in emphasis and intensity, depending on their specific circumstances) is consistent monetary, credit, fiscal, and trade policies and appropriate income or wage policies, combined with policies to promote saving, investment, and the development of productive capacity.

But second, excessive reliance on the "automatic" effectiveness of macroeconomic price signals and reform has ironically led to underestimation of institutional weakness, of market failures (many markets are imperfect, segmented, or incomplete), and of the importance of externalities—and has on occasion induced an overdependence on the capacity of macroeconomic policy alone to trigger growth. Experience has indicated that even the analytically best-conceived policies can fail or not evolve properly in an adverse institutional context. Indeed, these structural problems make it all the more difficult to achieve sustained growth solely through price signals.

Thus, the two main lessons are the continuing need for the present return to orthodoxy (get the prices "right") and the need for a simultaneous departure from orthodoxy (the "right" prices are necessary but not enough). Given the way in which stabilization efforts and structural reforms interact, the increasing integration of macroeconomic scenarios, of institutions and regulatory frameworks, of factor markets, and of microeconomic behavior will probably become a more important feature of policy-making in the future.

An Aside: The East Asian Development Experience and Its Impact in Latin America

Already in the 1980s the newly industrialized countries of East Asia (Singapore, South Korea, and Taiwan, as well as Hong Kong) had attracted much attention in Latin America as "success stories" that offered important lessons for the region (Fajnzylber 1981). Indeed, proponents of export orientation and proponents of strong state intervention alike could find in the range of experiences of these East Asian countries many models worthy of imitation. In more recent years, numerous formal studies have been prepared to examine the success of the so-called high-performing Asian economies; among these studies, the best known is undoubtedly the World Bank's *East Asian Miracle* (World Bank 1993).

There of course exist differing interpretations as to the exact lessons to be drawn from these "success stories"—especially in terms of precisely how important export orientation and market orientation (or conversely, industrial policy) really have been (Fishlow et al. 1994). In addition, probably the obsession with the "Tigers," and especially Korea, was somewhat misdirected, given the important cultural, political, institutional, and economic differences both within that country group and especially between that region and Latin America. It should further be recalled that the shift from import substitution to export orientation in the East Asian countries occurred before globalization had so greatly reduced the margin of maneuver in the realm of policymaking, in the sense that the world is less tolerant today of gradual or selective approaches to trade liberalization.

Still, much can be learned from the Asian development experience of the past decades,[6] especially when the countries of Southeast Asia (Indonesia, Malaysia, the Philippines, and Thailand) are included. Indeed, the latter share many commonalities with numerous Latin American countries, and clearly, the potential exists for enhanced

---

[6] But a single unified "model" does not emerge. In his preface to the World Bank study, Lewis Preston, then president of the Bank, rightly pointed out, "The eight economies studied used very different combinations of policies, from hands-off to highly interventionist."

interregional cooperation and for an interchange of experiences. In fact (as can be observed from previous sections of the present essay), some of the conventional wisdom regarding elements of the success of the high-performing Asian economies are today being systematically applied in Latin America. The list includes the pursuit of increased macroeconomic stability (or in the words of the World Bank, "getting the basics right"), greater investment in human capital (still not matching the actual efforts observed in this regard in East Asia), increased domestic financial savings, and greater export orientation. In addition, proponents of assigning industrial policy a more central role in promoting development in Latin America can and do draw on numerous East Asian countries as their sources of inspiration.

Thus, a mix of orthodoxy and heterodoxy is also plainly present in the East Asian experience. The World Bank study states that "fundamentally sound development policy was a major ingredient in achieving growth…but these fundamental policies do not tell the entire story. In most of these economies, in one form or another, the government intervened—systematically and through multiple channels—to foster development, and in some cases the development of specific industries" (World Bank 1993, p. 5).

Implications of Current Trends for the Future

From earlier comments here, the reader can deduce that the cycle on development thinking has reached its apex in the direction of orthodoxy and is now gradually coming back. It remains to be seen whether we are at the brink of a dramatic shift comparable to the two earlier described deviations or (as seems more probable) at the brink of a more modest adjustment of prevailing trends. Whichever the case, the sum of the foreseeable adjustments should have a profound impact on patterns of growth, leading to an important differentiation between the region's development experience during the second half of the 1990s versus the experience during the first half of the decade.

How can those adjustments be characterized, and what are their implications for the future trends in development thinking and policies? Let us draw on some of the earlier discussed points to put forward some thoughts in regard to six selected issues, while avoiding covering the territory assigned to other analysts to examine elsewhere in the present volume.

The first of these six ideas concerns the earlier mentioned notion of economic thinking as being subject to cycles. Little reason exists for believing that the clear shift toward market-based reforms will evolve toward some immutable paradigm. On the contrary, some of the insufficiencies of economic performance, which rightly or wrongly are attributed to the implementation of market-based policies alone, have already given rise to some revisionism, or at least to some questioning of the current conventional wisdom, especially in the realm of whether the pendulum moved too far in the direction of expecting that the "right" prices, by themselves, would lead to sustainable growth with financial stability and with ever-improving equity.

This observation is not to suggest a return to lapsed policies of the past, which would be incompatible with the way the international economy functions today. In other words, it is reasonable to assume that globalization will dictate certain norms of international behavior in terms of macroeconomic policymaking, and probably this reality is all to the good, because policy persistence is by itself valued (in comparison to wild swings in policymaking) as part of the context of stability that countries need to project in order to compete for resources and markets in the international economy. What is likely to emerge, however, is a shift in emphasis from short-term macroeconomic management to medium-term development strategies, as well as a redefinition of the role of public policy in meeting key development objectives, such as improved productivity (at the level of the firm as well as systemically), environmental sustainability, and improved income distribution. In short, we can look forward to the mix of orthodoxy and heterodoxy mentioned previously, which means combining stable and coherent macroeconomic management with a new form of intervention at the microeconomic and mesoeconomic levels. There exist different variants of this more pragmatic approach, which some authors have branded "neo-structuralist" (Fishlow 1985, Sunkel 1991). Indeed, ECLAC itself has been advocating such an approach since 1990 in its major publications (1990, 1992, 1994, 1996).

Looking to the future, the direction and content of policymaking in general will change when a clearer medium-term vision is brought into play. As stated, the objective of maintaining macroeconomic equilibriums over time will in all likelihood not be abandoned, but greater emphasis will probably be put on ensuring that the process of achieving stability does not detract from the efficient allocation of resources required to expand the production frontier. Macroeconomic stability will be understood to involve not only low inflation and fiscal balance but also a sustainable current-account deficit, a level of domestic saving sufficient to sustain investment, maintenance of an appropriate real exchange rate, and a level of aggregate demand consistent with full utilization of existing production capacity. Policymakers will presumably strive for progress on all fronts at the same time, without overemphasis on any one of these goals at the expense of the others.

The relative orthodoxy that will mark macroeconomic management will in all likelihood be complemented with a more "activist" stance on the part of governments. This activism will be manifested in increased selective policy interventions at the microeconomic level in order to meet specific objectives of development, such as attaining international competitiveness, maintaining price stability, and achieving greater social equity. In other words, public policy will not be limited to maintaining overall macroeconomic consistency; there will be more emphasis on productive development policies. These policies might include, for example, support of information networks, strengthening of the mechanisms of business cooperation, protection of intellectual property, promotion of research centers and of extension services for the technology specific to a given sector, adoption of international norms and standards, and promotion of occupational training and education.

In the same vein, we can anticipate greater selective interventions to mobilize national savings and to channel them toward productive investment. Reliance on the market alone (through interest rates) has not led to sufficient savings-to-GDP ratios; this fact has also hindered the achievement of higher investment-to-GDP ratios. To attain adequate levels of savings and investment, stable macroeconomic management will need to be complemented by effective incentives and appropriate institutions. We can expect to see greater efforts at fostering institutional saving (including reforms in the pension and tax incentive systems), improvement and deepening of financial systems, development of well regulated and well supervised financial institutions and instruments, and greater investment capital access for previously excluded production sectors.

The second idea we should like to reemphasize is this: the clear shift that has taken place in the last decade toward a greater specialization in the export of industrial and even basic commodities is in fact a two-edged sword. On the one hand, it makes sense for the region to base its growth on the exploitation of its fairly generous endowment of natural resources, especially since the application of technological innovations has in general improved the international competitiveness of most of these goods and since accordingly, the region is gaining a greater share of the market. On the other hand, there exist some similarities here to the international division of labor as perceived by ECLA/ECLAC in 1949; it would be an irony if we came full circle to the realization that in the global economy, developing countries (or at least Latin American and Caribbean countries) are to specialize in commodities subject to a low elasticity of demand on world markets and therefore are to be caught once again in a low-productivity trap. One of the main objectives of what we call *transformación productiva*[7] is to move in the direction of economic activities with a higher value added and a higher growth potential: that is, the pursuit of dynamic comparative advantages. Hence, the selective policy interventions alluded to earlier will probably move in the direction of the development of clusters of activities around the industrial commodities that Latin America is currently excelling in,[8] establishing both forward and backward linkages aimed at increasing sophistication and value added.

The third idea that is now in order was only briefly touched upon in our earlier comments. It is that environmental issues will loom ever larger in the Latin American policy agenda in the years ahead. More likely than not, growth will depend in large measure on the efficient and environmentally rational exploitation and processing of natural resources (ECLAC 1991). Further, it is already clear that the link between environmental standards and trade is becoming an increasingly important issue in international economic relations; it would be preferable for the countries of the region to adopt a proactive strategy rather than to expose themselves to a possible new form of protectionism. Thanks to the impact that the World Conference on Environment and Development of 1992 had on public awareness and thanks even more to the proliferation of nongovernmental organizations (some of them quite influential), the issue of environmental protection has gained importance in the realm of policymaking. Still, the old perception of a conflict be-

---

[7] This term is not easily translated into English. ECLAC's official translation, which is not wholly satisfactory, is "the changing of production patterns."
[8] These are derivatives of fisheries, forestry, mining, petroleum, energy, and agriculture.

tween growth and environmental protection has not been totally eclipsed; policymakers have not at this point yet been entirely persuaded that the two are not necessarily incompatible and could even reinforce each other.

Fourth, another increasingly important ingredient in policymaking in the next few years will be in the realm of trying to reconcile unilateral trade liberalization measures with formal intraregional and even intrahemispheric trade agreements (ECLAC 1994b). In the past few years, regional cooperation has been promoted without compromising the commitment of most countries to global trade liberalization; in this, they have been relatively successful. But just as regionalism has the capacity to contribute to the building of a more open international economy, it also at the same time entails the risk of contributing to the fragmentation of the world economy or of the region into "blocs." Therefore, several alternative scenarios for the future can be imagined regarding the new generation of trade agreements, ranging from a region fractured into four or five subregional groupings to a hemisphere-wide free-trade area. It is too early to tell which scenario will prevail, although one would hope that the present subregional arrangements will become stepping-stones to the latter scenario. At any rate, the topic will certainly occupy an important place in the region's development agenda for the rest of the present decade and probably well into the next century.

Fifth, there is no question that the single most important unfinished task of the postwar period in Latin America is that of resolving the equity problem. Given the increasing disparities among different segments of the population and given these disparities' impact on political interaction in the more-plural societies, this issue will certainly have to be addressed in a more systematic manner than in the past. Employment generation will become one of the paramount objectives of public policy, which brings us back not only to the need for higher investment-to-GDP ratios and for higher rates of growth but also to the need for incentives to promote labor-intensive activities that can at the same time be competitive and that can in general foster higher levels of productivity. Greater attention can also be expected to be given to expenditures earmarked for health and (especially) for education, the latter sector constituting the clearest potential route to the ideal of equality of opportunities. The whole matter of participatory development—which has received greater attention in Asia than in Latin America (Ghai 1988, Schneider 1995)—will no doubt be revisited. Further, improvement in the management of social policies (including the targeting of expenditures toward the most vulnerable segments of the populations) will become increasingly important. Even the old debate on the merits of land reform—which had virtually disappeared from the development agenda until quite recently (it is on the front burner again in Brazil)—may receive a new hearing, at least in some countries.[9]

Inequity has, of course, been a permanent feature of Latin American development. But now some reason exists for believing that real progress can be achieved on this front,

---

[9] If this comes about, land reform will probably be more "market friendly" than in the past—that is, rather than outright expropriation, the emphasis will be on financing the orderly transfer of property rights.

especially if higher growth rates are attained. Population growth rates are declining quite rapidly (although less so among the poorest segments of the population), and the impact of this trend on the demand for public services and on the number of entrants into the work force will be felt in the coming years. In addition, the increasing attention many countries have been devoting to quantitative and qualitative aspects of education—in combination with intensive investment in human capital, to ensure that work skills keep pace with technical progress—should yield tangible paybacks in the beginning of the coming century. Furthermore, the explosion in grass roots organizations in recent years, combined with the consolidation of democratic and participatory political systems, should diversify the structure of pressure groups, currently biased in favor of "big business."

Sixth (and last) among the ideas we should like to reemphasize here is the following: few people in the region are contemplating a return to heavy-handed governmental intervention or official efforts trying to "pick winners," but the public-policy agenda will be ample, complex, and demanding nonetheless. Reform of the public sector will be very high on the development agenda, simply to enhance the capacity of governments to improve the quality of their own performance—presumably with much greater accountability than in the past, if the trend toward democratization is to be taken seriously. Nevertheless, the debate will continue, and voices in favor of orthodoxy will persist, arguing that every public-policy intervention should be viewed with caution. To be consistent with the idea of cycles in economic thinking, perhaps the rising trend toward greater policy intervention will be the seed for the next shift in policy (sometime in the year 2020?) in the direction of greater orthodoxy!

To conclude on a somewhat optimistic note, if these trends in development thinking and policymaking are followed, one could argue that most Latin American countries can look forward to improved performance, both in terms of growth and in terms of equity. In other words, the learning process of the 1980s and 1990s can prove to be an important path to development as the region enters the next millennium. The pragmatic environment that currently surrounds policymaking should be an important asset in this endeavor. The same can be said for the increasing creativity and entrepreneurial spirit that the region's private sector has shown in recent times. Further, the consolidation of economic interdependence within the region, led by a new generation of formal integration commitments, will have the effect of mitigating the region's vulnerability to external shocks and even of giving it greater capacity to influence events at the global level. The fact that Latin America and the Caribbean will, by the year 2000, have a population of 515 million inhabitants with middle levels of annual per capita income (an average of roughly $3,800) makes the region an attractive market in its own right.

To be sure, progress will not be linear, nor will it be evenly distributed among countries, within countries, or among different strata of the population. Further, many of the problems that the region faces and that seem to be intractable—urban sprawl, personal insecurity, environmental degradation, pervasive poverty, deterioration of physical infrastructure—will take a long time to overcome. Still, on balance, there has occurred and there continues to occur movement in a positive direction.

REFERENCES

Birdsall, N., and C.E. Lozada. "Recurring Themes in Latin American Economic Thought: From Prebisch to the Market and Back." In *Securing Stability and Growth in Latin America.* Paris: OECD Development Center, 1996.

Bruno, M., G. Di Tella, R. Dornbusch, and S. Fischer, eds. *Inflation Stabilization: The Experience of Israel, Argentina, Brazil, Bolivia, and Mexico.* Cambridge: The MIT Press, 1988.

ECLAC/CEPAL (Economic Commission for Latin America and the Caribbean). *Strengthening Development: The Interplay of Macro- and Microeconomics* (LC/G.1898(SES.26/3)). Santiago: ECLAC, 1996a.

_____. *The Economic Experience of the Last Fifteen Years: Latin America and the Caribbean 1980–1995* (LC/G.1925(SES.26/17)). Santiago: ECLAC, 1996b.

_____. *Social Panorama of Latin America* 1995 (LC/G.1886-P). Santiago: ECLAC, 1995.

_____. *Latin America and the Caribbean: Policies to Improve Linkages with the Global Economy* (LC/G.1800/Rev.1-P), SES.25/3)). Santiago: ECLAC, 1994a. (United Nations publication, Sales No. E.95.II.G.6).

_____. *Open Regionalism in Latin America and the Caribbean: Economic Integration as a Contribution to Changing Production Patterns with Social Equity* (LC/G.1801/Rev.1-P). Santiago: ECLAC, 1994b. (United Nations publication, Sales No. E.94.II.G.3).

_____. *Social Equity and Changing Production Patterns: An Integrated Approach* (LC/G.1701/Rev.1-P). Santiago: ECLAC, 1992. (United Nations publication, Sales No. E.92.II.G.5).

_____. *Sustainable Development: Changing Production Patterns, Social Equity and the Environment* (LC/G.1648/Rev.2-P). Santiago: ECLAC, 1991. (United Nations publication, Sales No. E.91.II.G.5).

_____. *Changing Production Patterns with Social Equity: The Prime Task of Latin American and Caribbean Development in the 1990s* (LC/G.1601-P). Santiago: ECLAC, 1990. (United Nations publication, Sales No. E.90.II.G.6).

_____. *Economic Survey of Latin America* 1949 (E/CN/12/0164/Rev.1). New York: ECLAC/UN, 1951. (United Nations publication, Sales No. 1951.II.G.1).

Corbo, V. "Problemas, teoría del desarrollo y estrategias en América Latina". *Estudios Públicos* 32 (1988).

Corden, M.W. "The Structure of a Tariff System and the Effective Protective Rate". *Journal of Political Economy* 74 (3) (1996).

Dornbusch, R., and S. Edwards. *The Macroeconomics of Populism in Latin America.* (*Policy, Planning, and Research Working Papers* 316.) Washington, D.C.: World Bank, 1989.

Dornbusch, R., and S. Fischer. "Moderate Inflation." *The World Bank Economic Review* 7 (1) (1993).

Dornbusch, R., and A. Werner. "Mexico: Stabilization, Reform, and No Growth." (*Brookings Paper on Economic Activity* 1.) Washington, D.C.: Brookings Institution, 1994.

Edwards, S. "The Disturbing Underperformance of the Latin American Economies." Inter-American Dialogue Plenary Meeting. Washington, D.C., May 1996.

Fajnzylber, F. "Some Reflections on South-East Asian Export Industrialization." *CEPAL Review* 15 (E/CEPAL/G.1187). Santiago: ECLAC, 1981.

Fishlow, A. "The State of Latin American Economics." *Report on Economic and Social Progress in Latin America* 1985. Washington, D.C.: Inter-American Development Bank, 1985.

Fishlow, A., C. Gwin, S. Haggard, D. Rodrik, and R. Wade. *Miracle or Design? Lessons from the East Asian Experience.* (*ODC Policy Essay* 11.) Washington, D.C.: Overseas Development Council, 1994.

Ffrench-Davis, R., D. Titelman, and A. Uthoff. *International Competitiveness and the Macroeconomics of Capital Account Opening.* (*ECLAC Working Paper* 29.) Santiago: ECLAC, 1994.

Ghai, D. "Participatory Development: Some Perspectives from Grass-Roots Experiences." (*UNRISD Discussion Paper* 5.) New York: United Nations Research Institute for Social Development, 1988.

Krugman, P. "Toward a Counter-Counterrevolution in Development Theory." *Proceedings of the World Bank Annual Conference on Development Economics.* Washington, D.C.: World Bank, 1992.

Morales, J.A., and J. Sachs. "Bolivia's Economic Crisis." In J.D. Sachs, ed., *Developing-Country Debt and the World Economy.* Chicago: University of Chicago Press, 1988.

Ramos, J. *Neoconservative Economics in the Southern Cone of Latin America, 1973–1983.* Baltimore: The Johns Hopkins University Press, 1986.

Sachs, J., A. Tornell, and A. Velasco. "The Collapse of the Mexican Peso: What Have We Learned?" (*Discussion Paper* 1724.) Cambridge: Harvard Institute of Economic Research, 1995.

Schneider, H. *Participatory Development: From Advocacy to Action.* Paris: OECD Development Center, 1995.

Scobie, G., ed. *Macroeconomic Policy Reforms, Poverty, and Nutrition.* Ithaca: Cornell University Press, 1990.

Sunkel, O., ed. *El Desarrollo desde Dentro: Un Enfoque Neoestructuralista para la América Latina. México, D.F.:* Fondo de Cultura Económica, 1991.

Taylor, L. "Polonius Lectures Again: The World Development Report, the Washington Consensus, and How Neoliberal Sermons Won't Solve the Economic Problems of the Developing World." *The Bangladesh Development Studies* 20 (2 and 3.) (1992).

_____. *Varieties of Stabilization Experience: Toward Sensible Macroeconomics in the Third World.* Oxford: Clarendon Press, 1988.

Viner, J. *International Trade and Economic Development.* Oxford: Clarendon Press, 1953.

World Bank. *The East Asian Miracle.* Oxford: Oxford University Press, 1993.

Helio Jaguaribe[1] on Gert Rosenthal's Paper

Economic Development in Latin America and the Need for a Theory of Functional Elites

Under the title "Development Thinking and Policies in Latin America and the Caribbean: Past and Future," Gert Rosenthal has written an excellent paper in which he presents the main traits of economic development thinking and practice in Latin America since the Great Depression. In his concluding considerations, Rosenthal indicates the direction he thinks development practice will take in Latin America and the Caribbean at the turn of the present century.

Rosenthal's paper is a very good brief assessment of the question it deals with and an authoritative indication of the extent to which ECLAC has been able to revise its economic theories of the Prebisch era and creatively adjust its thinking to present world conditions. Rosenthal's guiding principle for that attempt is his idea that economic thinking follows, like the economic process itself, a sort of Kondratieff long cycle, in which liberal economic ideas of *laissez-faire* and *dirigiste* economic ideas of planning tend to succeed each other. Accordingly, he suggests that after the predominance of *dirigisme* from the 1930s to the 1980s, orthodox liberal *laissez-faire* views came to prevail from the 1980s to the present, and that now indications are emerging of a critical revision of *laissez-faire* liberalism. ECLAC is participating in that cautious revision of "neoliberalism" with its "pragmatic neostructuralist" approach.

Rosenthal's paper presents an objective description of the evolution of the ideas and practices in Latin America in the area of economic development. It is a policy-oriented paper as one would expect from the Executive Secretary of ECLAC, and not an academic discussion of theories. But the already excellent presentation would have perhaps gained if it had contained a few more quantitative data. A brief differentiation among the distinct cases of Mexico, Central America, and South America would also have been welcome. The author's suggestion of a Kondratieff long wave in economic thinking as well as in the economic process is interesting and left one wishing for further elaboration.

In what concerns Rosenthal's conclusions, this writer is inclined to agree with all of them, but at the same time, they do require two qualifications. The first qualification is

---

[1] Instituto de Estudos Políticos e Sociais, Rio de Janeiro, Brazil.

intrinsic to Rosenthal's own thesis—that is, his correct emphasis on the necessity of increasing the international competitiveness of the Latin American productive sector in order to prevent the process of globalization from forcing Latin America to return to its former role of producer of the world's raw materials. The second qualification goes beyond the concepts presented by Rosenthal's brief analysis and concerns the necessity of reaching a deeper and broader understanding of the whole range of issues associated with economic development. Let us quickly consider both of these issues.

Pragmatic Liberalism

Rosenthal's brief paper does not go into specific detailed treatment of the crucial issue of the low international competitiveness of most of Latin America's industrial activities. Middle-level economies, such as those of the more developed Latin American countries, are confronted during the process of globalization with a very prickly dilemma: if they adopt protectionist measures to preserve their industrial capacity, then they will pay a growing price in obsolescence, and they will increase their own backwardness; but if they completely open up their economies, then they will suffer broad disindustrialization and a corresponding increase in unemployment. What can be done?

One emerging conviction is that a policy of "fine-tuning" is required, combining selective and temporary protectionist measures (for sectors that present satisfactory conditions for acquiring international competitiveness) with a general policy of overall trade liberalization. This approach could be called "pragmatic liberalism." Pragmatic liberalism is the actual policy of the developed countries, despite their rhetorical commitment to full liberalization. The agricultural policy of the European Union and the quota practices of the United States are expressions of "pragmatic liberalism." Pure liberalism is an exportable doctrine for use by third-world innocents.

An *efficient* pragmatic liberalism, however, requires a delicate policy touch. First of all, objective conclusions must be reached with respect to those productive sectors that are capable, if given appropriate assistance, of reaching an international level of competitiveness. Secondly, it is also necessary to acquire critical sectorial mass in order to be able to manage such a policy; for instance, the European Union's total agricultural sector provides a critical mass for EU agricultural policy that an isolated European country (France, for instance) could not provide by itself.

Therefore, a Latin American free-trade area or, better still, a regional common market is essential for an efficient pragmatic liberalism. Rosenthal's paper bypasses that requirement and favors a hemispheric free-trade area, instead of MERCOSUR and its South American expansion. A cautious and efficient pragmatic liberalism designed for promoting promising sectors to their level of international competitiveness is the only way by which Latin America will be able, in time, to participate in the process of a globalized economy without reverting to the region's pre-1930 semicolonial status. Accepting NAFTA in the South American free-trade area before satisfactory international competitiveness is achieved would prevent reaching that target.

Elite Functionality

The second qualification, as mentioned earlier, concerns the necessity of reaching a deeper and broader understanding of the process of economic development. That process has been conceived of initially in purely economic terms. Underdevelopment would be the result of insufficiency of capital and inadequacy of technical training. More-recent theories, however, acknowledge the great complexity of the problem and provide room for cultural and political factors. But a central question still remains unsolved: why, given the availability of satisfactory economic models and strategies, do underdeveloped countries wishing to promote their development not succeed in achieving it? Why Africa?

Here enters what could be called the theory of "functional elites." The question really requires thorough and systematic treatment that cannot be given here; for the present purposes, suffice it to say that the theory starts with the acknowledgment that the maintenance of social elites—both historically and contemporarily for a given sociohistorical context—has a cost, which is a relatively fixed one.

In primitive economies and even in relatively developed rural economies (such as in contemporary Africa), the economic surplus produced by a society is totally absorbed by the cost of maintaining that society's respective elite. That is why not much economic development occurred in ancient empires, and that is also why practically no economic development occurred in the European Middle Ages. Finally, the mercantile revolution and later the industrial revolution produced such an increase in the economic surplus that it became possible to reinvest a good portion of this capital productively even after attending to the maintenance of the elites. A key question then is how a society can accumulate an economic surplus such that it can look after the cost of maintaining its elite and still have a capacity for productive investment.

But on the other hand, according to the theory of functional elites, elites themselves can actually become functional and not remain simply status-enjoying, as most elites have been and many continue to be. This functionalization of the elite can happen under two different sets of conditions. One set occurs when elites, pushed by political motivation, decide to assume personal sacrifice for the benefit of their country, as did the Japanese Meiji elite in the last quarter of the nineteenth century or Mustapha Kemal's "Young Turks" in Turkey after World War I; Frederick the Great's Junkers were an earlier historical example of such a politically motivated elite. The alternative set of conditions for functionalization of an elite occurs when an elite shifts from sheer status enjoyment to productive activities and tries to get independently rich through business, as has been the case of the British elite since the late eighteenth century—as against the parasitical behavior of their French contemporary counterparts. In fact, in France only the bloody French Revolution and the Napoleonic upheaval permitted the upward movement of the third estate or common people, who themselves entered business activities, which resulted in the economic development that occurred in France during the second half of the nineteenth century.

Economic development implies two distinct dimensions: one concerns such a conversion of merely status-enjoying elites into functional elites; the other dimension concerns the selection and application of appropriate development models and strategies. Interesting in that respect is the case of the Russian Bolshevik elite, which had a strong political motivation for economic development but which adopted an inadequate model. Economic theory has achieved a high level of sophistication concerning development models and strategies for a large variety of possible situations and conditions. So the thing that is really lacking now is a better understanding of the functional-elite question and of (what is still more complicated) how the status-enjoying elites can be motivated to become functional ones.

In effect, most of the remaining problems of development in today's world are concerned at some level with the question of converting status-enjoying elites into functional elites. This is the case of practically all the African countries, and it continues to be a problem in Latin America as well. The ideal solution is the combination of political motivation with incentives toward entrepreneurship.

Since the administration of Kubitschek, Brazil has been an interesting example of political motivation of the elites combined with increasing development of entrepreneurship by the elites. This process is what explains Brazilian development during the last few decades. The problem, however, is that in societies, nothing is absolutely stable. A positive political motivation of the elite as observed in the Brazil of Kubitschek and today around Fernando Henrique Cardoso has not totally eliminated nonfunctional forms of political activity. Although the traditional status-enjoying elites have practically disappeared, with only a few survivors in backward areas of the Brazil's Northeast, even now various parasitical forms of politics for self-serving purposes or politics restricted to pure corporative or sectorial interests carry great weight in the Brazilian Congress and exercise a distorting and retarding influence over the effort to modernize the country's institutions.

The agencies involved in the international promotion of development must take into account the need to convert status-enjoying elites into functional ones. Two important measures are within reach of these agencies. One measure is to promote managerial training of local elites, stimulating them to become entrepreneurs and helping them in such an endeavor; market economies, over and above the advantages described by neoliberals, have the decisive advantage of being able to open up an attractive functional alternative to local elites. The second measure for promoting the formation of functional elites is to support the activities of centers of critical thinking in developing countries, thus contributing to reducing the maneuvering space available to existing parasitical forms of politics.

Ignacy Sachs[1] on Gert Rosenthal's Paper

Overcoming Growth without Development?

As a devotee of ECLAC by affinity and affection, the present author is happy to see that the commission is resisting the "restoration of the neoclassical paradigm" (A. Barros de Castro 1995),[2] in keeping with its tradition of independent development thinking, at this juncture somewhat clumsily designated as "pragmatic neostructuralism." In his dense paper, Gert Rosenthal traces a cogent and disturbing picture of the problems affecting the countries of the region in the aftermath of stabilization programs and liberalization reforms, known under the code misnomer of the "Washington consensus."

In the short run, the stabilization programs—operating in different countries with diverse mixes of orthodox and heterodox instruments—succeeded in curbing inflation, a prerequisite for resuming development. But the social cost of stabilization has been very high—indeed, excessive, according to the proponents of "adjustment with a human face." More importantly, the internal and external liberalization reforms[3] deeply affected[4] the institutional and economic structures of the countries concerned, exposing them to the "magic of the market." The scope of state intervention has been reduced, and a shift has occurred from import substitution and public investment more toward exports and private investment as the main engines of growth. The results, judging from Gert Rosenthal's paper, are worrisome. They read like a catalog of obstacles on the road to resumed development:

- vulnerability to unpredictable international capital movements,[5] currency overvaluation, usurious interest rates (favoring financial speculation but paralyzing productive investment), and disarray of financial institutions
- fiscal imbalance
- foreign-competition damage to industries working for the domestic market (in particular small and medium-sized enterprises), and displacement of small traders by supermarkets and shopping malls

---

[1] Ecole des Hautes Etudes en Sciences Sociales, Paris.
[2] In H. Singer's terms, it is the "neoclassical, monoeconomic counterrevolution."
[3] Yves Berthelot's paper elsewhere in the present volume points to the unnecessarily high social costs of transition in Eastern Europe.
[4] Liberalization has advanced much more than has globalization. Rubens Ricupero's report to the ninth session of UNCTAD rightly speaks of a liberalized and globalizing economy (1996).
[5] For a warning about the risks involved in the absence of regulation of financial markets, see the interview of George Soros in *Veja* (Brazil) (May 1, 1996; pp. 6–10).

- growing unemployment and underemployment because of insufficient rates of overall growth, suppression of jobs in the rapidly modernizing competitive sector (manufacturing industries, banking, and modern services), and lack of fine-tuned employment policies in the rural sector, in social services,[6] and in resource-conserving activities (energy, water and resource conservation, recycling, maintenance of the stock of infrastructure, equipment, built environment)
- continued worsening of income distribution
- lack of industrial policy (in contrast with the East Asian Tigers)
- return in foreign trade to traditional areas of comparative advantage, with some similarities between the present international division of labor and the one analyzed by ECLA/ECLAC in 1949.

All of these negatives combine to accentuate the *structural heterogeneity* of the region's productive systems, with widening differences in productivity between large world class firms and the many activities lagging behind. This tendency may be a worldwide trend nowadays. The dualization processes also affect the industrial countries, a far cry from the long-harbored illusion that the transposition of Western models would bring about the progressive homogenization of Southern economies and societies. Instead, we are faced by a kind of "third-worldization" of the entire planet with the specter of social apartheid looming in the background. Also, the sluggish rates of economic growth in Latin America reflect a general phenomenon, concomitant with the restoration of the classical paradigm. In the 1960s, the world economy grew at 5 percent per year; in the 1970s at 3.6 percent; in the 1980s at 2.8 percent; and in the first half of the present decade at barely 2 percent. In two decades, capitalism lost 60 percent of its momentum (Thurow 1996, p.2).[7]

Whatever the mix of internal and external causes, the important indication is that Latin America right now is moving in the opposite direction from development, experiencing in structural terms *growth without development.* Latin American rates of growth, with the exception of Chile's, are too low to arrest the deterioration of the employment situation, and the income gap between rich and poor is growing again (even though the elimination of the inflationary tax meant an increase in real incomes for the working people, immediately reflected in their consumption).

In other words, Latin America is again resuming a kind of perverse growth-through-inequality known in the past as *excluyente y concentrador,* with three main differences. First, inflation has been brought under control, with important social and psychological effects; for the time being, people seem prepared to trade off growth and (for many) real income for stability (but for how long?). Second, consumerism is the dominant ideology, even among modest people, and there exists a strong preference for imported goods, whatever their utility, quality, and even price (in many cases, imported goods are cheap-

---

[6] See on this point Sachs (1994, 1995). In his contribution to the present volume, Paul Streeten insists on the possibility of employing more service workers in the currently despised or neglected public sector.
[7] For the United States, see J. Madrick (1995).

er than the locally made ones, and in other cases they are more expensive, yet the craze for "foreign made" proves stronger than national pride or economic calculus). Third, the external environment is shaped by the processes of globalization, the impact of which calls for a careful assessment.

Globalization is glorified by some and condemned without appeal by others, but the plain reality may not be quite so dramatic. Globalization presents, obviously, positive aspects at the same time as it considerably restricts the freedom of nation-states by imposing a new international order (disorder? straightjacket?). Its mixed nature is compellingly described by several authors, in particular in the excellent papers by Paul Streeten and Aldo Ferrer in the present volume. Paul Streeten notes that "the perception is of a greater degree of globalization and integration than has in fact occurred" and that reports on the death of nation-states are premature.

In any case, the tactic for successfully overcoming the negative impacts of globalization is to reject what Ferrer calls "the fundamentalist vision of globalization" and the tyranny of foreign markets.[8] National spaces still account for 80 percent of world output, internal savings account for more than 90 percent of investment, and 9 out of every 10 workers serve domestic markets.[9] Says Ferrer, "The application of policies based on the fundamentalist view of globalization points to paths leading in exactly the opposite direction. Resource allocation and income distribution, capital formation, and the incorporation of technology revolve around transnational hubs that are increasingly distanced from local realities. This distancing leads to widening gaps in the social system, the destruction of a large part of the productive capacity built up in the past, increased poverty, and social inequalities." More than ever, Latin American countries ought to engage into "growth from within" (*crecimiento desde adentro*), overcoming in this way the false dichotomy between inward-led and outward-led growth and defining their own (and original) strategies of development based on *self-confidence* and *autonomy* (Cardoso 1993).[10]

Ferrer's cogent analysis is perhaps somewhat at odds with Rosenthal's treatment of globalization as being more a part of the solution than as being part of the problem. Rosenthal's well-taken points about the centrality of employment policy, the need to reopen the unfinished agenda of land reform, and the pursuit of sustainable development do run the risk of remaining largely rhetorical unless the countries of the region recog-

---

[8] Compare A. Ferrer: "the so-called evidence of the sovereignty of markets is a self-fulfilling prophecy." Streeten considers that unregulated markets can be both inefficient and cruel. Enrique Iglesias (1996) puts in doubt the capacity of the markets to solve the social problems of Latin America with the urgency required because of the impatience of the society.

[9] A similar argument in the context of the United States has been developed by Paul Krugman (1994). For a critique of competitiveness as ideology, see the report of the Group of Lisbon (1996) cosigned by L.J. Emmerij. M. Dubey (1996) provides a critical assessment of the Uruguay Round from the Indian Perspective.

[10] Deepak Nayyar (1995), in his presidential address to the Indian Economic Association, considers that only the countries that have laid the requisite foundations for industrialization and development stand a chance in the globalization game. For this, strategic forms of state intervention are essential. The same is true of nation-states in industrial countries. According to E.B. Kapstein (1996), the disaffected workers there need the national-state "as a buffer from the world economy."

nize that their present paths are socially, even more than environmentally, unsustainable (Guimarães 1995).

To reverse this trend, a bold vision is necessary, in sharp contrast with the dismal state of contemporary economic thought (see on this point Heilbroner and Milberg 1995). In Latin America an important step in this direction would consist of revisiting and assuming the legacy of the ECLAC approach, often too hastily dismissed as belonging to a long-gone historical phase. The writings of Raúl Prebisch, Anibal Pinto, Celso Furtado, Osvaldo Sunkel, Fernando Fajnzylber, and many others contain a wealth of pertinent insights, ideas, and propositions that apply quite well to the present situation. A reevaluation of this body of literature is in order.

The most urgent task facing us is to design national strategies[11] of "development from within" (O. Sunkel), going beyond "proximate macroeconomic stability" (G. Ranis). This approach calls for overcoming economic reductionism (E. de Kadt), blending ECLAC's intellectual legacy with the emerging new paradigms encompassing the social and environmental dimensions[12] and reestablishing the centrality of employment (in particular, of self-employment in family agriculture) as the entry point in the design of these strategies. The objectives of such strategies ought to be redefined in terms of effective appropriation by the broader *totality* of human rights—political, civic, social, economic, and cultural—along the "gala" approach (A. Sen).[13]

---

[11] On the importance of national strategies and the preeminence of the internal order over the international order, see the papers of J. Toye and R. Hirono in the present volume.

[12] The concept of sustainability has six pertinent dimensions: social, ecological (capital of nature), environmental (nature as a sink), economic, cultural, and spatial.

[13] Should we speak of an ecosocioeconomy of total development? The adjective *total* is shorthand for *all* the pertinent dimensions of development. It refers to the systemic interdisciplinary analytical approaches based on the cybernetic notion of the "whole" and is proposed here by analogy with the concept of total history.

REFERENCES

Barros de Castro, A. "El Estado, la Empresa y la Restauración del Paradigma Neoclásico." *Revista de la Cepal* 58, 1996.

Cardoso, F.H. *As Idéias e Seu Lugar: Ensaios sobre as Teorias do Desenvolvimento.* Petropolis: Vozes, 1993.

Dubey, M. *An Unequal Treaty: World Trading Order after GATT.* New Delhi: New Age International Limited Publishers, 1996.

Guimarães, R. "El Desarrollo Sustentable: Propuesta Alternativa o Retórica Neoliberal?" *Revista EURE,* XX (6) (1994), Santiago de Chile.

Heilbroner, R., and W. Milberg. *The Crisis of Vision in Modern Economic Thought.* Cambridge: Cambridge University Press, 1995.

Iglesias, E. Conférence Annuelle de la Fondation F. Perroux. Paris, 1966.

Kapstein, E.B. "Workers and the World Economy." *Foreign Affairs* 45 (3) (1996).

Krugman, P. *Peddling Prosperity.* W.W. Norton, New York: W.W. Norton, 1994.

The Group of Lisbon. *Limits to Competition.* Cambridge, Mass.: MIT Press, 1996.

Madrick, J. *The End of Affluence: The Causes and Consequences of America's Economic Dilemma.* New York: Random House, 1995.

Nayyar, D. "The Past in Our Present." Presidential Address to the Indian Economic Association. Candigarh, 1995.

Ricupero, R. *Globalization and Liberalization: Development in the Face of Two Powerful Currents.* Report of the Secretary-General of UNCTAD to the Ninth Session of the Conference, 1996.

Sachs, I. "Population, Développement et Emploi." *Revue Internationale des Sciences Sociales.* Paris: UNESCO, 1994.

_____. "Scarching for New Development Strategies: The Challenges of the Social Summit. *MOST Policy Paper* 1. Paris: UNESCO, 1995.

Thurow, L. *The Future of Capitalism.* New York: William Morrow and Co., 1996.

Akio Hosono[1] on Gert Rosenthal's Paper

Development Thinking and Policies in Latin America and the Caribbean: Past and Future

In his highly insightful and stimulating article, Gert Rosenthal examines the shifts or cycles in policymaking over time. He suggests that the cycle of development thinking in Latin America has reached its apex in the direction of orthodoxy and that it is now gradually coming back in the other direction.

Behind this shift in the mid-1990s, are several new factors that have characterized the recent development of the world economy. First of all, we must take into account the irreversible globalization trend accompanied by simultaneous regional and subregional processes. Globalization is not yet clearly defined, and its real impact on individual countries, especially developing countries, has not yet been comprehensively analyzed. Even so, its importance is widely recognized among economists and political leaders.

The second factor is the increasingly wide appreciation of the East Asian economic success. The interest regarding that region's success is now widespread, and a number of organizations are searching for a new paradigm of development strategies taking into account the Asian experiences.

The third factor is a growing global concern about certain problems related to the past development process. The most important of the problems is the deterioration of the environment. The persistent phenomena of poverty and social inequality are also becoming major concerns. In other words, values other than growth and efficiency—such as environmental conservation, equity, participation, poverty reduction, good governance, and the like—are now increasingly considered to be of high priority (OECD 1996). In this regard, the "New Global Partnership for Development" agreed upon at the Lyon Summit in 1996 could be an important approach:

> This new partnership should set its sights on enabling all developing countries, whatever their stage of development, to share and participate in the benefits of globalization. To that end, it should take the achievement of sustainable development as its fundamental objective. Goals should include the reduction of poverty and social inequities, the respect of internationally recognized labor stan-

---

[1] Institute of Policy and Planning Sciences, University of Tsukuba, Japan.

dards, protection of children, a strengthened civil society, protection of the environment, improved health and education. (Lyon Summit Economic Communiqué, 1996)

The present comments will focus on the "implications of current trends for the future," the concluding part of Rosenthal's article, bearing in mind the three aforementioned factors. Regarding the first point of Rosenthal's concluding remarks, it is indeed clear that "public policy will not be limited to maintaining overall macroeconomic consistency; there will be more emphasis on productive development." Especially important is his observation that "to attain adequate levels of savings and investment, stable macroeconomic management will need to be complemented by effective incentives and appropriate institutions."

One aspect not explicitly discussed in the concluding part of Rosenthal's article is the role of small and medium enterprises. The present author has emphasized this particular aspect in a recent study as follows:

The policy on small and medium enterprises (SMEs) appears to be crucial, because these enterprises reinforce competition in the market. In Japan, Taiwan (province of China) and later Korea and other East Asian countries, a large number of SMEs have entered the market and vitalized it. Many major companies today started as SMEs and achieved remarkable growth over a relatively short period of time. (Hosono and Saavedra, forthcoming)

Regarding the role of SMEs in Japan and other East Asian countries, the World Bank report says: "The HPAEs (high-performing Asian economies) benefited from a profusion of small and medium-sized enterprises (SMEs). The large number of SMEs generally reflected market forces rather than government intervention" (World Bank 1993, p. 161). This World Bank report notes the large effects of SMEs on employment and on workers' real income, and hence the SMEs'contribution to "shared growth" is emphasized. For this reason the policy of SME promotion is included in the chapter discussing the "institutional basis for shared growth."

In the East Asian economies, several experiences confirm the importance of the role of the SMEs. Where not enough SMEs exist to play fully the role of serving as excellent, stable, and reliable suppliers of parts and components for the rest of the manufacturing industry, then considerable weakness is experienced in the capability of certain industries. This is what occurred in the case of the Republic of Korea—so much so, in fact, that when that country realized what was happening, it instituted a strong policy designed to foster the development of small and medium-sized enterprises to supply parts and components. In contrast with Korea, sustained development of SMEs is observed in Taiwan, where several manufacturing sectors based on SMEs, such as the personal computer industry, have attained very high competitiveness and a large share in the world market.

With respect to the availability of SMEs as supporting producers of parts, components, services, and other basic industrial materials and machinery, some countries, especially smaller ones, would prefer to internalize the externalities of other countries (particularly neighboring countries), counting on their neighbors' already established support-oriented small and medium-sized producers. In this case, trade liberalization and the efficiency of trading companies are crucial.

Several efforts have recently been made in Latin America to study the importance of SME policy and to identify some practical measures to promote SMEs without distorting the market, but instead strengthening it. For instance, a roundtable on credit guarantee systems was held by the IDB with special reference to SMEs ("Roundtable on Credit Guarantee Systems: International Experiences and Lessons for Latin America and the Caribbean," June 1995).

With respect to the second point of Rosenthal's concluding remarks, a very important concept is that of promoting "clusters of activities around the industrial commodities that Latin America is currently excelling in." Developing clusters means establishing both forward and backward linkages aimed at increasing sophistication and value added. Research recently conducted by Professor Kotaro Horisaka and the present author and based on around two hundred cases of international business activity (trade and investment) of Latin American enterprises does confirm the importance of "clusters of activities around industrial commodities" (Horisaka and Hosono 1996). This research found that Latin American companies fuel their international development by using the advantages they have, including the abundant natural resources of the countries in which they are located, and their expertise in developing and processing such resources, as well as their superiority or competitive edge in marketing processed natural resources and industrial commodities internationally. Further study and deeper understanding of the "clusters of activities in Latin America" could be highly relevant.

As for the third point of Rosenthal's concluding remarks, there indeed exists growing recognition that environmental awareness and economic development are not necessarily incompatible and that they could in fact reinforce each other. Development of environment-friendly technologies and experience in some industrial countries, including Japan, could contribute to supporting similar efforts in the Latin American countries. ECLAC has made important contributions in this area by proposing developmentally and environmentally integrated approaches in Latin America. The ECLAC publication *Sustainable Development: Changing Production Patterns, Social Equity and the Environment (1991)* is particularly relevant.

Regarding the fourth point of Rosenthal's concluding remarks, the following statement is extremely significant:

> Another increasingly important ingredient in policymaking in the next few years will be in the realm of trying to reconcile unilateral trade liberalization measures with formal intraregional and even intrahemispheric trade agreements.... It should be pointed out that just as regionalism has the capacity to contribute to the building of a more open international economy, it also at the same time entails the risk of contributing to the fragmentation of the world economy or to the fragmentation of the region into "blocs".

Such a possibility of fragmentation into blocs is precisely the anxiety of APEC, of which Mexico and Chile are members, and it is the reason that APEC maintains its firm stance in consolidating open regionalism. And ECLAC itself also explicitly addressed this aspect in its 1994 report *Open Regionalism in Latin America and the Caribbean: Economic Integration as a Contribution to Changing Production Patterns with Social Equity.* Regarding Rosenthal's concern about the reconciliation of unilateral trade liberalization with formal regional trade agreements, as well as such agreements' substantive contribution to building a more open international economy, APEC's unique approach of unilateral concerted action in the framework of its open regionalism, called the "Asia Pacific Approach," deserves to be given more attention and to be shared, as far as possible, by countries that are not members of APEC. The following statement of the Osaka Declaration seems important in this respect:

> We emphasize our resolute opposition to an inward-looking trading bloc that would divert from the pursuit of global free trade, and we commit ourselves to firmly maintaining open regional cooperation. We reaffirm our determination to see APEC take the lead in strengthening the open multilateral trading system. We trust that enlarged participation by APEC economies in the WTO would facilitate greater regional cooperation. We will explore joint initiatives under the WTO, including preparations for the Ministerial Meeting in Singapore. Ensuring that APEC remains consistent with the WTO Agreement, we will achieve trade and investment liberalization steadily and progressively.
>
> We are pleased to announce that each of us has brought a package of initial actions demonstrating our firm commitment to achieving liberalization and facilitation. These voluntary actions will spur and inspire APEC liberalization. They also represent the first wide-ranging initiatives to accelerate the implementation of our Uruguay Round commitments and to deepen and broaden the outcome of the Uruguay Round through, for example, acceleration of tariff reductions, early implementation of WTO agreements, and pursuance of deregulation. Together with these measures, our collective actions, including harmonizing and enhancing the efficiency of customs procedures and promoting mutual recognition and improving conformity assessment capabilities, will yield immediate and tangible benefits for business. We urge non-APEC economies to follow suit and help advance global trade and investment liberalization.

This same fourth point of Rosenthal's remarks strongly relates to the dynamic intraregional trade and investment that is expected to take place in Latin America and the Caribbean in the future. The pattern of dynamism that characterizes East Asian intraregional economic activities is now frequently described as resembling "flying wild geese." The pattern captures a phenomenon in which a group of economies, closely and synergistically interacting with one another through trade and investment, advance together, led by a dominant economy as the major provider of technology, complementary inputs, and markets. In this process the flock economies mutually benefit from the competitiveness-enhancing effects of the activities of transnational corporations (TNCs'), particularly from TNCs' role as agents of comparative-advantage recycling (Rowthorn 1996, Watanabe 1990).

What type of dynamism is observed in the Americas? The flying-wild-geese pattern appears to be rather weak here. Instead, some other factors that stimulate intraregional trade and investment can be identified. One example of this is the formation of clusters of activities around successful industrial commodities to which we have already referred (Horisaka and Hosono 1996). We shall have to study more closely why different types of dynamism are observed in these two regions and why the ratio of total exports to GDP is much higher in East Asia than in Latin America.

Another aspect related to the future scenario of globalism and regionalism mentioned in the fourth point of Rosenthal's paper is the potentiality of cross-Pacific economic relations and cooperation. On both sides of the Pacific we find dynamic growth centers and emerging markets: East Asia and Latin America. Chile's success in penetrating Asian markets is now well known, and other countries are making efforts in the same direction. Perú and Colombia, for instance, are strongly interested in participating in APEC. In order to promote cross-Pacific economic relations and cooperation, the following four issues are crucial:

- The Cross-Pacific liberalization process. This issue is important also for the future global trade system and is closely related to the concerns covered in Rosenthal's fourth point.
- Trade and investment regime building in APEC and in the Americas. In addition to trade liberalization regulations, many other rules and standards on trade and investment should be established through consultations in APEC and in the Americas, such as intellectual-property rights, safeguards, antidumping duties, dispute settlement, rules of origin, trade-related investment, environment, labor conditions, and the like (Morrison 1996).
- Realistic measures and modalities to facilitate cross- Pacific economic relations (in other words, to cross-extend dynamism on both sides of the Pacific). Although trade liberalization and regime building would be the necessary conditions for encouraging such economic relations, one could think of many other measures and modalities to facilitate them.
- Cross-Pacific cooperation for development. In order for all participating economies to be able to realize benefits from the process, it is necessary to strengthen cross-Pacific cooperation for development. In APEC, the importance of cooperation was reaffirmed at the Osaka meeting, and the creation of Partners for Progress in the APEC Secretariat was approved.

As for the fifth point discussed in the concluding remarks of Rosenthal's article, most of his observations are quite good. Rosenthal presentation here focuses on the equity question—including employment, health, education, and participatory development—

and has several points in common with the OECD's new approach: *Shaping the 21st Century: The Contribution of Development Cooperation*, adopted in May 1996 by the High-Level Meeting of DAC and establishing concrete goals with respect to poverty reduction and the field of social policies (OECD 1996).

In summary, Gert Rosenthal's paper provides an excellent review of development thinking and policies evolved over time in Latin America and the Caribbean, as well as an insightful analysis of lessons learned and their implications for the future.

REFERENCES

ECLAC. *Sustainable Development: Changing Production Patterns, Social Equity and the Environment.* Santiago: ECLAC, 1991.

_____. *Open Regionalism in Latin America and the Caribbean: Economic Integration as a Contribution to Changing Production Patterns with Social Equity.* Santiago: ECLAC, 1994.

G 7 Lyon Summit Economic Communiqué. *Making a Success of Globalization for the Benefit of All.* 1996.

Horisaka, K., and A. Hosono. *The Latin American New Multinationals,* Tokyo: Nihon Hyouronsha, 1996 (in Japanese).

Hosono, A., and N. Saavedra. *The East Asian Miracle and Development Strategy.* Forthcoming.

Morrison, C. "Regime Building in Asia Pacific and the Dangers of Regulatory Rift in US-European Relations." Mimeo. 1996.

OECD. *Shaping the 21st Century: The Contribution of Development Co-operation.* 1996.

Rowthorn, R. "East Asian Development: The Flying Geese Paradigm Reconsidered." UNCTAD Conference on East Asian Development: Lessons for a New Global Environment. Mimeo. Geneva: UNCTAD, 1996.

Watanabe, T. "The Era of the Western Pacific." Tokyo: Toyo Keizai Simposha, 1990 (in Japanese).

World Bank. *The East Asian Miracle: Economic Growth and Public Policy.* Oxford: Oxford University Press, 1993.

Catching up with the West: A Perspective on Asian Economic Development and Lessons for Latin America

Ajit Singh[1]

The present paper reviews and assesses Asian economic development in the recent post-1980 period, as well as over the somewhat longer time span since World War II. Our chief purpose here will be to draw analytical and policy implications from this Asian development experience—a challenging but pleasant task in that (at least as conceived of in narrow economic terms such as growth of per capita income) the Asian story is, generally speaking, one of outstanding success. Indeed, it would be no exaggeration to say post-World War II economic expansion in a number of Asian countries makes them examples of the most successful industrialization and fast growth over a sustained period in the entire history of mankind. Japan in 1950 produced less than 5 million tons of crude steel per annum and only around 30,000 motor vehicles of all types; the U.S. output at that same time was nearly 90 million tons of steel and approximately 7 million automobiles per year. By the mid-1970s, the Japanese had caught up with the United States in the production of steel and had replaced West Germany as the world's largest exporter of cars. By 1980, Japan had overtaken the United States to become the largest producer of automobiles in the world.

The Japanese experience has by no means been unique. Japan's approach has been methodically emulated by countries like Korea and Taiwan, with results that have been perhaps even more spectacular. The Korea of 1955 was unequivocally backward industrially. Its net value of per capita manufacturing output per year was US$8, similar to the level of US$7 in India but much less than the Mexican level of US$60.[2] Since 1955, Korea has managed to transform itself from being largely an agricultural society to being the next-to-most advanced country in the world (through its company Samsung) in electronic memory chip (DRAM) technology. Furthermore, by the year 2000, Korea is expected to become the fourth largest car producer in the world. Nothing could be more illustrative of the changing map of world industry than the fact that, reversing historic

---

[1] University of Cambridge.
[2] Maizels (1963), cited in Amsden and Hikino (1994).

roles, a hitherto developing country like Korea has become a chief foreign direct investor in the heart of the industrial West—namely, in the United Kingdom.[3]

The 1980s have been rightly termed the "lost decade" for countries on the other two developing continents—that is, for Latin America and for Africa. Notwithstanding the enormous setbacks to development on those two continents and despite the slowdown of economic growth in the world as a whole, the Asian industrialization and catch-up drive has continued unabated in the 1980s and into the 1990s. As we shall see later, economic expansion in Asia during this period has not been confined to just a few countries but has been widespread. It has involved the elevation of standards of living for billions of people—much of the human population, in fact.

To try to understand and make analytical sense of this extraordinary Asian drama is indeed a heartening task—but a rather vast one as well. Furthermore, no consensus exists on what might be the right lessons to be learned from the East Asian or Southeast Asian experience, let alone on whether or not such lessons might be applicable elsewhere, especially in view of the new conditions of the liberalized and globalized world economy. Therefore, to keep the present essay within manageable limits, its analytical aspect will be confined to an examination of a small number of relevant issues.

Specifically, the paper will concentrate on the extraordinarily high rates of savings and investment—particularly those of the private corporate sector—of these highly successful Asian economies. In fact, the corporation itself and the relationship between the corporation and the government will receive special analytical attention.

These emphases on the corporation, on savings, and on investment not only are more significant for the emerging post-Uruguay Round global economic order but also provide the microeconomic dimension that is normally missing from the vast literature in this field. Such emphases are also more directly relevant for any lessons that might be drawn specifically for the Latin American economies.

Before proceeding on to our detailed analysis of the aforementioned subset of issues, however, let us first examine in quantitative terms the main features of Asian economic development within a broad comparative international perspective, and then let us briefly outline the whole range of important analytical and policy questions raised by this extraordinary record.

Asian Economic Development in a Comparative International Context

Some important features of Asian economic development over the last three decades or so are summarized in Tables 3.1 to 3.6. Special attention should be given to the following six points that emerge from these tables as well from other available information not reproduced here.

---

[3] The Korean giant LG Group recently decided to install a factory in Wales and invest US$2.6 billion. This is apparently the largest single investment in the European Union from outside the member states. (See also *The Economist* (July 13, 1996) (p. 24).

TABLE 3.1. Trends in Sectorial Production Performance:
Regions and the World, 1965–1994

(Average annual percentage growth)

	GDP			Industry			Agriculture		
	1965–1980	1980–1990	1990–1994	1965–1980	1980–1990	1990–1994	1965–1980	1980–1990	1990–1994
Low-income economies *(excluding China and India)*	4.8	2.9	1.4	8.0	2.7	-0.7	2.4	2.0	1.5
Middle-income economies	6.3	2.5	0.2	6.7	2.3	1.3	3.4	2.4	0.9
Latin America	6.0	1.6	3.6	6.3	1.3	2.9	3.1	1.9	2.3
Sub-Saharan Africa	4.2	2.1	0.9	7.2	0.5	-0.2	2.0	2.1	0.7
South Asia *(including India)*	3.6	5.2	3.9	4.3	6.5	3.8	2.5	3.0	2.7
East Asia *(including China)*	7.3	7.8	9.4	10.8	10.2	13.4	3.2	4.8	3.6
All low-and middle-income economies	5.9	3.2	1.9	6.8	3.8	4.6	2.9	3.2	1.9
High-income economies	3.8	3.2	1.7	—	2.1	—	—	2.3	—
United States	2.7	3.3	2.5	1.7	2.9	—	1.0	4.0	—
Japan	6.6	4.0	1.2	7.4	5.2	0.7	-0.6	0.4	-2.8
Germany	3.3	1.9	1.1	2.8	0.0	—	1.4	1.6	—
World	4.1	3.1	1.8	—	2.4	—	—	2.8	—

Source: World Bank *(World Development Report)* (1992, 1996).

First, as Table 3.1 indicates, in the last fifteen years the developing countries of East Asia have been by far the most dynamic region of the world economy. Although the East Asian economies grew very fast even in the previous fifteen years (1965–1980), the gap between their growth rates and those of other developing regions, such as Latin America, was then relatively small (7.3 percent versus 6 percent for Latin America). But in the 1980s, economic growth collapsed in Latin America (from 6 percent per annum to 1.6 percent per annum), while there occurred a trend increase in East Asian economic growth to 7.8 percent per annum.

Second, disaggregated data by sector (Table 3.1) suggest that it was not so much the poor agricultural performance but rather the abysmal industrial performance that was responsible for the collapse of economic growth in Latin America in the 1980s. Nevertheless, East Asia did record particularly strong agricultural growth during that decade.

Third, in reflecting on East Asian economic expansion, the Chinese economy, because of the size of the country's population, deserves special consideration. As disaggregated data for individual countries in Table 3.2 show, the Chinese economy expanded at a rate of nearly 10 percent per annum in the 1980s, a shade below the Korean pace. In the 1990s, the Chinese growth rate has been even higher than Korea's. When a country such as South Korea grows at 10 percent a year for fifteen years, this growth is an extraordinary achievement for the world to note; however, when China, with its billion people, achieves a similar growth rate, this feat is not just an extraordinary but an epoch-making event.

TABLE 3.2. GDP Growth Rates in Asian and Latin American Countries, 1955–94
(Annual percentage)

	1955–1960	1960–1970	1970–1980	1980–1990	1990–1994
Asia					
China	—	5.2	5.8	9.5	12.9
India	—	3.4	3.6	5.3	4.8
Indonesia	—	3.9	7.6	5.5	7.6
Korea	4.5	8.6	9.5	9.7	6.6
Malaysia	4.0	6.5	7.8	5.2	8.4
Pakistan	3.4	6.7	4.7	6.3	4.6
Philippines	4.4	5.1	6.3	0.9	1.6
Sri Lanka	—	4.6	4.1	4.0	5.4
Taiwan, POC	—	—	—	—	—
Thailand	6.8	8.4	7.2	7.6	8.2
Median	4.4	5.2	6.3	5.3	6.6
Latin America					
Argentina	3.1	4.2	2.2	-0.4	7.6
Bolivia	—	5.2	4.8	-0.1	3.8
Brazil	5.5	5.4	8.4	2.7	2.2
Chile	4.0	4.5	2.8	4.1	7.5
Colombia	3.8	5.1	5.9	3.7	4.3
Ecuador	4.5	—	8.8	2.0	3.5
Mexico	5.9	7.2	5.2	1.0	2.5
Peru	4.1	4.9	3.0	-0.3	4.2
Venezuela	6.3	6.0	5.0	1.0	3.2
Median	4.3	5.1	5.0	1.0	4.2

Sources: World Bank *(World Development Report)* (1982, 1991, 1996)
   UN *(Yearbook of National Accounts Statistics)* (1966).

Fourth, turning now to the other main populous Asian country, India's performance until 1980 was relatively poor by international standards. Nevertheless, since 1980 there has occurred a marked improvement: during the 1980s, India was one of the few countries in the world to have achieved a significant trend increase in its growth rate. Some subsequent deterioration did occur in India's performance between 1990 and 1994, but if we include the data for 1995—when the economy grew at 7 percent a year and industry for the first time achieved growth rates similar to those seen in the East Asian NICs—then India's overall picture for the 1990s becomes quite positive.

Fifth, apart from the important differences in the pace of economic development between the East Asian countries and the South Asian countries like India, it is also customary and analytically useful to distinguish between two of the subgroups of countries within East Asia itself—specifically, between Northeast Asian (Japan, Korea and Taiwan)[4] and Southeast Asian (Malaysia, Thailand, Indonesia)[5] countries. The Southeast Asian countries have followed rather different economic policies from those followed in the

---

[4] Korea and Taiwan are also referred to as the "first-tier" NICs.
[5] These are also referred to as "second-tier" NICs.

Northeast Asian nations, but they have been just as successful as the latter during the past decade. Nevertheless, in this context UNCTAD (1996) observes that although the recent economic record of these two East Asian groups is indeed similar, taking a longer perspective reveals a significant performance gap between the groups. The exact result will depend on which periods and which countries have been considered, but the annual per capita GDP growth rates of Japan and the first-tier NICs have, on average, been roughly 2 percentage points higher than those of the second-tier NICs over the last three decades or so. The cumulative impact of this growth gap over 30 years is significant. For instance, Malaysia's per capita income in 1961 was almost three times that of Korea and almost twice that of Taiwan (Malaysia then included Singapore, so purely "Malaysian" income would have been somewhat lower), and it remained higher than Korean per capita income until 1981; but by 1993 it was less than half that of Korea and about one-third that of Taiwan.[6]

Sixth, the Asian countries' excellent record of economic growth during the last fifteen years with relatively low inflation (Table 3.3) has certainly translated into impressive increases in living standards, real wage, and employment and into reductions in poverty. Table 3.4 provides GDP growth rates for groups of developed and developing countries on a per capita basis. Further adjustments to these figures (for terms of trade and for net factor payments abroad) suggest that during the 1980s average per capita income in Asian countries rose by 50 percent. This figure contrasts with a decline of 15 percent in Latin America and 25 percent in Sub-Saharan Africa (UN 1990).

ILO (1995) provides evidence that in the 1980s, in the fast-growing Asian economies such as Taiwan, Korea, Singapore, and Malaysia, labor shortages emerged and there occurred significant immigration of labor from neighboring low-income countries. Manufacturing employment rose at a rate of more than 6 percent per annum during this decade in these dynamic economies, and real earnings increased at an average rate of 5 percent per annum.

With respect to poverty, available evidence for the 1980s on individual fast-growing NICs suggests sizable reductions in its incidence. Thus, in China the incidence of absolute poverty fell from 28 percent of the population in 1980 to 10 percent in 1990; in Indonesia the corresponding reduction was from 29 percent to 15 percent; in the Republic of Korea poverty declined from 10 percent to 5 percent; and in Malaysia it went from 9 percent to 2 percent (Singh 1994c).

A remarkable feature of East Asia and Southeast Asian development during the relevant period has been that not only has the rate of growth been very high but also income distribution has become more rather than less equal. The World Bank (1993) notes, "For the eight HPAEs, rapid growth and declining inequality have been shared virtues, as comparisons over time of equality and growth using Gini coefficients illustrate."[7]

---

[6] See also UNCTAD 1996a (page 13).

[7] It will be argued later that this conclusion of declining inequality may require some important qualifications.

TABLE 3.3. Rates of Inflation in Asian and Latin American Countries, 1960–94

(Average annual percentage growth of consumer price index)[1]

	1960–1970	1970–1980	1980–1990	1990–1994
Asia				
China	—	—	5.8	10.8
India	7.1	8.5	7.9	10.1
Indonesia	—	20.5	8.4	7.4
Korea	17.4	19.8	5.1	6.3
Malaysia	-0.3	7.5	1.6	3.7
Pakistan	3.3	13.5	6.7	10.8
Philippines	5.8	13.2	14.9	9.6
Sri Lanka	1.8	12.6	11.0	9.5
Taiwan, POC	3.5	12.2	—	
Thailand	1.8	9.9	3.3	4.4
Median	3.4	12.6	6.7	9.5
Latin America				
Argentina	21.7	130.8	395.1	27.6
Bolivia	3.5	22.3	318.2	10.9
Brazil	46.1	36.7	284.4	1,231.5
Chile	33.2	185.6	20.5	15.3
Colombia	11.9	22.0	24.8	23.8
Ecuador	—	14.4	36.7	41.0
Mexico	3.6	19.3	70.4	13.1
Peru	10.4	30.7	233.7	83.0
Venezuela	1.3	12.1	19.3	34.2
Median	11.1	22.3	70.4	27.6

Sources: World Bank *(World Development Report)* (1982, 1992, 1996).
[1]GDP deflator for 1980-1990 and 1990-1994.

The highly positive East Asian record stands in striking contrast to that of Latin America and Sub-Saharan Africa in the recent period. ILO (1995) reports that in Latin America between 1980 and 1992, there occurred a steady fall in modern-sector employment, with paid employment falling at a rate of 0.1 percent per annum during the 1980s. This situation reversed the trend of the previous three decades, when steady economic growth had led to a significant expansion of modern-sector employment. In most Latin American countries, the average real wage fell during the 1980s, recovering in only a few countries toward the end of the decade. The minimum wage fell on average by 24 percent in real terms across the region, and average earnings in the informal sector declined by 42 percent.

Analytical and Policy Issues

The central analytical and policy question raised by East Asian economic experience is, of course, "What are the causes of the fast economic growth in these countries?" No consensus exists as to the correct answer to this question. Indeed, there has emerged instead

TABLE 3.4. Growth in Real Per Capita GDP in Developed and Developing Countries, 1974–93
(Average annual percentage growth)

	1974–1983	1983–1989	1989–1993
Group of Seven	1.4	3.0	1.2
United States	0.8	2.7	0.1
Japan	2.5	4.0	3.4
European Community	1.6	2.7	1.4
Asian Developing Countries	3.2	5.6	4.5
Middle East and European Developing Countries	-0.6	-2.1	2.9
Latin America	0.5	0.4	0.3
Africa	-0.3	-0.4	-1.0

Source: IMF (1994).

a continuing controversy in which the two protagonists are the World Bank together with some orthodox economists on the one side and on the other side, a number of academic economists, not all of them heterodox.[8] This debate is important for two reasons: first, because the World Bank professes to base its policy recommendations for countries around the globe on what it regards as the lessons to be drawn from the experience of these highly successful East Asian countries; and second, because from an analytical point of view, the debate is clearly of central importance, precisely because of the fast growth of these economies over a sustained period. Thus, the resolution of this pivotal debate would inevitably have an important bearing on our general ideas on growth and development.

With the publication of the World Bank's *The East Asian Miracle* (1993), there has occurred some useful narrowing of differences between the two sides, but there remains a wide gulf on a range of significant issues. These issues have been reviewed and commented on in Singh (1995a). The more important ones are the following:

- the question of the effectiveness of industrial policy
- the issue of "openness": how open were the East Asian economies during their periods of fast growth?
- the nature of competition in the domestic product market and capital market
- the role of savings and investment in East Asian economic growth
- the question of why the Asian countries did not have a debt crisis while the Latin American countries did
- the relationship among technology policy, industrial policy, and international competitiveness
- the relationship among the "fundamentals," macroeconomic stability, and industrial policy

---

[8] See World Bank (1991 and 1993), Amsden (1994a), Fishlow *et al.* (1994), Ito and Krueger (1995), and Singh (1994b and 1995a).

An analysis and resolution of the foregoing issues will help determine the right lessons to be learned from the East Asian economic model or models. In addition, the economic record of the East Asian countries raises four other significant issues. Let us quickly outline each one.

First, can the Asian experience be replicated? Apart from anything else, it is suggested that the international economic environment is totally different today from that in which the East Asian NICs achieved their formidable success. For instance, in the emerging post-Uruguay Round world trading order, many of the interventionist industrial and commercial policy instruments used by Japan, Korea, and other countries will no longer be permissible.[9]

Second, is fast East Asian economic growth sustainable, in the direct, narrow sense of the term? The subject draws its significance from the slowdown in the Japanese economy in the 1990s (which may be expected to have adverse effects on economic growth in other countries in the region) and from the existence of large current-account deficits of the second-tier NICs and hence these economies' vulnerability to capital outflows. It will be recalled that prior to 1980, countries like Brazil had been growing fast for a considerable period. Then suddenly Brazil, Mexico, and the rest of Latin America stumbled into a decade-long crisis. In the current Asian situation, given their present vulnerability to surges of capital inflows and outflows, what is there to stop a similar fate from being visited upon the Southeast Asian NICs?

Third, an alternative view is that there now exists among the East Asian and Southeast Asian countries a large degree of economic cooperation that has fostered a regional dynamic which has acquired an autonomy of its own. These factors, it is suggested, would allow the Asian countries to sustain high rates of economic growth regardless of the condition of the world economy, including the condition of the economy of Japan. Indeed, some would argue that currency appreciation and slower economic growth in Japan actually actively help developing East Asian countries by leading to greater Japanese FDI in those countries.[10]

Fourth, special analytical issues are raised by the epoch-making Chinese record—specifically, if freely functioning internal and external markets are essential to economic growth (as the Bretton Woods Institutions routinely insist), then how have the Chinese been able to grow so fast with such low levels of development of their capital and labor markets and with their highly segmented product markets? Similarly, the Chinese experience raises the important question of whether privatization of the means of production is at all necessary for the adequate (from the perspective of achieving fast economic growth) development of markets.[11]

---

[9] See also Singh (1996a), ODI (1995), UNCTAD (1995), Greenaway and Milner (1995), and Agosin, Tussie, and Crespi (1995).

[10] See also UNCTAD (1996).

[11] For the view of the Bretton Woods Institutions on the necessity of free and flexible markets for fostering economic growth, the classic statement is World Bank (1991). For the difficulties that the Chinese experience over the last 15 years creates for this thesis, see Singh (1994a and 1996c).

TABLE 3.5. Investment Performance of Asian and Latin American Economies, 1955–94
(Gross domestic investment as percentage of GDP)

	1955–1965	1965–1973	1973–1980	1980–1989	1990–1994
Asia					
China	—	—	—	—	—
India	—	18.4	22.6	23.9	23.9
Indonesia	—	15.8	24.5	30.4	—
Korea	14.3	25.1	31.8	31.2	36.7
Malaysia	14.2	22.3	28.7	32.2	34.6
Pakistan	—	16.0	16.5	18.8	19.7
Philippines	11.4	20.6	29.1	21.7	23.1
Sri Lanka	14.0	15.8	20.6	25.8	23.0
Thailand	17.6	23.8	26.6	26.7	40.7
Median	14.2	19.5	25.5	26.3	28.9
Latin America					
Argentina	19.7	19.8	21.8	15.5	16.7
Bolivia	16.7	25.4	24.9	12.2	15.4
Brazil	16.4	26.1	26.2	21.5	20.5
Chile	11.3	14.4	17.4	18.1	25.3
Colombia	18.9	18.9	18.8	20.4	18.3
Ecuador	14.8	19.0	26.7	23.2	20.6
Mexico	15.1	21.4	25.2	23.1	22.4
Peru	22.4	27.7	28.9	26.2	21.5
Venezuela	22.0	29.3	32.6	22.0	16.3
Median	16.7	21.4	25.2	21.5	20.5

Sources: World Bank (WDR) (1991), UN (YNAS) (1966), Asian Development Bank (1995), ECLAC (1995).

These are all large questions and cannot be properly treated within the confines of the present paper. The rest of the paper will duly limit itself to exploring a relatively narrow issue—namely, "What are the right lessons to be drawn from the Asian experience in terms of savings and investment, and how have the East Asian economies been able to achieve such high rates of savings and investment, particularly in the private corporate sector?" Addressing this issue will involve, among other things, an analysis of the relationship among government, the corporation, and the financial system in these exemplar economies.

Our analysis therefore will diverge from the old debate about industrial policy and getting prices "right" or "wrong." It is intended to shed some needed light on an important dynamic aspect of the East Asian experience and also to generate useful implications for Latin American countries afflicted with the problem of low rates of savings and investment.

Savings, Investment and Total Factor Productivity Growth in East Asia
The successful East Asian countries are today characterized by very high rates of savings and investment, but this was not always the case. As indicated in Tables 3.5 and 3.6 (which report investment and savings rates for nine Asian and nine Latin American coun-

TABLE 3.6. Domestic Savings in Asian and Latin American Countries, 1955–94

(Gross national savings as percentage of GDP)

	1955–1965	1965–1973	1973–1980	1980–1989	1990–1994
Asia					
China	—	—	—	—	—
India	—	17.9	22.3	21.5	20.8
Indonesia	—	13.7	24.6	27.6	—
Korea	3.3	21.5	26.4	32.8	35.1
Malaysia	23.3	21.6	29.4	29.3	29.5
Pakistan	11.8	—	10.9	14.8	17.6
Philippines	10.9	20.6	24.3	17.6	18.1
Sri Lanka	13.5	14.6	13.5	15.6	12.7
Thailand	16.7	22.6	21.5	22.6	34.1
Median	12.7	20.6	23.3	22.1	26.8
Latin America					
Argentina	18.9	19.7	21.2	11.2	17.1
Bolivia	8.1	29.2	18.2	2.0	6.3
Brazil	16.0	24.3	21.7	19.7	20.4
Chile	10.8	12.9	12.2	9.7	24.4
Colombia	18.8	17.2	19.2	17.4	21.3
Ecuador	15.4	16.3	21.2	16.6	19.4
Mexico	14.6	19.9	21.3	21.3	17.2
Peru	20.9	27.2	24.9	22.0	18.9
Venezuela	32.0	30.0	34.5	23.6	19.8
Median	16.0	19.9	21.3	17.4	19.8

Sources: World Bank *(WDR)* (1991), UN *(YNAS)* (1966), Asian Development Bank (1995), ECLAC (1995).

tries), in the 1990s the median Asian economy has saved and invested nearly 30 percent of its GDP as compared with a figure of about 20 percent for the Latin American countries, even though in the 1950s and early 1960s, the Latin Americans saved and invested appreciably more than did the Asians. Between 1955 and 1965, domestic savings in Korea were only 3.3 percent of GDP compared with more than 35 percent in the 1990s.

UNCTAD (1994) notes in regard to Japan that gross domestic fixed capital formation in that country increased from 24 percent of GNP in the early 1950s to almost 40 percent in the 1960s. The ratio of private equipment investment to GNP doubled between the early 1950s and the late 1960s, reaching 17 percent. In terms of purchasing-power-parity Summers-Heston data, Young (1994) estimates that between 1960 and 1980, the ratio of gross fixed investment to GDP doubled in Taiwan, tripled in Korea, and quadrupled in Singapore.

Studies by Young (1994) and Lau and Kim (1994) have established the primacy of the accumulation process in accounting for fast economic growth in the East Asian countries within the "growth-accounting" framework. These contributions show that the rapid economic expansion achieved by these countries cannot be attributed to their faster growth of total factor productivity (TFP), or the so-called "residual" that is loosely identified with "technical progress" in such analysis. Young's empirical results suggest that Korea and Taiwan had lower TFP growth than did Bangladesh over the period 1970–1985. In other words, in terms of TFP methodology, most if not all of the economic growth of countries like Korea can be explained by the fast expansion of factor inputs, including (among other things) inputs arising from very high rates of capital accumulation.

An interesting neoclassical interpretation of these new empirical findings on TFP growth in East Asia is provided by Krugman (1994). He argues, on the basis of these results, that the high growth rates of the East Asian miracle economies are not sustainable. In his view, this unsustainability stems from the fact that it is unrealistic to expect countries that are already investing 40 percent of their GDP to be able to raise their rate of investment much higher still. Krugman goes on to point out that these countries similarly already have highly educated and high-quality labor forces, which limits the scope for further improvement in these spheres also. In these circumstances, without technical progress, eventual decreasing returns to investment will supposedly set in and limit the growth potential of these economies.

This view is, however, not the only possible interpretation of the observed phenomena. For instance, in the tradition of the classical economists and in that of Kaldor (1965 and 1967), it is suggested by Akyuz and Gore (1996) and by Singh (1996b) that on the contrary, high rates of investment actually lead to greater turnover of machines and therefore to faster technical change, greater learning by doing, more and quicker product development, and hence greater international competitiveness. Therefore, in this alternative non-neoclassical analysis there is no reason that eventual decreasing returns should set in within a situation of high rates of investment.[12]

The finding of low or zero TFP growth in the East Asian economies has also been interpreted by some economists to suggest that there is nothing "miraculous" about these countries' growth, since it can all be explained by the accumulation of physical and human capital. A simple neoclassical story ascribes the growth basically to sound "fundamentals." It is suggested that prudent macroeconomic management (and its consequent low rates of inflation and low fluctuations of the exchange rate) coupled with good initial conditions (land reform, favorable human-capital endowment) led to fast growth of household incomes, which in turn generated high rates of savings and investment. In this account, some countries were subject initially to financial repression (for instance, Korea in the mid-1960s), but once this repression was eliminated and real interest rates became positive, then household savings rose further, as did investment.[13]

---

[12] The fact that a country has zero TFP growth does not mean that the country has achieved no technical progress, in the ordinary usage of these terms. This fact becomes obvious when one considers that notwithstanding the absence of TFP growth, the Korean economy, for example, has been continuously producing and exporting an increasingly sophisticated range of products over the last three decades. For conceptual critiques of the neoclassical production function and its analysis of "technical progress," see (among others) Kaldor (1961) and Scott (1989).

[13] World Bank (1993) is a considerable improvement on this orthodox neoclassical analysis. It acknowledges that governments in these fast-growing East Asian countries adopted a host of measures to raise the levels of both savings and investment, as well as to influence the allocation of investments. It accepts that fast-growing East Asian countries did not eliminate financial repression.

The upcoming analysis, following the work of Akyuz and Gore (1996) and Singh (1996b), presents a more complex view of the accumulation process in East Asia. It stresses the essential role of profits in providing both the inducement to invest and the means to pay for the investment. Profits are also, of course, a consequence of investment. The propensity to save out of profits is greater than the propensity to save out of other sources of income, so therefore, higher profits also lead to higher savings. This investment-profitability-savings nexus was not, however, a spontaneous outcome of the invisible hand of the market or simply a result of "sound fundamentals," but rather of government policy measures and the government-business interactions central to generating and sustaining the nexus. At the aggregate level, the net results were a great increase in the propensities to save and invest and the ex ante equality of savings and investment at high rates of economic growth.

This conceptualization of the East Asian experience is very much in the Kaldorian tradition. Instead of static resource allocation and getting prices right or wrong, it emphasizes the dynamics of the accumulation process (mediated through high profits), the associated technical change, and the resultant growth of productivity. The argument is illustrated in the upcoming sections by considering the cases of Japan and South Korea.

Investment, Profits and Savings in Japan in the High-Growth Period (1950–1970)

The period of postwar Japanese economic history most relevant from the perspective of today's developing countries is the 1950s and 1960s. It was a high-growth period, and at the beginning of the period, the level of industrialization of Japan was not very different from the level prevailing in today's semi-industrial countries. Indeed, the value of Japanese exports in 1952 was lower than the value of those of India (Krueger 1995).

During these two decades from 1950 to 1970, the Japanese economy expanded at a rate of 10 percent per annum; the country's industrial output rose by 13 percent per annum; and Japan's share in total world exports of manufactures increased by 10 percentage points. These extraordinary growth rates were accompanied by extremely high rates of investment and savings, as the data in Tables 3.7 and 3.8 show. In the absence of readily available data on developing countries, the two tables provide comparative statistics only on industrial countries; nevertheless, information that exists for other than industrial economies also suggests that Japanese investment and saving rates during this period were among the highest in the world, including all of the developed, developing, or centrally planned economies.

Two further points in relation to the Japanese savings and investment history require particular attention. The first—and it is a central point—is that most of this high investment occurred in the private sector and in the corporate economy; because of government's relatively small size, the official sector's share of total investment in Japan was quite low compared with government's investment share in other countries. The second point is that savings rates in each sector of the Japanese economy (household, corporate,

TABLE 3.7. Gross Fixed Investment Ratios in Japan and Other Countries, 1953–72

(Percentage of GDP at constant prices)

	Total Fixed Capital Formation	Excluding Residential Construction	Trend Increase in Total Share[1]
Japan	31.8	26.2	1.11
France	23.0	17.1	0.66
Germany	25.1	19.4	0.25
Italy	20.2	14.2	(0.03)
United Kingdom	17.3	14.1	0.40
United States	17.0	12.8	(-0.02)
Soviet Union	17.0	12.8	0.28[2]

[1] Annual increase of total gross fixed investment in GNP obtained by fitting linear time trends to the data. Figures in brackets are statistically not significant, at the 5% confidence level.
[2] Total fixed investment as a share of NMP (1950 to 1969)
Source: Boltho (1975).

TABLE 3.8. Gross Savings Ratios in Japan and Other Countries, 1953–72

(Percentage of GDP at current prices)

	Total	Household[1]	Corporations[2]	Government
Japan	36.9	15.8	13.5	7.8[2]
France	25.0	10.2	10.4	4.3
Germany	27.1	9.6	11.2[3]	6.3
Italy[4]	23.4	12.6	9.7[3]	1.1
United Kingdom	18.3	5.0	8.8	4.3
United States	18.0	8.0	7.7	2.4[2]
Finland	28.4	10.0	9.6	8.9
Netherlands	27.1	9.1	12.9[3]	5.1
Switzerland[5]	28.3	12.6	10.2	5.4

[1] Including unincorporated enterprises.
[2] Including public corporations.
[3] Including depreciation allowances of unincorporated enterprises.
[4] From 1961 to 1972.
[5] From 1953 to 1969.
Source: Boltho (1975).

and government) were higher than the comparable sectorial savings rates of all the other industrial countries appearing in Table 3.8.[14]

Table 3.9 suggests that Japanese net manufacturing profits as a proportion of manufacturing output were generally much higher than those of other industrial countries. In 1970, for instance, the Japanese ratio was actually more than twice as high as the ratios recorded in the United Kingdom and the United States in that year and nearly twice as high as those recorded in Germany and Italy.

---

[14] The only exception to this statement is that Finland's government savings level was slightly higher than that of Japan.

TABLE 3.9. Ratio of Net Profit to Net Value Added: Manufacturing Sector of Japan and Other Countries, 1955–72

(Percentages)

		1955	1960	1965	1970	1972
Canada	P/Y	30.8	27.2	27.9	22.7	25.3
United States	P/Y	23.2	21.5	24.8	17.1	20.1
Japan	P/Y	36.6	44.7	37.0	40.9	35.4
Germany	P/Y	36.8	33.3	28.9	24.8	19.8
Italy	P/Y	30.9	31.6	23.1	22.5	20.1
Sweden	P/Y	25.0	26.2	23.1	26.8	20.4
United Kingdom	P/Y	29.6	25.2	24.9	18.4	19.3
Australia	P/Y	22.4	21.5	28.1	26.6	22.3
Netherlands	P/Y	40.4	34.5	30.5	29.4	29.3

Note: P = Net Operating Surplus   Y = Net Value Added

The Role of the Japanese State

These high Japanese profit ratios arose to a large extent as a result of the heavy state intervention that guided the Japanese economy during the period in question. The government's objectives with respect to such intervention were fully articulated in a number of government documents, one of the most important of which was the "Five-Year Plan for Economic Independence," issued in 1955 following the end of U.S. occupation. The plan emphasized the interlocking triad of "growth, investment, and exports." High rates of investment were viewed as necessary in order to develop modern industry and to shift labor from low-productivity to high-productivity sectors. Similarly, national savings had to be mobilized in order to fund this needed investment; the country could not rely simply on foreign aid to finance its investment needs (hence the words "economic independence" in the title of the plan). Similarly, exports were necessary in order to pay for the required imports of raw materials, machinery, and technology; this export orientation was thought to be particularly important for a country that was not well endowed with natural resources and that no longer had an empire to provide it with such materials.

The foregoing perception of Japan's situation was not just a vision of the planners but was also widely shared by the public, as exemplified by the popular slogan of the period: "Prosperity through exports and stability through savings." The overall vision was translated into practice by different branches of the government in different ways. Ackley and Ishi (1976, pp. 160–61) provide a useful and instructive account of the vision's *macroeconomic* implications as perceived by the relevant government agencies. These macroeconomic implications, according to the two authors, included the following five:

- government tax and expenditure policies that would encourage savings, investment, and exports, including heavy governmental investment in productive (but not in social) capital

- a monetary policy involving interest rates and easy credit designed to stimulate highly capital-intensive private investment (but not housing or consumer durables) and to provide an indirect form of export subsidy
- a significant role for the government as financial intermediary, to ensure that adequate amounts of both personal and governmental savings flowed to the favored kinds of investments
- the encouragement of rapid growth of aggregate demand so long as the current account of the balance of payments remained positive and export prices did not rise; the readiness to check expansion of demand whenever the continuation of either of these conditions was threatened; and the willingness to tolerate rising domestic prices, especially if they supported import-competing domestic production or did not significantly encourage imports of consumer goods
- the implicit readiness to sacrifice stability for growth.

To put it another way, the government had two main proximate objectives: to attain current-account equilibrium at as high a growth rate as possible and to increase the private sector's propensities to invest and save so as to raise substantially the economy's long-term growth rate. At the microeconomic level, the government sought to pursue its macroeconomic objectives by building up the strength and capabilities of individual corporations so that these could compete in the international marketplace with their counterparts from advanced countries. For this purpose a number of measures were taken that directly helped increase the amount of resources available for corporate investment. These measures were coupled with a range of indirect policies that positively influenced the external environment of the corporate sector and thereby also helped raise profits. All of these microeconomic policy measures have been discussed in detail in Singh (1996b) and will therefore simply be summarized here.

The first such policy measure related to corporate fiscal incentives. In fact, the direct policy instruments used by the government to promote corporate growth included quite a wide range of such fiscal incentives. Tsuru (1993) notes that by the mid-1970s Japanese corporations had available to them more than 25 tax-free reserves, including reserves for price fluctuations, for overseas market development, and for overseas investment losses.

The second policy measure had to do with domestic competition. One of the most important indirect policy measures was the lax enforcement of antitrust laws, thereby helping corporations to earn above-normal profits. Antitrust laws in Japan are regarded not as an end in themselves but as an integral part of government's overall industrial policy. The laws are enforced by the Fair Trade Commission, which has much less power (and this was particularly true during the high-growth period) than does MITI, the agency in control of industrial policy. MITI displayed important anticompetitive biases: it favored large firms in the belief that this approach was essential for competing in international markets and it disapproved of "excessive 'competition'" because of potential price wars that might diminish the corporate inducement to invest.

During the high-growth period, MITI encouraged a variety of cartel arrangements in a wide range of industries—export and import cartels, cartels to combat recession or excessive competition, rationalization cartels, and the like.[15] Although these cartels were formed for specific periods and were not always fully effective, they nevertheless restricted competition considerably in the domestic product market. Interestingly, however, MITI implemented these anticompetitive actions simultaneously with vigorous encouragement of domestic oligopolistic rivalry among the large firms and with the promotion of international competitiveness. MITI's purpose in these endeavors was not to achieve Pareto efficiency or to maximize consumer welfare but rather to promote rapid technological progress and fast growth of productivity in the industrial sector. Okimoto (1989) notes that in general, the decision as to whether to promote or to restrict competition depended on the nature of the industry and on the industry's life cycle stage. During the developmental phase of a young industry, the government discouraged competition but when this same industry became technologically mature, competition was allowed to flourish, and later, when the industry was in competitive decline, the government again discouraged competition and attempted to bring about the careful rationalization of that industry.[16]

The third policy measure was import control policy. During the rapid-growth period, the government effectively protected industry from external competition by using both tariff and (particularly) nontariff measures. In the 1960s the government did start on a program of eliminating or relaxing protective measures in order to conform to OECD norms, but protection remained highly effective even until the end of the 1970s. As late as 1978, manufactured imports constituted only 2.4 percent of the Japanese GDP; the corresponding proportion in Britain and other countries of the EEC was five to six times larger. Even in the United States—which traditionally, because of its continental size, has a relatively closed economy—the volume of imported manufactured goods in the late 1970s was proportionally almost twice as large as in Japan (see CEPG 1979).

The fourth policy measure had to do with low interest rates and policy-based finance. The government implemented a general policy of low interest rates and provided (through so-called policy-based finance) preferential rates for MITI's favored firms and industries. These rates lowered the cost of capital, helped increase corporate resources for investment, and induced firms to invest according to government's priorities.[17]

The fifth policy measure was related to "administrative guidance" and to the coordination and sequencing of investment. The government used important specific measures for raising and maintaining at a high level the corporate propensity to invest. Through "administrative guidance," MITI performed the important task of seeking to

---

[15] According to Caves and Uekusa (1976b), in the 1960s cartels accounted for 78.1 percent of the value of shipments in textiles; 64.8 percent in clothing; 50.0 percent in nonferrous metals; 47 percent in printing and publishing; 41.2 percent in stone, clay, and glass; 37.2 percent in food products; and 34.5 percent in steel products.

[16] For a fuller discussion of the issues raised, see Amsden and Singh (1994).

[17] Shinohara (1982); JDB/JERI (1993).

preclude any potential problems brought about by coordination failure—problems that, of course, are ubiquitous in the real world of incomplete and imperfect markets. This administrative guidance was especially in evidence during Japan's high-growth period; what in effect MITI did at that time was to guide and orchestrate the investment and technological races occurring among oligopolistic firms in the favored industries. Such races were carefully controlled by MITI because, otherwise, excess capacity might have been created that would have adversely affected the future corporate inducement to invest. Thus, in a number of industries (for instance, steel) that were undergoing large investment programs, the government "guided" firms not to invest all at the same time but rather to establish new capacity by turn. The government's role in Japan, unlike the case in Soviet-type planning, was one of "guidance" of the private corporate sector rather than of "command." MITI's coordinating role was performed through extensive consultations with trade associations and through what is known as the "deliberations councils."[18] Lockwood (1965, p. 149) observes the following:

> The industrial bureaus of MITI proliferate sectorial targets and plans; they confer, they tinker, they exhort. This is the economics by admonition to a degree inconceivable in Washington or London. Business makes few major decisions without consulting the appropriate governmental authority; the same is true in reverse."[19]

In general, the five policy measures that we have just outlined led to greater rents and profits for the private corporate sector than would otherwise have been the case. These profits enabled Japanese firms to undertake high rates of investment, to improve the quality of their products, and also to capture markets abroad. The latter was of particular importance to firms, since in return for its favors (protection, policy-based finance), MITI often imposed on them certain export and world market share performance targets.[20]

To sum up, the most important factors that distinguished Japanese governmental policies at the level of firm and industry from those of other *dirigiste* economies included the following:

- emphasis on exports
- enforcement of strict performance standards
- maintenance of oligopolistic rivalry among large firms in mature industries as opposed to promotion of single "national champions" (which many countries are prone to do)[21]
- maintenance of a close relationship between government and business.

---

[18] See also JDB/JERI (1993) and World Bank (1993).
[19] Quoted in Caves and Uekusa (1976a, p. 487).
[20] Other kinds of performance standards were also asked for, most notably those involving technological upgrading. See also Amsden and Hikino (1994).
[21] See also Boltho (1985).

Profits and Savings in Japan

The foregoing account of the government's role in sustaining Japan's investment-profits-exports nexus has not considered in any detail the question of savings. As noted earlier, each sector of the Japanese economy saved more than did its counterparts elsewhere in the world. High profits and strong corporate inducement to invest were clearly, at least in part, responsible for high corporate savings; the Japanese financial system itself (see following section) also played a significant part in facilitating such corporate savings.

In addition to encouraging corporate investment and savings, the high profits in the Japanese economy were also in part responsible for the high savings propensities of the Japanese household sector.[22] In Japanese national accounts, unincorporated businesses are included in the household sector. During the 1950s and 1960s, the incidence of such businesses in the Japanese economy was much greater than in other industrial countries. In view of the intense competition these unincorporated enterprises face, their natural propensity to save and invest out of profits tends to be very high. Another reason for the high savings propensities of the Japanese household sector concerns workers' bonus payments. These payments, which were directly linked to profits, constituted 16 percent of workers' annual incomes in the relevant period. During the 1950s and 1960s, the workers apparently regarded these bonuses as windfall incomes, out of which they had a higher propensity to save than out of their regular incomes (UNCTAD 1994).[23]

The Corporation and the Financial System in Japan

Our evidence of the high level of Japanese profits by comparative international standards has thus far been of a macroeconomic kind: the share of manufacturing profits in total manufacturing output. We have not yet considered microeconomic data on the rates of return achieved by individual Japanese manufacturing corporations. Here an apparent anomaly emerges that highlights the important complementary role of the financial system in sustaining the investment-profits-saving nexus in the Japanese economy during the high-growth period.

Comparative data on corporate rates of return in the United States (for example) and in Japan indicate that, unlike the greater share of profits in total manufacturing value added in Japan, the individual U.S. rates of return per firm were considerably greater than those earned by Japanese corporations. Kojima (1995) reports that between 1960 and 1964, the average rate of return of U.S. manufacturing firms was 6.3 percent per annum and that of Japanese corporations was 3.2 percent; for the period 1965 to 1969 the corresponding figures were 6.9 percent for U.S. firms and 3.3 percent for Japanese. These

---

[22] Akyuz and Gore (1996) and UNCTAD (1994).

[23] There exist several other factors that can, to some degree, account for the high savings propensities of the Japanese household sector (Maddison 1992, Kojima 1995, and IMF 1995). These factors include the fast rate of growth of household incomes, the age and employment structures of the population, and the lack of publicly provided social security. Moreover, low income elasticity of demand for foreign goods, the low level of development of financing and credit facilities for consumers, and formal and informal controls on imports of consumer durables can also be expected to have played a significant part in keeping household consumption low. See Felix (1994).

differences in observed rates of return could in principle have arisen simply from differences in accounting conventions between the two countries or other similar factors. But, detailed work by Blaine (1993) on this issue indicates that even if the data are corrected for such differences, the U.S. rates of return would still be greater than those of the Japanese firms.

The lower Japanese profitability at the microeconomic level (relative to the United States) is not necessarily inconsistent with the much higher share of profits in aggregate output in the former country as compared with the latter. Indeed, many economists regard it as a virtue of the Japanese financial system that allows Japanese firms to continue to survive and to invest even when their rates of return are very low. Moreover, the implied lower "hurdle rate" allows Japanese managers to undertake investments that U.S. firms would find unacceptable. For all the reasons outlined earlier, this capability gives Japanese corporations a competitive advantage.

Singh (1995c) refers to Dertouzos *et al.* (1989), who regarded this factor as a major reason that U.S. firms lost out to the Japanese corporations in the U.S. home market in a wide range of electronic products. Research showed that when a Japanese firm entered one of these markets, there occurred a fall in the rate of return of the existing U.S. firms in the industry because of greater competition. This decline often resulted in the U.S. firms' leaving that industry fairly quickly and in their diversifying and investing their resources elsewhere because they could not accept such low returns. Japanese companies were, however, able to sustain these low rates of return for long periods.

Similarly, comparative survey data on managerial objectives repeatedly show that, unlike their American counterparts, Japanese corporate managers are much more interested in pursuing market share than in earning a high rate of return on assets or in increasing the wealth of the shareholders (Abegglen and Stalk 1995, Kojima 1995). This all raises the important question as to why Japanese managers are able to ignore performance variables commonly used in the United States or the United Kingdom, such as movements in share prices or changes in earnings per share since the last financial statement.

The answer lies essentially in the differences in the nature of the financial system in Japan compared with that in Anglo-Saxon countries. Two aspects of the Japanese financial system are particularly relevant in this respect: the absence of hostile takeovers and the long-term relationships that typically exist between the leading Japanese corporations and their respective "main banks" in the *keiretsu.*

Hostile takeovers are rare in Japan for many reasons. Among the most important of these are the method of distribution of shareholdings in the large Japanese corporations and the relatively greater effective power of stakeholders versus shareholders. In such corporations, typically three-fourths of the shares are held in the "safe hands" of the company's suppliers, buyers, main bank, and other such stakeholders. Only one-fourth of the shares are owned by outside shareholders, who in any case do not effectively have the protection or rights available to minority shareholders in the United States or the United Kingdom.

These factors make it virtually impossible to mount a hostile takeover bid against a large Japanese corporation,[24] which helps to insulate Japanese managers from the "short-termism" to which Anglo-Saxon managers are subject.[25] The latter are obliged to pay constant attention to changes in earnings per share every quarter, for if earnings do not come up to the stockmarket's expectations, the firm in question may become subject to the danger of takeover.

In contrast, the Japanese corporations have long-term relationships with their lead banks.[26] These institutional features enable Japanese managers to worry very little about the verdict of the stock market, to pursue long-term strategies (such as increasing their market share) quite aggressively, and to reinvest most of their firms' profits rather than paying out large dividends.[27]

The aforementioned characteristics of the relationship between the corporation and the financial system in Japan complemented government policies in the 1950s and 1960s in maintaining the investment-profit-savings nexus. And in fact, the structure of the financial system itself was not independent of government policies. Evidence exists that after World War II, the government deliberately adopted a number of measures that helped consolidate the existing bank-based financial system rather than establishing a financial system based on the stock market.[28]

The Government, the Corporation and the Financial System in Korea

The relationship between government and corporations and the relationship between corporations and the financial system were even more important in Korea than in Japan in terms of initiating and maintaining high corporate and overall investment and savings rates. Let us examine three substantive reasons for this fact.

First—as suggested by available comparative flow-of-funds data for developing countries (Honahan and Atiyas 1993)—unlike the case of Japan, all of the economic sectors of Korea do not have higher savings rates than do all of the economic sectors of other countries. The high overall savings rate of the Korean economy is essentially the result of Korea's very high level of corporate savings relative to corporate savings levels in other countries. Countries like India and Turkey, for instance, have larger household savings rates than does Korea (India 14.8 percent, Turkey 11.5 percent, Korea 10.3 percent). But

---

[24] See also Odagiri (1994), Odagiri and Hase (1989), and Singh (1995c).

[25] There exists a large literature on the stock market and on the short-termism that it typically engenders. For a recent review, see Singh (1995c). See also Stein (1988, 1989); Cosh, Hughes, and Singh (1990); Porter (1992); Kojima (1995); Froot, Perold, and Stein (1992); and Jacobson and Aaker (1993). For an opposite point of view on the subject, see Marsh (1990).

[26] Instead of the takeover mechanism, managers in the Japanese system are subject to internal organizational and other types of disciplines. See also Aoki (1990), Odagiri (1994), and Aoki and Dore (1994).

[27] Dore (1985) points out that in some years the total dividend payments by Japanese corporations were less than the aggregate amounts managers spent on their perks and entertainments. He also notes from a sociological perspective the relatively low social status of the stock market in the Japanese society. The top graduates in the University of Tokyo—an elite institution—still prefer to have careers with the government or with the corporations rather than with the stock market or with institutions connected with the stock market.

[28] See also Aoki and Patrick (1994), and Rajan (1996).

business savings in Korea have been 8.3 percent of GDP compared with 3.4 percent in Turkey and 1.8 percent in India.[29]

Second, the history of Korean development during the last three decades is the history of the expansion and diversification of the *chaebol*—the huge conglomerates that produce a wide range of industrial and consumer products. A few of these very large firms have dominated the Korean economy throughout the entire period. The top ten *chaebol* accounted for 21 percent of total Korean manufacturing sales in 1977 and for 30 percent in 1985. By 1989, the share had declined slightly to 27 percent. At the international level, the 500 largest industrial companies in the world in 1990 included 11 Korean companies (the same number as from Switzerland) whereas in the 1960s there had been no Korean company at all on that list. The government played a central role in the creation and development of the *chaebol*.

Third, because of the low initial level of Korean development relative to that of Japan, the Korean state has been much more deeply and directly involved in all spheres of the economy, particularly in building up the competitive strength of Korean corporations. As a result of democratization and the continuing pressure from industrial countries to liberalize the Korean economy, the government's influence has declined compared with what it was in the high-growth period of the economy (1965–1985), but that influence is nevertheless still substantial. In any event, the following analysis, as in the case of Japan and for similar reasons, will concentrate on the earlier high-growth period.

The Role of the State in Korea: A Comparison with Japan

Rapid economic development and industrial catch-up in Korea began with the military coup[30] by General Park and very much bear the stamp of his economic philosophy. Applying what he regarded as the lessons of Japanese economic development, Park made the large private corporation the main vehicle for "late industrialization" in Korea. But Park also thought that to ensure that private business would act in the social interest, it needed careful and constant guidance from the government, particularly at Korea's particular stage of development.

The government in Korea followed policies broadly similar to those implemented in Japan in the latter's own quest for rapid economic growth. But there were significant differences, five of which we shall now briefly examine.

First of all, in Korea far more than in Japan, government played a direct role in helping to create large conglomerate organizations by promoting mergers and directing the entry and exit of firms according to the requirements of technological economies of scale and world demand conditions. A pertinent U.N. publication (1993) notes the following with respect to Korean industrial structure:

---

[29] As Honahan and Atiyas readily admit, the comparative "flow-of-funds" data on which these ratios are based are far from perfect. Apart from the deficiencies of the data themselves, the statistics do not refer to the same periods for the three countries: the Korean figures are averaged over the period 1980–1984, while those for India and Turkey cover the years 1970–1982 and 1970–1981 respectively. But these appear to be the best data we have.

[30] General Park Chung-Hee seized power in 1961. He later became president and was assassinated in 1978.

Such a structure is the deliberate creation of the government, which utilized a highly interventionist strategy to push industry into larger-scale, complex, technologically demanding activities while simultaneously restricting FDI inflows tightly to promote national ownership. It was deemed necessary to create enterprises of large size and diversity, to undertake the risk inherent in launching high-technology, high-skill activities that would remain competitive in world markets. The *chaebols* acted as the representatives and spearheads of the government strategy: they were supported by protection against imports and TNC entry, by subsidized credit, by procurement preference, and by massive investments in education, infrastructure, and the science-technology network.

Second, although on the face of it Japan and Korea have similar group banking systems, there exists a crucial difference between the two. For much of the high-growth period, the Korean financial system was effectively under state control, whereas the Japanese banks, although subject to government influence and guidance, were nevertheless private. In the Korean case, in which the main bank is state controlled, the relationship between the group and the bank becomes rather different; it provides the state with an extra degree of information and control over corporate activities than would otherwise be the case. Lee (1992) suggests that what the Korean government did in effect was to create an internal capital market for allocation of investment resources. Following Williamson (1975), Lee argues that in view of the various imperfections of a free capital market, particularly in a country at Korea's stage of development, an internal market of this kind may be more efficient.

Third, there also exists a significant organizational difference between the Japanese *keiretsu* and the Korean *chaebol*. Following the dissolution of the *zaibatsu*, the ownership of large Japanese corporations is not in the hands of families but instead is widely dispersed, leading to the separation of ownership from control and thus producing the complete professionalization of the management function. In contrast, in Korea company ownership still resides predominantly in entrepreneurial families; consequently, family members have often occupied the top managerial jobs, and the professionalization of management has been a slow process (Amsden 1989).

Fourth, Singh (1996b) notes that as in Japan, the government in Korea played a critical role in enhancing and maintaining at a high level the corporate inducement to invest. But, in Korea the state was not just a referee or ringmaster in orchestrating investment races but also a nursemaid and fairy godmother to the *chaebol*. During the 1970s when the government implemented its extremely ambitious "heavy and chemical industry" (HCI) program, the state became virtually a co-partner with the leading *chaebol* and actually "socialized" the risks involved.

These technological and market-related risks in the production and sale of sophisticated new products were indeed formidable for the Korean private corporations. Left to themselves, private firms might not have undertaken these risky investments at all. But goaded by the government and provided with finance at subsidized rates through the nationalized banking system, the fiercely competitive top *chaebol* were more than willing to participate fully in these new ventures. This approach is well illustrated by the story of the production of microwave ovens by the Korean company Samsung Industries, as told by an institution, the World Bank, not particularly known for its support of the state nursemaiding of industrial production (World Bank 1993, p. 130):

> The government's Economic Development Board was a key player in Samsung's success. Government officials were keenly aware that the Republic of Korea could not rely forever on low-wage manufacturing. Just as the United States had lost countless textile industry jobs to Korea, they reasoned, so Korea would one day find it could no longer compete for labor-intensive manufacturing jobs with low-wage neighbors such as China and Indonesia. To prepare for that day, government officials, working in consultation with the private sector, developed incentives for new knowledge- and capital-intensive industries. Incentives varied widely and included the government's building industrial parks, subsidizing utilities, giving tax rebates for exports, and making cheap loans for investment in new products. By 1980, urged forward by subsidies and incentives, Korean industry had moved into steel, ships, and even cars and was about to leap into world class electronics.
>
> Samsung made good use of these measures; company managers met frequently with government officials to trade ideas and projects. Even so, penetrating the world microwave market dominated by Japan was no easy task. By the late 1970s, when global production hit 5 million per year, Samsung had made a total of only 1,460 microwave ovens. The company's first break came in 1980, when a U.S. department store, looking for cheaper substitutes, ordered several thousand ovens. Soon production had risen to 100 thousand. When General Electric, unable to keep pace with the Japanese competition, decided to stop manufacturing microwaves itself and import the ovens under its own label instead, Samsung was a logical choice. The company has never looked back, and it now exports the ovens under its own name as well as buyers' labels.

Fifth, although the industrial strategies of both Japan and Korea emphasized exports, the Korean authorities have pursued this objective much more vigorously. In Japan's high-growth period, the share of exports in GDP increased only to a small degree, from 6.5 percent in the early 1950s to less than 9 percent in the early 1970s. Korean exports, on the other hand, rose from less than 5 percent of GDP in 1963 to nearly 35 percent in 1980 (Krueger 1995).

Investment, Savings and Profits in Korea

Very little statistical information is available on comparative profits and rates of return for developing countries. Nevertheless, recent research by Jang (1995) on Korean profits at the macroeconomic level indicates that the profit share (gross manufacturing profits as a proportion of gross manufacturing output) during the 1963–1975 period was quite high, ranging between 40 percent and 45 percent. In the late 1970s, the share began to decline, and in the 1980s it ranged between 30 percent and 39 percent. The reasons for this decline must lie partially in the tighter labor market conditions and in the increasing power of workers and trade unions, especially in the period leading up to democratization in 1989. In any event, as in the case of Japan, Korean profits (particularly during the high-growth period) were higher than what they would have been without government policies of protection against imports and in the absence of adequate domestic competition policies and interest subsidies.[31]

We have already analyzed the role of government and the financial system in inducing and sustaining high corporate investment rates in the Korean economy. We turn now to the important question of savings. How did the Korean domestic savings ratio rise from 3.3 percent of GDP during the 1955–1965 period to almost 35 percent during the 1980–1995 period? In the 1960s and 1970s, foreign savings played a major but waning role in Korean economic growth, and by the 1980s, foreign savings had become negative (that is, Korea was running a current-account surplus). Meanwhile, domestic private savings had greatly increased as a consequence of rising savings both in the corporate and personal sector. The notable growth in corporate-sector savings was largely the result of Korean firms' high corporate investment rates and high retention ratios. The government, through its anti-consumption policies, was also involved in helping raise the personal or household sector's propensity to save: official anti-consumption policies included prohibitive nontariff and tariff barriers on imported luxury goods, as well as instructions to the banks (largely state owned) not to extend consumer credit. One result of these policies was a very low automobile ownership rate in Korea. Chang (1994, p. 109–10) observes the following:

> Despite Korea's being a major exporter of passenger cars, Koreans have owned far fewer passenger cars than have people in other developing countries with a comparable income level.... Given such a clear (stated and revealed) anti-consumption bias, Korean macroeconomic policy may be more appropriately understood as "investment management" rather than as "aggregate-demand management."

It could perhaps be argued that the rise in personal or household savings has been entirely the result of the growth in household incomes and that it has had little to do with the government's anti-consumption policies. But although rising per capita incomes were no doubt important in increasing the propensity to save, UNCTAD (1994) rightly notes that income growth is not translated automatically into high savings growth. And in fact, relatively little increase occurred in the average savings ratios of many leading Latin American countries from 1960 to 1980 despite a fairly fast increase in per capita incomes; similarly, in the 1990s, although Latin American growth has revived, there has occurred no concomitant increase in the savings rate in many of those countries (Edwards 1995).

---

[31] Nevertheless, even more than in Japan, the government in Korea encouraged fierce rivalry among large oligopolistic firms and enforced strict performance standards on firms receiving any state benefits. Moreover, during the 1980s the government of Korea embarked on a gradual program of liberalization as well as of greater competition in the domestic markets. For a fuller discussion, see Amsden and Singh (1994).

Korean savings seem also to have been invariant to changes in real interest rates. For much of the high-growth period in Korea there was considerable financial repression, and yet savings continued to rise (Dornbusch and Park 1987, Cho and Khatkhate 1989).

Savings in Korea during the high-growth period would have been positively affected by the high level of corporate profits for the same reasons mentioned earlier with respect to Japan. During the 1970s, bonus payments to workers constituted between 14 percent and 33 percent of the total Korean wage bill, a somewhat higher figure than that cited for Japan. As in Japan, profits of unincorporated enterprises in Korea are included in the household sector; as explained earlier, the propensity to save out of such profits and to invest is likely to be very high.

Overview of the Japanese and Korean Processes

Our analysis of the accumulation process in Japan and Korea has emphasized the significance of government policies, of government interactions with business, and of the relationships between corporations and the national financial system. These policies, interactions, and relationships have been critical in the operation of the observed virtuous circle of high investment, high profits, and high savings in these economies during their earlier periods of very fast economic growth.

The workings of the investment-profits-savings nexus in the two exemplar East Asian economies may be contrasted with the situation in Latin American countries and in the former USSR. Evidence exists (Palma 1996) that the profits in many Latin American economies have also been high, but these high profits have not led to either higher investment rates or higher savings rates. In the former Soviet Union, on the other hand, there have been high rates of investment and savings, but these were not related to market-generated profits; such investment has therefore not had the same large positive impact on economic growth as that experienced by the East Asian economies.[32]

Implications for Development Thinking

We shall now bring together the various threads of our discussion in order to examine the latter's implications for development thinking and practice, with an eye to determining what useful policy lessons, if any, can be drawn from this analysis for the Latin American countries in their present circumstances.

With regard to development thinking, the first point that emerges from the present essay concerns the role of large domestically owned third-world firms in economic development. This subject has received very little attention in the development literature. The literature does emphasize capital accumulation but studies it by and large only at the macroeconomic level. And although the question of investment allocation is indeed ex-

---

[32] Akyuz and Gore (1996) critically note that "East Asian NIEs have been able to avoid the kind of problems associated with Soviet-type investment not based on profits, as well as the Latin American phenomenon of profits without investment." With respect to the Soviet Union, Delong and Summers make a similar point in explaining why high investment rates in plant and equipment in that regime did not generate the same degree of economic growth as in the market economies.

amined at a microeconomic level, that examination is carried out within the context of cost-benefit analysis of investment projects. The fact is that economists have been slow to recognize that industrialization and development are actually carried out by firms, organizations, and management. We have not as yet begun to develop an analytical perspective on the nature and role of these entities in carrying out industrial development. For instance, there exists no theory of the third-world firm. Is a large third-world firm much like a large firm in the advanced countries, or do there exist important differences between the two?

To comprehend the reality of intercountry differences in corporations, one need only consider Aoki's (1990) work on the differences between Japanese and Anglo-Saxon firms. Aoki has emphasized the differences between the two groups of companies with respect to their relationships with workers, their managerial cultures, their relationships with finance providers, their relationships with suppliers and subcontractors, and their ownership patterns. He has formalized these differences into a distinct theory of the Japanese firm.

Indeed, very important differences exist between large U.S. and Western European firms and those in other areas of the world both today and in the past when the more developed countries themselves were industrializing. It is a remarkable fact that the large private third-world firms tend to be organized as highly diversified industrial groups operating in a number of unrelated fields—that is, they are what might be called "irrational" conglomerates. This kind of "group" business organization seems to have arisen in countries of diverse cultures, institutions and historical development. Such widely diversified business groups constitute the leading firms in India, Korea, Mexico, Brazil, Argentina, and many other countries. Of the 31 largest private industrial enterprises in the semi-industrial countries in 1987, some 27 were diversified groups that were mostly family controlled (Amsden and Hikino 1994).

Large third-world firms have been increasing their share of world output. In 1962 there existed only four such firms (two from South Africa, one from India, and one from Turkey) among the world's 500 largest industrial enterprises. By 1992 this number had risen to 33, which included 12 Korean companies.[33]

The special characteristics of contemporary giant third-world firms need systematic research. How, for instance, do large Latin American "groups" differ from Asian "groups"? Is it true as some students suggest, that in the typical Latin American "group," corporations control the group bank, while it is the other way around in East Asia?

Our second point relates to the fact that the main part of the present study has emphasized the high corporate rates of savings and investment in East Asian economic development. Apart from its own intrinsic interest, this emphasis is also significant for another important analytical and policy reason. It will be recalled that the recently concluded Uruguay Round agreements have, in addition to promoting trade liberalization, also extended multilateral rules and disciplines to a number of important policy areas

---

[33] The source of these data is Amsden and Hikino (1994).

affecting industrial development and competitiveness with regard to both goods and services. As noted earlier, such policies—generally defined as industrial policies—have been extensively used by fast-growing East Asian countries to foster exports and to achieve rapid structural change and economic growth. A number of these policies, however, will fall foul of the aforementioned new agreements, particularly in respect to provisions on trade-related investment measures (TRIMS) (see also Singh 1996a). This limitation could seriously handicap developing countries that wish to emulate the example of the successful East Asian economies.

There is, however, a way out of this predicament. Even though the post-Uruguay Round trading regime may restrict the use of a number of industrial-policy instruments with respect to export promotion and import control, it does not regulate government policies toward domestic savings and investment. In analytical terms, the focus on raising the propensities to save and invest can be regarded as an alternative way of enhancing a country's long-term international competitiveness.

Historically, the East Asian governments have promoted international competitiveness by following both sets of policies simultaneously—that is, their normal industrial and commercial policies with respect to exports and imports, as well as policies that specifically enhance savings and investment. This pursuit of complementary means to attain the same ends would appear to be the optimal policy stance, for even if one set of measures does not fully succeed, the other set may work better and help achieve the objective. But, if the WTO regime in time effectively rules out traditional industrial policy, the other policy measures acting on the propensities to save and invest can by themselves still promote technical change and international competitiveness, particularly for the more developed of the industrializing countries (for example, Malaysia, Korea, or Thailand).

The third implication that our analysis of savings, investment, and profits has for development thinking concerns income distribution and wealth distribution. A striking aspect of the success of the exemplar East Asian countries is that they have been able to achieve fast economic growth while maintaining a relatively equitable distribution of income. Nevertheless, an important question is, "What has happened to wealth distribution?" It is well known that in Japan and Korea, the land reform under U.S. auspices led to a relatively equitable initial distribution of income and wealth. But in these countries' subsequent industrialization, the level of corporate profits, savings, and investment increased enormously. Industrial concentration may not have increased, but it has remained high (Amsden and Singh 1994). One would expect in these circumstances that, other things being equal, wealth distribution in the urban economy will become more unequal. UNCTAD (1994) suggests that there exists indirect evidence that this scenario has in fact already occurred. If so, it may be necessary to revise extant political-economy interpretations that assume that neither income distribution nor wealth distribution has worsened in the East Asian economies.[34]

---

[34] See for example Alesina and Perotti (1996), or Alesina and Rodrik (1994a).

The question of wealth distribution in these countries therefore requires systematic research. If wealth distribution—despite high corporate profits, savings, and investments—did not become more unequal over time, then what market or nonmarket mechanisms prevented that? If it did become more unequal, then what are the implications for the political economy of these countries? In principle it is quite possible that even if there is no trade-off between growth and income inequality, there may well be one between growth and wealth inequality.

Lessons for Latin America?

Let us turn now to the more difficult question: What are the lessons of the East Asian story for Latin American countries? Can the Latin Americans learn anything from the East Asians about such things as how to improve their corporate savings and investment record? This whole issue of lessons to be learned is a complex one. The results of the East Asian experience are clear enough, but there does not appear to exist at present the appropriate political conjuncture for Latin Americans to be willing either to heed such advice or to learn from that experience.

The present Latin American political conjuncture—at which most governments in the region are in one form or another following the Washington consensus and abandoning long-held *dirigiste* policies—coincides with a broader movement in the world economy toward liberalization and globalization. In this overall context, the following points in relation to the relevance of the East Asian experience for Latin America are perhaps significant.

First, the successful East Asian countries clearly have not followed the "market-friendly" approach as enunciated in its classic form in World Bank (1991). "Market-friendliness" can mean all things to all people. In order, therefore, to prevent the concept from degenerating into a mere tautology, the World Bank (1991), to its credit, has defined the "market-friendly" governmental stance fairly precisely as follows: a) intervene reluctantly, b) apply checks and balances, and c) intervene openly.[35] As is evident from the discussion in the present paper as well as from much scholarship in this area,[36] the East Asian governments did not intervene reluctantly: rather, they pursued vigorous and purposeful industrial policies.[37] Nor did they intervene openly or transparently, as evidenced by the widespread use of administrative guidance. They did, however, apply checks and balances in the form of performance standards (notably with respect to exports) in return for subsidies and other government concessions. In relation to corporate investment and savings, the government again, as seen in previous sections, had a major role in raising and maintaining at a high level the corporate propensity to invest. It used, among other things, financial policy and policy on trade and competition to create

---

[35] There occurred some confusion on this point at the conference, when one of the participants wrongly thought that this was the present author's definition of "market friendly" rather than that of the World Bank (1991).

[36] See Amsden (1989), Wade (1990), and Singh (1995a and 1995b).

[37] There exists dispute about the effectiveness of industrial policy, but most economists—including the World Bank (1993)—do accept that such *dirigiste* policies were actually implemented by the successful East Asian States.

"rents" that boosted corporate profits; it also took steps to ensure that such rents were not consumed but translated instead into investment. With the blessings of the government, if not with its outright control, the financial system worked in such a way that business managers were able to pursue long-term investment strategies rather than being constrained by short-term goals of profitability and earnings per share. Thus, these prolonged high corporate investment rates that have been so crucial to East Asian growth were not simply the result of getting the macroeconomic fundamentals right and of achieving low and stable inflation, but rather the outcome of a visible process of government intervention.

Second, in the current world context of liberalization and globalization, the East Asians have been reluctant liberalizers. Contrary to the thrust of the Bretton Woods Institutions, the East Asian countries during the last three decades have not sought close integration with the world economy but have instead sought what the present author has elsewhere termed a "strategic integration"[38]—that is, they have integrated to the degree to which and in the spheres in which it was in their interest to do so. Thus, they have traditionally been open with respect to exports but not so open with respect to imports. As noted in the first part of the present essay, by the year 2000 South Korea is expected to become the fourth-largest car producer in the world, and it already has sizable exports to the United States and Western Europe; yet in 1995 Korea itself imported only four thousand cars. Many students of the Japanese economy would endorse the following recent complaint[39] (although somewhat self-serving) from the Federation of Swedish Industries concerning the "Asian way" of doing business:

> ...it is necessary to face the new challenges presented to the present international trading system by "the Asian way" of regulation and of business. So far this challenge has been encountered mainly in relation to Japan, which has adhered to (almost) every letter in the GATT agreement, and at the same time managed to circumvent the spirit of the agreement by maintaining various formal and informal nontariff barriers to imports, which have resulted in continued large surpluses. Only recently have these barriers begun to be dismantled, but the surplus is still large. These barriers combined with structural surpluses have shaken the confidence of the general public and of many economic operators in the fairness of the system, and contributed to continuous and rising pressures for increased protection in Europe and in North America from sectors which feel hurt by such policies. We also see the Koreans and the Chinese emulating important parts of the Japanese practices, while the records of Southeast Asian nations are more mixed.[40]

The East Asians have similarly been less than enthusiastic in implementing financial liberalization.

---

[38] See also Singh (1994b).
[39] See for example Johnson, Tyson, and Zysman (1989).
[40] See Hagdahl and Ekdadl (1996, p. 11).

Third, in relation to both trade liberalization and financial liberalization, the contrast between the East Asian and the Latin American countries could not be more striking: the Latin Americans have enthusiastically reduced tariffs and other trade barriers as well as capital controls.[41] The central issue now is whether or not the liberalization experiment will succeed in terms of evoking an adequate supply response. Although the jury is still out, thus far the evidence is not very favorable to the Washington consensus. Despite the huge capital inflows in the 1990s,[42] the Latin American growth rate in the first half of the decade has been only about 3 percent per annum, or roughly half the long-term rate (6 percent per annum between 1965 and 1980, as shown in Table 3.1) that was achieved in the bad old days of *dirigiste* policies. More importantly, the recent growth rate is also coincidentally less than half the rate required (based on past statistical relationships) in order to provide remunerative employment for merely the new entrants into the fast-growing Latin American labor force.[43] Similarly, in relation to corporate profits and investment, Palma (1996) reports for a sample of six Latin American countries for which he had comparable data that although the share of profits in GNP in these economies increased by 10 percentage points (from 50 percent to 60 percent) with the recovery that started in 1987, corporate savings and investment hardly increased at all. Evidence exists also that the commodity composition of Latin American exports is moving in the adverse direction—that is, toward those products for which world demand is expected to grow slowly.[44]

It would appear to an observer of Asian economic development that the precipitate and uncontrolled trade liberalization that occurred in Latin America in the 1980s was probably not well timed. This trade liberalization took place when Latin American industry was competitively weak from the low levels of investment during the debt crisis. The situation seems to have been made doubly difficult for the real economy in many countries by the financial liberalization implemented toward the end of that same decade. In the wake of the financial crisis that overwhelmed Mexico in December 1994, Latin American economies have already paid a heavy price for this financial liberalization in terms of loss of output. Portfolio investment and stock markets have played a key role in the internal and external financial liberalization that has taken place. Apart from the macroeconomic effects of financial liberalization, it is arguable that the consequent growing hegemony of the stock market in these economies may, at the microeconomic level, hinder rather than help industrialization and economic growth. Long ago Keynes (1936, p. 139) observed that "when the capital development of a country becomes the by-product of the activities of a casino, the job is likely to be ill done." Enormous fluctuations have occurred on the Latin American stock markets in the recent period unre-

---

[41] For an interesting analysis of the reasons for the Latin American enthusiasm for liberalization, see Rodrik (1994b) and Krugman (1995).

[42] During the period 1992–1994, net capital inflows into Latin America reached 5 percent of GDP (at current prices), exceeding the previous historical peak figure of 4.5 percent (1977–1981). See also Devlin et al. (1995).

[43] See also Singh and Zammit (1995).

[44] UNCTAD (1996b).

lated to any changes in the fundamentals,[45]—which would appear to confirm Keynes' characterization of such markets as casinos. Even if Latin American industry can bear the burden of trade liberalization, the added weight of financial liberalization may prove to be crippling.[46]

Still, in any case, the jury on the supply response and the real economy is still out. But if adequate supply response does continue to be elusive, at what point will the architects of the Washington consensus be willing to admit that the experiment has failed?

Postscript

In response to the foregoing question, which concluded the present paper as it was actually presented at the conference, John Williamson, in an intervention, provided a clear answer: he thought that five more years were needed for properly assessing the validity of the policy program prescribed by the Washington consensus. Andrés Bianchi, in making an eloquent intervention in support of John Williamson's plea that more time is required, pointed out that the Latin American country in which these ideas have been implemented the longest is Chile, where they have in fact been extremely successful. And in a commentary on the original paper, Professor Francis Lui drew attention to the case of Hong Kong as an East Asian example of fast economic development that did not require dirigiste policies.

These and other interventions and comments were very helpful, as they allow us now to explore a bit further the ideas put forward in the final section of our original essay. It will be useful to begin by commenting briefly on the cases of Chile and Hong Kong before directly discussing John Williamson's idea of allowing "five more years" for the neoliberal program.

Chile

Andrés Bianchi is of course quite right to draw attention to the case of Chile, which alone among Latin American economies has achieved successful economic growth over the last ten years. The Chilean example, however, immediately raises the question, "Why has that particular country's real economy responded successfully and adequately to Washington consensus policies while the economies of the other countries of the region have not?" Leaving aside for now the question of the long-term sustainability of the Chilean model, Chile's success suggests the Chilean political economy may have unique aspects not present in other Latin American countries. Thus, even if the Chilean model were found to be sustainable, it might not be replicable in other countries on the continent.

The two primary unique features of the Chilean political economy that come immediately to mind are the Pinochet military dictatorship that assumed power in 1973 and the associated early introduction of the neoliberal model in that country. The latter

---

[45] El-Efrain and Kumar (1995) report that between 1983 and 1993, stock market volatility in Mexico was nearly fifteen times as large as that in the United States or Japan. See also Smith and Walter (1996) and Calvo *et al.* (1996).

[46] For a fuller discussion of the issues raised in this paragraph, see Singh (1997a and 1997b).

involved internal and external liberalization, including, notably, the destruction of the power of the trade unions and the consequent more or less complete deregulation of the labor market. In the external sphere, Chile abolished all nontariff barriers and over a relatively short period thereafter reduced tariffs to an average level of 10 percent.[47] This regime of more or less free trade was combined with the liberalization of capital movements. In the event, the neoliberal model was not successful in the first decade of its operation. During the 1978–1981 period, unregulated capital flows resulted in a huge surge of loans from abroad, contracted mainly by the private sector. This capital influx led to an unsustainable appreciation of the currency, and the ensuing financial crisis resulted in a huge 15 percent reduction in GDP during the depression of 1982–1983.

The recovery from the depression and the fast economic growth of the 1980s were greatly facilitated by the rise in copper prices in 1987 and by another surge in capital inflows (which began in Chile somewhat earlier than in other Latin American countries).[48] Importantly, these favorable external shocks were translated into sustained growth by two major basic factors: exchange rate management and a relatively unregulated labor market.

With respect to the first factor, the government of Chile, having learned the hard lessons of the previous surge of capital inflows, has in the recent period adopted highly pragmatic and interventionist policies toward such inflows and toward the management of the exchange rate. Government now fully recognizes that it is important for exports and for the real economy that a competitive real exchange rate be maintained, and it acknowledges that the exchange rate level cannot simply be left to market forces. Consequently, Chilean authorities have adopted policies to influence both the level and the composition of capital inflows, encouraging long-term inflows such as FDI and discouraging speculative short-term capital flows. Ffrench-Davis, Agosin, and Uthoff (1995) note that the government has used four basic instruments to neutralize any effects that, as a result of the influx of short-term capital, may be inconsistent with the objectives of Chile's export development strategy. These instruments are the following: the application of taxes and reserve requirements to capital inflows; an exchange rate policy based on dirty floating of the exchange rate in relation to a reference value pegged to a basket of currencies; open-market operations to sterilize the monetary effects of exchange rate dealings; and the prudent supervision of financial markets.

The second major factor that has been important to the Chilean success and to the authorities' ability to maintain a competitive real exchange rate derives from the fact that the labor markets in Chile are more unregulated and "flexible" than in other countries. Consequently, unlike a number of other Latin American economies, Chile does not have

---

[47] Chile has had two trade liberalization programs since 1973: a radical scheme in the years 1974–1979 and a more moderate one in 1985–1991. The 10 percent uniform tariff introduced under the first program remained in force until 1982. After being raised to 35 percent in 1984, import duties were reduced to 20 percent in 1985, to 15 percent in 1988, and to 11 percent in 1991 (ECLAC 1995).

[48] The rise in copper prices not only helped alleviate the balance-of-payments constraint but also (because the copper sector was state owned) made a sizable contribution toward correcting the fiscal disequilibrium. Copper exports rose from 5.2 percent of GDP in 1981 to 14.1 percent in 1987–1988. See also Frenkel (1995).

TABLE 3.10. Sectorial Orientation of Exports of Selected Developing Countries, 1990
(Share in total exports of goods in fast-growing OECD import sectors*)

Country		Country	
Hong Kong	91.0	Mexico	61.2
Taiwan, POC	83.9	Tunisia	57.9
Singapore	83.3	Morocco	49.8
Republic of Korea	82.0	Turkey	49.4
Thailand	66.7	Indonesia	39.5
Malaysia	60.8	Argentina	20.9
Brazil	35.5	Colombia	16.0
		Chile	12.3

Source: (UNCTAD) 1996b). Original source: ECLAC, Database on Comparative Analysis of Nations.
* A fast-growing OECD import sector is defined as one in which imports into OECD countries as a proportion of total OECD imports rose from 1963 to 1990.

to use the nominal exchange rate as an anchor to reduce inflationary expectations. (Such policies, experience suggests, inevitably lead to real appreciation of the currency during episodes of capital surges.)

Notwithstanding Chile's undoubted success both in exports and overall economic growth in the last ten years, important questions arise regarding how good an example that economy is for other countries to emulate and regarding the sustainability of the Chilean export performance. Chile's exports are essentially based on local natural resources and are largely unprocessed. Compared with the levels set by the Asian NICs, Chile's manufactured exports are insignificant: only $1.3 billion in 1992 versus, for example, $70 billion for Taiwan the same year. Taiwan's population is about one-third larger than that of Chile, but even on a per capita basis, Chile's exports were $96 per capita and Taiwan's $3500.

Furthermore, as Table 3.10 suggests, the structural composition of Chilean exports is the most unfavorable among the 15 leading industrializing countries in the sample. Only 12 percent of Chile's exports to the OECD countries go to the 20 dynamic sectors in which demand is growing fastest. The corresponding figures for the first-tier Asian NICs (Hong Kong, South Korea, Taiwan) are all at least 80 percent. Chile is often compared with the second-tier NICs (Indonesia, Malaysia, Thailand), in terms of its export achievement; however, the shares of the latter countries' exports going to the most dynamic sectors of OECD demand are 40 percent (Indonesia), 61 percent (Malaysia), 67 percent (Thailand). Indeed, Table 3.10 suggests that among the Latin American countries the Mexican (61 percent) and Brazilian (36 percent) export structures are much more dynamic than that of Chile.

Of course, it could be argued that despite an unfavorable structural composition of its exports, a country can still achieve fast expansion by increasing its export share even in slow-growing markets—which is in fact exactly what Chile has done over the last decade or more. This approach will, however, become more difficult in the future as Chilean real wages rise: not only do most Chilean exports go to sectors in which demand growth is slow but also in many of those exports, the scope for further productivity im-

TABLE 3.11. Dynamism and Competitiveness of Exports from Selected Asian and Latin American Developing Countries, 1990

(Percentages)

	H/C	L/C	H/U	L/U
Republic of Korea	82.9	17.1	0.0	0.0
Taiwan, POC	83.8	15.2	0.0	0.0
Hong Kong	43.8	6.3	47.2	2.7
Singapore	83.4	16.0	0.0	0.6
Malaysia	60.7	39.3	0.0	0.0
Indonesia	43.8	6.3	47.2	2.7
Thailand	66.6	31.3	0.0	2.3
Mexico	59.1	34.4	2.0	4.5
Brazil	33.7	53.3	1.8	11.2
Argentina	17.6	36.8	3.3	42.3
Chile	11.4	46.7	0.9	41.0

Source: Adapted from UNCTAD (1996b).
See note in UNCTAD *Trade and Development Report* (1996b, p. 127).

provements may be limited. Data presented in Table 3.11 suggest that of the more than 80 percent of Chilean exports that go to the less dynamic sectors, in about half of these Chile was increasing its market share while in the other half, the Chilean share was declining. (In the small dynamic portion of its exports, Chile did have a rising market share). By way of contrast, in the case of Korea, not only were most (82 percent) of its exports in the dynamic sectors (see Table 3.10) but also that country had an increased market share in 83 percent of these dynamic products (Table 3.11). In general, the essential explanation for the export dynamism of Asian NICs lies in their purposive industrial-policy program to upgrade their respective industrial and export structures continuosly as real wages rise. This approach accords with the "flying-geese" pattern of development ascribed to the Asian countries.[49] Chile has also upgraded its exports over the last twenty years, but the improvements have been confined to restructuring within the slow-growing sectors rather than pursuit of a progressive movement toward the more dynamic sectors. Lall (1995, p. 151) observes the following:

> ...despite two decades of stringent policy reforms intended to free its economy from government intervention, Chile has failed to transform its manufacturing sector into an engine of export growth. It has not been able to "do a Taiwan China." It is not that Chile lacks the human resources it needs to develop its industrial exports. It has one of the best educational systems in Latin America, as well as a base of entrepreneurship and substantial experience with industrialization as far back as the nineteenth century.... The presence of human capital has helped Chile in boosting resource-based exports, but the creation of new competitive advantages in industry has been severely constrained, in the absence of policy support, by the learning costs inherent in upgrading and deepening industry.

---

[49] There exists a large literature on this subject. For a recent review, see Rowthorn (1996).

Hong Kong

Hong Kong certainly is an example of an East Asian state that has followed broadly *laissez-faire* policies with regard to trade and capital flows and has achieved fast economic growth. Nevertheless, as in the case of Chile, certain special features of the Hong Kong situation require attention.

Hong Kong started with the enormous advantage of a pool of skilled labor and entrepreneurs with capital who migrated from Shanghai after the Chinese revolution. Furthermore, Hong Kong has long been an entrepôt city with well-established firms possessing considerable export capabilities. There has therefore existed much less need than in other NICs for the government to intervene to build up production and export capacities.

Even so, Hong Kong has not been as successful as some of the other Asian NICs in upgrading its industrial and export structures. More than 90 percent of Hong Kong's exports are in the dynamic sectors (Table 3.10), but in about half of them Hong Kong has been losing its market share (Table 3.11). Rising real wages in the colony have led to the relocation of its industry abroad (mainly to mainland China). Consequently, Hong Kong has suffered massive deindustrialization in the last ten years, with a 35 percent fall in manufacturing employment. Hong Kong's decision makers are apparently deeply concerned about the erosion of the city's industrial base. The *Financial Times* (1993) noted the following in its survey of Hong Kong:

> The *laissez-faire* prop against which the Hong Kong government has leaned since 1841 has prevented it from adopting the ambitious strategies that have spawned the computer components and telecommunications products of Singapore, South Korea and Taiwan. But as Hong Kong continues to evolve into a financial and services centre, the pressures of some of the highest land and labor costs in Asia appear to have given the government second thoughts about its stance.... The government is taking serious measures to encourage the inflow of overseas technologies, so that Hong Kong can retain some kind of industrial base.... The government has toned down its *laissez-faire* inclinations to permit a new applied research and development scheme. This is a $HK 200m. fund that will match the investment of any start-up company that fulfills certain criteria, in exchange for an equity stake. This represents the first step toward direct government funding for research and development, and by implication, the creation of a government industrial policy.[50]

Even despite the deindustrialization, the Hong Kong economy has continued to prosper, because the colony has been able to shift from manufacturing into high-value financial services. It is perfectly possible for a city-state with a small population and an increasingly industrialized hinterland to exist largely, if not entirely, on the basis of the production and export of services. But for most countries, this model is normally not feasible because of the high income elasticity of demand for manufactures and the much

---

[50] Quoted in Lall (1995, p. 139).

more limited scope for the exports of services relative to that of exports of industrial products.[51]

"Five More Years"

At one level, John Williamson's suggestion that the Washington consensus (WC) program requires five more years to show its full results perhaps seems reasonable. The program embodies enormous institutional changes domestically (a much-diminished role for the state and a correspondingly far larger space for the markets to function freely) and great changes also in the external sphere (a move away from a "sheltered" economy toward greater openness and toward much closer integration with the world economy). It clearly takes time for economic agents to accept and adapt to far-reaching environmental changes of this type and magnitude.

Unfortunately, however, the WC program is not a mere scientific experiment to advance the cause of economics or of social science but a reality that affects the actual lives and well-being of hundreds of millions of people. Citizens of Mexico, for example, have already waited for more than ten years; Mexico, after all, has been Washington's star pupil ever since the beginning of the debt crisis in the early 1980s. The Mexican people and those in a number of other Latin American countries may simply not be prepared to wait for another five years, particularly if the program continues not to work in terms of real economic growth, jobs, and poverty alleviation. The result may then be another violent pendulum swing that could go too far in the other direction and thereby jeopardize such gains as the WC has secured in the sphere of stabilization (for instance, the correction of fiscal disequilibriums in many countries). Two leading proponents of the WC reform, Burki and Edwards (1996),[52] have recently noted the following:

> The slow recovery of the...(Latin American) economies is troublesome for a number of economic, social and political reasons. In many countries, modest economic performance over the last few years is generating impatience and a sense of disappointment with the reform process. An increasing number of people are disillusioned and beginning to look at alternative policies. Although this disenchantment has not been translated into an activist "anti-reform" movement, it is slowly generating "reform-skepticism." What makes this particularly disturbing is that the reform-skeptics do not have a coherent plan and tend to offer an assortment of mutually inconsistent policies with an unmistakable populist flavor.

Burki and Edwards go on to suggest the following:

> The sluggish behavior of...(Latin American) labor markets—low wages and slow employment creation—constitutes one of the gravest concerns of Latin American populations and has serious economic, social and political con-

---

[51] See also Singh (1977 and 1987), and Rowthorn and Wells (1987).

[52] Mr. Shahid Burki is the Regional Vice-President for the Latin American and Caribbean Region at the World Bank. Professor Sebastian Edwards is a consultant to the World Bank.

sequences. It contributes to poverty—many of the poor are unemployed, or employed at very low wages in the informal sector—and it erodes the political support for reformist governments. There is some preliminary evidence suggesting that in many—if not in most—Latin American countries the positive impact of lowered inflation on political support is beginning to fade and voters are now demanding improved performance in terms of higher growth, wages and employment. If these are not delivered, it is likely that voters will begin to desert the reformist ranks, increasing the risk of populist relapse.

If in the light of the foregoing considerations five years would appear to be too long to wait, then can anything be done in the interim? Burki and Edwards prescribe a continuation of the reform process toward its next phase. They acknowledge that these "institutional second-generation" reforms are technically very difficult and are likely to take time to be implemented and to generate their beneficial effects. Countries will tend to proceed cautiously and are likely to make mistakes. This process may generate frustration and, at times, disenchantment. A great deal of leadership and consensus building will be needed to push forward with the much needed next phase of the reform process. Specifically, for the two World Bank economists the next phase of the WC would give priority to the reform of the labor market and of the educational and health systems, and above all it would redefine the role of the state. The latter, in this conception, would essentially be a "night watchman," if not a "minimalist" state.

Although the Burki and Edwards assessment of the gravity of the present situation is well taken, there do exist difficulties with their diagnosis and remedies. Two points are particularly problematical. The first point is that the two authors ascribe low wages and the rise in unemployment and underemployment in Latin American countries largely to the rigidities of the labor market—a conclusion that is difficult to accept in the light of evidence over the last 15 years. In static terms, there may well exist many rigidities and imperfections in Latin American labor markets, but it is important to appreciate that over time these labor markets have responded well and quickly to economic changes. Real wages fell by as much as 50 percent in countries like Mexico during the economic downturn of the 1980s and rose somewhat in the subsequent upturn. In other words, labor markets have been dynamically flexible. True, real wages in Mexico or in other countries have not been as flexible as in Chile. But even if that degree of wage flexibility were desirable for most Latin American countries, it would not be feasible in their present democratic context.

The second main difficulty with the Burki-Edwards proposals is that these proposals involve further institutional changes likely to be a long time in coming. The proposed "second-generation" reforms do not address the question of people's present frustrations and impatience with the WC policies—a central issue that the two authors themselves highlight, as seen earlier.

In the spirit of stimulating a constructive debate, the present essay proposes a rather different course of action. The underlying hypothesis here is that under the aegis of the WC, the Latin American countries opened up too much and too suddenly to the international economy, both in the financial and product markets, and were unable to sustain a desirable current-account position at the socially necessary GDP growth rate of 5 percent to 6 percent per annum. This hypothesis is motivated by the Asian experience and the analytical considerations presented in the main body of the present paper.

If this analysis is correct, then as a minimum the Latin American countries should carefully control financial flows. The volatility of unregulated international capital flows leads to fluctuations in exchange rates and stock market prices. The interaction between these two inherently unstable markets often leads to a negative feedback loop that in turn generates fluctuations in real economic variables (consumption, investment, exports, and the like). All of this creates an unstable and uncertain economic environment that inevitably affects the private sector's inducement to invest. Further, in view of the apparently high income elasticity and low price elasticity of the demand for imports by Latin American consumers, the speed and the degree of trade openness thus far implemented also need to be questioned. The latter measures may have assisted stabilization, but they have evidently not been helpful to Latin American industry. The result is that many Latin American economies are running sizable current-account deficits even when they are operating well below their productive potential or the socially necessary growth rates. Thus, some import controls—particularly against luxury products—not only will be directly helpful to the real economy by alleviating the balance-of-payments constraint but also may help to raise the propensity to save. Taylor and Piper (1996) note that during the recent period, under the combined impact of trade liberalization and financial liberalization Mexican private savings have fallen from 15 percent of GDP to 5 percent.

To sum up, instead of a doctrinaire pursuit of more or less free trade and of virtually unimpeded capital flows, what is being proposed here to assist the Latin American real economy in the short to medium term is a set of pragmatic policies. These policies will involve, among other things, a considerable regulation of external-capital flows and preferably also a relatively modest degree of control over imports. Unfettered capital markets and unrestricted trade liberalization would not appear to represent the optimal degree of openness for most Latin American economies at the present juncture.

REFERENCES

Abegglen, J.C., and G.C. Stalk. *The Japanese Corporation.* New York: Basic Books Inc., 1995.

Ackley, G., and H. Ishi. "Fiscal, Monetary and Related Policies." In H. Patrick and H. Rosovsky, eds., *Asia's New Giant: How the Japanese Economy Works.* Washington, D.C.: The Brookings Institution, 1976.

Agosin, M., D. Tussie, and G. Crespi. "Developing Countries and the Uruguay Round: An Evaluation and Issues for the Future". In *UNCTAD (1995).*

Akyuz, Y., and C. Gore. "The Investment-Profits Nexus in East Asian Industrialisation." *World Development* 24, 3 (March 1996).

Alesina, A., and R. Perotti. "Income Distribution, Political Instability and Investment." *European Economic Review* 40, 6: 1203–28 (1996).

_____, and D. Rodrik. "Income Distribution and Economic Growth: A Simple Theory and Some Empirical Evidence." In Alex Cukierman, Zvi Hercovitz and Leonardo Leiderman, eds., *The Political Economy of Business Cycles and Growth.* Cambridge: MIT Press, 1993.

Amsden, A. *Asia's Next Giant.* New York: Oxford University Press, 1989.

_____. "Review of World Bank, 1993." *World Development* 22, 4 (1994a).

_____. "Big-Business-Focused Industrialisation in South Korea." In A.D. Chandler, T. Hikino and F. Amatore, eds., *Big Business and the Wealth of Nations in the Past Century, 1880s–1980s.* Cambridge: Cambridge University Press, 1994b.

_____, and T. Hikino. "Project Execution Capability, Organizational Know-How and Conglomerate Corporate Growth in Late Industrialization." *Industrial and Corporate Change* 3 (1994).

_____, and A. Singh. "The Optimal Degree of Competition and Dynamic Efficiency in Japan and Korea." *European Economic Review* 38, 3/4: 941–51 (April 1994).

Aoki, M. "Toward an Economic Model of the Japanese Firm." *Journal of Economic Literature* XXVIII: 1–27 (March 1990).

_____, and R. Dore. *The Japanese Firm: The Sources of Competitive Strength.* Oxford and New York: Clarendon Press, 1994.

_____, and H. Patrick. *The Japanese Main Bank System: Its Relevance for Developing and Transforming Economies.* Oxford: Oxford University Press, 1994.

Asian Development Bank. *Key Indicators of Developing Asian and Pacific Countries* XXXVI. London: Oxford University Press, 1995.

Blaine, M. "Profitability and Competitiveness: Lessons from Japanese and American Firms in the 1980s." *California Management Review* 36: 48–74 (Autumm 1993).

Boltho, A. *Japan: An Economic Survey 1953–1973.* London: Oxford University Press, 1975.

_____. "Was Japan's Industrial Policy Successful?" *Cambridge Journal of Economics* 9, 2 (June 1985).

Burki, S.J., and S. Edwards. *Dismantling the Populist State: The Unfinished Revolution in Latin America and the Caribbean.* World Bank Latin American and Caribbean Studies. Washington D.C.: World Bank, 1996.

Calvo, G.A., L. Leiderman, and C.M. Reinhart. "Inflows of Capital to Developing Countries in the 1990s." *The Journal of Economic Perspectives* 10, 2: 123–39 (1996).

Caves, R.E., and M. Uekusa. "Industrial Organization." In Hugh Patrick and Henry Rosovsky, eds., *Asia's New Giant*. Washington, D.C.: The Brookings Institution, 1976a.

____. *Industrial Organization in Japan*. Washington, D.C.: The Brookings Institution, 1976b.

CEPG (Cambridge Economic Policy Group). *Economic Policy Reviews* 5 (1979).

Chang, Ha-Joon. *The Political Economy of Industrial Policy.* New York: St. Martins Press, 1994.

Cho, Y.D. "Financial Factors and Corporate Investment: A Microeconometric Analysis of Korean Manufacturing Firms." Ph.D. Dissertation. University of Oxford, 1995.

Cho, Yoon Je, and D. Khatkhate. "Financial Liberalisation: Issues and Evidence." *Economic and Political Weekly* 20 (May 1989).

Cosh, A., A. Hughes, and A. Singh. "Takeovers and Short-Termism in the UK." *Industrial Policy Paper* 3. London: Institute for Public Policy Research, 1990.

De Long, B., and L.H. Summers. "How Robust is the Growth-Machinery Nexus?." In M. Baldassari, L. Paganetto, and E. Phelps, eds., *International Differences in Growth Rates*. New York: St. Martins Press, 1994.

Dertouzos, M., R. Lester, and R. Solow, eds., *Made in America*. Cambridge: The MIT Press, 1989.

Devlin, R., R. Ffrench-Davis, and S. Griffith-Jones. "Surges in Capital Flows and Development: An Overview of Policy Issues in the Nineties." In R. Ffrench-Davis and S. Griffith-Jones, eds., *Coping with Capital Surges: The Return to Finance in Latin America*. Lynne Rienner, Boulder and London: Lynne Rienne, 1995.

Dornbusch, R., and Y. Park. "Korean Growth Policy." *Brookings Papers on Economic Activity* 2 (1987).

Doyukai, K. "Kigyo Hakusko, 1985: Saika no Jidai." (Report on Japanese Firms, 1985: The Age of Differentiation.) Cited in Kojima, 1995.

ECLAC. *Statistical Yearbook for Latin America and the Caribbean*. Santiago: ECLAC, 1995.

Edwards, S. "Why Are Savings Rates So Different Across Countries?: An International Comparative Analysis." *NBER Working Paper* 5097. New York: National Bureau of Economic Research, 1995.

El-Erian, M.A., and M.S. Kumar. "Emerging Equity Markets in Middle Eastern Countries." Paper presented at the World Bank Conference on Stock Markets, Corporate Finance and Economic Growth. Washington, D.C. (February 1995).

Felix, D. "Industrial Development in East Asia: What Are the Lessons for Latin America?" *UNCTAD Discussion Paper* 84. Geneva: UNCTAD, 1994.

Financial Times. "Survey of Hong Kong." May 4, 1993 (p. 6).

Fishlow, A., C. Gwin, S. Haggard, D. Rodrik, and R. Wade. *Miracle or Design: Lessons from the East Asian Experience*. Washington, D.C.: Overseas Development Council, 1994.

Frank, J., and C. Mayer. "Capital Markets and Corporate Control: A Study of France, Germany and the UK." *Economic Policy* (1990).

Ffrench-Davis, R., M. Agosin, and A. Uthoff. "Capital Movements, Export Strategy and Macroeconomic Stability in Chile in the Nineties." In R. Ffrench-Davis and S. Griffith-Jones, eds., *Coping with Capital Surges: The Return to Finance in Latin America.* Lynne Rienner, Boulder and London: Lynne Rienner, 1995.

Frenkel, R. "Macroeconomic Sustainability and Development Prospects: Latin American Performance in the 1990s." *UNCTAD Discussion Paper.* Geneva: UNCTAD, 1995.

Froot, K.A., A.F. Perold, and J.C. Stein. "Shareholder Trading Practices and Corporate Investment Horizons." *Journal of Applied Corporate Finance* 5: 42–58 (Summer 1992).

Greenaway, D., and C. Milner. *The Uruguay Round and Commonwealth Developing Countries: An Assessment.* Report to the Commonwealth Secretariat. February 1995.

Hagdahl, T., and H. Ekdahl. "Market Access in High-Growth Asian Markets." *Trade Policy* 3 (June 1996). (Federation of Swedish Industries.)

Honohan, P., and I. Atiyas. "Intersectoral Financial Flows in Developing Countries." *The Economic Journal* 103: 666–79. (May 1993).

ILO. *World Employment Report.* Geneva: ILO 1995.

ILO. *Employment Policies in a Global Context.* Report V. Geneva: ILO 1996.

IMF. *World Economic Outlook.* May 1995.

Ito, Takatoshi, and A. Krueger. *Growth Theories in Light of the East Asian Experience.* Chicago, London: The University of Chicago Press, 1995.

Jacobson, R., and D. Aaker. "Myopic Management Behaviour with Efficient, but Imperfect, Financial Markets: A Comparison of Information Asymmetries in the US and Japan." *Journal of Accounting and Economics* 16: 383–405 (1993).

Jang, Ha Won. "Phases of Capital Accumulation in Korea and Evolution of Government Growth Strategy, 1963–1990." Ph.D. dissertation. University of Oxford, 1995.

Japan Development Bank and Japan Economic Research Institute (JDB/JERI). *Policy-Based Finance: The Experience of Post-War Japan.* Final Report for the World Bank, 1993.

Johnson, C., L. Tyson, and J. Zysman. *Politics and Productivity.* New York: Harper Business, 1989.

Kaldor, N. "Capital Accumulation and Economic Growth." In F. Lutz, ed., *Theory of Capital.* London: Macmillan, 1961.

_____. *Causes of the Slow Rate of Economic Growth in the United Kingdom.* Cambridge: Cambridge University Press, 1965.

_____. *Strategic Factors in Economic Development.* New York: Cornell University Press, 1967.

Kojima, K. "An International Perspective on Japanese Corporate Finance." *RIEB Kobe University Discussion Paper* 45. March 1995.

Krueger, A.O. "East Asian Experience and Endogenous Growth Theory." In T. Ito and A. Krueger, eds., *Growth Theories in Light of the East Asian Experience.* Chicago, London: The University of Chicago Press, 1995.

Krugman, P. "The Myth of Asia's Miracle." *Foreign Affairs* (pp. 62–78) (Nov./Dec. 1994).

_____. "Dutch Tulips and Emerging Markets." *Foreign Affairs* 74, 4: 28–44 (July/Aug. 1995).

Lall, S. "The Creation of Comparative Advantage: Country Experiences." In Irfan Ul Haque, ed., *Trade, Technology and International Competitiveness.* Washington, D.C.: World Bank, 1995.

Lau, L.J., and J. Kim. "The Sources of Growth of the East Asian Newly Industrialising Countries." *Journal of the Japanese and International Economies* (1994).

Lee, C.H. "The Government, Financial System and Large Private Enterprises in Economic Development of South Korea." *World Development* 20(2): 187–97 (1992).

Lockwood, W.W. "Japan's New Capitalism." Chapter 10. In Lockwood, ed., *State and Economic Enterprise in Japan.* Princeton: Princeton University Press, 1965.

Maddison, A. "A Long Run Perspective on Saving." *Scandinavian Journal of Economics* 94, 2: 181–96 (1992).

Maizels, A. *Industrial Growth and World Trade.* Cambridge: Cambridge University Press, 1963.

Marsh, P. *Short-Termism on Trial.* London: Institutional Fund Managers Association, 1990.

Odagiri, H. *Growth Through Competition, Competition Through Growth: Strategic Management and the Economy in Japan.* Oxford: Clarendon Press, 1994.

_____, and T. Hase. "Are Mergers and Acquisitions Going to Be Popular in Japan Too? An Empirical Study." *International Journal of Industrial Organisation* 7, 1 (1989).

Okimoto, D.I. *Between the MITI and the Market.* Palo Alto: Stanford University Press, 1989.

Overseas Development Institute. "Developing Countries in the WTO." Briefing Paper 3. London: ODI, May 1995.

Palma, G. "Whatever Happened to Latin America's Savings? Comparing Latin American and East Asian Savings Performances." Study 9. Geneva: UNCTAD, 1996.

Porter, M.E. "Capital Disadvantage: Americas Failing Capital Investment System." *Harvard Business Review* (pp. 65–82) (Sept./Oct. 1992).

Rajan, R.G. "Review of M. Aoki and H. Patrick, eds., *The Japanese Main Bank System: Its Relevance for Developing and Transforming Economies. Journal of Economic Literature* XXXIV (Sept. 1996).

Rodrik, D. "King Kong Meets Godzilla: The World Bank and the East Asian Miracle." CEPR Discussion Paper 944. London: Center for Economic Policy Research, 1994a.

_____. "The Rush to Free Trade in the Developing World: Why So Late? Why Now? Will It Last?" In S. Haggard and S.B. Webb, eds., *Voting for Reform: The Politics of Adjustment in New Democracies.* New York: Oxford University Press, 1994b.

_____. "Getting Interventions Right: How South Korea and Taiwan Grew Rich." *Economic Policy* (April 1995).

Rowthorn, R. "East Asian Development: The Flying Geese Paradigm Reconsidered." UNC-TAD Study 8. Geneva: UNCTAD, 1996.

_____, and J.R. Wells *De-Industrialization and Foreign Trade.* Cambridge: Cambridge University Press, 1987.

Scott, B. *A New Theory of Economic Growth.* Oxford: Oxford University Press, 1989.

Shinohara, M. "Patterns and Some Structural Changes in Japan's Post-War Industrial Growth." Chapter 9. In L. Klein and K. Ohkawa, eds., *Economic Growth: The Japanese Experience since the Meiji Era.* Homewood, Illinois: Richard D. Irwin Inc., 1968.

Singh, A. "UK Industry and the World Economy: A Case of De-Industrialization?" *Cambridge Journal of Economics* 1: 113–36 (1977).

_____. "Manufacturing and De-Industrialization." In *The New Palgrave: A Dictionary of Economics*. London: Macmillan, 1987.

_____. "Du Plan au Marché: La Reforme Maitrisée en Chine." *Revue Tiers Monde* XXXV, 139 (July/Sept.1994a).

_____. "Openness and the 'Market-Friendly' Approach to Development: Learning the Right Lessons from Development Experience." *World Development* 22, 12 (Dec. 1994b).

_____. "Growing Independently of the World Economy: Asian Economic Development since 1980." *UNCTAD Review*. Geneva: UNCTAD, 1994c.

_____. "The Causes of Fast Economic Growth in East Asia." *UNCTAD Review*. Geneva: UNCTAD, 1995a.

_____. *Corporate Financing Patterns in Industrializing Economies: A Comparative International Study*. IFC Technical Paper 2. Washington, D.C.: World Bank, 1995b.

_____. "The Anglo-Saxon Market for Corporate Control, the Financial System and International Competitiveness." University of Cambridge Department of Applied Economics *Working Paper* AF16. 1995c.

_____. "Competitive Markets and Economic Development: A Commentary on World Bank Analyses." *International Papers in Political Economy* 2, 1 (1995d).

_____. "The Post-Uruguay Round World Trading System, Industrialisation, Trade and Development." In *Expansion of Trading Opportunities to the Year 2000 for Asia-Pacific Developing Countries*. (pp. 147–88). Geneva: UNCTAD, 1996a.

_____. "Savings, Investment and the Corporation in the East Asian Miracle." UNCTAD Study 9. Geneva: UNCTAD, 1996b.

_____. "The Plan, the Market and Evolutionary Economic Reform in China." In A. Abdullah and A.R. Khan, eds., *State, Market and Development: Essays in Honour of Rehman Sobhan*. Dhaka: The University Press Limited, 1996c.

_____. "Liberalization and Globalization: An Unhealthy Euphoria." Forthcoming in J. Michie and J. Grieve Smith, eds., *Employment and Economic Performance*. 1997a.

_____. "Stock Markets, Financial Liberalization and Economic Development." Forthcoming in *Economic Journal*. 1997b.

_____, and A. Zammit. "Employment and Unemployment, North and South." In J. Michie and J.G. Smith, eds., *Managing the Global Economy*. Oxford: Oxford University Press, 1995.

Smith, R.C., and I. Walter. "Rethinking Emerging Market Equities." Conference on the Future of Emerging Market Capital Flows. New York University (May 1996).

Stein, J. "Takeover Threat and Managerial Myopia." *Journal of Political Economy* 96: 61–80 (1988).

_____. "Efficient Capital Markets, Inefficient Firms: A Model of Myopic Corporate Behaviour." *Quarterly Journal of Economics* 104: 655–69 (1989).

Taylor, L., and U. Piper. "Reconciling Economic Reform and Sustainable Human Development: Social Consequences of Neo-Liberalism." *Discussion Papers Series*. New York: UNDP, 1996.

Tsuru, S. *Japan's Capitalism: Creative Defeat and Beyond.* Cambridge: Cambridge University Press, 1993.

UN *Yearbook of National Accounts Statistics.* Geneva: UN, 1966.

_____. *World Economic Survey.* New York: UN, 1990.

_____. *Transnational Corporations from Developing Countries.* New York: UN, 1993.

UNCTAD. *Trade and Development Report.* Geneva: UNCTAD, 1994.

_____. *International Monetary and Financial Issues for the 1990s: Research Papers for the Group of Twenty Four VI.* Geneva: UNCTAD, 1995.

_____. "East Asian Development: Lessons for a New Global Environment." Study 10. Geneva: UNCTAD, 1996a.

_____. *Trade and Develpoment Report.* Geneva: UNCTAD, 1996b.

Wade, R. *Governing the Market.* Princeton: Princeton University Press, 1990.

Williamson, O.E. *Markets and Hierarchies: Analysis and Antitrust Implications.* New York: The Free Press, 1975.

World Bank. *The Challenge of Development: World Development Report.* Washington, D.C.: World Bank, 1991.

_____. *The East Asian Miracle.* Oxford: Oxford University Press, 1993.

_____. *World Development Report.* Washington, D.C.: World Bank, various years.

Young, A. "Lessons from the East Asian NICs: A Contrarian View." *European Economic Review* 38, 3/4 (April 1994).

Keijiro Otsuka[1] on Ajit Singh's Paper

Catching up with the West: A Perspective on Asian Economic Development and Lessons for Latin America

Dr. Singh's article addresses the important issue of how the East Asian economies have been able to achieve high rates of savings and investment in the course of their miraculous economic growth. Special attention is paid to the relationship between government policies, the corporation, and the financial systems characterizing Japan and Korea. The role of profits in providing the incentives to invest as well as the means to pay for this investment occupies a central place in the analysis.

Singh argues that the pre-1970s high profit rates in Japan were generated to an extent by heavy state interventions such as tax concessions, restriction of domestic competition, trade protection, and low-interest policies; the high profits in turn induced high investment and stimulated high savings. The story of Korea is similar but is characterized by stronger government interventions as reflected in the promotion of the large *chaebol* enterprises and the active role played by state-owned banks. Basically these arguments seem sound and appear to be largely consistent with the existing literature on East Asian economic development—even though the present commentator in no way claims to be a specialist on savings and investment, financial markets, or corporation structures in East Asia.

There does arise, however, one clear objection to Dr. Singh's argument in the final section on "Lessons for Latin America?" in which he says that "it is clear that the successful East Asian countries have not followed the 'market-friendly' approach." Needless to say, the validity of this statement depends on the definition of "market friendliness." Logically speaking, a policy is market friendly if it facilitates or supplements the functioning of markets. As Pranab Bardhan's paper strongly suggests, direct credit allocation and other interventions in financial markets may be market friendly in the light of this definition, as financial markets are inherently imperfect because of imperfect information. In fact, without appropriate government interventions, imperfect information will result in adverse selection and moral hazard. An important point is that interventionist policies in financial markets do not necessarily imply suppression of market forces; they could

---

[1] International Food Policy Research Institute and Tokyo Metropolitan University.

actually support such forces. Therefore, Dr. Singh's argument could possibly give a misleading impression regarding the lessons to be learned from East Asia.

There are certain other issues that Dr. Singh did not adequately address but that are of essential importance and relevance in understanding the high profits, investments, and savings in East Asia. The first comment that comes to mind is centered on the importance of the process of catching up through the importation of advanced technology from the West. In fact, this process has been so important that the term "catching up" in the context of East Asia immediately connotes the successful introduction of modern technology. Dr. Singh does not address the issue of technology except for alluding to the recent work of Young (1994) and Lau and Kim (1994), which demonstrates the small contribution by total factor productivity (TFP) growth to the overall growth of the East Asian economies. The author argues that "the rapid economic expansion achieved by these countries cannot be attributed to the faster growth of their TFP, or the so-called 'residual' that is loosely identified with 'technical progress' in such analysis.... In other words, in terms of TFP methodology, most if not all of the economic growth of countries like Korea can be explained by the fast expansion of factor inputs, including (among other things) capital inputs arising from very high rates of capital accumulation." This statement is perhaps somewhat misleading. How did East Asian economies such as Japan and Korea sustain such heavy investments without facing declining profit rates if technical progress was unimportant? If technology is stagnant and the capital-labor ratio increases, the profitability of investment is bound to decline. The fact that these economies have sustained heavy investment and high profit rates strongly indicates the critical importance of continuous inflows of new technologies that have induced and sustained high rates of investment. In the view of many analysts, MITI's ostensibly interventionist policies were in fact geared toward the successful importation of advanced technology, and a large part of investment in industry was directed to the installation of new equipment embodying new technologies. Without the analysis of technology imports, the analysis of investment and its profitability in the context of East Asia will be incomplete.

Our next comment on the paper relates to our previous comment. The author claims that profitability plays a central role in the analysis of investment behaviors, but his analysis of the determinants of profitability is not really adequate. The profit rates in Japan are analyzed only for the period from 1955 to 1972, when the profitability had been high and largely stable (see his Table 3.9). What happened to the profitability of investment in Japan after 1972 when government policies were more liberalized? What were the major factors precipitating these changes, if any, in profitability? The relevance of the proposed analytical framework can be examined more clearly when profitability changes rather than when it is stable. In the case of Korea, the author mentions declining trends in the profit rate and profit share from 1978 to 1990 without explaining these downward movements. Was this decrease the result of the declining intervention of the government, as implied by the main thesis of the article? The credibility of the analytical framework may be questioned because of the lack of rigorous analysis on this key issue.

Our final comment here concerns the relevance of the first implication for development thinking mentioned in Singh's paper—namely, the role of large domestically owned third-world firms in economic development. The author's point that "the special characteristics of contemporary giant third-world firms need systematic research" is not necessarily wrong, but why is this issue a major implication? He points out the critical role played by the large *chaebol* firms in Korea, but he does not examine the importance of large firms in Japan and other East Asian countries. Actually one of the unique characteristics of the Japanese and Taiwanese economies is the small size of their enterprises. The number of workers per establishment in manufacturing has been declining in both Japan and Taiwan throughout the 1970s and 1980s and reached less than 20 in 1991. It was small enterprises linked by a network of subcontracts that contributed to the growth of export-oriented manufacturing in these countries. The network of subcontracts is supported by the low transaction cost associated with long-term transactions and the existence of social capital, which honors honest behaviors and sanctions deviating behaviors.

The case of Korea is contrasting in the sense that the size of enterprises has been far larger. In fact, the average number of workers per establishment increased until the mid-1970s, reflecting the policies to promote the large firms, as pointed out in the paper. But an important observation here is that the number of workers per firm in Korea has also been decreasing significantly since the mid-1970s. In this process, the role of subcontracting has become more prominent, and access to credit by medium and small enterprises has been improved. Although it is too early to draw definite conclusions, apparently the industrial structure in East Asia is increasingly characterized by the large number of small enterprises rather than by the small number of large enterprises. In all likelihood, the applicability of East Asian experience for other regions needs to take this aspect into account.

In short, although Singh provides a careful review of the development experience of Japan and Korea in the sphere of investment and savings with special attention to the role of government, the analysis seems incomplete because of the exclusive focus on a narrow range of issues. Another difficulty is the lack of rigorous statistical analysis supporting or refuting the proposed claims. In order to clarify further the issues addressed in this study, more micro-based disaggregated statistical analysis with a larger information base would be useful.

Francis T. Lui[1] on Ajit Singh's Paper

Catching up with the West: A Perspective on Asian Economic Development and Lessons for Latin America

Professor Ajit Singh's paper is an authoritative survey and analysis of the success stories of East Asian countries, with particular emphasis on Japan and South Korea, written with a perspective on what Latin American countries can learn from the East Asian experience in economic development. This commentator agrees with much of what Professor Singh has said about the underlying causes of the high growth rates of Japan and South Korea. Nevertheless, because a commentator's role is to offer critical comments, we shall focus here on issues on which some degree of disagreement exists with Professor Singh's viewpoint.

Professor Singh, using Japan and South Korea as examples, argues that the successful East Asian countries have not followed the "market-friendly" approach. Instead, their growth is seen as the outcome of a vigorous process of active government intervention. The underlying conceptual presumptions are that the dynamic efficiency of the accumulation process—involving more investment, which leads to greater learning by doing and ultimately to faster growth—is more important than static allocative efficiency and that government interventions, implemented properly, may stimulate the former, even though perhaps at the expense of the latter.

A number of questions can be raised here. Are interventionist policies the only route that the more successful East Asian countries have followed? Is there more diversity of experience in the development process of these countries? Is it possible that a country can attain dynamic efficiency without sacrificing static efficiency?

Active government involvement has worked reasonably well in Japan and Korea, as demonstrated by the paper, but it is not clear that this path is the unique or superior route to higher growth. The case of Hong Kong provides a counterexample of an experience diametrically opposite to that of Japan and Korea. From the methodological point of view, counterexamples are important because they show us the limitations of a theory. As we shall argue later, the recent phenomenal success of China also does

---

[1] Hong Kong University of Science and Technology.

not support a belief in the superiority of active interventionist policies in economic development.

Hong Kong's case provides an interesting contrast to those of Japan and Korea in several respects. Let us begin by looking at a few basics. First, Hong Kong must be classified as an economy which has attained at least the same level of success as the other three dragons of Asia. It has few or even no natural resources, its land is severely limited in supply, it did not have a well-educated labor force at the beginning phase of its development, and it has gone through a large number of major political and economic shocks—yet its per capita real GDP has gone up by a factor of almost 10 during the past 40 years. Measured in purchasing-power-parity terms, its per capita GDP in 1993 was the world's third highest. Its growth rate has remained high even in recent years, and its per capita income is expected to surpass that of Switzerland soon. Second, the path of "positive non-interventionism" has been the hallmark of Hong Kong's economic policy. Third, as will be seen from the following discussions, Hong Kong's saving and investment rates are lower than but comparable to those of Japan and Korea even though its development process appears to be different. Some comparisons will show that the free-market system has worked very well in Hong Kong.

Japan follows a protectionist policy in trade, as demonstrated by the extremely small value of imports as a share of GDP; Hong Kong, on the other hand, is arguably the freest port in the world, with both exports and imports bigger than the GDP. Japan has credit rationing and subsidization; these are by and large absent in Hong Kong. Profit margins in Japanese corporations are very low by world standards; investments are profit driven in Hong Kong, where the annual average rate of return to capital is in the neighborhood of 23 percent. The financial system and ownership structure in Japan, as Professor Singh has argued, have induced willingness on the part of firms to make long-term strategic investments; Hong Kong does not have the same system or structure, but judging from the continuous structural shifts in Hong Kong's economy, one can see that it is very flexible in responding to the changing economic environment.

Korea restricts FDI so as to protect local ownership; capital flow is almost completely free in Hong Kong.[2] The government in Korea has intervened heavily to encourage export-led growth; the government's role in supporting trade in Hong Kong does not really go much beyond that of a liaison agency, yet Hong Kong's exports, both in absolute amount and as a share of GDP, are bigger than those of Korea. Industrial parks have been adopted in Korea; Hong Kong also has a few industrial parks, but they are nothing more than some pieces of land that the government has zoned for industrial purposes, and there is no significant government involvement in these parks. Hong Kong has chosen to follow the alternative policy of training people for its industries by expanding tertiary and technical education rather than by directly supporting industries. Korea's growth owes a

---

[2] When currency speculators attempt to attack the Hong Kong dollar, the Hong Kong Monetary Authority does have a policy of raising the short-term interest rate so as to redirect the flow of capital. This is an interventionist policy but not a restriction on capital flows.

lot to the expansion of existing firms, especially of the giant corporations, and entrance of new entrepreneurs has been unimportant; quite the contrary has been true for Hong Kong, where the economy has been able to produce a lot of entrepreneurs, where a large proportion of the leading entrepreneurs (at least two of them among the richest top ten in the world) are of modest origin and where new business opportunities with China since the early 1980s have enabled a large number of small Hong Kong companies to grow into multinational corporations.

So the experience of Hong Kong appears to constitute an effective counterexample to show that active interventionist policies are not the only path that successful East Asian countries have followed. The free-market approach of Hong Kong can support a similarly high rate of growth, and perhaps there even exists greater allocative efficiency there owing to the fact that prices are not distorted. The TFP estimates in Young (1994) seem to support the view that Hong Kong has actually done better in TFP growth than have the interventionist economies of South Korea, Taiwan, and Singapore. The average annual growth rates of TFP in these three dragons are 1.4 percent, 1.5 percent, and 0 percent; even though annual R&D investment in Hong Kong is below .1 of 1 percent of GDP, Hong Kong's TFP growth rate of 2.5 percent is higher than in the other dragons.[3]

The foregoing discussion does not imply that government has had no role in the economic development of Hong Kong. The government does spend a lot on infrastructure. Education, health care, and public housing are among the most heavily subsidized in the world, and these subsidies do not seem to have hampered growth in any significant way.

To some extent, recent experience in China also casts doubt on the necessity of government interventions to promote growth. For instance, from 1978 to 1985, real agricultural output in China went up by more than 70 percent. McMillan, Whalley, and Zhu (1989) have shown that three-fourths of that increase was the result of privatization of property rights and that the remaining one-fourth was the result of liberalization of the market. Indeed, much of the growth in the so-called Pearl River Delta in South China, now often referred to as the fifth dragon, has been the result of the emulation of the entrepreneurial and free-market style of Hong Kong. What are the right lessons to be learned from East Asia? Free market or government interventions? This question has not yet been fully answered.

---

[3] Lau and Kim (1994) have made a much lower estimate for the TFP for all the four dragons. According to them, the TFP of Hong Kong is about one-sixth that of the United States. Given that the stock of human capital in Hong Kong is much lower than in the States and that this stock of physical capital in Hong Kong is unlikely to become much larger, it is difficult to accept this result when one further observes that these two economies have roughly the same level of per capita income. Felipe (1996) has estimated that the TFP of Hong Kong is not significantly different from that of the United States.

REFERENCES

Felipe, J. "Total Factor Productivity and Technological Level in Singapore and Hong Kong." Working Paper. Hong Kong: Hong Kong University of Science and Technology, 1996.

Lau, L.J., and Jong-II Kim. "The Sources of Growth of the East Asian Newly Industrialized Countries." *Journal of the Japanese and International Economies* (5–71): 23 (1994).

McMillan, J., J. Whalley, and Lijing Zhu. "The Impact of China's Economic Reforms on Agricultural Productivity Growth." *Journal of Political Economy* 97 (August 1989).

Young, A. "Lessons from the East Asian NICs: A Contrarian View." *European Economic Review* 38, 3/4 (April 1994).

The Political Economy of Development Policy: An Asian Perspective

Pranab Bardhan[1]

> *If the state is strong it will crush us;*
> *if it is weak, we will perish.*
>
> —Paul Valéry

In the traditional development literature that emphasized market failures and prescriptions whereby government might fix these failures, the state was often viewed as floating in some behavioral and organizational vacuum. This perception made it easy for economists to charge the state with the duty of maximizing social welfare and then to use this charge for blanket endorsements of indiscriminate state intervention—the adverse effects of which, for both economic growth and distribution, have been painfully obvious in many countries over the last two or three decades. The public-choice literature that grew in part as a reaction to this poorly demarcated model of the state drew pointed attention to how, by engaging in rent-seeking activities, the regulatory, interventionist state spawned an enormous waste of resources, over and above the standard economic losses stemming from the misallocation effects of policy-induced distortions. The literature in development economics has now come full circle from the unquestioning dirigisme of the early days to the current gory accounts of government failures all around. In the present paper we shall draw upon the Asian experience, with the contrasting cases of East Asia and South Asia, to point to a more nuanced role of the state and to a more complex political economy of development policy than what usually underlies most partisan debates on the subject.

Both sides in the different partisan development policy debates clearly have their own definitive ideas of what constitutes "good" or "bad" policy. Much of policy economics gives the impression that governments follow "bad" policy primarily because they have been given bad advice; much of the political-economy literature tells us that governments follow "bad" policy because they are subservient to interest groups that block economic progress; the public-choice literature blames the lobbies and the rent-seeking special interests; the leftists blame the dominant elite classes and coalitions; still others refer to the plundering dictators in "predatory" states. There exist obvious elements of truth in all of these viewpoints: governments do sometimes get bad advice, and they are sometimes hampered by marauding lobbies and oligarchic predation.

---

[1] University of California at Berkeley.

But even so, the overarching question remains: Is it logically not still in the interest of the powerful forces (classes, interest groups, or dictators) to pursue basic policies that will help overall economic growth and thus enlarge the total pie that they can then lay their grubby hands on? And even when consensus does exist, on the constituent elements of good basic policy, why do some states find it difficult to effectuate these desired elements and why can even policies that are ostensibly similar have very different outcomes in different countries? Apparently an intricate market coordination problem exists here that many states, despite perhaps even the best advice and the best intentions, fail to resolve—a problem however, that some of the East Asian states have succeeded in overcoming.

In the present article we shall briefly analyze this coordination problem, explore some of the preconditions for success or failure in resolving it, and focus on elements of state capacity and governance structure and how they may be affected by distributive conflicts.[2] There exist, of course, many context-specific social-historical or geopolitical factors and other path-dependent forces that can help explain the divergent trajectories of different state policies and their outcomes in different countries. But here we abstract from many of them and focus on an extremely narrow set of political-economy issues at the level of sweeping generality.

Strong and Limited Government

Despite all the controversies in development policy thinking, some consensus exists in the sense that a successful policy package has to contain as a minimum some policies toward macroeconomic stability and fiscal discipline and some microeconomic policies toward securing property rights and providing a predictable and reliable legal and contractual structure. Most developing countries have not been able to provide this minimum package on any sustained basis. Nevertheless, four East Asian states—South Korea, Taiwan, Hong Kong, and Singapore—have been remarkably successful in this respect, as have Japan in its postwar reconstruction and development phase and also, but to a somewhat lesser extent, the high-growth economies of Southeast Asia (Malaysia, Indonesia, and Thailand).

In the literature on the new institutional economics, the prevailing view about the state is that it has to be strong enough to be able to provide the aforementioned minimum policy package and yet has to commit credibly to not making confiscatory demands on the private sector. The recommendation is for a "strong but limited" government: strong and resolute enough to resist the inevitable political pressures from all sides for market intervention (and certainly far from being the minimalist government called for

---

[2] In the last three years there have been at least four major studies on the lessons of the East Asian success story in development: World Bank (1993), Fishlow et al. (1994), Aoki et al. (1996), and Campos and Root (1996). Despite some differences, there is a remarkable measure of agreement among these four studies, and in the present paper we ourselves have a lot in common with the intersection of these studies. But our emphasis here is on coordination problems and on how they may be exacerbated by distributive conflicts. This, of course, has links with the common emphasis on East Asian "shared growth" in all the four studies.

in classical liberalism) and at the same time willing to constrain itself from interfering with market-led growth. The pursuit of this combination of qualities poses a major dilemma of political governance, in that strong states often become interventionist and confiscatory. And in fact, very few states have succeeded in fully resolving this dilemma. North and Weingast (1989) do cite the historical case of the Glorious Revolution in England in 1688, which by fostering political institutions constraining the country's strong king, actually enhanced his commitment to securing private-property rights and thus fostered economic growth. And Root and Weingast (1996) describe the successful East Asian cases as modern-day examples of strong but limited government.

But some might say that in the successful cases of East Asian development (including that of Japan), the state has in general really played a much more active role than the role described by the definition of "strong but limited" government and that it has sometimes intervened, particularly in the capital market, in subtle but decisive ways, using regulated credit allocation (occasionally threatening withdrawal of credit in not-so-subtle ways) to promote and channel industrial investment, underwriting risks and guaranteeing loans, establishing public development banks and other financial institutions, encouraging the development of the nascent parts of financial markets, and nudging existing firms to upgrade their technology and to move into sectors that fall in line with an overall vision of strategic developmental goals. And as Gerschenkron (1962) notes, the state played a much more important role for the development of the capital market in the late industrializers of Europe than it had played in England.

The usual credit market and equity market imperfections that are described in the literature on imperfect information[3] are severe in the early stages of industrial development. The investment in learning by doing is not easily collateralizable and is therefore particularly subject to the high costs of information imperfections. For firms waiting in the wings, learning by experimentation gives rise to externalities difficult to internalize without some coordination. Even established and successful mercantile firms, more used to short-horizon trading, often have limited capacity to pool risks and to mobilize the capital of the society at large for their high-risk, high-return industrial ventures.

There do exist, of course, scattered cases in developing countries of coordination and mutual support among merchant families, facilitating the transition to the industrial economy without much help from the government. For instance, in regard to nineteenth-century India, Bayly (1983) cites an important case:

> In Ahmedabad, the one case of a "traditional" merchant city which industrialized from inside, it was several of the leading families who controlled resources and status within the trade guilds who went into the cotton mill ventures. No small man could go it alone. But if the leaders of the community who could themselves call on a wide range of security and information made the initial move, the others would follow.

---

[3] For a general discussion on the role of the state in financial markets, see Stiglitz (1993).

But more often, private-sector coordination in investment and in risk taking on the part of merchant families has been missing. Coordination facilitates "strategic complementarities" and positive feedback effects that result in multiple equilibriums.[4] Coordination is particularly important when externalities of information and the need for a network of proximate suppliers of components, services, and infrastructural facilities with economies of scale make investment decisions highly interdependent and make raising capital from the market for a whole given complex of activities particularly difficult.[5] In East Asia (with the possible exception of Hong Kong), the state has played an important role in resolving "coordination failure," much beyond the "positive noninterventionism" prescribed in the literature on the new institutional economics.

In this process—as Aoki, Murdock, and Okuno-Fujiwara (1996) have emphasized—the state has often enhanced the market instead of supplanting it;[6] it has induced private coordination by providing various kinds of cooperation-contingent rents. In the early stages of industrialization, when private financial and other related institutions were still underdeveloped and coordination was not yet self-enforcing, the East Asian state created opportunities for rents conditional on performance or outcome (in mobilization of savings, commercialization of inventions, export "contests," and so on) and facilitated institutional development by influencing the strategic incentives facing private agents through an alteration of the relative returns to cooperation in comparison with the adversarial equilibrium.

One should not, of course, underestimate the administrative difficulties of such aggregate coordination, and the issues of micromanagement of capital may be much too intricate for the current institutional capacity and information-processing abilities of many a state in Africa, Latin America, South Asia, and even East Asia (if one thinks of the Philippines, for example).[7] One should also be wary about the moral-hazard problems (affecting incentives to invest wisely and repay loans promptly) and about the political pressures for bailout or for throwing good money after bad (that is, after already-sunk investment in large projects that are doing badly) that a state-supported financial system inevitably faces. This is the "soft-budget constraint" problem of refinancing in centralized credit systems formally analyzed by Dewatripont and Maskin (1993). Although government-supported development banks (such as France's Crédit Mobilier in the nineteenth century and its later Crédit National, Germany's Kreditanstalt für Wiederaufbau, Japan's

---

[4] This has a long history in the postwar development literature, from Rosenstein-Rodan (1943) to Murphy, Shleifer, and Vishny (1989). For more-recent theoretical contributions to this literature, see the special issue on "Increasing Returns, Monopolistic Competition, and Economic Development" in the Journal of Development Economics (April 1996).

[5] For an account of the great financial difficulties faced by enterprising groups like the Tatas at Jamshedpur or by Walchand at Visakhapatnam in pre-Independence India, see Ray (1979).

[6] In Taiwan, of course, a large part of the industrial economy was owned and controlled by the party-state. Even today, KMT runs many enterprises.

[7] As the example of Japan in recent years shows, when the technologies become more complex and the exploration of new technological opportunities becomes highly uncertain, the state loses some of its efficacy in guiding private-sector coordination, as pointed out by Aoki, Murdock, and Okuno-Fujiwara (1996).

Development Bank, and the Korea Development Bank) have indeed played a crucial role in long-term industrial finance in past and recent history, the experience with such banks in other developing countries (say, in India or Mexico) has been mixed at best. Armendariz de Aghion (1995) has suggested that the efficiency of government sponsorship can be enhanced if conditions like targeting of development bank intervention (thus helping acquisition of specialized expertise in financing projects in particular sectors), co-financing arrangements (thus helping risk diversification and dissemination of expertise), and/or co-ownership with private financial institutions are attached to government sponsorship.

What State and Why

We have discussed the importance of the role of the state as a coordinator and have hinted at the administrative and political difficulties inherent in playing that role. But some basic questions must be addressed. Why would the state leadership be interested in playing such an active role in the development process? What is in it for the state? Should the state not be interested instead in maximizing its own loot? In this vein, Robinson (1995) quotes the Kenyan dissident leader Oginga Odinga commenting on the economic policies of President Daniel Arap Moi: "If your mouth is the only mouth on the udder of the cow, you do not care if the cow becomes smaller." Of course, this attitude implicitly assumes a short time horizon (or "satisficing") in the objective function of the ruler (or the ruling clique). On the other side, there have also been some cases in the history of state-led industrialization in the last century and a half (starting with the classic case of Meiji Japan) in which the impulses that shaped major policies and actions by the state elite were fueled not merely by motives of self-aggrandizement but also by some larger organizational goals or nation-building mission.

Even if one posits rational and solely self-interested economic actors at the helm of the state, McGuire and Olson (1996) have argued that such actors may have incentives to take an "encompassing interest" in the productivity of society as a whole and to take into account the deadweight losses from unduly onerous governmental impositions on society's overall productive capacity. McGuire and Olson point to the smaller distortionary effects of the "stationary bandit" regime by rational autocrats as opposed to the greater distortion caused by the state as "roving bandit" (that is, the state as *organized* crime has more at stake in the prosperity of its subjects than does the state as petty, decentralized theft). They also argue that a majoritarian democracy (even with no scruples about robbing the minority, but with a stake in the market economy) will similarly have an encompassing interest in nonconfiscatory policies.

Formally speaking, the rulers in McGuire and Olson (1996) maximize their own objective function subject to the reaction function of the ruled (although McGuire and Olson do not formulate their problem quite this way), and so in the process these rulers internalize the economic cost of their impositions in accordance with these impositions' effect on that reaction function. Such ruler is thus taken to constitute a Stackelberg leader. In contrast, one can say that the weak or the "soft" state is a Stackelberg follower.

The "soft" state, instead of committing to particular policies, merely reacts to the independent actions and demands of private actors such as special-interest groups. Thus, it is easy to see[8] that compared with the "strong" state ("strength" defined as ability to precommit credibly), the "soft" state will perform many scattered and undesirable interventions (creating distortions by seeking to generate rent for the various lobbying groups) and by the same logic, too few desirable interventions (as in alleviating market failures or the kind of coordination failures we have alluded to earlier), since the "soft" state does not internalize or have an encompassing stake in the overall effects of its own policies. So the distinction between a "strong" state (as in much of East Asia) and a "soft" state (as in much of Africa, South Asia, or Latin America) is not in the extent of intervention but in its *quality.* (For a discussion of the issue of quality of intervention, see Bardhan [1990]). Therefore, the beneficial effects of a "strong" state go beyond those created by the ideal of "strong but limited government" of the new institutional economics.

An important example of the ability of the strong state to precommit like the Stackelberg leader relates to the popular infant-industry argument for protection. By the very nature of this argument, such protection is granted for a short period until the protected industrial infant can stand on its own feet. But in most countries, infant industry protection faces the time inconsistency problem: when the initial period of protection nears its completion, the political pressures for the protection's renewal become very strong, and under a "soft" state regime, the infant industry all too often degenerates into a geriatric protection lobby. In the recent history of the strong states of East Asia, however, there have occurred some remarkable instances of the government's withdrawing the protection for an industry after the lapse of the preannounced time span, letting the industry sink or swim in international competition.[9]

The Quality of State Intervention

The difficult issue now becomes how to determine the factors that predispose a state or a political coalition to have an "encompassing interest" in the economic performance of the country as a whole—or to put it differently, to determine what helps in the making of a strong state. There exist many path-dependent factors (deeply historical, cultural, and geopolitical) that affect the process of formation of a strong or a weak state. But certain patterns decipherable from a comparison of East Asia with South Asia may be important from the point of view of the political economy of a so-called developmental state.

Many political scientists, for instance, have pointed to the remarkable insulation enjoyed by the technocratic elite in charge of policymaking in the successful East Asian states from the ravages of short-run pork barrel politics (leaving aside for the time being

---

[8] For a simple but illuminating demonstration of this result, see Rodrik (1992).

[9] For an example of how the government in Taiwan imposed an import ban on VCRs in 1982 (to help out two of the main domestic electronic companies) and withdrew it after eighteen months when the companies failed to shape up to meet international standards, see Wade (1990). Jeff Nugent has pointed out that with the recent advent of democracy, some of these precommitments have become somewhat weaker—as, for example, in the case of the promised withdrawal of protection of small manufacturing enterprises against competition from the *chaebol* in South Korea.

special policies affecting certain relatively small sectors such as protected rice farmers). The role played by powerful semiautonomous technocratic organizations like the Economic Planning Bureau in South Korea and the Industrial Development Bureau in Taiwan has been cited in support of this argument. Of course, authoritarianism is neither necessary for creating such insulation (examples: many sectors in Austria, Scandinavia, or postwar Japan) nor sufficient for creating it (examples: many states in Africa and Latin America in recent history). Among the enabling conditions for this insulation, Evans (1995) does emphasize Weberian characteristics of internal organization of the state such as highly selective meritocratic recruitment and rewards for long-term careerism in members of the bureaucracy. In post-independence India (where these Weberian characteristics are present to a reasonable degree), insulation is also nurtured through the mechanisms of promotion and transfer: the strong officers' unions in the Indian administrative services make sure that once recruited, officers are regularly promoted (more on the basis of seniority than performance). Powerful politicians may not be able to sack them but can still make life unpleasant by getting them transferred to undesirable jobs and locations. Furthermore, the institutionalized practice of rapid turnover in a given slot in the Indian administrative hierarchy inhibits the process of officers' acquisition of specialized expertise in any particular area.

In Latin America in general (or in the Philippines in East Asia), appointments in the bureaucracy are more often matters of political patronage than in India[10] or in much of East Asia. Geddes (1994), in an analysis of the obstacles to building state capacity in Latin America, shows how in the recent history of that continent the political leaders have frequently faced a dilemma between their own need for immediate political survival, buying political support with patronage in appointments to economic-management positions, and their longer-run collective interest in overall economic performance and regime stability.

Insulation of the technocratic elite, however, can have very real efficiency costs. In addition to causing a loss of localized information and accountability (to which we shall come back later), bureaucratic insulation also can make it difficult to attain flexibility in dealing with changes in technical and market conditions (and may thus work against risk taking) and also in correcting wrong decisions. This desirable flexibility has been achieved in East Asia by fostering a dense network of ties between public officials and private entrepreneurs through deliberative councils (as in Japan or South Korea) or through the tightly knit party organization (as in Taiwan), allowing operational space for negotiating and renegotiating goals and policies and for coordinating decisions (and expectations) with remarkable speed. Such government-business relations (with the state retaining its privileged position as a senior partner in the relation) not merely facilitate the sharing of information and risks but also provide a framework for compromise and for rent sharing within the business elite. Evans (1995) has described this networked insulation of the top

---

[10] Even in India, appointments to the boards of public-sector corporations in provincial governments are often political sinecures.

bureaucracy as the "embedded autonomy" of the state, which he regards as key to the success of the East Asian state.

But is such "embedded autonomy" of the state elite feasible in societies that are internally more heterogeneous and unequal than are Japan, South Korea, or Taiwan? As we know from Olson (1965), internal heterogeneity makes collective-action problems more difficult. The relevant collective-action problem here is that of formulating cohesive developmental goals with clear priorities and that of avoiding prisoners' dilemma deadlocks in the pursuit of even commonly agreed-upon goals. Intercountry societal differences in rule obedience and organizational loyalty (for a discussion of the multiple equilibriums in different countries' evolution processes, see Clague [1963]) do of course matter in this context (palpable differences exist in this respect between Northeast Asia and South Asia), but it is also very important to keep in mind the different backgrounds of structural conflict in civil society. When wealth distribution is relatively egalitarian, as in large parts of East Asia (particularly through land reforms and widespread expansion of education and basic health services), it is easier to enlist the support of most of the country's social groups (and to isolate the radical wings of the labor movement and petty bourgeoisie) in making short-run sacrifices and coordinating on growth-promoting policies.[11] There exists some broad evidence[12] that inequality and other forms of polarization can make it more difficult to build a national consensus about policy changes in response to crises and can result in instability of policy outcomes and insecurity of contractual and property rights.

When a society is extremely heterogeneous and conflict ridden, as in India, and no individual group is powerful enough to hijack the state by itself, then the democratic process tends to install an elaborate system of checks and balances in the public sphere and meticulous rules of equity in sharing the spoils, at least among the divided elite groups. (For an analysis of the developmental gridlock in India as an intricate collective-action problem in an implicit framework of noncooperative Nash equilibriums, see Bardhan 1984.) There may exist what is called institutionalized suspicion in the internal organization of the state (in the Indian case, enhanced no doubt by the legacy of the institutional practices of the colonial rulers suspicious of the natives and by the even-earlier legacy of the moghul emperors suspicious of the potentially unruly *subadars* and *mansabdars*), manifested in a carefully structured system of multiple veto powers. The tightly integrated working relationship of government with private business that the "embedded autonomy" of Evans involves is indeed very difficult to contemplate in such a context. The cultural distance between the "gentleman (or lady) administrator" and the private capitalist is rather large in India (although it has been declining in recent years). Much more importantly in the Indian context of a plurality of contending heterogeneous groups, any close

---

[11] Campos and Root (1996) emphasize this point: "In contrast with Latin America and Africa, East Asian regimes established their legitimacy by promising shared growth so that demands of narrowly conceived groups for regulations that would have long-term deleterious consequences for growth were resisted. In particular, broad-based social support allowed their governments to avoid having to make concessions to radical demands of organized labor."

[12] See Keefer and Knack (1995).

liaison and harmonizing of the interests of the state with those of private business would raise an outcry of foul play and strong political resentment among the other interest groups (particularly among organized labor and farmers), the electoral repercussions of which the Indian politicians can afford to ignore much less than can the typical East Asian politician. Thus, cozy relations between the state and private capital remain inherently somewhat suspect in such political regimes in general—but not without a degree of interesting sectorial variability. In some sectors in the Indian economy, for instance, shared vision and some consensus building on encompassing development projects have not been absent, and it is very important to study the preconditions and modalities of such instances. The comparative study in Evans (1995) of the emerging relationships between the state and private industrialists in Korea, Brazil, and India in the information technology sector (electronics and telecommunications) is thus quite instructive.

The general theory of bureaucracy suggests[13] that it is difficult to devise work contracts granting high-powered incentives for civil servants because primarily of what is called a "common-agency" problem (that is, the civil servant has to be the agent of multiple principals) or a multitask problem (meaning that he or she has to pursue multiple goals, many of which are hard to measure). Under low-powered incentives for civil servants, the latters' "capture" by interest groups is considered very likely, and in structuring bureaucratic organizations, the likelihood of such capture is usually taken into account in the form of checks and balances in the allocation of control rights and as some bit of multiple veto power systems, even in societies less conflict ridden than India. But these institutional devices create their own opportunities for a kind of "inefficient" corruption. A multiple veto power system makes centralized collection of bribes in exchange for guaranteed favors very difficult: one high official in New Delhi is reported to have told a friend, "If you want me to move a file faster, I am not sure I can help you but if you want me to stop a file, I can do it immediately." This ability to "stop a file" at multiple points (a system often originally installed to keep corrupt officials in check) may result in increasing inefficiency as well as a rise in the number of bribes. In general, centralized corruption (as in South Korea or Taiwan) actually has fewer adverse consequences for overall efficiency than does decentralized bribe taking, since in the former case the bribee will internalize some of the distortionary effects of corruptions. Shleifer and Vishny (1993) have used a similar argument in explaining the increase in "inefficient" corruption in post-Communist Russia compared with the earlier regime of centralized bribe collection by the Communist Party.

An important aspect of the quality of state intervention in East Asia has to do with the use, by and large, of clear, well-defined, preannounced rules regarding performance criteria. In South Korea, for example, the heavy involvement of the state in directing investment through credit allocation has been successful largely because of the state's strict adherence to the criterion of export performance. Through this precommitment device, the strong Korean state has used the vital disciplining function of foreign competition in

---

[13] See Wilson (1989), Tirole (1994), and Dixit (1995).

encouraging quick learning and consciousness of cost and quality among domestic enterprises, something that is conspicuously absent in many other interventionist regimes
(even though the Korean state, at least until the 1980s, shared with the latter regimes
many of the restrictive policies on imports and foreign investment).

While it is easy to see that transparent and preannounced rules rather than discretion
and credible commitment devices can be very important for efficiency and long-term investment, particularly in states prone to "capture", one should also keep in mind, as
Laffont and Tirole (1994) indicate, that commitment may allow the government in one
period to bind governments in subsequent periods to a rent-generating contract with a
firm with which the politicians in the former government have colluded but which is not
beneficial for the country as a whole.[14] In a multiperiod model, if the state actors who behave like a Stackelberg leader with a presumed encompassing interest have some chance
of being thrown out of office (in future elections or otherwise), commitment may act as
a rent-perpetuating device. While Laffont and Tirole correctly point out that concern of
the incumbent government for reelection will reduce the probability of collusion, elections are after all highly imperfect as disciplining devices.

Thus, the "strength" of a state in the sense of its ability to commit itself credibly to
developmental goals is clearly not sufficient to ensure development. It may not even be
necessary: the remarkable economic success of Italy over three decades (until very recently), despite a notoriously weak and corrupt government heavily involved in the economy, is an obvious counterexample. Nevertheless, the overall correlation between growth
performance and state "strength" (in the sense defined earlier) is probably quite robust.
It is, of course, possible that economies in their most successful phases have less political
conflict (most groups are doing well without political exertion, and the few losing
groups are bribed), and therefore their governments have an appearance of "strength" in
that their commitments are not challenged or reversed by political action. Such a situation may have caused a selection bias here and constitutes an important issue that needs
to be examined with detailed historical data; but the determined way the Korean state has
handled various macroeconomic crises, say, in the 1970s (the two oil shocks, massive foreign debt, inflation, and so forth) does strongly suggest that the Korean state's "strength"
is not just a reflection of the success of the economy.

In most situations, states are neither Stackelberg leaders nor Stackelberg followers.
Neither the state actors nor the private interest groups usually have the power to define
unilaterally the parameters of their action. Both may be strategic actors with some
power to influence the terms, and the outcome of the bargaining game will depend on
their varying bargaining strengths in different situations. In this context it may be important to point out a major inadequacy in the analysis of "encompassing interest" by
McGuire and Olson (1996). In that model, the power of the ruler to collect taxes or rents
is invariant with respect to the policies to promote productivity. But some of the latter

---

[14] In India this kind of argument was cited in the recent political controversy around the Enron power project in
Maharashtra.

policies may change the disagreement payoffs of the ruled if one thinks of it as bargaining game. As Robinson (1995) has emphasized, it may not be rational for an autocrat to carry out institutional changes that safeguard property rights, law enforcement, and other overall economically beneficial structures if in the process his rent-extracting machinery has a chance of being damaged or weakened. The autocrat may not risk upsetting the current arrangement for the uncertain prospect of a share in a larger pie. For some of the "stationary bandits" in this century (the Duvaliers in Haiti, Trujillo in the Dominican Republic, Somoza in Nicaragua, Mobutu in Zaire, and so on), who systematically plundered and wrecked their economies for excruciatingly long periods, this may have been a serious consideration.

McGuire and Olson (1996) are in the grand tradition of theorists of public choice and the new institutional economics in which all state-mandated redistribution is dismissed as mere unproductive rent creation. They ignore the possibility of some redistributive reform that—even if carried out by a state motivated entirely by considerations of improving its base of political support—may help in increasing productivity and even in creating socially more-efficient property rights. The so-called efficiency-equity trade-off that is central to much of standard policy economics is often really false or exaggerated. Many opportunities exist for cooperative problem solving that are forgone by societies that are sharply divided along economic lines. Barriers faced by the poor in the capital markets (through their lack of the collateralizable assets that borrowers need in order to improve the credibility of their commitment) or in the land market (where the landed oligarchy blocks efficiency-enhancing redistribution of land to more-productive small farmers) sharply reduce a society's overall potential for productive investment, innovation, and human-resource development. The East Asian states[15] have succeeded in realizing a large part of their potential through redistributive reforms that facilitated some measure of social consensus behind ambitious economic programs (or a superior bargaining outcome, if one thinks in terms of a bargaining model)—and not because Park Chung Hee and his successor dictators in Korea or the KMT in Taiwan were "stationary bandits" with a much larger stake in fattening the economy than such bandits had elsewhere. The extreme inequality within Latin American countries has made coordination on common programs of short-run sacrifices and compromises (social "pacts") for long-run development much more difficult to sustain.

Accountability and Legitimacy

When state leadership and the private interest groups are pitted against one another in a bargaining setup, it is important to strengthen the accountability mechanisms on both sides, as Przeworski (1995) emphasizes. On the one hand, credible commitment devices

---

[15] It is important to include the case of China in this statement. One can argue that the market discipline and the hard-budget constraint that—according to Montinola, Qian, and Weingast (1995)—have contributed to the success of decentralized development in China (led by the Village and Township Enterprises) were rendered politically tolerable by the secure social safety net made possible by the highly egalitarian redistribution of private access to land that the post-1978 decollectivization has effectively implied for the rural population.

and rules (including constitutional safeguards) may be necessary to insulate some of the government's economic decision-making processes from the pork-barrel politics of private special-interest groups. And on the other hand, certain institutional arrangements (such as an independent office of public accounting and auditing, an election commission with powers to limit [and enforce rules on] campaign contributions and to conduct fair elections, citizens' watchdog committees providing informational and monitoring services, and an office of local ombudsmen with some control over the local bureaucracy) can help in limiting the abuse of executive power and in providing a system of punishments for undesirable government interventions in the economy and rewards for desirable interventions. In countries like India where most of the economy is still in the informal sector and dispersed in far-flung villages, such accountability mechanisms have to be reinforced by informal institutions at the local community level. We shall illustrate this need by drawing upon the Indian experience, although the issues are more general.

The ideological state-versus-market debates, focusing on the larger market-related and governmental failures, have often overlooked the serious failures of local self-governing institutions and the associated lack of accountability and legitimacy at the local level. The state may be the body that spends vast sums of money on irrigation, education, health, and subsidized credit, but the programs themselves are usually administered by a distant, uncoordinated, and occasionally corrupt bureaucracy, insensitive and unaccountable to the local people; often only a very little of the planned benefit reaches the intended beneficiaries of the programs. For instance, one reason that public investment in irrigation has been more effective in Korea than in India is—as Wade (1994) has indicated—that the Indian canal systems consist of large, centralized hierarchies in charge of all functions but in the Korean canal systems, implementational and routine maintenance tasks are delegated to the respective Farmland Improvement Association in each catchment area, staffed by local people, knowledgeable about local conditions and continually drawing upon local trust relationships.

In water management as well as in other local public projects (such as environmental protection, prevention of soil erosion, regulated use of forests and grazing land, and public health and sanitation), the local community level institutions that might play a vital role in providing an informal framework of coordination for design and implementation are largely missing in many parts of India. Evidence exists, for instance, that the serious problem of absenteeism of teachers in India's village public schools and of doctors in its rural public clinics would be significantly lessened if these professionals were made accountable to the local community rather than to a centralized bureaucracy. Furthermore, subsidized credit is administered through governmental and semigovernmental agencies that do not have enough local information about the borrower and so insist on levels of collateral that exclude many of the potentially productive poor; these agencies do not have access to the systems of peer monitoring and social sanctions that local community institutions can provide.

This local institutional failure is an example of the severity of collective-action problems in India. Evidently, the extreme social fragmentation in India, intensified by the exigencies of pluralist politics, makes cooperation in community institution building much more difficult than in socially homogeneous Korea, Taiwan, and Japan. There also exists scattered evidence that community level institutions work better in enforcing common agreements and cooperative norms when the underlying property regime is not too skewed and when the generated benefits are more equitable shared. Putnam's (1993) study of the local variations across Italy also suggests that "horizontal" social networks (that is, those involving people of similar status and power) are more effective in generating trust and norms of reciprocity than are "vertical" networks. One beneficial by-product of land reform, underemphasized in the usual economic analysis, is that such reform, by changing the local political structure in the village, gives more "voice" to the poor and induces them to get involved in local self-governing institutions and management of local public goods. In Indian social and political history when in situations of extreme inequality local organizations have been captured by the powerful and the wealthy, instances of subordinate groups appealing to supralocal authorities for protection and relief have not been uncommon: the intervention by the long arm of the state even in remote corners of rural India has been in such cases by invitation, and not always by arbitrary imposition.

In the present study we have emphasized the critical coordination role of the state beyond that of ensuring property rights and guaranteeing contract enforcement as prescribed in the literature of the new institutional economics. Drawing upon the experience of East Asia and South Asia, we have tried to examine the factors that potentially predispose a state to have an encompassing interest in the overall economic performance of the country and the conditions under which the state frequently fails. Governance capacity often depends on the resolution of some collective-action problems, which in turn are related to strategic distributive conflicts among different groups in society. These collective-action problems arise both at the level of the state (and underly the difficulty of breaking out of the policy deadlock of which inefficient interventionism is only a symptom) and at the local level (and make provision and management of crucial local public goods highly inefficient).

REFERENCES

Aoki, M., Murdock, and M. Okuno-Fujiwara. "Beyond the East Asian Miracle: Introducing the Market Enhancing View." In M. Aoki, H. Kim, and M. Okuno-Fujiwara, eds., *The Role of Government in East Asian Economic Development: Comparative Institutional Analysis.* New York: Oxford University Press, 1996.

Armendariz de Aghion, B. "Development Banking." DEP 64. London: School of Economics, 1995.

Bardhan, P. *The Political Economy of Development in India.* Oxford: Basil Blackwell, 1984.

_____. "Introduction to the Symposium on the State and Economic Development." *Journal of Economic Perspectives.* (Summer 1990).

Bayly, C.A. *Rulers, Townsmen and Bazaar: North Indian Society in the Age of British Expansion 1770–1870.* Cambridge: Cambridge University Press, 1983.

Campos, E., and H.L. Root. *The Key to the East Asian Miracle: Making Shared Growth Credible.* Washington, D.C.: Brookings Institution, 1996.

Clague, C. "Rule Obedience, Organizational Loyalty, and Economic Development." *Journal of Institutional and Theoretical Economics* (1993).

Dewatripont, M., and E. Maskin. "Centralization of Credit and Long- Term Investment." In P. Bardhan and J. Roemer, eds., *Market Socialism: The Current Debate.* New York: Oxford University Press, 1993.

Dixit, A. *The Making of Economic Policy: A Transaction Cost Politics Perspective.* Cambridge, Mass.: MIT Press, 1995.

Evans, P. *Embedded Autonomy.* Princeton: Princeton University Press, 1995.

Fishlow, A., C. Gwin, S. Haggard, D. Rodrik, and R. Wade. *Miracle or Design? Lessons from the East Asian Experience.* Washington, D.C.: Overseas Development Council, 1994.

Geddes, B. *Politician's Dilemma: Building State Capacity in Latin America.* Berkeley: University of California Press, 1994.

Gerschenkron, A. *Economic Backwardness in Historical Perspective.* Cambridge, Mass: Belknap, 1962.

Keefer, P., and S. Knack. "Polarization, Property Rights and the Links between Inequality and Growth." Unpublished. 1995.

Laffont, J.J., and J. Tirole. *A Theory of Incentives in Procurement and Regulation.* Cambridge, Mass.: MIT Press, 1994.

McGuire, M.C., and M. Olson. "The Economics of Autocracy and Majority Rule." *Journal of Economic Literature* (March 1996).

Montinola, G., Y. Qian, and B.R. Weingast. "Federalism, Chinese Style: The Political Basis for Economic Success in China." *World Politics* (October 1995).

Murphy, K., A. Shleifer, and R. Vishny. "Industrialization and the Big Push." *Journal of Political Economy* (October 1989).

North, D.C., and B.R. Weingast. "Constitutions and Commitment: Evolution of Institutions Governing Public Choice." *Journal of Economic History* (December 1989).

Olson, M. *The Logic of Collective Action: Public Goods and the Theory of Groups.* Cambridge,

Mass.: Harvard University Press, 1965.

———. *The Rise and Decline of Nations: Economic Growth, Stagflation, and Social Rigidities.* New Haven: Yale University Press, 1982.

Przeworski, A. "Reforming the State: Political Accountability and Economic Intervention." Unpublished. New York University, 1995.

Putnam, R.D. *Making Democracy Work: Civic Traditions in Modern Italy.* Princeton: Princeton University Press, 1993.

Ray, R.K. *Industrialization in India: Growth and Conflict in the Private Corporate Sector 1914–47.* Delhi: Oxford University Press, 1979.

Robinson, A. "Theories of 'Bad Policy'." Unpublished. 1995.

Rodrik, D. "Political Economy and Development Policy." *European Economic Review* (April 1992).

Root, H.L., and B.R. Weingast. "The State's Role in East Asian Development." In H.L. Root, *Small Countries, Big Lessons: Governance and the Rise of East Asia.* Hong Kong: Oxford University Press, 1996.

Rosenstein-Rodan, P. "Problems of Industrialization of Eastern and Southeastern Europe." *Economic Journal* (June-September 1943).

Shleifer, A., and R. Vishny. "Corruption." *Quarterly Journal of Economics* (1993).

Stiglitz, J.E. "The Role of the State in Financial Markets." *Proceedings of the World Bank Annual Conference on Development Economics* (1993).

Tirole, J. "The Internal Organization of Government." *Oxford Economics Papers* (1994).

Wade, R. *Governing the Market: Economic Theory and the Role of the Government in East Asian Industrialization.* Princeton: Princeton University Press, 1990.

———. "State Effectiveness as a Function of State Organization and Social Capital." Unpublished. Sussex University, 1994.

Wilson, J.Q. *Bureaucracy: What Government Agencies Do and Why They Do It.* New York: Basic Books, 1989.

World Bank. *The East Asian Miracle: Economic Growth and Public Policy.* New York: Oxford University Press, 1993.

Francis T. Lui[1] on Pranab Bardhan's Paper
The Political Economy of Development Policy: An Asian Perspective

The paper by Professor Bardhan was both interesting and enjoyable. Although Professor Bardhan chose here to abstain from any formal mathematical modeling, the paper's rich ideas and insights are more than enough to stimulate a large number of research programs on economic development, organization theory, and political economy. Drawing lessons from comparisons between East Asia and South Asia, the paper offers a new perspective on the role of the state in economic development. This perspective is useful because it alerts us to some fundamental issues often neglected in the literature of endogenous growth and institutional economics.

The basic theme of the paper is that there may exist a correlation between a country's growth performance and the "strength" of the state. A state is strong if the "quality" of its intervention is good. It should be able to provide people with at least a minimum policy package of macroeconomic stability, fiscal restraint, and a reliable legal system and at the same time be able to resist political pressures for undesirable market interventions. More importantly, it should have at heart the "encompassing interest" of the country as a whole so that it can credibly precommit itself to resolving the "coordination" failures of the market. The author believes that coordination difficulties are major obstacles to growth.

A regime ruled by a rational "stationary bandit" or by a majoritarian democracy may be guided by an encompassing interest in the economic health of the country. Nevertheless, there still remains the question of what conditions are needed so that the coordination problem can be solved more easily. Among others, inequality and polarization within a society make it difficult to build consensus about policy changes and are therefore seen as important obstacles to resolving the coordination problem. They consequently hurt growth.

The identification of inequality or heterogeneity among a country's people as a factor affecting growth is a useful approach. The relationship between growth and inequality has always been a controversial subject. One can easily formulate a class of models that

[1] Hong Kong University of Science and Technology.

generates results working in the opposite direction. To illustrate, let us use Hong Kong—the East Asian economy that this writer is most familiar with—as an example to show that static inequality in income distribution does not necessarily reduce growth.

Hong Kong's growth has been so high that its per capita income level has increased almost tenfold during the last forty years. Yet Hong Kong's Gini coefficient based on 1991 census data was as high as 0.48. Even though this figure may be reduced to about 0.4 once we take into account the substantial amount of redistributive subsidy spent on massive public housing programs, Hong Kong's static income distribution is still generally regarded as rather unequal.[2]

Moreover, the Gini coefficient has been on the increasing trend of the Kuznets inverted U-shaped curve for a long time. Although more recently, heterogeneity in earnings has occasionally caused some social problems, these problems are far from being able to pose serious challenges to society. The majority still seems to be holding on to middle class values.

The important thing to recognize is that equality of opportunity, rather than of income, has been working well. The extensive system of student loans and scholarships has made it possible for talented students of any income class to enter universities, which constitute the most important channel for upward social mobility. The free-market environment is also conducive to building an entrepreneurial spirit, which further reduces barriers to social mobility. The huge income differential between the poor and the rich has created strong incentives for the former to strive harder. This situation enhances rather than reduces growth. One can go further to argue that the achievements of the most talented will raise the general productivity of society, thereby benefiting not only themselves but also the less fortunate. When the poorer people see that they have a chance to get richer, they tend to be less envious of the more successful. Heterogeneity in income does not complicate the coordination problem when people are mobile in a free-market economy.

The paper points out that the technocratic elite in charge of policymaking in East Asian countries has been remarkably insulated from politics. This factor may also help to make a state strong. To achieve insulation, some conditions are necessary, including highly selective meritocratic recruitment, long-term career rewards, rapid job turnover, extensive connections between bureaucrats and business people so that information and risks can be shared, and compromises on who should get rents. Again, using Hong Kong as the point of reference, one can easily verify that all these necessary elements are pervasive there. Why do the successful East Asian countries all share these diverse characteristics? Each country seems to be able to develop them on its own, without the need to

---

[2] The Gini coefficient is not necessarily a good measurement of inequality. If everybody's income level is the same, the Gini is zero. If one person among this group gets rich, the Gini increases. If more become rich while others remain poor, the Gini is even higher. The Gini may become zero again when everybody has become rich. When half the people are rich and half are poor, is it less equitable than the case when one is rich and all others are poor? Hong Kong's high Gini coefficient may be the result of the pattern that more and more of the poorer people have become rich.

import them from others. Is it because they also share the same cultural values or is it because of some other factors we have not identified? The answers to these questions are elusive but need to be sought if other countries want to emulate the East Asian successes.

Insulation of a country's bureaucrats requires the political neutrality of its civil servants. But most of the successful East Asian countries are now in the process of achieving a greater degree of democratization. Vote-hungry politicians may exert great pressure on civil servants to take certain stands. Sometimes, civil servants in the executive branch of the government may need to make political compromises in order to get support from the politicians. Will the civil servants in these countries be able to maintain their neutrality in the face of public pressure? What institutions are needed so that bureaucratic neutrality can be better protected? These are also important questions that need to be addressed.

REFERENCE

McGuire, M.C., and M. Olson. "The Economics of Autocracy and Majority Rule." *Journal of Economic Literature* (March 1996).

Keijiro Otsuka[1] on Pranab Bardhan's Paper

The Political Economy of Development Policy: An Asian Perspective

In this extremely insightful article, Professor Bardhan develops an integrated model of the political economy of development policy by synthesizing recent theories of institutional economics and political economy with the contrasting development experiences of East Asia and South Asia. According to conventional wisdom, in order to achieve economic development government must ensure macroeconomic stability, establish efficient legal systems to facilitate economic transactions, and provide social infrastructures. In addition, both the experience of East Asia and the economic theories of transaction costs and imperfect markets strongly suggest the importance of policies to coordinate and promote private investments so as to support infant industries by such means as direct credit allocations and the operation of development banks. This new paradigm of economic development differs from the old one that naively identified government intervention with government failure.

Professor Bardhan argues that only "strong government," which is defined as one with the ability to commit itself credibly to long-term development goals, chooses and enacts appropriate policies, whereas "weak government" is prone to failure as it is easily influenced by the pressure of interest groups. This point is relevant and amply supported empirically.

The article then explores the question of what determines the "strength" of government. One of the answers is that only homogeneous or "equal" societies—such as Japan, Taiwan, and Korea—can help support strong developmental government. In contrast, interest groups tend to control politics in domestically heterogeneous and unequal societies. Another unfavorable consequence of unequal societies is the absence or weak functioning of communal institutions, which are capable of enforcing social rules and regulations regarding economic transactions, property rights, and the provision of local public goods. Inefficient bureaucracy dominates in local politics in the absence of communal institutions.

Thus, Bardhan attributes at least part of the success of economic development in East Asia to the homogeneity of the society there and part of the relative difficulty in South Asia to the heterogeneity there. This assertion is basically sound.

---

[1] International Food Policy Research Institute and Tokyo Metropolitan University.

In the view of the present writer, two additional features of East Asian economies that are also conducive to development, are the low transaction cost associated with long-term transactions there and the existence of social sanctions, in which trust and reputation play a central role. The low transaction cost is manifested in efficient inter-enterprise transactions involving parts and intermediate products, in the effective labor management of enterprises, and in the relatively corruption-free bureaucracy. There is no question but that the homogeneity of societies provides the basis for the low transaction costs.

Thus, the homogeneous society supports "strong" government and efficient institutions—the two critical components of economic development. An ultimate question of development then is what determines the homogeneity of the society. History and path-dependence "explain" an important part of the story. Certain economic and political forces also contribute to the formation of more homogeneous or equal societies. In this connection, Bardhan argues that the "East Asian states have succeeded in realizing a large part of their potential [for development] through...redistributive reforms." An important redistributive reform in developing countries is land reform. Thus, Bardhan's political-economy model stimulates renewed interest in land reform, which has obvious relevance for development in Latin American countries.

But do we really have enough evidence to support the hypothesis that land reform has resulted in accelerated development through the establishment of strong community institutions and support of strong government? The answer is that we do not. Japanese rural societies are indeed known for strong social ties and community relations, which have undoubtedly contributed to the efficient management of communal irrigation and forests and the effective enforcement of property rights and contracts; but such rural institutions have existed for centuries in Japan. And it is indeed true that Japanese farmers have supported strong government; but they have done so as an interest group demanding heavy protection for agriculture. Further, the Japanese economy grew fairly rapidly even before the war, when distribution of land was much less equal. In East Asia, aside from Japan, Taiwan, and Korea, land reform has been implemented effectively in the Philippines, but in the latter, little if any significant change occurred in communal institutions after that reform.

Thus, the importance of redistributive policies for economic development is perhaps overemphasized in the article. In contrast, the role of schooling and education deserves more attention. In analyzing the role that schooling plays in economic development, it is important to emphasize both the acquisition of academic knowledge and the acquisition of the ability to interact and cooperate with other people. The economic theory of human capital pays attention only to the acquisition of knowledge, even though the more social aspect of schooling is also important and is deeply related with transaction costs. Indeed, in practice, the ability to coordinate teamwork, the capacity to deal with trade partners, and a reputation for respectable and reliable behavior are prerequisites for leadership in modern organizations, particularly in the context of East Asia. The acquisition of such ability and traits is an integral part of schooling. In other words, schooling in East Asia contributes to the formation not only of human capital but also of social capital. Social capital, in turn, facilitates economic transactions and improves organizational efficiency by enhancing social solidarity and homogeneity. One can, of course, argue that this important role of schooling cannot be realized without the underlying support of a strong government.

The homogeneity of a society is subject to change. Kuznet's inverted-U hypothesis of income distribution suggests the interdependence between development and equity—or between development and homogeneity, in our context. The story of Taiwan, which achieved greater equity with rapid economic development, is well known. The problem is that the mechanism by which equity changes with economic development is underresearched. Actually we do not know the answer to the most rudimentary question of whether and to what extent the inverted-U hypothesis holds in reality.

It is no exaggeration to say that our empirical knowledge about economic development in general, and about the East Asian development model in particular, is deplorably meager. Professor Bardhan's article provides a logical and valuable analytical framework for the examination of the political economy of economic development based firmly on economic theories and casual empiricism and should stimulate empirical research from a fresh perspective.

Economic Policy and Performance in Capitalist Europe[1]

Angus Maddison[2]

The present paper deals with 16 European capitalist countries and tries to put their economic and social development into comparative and historical perspective. It is in three parts. The first part emphasizes distinctive features that characterize the long-term performance of this group and differentiate it from the rest of the world. The second part examines major development phases and economic-policy fashions that these countries experienced from 1820 to 1973. The third part deals with economic performance and social development since 1973 and with the nature of the forces that have transformed the "establishment view" of economic-policy goals.

Long-Run Considerations

In terms of basic institutions and economic policy, the European capitalist sample group is reasonably homogeneous. The basic core consists of 12 countries (Austria, Belgium, Denmark, Finland, France, Germany, Italy, the Netherlands, Norway, Sweden, Switzerland, and the United Kingdom) with a range of per capita incomes that goes from 1.3 to 1. Among the four peripheral European capitalist countries (Greece, Ireland, Portugal, and Spain) the income range is from 1.4 to 1. Some 14 of the 16 countries in our sample are members of the European Union.

By world standards they are all relatively rich, and most have been so for the past two hundred years. For them, economic growth is nothing new. In the protocapitalist period they had more than four centuries of very modest (0.2 percent a year) growth in per capita income, and they have experienced significantly faster income growth (1.5 percent a year) in the capitalist epoch since 1820 (see Table 3.12). In the protocapitalist period they pulled ahead of the rest of the world, so their income levels were already twice the world level in 1820. The lengthy protocapitalist apprenticeship was required in order to build the institutional basis of modern capitalism. Legal protection of property rights, enforceable contracts, and techniques of corporate and financial organization are elements assumed to be quickly transferable nowadays to the rest of the world, but speedy malleability has not been a characteristic of Europe itself.

[1] I am grateful for comments and suggestions from Charles Maddison, Irma Adelman, and participants in the September 1996 IDB Conference on Development Thinking and Practice.
[2] University of Groningen, Netherlands.

**TABLE 3.12.   Comparative Performance of Capitalist Europe
and Other Economic Areas, 1400–1996**

	1400	1820	1950	1996	1400–1820	1820–1996
	Population (000s)				Annual average compound growth rates	
Capitalist Europe	42,000	127,347	285,143	372,400	.26	.61
Latin America	10,000	15,754	127,160	396,327	.11	2.00
USA	1,000	9,981	152,271	265,788	.55	1.88
China	72,000	381,000	547,000	1,219,084	.40	.66
Japan	12,700	31,000	83,563	126,063	.21	.80
World	320,000	1,068,000	2,512,211	5,636,578	.29	.95
	GDP per capita (1990 international $)					
Capitalist Europe	(530)	1,222	4,666	17,097	.20	1.51
Latin America	(450)	715	2,614	5,602	.11	1.18
USA	(450)	1,262	9,573	23,196	.25	1.67
China	(575)	575	525	2,820	.00	0.91
Japan	(575)	704	1,873	19,974	.05	1.92
World	(500)	669	2,119	5,200	.07	1.17
	GDP (million 1990 international $)					
Capitalist Europe	(22,260)	155,634	1,330,514	6,366,837	.46	2.13
Latin America	(4,500)	11,264	332,379	2,220,052	.22	3.05
USA	(450)	12,595	1,457,624	6,165,120	.80	3.58
China	(41,400)	219,075	287,175	3,457,816	.40	1.57
Japan	(7,303)	21,831	156,546	2,517,991	.26	2.73
World	(160,000)	714,700	5,372,330	29,310,207	.36	2.13

Source: Maddison (1995a). GDP 1820–1992 updated to 1996 from OECD and ECLAC sources, China from Maddison (1997). 1400 very crude guesstimates backcast from 1820 levels, mainly from Maddison (1997). Population 1820–1996 from Maddison (1995a). Population 1400, Japan from Taeuber (1958) p.20 interpolated between her estimates for 1185–1333 and 1572–91; US and Latin America from sources cited in A. Maddison, "The Historical Roots of Modern Mexico, 1500-1940" in Maddison (1995b); China from Maddison (1997). For a discussion of alternative estimates of American population before Columbus, see Daniels (1992).

The European family pattern has been different from that in most other parts of the world. Fertility rates were lower than elsewhere and dropped as mortality rates dropped. Since 1820, population growth has averaged 0.6 percent a year, compared with 2.0 percent in the Americas and 1.3 percent in Africa. Since 1973, population has grown by only 0.3 percent a year in the core and 0.7 percent in the European periphery. Smaller family size has favored investment in human capital and has enhanced the capacity to finance investment in physical capital.

These countries have played a dominant role in the development of world trade since the end of the fifteenth century, when they pioneered the routes to America and Asia. From 1820 to 1913, they accounted for significantly more than half of world exports. In 1992 the proportion was still 45 percent, even though their share of world population was only 7 percent. This openness of their economies brought them gains in efficiency through specialization and added to economic dynamism by providing ready access to

TABLE 3.13. Ratio of Commodity Exports to GDP, 1820–1992

(At 1990 prices)

	1820	1913	1950	1992
European Capitalist Core	2.5	16.3	9.4	29.7
Spain	1.1	8.1	1.6	13.4
Latin America	n.a.	9.5	6.2	6.2
USA	2.0	3.7	3.0	8.2
World	1.0	8.7	7.0	13.5

Source: Maddison (1995a), p. 38

new products and processes. In the nineteenth century, only the Netherlands and the United Kingdom were committed to free trade, but the others were only mildly protectionist. A major setback occurred from 1929 to 1950, when the policies of these countries moved closer to the prescriptions of Hjalmar Schacht than to those of Adam Smith. After 1950, trade expanded hugely as policy was liberalized. By 1992, merchandise exports in the European core averaged nearly 30 percent of GDP and in the periphery about 24 percent. Table 3.13 gives a striking illustration of the difference between capitalist Europe and Latin America in this respect: between 1950 and 1992 the commodity exports of the capitalist core rose from 9 percent of GDP to 30 percent, but in Latin America the export ratio averaged 6 percent of GDP in 1950 and was still the same in 1992.

The most fundamental characteristic of Western Europe that favored development was the recognition of the human capacity to transform the forces of nature through rational investigation and experiment. Thanks to the Renaissance and the Enlightenment, Western elites gradually abandoned superstition, the belief in magic, and unthinking submission to religious authority. The Western scientific tradition that underlies the modern approach to technical change and innovation had clearly emerged by the seventeenth century and began to impregnate the educational system. Circumscribed horizons were abandoned, and the quest for change and improvement was unleashed.

This situation was very different from that prevailing in Asia. Even J. Needham (1981, p. 9), the main chronicler of Chinese technological precocity and a noted sinophile, has clearly acknowledged this Western achievement: "When we say that modern science developed only in Western Europe in the time of Galileo during the Renaissance and the scientific revolution, we mean, I think, that it was there alone that there developed the fundamental bases of *modern* science, such as the application of mathematical hypotheses to Nature, and the full understanding of the experimental method, the distinction between primary and secondary qualities and the systematic accumulation of openly published scientific data."

The immediate payoff from this change was rather meager, and most innovation in the protocapitalist period came from practical experience and from learning by doing. But the potential for the acceleration of technical progress through application of the experimental approach was substantially augmented in the nineteenth century, when the

TABLE 3.14. Productivity and Per Capita GDP Growth Performance of Lead Countries, 1820–1992

	1820–1870	1870–1913	1913–50	1950–73	1973–92
Total factor productivity (proxy for rate of progress at technical frontier)					
UK	0.15	0.31			
USA		0.33	1.60	1.72	0.18
Labor productivity					
UK	1.16	1.13			
USA		1.88	2.48	2.74	1.11
Per capita GDP					
UK	1.2	1.0			
USA		1.8	1.6	2.4	1.4

Source: Maddison (1995a), pp. 62 and 441–2.

Table 3.15. Levels of Performance in Lead Countries, 1820–1992

	1820	1870	1913	1950	1973	1992
Labor productivity (1990) int. $ per hour worked)						
UK	1.48	2.64	4.28	7.86	15.92	23.98
USA	1.33	2.3	5.12	12.68	23.60	29.10
GDP per capita (1990 int. $)						
UK	1,703	3,164	4,878	6,847	11,992	15,738
USA	1,287[a]	2,459	5,312	9,582	16,608	21,558
Stock of machinery and equipment per person employed (1990 int. $)						
UK	238	857	2,021	4,699	13,893	23,095
USA	281	1,367	6,932	15,120	26,259	39,636
Stock of nonresidential structures per person employed (1990 int.$)						
UK	2,973	6,254	7,404	7,556	21,464	41,797
USA	3,503	10,294	37,905	42,673	59,461	72,625
Years of formal education per person employed						
UK	2.00	4.44	8.82	10.60	11.66	14.09
USA	1.75	3.92	7.86	11.27	14.58	18.04

Source: Maddison (1995a). The figures for education are weighted: primary education is given a weight of 1, secondary 1.4, and higher 2 in line with evidence on relative earnings.
a) Excludes indigenous population (who are included in the figure in Table 3.12).

gradual infiltration of the scientific approach into educational systems facilitated the absorption and adaptation of technical change.

In the course of the nineteenth century, the main locus of technical progress was Western Europe, particularly the United Kingdom, but the United States began to take over in the twentieth century (Table 3.14 and Table 3.15). From 1913 to 1973, U.S. per-

TABLE 3.16. Labor Productivity (GDP per hour worked), 1870–1992
(U.S. level = 100)

	1870	1913	1950	1973	1992
Austria	62	57	32	65	83
Belgium	94	70	48	70	98
Denmark	67	66	46	68	75
Finland	37	35	32	57	70
France	60	56	45	76	102
Germany	70	68	35	71	95[a]
Italy	46	41	34	66	85
Netherlands	103	78	51	81	99
Norway	48	43	43	60	88
Sweden	54	50	56	77	79
Switzerland	77	63	69	78	87
UK	115	86	62	68	82
Arithmetic Average	**69**	**59**	**46**	**70**	**87**
Greece			20	46	59
Ireland			30	43	71
Portugal			20	42	48
Spain			21	46	69
Arithmetic Average			**23**	**44**	**62**
Argentina			49	47	41
Brazil			19	24	23
Chile			37	38	37
Colombia			22	25	27
Mexico			24	33	29
Peru			23	27	15
Venezuela			71	82	58
Arithmetic Average			**35**	**39**	**33**

Source: Maddison (1995a), p. 47.
[a] Figure refers to West Germany; including East Germany, it would be 85.

formance improved much faster than had that of the United Kingdom in the nineteenth century (as measured by the growth rate of total factor productivity). This acceleration in the United States was achieved by a massive and systematic research and development effort by corporations and government and was helped by unusual economies of scale in production of new standardized products. From 1913 to 1950, European policy and circumstances were not propitious for exploiting the opportunities of this new American technology, and a very substantial productivity gap emerged between Western Europe and the United States. Since 1950 there has occurred a very impressive process of European catch-up. The technological gap is now much smaller than in 1950, and Europe operates much nearer to the productivity frontier (see Table 3.16). In terms of labor productivity, the leading European countries are France, the Netherlands, and Belgium. Germany is popularly supposed to be the star performer, but it was never the European leader and has ranked level with Italy since aborbing East Germany.

The capitalist European countries are often called "industrial." This appellation is based on a historical fallacy that goes back to Ricardo, who regarded manufactures as the

TABLE 3.17. Proportion of Employment by Major Economic Sector, 1870–1995
(Percent of total employment)

	Agriculture, Forestry, and Fishing	Industry	Services
	12 core countries of capitalist Europe		
1870	50.2	26.4	23.4
1950	24.7	38.1	37.2
1973	9.7	38.5	51.8
1995	4.5	27.3	68.2
	4 countries of capitalist periphery		
1950	19.7	22.3	28.0
1973	27.0	32.3	40.7
1995	11.3	29.7	59.0

Sources: Core countries 1870-1973 from Maddison 91991), pp. 248-9, 1995 from OECD Quarterly Labour Force Statistics 1, 1996. Periphery 1950 from Mueller (1965), p. 39; 1973 from OECD, Labor Force Statistics.

sole locus of technical progress and who took as dim a view as did Malthus of the potential for improvement in and through agriculture. In the past, economic historians have given excessive emphasis to the notion of an industrial revolution. Many policymakers have been in thrall to these dead economists and economic historians. As a result, a wide swath of politicians—from Stalin to Harold Wilson—has diverted resources toward or has showered subsidies on what they considered the leading sector of the economy: industry. Another group has lavished subsidies on what they presumed to be a backward peasantry.

In the nineteenth century, technical change was probably fastest in industry and transport and was slower (but not negligible) in agriculture. Since World War II, however, productivity has grown faster in agriculture than in industry (see Maddison 1991, p. 150).

Over time, the production structure of the capitalist countries of Europe has changed dramatically (see Table 3.17). In 1870 about half the employed population of the core countries was engaged in agriculture and about one-fourth each in industry and in services. The agricultural share has fallen dramatically and is now less than 5 percent; the service share has risen to more than two-thirds; and the industrial share peaked at around 38 percent in the 1950–1973 period and has now fallen back very substantially to a level not very different from that of 1870. Similar tendencies operated in the European capitalist periphery, with some delay: in 1950 these countries had an employment structure similar to that in the core countries in 1870, but now they have converged much closer to the richer countries. Their lead sector is services, with a falling labor force share engaged in industry and with little more than one-tenth of the labor force engaged in agriculture.

These changes have been influenced by the pattern of technical change, but they were also influenced by changes in consumer demand as incomes rose, the share and pat-

TABLE 3.18. Growth of GDP in Constant Prices, 1820–1996

(Annual average compound growth rates)

	1820–1870	1870–1913	1913–1950	1950–1973	1973–1996
Austria	1.4	2.4	0.2	5.3	2.3
Belgium	2.2	2.0	1.0	4.1	1.9
Denmark	1.9	2.7	2.6	3.8	1.9
Finland	1.6	2.7	2.7	4.9	2.1
France	1.3	1.6	1.1	5.0	2.1
Germany	2.0	2.8	1.1	6.0	2.1
Italy	1.2	1.9	1.5	5.6	2.4
Netherlands	1.9	2.2	2.4	4.7	2.2
Norway	1.7	2.1	2.9	4.1	3.5
Sweden	1.6	2.2	2.7	3.7	1.5
Switzerland	n.a.	2.4	2.6	4.5	1.1
UK	2.0	1.9	1.3	2.9	1.8
Arithmetic Average	**1.7**	**2.2**	**1.8**	**4.6**	**1.9**
Greece	n.a.	n.a.	1.4	7.0	2.1
Ireland	0.7	0.5	0.6	3.2	3.9
Portugal	n.a.	1.3	2.2	5.7	2.6
Spain	1.1	1.7	1.0	6.8	2.4
Arithmetic Average	**0.9**	**1.2**	**1.3**	**5.7**	**2.8**
USA	4.2	3.9	2.8	3.9	2.5

Sources: Maddison (1995a), Appendix B, pp. 148–53, updated to 1994 from OECD, *National Accounts* 1960–1994 1, Paris 1996, with estimates for 1995 and projections for 1996 from OECD, *Economic Outlook,* June 1996.

tern of government consumption, the share of foreign trade, the investment rate, the depletion of natural resources, and government policies to subsidize or protect particular activities.

Phases of Development and Fashions in Policy, 1820–1973

Within the capitalist epoch, the momentum of growth has varied considerably, and so have fashions in economic policy. We can distinguish five major phases of development since 1820. Our main interest is in the last phase, from 1973 onward, but it will be useful to say something first about the other four in order to provide some sense of perspective.

From 1820 to 1870 these countries experienced very substantial growth, by previous standards (Table 3.18). They were all involved in this growth process. The earlier notion that there occurred a staggered succession of takeoffs in this group is not correct. The dynamics of productivity growth were not as intense as was later the case, but there nevertheless occurred a very rapid growth of trade. The lead country, the United Kingdom, exercised a diffusionist influence through its policies of free trade.

The second major phase, from 1870 to 1913, was one of faster technical progress and of quickened per capita income growth (Table 3.19 and Table 3.20). There were no major armed conflicts or great differences of economic regime among the countries.

TABLE 3.19. GDP Per Capita, 1820–1996

(1990 international dollars)

	1820	1913	1950	1992
Austria	1,295	3,488	3,731	17,755
Belgium	1,291	4,130	5,346	17,859
Denmark	1,225	3,764	6,683	19,701
Finland	759	2,050	4,131	15,771
France	1,218	3,452	5,221	18,335
Germany	1,112	3,833	4,281	18,998
Italy	1,092	2,507	3,425	16,985
Netherlands	1,561	3,950	5,850	18,038
Norway	1,004	2,275	4,969	20,211
Sweden	1,198	3,096	6,738	17,161
Switzerland	n.a.	4,207	8,939	20,905
UK	1,756	5,032	6,847	17,264
Arithmetic Average	**1,228**	**3,482**	**5,513**	**18,249**
Greece	n.a.	1,621	1,951	10,626
Ireland	954	2,733	3,518	14,546
Portugal	n.a.	1,354	2,132	11,765
Spain	1,063	2,255	2,397	13,223
Arithmetic Average				
for Capitalist Europe	**1,009**	**1,991**	**2,500**	**12,540**
Argentina	n.a.	3,797	4,987	8,072[a]
Brazil	670	839	1,673	4,979[a]
Chile	n.a.	2,653	3,827	8,261[a]
Colombia	n.a.	1,236	2,089	5,552[a]
Mexico	760	1,467	2,085	4,660[a]
Peru	n.a.	1,037	2,263	3,416[a]
Venezuela	n.a.	1,104	7,424	8,381[a]
Arithmetic Average	**715**	**1,733**	**3,478**	**6,189[a]**
USA	1,287[b]	5,307	9,573	23,188

Sources: Maddison (1995a) updated from OECD *National Accounts 1960–1994*, OECD *Economic Outlook* (June 1996), and ECLAC 1995.
[a] 1995; [b] excludes indigenous population

Virtually all of them adopted the gold standard. There existed international mobility of labor—with large labor migrations from Europe and with large exports of capital to the rest of the world. At that time the capitalist European countries felt that their power and income would be advanced by having colonial possessions, and so there existed competition for power in Africa and in Central Asia, operating to some extent as a safety valve for conflicts that might otherwise have occurred within Europe. A that time governments did not feel the need for activist policies to promote economic growth; they assumed that the free operation of market forces in conditions of monetary and financial stability would automatically lead to something like an optimal allocation of resources. There existed limited suffrage, trade unions were weak, and wages were flexible. Low taxes and free labor markets were felt to be the best stimulus to investment. Domestic policy was inspired largely by principles of fiscal responsibility and sound money. There occurred no net change in the general price level from 1870 to 1913: prices fell until the 1890s and

TABLE 3.20. Growth of Per Capita GDP in Constant Prices, 1820–1996

(Annual average compound growth rate)

	1820–1870	1870–1913	1913–1950	1950–1973	1973–1996
Austria	0.7	1.5	0.2	4.9	2.0
Belgium	1.4	1.0	0.7	3.5	1.8
Denmark	0.9	1.6	1.6	3.1	1.7
Finland	0.8	1.4	1.9	4.3	1.7
France	0.8	1.5	1.1	4.0	1.5
Germany	1.1	1.6	0.3	5.0	1.6
Italy	0.6	1.3	0.8	5.0	2.2
Netherlands	1.1	0.9	1.1	3.4	1.5
Norway	0.5	1.3	2.1	3.2	3.0
Sweden	0.7	1.5	2.1	3.1	1.1
Switzerland	n.a.	1.5	2.1	3.1	0.7
UK	1.2	1.0	0.8	2.4	1.6
Arithmetic Average	**0.9**	**1.3**	**1.2**	**3.8**	**1.7**
Greece	n.a.	n.a.	0.5	6.2	1.4
Ireland	1.2	1.0	0.7	3.1	3.2
Portugal	n.a.	0.5	1.2	5.7	1.9
Spain	0.5	1.2	0.2	5.8	1.8
Arithmetic Average	**0.9**	**0.9**	**0.7**	**5.2**	**2.1**
Capitalist Europe	0.9	1.3	1.1	4.1	1.8
USA	1.3	1.8	1.6	2.4	1.5

Sources: Maddison (1995a), p. 62, revised and updated to 1996. GDP to 1994 from OECD, *National Accounts 1960–1994*, Paris 1996, with estimates for 1995 and projections for 1996 from OECD, *Economic Outlook*, June 1996, p. A-4. Population from Maddison (1995a), Tables A-3a and A-36 to 1994. It was assumed that rates of poulation growth 1994–96 were the same as for 1992–94.

rose somewhat thereafter. Taxes and government expenditures were low and generally in balance; spending was confined mainly to making provision for domestic order and for national defense. Social spending was small, generally covering only elementary education and preventive health measure, although Bismarck began to provide pensions and welfare payments in Germany in the 1880s, and Lloyd George introduced similar measure in the United Kingdom in 1909. There existed no international organizations like the OECD, IMF, BIS, and GATT to manage a "world system."

Performance in that 1870–1913 phase in the European capitalist countries was probably close to potential. At that time, technical progress was not as fast as it was later to become, and Europe was exporting its surplus capital and labor mainly to areas of recent settlement, where natural-resource endowments were greater.

The two phases that followed were very different both from the 1870–1913 phase and from each other. In the 1913–1950 phase, the European economies were deeply disturbed by wars, depression, beggar-your-neighbor policies, and the strains of adjusting to the Cold War; it was a bleak age, in which the countries' potential for accelerated growth was frustrated by a series of disasters. By contrast, the 1950–1973 phase was a golden age in which a backlog of missed opportunities was successfully exploited.

Generally speaking, the entire 60 years from 1913 to 1973 were abnormal; in some ways, experience in the 1870–1913 phase is more relevant in assessing the comparative adequacy of performance since 1973. The latest phase has been closer to the 1870–1913 phase in respect to per capita income growth and to policy aspirations than it has been to either the bleak age or to the golden age.

It is not worth dwelling here on the 1913–1950 phase in any greater detail. The reasons for setbacks to European growth during that time have been well documented.

In contrast, the years 1953 to 1973 were a golden age of unparalleled prosperity. Per capita income rose by 3.8 percent a year in the core countries and by 5.8 percent per year in the European periphery, and GDP per man-hour rose by 4.7 percent and 5.7 percent. There took place a very significant degree of catch-up to U.S. levels of performance. Not only did there exist unusual opportunities from the productivity backlog but also progress at the technical frontier continued to grow quickly. European savings rates were higher than ever before but were absorbed by very high rates of domestic investment. Europe attracted very substantial net migration from the rest of the world.

Major changes in policy made it possible to seize these opportunities. The first of these policy changes was the remarkable revival of liberalism in international transactions. Barriers to trade and payments that had been enacted in the 1930s and during the war were removed. The new-style liberalism was buttressed by effective arrangements both for articulate and regular consultations among Western countries and for mutual financial assistance. Trade was freed by the abolition of quantitative restrictions in OEEC and by the reduction of tariffs on a regional basis in the EC and EFTA and, more globally, in the GATT. Export volume rose sevenfold (Table 3.21). Increased exports were a major force in sustaining the growth of demand and productivity and in keeping prices in check.

The fundamental innovation in domestic policy was the commitment to full use of resources. In the 1950–1973 phase the average unemployment rate in the core countries was only 2.4 percent of the labor force, and in the periphery it was only 3.6 percent (Table 3.22). In Scandinavia and the United Kingdom, the gospel of fiscal activism and primordial commitment to full employment had been propounded by Keynes, Lundberg, and Myrdal and gained wide postwar acceptance in academic, political, and bureaucratic milieux. In France, the objective of full resource use derived from the strong commitment to growth and supply side stimuli in the planning process. Germany gave greater emphasis to price stability and work incentives than to buoyant domestic demand but proclaimed the full-employment goal in its Stabilization Law of 1967; in any case, it achieved fuller employment than most countries by export-induced growth.

Until 1971 these countries had the dollar as their monetary anchor. The fixed-rate exchange system derived from the wartime Bretton Woods commitments. Exchange stability was easier to attain in a period in which there existed significant controls on capital movements.

Policy was also helped by the moderation of price increases. The general goal of governments was not price stability but to keep the pace of increase within limits that did not put too great a strain on competitiveness. When the outcome of demand management

TABLE 3.21. Growth in Volume of Merchandise Exports, 1820–1996
(Annual average compound growth rates)

	1820–1870	1870–1913	1913–1950	1950–1973	1973–1996
Austria	4.5	3.5	-3.0	10.7	6.4
Belgium	5.4[a]	4.2	0.3	9.2	4.3
Denmark	1.9[b]	3.3	2.4	6.9	4.1
Finland	n.a.	3.9	1.9	7.2	4.0
France	4.0	2.8	1.1	8.2	4.3
Germany	4.8[c]	4.1	-2.8	12.4	3.7
Italy	3.4	2.2	0.6	11.6	5.5
Netherlands	n.a.	2.3[d]	1.5	10.4	4.0
Norway	n.a.	3.2	2.7	7.3	6.8
Sweden	7.0[e]	3.1	2.8	6.9	4.1
Switzerland	4.1	3.9	0.3	8.1	2.6
UK	4.9	2.8	0.0	3.9	4.2
Arithmetic Average	**4.4**	**3.2**	**0.7**	**8.6**	**4.5**
Greece	n.a.	n.a.	n.a.	11.9	5.6
Ireland	n.a.	n.a.	n.a.	6.8	9.4
Portugal	n.a.	n.a.	n.a.	5.7	8.3
Spain	3.7[f]	3.5	-1.6	9.2	8.8
Arithmetic Average	**3.7**	**3.5**	**-1.6**	**8.4**	**8.0**

Sources: Maddison (1995a), pp. 74 and 236, updated to 1996 from OECD, Economic Outlook, June 1996, Annex Table 39. The figures are not adjusted to exclude the impact of frontier changes.
[a] 1831–70; [b] 1844–70; [c] 1840–70; [d] 1872–1913; [e] 1851–70; [f] 1826–70

policy was unclear, the tendency was to take the upside risk. This was most clearly the case in France, which looked to devaluation as compensation.

The average rise in consumer price indexes from 1950 to 1973 was about 4 percent a year in the 16 countries. The rate of price increase might well have been faster at such high levels of employment, but stability was helped by the fixed-rate exchange system, the impact of foreign trade in stimulating competition, the stability of primary commodity prices because of U.S. farm surpluses, and the large oil reserves and political weakness of Middle Eastern countries. Large flows of labor from farming and immigration helped to keep down wage pressure, and levels of social tension were low because of the creation of the welfare state. Finally, expectations had not adjusted to continuous inflation. Friedman (1968) suggested that expectations would become more adaptive and decidedly more explosive unless unemployment increased.

Eventually the collapse of the monetary anchor, the erosion of the special factors that had mitigated price increases, and the OPEC shock all operated simultaneously in the early 1970s in a way that forced a change in the overall emphasis of domestic policy.

The 1973–1996 Phase: A Return to Capitalist Normalcy?

The Slowdown in Performance of the Core Countries

In the latest phase of European capitalist development, growth has been very much slower than in the golden age. The slowdown has affected all major indicators. In the 12 core

TABLE 3.22. Unemployment as a Percentage of the Labor Force, 1920–1996

	1920–29	1930–38	1950–73	1974–83	1984–95	1996 projected
Austria	6.0[a]	12.8	2.6	2.3	5.0	6.2
Belgium	1.5[b]	7.9	3.0	8.2	11.3	13.2
Denmark	8.1	10.9	2.6	7.6	9.9	9.2
Finland	1.6	3.7	1.7	4.7	8.9	16.4
France	1.7[c]	3.5[d]	2.0	5.7	10.4	12.1
Germany	3.9	7.9	2.5	4.1	7.9	10.3
Italy	1.7[e]	4.8[f]	5.5	7.2	9.8	12.1
Netherlands	2.3	7.8	2.2	7.3	7.4	7.0
Norway	5.6[b]	7.3	1.9	2.1	4.2	4.3
Sweden	3.2	5.0	1.8	2.3	4.0	7.6
Switzerland	0.4[e]	2.7	0.0	0.4	1.8	4.2
UK	7.5	10.4	2.8	7.0	9.0	7.9
Arithmetic Average	**3.6**	**7.1**	**2.4**	**4.9**	**7.5**	**9.2**
Greece	n.a.	n.a.	4.6[g]	3.2	8.2	10.2
Ireland	n.a.	n.a.	5.2[g]	8.8	15.3	12.4
Portugal	n.a.	n.a.	2.4[g]	6.5	6.4	7.4
Spain	n.a.	n.a.	2.9[g]	9.1	20.1	22.9
Arithmetic Average	**n.a.**	**n.a.**	**3.6[g]**	**6.9**	**12.5**	**13.2**
USA	4.8	18.2	4.6	7.4	6.4	5.5

Sources: First 12 countries 1920–73 from Maddison (1991), Appendix C; 1974–83 from OECD, *Labor Force Statistics;* 1984–96 from OECD, *Economic Outlook,* June 1996, annex Table 21. European periphery 1960–83 from OECD, *Labor Force Statistics,* 1984–96 from OECD, *Economic Outlook,* June 1996.
[a] 1924–9;   [b] 1921–9;   [c] average of 1921, 1926, and 1929;   [d] average of 1931, 1936, and 1938;   [e] 1929 only;   [f] 1935–36 not available; [g] 1960–73.

countries, per capita GDP growth has averaged 1.7 percent a year from 1973 to 1996 compared with 3.8 percent from 1950 to 1973; the smallest proportionate decline has occurred in Norway and the United Kingdom. There also has occurred a significant drop in population growth; on average, population growth was only 0.3 percent a year from 1973 to 1996, compared with 0.8 percent from 1950 to 1973, reflecting the recent widespread fall in fertility. The deceleration in labor productivity growth has been less marked than the decline in per capita output: total GDP growth has averaged 1.9 percent a year in the 1973–1996 phase as compared with 4.6 percent in the 1950–1973 phase.

The recent decline is less discouraging if it is compared with growth before the golden age. In the relatively prosperous and peaceful 1870–1913 phase, per capita income growth was somewhat slower on average than in the 1973–1996 phase. Only Sweden and Switzerland have performed worse than in that earlier period. France and Germany have had the same growth as from 1870 to 1913, and the rest all did better.

It was inevitable that performance would decline significantly after the golden age. In that period, unique opportunities for rapid catch-up with the United States were available and were seized, and the rate of technical progress in the lead country (as measured against U.S. total factor productivity) was then very much faster than has since been the case. Some scope for catch-up still existed in the 1973–1996 phase, but this possibility has now been almost fully eroded. If the rate of progress at the technical frontier is as slow in future as it has been from 1973 to 1996, the process of growth retardation may be even more marked in years to come.

Competition in Foreign and Domestic Markets

Foreign trade in the core countries has grown more slowly in recent times than in the golden age, but foreign-trade volume has decelerated less than has GDP. Commodity exports have grown faster than from 1870 to 1913 (except in Germany and Switzerland), and at about the same rate as in the 1820–1870 phase; the same is more or less the case for commodity imports. Here again, this slower progress has not been surprising. The 1950–1973 phase was one of very large reductions in trade barriers because of OEEC, GATT, and EEC action programs. The successful completion of the Uruguay Round and the establishment of the World Trade Organization mean that some further liberalization of trade is feasible, but its impact on commodity trade will necessarily be mild in these core countries because trade barriers there are already low.

It is not so easy to monitor or measure development of international trade in services. This is a pity, as services are now such a large part of economic activity. In these countries, about two-thirds of employment and GDP is derived from services, but service exports average only 8 percent of GDP. Roughly speaking, service exports are less than 12 percent of service output, whereas commodity exports are about 80 percent of value added in the commodity sector.

In 1985, the European Union launched a major campaign to remove internal barriers by January 1993, mainly to augment possibilities for trade and specialization in services. The ratio of trade in services has risen only slightly since 1985, as very substantial barriers remain in areas like telecommunications and air transport, in which consumers obviously have a good deal to gain from more-effective international competition.

EU trade policy action was the major element reinforcing market forces in most of the countries, but in the United Kingdom, the Thatcher government went much further than any other in its promarket activism. This activism comprised deregulation, including the complete abolition of exchange controls in 1979, the legal reduction of trade union powers (including direct action to break union power in the miners' strike of 1984 and increased freedom to entrepreneurs to hire and fire workers), and a sweeping program to privatize public enterprises (in telecommunications, steel, air transport, rail transport, and the production and distribution of coal, gas, electricity, and water supplies). The only other effort on this scale was the dismantling of the socialist economy of East Germany after it became part of the Federal Republic in 1990. France experienced a move in the opposite direction in 1981, when the Mitterrand government nationalized banks and other important enterprises; this trend was generally reversed by privatization in the Chirac, Balladur, and Juppé administrations, but French privatization has not been as extensive as in the United Kingdom. The continental countries experienced no real counterpart to British action in freeing labor markets, although there have been some very recent moves in this direction in Germany.

In line with EU policy, those countries that still had them finally eliminated controls on capital movements in July 1990 (Ireland, Spain, and Portugal followed in 1992 and Greece in 1994). The positive impact on efficiency of resource allocation was probably greatest in British capital markets, but capital liberalization also had negative effects by increasing the scope for speculative capital movements.

Thus, the European core countries have pushed their economies closer to the technological frontier in this new period of capitalist normality and have enlarged somewhat the degree of market freedom to facilitate microeconomic efficiency in most sectors of their economies (most notably in the United Kingdom). In the case of agriculture, no significant progress has been made to remove the elaborate network of subsidies and controls that has kept markets rigged. In 1993, total transfers per full-time equivalent farm worker were $15,400 in the EU, $17,000 in Austria; $24,200 in Finland; $38,900 in Norway; $24,500 in Sweden; and $29,600 in Switzerland (see OECD 1994, p. 124).

The Rise in Unemployment and the Change in the "Establishment View" of Economic-Policy Objectives

The major respect in which economic performance has worsened can be seen in the evidence on unemployment. In 1996 the average unemployment rate in the core countries was around 9.2 percent, which is higher than that in the depressed years of the 1930s and nearly four times the average rate in the golden age. Except for Denmark, the Netherlands, and the United Kingdom, the situation has been steadily worsening and shows signs of deteriorating still further. Unemployment rates in Europe are now much higher than in the United States, reversing the situation that existed in the golden age.

The major reason for the rise in unemployment has been the change in macropolicy objectives. To some extent this change has been dictated by events, but it also reflects a basic ideological switch.

Erik Lundberg (1968, p. 37) characterized the "establishment view" in the 1960s as follows:

> In the postwar period, the achievement of full employment and rapid economic growth has become a primary concern of national governments. Such policy targets certainly did not guide government activities during most of the interwar period—instead, there were various policy aims that today would largely be considered as either intermediate, secondary, irrelevant, or irrational targets, such as the restoration or preservation of a specific exchange rate, the annual balancing of the government budget, and the stability of the price level at a prevailing or previously reached niveau.

The establishment wisdom has now reverted completely to the old-fashioned religion. The pursuit of full employment and rapid economic growth has been jettisoned, and ancient goals have been embraced with crusading zeal.

The initial switch in emphasis had considerable conjunctural validity. In the early 1970s, the Bretton Woods system of fixed exchange rates collapsed. The dollar was floated in 1971, and policymakers felt disoriented without a monetary anchor. This all happened at a time at which there already existed a climate of inflationary expectations. These expectations greatly augmented by the OPEC price shock (which also produced serious payments problems). It was felt that accommodation of inflation beyond a certain point would lead to hyperinflation and that the latter would threaten the whole sociopolitical order. This was the "razor's edge" theorem. Incomes policies had been discredited, so disinflation was given strong priority. It was not easy to break inflationary momentum quickly. Further inflationary pressure was created by the second OPEC shock in 1980 and by the surge in other commodity prices. With honorable exceptions like Tobin and Modigliani, the Keynesians threw in the towel, and politicians sought intellectual sustenance from Friedman, Hayek, and the neo-Austrians who regarded unemployment as a useful corrective. The rational-expectations school further sapped confidence in the usefulness of discretionary policy action. The establishment decided that if simple rules were followed long enough, the economy would be self-regulating. Responsibility for economic-policy action should move from ministers of finance to central bankers.

The switch from old to new modes of policy thinking has been most dramatic in the United Kingdom—the former Keynesian heartland. Another big switch occurred in France in 1983; after a couple of years of nationalizing major enterprises, encouraging wage increases, and carrying out devaluations (three), the Mitterrand government embraced the new orthodoxy, and France has since followed a policy of "competitive disinflation" with defense of the exchange parity as the primary objective (see Blanchard and Muet 1993 for a detailed analysis of French policy). With some delay, there has also occurred a major change in objectives in Sweden. In other countries the change has been less dramatic but nonetheless substantial.

From 1983 onward, these deflationary policies have been quite successful (Table 3.23). The rate of price rise dropped very sharply, and the power of OPEC was broken through the price increases' impact in inducing energy economy and in stimulating non-OPEC oil output.

From 1973 to 1983, inflation in the core countries averaged 9.4 percent, but from 1983 to 1995 this figure was reduced to 3.8 percent—significantly lower than in the golden age in most countries. For 1996, the average rate is expected to be only 1.8 percent (OECD, June 1996).

At the end of the 1980s, the new orthodoxy was reinforced by the adoption of the objective of creating a monetary union. The creation of such a union was not a new idea. It had been advocated within the EEC by the 1970 Werner Report, but this objective was abandoned when the "snake" system (precursor of the EMS) collapsed in 1976. The EMS was created in 1979 to establish an area of exchange stability. From 1987 to 1992, it achieved reasonable success. As a result, the objective of monetary union was disinterred and put forward in the Delors report of 1989. That report reiterated the importance of policy objectives that Lundberg had qualified as secondary or irrational in 1968. It made no mention of employment or growth objectives, nor did it give serious consideration to the institutional, social, or economic costs involved in enforcing convergence in

TABLE 3.23. Average Rates of Peacetime Change in Consumer Price Level, 1870–1996
(Annual average compound growth rates)

	1870-1913	1920-38	1950-73	1973-83	1983-95	1996 projected
Austria	0.1[a]	2.1[b]	4.6	6.0	3.0	1.9
Belgium	0.0	4.4[c]	2.9	8.1	2.8	2.0
Denmark	-0.2	-2.0	4.8	10.7	3.4	2.1
Finland	0.6	0.5	5.6	10.5	4.1	0.6
France	0.1	3.6	5.0	11.2	3.3	1.8
Germany	0.6	-0.1[d]	2.7	4.9	2.4	1.7
Italy	0.6	0.3	3.9	16.7	6.1	4.2
Netherlands	0.1	-2.9	4.1	6.5	1.9	1.7
Norway	0.6	-3.1	4.8	9.7	4.6	1.3
Sweden	0.5	-2.7	4.7	10.2	5.8	1.5
Switzerland	n.a.	-2.8	3.0	4.3	2.9	0.7
UK	-0.2	2.6	4.6	13.5	4.8	2.6
Arithmetic Average	**0.2**	**-0.1**	**4.2**	**9.4**	**3.8**	**1.8**
Greece			3.7	18.8	16.2	8.6
Ireland			4.3	15.7	3.6	1.8
Portugal			3.2	22.6	11.8	3.2
Spain			4.6	16.4	6.5	3.6
Arithmetic Average			**4.0**	**18.4**	**9.5**	**4.3**
USA						

Sources: 1870–1973 from Maddison (1991), p. 174; 1973–83 from Maddison (1995a), p. 84; 1983–95 from OECD, *Economic Outlook*, December 1996, Annex Table 16, 1996 projection from Annex Table 15.
[a] 1874–1913; [b] 1923–38; [c] 1921–38; [d] 1924–38

price, wage, monetary, and fiscal behavior. Such convergence would of course have been expansionary if Greek standards had been the target, but it was clear that the new anchor was expected to be the deutsche mark. The major economic gain from union would be a reduction in transaction costs and some possible improvement in economic stability. It was also argued that monetary union was necessary for "completing" the single market.

The arguments for monetary union were set out more elaborately in the EC report *One Market, One Money* (1990). That report was basically one-sided salesmanship disguised as scholarship; it paid no serious attention to the costs or risks involved. Nevertheless, the proposal was adopted by the EC in 1991, and the Maastricht Treaty of European Union was ratified in 1993. The European Monetary Institute was installed in Frankfurt in 1994 (with an endowment of 616 million ECU), to be responsible for creating a European Central Bank.

The guidelines for monetary union were based on the assumption that countries should converge toward German standards of price and exchange rate stability. Countries were required to hold their currencies within a narrow band for at least two years, to achieve a high degree of price stability, and to attain a "sustainable fiscal position"—that is, to keep fiscal deficits below 3 percent of GDP and to reduce public debt to less than 60 percent of GDP.

TABLE 3.24. Average Government Fiscal Outcome as Percent of GDP, 1960–1996

	1960–73	1974–81	1982–89	1990–95	1996 projected
Austria		-2.0	-1.5	-2.7	-4.3
Belgium		-7.1	-8.9	-6.0	-3.2
Denmark		-1.4	-2.1	-2.6	-1.5
Finland		2.3	3.0	-3.6	-2.9
France	0.5	-0.9	-2.4	-4.1	-4.1
Germany	0.6	-3.1	-1.7	-3.0	-4.1
Italy		-11.3	-11.2	-9.4	-6.7
Netherlands	-0.5	-2.8	-5.2	-3.6	-2.6
Norway		2.9	4.7	0.5	5.4
Sweden		-0.2	-0.9	-6.0	-3.8
UK	-0.8	-3.9	-1.7	-5.1	-4.8
Arithmetic Average	**-0.1**	**-2.3**	**-2.3**	**-3.8**	**-2.7**
Greece		n.a.	-9.9	-12.6	-8.2
Ireland		n.a.	-8.7	-2.4	-1.5
Portugal		n.a.	-6.3	-5.5	-3.8
Spain		-1.8	-4.7	-5.6	-4.8
Arithmetic Average		**n.a.**	**-7.4**	**-6.5**	**-4.6**

Sources: General government financial balances from OECD *Economic Outlook*, December 1996, Annex Table 30 for 1979–96, earlier issues for 1978–81. 1960–73 from Maddison (1991), p. 183.

The path to monetary union has not been smooth. In 1992 there occurred a major currency crisis. After a costly defense of their existing exchange rates, there occurred a number of devaluations and an exit of Italy and United Kingdom from the EMS. In 1993 new pressures on the franc led the EMS authorities to widen the permitted fluctuation band from 2.25 percent to 15 percent. The other Maastricht criteria have not been met by most of the potential members. It is therefore impossible to predict when or whether it will be a monetary union, who will be members, and whether it will be as irrevocable as expected. It is clear, however, that official endorsement of the objective has reinforced the deflationary bias in policy and has contributed heavily to the increase in European unemployment.

The Fiscal-Monetary Policy Mix

Although the intent of government policy has been substantially deflationary for a prolonged period over the past two decades, fiscal freedom has been markedly constrained by the very substantial welfare state provisions inherited from the golden age (Table 3.24 and Table 3.25). Budget deficits have been bigger since 1974 than in the golden age. When unemployment increased, transfer payments were triggered automatically. In many cases, people who left employment and dropped out of the labor force also got substantial benefits—for instance, they were urged to retire early or to acquire "handicapped" status. There has also occurred a steady buildup of pension benefits because of the aging of the population. By 1990, government transfer payments averaged 19.2 percent of

TABLE 3.25. Total Government Expenditure as Percent of GDP at Current Prices, 1913–1992

	1913	1950	1973	1992
France	8.9	27.6	38.8	51.0[b]
Germany	17.7	30.4	42.0	46.1[b]
Netherlands	8.2[a]	26.8	45.5	54.1
UK	13.3	34.2	41.5	51.2
Average	12.0·	29.8	42.0	50.6

Source: Maddison (1995a), p. 65.
[a] 1910; [b] 1990.

Table 3.26. Long-Term Bond Yields in Real Terms, 1960–1995

	1960–73	1974–81	1982–89	1990–1995
Austria	n.a.	3.09	4.08	4.17
Belgium	2.41	2.76	5.65	5.60
Denmark	1.15	5.19	7.30	6.67
France	1.64	-0.57	5.37	6.13
Germany	3.72	2.95	4.83	4.08
Italy	1.32	3.50	4.94	5.90
Netherlands	1.09	2.04	5.54	5.40
Sweden	1.36	-0.46	4.71	5.85
UK	2.52	-1.30	4.60	5.00
Arithmetic Average	**1.90**	**1.13**	**5.22**	**5.42**
Spain	n.a.	n.a.	4.74	6.06

Sources: 1982–95 from OECD, *Economic Outlook,* June 1996; 1960–81 from IMF *International Financial Statistics,* 1986 issue for bond yields; OECD *National Accounts 1960–94* for GDP deflators.

GDP in the core countries (ranging from 12 percent in Finland, Switzerland, and the United Kingdom to highs of 28 percent in the Netherlands and 23 percent in France) and were as high as government consumption. In the periphery countries, transfers were 14.5 percent of GDP (Alesina and Perotti 1995).

The deflationary intent of government policy can thus be seen more clearly in the level of real interest rates. These rates have been very much higher in the period of moderate price increases since 1982 than they were in the golden age (see Table 3.26).

The Social Impact of Government Policy

It is difficult to assess the social impact of government policy in the phase since 1973. Per capita income has risen in all the countries at rates that are disappointing only by the standards of the golden age. Income levels in the core countries are high enough for the latter to be regarded as rich by most of the rest of the world. Standards of health, life expectancy, and education are much better than those that most other countries enjoy. The periphery can hardly be considered as poor and receives financial aid from the core coun-

TABLE 3.27. Net Receipts from EC Budget in 1991 as Percent of GDP

Ireland	6.43	Belgium	0.29
Greece	4.18	UK	-0.08
Portugal	2.43	Italy	-0.14
Luxembourg	1.82	Netherlands	-0.23
Spain	0.49	France	-0.25
Denmark	0.33	Germany	-0.63

Source: Artis and Lee (1994), p. 381, for Community expenditure. Country contributions to EC budget from UK White Paper, *Statement on the 1994 Community Budget*, HMSO, March 1994. GDP from OECD, *National Accounts 1960–94* with dollars converted at 1.2405 to the ECU from IMF, *International Financial Statistics*. In 1991 about 59 percent of disbursements went to agriculture, about 30 percent to structural operations and internal policies, about 4.4 percent for foreign aid, and 7.2 percent for administration and reserves.

tries that is extremely generous in comparison with the aid received by the developing world (see Table 3.27).

The rise in unemployment is the major blemish on the recent performance of these countries. Unemployment's income consequences are significantly cushioned by transfer payments, but there is, of course, income loss, accompanied by a good deal of anxiety for the unemployed and their families.

Significant changes have occurred within the labor force itself (see OECD, *Employment Outlook* 1995, p. 204). Between 1973 and 1992, the core countries' average activity rate for males (defined as total employment divided by the population of age 15 to 64) fell from 85.9 percent in 1973 to 75.3 percent in 1992. This decline reflects a rise in scholarity, earlier retirement, and the discouraged workers who have given up hope of employment. On the other hand, with the decline in family size and the increase in temporary or part-time employment opportunities, the average activity rate for women rose from 48.7 percent to 63.7 percent during those same 20 years. The gender breakdown of the labor force has therefore become much more equal and has increased the proportion of couples comprising two earners. In the core countries, the average activity rate for both genders combined is about the same as in 1973. In the periphery, male activity rates have fallen a good deal more than in the core countries; female activity has risen in the periphery but is still well below that in the core. The total activity rate has fallen significantly in Ireland and Spain, reflecting a significant discouraged-worker effect, as well as very high unemployment.

Significant changes have also occurred in marital patterns in capitalist Europe. Changes in the tax and transfer systems have facilitated a rise in the proportion of informal cohabitation instead of marriage. In this connection, there has occurred a substantial rise in single parenthood; the latter phenomenon has triggered substantial welfare payments, which would have been smaller if traditional family habits had not eroded.

A recent OECD report (Atkinson, Rainwater, and Smeeding 1995, p. 40) shows that in 11 core countries in the mid-1980s, the average level of disposable income per equivalent adult (after tax and transfers) in the top decile was three times that in the bottom decile, as compared with the very high ratio of nearly six in the United States. In the core countries, the most unequal income distributions were in Italy, the United Kingdom, and

France. In the periphery, inequality was greater in Ireland than in Italy. The survey also analyzed changes in income distribution over time for different subperiods. For the United Kingdom, the trend to greater inequality between 1978 and 1990 was very marked, and there occurred milder inequality increases in Norway and in the Netherlands. Significant declines in inequality took place in Finland and in Italy, as well as somewhat lesser declines in France and in Germany.

Experience of the European Periphery since 1973

The most encouraging feature of performance in the capitalist periphery after 1973 has been the continuing rapid growth of commodity exports; the average growth of 8.8 percent a year during the present phase is little different from that in the golden age. In terms of labor productivity, these countries have also done well; with an average growth of 3 percent a year, they have performed better than the core countries. Unfortunately, their unemployment experience has been a good deal worse.

They have also been much less successful than the core countries in combating inflation; from 1973 to 1981 their average inflation rates were twice as high, and the discrepancy has been even bigger in the 1983-1995 subperiod.

Despite substantial transfers from the EU (6.4 percent of GDP in Ireland, 4.2 percent in Greece, 2.4 percent in Portugal, and 0.5 percent in Spain), the peripheral countries have experienced major problems in coping with the approach to monetary union. Between 1990 and 1995, successive devaluations lowered the value of their currencies relative to the deutsche mark by 39.4 percent in Greece, 27.5 percent in Spain, 15.8 percent in Portugal, and 14 percent in Ireland. Their budget deficits (except for that of Ireland) have been higher on average than in the core countries.

Conclusions on 1973–1996 Performance

By comparison with the rest of the world, the European capitalist group as a whole has not done too badly since 1973, but it nevertheless has performed below potential. It has had unnecessarily high levels of unemployment, as well as macropolicy objectives that have given too much emphasis to price stability and to exchange rate convergence.

The most puzzling aspect of policy in capitalist Europe in the 1990s has been the obsession with closer integration within West Europe. The original political motive for Western European integration was to reduce the likelihood of future armed conflict within the group and to strengthen the group's position in the Cold War. The first objective was achieved years ago, thanks to the NATO alliance. The Cold War ended in 1990, and one might have expected West Europeans to welcome the newly liberated East Europeans into the capitalist fold. Instead, Western Europe has concentrated on building institutions that actually make it more difficult to integrate with the East. Furthermore, the amount of financial aid to the latter has been very modest: from 1991 to 1994, the EU spent only $1.1 billion a year on aid to Eastern Europe. In addition, the total of the bilateral programs has been meager compared with the $41.7 billion a year going to West European farmers and with the $22.6 billion a year in structural subsidies going to areas of Western

TABLE 3.28. Votes in EU Council of Ministers, 1996

	Votes	Population (000s)	Inhabitants per Vote (million)
Austria	4	8,219	2.054
Belgium	5	10,045	2.009
Denmark	3	5,231	1.744
Finland	3	5,094	1.698
France	10	58,680	5.868
Germany	10	68,816	6.882
Greece	5	10,519	2.104
Ireland	3	3,587	1.196
Italy	10	58,369	5.837
Luxembourg	2	404	.202
Netherlands	5	15,597	3.119
Portugal	5	9,952	1.990
Spain	8	39,278	4.910
Sweden	4	8,935	2.234
UK	10	58,745	5.875
Total	**87**	**361,471**	**3.615**

Sources: Votes from *The Economist* (3.3.96). P. 25. Population from OECD *Quarterly Labor Force Statistics,* 1994 figure extrapolated to 1996 using the 1993–4 rate of increase.

Europe that are already much more prosperous than the East. Trade has expanded rapidly with Eastern Europe, but "sensitive" areas like agriculture, steel, textiles, and chemicals still provide only restricted opportunities. Closer integration with the East will require restructuring of the EU's voting rights (Table 3.28) and budget. This change will obviously pose serious political problems, but the tediously slow welcome to the East is difficult to fathom.

REFERENCES

Alesina, A., and R. Perotti. "Fiscal Adjustment: Fiscal Expansions and Adjustments in OECD Countries." *Economic Policy* (October 1995).

Artis, M.J., and N. Lee. *The Economies of the European Union.* Oxford: Oxford University Press, 1994.

Atkinson, A.B., L. Rainwater, and T. Smeeding. *Income Distribution in OECD Countries.* Paris: OECD, 1995.

Bjerke, K., and N. Ussing. *Studier over Danmark Nationalprodukt 1870–1950.* Copenhagen: Gads, 1958.

Blanchard, J.B., and P.A. Muet. "Competitiveness through Disinflation: An Assessment of the French Macroeconomic Strategy." *Economic Policy* (April 1993).

Carreras, A., ed. *Estadísticas Históricas de España: Siglos XIX–XX.* Madrid: Fundación Banco Exterior, 1989.

Daniels, J.D. "The Indian Population of North America in 1492." *William and Mary Quarterly* (1992).

ECLAC. *Preliminary Overview of the Latin American and Caribbean Economy.* Santiago: ECLAC, Dec. 1995.

European Community. *Report on Economic Monetary Union in the European Community (Delors Report).* Luxembourg: EU, 1989.

————. "One Market, One Money." *European Economy* 44 (October 1990).

Friedman, M. "The Role of Monetary Policy." *American Economic Review* (1968).

Hjerppe, R. *The Finnish Economy 1860–1985.* Helsinki: Bank of Finland, 1989.

Kausel, A. *Österreichs Volkseinkommen 1913 bis 1963.* Vienna: Österreichisches Institut für Wirtschaftsforschung, 1965.

Lundberg, E. *Instability and Economic Growth.* New Haven: Yale University Press, 1968.

Maddison, A. "Economic Stagnation since 1973. Its Nature and Causes: A Six Country Survey." *De Economist* 4 (1983). (Reprinted in Maddison, 1995b.)

————. *Dynamic Forces in Capitalist Development.* Oxford: Oxford University Press, 1991.

————. *Monitoring the World Economy 1820–1992.* Paris: OECD Development Center, 1995a.

————. *Explaining the Economic Performance of Nations: Essays in Time and Space.* Elgar, 1995b.

————. *Chinese Economic Performance in the Long Run.* Forthcoming 1997.

Needham, I. *Science in Traditional China: A Comparative Perspective.* Cambridge, Mass.: Harvard University Press, 1981.

OECD. *Agricultural Policies, Markets, and Trade: Monitoring and Outlook 1994.* Paris: OECD, 1994.

OECD. *Employment Outlook* (June 1995).

OECD. *Economic Outlook* (July 1996).

Olgaard, A. *Growth, Productivity and Relative Prices.* Copenhagen, 1966.

Taeuber, I.B. *The Population of Japan.* Princeton: Princeton University Press, 1958.

Irma Adelman[1] on Angus Maddison's Paper

Economic and Social Performance of Capitalist Europe: An Interpretative Commentary

Angus Maddison's paper succeeds admirably in providing a brief and yet very insightful, empirically based overview of the economic history of sixteen successful industrialized countries. From personal experience, the present writer can affirm that such a tour de force is indeed very difficult to achieve. Naturally, the scope of his paper does not permit Professor Maddison to dwell on the systematic differences among industrialization paths adopted by different subgroups of European countries: the early export-led industrial growth paths of the firstcomers (France and Great Britain); the import-substituting industrialization paths adopted by the later industrializers (Germany, Italy, and Russia); and the balanced-growth, open-economy paths pursued by small countries (Belgium, Denmark, the Netherlands, Sweden, and Switzerland). Nor does Maddison discuss in any detail how the European countries' development processes and development environments differed from those of current developing or East Asian countries. But this aspect is not what we shall be focusing on in the present comments.

Rather, let us devote our discussion here to underscoring some of the development-policy-relevant themes hinted at but not fully developed in Maddison's paper. Our comments will be based on systematic comparative historical work carried out by Cynthia Morris and the present writer, entitled *Comparative Patterns of Economic Development, 1850–1914* (1988), as well as on personal experience with successful East Asian economic development. Of course, drawing policy conclusions from development evidence applying to earlier periods is subject to obvious qualifications. Historical experiences cannot provide detailed prescriptions for contemporary development because of the differing international, technological, demographic, and political contexts in which historical growth and contemporary growth take place. Maddison therefore showed commendable caution, which we shall not emulate here, in not drawing policy conclusions from his stylized historical portrayals of economic development.

First, a reading of the economic history summarized by Maddison suggests that institutional readiness for capitalist economic growth is key to economic development, because it provides the conditions that enable technical progress and export expansion to induce widespread economic growth. The varied experiences of European countries during the industrial-revolution period and those of developing countries during the

---

[1] University of California, Berkeley.

golden age of economic growth underscore this point: those European countries that had achieved widespread economic growth by the end of the nineteenth century started with institutions better equipped for technological change than did either the European dualistic-growth later industrializers or the developing countries of the 1950s (Morris and Adelman 1989, Kuznets 1958). They already had large preindustrial sectors well endowed with trained labor and entrepreneurs; governments that protected private property, enforced private contracts, and acted to free domestic commodity and labor markets; and leaderships responsive to capitalist interests that adopted trade, transportation, and education policies fostering technological progress in either industry (the early industrializers) or agriculture (the balanced-growth countries). Similarly, those developing countries that in the 1950s were institutionally most advanced were the ones that benefited most from the growth impetus imparted by import demand from the OECD countries during the golden era of economic development. They had an average rate of economic growth 50 percent higher than that of the average non-oil country at the next-highest, intermediate, level of socio-institutional development (Adelman and Morris 1967). Furthermore, by 1973 the overwhelming majority of the countries that were institutionally most developed in 1950 had become either NICs or developed countries, while none of the countries that had lower levels of socio-institutional development had become NICs.

Second, government economic policies do matter—particularly with respect to domestic institutional structure, trade, commerce, industry, agriculture, investment, and macroeconomic management. (This point would hardly be worth making were it not for the now Nobel-prize-hallowed rational-expectations school). As evident from Angus's paper, when, in the golden-age 1950–1973 phase, the OECD countries focused on economic growth, they got it. Similarly, when, after 1973, they focused on economic stabilization, deliberately sacrificing economic growth and employment, they also got that. Along the same vein, during the nineteenth century, developing countries that had sufficient political autonomy from their colonial rulers to be able to set their own economic policies so as to benefit domestic industrialization (Australia, Canada, and New Zealand) were able to translate the growth impulses from export expansion into widespread economic development; by contrast, those countries that were politically and economically so dependent on the center that they had no control over domestic economic policies (India and Burma) achieved only dualistic, enclave, sporadic growth (Morris and Adelman 1988, chapter 6).

A corollary from the importance of government policy, hinted at but not emphasized by Maddison, is that the nature of the state and its relation to civil society also matter. Both historically and more recently, the structure of power in the government has determined the choice of policy thrust. Political history and economic history are closely related, as references in Maddison's paper to Thatcher-omics indicate. When the landed political elites were modernizing (as in Germany and Japan), the industrializers of the late nineteenth century invested in education, agricultural extension, and credit policies favoring family-owned farms; these, in turn, permitted technological improvement in agriculture and the development of a home market for industry. By contrast, where (as in Italy and Russia) the large-estate owners that held political power were status quo oriented, they did little for education and agriculture, growth was dualistic, and poverty and illiteracy were rampant. Political institutions' critical importance to widespread economic development is also confirmed by the contrast in development paths, evident during the nineteenth century, among European-settled land-abundant overseas territories—between Australia and New Zealand, on the one hand, and Argentina and Brazil, on the other. Thus, nineteenth-century economic history strongly confirms that political institutions do matter to the successful spread of economic development.

The crucial importance of the political complexion of government is also confirmed in postwar developing countries. Systematic quantitative analysis of economic and institutional forces in economic development in the early 1960s (Adelman and Morris 1967) shows that specific leadership commitment to economic development was the major institutional factor differentiating between the more and the less economically successful nations in the group of countries, mostly Latin American, that had already achieved high levels of socio-institutional development. This point is further reinforced by reference to East Asia, where no correct reading of the role of the government in the economy is compatible with a view that Japan, Korea, Singapore, and Taiwan were neoliberal states.

But another corollary and caveat derived from the importance of government policy to economic development is the fact that a strong state that adopts self-serving, or simply misconceived economic policies and/or institutions can generate economic disaster. The last twenty-five years of indifferent economic growth in most of Latin America and in the nondefense sector of the former Soviet Union underscore this point. A nonactivist government would be preferable to a strong government promoting bad policies.

Nevertheless, these are not the only alternatives. The economic histories of Japan, the four little tigers, the seven flying geese, and post-1980 China suggest rather strongly that the combination of a developmental state with good economic policy is unbeatable. Their experience underscores that a technocratically influenced developmental state, with an economically literate meritocratic bureaucracy, is key to long-run success in economic development.

Is a strong autocratic state necessary to the adoption and maintenance of good economic policies? European growth during the golden age suggests that it is not. But the experience of the ultimately successful European latecomers to the industrial revolution, in which strong national leaders transformed institutions and engaged in aggressive industrial policies, does indicate that a strong state is needed in order to initiate economic development. Perhaps most importantly, as the literature on bureaucratic authoritarianism emphasizes, a state with a certain degree of autonomy from pressures emanating from entrenched economic elites is necessary in order to implement switches among policy regimes (say, from import substitution to export-led economic growth) or to engineer fundamental changes in economic institutions, such as land reform. Such policy regime switches—which, as emphasized later, are necessary to successful long-run economic development—inflict inescapable injuries upon some entrenched economic interests, such as entrepreneurs and workers in the protected import-substituting enterprises, while only promising to confer potential benefits on other groups, such as the would-be exporters and their workers (with such promised benefits manifesting only after the latters' painful restructuring to become export competitive). Popular support for major policy regime switches is therefore unlikely, especially over a time frame long enough for the new policy regime to become effective. Repeated abortive trade liberalization efforts in Latin America and recent elections of communist leaders in some reforming Central European countries underscore this point. A government with substantial autonomy and credibility is therefore required for successful long-term economic growth. But such autonomy need not arise from repression of popular participation and civil rights. As long as the government is perceived as acting in the public interest, the requisite autonomy can be bestowed upon the government by independent popular support (such as that enjoyed by governments led by national liberators or war heroes), or by the government's general credibility gained through successful economic and political leadership, or by popular values supporting strong hierarchic leadership roles (such as Confucianism) or arising from a perceived external threat to the country's national survival.

Third, trade policies and the international trade and payments regimes are critical for economic development. But as Maddison correctly points out and the East Asian development successes reinforce, this fact does not mean that, within countries, free-trade policies are either necessary or optimal for industrialization. In nineteenth-century Europe and Japan, tariffs were usually the cornerstone of industrialization policies; nowhere except in Britain did initial factory-based industrialization occur without some tariff protection. Thus, the historical record of successful industrialization before World War I suggests that List and Schacht, rather than Adam Smith and Ricardo, provide the appropriate guidelines for commercial policy in countries pursuing economic development.

A correct reading of the practice of the successful industrializers, both historically and in current East Asia, indicates that *export orientation* rather than free trade constitutes the critical ingredient of successful development policy. Historically, export expansion systematically speeded economic growth everywhere. But this export growth led to widespread economic development only where agriculture was at least moderately productive and where modernizing governments fashioned institutional conditions favorable to technological improvements and undertook investments in education and transport favorable to the development of a domestic market. Except for the firstcomers to the industrial revolution, European countries did not adopt free-trade policies; rather, they obtained their start on industrialization with tariffs and quantitative import controls (Morris and Adelman 1988, chapter 6).

Similarly, both Korea and Taiwan engaged in import substitution policies at the same time as they pursued export-led economic growth. But unlike the Latin American countries, they used quantitative import controls, more than tariffs and effective exchange rates, to achieve their selective industrial policies. They were thus able to maintain incentives for exports at the same time as they pursued selective import substitution.

Indeed, quantitative import controls, which granted exporters a sheltered domestic market, were one of the mechanisms that made export orientation profitable to exporting firms. During the heyday of export-led growth in Korea (1967–1973), there were about 15 thousand commodities on the prohibited list for import. And in Taiwan, quantitative constraints on imports were specified not only by commodity but also by country of origin, with most labor-intensive imports from other developing countries barred in order to shelter infant consumer manufactures from foreign competition. The critical difference between the second import substitution phase into heavy and chemical industries in these two East Asian countries and the same phase of import substitution in Latin America was that from the very beginning, the East Asian heavy and chemical industries were expected to export a large share of their output and thereby forced to become export competitive.

As to the payments and trade regimes, as Angus Maddison hints in his current paper and has emphasized elsewhere (Maddison 1982), periods of exchange rate stability—under either the gold standard or the golden-age Bretton Woods system of fixed exchange rates—were uniformly associated with high worldwide economic growth; by contrast, periods of widely fluctuating exchange rates, as during most of the 1914–1950 phase and the years since 1973, were and have been associated on average with slow economic growth. Similarly, liberal international trade regimes were associated with high rates of economic growth while protectionist regimes were associated with slow growth.

There is little emphasis on investment and its structure in Maddison's paper, perhaps because of space limitations. Rather, the impression one emerges with is that the critical historical component of successful economic growth was not investment per se but productivity and that the level of productivity in the use of resources, both newly accumulated and existing, and this productivity's rate of increase through technological change and resource reallocation among sectors were the crucial ingredients of long-term economic growth. In support of Maddison's thesis, recent cross-country studies do suggest that in the demand-constrained growth regime of the post-1973 period, the association between investment and economic growth in developing countries has indeed been weak. Further support for the relative unimportance of investment can be found in the growth of the ultimately unsuccessful high-investment economies of the former Soviet Union and Central Europe; they had little to show for their investment because of low TFP growth. And like Maddison historically, Krugman finds that there exists a close association currently between total factor productivity (TFP) growth and rates of growth of GNP, just as classical Kuznets-Abramowitz-Dennison-Solow and endogenous-growth theories would suggest.

Nevertheless, the results obtained by Mrs. Morris and the present writer are at variance with the suggestion that investment is relatively insignificant for economic development. Technological dynamism was important in explaining contrasts in rates of economic growth during the nineteenth century in our results as well. But we found that investment in human capital and transportation also made a significant difference to economic development. Indeed, in our statistical analyses, human-resource development was critical to technological dynamism in both industry and agriculture. No country achieved successful economic development before 1914 without adult literacy rates above 50 percent. And literacy was a foremost variable discriminating among the more and the less successfully developing countries during the nineteenth century (Morris and Adelman 1988, p. 211). Similarly, in our results, breakthroughs in inland transportation were necessary to advance agriculture in countries starting with severe transportation bottlenecks and having land institutions, human resources, and political structures that provided the potential for economic growth (Morris and Adelman 1988, chapter 5). Only where the structure of investment in transport accorded priority to domestic trade were technological improvements in food agriculture likely.

The evolution of the East Asian miracle countries also benefited from exceptionally high levels of human-resource development. Indeed, starting from low levels of education and literacy (the legacy of Japanese colonialism), Korea and Taiwan had by the mid-1960s already attained levels of scholarization that were triple the Chenery norm for their levels of per capita GNP. And in Korea, university enrollment rates exceeded those of Great Britain. The East Asian miracle growth countries had both high rates of accumulation and high rates of economic growth. Indeed, Paul Krugman (1995) and Larry Lau (1996) both find that in Taiwan and Korea almost all economic growth has, so far, been the result of exceptionally high accumulation rates of physical and human capital accumulation and that the contribution of TFP growth to income growth has been negligible.

Finally, institutional and policy malleability are key to sustaining economic development in the long run. This point is not implicit in Maddison's paper but rather emerges from nineteenth century comparative analyses (Morris and Adelman 1988, chapter 8) and is reinforced by the Asian-miracle countries' fifty-year experience with successful economic development. The aforementioned historical study indicates that institutions and policies good for initiating economic growth were generally not appropriate for the continuation of that growth. For instance, in the land-abundant non-European countries, foreign-dominated political institutions were a powerful force for the market-oriented institutional change that initiated strong primary-export expansion. But the institutions that were good for export growth brought about neither systematic agricultural improvements nor consistently rising standards of living. For ultimate success, the domestic economic institutions had to be transformed so that widely shared growth could ensue and a domestic market for manufactures could emerge. This growth and market creation required political transformation as well. In fact, at first, the establishment of political stability and political support for the promulgation of laws furthering market development was sufficient to promote rapid primary-export expansion. But unless the political institutions later adapted so as to provide support for the economic needs of rising domestic commercial and industrial classes, the translation of the initial impetus from exports into long-term economic development became blocked.

Similarly, in backward European countries, governments and international resource flows could initially substitute for the missing institutional adaptations eventually required for economic growth. At first, government demand for domestic manufactures could successfully substitute for deficient home markets; government finance and foreign-capital inflows could substitute for limited domestic savings and for inadequate financial institutions; and imports of skilled workers and technology could substitute for meager domestic human resources. But after a certain point, such substitutions became inadequate. To generate development, economic institutions had to change so as to make possible the domestic provision of the needed capital, skills, and broad-based domestic markets.

In the same vein, our results (Morris and Adelman 1988, chapter 5) suggest that agriculture's critical functions in countries' economic development tend to change as this development proceeds. Initially, agriculture must be capable of performing the Lewis function, of providing capital for industrialization. In this phase, agricultural institutions must primarily be suited to the initial mobilization of the agricultural surplus and to its transfer to the industrial sector; large estates, worked with semi-attached labor, were best suited for this phase. Later, agriculture must be capable of providing food to the growing urban sector and markets for urban manufactures. In this later phase, the institutional structure of agriculture, terms-of-trade policies, and investments in agricultural infrastructure must provide incentives for improvements in the productivity of food agriculture, and the agricultural surplus must be sufficiently widely distributed to permit widespread farmer income growth and broad-based increases in demand for domestically produced manufactures; at this stage, owner-operated farms of productivity and size sufficient to provide a marketable surplus were best.

In international trade, too, our results (Morris and Adelman 1988, chapters 4 and 8) suggest that development requires policies to shift so as to permit continuous change in the composition of domestic production and exports. This policy malleability requires dynamic adaptations in trade regimes. Commercial policies necessary to initiate industrialization (such as import substitution policies) are not necessarily good for industrialization's continuation, when shifts to export-led growth are needed in order to enhance scale and to provide the impetus for efficiency in production. In both Korea and Taiwan, the major thrust of government strategy with respect to trade and industrial policy shifted in rapid succession, with sometimes as little as four years spent in a given policy regime (Adelman 1996).

Not only economic institutions and primary policy thrust but also the major functions of government itself must shift as industrialization proceeds. Initially, the primary roles of government consisted of institution creation (both economic and political) and infrastructure build-up. The early industrializers and the balanced-growth countries built up their market institutions during the 400-year protocapitalist period. The governments of the European latecomers introduced the institutional changes required to strengthen responsiveness to market incentives during the early phases of the industrial revolution. The latecomers unified their countries and markets, as in Italy and Germany; eliminated legal barriers to trade and factor mobility, as in the Russian serf emancipation; created credit institutions and promoted joint-stock companies, as in Germany; and facilitated transactions, as in Italy and Spain.

Next, once the institutional and physical frameworks for development were established, the primary function of government consisted of the promotion of industrialization while raising the productivity of agriculture. The performance of this function entails an activist government role in the adoption of an industrial policy that promotes dynamically changing comparative advantage: from resource intensive, where appropriate, to labor intensive, to skill intensive, to high-level-manpower and capital intensive. This industrial sequencing needs to be implemented through the formulation of appropriately changing international trade and commercial policies and the consistent direction of government finance, government demand, government investment, and government incentives to this end. The general aim should be to make industries export competitive and to create a dynamic private sector. Nevertheless, in each phase, initially infant industry protection needs to be accorded to the key sectors; but this infant industry protection *must be* gradually withdrawn and replaced by pressures and incentives to export. In support of the industrialization effort and in order to feed the expanding urban population engaged in this effort, the productivity of food agriculture must be raised through investment in agricultural infrastructure and through technology and terms-of-trade policies leading to the increases in agricultural incomes necessary to boost home demand for domestic manufactures. This phase also involves a *mildly* expansionary macroeconomic regime bolstered by foreign-capital inflows in the form of investment and aid and combined with measures and institutional changes aimed at promoting domestic savings.

Finally, once the desired growth and savings habits are firmly entrenched in the entrepreneurial and household sectors, the scope of government policy should be curtailed. By and large, the government ought then to limit itself to providing the macroeconomic-policy framework for rational economic calculus and full resource utilization, for the promotion of economic and political competition for the provision of a safety net and the protection of the weak in the marketplace, and for the containment of the negative social externalities (safety related and environmental) inherent in unfettered profit maximization. That is, the appropriate role of the government in the final phase, but only in the final phase, should change to that prescribed by the current neoliberal, Reagan-Thatcher, Washington consensus. This phase has been attained by less than a handful of NICs and is not characteristic of even the current United States. The Clinton administration has in fact been pursuing an activist industrial policy aimed at accelerating the shift into a high-tech and service economy; an interventionist trade policy aimed at pushing agricultural, service, and technology exports through bilateral and multilateral negotiations and participation in global institutions; and an energetic human-resource investment policy aimed at generalizing the ownership of human capital and increasing its rate of accumulation.

The inescapable conclusion of all of this, based on both European and East Asian development history, is that had the neoliberal Washington consensus been enforced on the East Asian miracle countries during the 1950s, 1960s, and early 1970s, there would not have been an East Asian miracle.

Thus, it is evident from Maddison's paper as well as from our present discussion that the process of successful long-term economic development involves a systematically changing dynamic interaction among institutional change, technological progress, international trade and accumulation—an interaction in which government and its policies play a key role. The government must have sufficient autonomy to shift among policy regimes in accordance with changes in current economic-development requirements, present domestic conditions, and the existing international environment. Long-run success in economic development also requires that this dynamic reframing be consistent among all the processes and areas affected and that the surrounding international setting be receptive to and compatible with the major thrust of domestic change.

REFERENCES

Adelman, I. *Economic and Social Development in Korea 1945–1993.* Korea Development Institute, 1996.

_____, and C.T. Morris. *Society, Politics and Economic Development: A Quantitative Approach.* Baltimore: Johns Hopkins University Press, 1967.

Krugman, P. "The Myth of Asia's Miracle." *Foreign Affairs* 73(6): 62–78.

Kuznets, S. "Underdeveloped Countries and the Pre-Industrial Phase in the Advanced Economies." In Amar Narin Agarwala and S.P. Singh, eds., *The Economics of Development.* Oxford Press, 1958.

Lau, L. "Intangible Capital and East Asian Economic Growth." *Asian Pacific Journal of Economics* (forthcoming).

Maddison, A. *Phases of Capitalist Economic Development.* Oxford Press, 1982.

Morris, C.T., and I. Adelman. *Comparative Patterns of Economic Development, 1850–1914.* Baltimore: Johns Hopkins University Press, 1988.

_____. "Nineteenth Century Development Experience and Lessons for Today." *World Development.* (1989).

Wolf Grabendorff[1] on Angus Maddison's Paper

Lessons from Europe

A great deal can be learned from Professor Maddison's impressive paper, even though this writer must admit to certain difficulties in sharing that paper's particular conclusions. Not being an economist but nevertheless being very much aware of the goal of the present conference to apply some of the world's existing development thinking and practice to the current stage of development in Latin America, we would like to offer in this commentary some possible lessons from the development of continental Europe with regard to the political conditions in which European development has taken place, based on our great interest and continuing analysis of development in both Europe and Latin America.

Let us begin by stating that many of those European lessons should not and cannot be taught to Latin Americans, because recent European history has brought a great deal of suffering to mankind and also because with respect to economic policies and their institutional and political framework, it is not always even possible to apply lessons learned by some societies to other societies of different contexture and in a different stage of development. That having been said, this writer will now venture to offer three different lessons from recent European development experience, each of which we shall briefly discuss in turn:

- the importance of an internal consensus within the developing society
- the importance of the arbiter role of the state
- the importance of increasing integration.

Importance of Internal Consensus in a Developing Society

When talking about Latin America and its recent—and in some countries spectacular—efforts at economic development, invariably the Washington consensus comes up. But very seldom do observers seem to take into account the fact that this is a consensus entirely external to Latin American society and that this consensus has in the best of cases only the support of the economic elite in some countries. It seems obvious that when it was formulated, nobody took the precaution to try to figure out the internal costs—be they economic or social, but in the end almost certainly political—of the measures foreseen in that consensus. One is tempted to quote Argentina's former Minister of Economic Affairs Domingo Cavallo, who said with regard to the cost of implementing all the nec-

---

[1] Director of the Institute for European–Latin American Relations (IRELA), Madrid.

essary adjustment measures in his country and its resultant macroeconomic successes, "Unfortunately, nobody lives in the macroeconomy!"

In contrast, the importance of an internal consensus, which in some European countries has gone so far as to express itself in social pacts, can be seen in a number of elements that, taken together, appear as a set of ground rules on which voters can agree or disagree on election day. These ground rules consist of strong policy guidelines, elaborated by the government in dialogue with the social forces, by which the social and economic actors have to play. The existence of strong countervailing interests—not only those of business and labor but also those of regional and municipal governments and their institutions, along with those of a diversified private sector in which national and transnational interests compete side by side—is considered to be of primordial importance. In the best of cases, the outcome of such an internal consensus for economic policymaking is an active bargaining policy plus additional social measures, which together constitute the very idea of a social market economy. Such an economy is also based on the strengthening of the internal market (which in the European case is no longer a national one) through employment and consumer protection measures and the strengthening of domestic savings through appropriate fiscal policy designed to avoid too much dependence on external capital flows.

Many economists argue that such an economic system is bound to lead to low growth and is characterized by an equally low capacity to adapt to economic change. At the same time, it provides a high degree of behavioral predictability and certainly tends to be strong in terms of its acceptability to large majorities of the people affected.

Importance of the Role of the State

In a time of heated debate about the need for a lean state not only in Latin America but also in Europe, it seems perhaps very unfashionable to argue for a high profile of the state in the economy. Nevertheless, the experience of entrepreneurs who have to deal with the inefficiency and unpredictability of policymaking in weak states (as in most transition economies)—which has been characteristic of their dealings with the majority of Latin American states—seems to demonstrate that the latter case constitutes by no means a good condition for economic development.

The Asian experience of continuous large public investment in human capital at all levels also serves to demonstrate, at least in this basic area, the importance of public institutions and public policies. The equally successful Asian experience of fostering high savings by tax incentives and other measures, in order to avoid undue reliance on external savings, is already taken as a model by many Latin American policymakers, and in some European countries the experiences with such policies have been as positive as in Asia.

Also important is the state's capacity to enforce an effective fiscal regime to correct the accumulation model of market forces and to channel resources not only into the areas mentioned but also into safeguarding the environment and into striving toward a model of sustainable development. The state's role as an arbiter between private interests and the public interest is invaluable, even though the officials who are voted into this arbitrative position should definitely be replaced periodically, in true democratic fashion. If the state abdicates its position of providing democratic legitimacy for a set of rules, economic or otherwise, economic development might still be around, but its benefits will extend only to the very few, who will have to guard themselves heavily against the very many who consider the formers' wealth and power as illegitimate. In that respect, the previous waves of the breakdown of democracy in Latin American countries cannot be dissociated from the fears of a comfortably established minority of being outvoted by a majority.

Importance of Increasing Integration

It may not be very convincing for a European commentator to stress the importance of integration, in view of the difficulties the European integration process has been faced with for a number of years and given the political upheavals that a continuing integration process has produced in many member states of the European Union. Nevertheless, there must be something attractive about this integration process, because otherwise the waiting line to get into the European Club would not be as long. Something similar could possibly be said about the increasing attractiveness of the MERCOSUR process in Latin America. In this regard, a shortcoming of many economists is that of viewing the integration process basically as a trade-related measure and little more.

From the present author's own obviously very European viewpoint, which might reflect lessons learned from some of the terrible events of European history, the most important factor of integration is the reduction of the potential for conflict, not only with neighbors but also far beyond the borders of each of the member states. The importance of the internal consensus within a given society can possibly be extended through long and difficult consultation processes to a number of other nations. The willingness to limit one's own sovereignty and to pool one's resources is a test case for any meaningful integration process. Here again, Latin America is still far away from consolidating such an experience, but there also exists a growing conviction that in an increasingly globalizing economy, competing with other areas will become ever more difficult in the absence of membership in a successful integration process that creates a wider platform. Such an integration process—and this is also the European experience—can be helpful in limiting external economic shocks, something Mexico has felt very clearly, even though NAFTA does not yet, strictly speaking, constitute an integration process.

The increasing bargaining power in trade-related disputes compensates handsomely for the partial loss of national sovereignty. In the global competition for bigger market shares and more investment, only large integrated economic spaces count as big players. In that respect, the lesson from Europe might indeed be helpful to MERCOSUR.

Conclusions

Returning now to the overall concept of development thinking and practice, the aforementioned three lessons from Europe will admittedly be viewed with suspicion by many. That fact in itself might be sufficient reason to doubt the applicability of such lessons to other regions in different stages of development, a point touched on at the beginning of the present commentary.

As the European Union is coming to grips with its widening process of extension toward East Europe, it will also have to reassess the underlying hypotheses of its own functioning and of the various concepts of its economic policymaking. Given the striking similarity of some of the transition processes in Latin America with some of those in Eastern Europe, especially with regard to economic policies to be pursued and new institutional mechanisms to be developed, the European Union might here find lessons to be learned from Latin America. The different stages of development thinking have been particularly fruitful in Latin America, even though the same thing cannot be necessarily said about many of that region's actual development practices. Practical cooperation between the European Union and MERCOSUR might create a broad field for exchanging experiences, which might then help the Europeans to adapt more skillfully to the future process of understanding and integrating the other part of Europe.

Lessons from Countries in Transition

Yves Berthelot[1]

Four *A Priori* Lessons

The former communist countries' transition process into market economics started with the fall of the Berlin Wall seven years ago and is still far from complete. Thus, the first lesson is that systemic changes take time.

The fall of the Wall marked the culmination of a chain of political and economic events and developments that confirmed that the economic activity of a country cannot be separated from the sociopolitical context in which it takes place and that these two factors in fact mutually influence each other. This is the second lesson.

The collapse of the centrally planned economies in the East coincided chronologically with the triumph of supply side economists in the West; this unfortunate coincidence led to a series of errors in the flow and content of advice provided to the emerging governments of Eastern Europe and in the policies they followed. In particular, the need for the state itself to manage the transition process was underestimated, and seemingly forgotten was the fact that there exist many different valid ways of conducting an efficient and sustainable market economy. Thus, the third and perhaps most important lesson to be drawn from the countries in transition is that at the heart of any development strategy there needs to be a proper division of responsibilities between government and market and that the balance between the two necessarily varies from one country to another.

Among its responsibilities, the state has to provide an essential public good—namely, a reasonably stable institutional and policymaking framework, together with an adequate flow of information, all of which help to minimize the negative impact of uncertainties on decisionmaking by economic actors. Ironically, the fourth lesson would therefore be that some form of medium-term planning should be reestablished.

The Legacy of the Communist Era

The legacy of the communist era is well known: an extremely centralized system of decision making, state ownership, and the ultimate sovereignty of planners over investments

---

[1] Executive Secretary, UN Economic Commission for Europe. The present paper draws heavily on the work of the secretariat of the UN–ECE, the Economic Commission for Europe, and particularly on the 1990, 1992, 1993, 1995, and 1996 issues of the Economic Survey for Europe. This publication is the work of a small team led by Paul Rayment, from whom I also borrowed ideas contained in his paper "The Hard Road to the Market Economy: Realities and Illusions," published in MOCT–MOST 5: 45–64, 1995, Kluwer Academic Publishers.

and prices. This system could not compete with market economies as it could not provide the right incentives. But even so, the population did benefit from a high level of education, which today remains an asset, as well as from job security and a very comprehensive social-security system.

In Eastern Europe and the Soviet Union, the policies followed in the 1980s could not successfully tackle any of the problems faced by the countries of the region. In fact, the economic decline actually dates back to the 1960s, when in order to maintain economic development, it was decided to shift from extensive growth to intensive growth. Rates of output growth continued to slow down in the 1970s despite a significant acceleration of investments, and productivity of both labor and capital fell steadily from the early 1970s. Borrowing from the West allowed the import of capital goods and consumer goods. The former did not help to improve productivity, and the latter delayed the fall in domestic consumption until the debt burden became unsustainable when interest rates became positive in the early 1980s. Because of the inefficiency of the production sector and the lack of marketing skills, exports became less and less competitive, and the unavoidable adjustment effort fell upon domestic demand: on consumption for a while and for much longer on investment. By 1989 the current-account deficit had been transformed into a small surplus, but the debt burden of Eastern Europe, even if small ($85 billion) compared with that of Latin America, was almost unbearable for some countries like Bulgaria, Hungary, and Poland.

The system's inefficiency—caused by chronic structural disequilibrium and severe problems of macroeconomic instability—was clear to some of the Eastern policymakers, and reforms were introduced in some countries in order to halt the economic decline. Enterprise managers were given more independence, and central control over wage setting was reduced. But this reform was not radical enough, mainly because the authorities retained considerable power to control the actions of individual enterprises and because the communist party continued to exercise ultimate authority over governmental and economic hierarchies and blocked any reform that might have reduced its privileges and undermined its interests. The incapacity of the communist parties of Eastern Europe and the Soviet Union to allow a sufficient degree of autonomy to the economic system caused their own ruin, in marked contrast to what has happened in China. The economic impasse led to the collapse of the region's political and economic systems. It would be interesting to understand why what seems to have been impossible in Europe has worked rather efficiently in China, but that is not the purpose of the present analysis. Let us go back to Europe for now and move to the transition period, which actually started when the communists lost power.

Five to Seven Years of Reform and the First Results

It is common practice, before describing the reforms and assessing their consequences, to remind the reader that each country represents a special case and that a distinction also should be made between Europe (Central and Eastern) and the CIS countries (including Russia), if only because the former had already experienced—and thus retained the memory of—a market economy and the latter had not and did not, and also because the former had been under a communist regime for less than fifty years and the latter for more than seventy. Differences in achievements are also the result of the initial conditions prevailing in each economy and of the degree of steadiness with which reforms were conducted. Some countries have followed a relatively continuous line despite political difficulties, while others have gone back and forth and not surprisingly have achieved less-positive results. The following subsections will describe in a general way the transition process, its results thus far, and the issues it raises.

The Initial Reform Program

The initial programs consisted of various combinations of stabilization measures, institutional reforms, and structural policies, including privatization. Monetary and fiscal restraint was aimed at reducing inflation, restoring financial equilibrium, and setting the stage for a stable macroeconomic environment. Liberalization of the external sector would help to establish correct relative prices and would impose a desired measure of competition on the domestic market. Resources were expected to flow from loss-making firms into profitable new activities, which would be undertaken and managed chiefly by newly emerging private entrepreneurs. The overall level of social welfare would rise, even though there would also be some "losers," especially in the sectors that had enjoyed exceptional privileges under central planning—namely, heavy engineering, metallurgy, mining, and the bureaucracy. But adjustment costs were expected to remain relatively limited, in part because of the substantial foreign direct investments that were expected to flow into the transition economies because of the attractiveness of the latters' low manpower costs and "virgin" markets.

It cannot be denied that the East European countries have come a long way since they started their transition to capitalism. Democratic and pluralistic political systems have been established in all of them, and there is little question of halting the present trend toward the market economy. The straitjacket of central planning and state controls has been dismantled. Prices have been liberalized as well as trade (although export duties and controls do still exist in CIS countries), domestic currencies are convertible, and consumers and producers are essentially free to make decisions according to their preferences. Inflation has been greatly reduced and endemic shortages eliminated. A large part of output is now produced in a dynamic private sector, and domestic markets offer a large variety of goods and services, comparable to that in Western countries. According to official national statistics, the nonstate sector's share in GDP already exceeds 50 percent in most countries, an indicator of the enormous distance they have covered since 1989, when the share was generally less than 5 percent (except in Poland, where it was around 30 percent because of largely private agriculture). Naturally, these statistics must be treated with some caution because the rules of statistical reporting and sectorial classification are not always clear and consistent, but the radical change in the ownership structure is clearly evident.

The governments of transition countries have also made considerable progress in in-

tegrating their economies into the global market economy. Most of these countries' foreign trade is now conducted with developed market economies at international prices and
in convertible currencies, and their international links have been further strengthened by
inflows of foreign direct and portfolio investment. Many new market institutions have
been established and developed, such as stock exchanges, monetary and credit instruments, antimonopolistic regulations, and bankruptcy legislation. By the end of 1994,
most East European economies had passed the low point of the economic recession. In
1995 the recovery was confirmed in Central Europe and was perceptible in some CIS
countries.

The results of the transformation this far lend credibility to recent claims that the
transition economies "have put the essential foundations of a market economy securely
in place."[2] The results also show that the countries' strategic decision to dismantle central planning and to organize their economies according to market rules and principles
was justified. But all these achievements notwithstanding, there have also been failures
and disappointments. In fact, after five years, capitalism in the transition economies is
still in its infancy: growing fast, but still immature and turbulent.

An Unexpectedly Severe Recession

Perhaps the most disturbing and unexpected outcome of the 1989 revolutions was the
"transitional recession," which depressed output and employment well below pretransition levels. The official statistics show that the cumulative contraction of output between
1989 and 1993 in the transition economies was on a massive scale not seen since the
Great Depression of 1929 to 1933. The recession was particularly dramatic in Bulgaria
and Romania, the two East European countries commonly considered as being the least
prepared for market reforms, and in nearly all the countries of the former Soviet Union.
Another common feature is that the cumulative fall of (gross) industrial output was larger, generally by more than a half, than the fall of GDP, and by the end of 1993 it exceeded
50 percent in the worst cases (Bulgaria, Romania, Russia, Ukraine, and the Baltic states).
In Central and Eastern Europe the resumption of growth in 1994 and more clearly
in 1995 was relatively strong in the traditional industrial sectors, showing that once the
restructuring is under way, the accumulated expertise can be mobilized.

What was surprising about the recession was not the fall in output itself, because
"some" recession had indeed been anticipated, but rather that the fall was so deep, so
widespread, and so persistent and that the subsequent adjustment on the supply side has
been so weak.

A number of possible explanations of the "transitional" recession have been suggested over the last few years.[3] They range from Keynesian demand deficiency to

---

[2] "Camdessus Discusses Progress in Transition Economies in Central and Eastern Europe," *IMF Survey* (Washington
D.C., January 1995) 21.

[3] See, for example, B. Chadha, F. Coricelli, and K. Krajnyak, "Economic Restructuring, Unemployment, and Growth
in a Transition Economy," IMF *Staff Papers* 40: 4 (Washington, D.C. December 1993). In this context, J. Kornai
coined the term "transformational recession" as something fundamentally different from a regular recession associated

Schumpeterian institutional interpretations, from concepts of structural rigidities and distortions typical of Soviet-type economies to views regarding the recession as a statistical artifact. No single one of them is fully convincing in itself, but considered jointly they do allow for some conclusions.

First, it should be noted that the recession was real and not imaginary. Clearly, the official statistics do tend to overestimate the extent of the actual fall in output, but it may also be argued that the margin of error is probably smaller than commonly believed.[4]

Second, the recession was the joint outcome of a combination of factors working from both the demand and the supply sides, including the loss of large chunks of economically viable capital stock (because of the rapid liberalization of imports and prices), the unexpected collapse of intra-CMEA trade, and the energy price shock for oil-importing countries. Stabilization programs' adverse impact on domestic demand also appears to have been quite substantial. With the benefit of hindsight, it can be argued that the stabilization policies were probably too restrictive, as they were guided by a mistaken judgment of the initial degree of macroeconomic disequilibrium.

Third, it might have been expected that the shift away from communism would release large "X-efficiency gains" that would generally work in favor of output expansion rather than output contraction.[5] The fact that these gains have not materialized underlines the excessive optimism that prevailed in 1989 as to the responsiveness of the supply side of the transition economies. Whether microsupply responses could have been stronger with a different set of policies is an open question.

Structural Unemployment

It is a well-established proposition of traditional comparative economics that the near-full employment levels observed under central planning were achieved artificially because of low work discipline and the ideological commitment to full employment and that they were further supported by low wages. Large-scale layoffs during the governmental transition were therefore predicted, but it was also assumed that rapidly increasing demand for labor in the expanding service and private business sectors would absorb most of the excess manpower in industry and that unemployment would therefore remain moderate. In reality, the jobless rate in most East European countries is well above 10 percent of the labor force and has remained high despite the emerging recovery of output.

---

with a normal, Western-type business cycle. (J. Kornai, *Transformational Recession: A General Phenomenon Examined through the Example of Hungary's Development*, Collegium Budapest, Institute for Advanced Studies, Discussion Paper 1, June 1993.) Similar views are also expressed by many other authors. See, for example, O. Blanchard, R. Dornbusch, P. Krugman, R. Layard, and L. Summers, *Reform in Eastern Europe* (Cambridge, MA, and London: The MIT Press, 1991).

[4] K. Rosati, "Output Decline during Transition from Plan to Market: A Reconsideration," *The Economics of Transition*, 2: 4 (Oxford, 1994), 419–41.

[5] In most general terms, the X-efficiency idea refers to the closing of the difference between actual and maximum output, the gains arising from better use of inputs for a given output, varying degrees of work effort and discipline by individuals, varying degrees of diverging interests in agent-principal relationships, inertial costs, and some other factors. For a more detailed exposition, see H. Leibenstein, *General X-Efficiency Theory and Economic Development* (New York and Oxford: Oxford University Press, 1978), 17–38.

An important message from labor market statistics is that not only are unemployment rates high in the transition economies but also that there has been only a small reduction in "excess employment" (as indicated by the difference between the cumulative change in GDP and the cumulative change in employment) between 1989 and 1994. In Bulgaria, Hungary, Poland, and Slovenia, employment levels have fallen broadly in line with the fall of output, thus leaving the initial level of overemployment practically unchanged; in all the other countries, but especially in the former Soviet republics and Yugoslavia, the level of overemployment has increased, with obviously negative implications for labor productivity and wages.

Since the major reason for high unemployment has been the "transitional" recession, the recovery might in principle have been expected at least to alleviate the problem. Unfortunately, the emerging recovery cannot be counted on to improve the labor market situation radically, because the flow of new jobs will most likely be broadly offset by new entrants to the pool of unemployed coming from schools, an overmanned agricultural sector, and shrinking state enterprises. As a result, the transition countries are likely to have to live with double-digit unemployment rates for several years to come. Nevertheless, in Poland and in some other Central European countries, the unemployment rate fell slightly in 1995 because of strong growth and despite significant gains in productivity.

Long-term and high rates of unemployment, however, involve serious risks. First, as more and more persons remain without a job for a long time, they will tend to drop out of the active labor force permanently because of a loss of skills. This "hysteresis" effect will thus reduce the potential output of the transition economies in the future and will put additional burdens on their fiscal expenditures on extensive social safety nets. The share of the long-term unemployed (more than 12 months without a job) in total unemployment has been gradually increasing in Eastern Europe and was nearly 50 percent on average in mid-1995 (and above 60 percent in Bulgaria). Another worrying fact is that there are more and more young people and school leavers among the unemployed—a tendency that carries a high risk of their remaining more or less permanently without a job. The implications are daunting: not only is the economy likely to suffer from the waste of manpower resources but also social and political stability may be endangered if too many people are unemployed for too long. There exist no simple solutions to this problem, but structural policies aimed at improving the workings of the labor markets and active labor market policies, including training and retraining programs, would appear to be priority areas for action. But there must also be a recovery to sustained, employment-creating rates of output growth if the inflow to the pool of unemployed is to be reduced significantly.

From Hyperinflation to Moderate Inflation

High rates of inflation and widespread shortages were characteristic of the final days of the central planning system. Transition's liberalization of prices and its initial devaluation of domestic currencies added to existing inflationary pressures. In fact, the "corrective" inflation in most countries greatly exceeded the levels foreseen in designing the stabilization programs. To restore fundamental price stability was thus one of the central objectives of the reformist governments. Experience has shown that reducing inflation from near-hyperinflationary levels to manageable proportions is a relatively easy task and can be done quickly with standard measures of financial restraint implemented within a credible and consistent program. But most of the East European countries that have succeeded in lowering inflation to the range of 20 percent to 40 percent per annum seem to be finding it very difficult to reduce it further to one-digit rates.

The persistence of inflation at so-called "moderate" levels cannot be easily explained with standard theories.[6] The growth of the money supply does not seem to have been a primary inflationary factor, because it has generally lagged behind the rise in the consumer price index in all Eastern European countries (except the Czech Republic, where, however, inflation is the lowest in the region), and even more so in Russia and the other CIS countries. Nor does there exist any uniform pattern in the inflationary impact of budget deficits; there does seem to exist a clear link between fiscal deficits and inflation in Russia and in Ukraine, but the evidence is less clear for East European countries (Hungary and Slovakia have had lower inflation rates and higher deficits than Poland or Romania). Wages have been kept under control throughout the region, generally increasing less than consumer prices (again, the exceptions include countries with the lowest inflation rates in the region).

Although inflation has been considerably reduced in Eastern Europe, it nevertheless varied in 1995 from 4 percent to more than 30 percent, remaining in double digits in Bulgaria, Hungary, Poland, Romania, and Yugoslavia. Such rates are likely to have an adverse impact on economic activity: interest rates, both nominal and real, are kept high, thus hampering economic recovery; uncertainty is maintained in the business sector and investment horizons are shortened; and social unrest may be provoked because of inflation's undesirable effects on income distribution.

The nature of the current "moderate" inflation appears to be different from that of the inflation observed in the initial stages of the transition when liberalization shocks, excess demand, and monetization of fiscal deficits played the most important roles. "Moderate" inflation seems to be caused chiefly by inertial mechanisms, such as various indexation schemes for wages and pensions, frequent foreign exchange rate adjustments, periodic increases of key commodity prices (mostly energy and food), and inflationary expectations. Attempts to stop such inflation with the standard instruments of tight monetary policy tend not to be very effective, especially when inflows of short-term capital boost the domestic money supply under pegged exchange rates (Czech Republic, Poland). A conservative monetary policy is still needed, but it should be combined with other measures that would dampen inflationary expectations through the breaking up of inertial mechanisms.

---

[6] R. Dornbusch and S. Fischer, "Moderate Inflation," *The World Bank Economic Review,* 7 (Washington, D.C. 1993), 1–44.

On the Way to Privatization

Policymakers in the transition economies were clearly aware of the systemic weaknesses of traditional state enterprises and seem to have recognized that, unreformed, these enterprises were likely to behave in a perverse way in a market environment because of the distorted structure of incentives facing not only managers but also banks, workers, and government agencies. In the initial stage, these dangers were to be avoided through rigid tax-based incomes policies, and thereafter through privatization. And yet the composition of the stabilization packages that were actually implemented in most countries suggests that they were based on an implicit assumption that the reaction pattern of state enterprises to the stabilization measures would be broadly similar to that observed in developed market economies. This may help to explain the lack of early reforms of state enterprises and banks and the slow pace of privatization. Indeed, instead of discontinuing inefficient production, laying off excessive manpower, and responding to market signals in a standard, profit-maximizing way, state enterprises preferred to raise prices, protect employment, and lobby heavily for government support and assistance.

Incomes policies, although instrumental in reducing inflationary expectations, proved to be only partially effective in imposing wage discipline and in keeping unemployment low. In many cases, incomes policies proved to be an impediment to restructuring and were often considered to be socially unfair and politically unacceptable. On the other hand, privatization proved to be much more difficult and time consuming than initially envisaged.

From the economic perspective, the role of privatization was to introduce efficient corporate governance and additional sources of funding for enterprises.[7] In addition, and in many cases primarily, it was seen as an important underpinning of the political transformation. Very broadly, two different privatization strategies were followed, both of which we shall now examine. The first strategy was based on the free distribution of state assets to the public at large, and the second strategy was based on a case-by-case "commercial" approach.

In the first case, the transfer of ownership rights can be carried out relatively fast, and the share of the nonstate sector in the economy is expanded "at the stroke of a pen." The main advantage of this method is essentially its speed. As for its contribution to the achievement of the economic objectives of privatization, it takes much longer for effective corporate governance to be established, since giveaway schemes create dispersed ownership with the dominance of passive owners. As a result, although managers are liberated from government supervision, they are not put under the control of new owners. Effective controls can be imposed only gradually, no matter how fast the formal ownership rights are distributed. A good illustration of the problem is provided by the results of privatization in the Czech Republic, widely regarded as the most successful in Eastern Europe. Even though the state managed to divest itself of more than half of its industri-

---

[7] P. Aghion and N. Stern (eds.), "Obstacles to Enterprise Restructuring in Transition," EBRD Working Paper 16 (London, December 1994).

al property within less than three years, the behavior of enterprises has in fact changed very little, if at all, because the new owners are either dispersed or, if they hold strategic stakes, are unable to exert the desired influence on managers because of a lack of information, conflict of interest, or general passivity. The privatized enterprises are thus "nonstate," but they are not yet fully private in the Western sense of that term. Moreover, only limited funds have been channeled to enterprises as a result of this method of privatization. Voucher privatization in Russia is another example of the rapid "formal" transfer of ownership away from the state that is followed neither by effective governance nor by an inflow of new capital.

Under the second strategy of a case-by-case "commercial" approach to privatization, when a state enterprise is sold to a new owner, corporate governance is immediately established, additional financing is often forthcoming, and the necessary adjustments begin to follow. But since the strategy does proceed case by case, it takes a long time to privatize a majority of state enterprises. The dilemma is therefore to choose between a wide and shallow "giveaway" privatization and a deep and narrow "commercial" privatization. Whichever alternative is selected, the process of economic restructuring will take years to complete.

One important lesson that can be drawn from the experience of the last five years is that a "mixed" strategy may be desirable, combining elements of free distribution and commercial sales. Another is that the rate at which corporate governance can effectively be established in newly privatized enterprises should be an important consideration determining the speed of the privatization process. As proper governance cannot be achieved overnight, a large number of enterprises will have to stay and operate under nonprivate ownership for some time. But to minimize losses from possible mismanagement, several steps can be taken. State enterprises should be legally remolded in order to create an economically desirable structure of incentives facing managers; this remolding can be done through "corporatization" and "commercialization," which would precede privatization proper. In addition, both the managers and members of the board should be offered a stake in their enterprise's future market value (for instance, a call option for shares to be issued in a future privatization), in order to prevent asset squandering and dissipation.

In the *länder* of the former German Democratic Republic, the "commercial" approach was followed, and as much importance was given to the choice of new management as to the search for new owners. The Treuhand, the organism in charge of privatization, considered that the previous management of any state enterprise would be incapable of carrying out the restructuralization and streamlining necessary to make the enterprise competitive. Privatization was conducted rapidly, and a massive inflow of capital flowed from other länder. Nevertheless, Eastern länder continued to lag far behind Western ones, and many qualified people migrated to the Western part of Germany, causing increased unemployment. One of the reasons for this lag was probably the introduction of the deutsche mark as the single currency, which undermined the competitiveness of enterprises that did not yet have the required level of productivity.

Lower wages did not compensate for this competitiveness lag. Clearly, behavioral changes and the good functioning of institutions do take time, even if financial, managerial, and technical support are provided without restriction.

The Late Reform of the Financial System

The need to overhaul the whole financial sector in the transition economies was fully recognized only when the banks and other financial institutions emerged as major obstacles to the process of reform. The main weaknesses of the financial sector included the following: absence of many important institutions of financial intermediation (such as pension funds, mutual funds, specialized savings and loans organizations, security firms, and equity and bond markets); the small capital base of the existing commercial banks; the excessive dependence of banks on a limited number of clients (mainly large state enterprises); the lack of experience in credit operations; and the absence or inadequacy of prudential regulations and bank supervision. Policymakers apparently did not fully realize that the reform of the financial system was an integral component in the creation of a market economy and that it should have been initiated at the very beginning of the transformation process.

The failure to reform the financial sector at the start of the transition has had a number of important implications. The most important is probably the rapid accumulation of bad loans in the commercial banks, a phenomenon common to all the transition countries.[8] Some of the bad loans are an inheritance from the regime of central planning, when state enterprises were largely unconstrained in their investment activities. But much more significant is the group of bad loans accumulated during the transition period, stemming from a lack of appropriate adjustment by enterprises and banks to the sudden change in the macroeconomic environment and from the protracted recession and the collapse of traditional export markets in former CMEA countries, which has led to many technical and actual insolvencies in the enterprise sector.

The problem of bad loans is now at the center of economic discussions in all the transition economies. Any efficient and lasting solution to the problem should combine two types of initiative. First, the existing stock of bad loans has to be dealt with through a comprehensive financial restructuring program. Second, the recurrence of bad loans (the flow problem) has to be forestalled, which implies a fundamental change in the behavior of economic organizations—which in turn requires a radical change in the structure of incentives faced by the managers of banks and enterprises.

Disappointing Volume and Distribution of Foreign Investments

From the very beginning of the transition process, the governments of Western countries and East European countries alike have envisioned foreign direct investment (FDI) as playing a key role in the restructuring and transformation of the former centrally planned

---

[8] The bad loans include nonperforming assets on banks' balance sheets, mostly in the form of overdue credits, extended to enterprises that for various reasons were unable or unwilling to service those credits.

economies. The initial optimism surrounding the potential role of FDI was based essentially on a number of perceived characteristics of the transition economies: an abundance of cheap skilled labor, geographical proximity to Western markets, the anticipation of a rapid growth of internal demand, and liberal commercial legislation. The balance after five years of transition looks rather modest. The actual volume of FDI in the transition economies has been much lower than expected and, in addition, has been very unevenly distributed across countries.

One possible explanation of this outcome is that foreign investors picked up the best companies in Eastern Europe, in terms of their market potential, their expected profits, and the risks involved, and are not in any hurry to invest in other, typically more debt-ridden and overstaffed, companies. But a more general explanation for the reticence of foreign investors is probably linked to more-systemic factors, such as the uncertain legal, political, and institutional environment. The delays, frequent changes, and occasional reversals of earlier government decisions on privatization have also created uncertainty by sending confusing signals to foreign investors, thus blocking an important channel for FDI.[9]

Apart from the limited volume of FDI inflows, FDI's distribution patterns may also be sometimes questionable. Casual observation and case studies suggest that FDI often tends to concentrate in sectors and branches with a relatively high potential for rent seeking that may arise from quasi-monopolistic positions or from special arrangements with the host governments of transition countries. Thus, foreign investment in East European car manufacturing was typically made conditional on the granting of special privileges to investors in the form of high customs tariffs (in Poland, for example). Similar phenomena may be at work in the attempts by large multinational companies to establish control over East European markets for tobacco products.[10]

The Need for Structural Reforms

Countries in transition are all confronted with essentially the same task of a massive reconstruction of their productive capacities. This task includes a substantial reallocation of resources and probably the closing down of many inefficient enterprises.

In this context, the slow pace of structural reforms raises serious concern. Political obstacles to the restructuring of state enterprises, the lack of funds for new investment and for the rehabilitation of existing plants, and the problems involved in the large-scale reallocation of resources all conspire to hold back the reforms and all contribute to high interest rates and inflation. Restructuring's actual or anticipated implications for the dis-

---

[9] The recent decision by Russia to restore partial state controls over already-privatized enterprises, or the *withdrawal* of the offer by Hungary to sell a state-owned hotel chain to an American consortium provide examples of "stop-go" policies *vis-à-vis* foreign investors.

[10] There appears to be little or no discussion of the welfare implications of allowing foreign companies to introduce modern advertising and distribution methods in the cigarette industry. Male mortality rates from smoking-related diseases in Eastern Europe and the former Soviet Union are the highest in the world, while those for females are among the lowest. See R. Peto *et al.*, *Mortality from Smoking in Developed Countries 1950–2000* (New York and Oxford: Oxford University Press, 1994).

tribution of income and wealth are also a cause of bitter political infighting in most transition countries, which is another factor slowing the progress of reforms.

Improving the functioning of an inefficient and underdeveloped financial sector is also taking a great deal of time and effort, and the burden of bad debts has negative repercussions on commercial banks' ability to finance the enterprise sector. Furthermore, the reform of public finances has not yet been completed, and the rapid increase of budgetary expenditures on social security threatens to upset the fragile stability of governmental budgets in the near future. Domestic public debt has been increasing in all countries, and in some of them it may soon reach alarming proportions.

In addition, the economic performance of the East European transition countries will depend heavily on continued export expansion if overdependence on foreign capital is to be avoided or (since such capital seems unlikely to be available in significant amounts anyway) if the balance of payments is not to be a constraint on growth. Satisfaction of the need for imports of new technology to support the restructuring process will depend largely on export growth. Exports' positive impact on growth may be extended and strengthened if better access to West European markets is granted for the transition countries. This expansion in turn may encourage an "outward-looking" FDI that can have a useful role in expanding exports over the longer term. Export growth can also be supported by export promotion efforts directed at the more dynamic economies in Asia and other parts of the developing world. This outreach effort will require improvements in the trading infrastructure of the transition economies.

The other major constraint on growth—and one likely to be increasingly encountered by all transition countries—is the relatively low rate of domestic savings, which limits the potential for domestically financed investment. The low savings rate stems in part from the currently low level of per capita incomes in these countries. Furthermore, a considerable part of the household savings accumulated in the pretransition period was wiped out by inflation and exchange rate changes. Policies to encourage more savings are urgently needed in the transition countries. Positive real interest rates on bank deposits are an important but not sufficient incentive. A variety of attractive and secure additional savings instruments needs to be further developed, such as mutual funds, pension funds, bonds, and equity shares. Also, accessibility of more-expensive goods (consumer durables, housing) could be increased through the development of financial instruments allowing people to save a larger proportion of their incomes in order to finance long-term purchases and investments (mortgages, consumer credits, and so on).

Return to the *A Priori* Lessons from Transition in Eastern Europe and the CIS

Moving from a centrally planned economy to a market economy means a dramatic change in the institutions governing society. The two first *a priori* lessons are therefore obvious: it takes time, and it requires a certain amount of popular support.

Indeed, institutions, even if they are poorly adapted and inefficient, can endure for a long period of time; they are simply taken for granted. Alternatively, the lack of information on alternative forms of institutions can lead to the maintenance of the *status quo*. Even if the need for change is recognized, there are many obstacles to overcome. When Machiavelli declared that "there is nothing more difficult to take in hand, more perilous to conduct, or more uncertain in its success than to take the lead in the introduction of a new order of things," he identified two reasons for failure: the determined resistance from those benefiting from the *status quo* and the lukewarmness of support from those who will benefit from the reform. The weak support by the benefited stems in part from a fear of hostility from those favoring the *status quo* and in part from uncertainty about the final result of the new order. If individuals are uncertain as to whether or not they will benefit from a reform, there may be a bias against the change even if the majority stands to benefit: the majority can vote against its own ultimate best interest.

As stressed by the Austrian school, institutions and behavior develop over extended periods. In a legal sense, institutions can be easily replicated, but the development of institutional effectiveness is a much slower process of learning and adaptation. This is the reason (without entering into a debate that is no longer valid) that transition economies could not have been "shocked" into suddenly being market economies. The previous system had produced very deeply entrenched behavior and habits; therefore, changes that in Western economies would have been a spontaneous reaction to constraints or incentives remained blocked. Differences between Europe (Central and Eastern) and the CIS countries in terms of the effective implementation of new rules and laws and the functioning of new institutions can be explained in part by differences in the number of years each group was under the central planning system.

When the reform process began in the transition countries, popular support was massive and was based on unrealistic expectations. The critique of the inefficiencies and failures of central planning seemed to be perfectly consistent with the demonstration effect stemming from the affluent markets of the Western economies: people expected that the substitution of capitalism for communism would be a rather simple exercise that would bring about a rapid improvement in the long-depressed standards of living of the East European populations. The reality was less rosy, as recession and unemployment hit all the countries in the region very hard. Elections in most Central and East European countries (but not in all the CIS countries, despite even more-painful situations there) have brought into power politicians closely linked to the former communist parties and have focused government concerns on the need to develop appropriate safety nets. The fact that the basic need for reforms was not questioned demonstrates that the shift to a market economy is irreversible but, at the same time, that democratic progress imposes on governments the need to pay closer attention to the concerns and expectations of the population. This understanding is likely to lead to a more balanced and better-thought-out set of reforms. The ongoing efforts to rethink the social security system in central Europe is one illustration of this new approach whereby governments are seeking genuine solutions to specific problems and are taking examples from foreign countries, not as models, but for the purpose of drawing appropriate lessons from them.

The belief that government must be removed from the economic scene as rapidly and as far as possible was grounded in the ideology of many of the advisers to Eastern governments and was catalyzed by the Anglo-Saxon model of liberalization, deregulation, and privatization that dominated the 1980s. The belief was caused also by the fear that the *nomenclatura* would try either to restore the previous regime or to impose a mixed economy too far removed from the type of market economy prevailing in the West. The weakening of the state, *de facto*, benefited the *nomenclatura*, which was in the best position to take advantage of the opportunities created by privatization and the inability of governments to enforce the rules.

The transition process entails huge responsibilities for governments. They have to build institutions, establish and enforce formal rules of competitive behavior, reduce the uncertainties that impede reform, and conduct structural reforms that may include investments to reduce bottlenecks in infrastructure and to provide public utilities. In so doing, government must be able to define clear objectives, to demonstrate a clear understanding of what is required in order to achieve these objectives, to consult with its social partners and to convince these partners and the electorate at large that it possesses or will soon acquire the necessary economic instruments to implement its program. The preceding sentence corresponds to the definition of "indicative planning" that has prevailed in France (with obvious adjustments) over the last fifty years.

Another way of putting it would be to recognize that because of the complexity of the reform process and the time involved in constructing working institutions, the drive toward a market economy must be spelled out in terms of a series of intermediate objectives and the interdependencies among these objectives must be set out in a transparent and comprehensible manner. This issue is related to sequencing. The literature on sequencing shows that the possibility of success in achieving a given objective may be increased by following one sequence of measures rather than another. In the worst case, an incorrect sequencing would destroy all chance of success. But the literature on sequencing may also be misleading insofar as it suggests alternative linear sequences of policy actions. The transition process, with economic and political reforms intertwined, requires simultaneous action on a number of interdependent issues in order for significant progress to be made. The task is therefore to identify key sets of interdependencies that, in turn, would help to identify those subjects of reform that should be given priority. Contrary to the philosophy of "shock therapy," what matters here is not the simultaneous beginning of a set of reforms but their simultaneous completion.

Contrasts with the Chinese Approach[11]

On the issue just addressed, the contrast with the Chinese experience is striking. Certainly, similar difficulties do exist in the European transition economies and in China. Two such shared difficulties, which are not negligible, are the delay in restruc-

---

[11] The Economic Commission for Europe has no in-house expertise of the Chinese reform process. The remarks contained in this paragraph are inspired by an excellent recent paper by Wei-Wei Zhang entitled "China: Economic Reform and its Political Implications," published by the Programme for Strategic and International Security Studies (PSIS), The Graduate Institute of International Studies, Geneva.

turing large conglomerates and the neglect of the financial sector (in both regions, this neglect constitutes a serious obstacle to the development of enterprises).

In China, however, the time factor is fully incorporated into the reform process and is used to convince the people of the advantages of a given reform without triggering vigorous opposition from those who have a vested interest in the *status quo*. For instance, the rural reform initiated in 1978 was achieved only in 1993, with the deletion from the Constitution of the article related to the "people's commune." The "responsibility system" that has gradually replaced the commune system was, in the beginning, an initiative taken by some poor villages and then progressively extended geographically and functionally (from the possibility of selling on the free market those products that exceeded producers' contractual quota to the later possibility of developing new productions and small enterprises).

Similarly, privatization was not made a key instrument of the Chinese reform. For existing enterprises the reform focused on gradually improving management and separating management from ownership. At the same time, the government encouraged the creation "from scratch" of a nonstate sector, particularly in the "special economic zones" and then in the "Economic and Technological Development Zone."

Wei-Wei Zhang[12] wrote, "A major reason for gradual extension of experience was political: any drastic and comprehensive reforms were the subject of ideological and political dispute. Reformers had to be pragmatic enough to understand that they would be unable to enforce reforms across the country unless they could prove the effectiveness of their reforms." Important lessons in pragmatism and time management can thus be drawn from the Chinese approach. The Chinese model is also a model for communist parties that want to stay in power while making the economy efficient—that is, to achieve what the East European and Soviet parties were unable to do.

Another specificity is the flow of capital, know-how, and business relations that China was able to mobilize in the Chinese communities abroad. In Europe only Poland, Armenia, and Albania have in some way been able to take advantage of their diaspora, but they were less wealthy and less ready to take the risk.

The Additional Uncertainty from Globalization

It is difficult to disentangle the transition-related problems faced by Eastern Europe from the problems related to those countries' insertion into a globalized economy, simply because that transition is taking place as the economies become global. Globalization clearly adds to the uncertainty and therefore to the length of the transition period, as there exists no established frame of reference to institutions that have already coped efficiently with the problems raised by globalization—in particular, the volatility of financial flows and the full-fledged competition among countries with very different living standards. It may also be argued that the adjustments imposed upon Western countries by globalization, as well as the opportunities it has opened for them, explain the limited

---

[12] See preceding footnote.

nature of the support given by them to the transition countries: investors had more-secure countries or operations in which they could invest, and Western governments had no significant public money to spare for helping the reform process.

Nevertheless, as is the case for developing countries, globalization also offers new opportunities. It provides advantages to low-cost qualified labor, through delocalization of production and also through allowing the development of service activities at a relatively low cost of entry, in that a computer and a telephone line can provide access to the entire world market. In economies in transition, the low level of telecommunications infrastructure development thus remains a serious handicap.

From our rapid review of the experience of the economies in transition, little is directly relevant to Latin America. Any lesson would more appropriately flow in the other direction, in regard to privatization, inflation control, debt management, and the inflow of foreign speculative capital. Even so, one valid general lesson does emerge: the need to have a vision, to stick to it, and to concretize it in a pragmatic and flexible way.

John Flemming[1] on Yves Berthelot's Paper
Lessons from Countries in Transition

This is the second time the present commentator has been called upon to compare Eastern Europe with Latin America. In March 1993 the annual meeting of the Inter-American Development Bank was held in Hamburg, and in light of the proximity of the ruins of the Iron Curtain, the EBRD cooperated in a joint sideshow. I was struck then by the similarity between the two regions in terms of total population and total income. One of the biggest differences then related to capital inflows, which were at least five times greater in Latin America; indeed, the sign of the net flows then, as since, was uncertain in Eastern Europe, particularly in the former Soviet Union (FSU).

Berthelot comments on the conventional distinction (which we too shall here invoke) between Central and Eastern Europe (CEE) on the one hand and CIS on the other, but he does not mention that Stalinist planning was homegrown in Russia and was identified there with victory in war and with successful expansion, while in the CEE, it was imposed by occupying forces aided by indigenous fellow travelers or quisling fifth columnists.

Although we shall be criticizing here several features of Yves Berthelot's paper, we do concur with him on the following two major points: first, at least some aspects of transition would have been better done gradually, thereby reducing the associated social costs; and second, few, if any, lessons can be derived from the transition process for application to the development process, or specifically, from Eastern European transition for Latin American development.

This second point of agreement may explain why Berthelot's paper concentrates on issues within the transition rather than on transition's lessons for development. Let us go one step farther and argue that established lessons from development—as reflected in other papers in the present volume, notably John Williamson's on the "Washington consensus"—support the first point (gradualness and reduced social costs) on which Berthelot and I are agreed, and so therefore let us ask why something that is seen by many as an uncontentious element in the "established consensus" on development is rejected by and for transition economies.

As already noted, our starting point is sympathetic to the UN-ECE line of Berthelot, Rayment, and the late Sasha Vacic, in the sense that transition could have been more gradual and had fewer social costs. We have summarized some of the apparent social costs in papers for the IMF and the IEA and while at EBRD argued for tariffication and

---

[1] Warden of Wadham College, Oxford. Formerly Chief Economist, EBRD.

phased elimination of inherited distortions rather than the instantaneous elimination of distortions as well as controls.

For instance, mortality increases in transition economies, particularly in Russia have been observed. This increase reflected not only average income falls but also markedly deteriorating income distribution and the breakdown of government-organized medical "support services." None of these factors applied in Germany's *Neue Länder*, yet mortality rose sharply there, too; perhaps transition itself is bad for the health?

Western European experience over two decades suggests that 10 percent unemployment may be the norm for the kind of society at which those in transition are aiming; by what standard is this "high," given the adjustments necessary in Eastern Europe? A good rule of thumb is that the shadow wage might fall linearly from the market wage to zero as unemployment rises from 10 percent to 20 percent. This criterion suggests serious divergences in few cases.

Berthelot suggests that equiproportionate falls in output and employment, as in Eastern Europe, imply "unchanged overemployment," although the standard "Okun's law" proposition for market economies would have productivity fall in recession; might one not have expected this even in a "transformational recession"? In the CIS, output has fallen more, and unemployment has risen less. Is this a case of badly falling productivity or of a well-clearing labor market (Layard/Richter)?[2]

Richard Jolly compared setbacks in developing countries to the Great Depression. Poland, the best of the transition economies, suffered a loss as large as Britain's modest one then, most of them can more than match the 30 percent U.S. loss, and in much of the FSU that judgment survives adjustment for statistical biases.

Berthelot says little about the statistical problems of measuring the output fall in transition economies. To the extent that it was concentrated on the military-industrial complex, there is a fascinating parallel with Kuznets's attempts to measure U.S. GDP growth in 1940. But as Berthelot says, the falls appear to have been across the board and not concentrated in particular "losing" sectors such as those using newly expensive energy. Although this does point to macropolicies, experience suggests that radical stabilization pays.

Those countries that stabilized prices most rigorously had the smallest cumulative output falls and the earliest recoveries. Possibly they were blessed in some special way that made both possible, but it is incumbent on critics of rapid stabilization to identify, or at least offer, hypotheses as to the identity of the blessing factor if they do not want us to conclude that stabilization should indeed be sharp. An inflation rate of about 75 percent per annum seems to have separated transition economies in recovery from those still falling.

Berthelot further suggests that output losses have been heavier than expected. Although he is correct, one might have been surprised that any were expected at all.

---

[2] P.R.S. Layard and A. Richter, 1995, "How Much Unemployment is Needed for Restructuring?" *Economics of Transition* 3 No. 1 pp. 39–58.

Conventional welfare economics teaches that where there is distortion there is scope for (dynamic) Pareto improvement, yet orthodox Western economists said, "Gee, your distortions are terrible. You'd better tighten your belts." Why?

Berthelot writes of "the loss of large chunks of economically viable capital stock because of the rapid liberalization of imports and prices." We have already indicated some sympathy for this view but would nevertheless put it very differently. First, it is not so much the dismantling of trade and price controls (that is, "liberalization") that may be at fault as the failure to influence the course of liberalized prices (for instance, by transitional protection or by employment subsidy). Second, liberalization does not destroy capital. At (low) liberalized prices (of some goods), using some capital may become unprofitable at old real wages. But one needs to notice three things: there must be as many winners in this process generated by changing effective relative prices as there are losers; reallocation of resources from losers to winners will raise aggregate output at the new (world) prices; and the market-clearing real wage may well fall. If this is impeded by social norms, statutory minimum wages, and so forth, it is jobs, not capital, that are destroyed.

Abolishing price controls in the face of previously repressed inflation inevitably gave the transition economies an inflationary impulse unrelated to current fiscal conditions or monetary growth. Attempts to eliminate the fiscal imbalances that had fed the repressed inflation encountered the offsetting, and often off-budget, effects of continued support for enterprises—support that in substance, if not in form, Berthelot approves. In transition economies lacking capital markets, the links between fiscal deficits, whether on current or capital account, and money creation are inevitably close, as emphasized by Heymann and Leijonhufvud,[3] who draw heavily on Latin American experience. That experience also reveals the difficulty of squeezing out the last 30 percentage points of inflation on which Berthelot comments.

Surprisingly, Berthelot does not comment on either nominal or real exchange rates in the transition economies. Poland's rate was initially fixed (in dollar terms) at a level that did not restrain domestic prices or costs but ensured supercompetitiveness. More generally, the real exchange rates when currency markets were first (partially) liberalized were quite extraordinarily low—to which the partial nature of the liberalization may have contributed. If nominal appreciation is implausible, moderate domestic inflation may occur even if monetary policy holds the exchange rate. Thus Russia's dollar rate was stable for much of 1993 while inflation (and thus real appreciation) ran at about 20 percent per month (or 800 percent over the year). Similarly, Estonia's virtual currency board commitment of monetary policy to its fixed deutsche mark exchange rate has not eliminated price inflation there.

We have already noted John Williamson's support for gradually phasing out effective protection in transition economies. Just as the local decision makers have been slow to adopt the protection, let alone its phasing out, they have also come rather slowly to adopt his exchange rate prescription. This, too, is one that the present commentator also

---

[3] *High Inflation* (Oxford University Press, 1995).

urged, without success, but it is now an important element of Hungary's March 1995 Adjustment and Stabilization Policy, on which Janos Kornai has just published a very positive interim report.[4]

Typically, stabilization policies are associated with reduced competitiveness. This was not true of Poland's 1991 program nor is it of Hungary's new one. Poland devalued and pegged. This strategy, for which there has been voiced some support at the present conference, is inferior to a Williamson crawling band even from the start, particularly because it is more compatible with appropriate interest rates, as Kornai stresses is now true in Hungary, putting less strain on interest arbitrage conditions—which remain relevant even where capital controls remain in place (which are less necessary for crawling bands than for fixed rates).

Berthelot's comments on privatization are somewhat puzzling. Efficient corporate governance exists nowhere, East or West. The trade-off between risk spreading through portfolio diversification and the concentration of ownership needed to prevent the discharge of the proprietorial role from becoming a public good has no known ideal. Private enterprises in the West are apparently no less merely "nonstate" than those of the Czech Republic. Berthelot seems to identify true privatization with owner-managers.

Nor is it easy to recognize any case-by-case "commercial" approach as contrasted with free mass distribution. Where has it been done and how are governance issues there resolved? If the enterprise becomes a wholly owned subsidiary, the governance problem is shifted to the holding company level; it is not resolved. Does Berthelot intend to hold up Poland's indecisiveness as, *ex post*, a model procedure?

Berthelot writes that the "accumulation of bad loans in the commercial banks" follows from "the failure to reform the financial sector." It is not so simple. We have argued that rapid movement to world prices left "losing" enterprises unable to pay the going real wage. They had to be closed (bankruptcy), subsidized or protected (fiscally), or given more credit (financially). The first would not be socially optimal if the market wage exceeded the shadow wage. Although the second would be preferable to the third, the third might be second best, and the second would in any case have required something other than "early financial-sector reforms." On the contrary, financial-sector reform was attempted (for instance, in Hungary) too soon—while enterprises were still operating at a loss for socially plausible reasons—and therefore had to be repeated, with damaging moral-hazard and credibility effects.

One of the recurring themes in our earlier discussion in 1993 was caution in relation to FDI, not only for its ability to undermine competitiveness on the way in and to undermine stability on its way out. We should be more concerned with contributions to national income than with domestic production. The direct contribution of foreign capital to domestic production accrues to foreigners. Under plausible conditions, but ignoring any associated technology transfer, domestic saving is ten times as effective in raising GNP as is FDI.

---

[4] J. Kornai 1995, "Dilemmas of Hungarian Economic Policy," DP No. 18, November 1995, Collegium Budapest.

Berthelot makes two references to FDI. First, he claims it strengthened international links, and later he says it was disappointing. These are not inconsistent, but the disappointment is the dominant factor, especially in the CIS. Latin American experience suggests that capital flight may be a necessary precursor of capital inflows. Eastern Europe, apart from Russia, saw relatively little flight. Admittedly, hopes of FDI as *deus ex machina* are always exaggerated, and he is right to stress the need for domestic savings as well as host country ambivalence. Countries complain of neglect, and they then legislate (unwisely) for fiscal incentives for FDI; if these are effective, they then complain of being exploited, and they cut back on the incentives. The list of "go-stop" episodes could be longer than he gives, including the Czech Republic. In any case, FDI and domestic savings are not alternatives in their effect on national income, which is more important to welfare than is GDP. What matters is openness to trade for the ideas it brings and to investment for their better adoption (see Jeff Sachs, BPEA 1995).[5]

Gustav Ranis said that we should be looking less at Japan's development after World War II than at its development following the Meiji restoration. Post-defeat reconstruction is indeed a very misleading model for postcommunist transition. In particular, Japan's priority allocation for the symbiotic development of energy and heavy industry was peculiarly inappropriate to the FSU. More generally, physical reconstruction offered abnormally high returns while expectations were lowered by defeat. Neither applied in Eastern Europe, where euphoria had to be transformed into despair before recovery could begin.

Eastern European neoliberalism included a rejection of industrial policy, despite the success of the less liberal policies of the Asian tigers that we drew to their attention but that certainly do not merit endorsement since there exists no cookbook recipe for the selection of the sectors to be promoted. At the very early stage of development, when the real exchange rate is typically very low, it may, in fact, be relatively unimportant which sector is selected. It may merely be unwise to attempt to advance on a broad front. The military metaphor is actually inappropriate. The typical developing country is too small for any concentration of its forces to elicit a strategic response from others. But although even this modified presumption may be appropriate to relatively unindustrialized countries in Asia and South America, it is less likely to apply to the overindustrialized economies of Eastern Europe deciding what to do with their ambivalent inheritance.

The ambivalence to FDI revealed by Central Europeans may be for the wrong reasons but is basically right. What is needed is an investment-friendly fiscal and regulatory regime.

What then of Berthelot's conclusions? Revisiting his opening remarks, we take those conclusions to be the following:

First, supply-siders were overrepresented among Western advisors to transition economies. But Jeff Sachs is not a supply-sider at home, and Balcerowicz and Klaus are less compromising (market) liberals (in the European sense), at least in their rhetoric, than most Western advisors.

---

[5] J. Sachs 1995, Brookings Papers on Economic Activity.

Second, the state has to manage the transition. This is a good point. But the question "Should we restructure enterprises before or after privatizing them?" is misplaced. At a minimum, the state must draw the boundaries of the lots to be auctioned. Klaus's prescription for restructuring—"Let the new owners decide"—is naively misplaced when the dispersed new owners, under his voucher privatization scheme, could not conceivably restructure without solving intractable problems of collective choice. Note that this, like "state desertion"[6] of enterprises, was a reflection of local, not imported, thinking. A related point Berthelot makes is that established state organs and personnel were not promising vehicles for market-oriented reforms.

Third, there exist different forms of market economy. This is also a good point, but it is one that perhaps was not really neglected, especially by international financial institutions. Certainly at EBRD we were acutely conscious that we could not say, "You must be democratic," or "Your democracy must choose our model economy." Indeed, we and others said, "Stop. Think. What about the Asian example?" The reply was, "We are Europeans and want the EC/EU model (or at least a model within that range)."

Fourth, medium-term planning should be established. Certainly consistency and predictability of institution building, fiscal regimes, and the like are desirable. But these governments are/were precarious. Gaidar used to say, "I don't know whether I shall be in charge next month." How could he offer medium-term-credible plans? My prescription for transitional protection stands only if its transitional nature can be made credible. This requires medium-term commitment. To that extent, Berthelot is certainly right. But credibility is not there for the asking. Elsewhere we have suggested ways in which it could be achieved by treaty commitments to other countries in transition or by international financial institutions' conditionality or by EU agreements. All of these have made medium-term arrangements for conditional SALs, phased trade liberalization, and so forth. Although they may reject the language of planning, the IFIs and their advisors do recognize the logic of medium-term commitments; but such commitments suffer serious feasibility problems.

All this brings us to the last point—transition and development. John Williamson has expressed sympathy for the transitional protection proposal for countries in transition, and progressive liberalization is part of his restated Washington consensus. Despite its thus being virtually conventional wisdom in the development context, it encountered persistent criticism and unyielding resistance both from other IFIs and from liberal policymakers in the region in the early 1990s (although it might be different now). Why the discrepancy?

---

[6] R. Portes and M. Nuti 1993, "Central Europe: The Way Forward" in R. Portes, ed., *Economic Transformation in Central Europe,* CEPR 1993.

Dragoslav Avramovic[1] on Yves Berthelot's Paper

Lessons from Transition:
The Case of Yugoslavia, 1994–1996

Three issues are considered here. First, what strategy was selected to cope with Yugoslavia's hyperinflation, with its decline in production, and with the external disequilibriums caused by the breakup of the country and by the international economic blockade? Second, how successful was that strategy and what would one do now if one could do it all over again? And third, what does one do next and what are the general lessons of this experience?

Strategy to Cope with Hyperinflation and Systemic Deficiencies

Yugoslav inflation—at 60 percent per day of price increases at its peak toward the end of 1993 and the beginning of 1994, which was higher than the German inflation of 1923 and a match for the Hungarian inflation of 1947—stemmed from a combination of factors. First, the sharp increase in government expenditures under war conditions—including care of the refugees and government support to workers unemployed because of economic sanctions and the breakup of the economy—had not been accompanied by the required additional fiscal effort. Second, no thought had been given to introducing measures of war economy—rationing, production planning, and incomes policy. Third, high industrial-financing costs resulting from rising interest rates early in the inflation had been counteracted by a reduction in the central bank's discount rate, which then had led to a massive increase in lending and an expansion in the money supply. Fourth, economic sanctions and the breakup of the country had led to deterioration of the terms of trade, capital flight, and a sharp increase in the price of foreign exchange, which in turn had influenced all other prices. We thus had in operation three gigantic inflationary engines reinforcing each other: government deficit spending, lending at interest rates below the rate of inflation, and pricing of foreign exchange pushed upward by factors beyond the country's control.

The strategy that was initially considered in the fall of 1993 was a combination of a gradual reduction of inflation and the introduction of privatization and import liberalization. The present writer did not find this to be the appropriate remedy. Price inflation had gone so far that domestic currency was losing properties of money: it was no longer a store of value or savings and was increasingly being pushed out as an accounting device

---

[1] Former Governor, Central Bank, Belgrade.

and a transaction money by rising inroads of the leading foreign currency—the German mark. Prices were rising so fast that increases in money incomes could not keep pace: we had reached a stage in which each additional injection of money was leading to a decline in the aggregate real value of money. The aggregate value of the money stock at the beginning of the inflationary process, in 1991, was equivalent to 2 billion marks; at the end of the process, in January 1994, this value was 40 million marks. Under these circumstances, there was no way in which we could reduce inflation except by eliminating it— that is, by moving to another, stable, currency. Gradual reduction of inflation was no longer possible. On the other hand, it did not seem that we could afford to move right away into import liberalization or obligatory privatization. Both import liberalization and obligatory privatization would have involved losses of jobs in the affected industries; these losses would have been superimposed on the losses possibly resulting from the halting of inflation through the reconstruction of the monetary system. Hence, the strategy that was finally decided upon consisted of the introduction of a new noninflationary currency, its partial convertibility to ensure its stability, and a swift movement to a balanced government budget so as to avoid any serious inflationary finance. The structural measures— opening up of the economy to foreign competition and establishment of competitive domestic conditions through privatization and de-administration of the economy— were to wait until the integrity of the financial system and of money was restored.

This strategy worked during the short run. The new currency was accepted: decisive here were that currency's link to the German mark and its partial convertibility, decontrol of all commodity prices except those for bread and rent, and swift moves to restore the budget balance. The link to the German mark was possible even at the very low level of exchange reserves and without foreign assistance, because the domestic money stock was so low in foreign currency that its convertibility was ensured. Prices could be decontrolled because there were plenty of stocks hoarded during the hyperinflation and money incomes were extremely low at the beginning of monetary reconstruction. Budget balance could be restored relatively quickly because government expenditures in real terms had fallen to an extremely low level in the final phase of the hyperinflation (pensions were running to the equivalent of only 5 marks a month) and were readjusted only slowly, while revenue improved both as a result of economic recovery as inflation stopped and as a result of fiscal measures designed to accelerate budget receipts. There existed virtually no deflationary pressure, as a result of stabilization. The new Yugoslav *dinar* was released through the government budget, the currency issue fully covered by the existing stock of foreign exchange and gold. A positive interest rate of 6 percent was introduced; the holders of inventories in trade and production facilities—facing a situation of rising real financing costs and no increase in prices as all goods markets were decontrolled— were compelled to sell goods from stocks; as stocks were being depleted, the manufacturers were induced to expand production, knowing that wage costs would never again be as low as in this initial phase of post-inflationary recovery (the average wage in January 1994, at the start of the reform, was 26 marks per month). Production picked up rapidly in industry as stocks were falling and money was kept stable in value. In agriculture, a deal was struck among the banks, the agricultural cooperatives, and the central-bank governor (the present writer): banks were to lend at no more than 9 percent per year (deposit rate of 6 percent plus margin), while agricultural cooperatives would persuade their members to sow and work in the fields, in exchange for the governor's promise that money values would remain stable (and thus the value of the crops) and interest costs moderate.

The first eight months, January to August 1994, sailed along as smoothly as in a dream. Prices were remarkably stable, without intervention; industrial production shot up 70 percent (albeit from a very low level); agricultural output and supplies were also up; and real wages and incomes generally recovered extremely rapidly. Furthermore, government revenue shot up, and we could announce, six months after the inauguration of the stabilization plan, that there would be no more financing of the government by the central bank; not only did we not use any of the slim foreign-exchange reserves with which we started but also we accumulated (that is, the central bank accumulated) a large amount, as some capital was repatriated and as a part of the population with foreign-exchange holdings parted with some of these holdings to supplement still-low *dinar* incomes. The reform was hailed as a "people's reform"—which was a source of great pride for the present commentator—because the new money was injected through the government budget rather than through banks, and as a result, it was the retired people, the impoverished government employees, and the recipients of welfare assistance who were the first to benefit from the improved real incomes. Had the banks been the main channels of distribution of new money in the form of advances (credits) to business and to rich individuals, it would have been more likely that a proportion would have leaked out into imports or capital flight. As it was, additional incomes were spent mostly on foodstuffs and other articles of prime necessity that were primarily domestically produced. We thus got a circular flow of income within the economy, resulting in rising production, rising consumption, and a temporary accumulation of foreign exchange.

Stabilization seemed perfect: no deflation, no unemployment, perfectly stable prices without controls, near-restoration of the budgetary equilibrium, recovery of production, and accumulation of foreign-exchange reserves—all achieved without a penny of foreign assistance, under conditions of economic blockade. The stocked goods reappeared on the market, foreign trade moved somewhat despite the blockade, and for more than six months it seemed a miracle had descended on Yugoslavia despite the war, the international sanctions, and the breakup of the country.

From a strategic viewpoint, it also seemed that a focus on one thing at a time (stabilization) was superior to spreading wide and thin—that is, attempting privatization and import liberalization as well. The present writer was always skeptical with respect to the Kornai-Sachs big-bang comprehensive anti-inflationary and systemic reform all at once: policymakers' long years of experience both in previous attempts at stabilization in Yugoslavia and in most developing countries' processes of adjustment had strongly suggested that stepwise reform was a better way. Even so, a big-bang prescription was in fact applied to the monetary system, by rejecting a gradual reduction of inflation in favor of all-at-once restoration of the integrity of money through the reconstruction of the monetary system. But the big-bang approach was not applied to the other two components of the Kornai-Sachs model—privatization and liberalization. This policy proved correct over the short run.

Setbacks

The first signs of strain in the stabilization process occurred in June 1994, when banks increased their demand for central-bank credits. One reason for this increase was a continuing growth of industrial production and the consequential increase in the demand for more working capital, which the banks were unable to supply because of weak deposit growth and the absence of capital inflow. Another reason was more serious: the repayment of loans granted by the banks at the beginning of stabilization to producing and trading firms was lagging behind schedule, indicating weakness in the banks' lending criteria and practices as well as failures of the borrowing firms to recover their costs.

Second, at about the same time, in June 1994, a letter received from a manufacturing firm in Novi Sad, Yugoslavia's third-largest town, noted the sharply rising prices of intermediate goods (steel, aluminum, packing materials, paints, and the like) and the rising interest costs in intra-trade of firms, which had not yet been reflected in price statistics but were nonetheless real and would threaten recovery.

Third, about August 1994, unpleasant news started coming in from the countryside, where agricultural-producer cooperatives were not being paid by the government purchasing agency for the crops delivered in June and July of 1994. It was the guaranteed price that had been promised, and the guarantee had to be met if the entire strategy was to be successful. Despite the commitment not to engage the central bank in any deficit financing of the state, we allowed credit for these agricultural purchases to be refinanced by the central bank. We also allowed some credit to be given by the central bank for the maintenance and repair of the electric-power network, initially at the request of the government of Crna Gora. (It was said half-jokingly at the time that 1994 was the first year in its history that Crna Gora had met all its budgetary expenditures out of its revenue.) We felt justified in extending central-bank credit for agriculture and electricity, the two vital sectors, in view of perfect price stability up to that point in the economy as a whole, but in retrospect it was a mistake, even though the credits were short term—one year. They were not repaid.

Fourth, the real crisis occurred in October 1994, when the price index shot up 1.4 percent in one month, to be followed by another 7 percent rise in November 1994. This price rise was accompanied by a sharp increase in the price of foreign exchange in the free market. Right from the start of the stabilization, in January 1994, there was a somewhat higher price of the mark, about 10 percent to 20 percent, in the free market, compared to the official parity of the national currency (1 dinar for 1 German mark). But this difference did not seem to lead to any major distortion or speculation in the market or in the economy generally. By October 1994, however, as domestic prices started increasing, the disturbance spread to the foreign-exchange market, and prices there shot up to 50 percent above official. The spell of the perfect Yugoslav monetary stabilization was broken, and we had at hand a serious foreign-exchange crisis as 1994 drew to a close.

Our immediate reaction to the crisis was to change the exchange rate to the market level: this would improve the capital side of the balance of payments and at the same time work in the direction of improving the current side by expanding exports and holding the demand for imports in check. This would have to go hand in hand with reasonable stringency of monetary policy and renewed efforts to stabilize the totality of government financial operations, including price supports and investment financing. But we could not convince the government that this was the best course to follow. We even had difficulty convincing the majority of the senior staff of the central bank, who should have known better. The fundamental reason for rejecting this course of action was fear of renewed massive inflation. Apparently, the experience of Yugoslavia with devaluations in the past has been bad: devaluations would be followed by renewed inflationary pressures, which in turn would require another devaluation. The reluctance to change the exchange rate, however, would lead to further distortions in the economy, rationing of foreign exchange and credit, very restrictive monetary policy, and ultimately stagnation and then devaluation in this case as well. The refusal of the government to agree to the change in the exchange rate—such an agreement between the government and the central bank is necessary, according to legislation—meant in practice that we had to resort to restrictive monetary policy throughout 1995. It was successful in the sense that some semblance of stability was preserved and the *dinar* continued to be an accepted and acceptable currency. But industrial production, after the leap that had occurred between January and October of 1994, was practically stagnant in the following twelve months, while prices continued to creep upward at an average rate of about 5 percent per month. Real wages, after a major increase in the first nine months of 1994, stagnated and fell during the following year.

Limits of Monetary Policy

Restrictive monetary policy during 1995 was successful in maintaining the stability of agricultural prices: output was satisfactory, and so were the movement and distribution of supplies. (This refers to raw agricultural products, including fruits and vegetables.) The competitive conditions in agriculture, which combines private and public ownership, were such that, with reasonable stability of the currency, a sufficient flow of production came to the market, even though price trends were against agriculture and the volume of agricultural credit was unsatisfactory.

The situation was the reverse in the industrial sector. Industrial prices were rising steadily, at the rate of 10 percent per month, throughout the stabilization period. Stringent monetary policy did not seem to have any effect on industrial prices. The commanding role in the industrial sector belonged to the "social" sector—that is, to the state-owned companies; it was these companies that had the role of price leader in industry. Whether because of inefficiencies that had to be compensated by price increases or because of excessive profit margins sought after by the firms or because of excessive tax burdens on them or because of excessive protection and widespread monopoly in the domestic market, or because of a combination of all these factors, pricing in industry proved immune to either stringent monetary policy or to government pressures to keep prices stable. By the middle of 1995 it was clear that new measures of stabilization, in addition to measures of monetary policy, were necessary if we were to achieve the stability of the economy, restart economic growth, and improve welfare.

Program 2: Adjustment and Restructuring

After a debate lasting some six months, first within the government establishment and then increasingly in public, the government adopted a series of measures proposed by the central bank and entitled Program 2. (Program 1 was that of January 1994 dealing with monetary reconstruction, described earlier.) Program 2 had four essential features.

First, the official exchange rate was changed to the level of the free-market rate (3.3 *dinars* for 1 mark, compared with 1:1 previously). At the same time, exchange restrictions were substantially liberalized: the *dinar* was made convertible into foreign exchange for commercial imports of goods and services, and individuals could buy foreign exchange for travel and other needs in limited amounts that would be, and were, progressively increased. The shackles of an overvalued exchange rate were now gone. At the same time, no overall domestic price increase occurred as a result of the change in the exchange rate, as this change in effect simply confirmed an already-existing market reality.

Second, a policy of trade liberalization was instituted. Some export restrictions were eliminated, import-licensing requirements for a group of products were abolished, and some simplification of the tariff structure was introduced. Import liberalization was essential, and continues to be so, in order to exercise competitive pressure on domestic industry. The process of trade liberalization has a long way to go. The existing protective structure has been built during a period of 50 years, and to dismantle it calls for a massive and sustained effort. Perhaps the greatest obstacle is the deep-rooted belief that any domestic production is "good" and any imports are "bad." There as yet exists insufficient realization that a small country—Yugoslavia has only 10 million people—must move in the direction of export-oriented development and that this calls for cheap and liberalized imports. Ideally, this realization will grow.

Third, interest rate policy was liberalized. The discount rate of the central bank was shifted upward to a positive value in real terms. All restrictions on banks' rates were removed. It had been learned that restrictions did not create conditions for either greater or cheaper credit, but the other way around. Interest rates in the free market were higher than ever—up to 1 percent per day—and the official market had ceased to exist, as the central bank had refrained from primary issues. Liberalization of interest rates resulted in some increases in saving in banks—the rate doubled in several months—but these are still very small amounts. The interest rate in the free market was cut in half as a result of the new policy, but the level continues to be formidable: 15 percent per month or 10 percent per month in real terms. This high interest rate reflects a still-existing fear of inflation, but it also results from the extremely low flow of savings and from the country's virtually nil capital inflow. The high cost of credit and capital is now our central problem, faced as we are by a dearth of working capital in industry and agriculture (and tourism) and by the poor state of maintenance and repair of the infrastructure.

Fourth, a policy of "democratization of property relations",—that is, privatization—was identified as of crucial significance for future growth and stability. The existing pattern of industrial ownership and control clearly is unsatisfactory. Not only it is associated with continuing price increases, but also it leads to a widespread "meltdown" of the social (or public) sector of the economy through transfers to private enterprise, representing a stripping away of assets on a substantial scale. Furthermore, losses in operations of many public enterprises are large and unsustainable. Yugoslavia had led the rest of the socialist world in market-oriented reforms in production and trade. It is now lagging in the reform of the organization and ownership of its industry. This reform is essential for the attraction of foreign capital, for repatriation into Yugoslavia of capital that had fled abroad, and for revival of incentives to produce, invest, and save within Yugoslavia. The future lies in widespread share ownership of public enterprises, of which a proportion, say 25 percent to 30 percent, would be held by workers (ESOP system) and another 20 percent by pension funds, in the initial distribution. The final distribution would, of course, be decided by the market.

Lessons

Three lessons can be drawn from the Yugoslav experience thus far. First, a clever macropolicy can result in substantial gains over the short run. A one-shot monetary stabilization can result in a release of stocks and hoarded cash and thus can attain stability quickly and painlessly, if it is designed in a fashion that rewards the use of readily available resources and penalizes their being held off the market. This was our experience in January 1994—Program 1. Devaluation can also bring about the use of extra resources if it is done in a way that simply confirms and extends the market reality. It will then improve the reserve position and lead to additional exports and to related income and employment gains, without the cycle of new inflation. This was our experience in November 1995—Program 2 although export progress has been slow because of the shortage of working capital and because of import restrictions abroad.

Second, clever macropolicy cannot substantially or directly influence the long-run position. This position depends on real factors—elasticity of foreign-capital inflow and the capacity to generate savings and to use them properly. Foreign-capital inflow depends on international politics with respect to public assistance and on the profitability and "climate" for private investment. In the competitive global market as it has now developed, individual borrowing countries have very limited freedom of action: they have to offer competitive terms to prospective lenders and investors—competitive with respect to the individual project, as well as to the sector in which that project is located and to the host economy as a whole, including its policies.

Third, governments in developing countries face a formidable conflict between the need for low taxation so as to permit private capital accumulation and growth and the need for high public expenditures on health, education, social safety nets and some indispensable public infrastructure as required by their population and geography. There exists only one way in which this conflict can be resolved, apart from foreign-capital inflows. This is to cut to the bone public expenditures on administration, security, and nonessential investment.

We managed to stabilize in Yugoslavia without deflation and without foreign assistance. But we cannot improve the social situation and grow without large foreign-capital inflows, government administration cutbacks, public-enterprise privatization, and widespread shared ownership by workers and pensioners.

Lessons from Japan: Industrial Policy Approach and the East Asian Trial

Katsuhisa Yamada[1]
Akifumi Kuchiki[2]

Overview

National Objectives

After the Meiji Restoration of 1868, the national objective of Japan was to catch up with the level of the advanced countries in Europe and America. Its slogans were *fukoku kyohei* (in a literal translation: "wealthy nation and strong army") and *shokusan kohgyo* ("promotion of industries"). The former policy of *kyohei* (strong army) was overemphasized, and Japan was led to a collapse. After World War II, Japan revised its policy from *hei* (army) to *heiwa* (peace) and made every effort for the nation's revival and its economic growth.

In the period immediately following World War II (1946–1947), Japan's production in the mining and manufacturing industries fell to one-fourth that of the prewar level (1934–1936). But by 1953, its production had recovered to prewar levels. In 1955, the living standard was also back to its highest prewar level. Then in 1956 the government-issued "Economic White Paper" declared that "the economy of Japan is no longer termed 'postwar!'" This supposedly meant two things: first, that reconstruction had come to an end and the rate of economic growth would slow down and second, that economic growth in the future would have to be attained by modernization and technological innovation.

Actually, although the second presumption proved to be correct, the first was wrong. Economic growth of an average annual rate of 10 percent had begun and would last for the following 15 years. The national objective of "let's catch up with the advanced countries in Europe and America" was still alive. In the years 1978–1980, Japan's per capita GNP reached a level comparable to those in Europe and America. More than one hundred years had passed from the Meiji Restoration and 35 years from the end of World War II to the year 1980. Putting the average level in Europe and America (United States, Canada, United Kingdom, West Germany, France, and Italy) at 100 percent, Japan's per

---

[1] President, Institute of Developing Economies, Tokyo.
[2] Senior Research Fellow, Institute of Developing Economies, Tokyo.

capita GNP was comparatively 23 percent in 1960 and 53 percent in 1970, which shows the remarkably rapid growth during the 20-year period after 1960.

In 1990, the per capita GNP paralleled that of the United States, in part because of changes in the dollar-yen exchange rate. The Japanese economy then stagnated in the first half of the 1990s. This stagnation may have been caused by a business cycle stage. At the same time, however, it may have had something to do with the fact that the Japanese economy had reached the same per capita level as the U.S. economy. In other words, "it had already become mature."

The year 1980 was also a turning point for Japan in another respect. Japan's position in the world economy reached a high of 10 percent of the entire world GNP. In periods in which the ratio was lower (3.6 percent in 1950, 4.4 percent in 1960, and 7.5 percent in 1970), it was taken for granted that Japan had passively accepted the trend of the world economy. But when the ratio reached 10 percent, Japan's behavior became very influential in the world economy, and the country had to change its economic policies to become more active. Coincidentally, interdependence in the world economy was growing stronger, and a global economy had arrived. Making an "international contribution as an economic superpower" became another national objective for the Japanese people.

The growth process of the Japanese economy from 1945 to 1980—and in particular the role of industrial policies during that period—could perhaps provide certain useful lessons for many developing economies. It might be interesting to take a look at some 1994 data on Latin America and East Asia (excluding Japan and China). The population of Latin America was 464 million; GDP was $1,200 billion; per capita GDP was $2,590; and their ratio to those of Europe and America was around 11 percent. The data for East Asia were 572 million population, $1,440 billion GDP, $2,520 per capita GDP, and 11 percent ratio vis-à-vis Europe and America. The two regions show similar figures. The corresponding figures for Japan were 126 million population; $4,700 billion GDP; $37,620 per capita GDP; and 157 percent ratio vis-à-vis Europe and America.

Industrial Policy and the Developmental State

Taking into consideration the circumstances described earlier, Professor Chalmers Johnson published a book in 1982 entitled *MITI and the Japanese Miracle: The Growth of Industrial Policy, 1925–1975* (Stanford University Press). His desire was to uncover the secrets of the high economic growth rate of Japan. At that time, the term "industrial policy" was not yet recognized in the United States. At most, industrial policy was understood as "the policy put into effect by MITI (the Ministry of International Trade and Industry) of Japan." There existed no industrial policy in the United States. In Europe— for instance in the United Kingdom, France, and Italy—there existed many state-owned enterprises not only in defense industries but also in others (such as steel, automobiles, and electronic machinery), and there existed various policies related to them. State-owned enterprises have not existed in the manufacturing sector of Japanese industries (except for tobacco and pure alcohol) since Yawata Steel was privatized in 1950. In this respect, except for the period during World War II and several years following it, Japan was and is a nation with an economic system based on the principles of private enterprise and market mechanisms, just like that of the United States.

At present, the term "developmental state" is used in contrast with the "market-friendly approach," and Japan is held up as a model of a "developmental state." This term implies a "government-led or antimarket economy" and can cause misunderstanding. It seems that the expression was originally derived from Professor Johnson's book, in which he states the following:

> A regulatory or market-rational state concerns itself with the forms and procedures (the rules) of economic competition, but it does not concern itself with what industries ought to exist and what industries are no longer needed. The developmental, or plan-rational state, by contrast, has as its dominant feature precisely the setting of such substantive social and economic goals, and the government gives greatest precedence to industrial policy.

When he concluded that MITI's industrial policy is one of the secrets for explaining Japan's high economic growth rate, he described the United States as a "regulatory state" and Japan as a "developmental state."

Dynamic Market Effectivization Approach

Japanese postwar industrial policies, particularly those before 1980, provide lessons for developing countries. Professor Johnson's analysis for the period 1925–1975 was almost correct. Nevertheless, special attention should be drawn as to how to interpret and apply the results of his analysis in the following five points.

First, although Johnson describes the Japanese approach with the term "plan rational," in reality Japan's system is based on "indicative planning" or on "showing visions."

Second, judging from the industrial policy adopted by MITI, it may be possible to consider Japan a developmental state. Nevertheless, Professor Kent Calder says the following:

> A strong developmental orientation has often prevailed at MITI, but other ministries such as the Ministry of Finance (MOF) and the Bank of Japan have often held a perspective closer to the American regulatory orientation than MITI's developmental stance (*Strategic Capitalism*).

Third, MITI's method is not based on a static idea but on a dynamic way of thinking. Japan has deployed different industrial policies according to the stage of its economic development and international situation. MITI holds in-house summer discussions every year on priority items in the following year's policy and presents a tentative plan to its Industrial Structure Council. The policy is determined after deliberation by the council. Appendix 1 shows changes in the priority items of MITI's policy in five-year periods from 1950 to 1997; for the sake of convenience, only large items are shown.

Before moving on to our fourth point, let us briefly review several items from the dynamic-efficiency point of view by pondering three points: What kinds of items appeared at approximately what time? Which items appeared at all times? How has the order of items changed? In the following, six items are given as examples.

"Promotion of trade" was always listed as a number-one item from 1950 to 1965, in recognition of Japan's being a "trade-based nation." This item has kept a high ranking thereafter but changed its form to "international development of the national economy" starting in 1970 and "positive contribution to the world economy" starting in 1980.

"Small and medium enterprises" have also consistently been considered an important item. Such enterprises are one of the basic components of Japan's industrial policy. In the earlier stage, the item ranked rather low, but in the period of high economic growth, it ranked first or second in importance (from 1962 to 1968). This was because the modernization of small business, which was one of the bottlenecks for the national economic growth, became a key subject. Recently (1995–1997), this item has been absorbed in the subject of overall industrial-structure transformation and business innovation.

"Consumer policy and people's quality of life" appeared on the list in 1960, was placed as second in importance in 1970, and has been sustained as a large item thereafter.

"Stable energy supply" (although not shown in Appendix I) was listed as seventh and last among those items selected in the summer of 1972 for the year 1973. It ranked fourth in the list prepared right before the first oil crisis in 1973. In the list of 1975, "stable energy supply" rose to number two. This was a hindsighted policy decision and reflected negligence. "Negligence" is written as *yudan* in the Japanese language, and its literal meaning is "to cut oil." Just when "energy" had again dropped in ranking (fifth place in the list of 1979), the second oil crisis took place, and so the item was pushed up to first place in the 1980 list.

"Technological development" had appeared as "promotion of industrial technology" in the lower part of the list every year since 1950 but ranked second in 1981 under the motto of "establishment of the nation on the basis of technology." This item has been holding on to second or third place since 1986, marking the existence of the present high-tech era.

"Industrial-pollution prevention" appeared in 1962 and ranked low at that time, but it was put at the top in 1973.

Moving on to our fourth more general point, MITI's authority in such fields as legislation, budget preparation, and tax systems was decreasing with the growth of the Japanese economy. Yet MITI has continued to play a key role in other fields. Former Prime Minister Kiichi Miyazawa expressed his opinion in *Bungei-Shunju* (July 1996), one of the most popular magazines in Japan:

> MITI, which held great power as did the Ministry of Finance, has been losing its power under the name of industrial liberalization. There was even a period when MITI's *raison d'être* was doubted. However, MITI officials seriously reconsidered their own *raison d'être* and have survived by reforming it into a government office for public service. A good example is JETRO (Japan External Trade Organization). This organization was originally established to promote Japan's export trade, but now holds the enhancement of imports as its primary goal. MITI has changed its role greatly.

Fifth, the role of government is to compensate for market failures. Hence, we can conclude that MITI's role is to make the market effective from the point of view of dynamic efficiency. We daresay therefore that Japan is a market-effective developmental state.

Japan's Case versus the East Asian Trial

The transition from controlled economy to market economy in postwar Japan is called "gradualism." The industrial policies adopted in the transition process and afterward are divided into four major stages as shown in Table 3.29: (I) the priority production program (1945–1950), (II) the industrial rationalization policy (1950–1960), (III) the system of cooperation between government and business (1960–1970); and (IV) the formulation of visions (1970–present). Government intervention in the private sector was effective until the third major stage. We shall discuss the relationship between the Japanese experience until the mid-1960s and the ASEAN experience since the latter half of the 1980s.

The export-processing zone system, or the Asian EPZ model, has been a main reason for the high economic growth in Malaysia and Thailand since the latter half of the 1980s. The differences between the ASEAN (Association of Southeast Asian Nations) system and the industrial policies of Japan are illustrated by the following two points.

The first is that ASEAN countries are relying on foreign direct investment (FDI) whereas Japan put priority on the promotion of domestic capital. The reasons that Japan adopted such a policy were that the industrial foundation already existed and that the international capital market was not as large as it is at present. These factors resulted in differences between Japan and ASEAN in terms of their industrial-promotion policies. For the ASEAN countries, favorable taxation policies, which are crucial for attracting FDI, have been relatively important. In contrast, in Japanese industrial policies, preferential financing for domestic investment, or credit allocation, played an important role; therefore, the role played by Japanese banks was essential.

The second point of difference is that while ASEAN countries have been export oriented since the latter half of the 1980s, Japan had long been export oriented, and at the same time had a strong trend of import substitution until the first half of the 1960s. Japan needed an industrial policy to strengthen the international competitiveness of its import substituting industries in the third stage when trade liberalization was under way. If we observe the present situation in ASEAN countries in this connection, it is necessary to promote supporting industries (including small and medium enterprises) and to foster human capital in order to strengthen the industrial linkage of local entrepreneurs with FDI.

Here we refer to the "market-friendly approach." The World Bank regards Malaysia, Thailand, and Indonesia as outstanding pupils in this regard. Motivated and stimulated by the introduction of FDI, these three nations have achieved high rates of growth in the last ten years, with export expansion and large increases in investment of plant and equipment in the private sector as two important factors. But in introducing FDI, the gov-

TABLE 3.29. Industrial Policies in Japan's Process of Transition to a Market Economy (1945–present)

	[I] (1945–50)	[II] (1950–60)	[III] (1960–70)	[IV] (1970–)
Industrial Policy	The Priority Production Program	The Industrial Rationalization Policy	The System of Cooperation between Government and Business	The Formulation of Visions
Economic System	direct control	indirect control	liberalization	free competition
Main Industries	coal steel	coal electricity shipping	steel petroleum refinery petrochemicals synthetic fiber machinery electronics	high-technology, etc.
Policy Measures	materials rationing	financing	merger and reorganization	deliberation councils for formulating visions
	price controls	tax reduction or exemption	investment coordination	
	Reconstruction Finance Corporation loans		production coordination	
	Price gap subsidies	price coordination		
			development of small-scale industries	

Note: Gradualism
(1) Strengthening of the supply side (the priority production program) (I)
(2) Private-sector development (the dissolution of big business groups)
(3) Macroeconomic stabilization (the Dodge line)
(4) Structural-adjustment program
(5) The industrial-rationalization policies (II)
(6) The system of cooperation between government and business (III)

ernments of these countries approved these foreign investments on the condition that the export ratio of the ensuing products had to be very large and that the ratio of local contents of these products had to be high; such a policy cannot really be considered as "market friendly."

Transition to a Market Economy in Postwar Japan through the Mid-1960s: Gradualism

The transition of the economy in postwar Japan from a controlled economy to a market economy can be characterized as "gradualism," as opposed to "shock therapy." The sequencing of the Japanese gradualist transition was as follows: strengthening of the supply side (priority production program) (I); private-sector development (dissolution of big business groups); macroeconomic stabilization (Dodge line); structural-adjustment program; industrial-rationalization policies (II); and the system of cooperation between government and business (III). Among these industrial policies, stages II (industrial rationalization) and III (cooperation between government and business) are subjects applicable to the present situation of developing countries; these were part of the whole process by which the economy of postwar Japan changed from a controlled economy to a market economy. Let us now examine Japan's entire postwar process in some detail, in accordance with the aforementioned list of gradual stages.

Strengthening the Supply Side (I) (1946–1948)

In Japan's postwar reconstruction period, it was deemed necessary to strengthen the coal and steel industries. The policy aimed to increase coal and steel production by giving priority to the steel industry in the allocation of coal, and then giving priority to the coal industry in the allocation of steel. The program's objective was to strengthen the capacity of basic raw-material supplies.

This policy was executed under direct control of the government. The measures included allocation of materials, financing from the Reconstruction Finance Bank, price gap subsidies, price control, and allotment of imported materials.

Production of steel and coal in 1947 hit a record high. And the production of mining and manufacturing industries in that year increased by 23 percent. In 1948, growth increased even further to 33 percent.

According to Y. Kosai (*Industrial Policy of Japan*), however, particular attention must be paid to the following point: since it was designed to overcome Japan's unusual situation immediately after the war, this import substitution policy (necessitated by the great shortage of foreign currency) is not properly applied to other countries under different circumstances.

Private-Sector Development (1946–1947)

In order to promote competition in the private sector, the *zaibatsu* (big business groups) were dissolved, and the antimonopoly law was enacted. The 10 groups that were designated for dissolution included Mitusi, Mitsubishi, Sumitomo, and Yasuda, and reorganization orders from General Headquarters (GHQ) were issued to 18 companies. For instance, the two giant trading firms Mitsubishi Corporation and Mitsui & Co., Ltd., were divided into l20 and 170 companies respectively. Through this process, family-controlled *konzerns* (multiple enterprises) ceased to exist. Competition was further promoted by the enactment of the aforementioned antimonopoly law.

Macroeconomic-Stabilization Policy (1948)

GHQ announced nine economic stabilization principles in December 1948, and upon arrival of the mission headed by Joseph Dodge in 1949, effective demand was cut by imposing a reduced budget. This policy was called the "Dodge line." He reformed the taxation system, reduced subsidies greatly, attained a balanced budget, and started a return to market principles. As a result, hyperinflation was controlled and the economy moved toward macroeconomic stabilization.

Structural Adjustment Program (1949–1951)

In order to return to market economy status, it was necessary to lift price controls and to set and unify the exchange rate. There had been about 63 thousand price-controlled items at the end of 1948, and that number was reduced to about 80 by the end of 1951. The multiple exchange rates that existed for price gap subsidies were unified, and a single exchange rate of 360 yen/U.S. dollar was established in 1949 to make international trade possible.

The Industrial Rationalization Policies (II) (1950–1960)

Industrial policies were introduced in this period. Key policy measures included preferential taxation (including the special depreciation scheme) (1951), import tax exemption for important machinery (1952), and the export income tax deduction (1953). Other measures included the low-interest credit allocated by the Japan Development Bank (which was established in 1951 and replaced the Reconstruction Finance Bank), the technology import approval system (based on foreign-currency allocations), and the import quota system implemented for the steel industry in 1950.

A distinctive feature in the 1950s was that the government targeted priority industries and designated priority enterprises. The process was controlled by the government to some extent, but it was not under government's direct management. Financing, or credit allocation, was particularly important because it aimed at fostering domestic capital. Financing from the Japan Development Bank played a key role in supplying funds to basic industries in the early stages.

The System of Cooperation between Government and Business (III) (1960–1970)

Trade liberalization went on throughout the 1960s. Liberalization of trade and foreign exchange was announced in 1960. In 1964, Japan joined the OECD (Organization for Economic Cooperation and Development) and lifted foreign-exchange restrictions. Trade liberalization was carried out in three steps from 1961 onward and exceeded 90 percent by 1964. Liberalization of capital was initiated in 1967 and was completed in 1973. An event that reflected the economic climate at the time was the rejection by the Japanese House of Representatives of the draft bill of a law to promote specially designated industries; this bill proposed to create priorities in taxation and financing for three types of industries, including automobiles, steel specialities, and petrochemicals.

As liberalization progressed, the promotion of heavy and chemical industries was carried out in the 1960s. During that period, cooperation and coordination arose between the government and business, in order to make Japanese enterprises more competitive in the face of liberalization. Macroeconomic management in the period was based on Keynesian economics (which claims that investment produces savings) and on Harrod-

Domar's theory (which implies that private investment in plant and equipment may create effective demand with a multiplier effect and increase supply capacity at the same time).

Japanese Industrial Policy since the Mid-1960s: The Formulation of Visions
Changes in Industrial Policies
Industrial policies have changed dramatically, particularly since the middle of the 1960s (and since the 1970s in the case of computers). Measures to restrict imports and promote exports were gradually lifted, and "the period of protective industrial policies" was over. Japan has reduced its tariff rates and today has a lower average tariff level than both the United States and the EU.

In recognition of its increasing role in the world economy in the 1980s, Japan made vigorous import promotion efforts, including shifting the emphasis of the activities of the Japanese External Trade Organization from export to import promotion. Policies have stressed the promotion of international cooperation in joint research and development efforts and investments to contribute to the revitalization of the world economy.

Basic Attitude behind Industrial Policies
The basic attitude behind Japan's industrial policies is to support the free-trade principle. For instance, several Japanese industrial sectors, such as textiles and the rubber footwear industry, were put under severe import pressure from other countries (particularly those in Asia) around 1980, but despite these industries' difficulties, the government of Japan did not extend help to them in the form of import protection.

Japan's industrial-policy tools are indirect and inductive in nature and are designed to stimulate competition-oriented private firms to make maximum use of their own initiative and entrepreneurship. Imperfections exist in the mobility of capital and of labor, in information flows, and in other areas. Furthermore, there exist external economies and diseconomies that cannot be adequately addressed by the functioning of the market mechanism alone. Herein lies the role of industrial policy: the role of industrial policy is to provide a framework in which market forces can better function.

Formulation of Visions: The "Soft Technology" of Public Administration
Among the tools of industrial policy, the formulation of visions is considered basic for the designing of policies (for example, the technopolis act of 1983[3]). There exist various kinds of visions: some cover the entire industrial structure, while others relate to specific problems such as industrial adjustment or energy.

Visions are not formulated by the government alone but also through open discussions of councils composed of representatives from various sectors, in addition to indus-

---

[3] The "technopolis" idea is one of the typical concrete proposals of the vision for the 1980s. This creates a new kind of city combining high-tech industries and habitat. This idea was legislated in 1983 and was implemented thereafter. From the standpoint of a policy objective view, the technopolis project represents regional development under the motto of a technology-based nation.

TABLE 3.30. Ministries' Share in Japan's General Accounting Budget (1950–1995)
(Percentages)

Fiscal Year	1950	1965	1980	1995
MITI	0.8	1.5	1.5	1.3
Ministry of Finance	15.1	4.2	14.5	22.8
Ministry of Agriculture, Fishery and Forestry	7.7	10.7	8.8	4.3
Ministry of Transportation	3.0	2.6	3.2	1.3
Ministry of Construction	9.6	13.2	10.0	7.9
Ministry of Welfare	5.4	13.8	18.9	19.7
Ministry of Education	2.4	12.5	10.1	7.9

Source: MOF.

trial circles, such as financial institutions, academia, journalism, labor, small business, consumers, and local public entities (the Industrial Structure Council is a typical one). In the case of the formulation of the vision for the 1980s, not only economists but also political scientists, sociologists, engineers, historians, writers, and even an author of science fiction were among the participants.

The vision formulation process and result—that is, the drafting of long-term perspectives—are crucial to the government-business interface and constitute the main role of MITI. Having a vision reduces uncertainty about the future and promotes brisk market activity and desirable competitive conditions. MITI is not in a position to intervene and control the activities of private companies but instead plays the role of advisor and consultant. MITI's financial budget is relatively small (see Table 3.30), and its legal authority is less than powerful. We might say that MITI makes free use of what can be called "soft" technologies of public administration, represented by a future-oriented way of thinking and a consensus-based process of policymaking.

Master visions are formulated at the beginning of each decade. Table 3.31 indicates the main orientations of these visions historically. MITI's vision for the 1970s indicated the importance of the computer industry or "mechatronics." Senior industrial schools and colleges, reading this information, increased the number of students admitted to departments specializing in data-processing technology four times from 1970 to 1979. The vision for the 1970s also used the term "knowledge intensification". In addition to referring to the computer industry, this term suggested that such an orientation was necessary in order to cope with various problems encountered in raising productivity. The desired approach was achieved by emphasizing knowledge factors in every industrial field. The vision for the 1970s was unable to predict the occurrences of the dollar shock in 1971 or the oil crisis in 1973, but the concept of "knowledge intensification" was helpful in recovering from these shocks.

One of the slogans of MITI's vision for the 1980s was a "technology-based nation." MITI recognized that creating technology was essential both for contributing to the world economy and for the economic security of the nation. The prevailing opinion around that time, however, was that there would be "no more technological revolution."

TABLE 3.31. Evolution of MITI's Visions (1960–1980)

	MITI's Vision for the 1960s (1963)	MITI's Vision for the 1970s (1971)	MITI's Vision for the 1980s (1980)
Direction	Heavy and chemical industrialization	Knowledge intensification	Creating and vitalizing knowledge
National goals	Stronger international competitiveness through pursuit of scale merit	Assurance of a full and rewarding way of life	Contributing positively to the international community
	Stable supply of inexpensive basic materials	Positive contribution toward international peace and development	Overcoming the limitations of natural resources and energy
	Sophistication of light industrial products, leading to expanded exports	Maintenance and enhancement of national creativity and dynamism	Attaining the coexistence of society's dynamism and an improved quality and comfort of life
	Elimination of friction arising during the process of progressive adjustment of the industrial structure		Establishing "technology-based nation"

Source: MITI.

Furthermore, expenditures on research and development as a percentage of GNP in Japan were 1.7 percent in 1977, the lowest among the advanced nations (Germany 2.3 percent, United States 2.2 percent, Britain 2.2 percent, and France 1.8 percent in 1977). MITI's vision targeted increasing this figure to 2.5 percent by 1985 and to 3.0 percent by 1990. These targets were attained exactly as MITI had indicated. Moreover, the government's share in research and development expenditures (which had been only 27 percent in 1977 compared with 50 percent in other advanced nations) decreased still further to 20 percent in 1990. Private companies stood out. The "technology-based nation" concept set a marker for Japan's business circles, as it vitalized their incentives and introduced the high-tech age by its announcement effect. The vision is mightier than the budget.[4]

Industrialization Policies in the ASEAN and ANIES Countries

The ASEAN and ANIES (Asian Newly Industrialized Economies) economies adopted an import-substituting industrialization policy that proved successful in the early stage of their economic development. But they were soon faced with a saturated market because

---

[4] As a result of stagnation of business activities in the first half of the 1990s, the ratio of R&D expenditures to GNP declined to 2.8 percent in 1994, which still represents the largest share among other nations (the United States 2.5 percent, Germany 2.5 percent, France 2.5 percent, and the United Kingdom 2.2 percent). Although the government share in total R&D expenditure increased to 22 percent in 1994, it was less than in other nations (the United States 36 percent, Germany 37 percent, France 46 percent, and the United Kingdom 32 percent).

of their population and income levels. Therefore, the ASEAN countries shifted toward an export-oriented policy as of the mid-1980s.

Malaysia: High Growth, Human-Resource Development, and Free-Trade Zones
Import substitution (1957–1967)

A first phase of import substitution was implemented moderately in Malaysia after independence in 1957. The World Bank proposed that Malaysia adopt a policy of replacing imports with domestic products, and the government followed that suggestion in general, but it did not control exchange rates, it imposed few limits on import volume, and it set relatively low import tariff rates.[5]

Export orientation (1968–1979)

In 1965, the government had put emphasis on import substitution of consumer goods, but the size of the domestic market was too small. As a result, the government then shifted toward an export-oriented policy as outlined in the 1968 investment incentives act. This act identified industries that exported finished and semifinished manufactured goods as priority industries to enjoy preferential treatment. This treatment was centered on their exemption from corporate tax payments for five to eight years. Other exemptions included the development tax (5 percent of profits), the 3 percent excess-profits tax, and the 40 percent corporate tax. In addition, in 1971 a law took effect to govern free-trade zones, which have essentially the same functions as export-processing zones.

Import substitution revisited (1980–1985)

Beginning in 1970 the Malaysian economy shifted its dependence from rubber and tin to palm oil and crude oil. Crude oil accounted for 30 percent of all Malaysian exports in 1985. Amidst this change, the government implemented the second phase of the import substitution policy in 1980. The plan to shift to heavy industries was launched by the establishment of the Heavy Industries Corporation of Malaysia (HICOM), and the investment priority was shifted to steel, cement, automobiles, chemicals, and other industries. But the country's macroeconomic stability worsened dramatically in the early 1980s: the shortage of savings exceeded 10 percent of GNP, the fiscal deficit was 20 percent of GNP, and the external current-account deficit amounted to 10 percent of GNP. The country's foreign debts kept growing, to exceed 40 percent of GNP in 1986, with the debt service ratio rising more than 15 percent. In 1985, the country suffered from its first negative economic growth since 1961.

Export orientation through introduction of FDI (1986–present)

This negative economic growth forced Malaysia to strengthen export-oriented industrialization. The nation's previous basic policy was called the "new economic policy," or

---

[5] Hirohisa Kohamá, Ippei Yamazawa, and Akira Hirata, eds., *Industrialization and Export Promotion Policies of Developing Countries* (Tokyo: Institute of Developing Economies, 1987).

NEP, and had been implemented after the 1969 ethnic riots. One of the primary goals of this policy which was also called the Bumiputra policy, had been the restructuring of the society to lessen economic disparity among ethnic groups and regions. Therefore, the country's priority for economic policy was equity rather than efficiency. In 1986, an export promotion act was adopted that shifted the priority in the government's economic policy from equity to efficiency, and the government authorized 100 percent capital ownership by foreign investors. In other words, a period of deregulation, privatization, and economic liberalization had begun.

The 1986 deregulation of foreign direct investment (FDI) was an epoch-making event in that it allowed full ownership of a company by foreign investors under certain conditions.[6] The conditions were either that the company export more than 80 percent of its products or alternatively, that the company export more than 50 percent of its products and employ more than 350 full-time regular workers.

This deregulation coincided with the period in which Japanese companies started to shift their production base to other countries because of the appreciation of the Japanese currency. This shift induced massive direct investment by Japanese firms, which was labeled the "historic Japanese opportunity." Foreign investors from Japan, Taiwan, and Korea invested in the free-trade zones in Malaysia during this period.

One major aspect of Malaysian industrialization was the designation of 12 industries as the leading sectors in the industrial master plan of 1986. Those designated in the non-resource category were electric/electronic manufactures, textiles/garments, machinery, transport equipment, and steel; the resource category included wood processing, rubber manufacturing, palm oil manufacturing, food processing, chemicals/petrochemicals, nonferrous metals and nonmetal manufactures. Under these arrangements, the Malaysian economy started its high-growth process as of 1988. This process did not follow the gradual-development pattern starting from textiles and processing to less labor-intensive industries. It instead tried to establish a high-tech sector at a stroke.[7] This is not the flying-geese pattern. Malaysia recorded high rates of economic growth after 1988, and per capita GNP reached US$2,500 in 1991. At this point, the next steps in the industrialization process emerged: one was the development of human resources, and the other was the fostering of supporting industries.

The economy's shortage of labor has been pointed out regularly and derives from the smallness of Malaysia's population (about 18 million). When the shortage of skilled and semiskilled workers became clear, it became necessary to develop human resources to meet the labor shortage in each industry. In the early 1990s, Malaysia supplemented human-resource development with labor supplies from Indonesia, Bangladesh, and other countries.

Another problem is that the link is weak between local firms and the foreign companies in the country's free-trade zones. This weakness can be solved by building bridges

---

[6] Takeshi Aoki, *Export-oriented Industrialization Strategy* (Tokyo: JETRO, 1994).
[7] Aoki, p. 51.

to export enclaves through the development of supporting industries. In this way, the country has in fact successfully dealt with the two major problems and has managed to maintain its high economic growth in the first half of the 1990s.

Thailand: Successful Introduction of FDI

Thailand's industrial modernization got under way with a series of liberalization steps taken in the late 1950s. These steps included abolishing the multiexchange rate system and doing away with large national corporations. The subsequent stages of the nation's industrialization can be divided into four phases.[8]

Import substitution (1960–1971)

Thailand's policy to replace imports with domestically produced goods was made explicit with the implementation of the new tariff law and the industrial-investment encouragement law, both of which took effect in 1960. The new tariff law aimed at raising tariff rates to protect domestic industries. The industrial-investment encouragement law gave preferential tax treatment to imported machinery, equipment, raw materials, and other intermediate goods for industrial use; this law was amended in 1962 to authorize preferential conditions for the so-called "priority" industries, and preferential tax breaks were granted to corporations within those priority industries (exemption from corporate income tax for five years; exemption from import tariffs on machinery, equipment, parts, and raw materials necessary to set up ventures; and reduction or exemption of all or part of import tariffs on other investment assets for five years).

The import substitution policy achieved a certain success: some Thai-made products fully saturated the country's domestic demand in the early 1970s.[9] On the other hand, the import of intermediate and capital goods increased as industrialization progressed, resulting in a sharp rise in the country's trade deficit from 1967 through 1970. Thus, the nation was forced to switch to a policy of export orientation.

Export orientation (1972–1976)

In 1972, the industrial investment encouragement law was again amended, and a new export promotion law took effect. Preferential conditions in the amended industrial-investment encouragement law included the reduction of or exemption from import tariffs and operating taxes for export-oriented corporations and the deduction of increased export sales from taxable corporate income.

The new export promotion law offered the following preferential conditions: tariff repayment on raw-material imports used in export goods; tax credit for the value of the portion of paid tariff and operating tax for raw materials used in export products; and

---

[8] Yukio Ikemoto and Warin Wonghanchao, eds., *Thai Economic Policy* (Tokyo: Institute of Developing Economies, 1988).

[9] *The Study of Japanese Cooperation in Industrial Policy for Developing Countries* (Tokyo: Institute of Developing Economies, 1994).

financing for export-oriented operations. But this policy change was not smoothly implemented, in part because of social unrest in the country.

Import substitution revisited (1977–1982)

In 1976, a coup led by Sagatt succeeded. The new administration formulated the fourth five-year plan (1977), aimed at the stabilization of the Thai economy. It allowed the protection of heavy industries producing intermediate goods and capital goods. At the same time, the administration placed priority on the development of exports, agro-industry, regional industries, and small businesses. Furthermore, it launched the East-Coast Development Program as a large-scale regional industrial plan.

Export orientation through the introduction of FDI (1983–present)

In the fifth five-year plan (1983), the government placed special emphasis on promoting FDI and allowed export companies to be fully owned by foreign investors. The Industrial Estate Authority of Thailand constructed industrial estates, and the first EPZ in Thailand was established at Bangchan near Bangkok in 1970. The Lad Krabang Industrial Estate, which was completed in 1979, functioned as an EPZ and was sold out in 1987. In addition, the government divided the country into three regions and encouraged investment in specific areas.

Thailand's high economic growth started in 1987, with successive annual growth rates of 9.5 percent, 13.3 percent, 12.3 percent, and 11.6 percent. During this period, drastic deregulation was implemented in the automobile and textile industries. With this high economic growth, various problems surfaced in the Thai economy, including infrastructure deficiencies, human-resource shortages, an income gap between urban areas and rural villages, and the need to promote small businesses.

Indonesia : Structural Adjustment under Deregulation

Import substitution (1966–1979, 1979–1982)

Compared with Thailand and Malaysia, Indonesia was late in launching its import substitution policy. Once the policy had been launched, however, policy duration was relatively long. The first phase of the policy lasted from 1966 to 1979 and can be subdivided into two subphases: 1966–1973 (introduction of selected foreign direct investment) and 1974–1979 (intensive protection of domestic industries).[10] In 1967, the foreign-investment law took effect, but from 1970 onward, the government grew more selective in choosing foreign partners, and the application of preferential conditions for foreign investors was limited to priority industries. Furthermore, from 1970 to 1973, some 44 industries were made ineligible to receive foreign investment.

Meanwhile, the country's oil revenue soared as oil prices rose in 1973. The period from 1974 through 1979 is considered to be a time of intensive protection of domestic

---

[10] Keiichi Oguro, "Development of Manufacturing and Unfolding of Industrial Policy," in *The Study on Japanese Cooperation in Industrial Policy for Indonesia* (Tokyo: Institute of Developing Economies, 1995).

industries. In 1974, the government decided to expand the scope of foreign-investment regulations to additional industries and to nationalize foreign-affiliated companies. Thus, the government implemented the second phase of its import substitution policy; this second phase lasted from 1979 to 1983. The government tried to achieve the nationalization of 52 basic industries such as petrochemicals and basic metals. Examples of other listed industries were steel, shipbuilding, aerospace, and automobiles; however, this plan was revised after oil prices fell in 1981.

Structural adjustment policy (1983–present)
In 1979, 1983, and 1986, the rupiah (the nation's currency) was drastically devalued. This devaluation greatly influenced Indonesia's switch to an export-oriented policy. In 1983, the country began to change its economic policy, as it adopted a structural adjustment policy recommended by the International Monetary Fund and the World Bank in order to receive the structural adjustment lending extended by those institutions. Malaysia differs from Indonesia in this regard, in that Malaysia did not receive structural adjustment lending.

Deregulation was implemented in all sectors of the Indonesian economy, including the financial sector. The country's import-licensing system and other systems were also largely deregulated, and since then the country has continued these deregulation measures. Two export-processing zones were established in 1986 and in 1992, and the government allowed the establishment of foreign owned companies in limited areas. Indonesia did not implement preferential conditions for foreign investment in terms of taxation, financing, and other areas (unlike Malaysia and Thailand).

In 1994, the government authorized 100 percent capital ownership by foreign investors, which led to a drastic increase in foreign direct investment and a higher rate of economic growth.

Korea: On Its Way to Becoming an Advanced Nation[11]
Import substitution (until 1961)
In the post-Korean War recovery period until 1961, the government of Korea implemented an import substitution policy, mostly in the area of consumer goods, with priority on sugar, fertilizer, spun yarn, cement, glass, and other similar industries. But this policy soon reached a saturation point because of the small size of the domestic market and because the country's economic growth was constrained by the external current-account balance. Therefore, the country was forced to change its policy.

Export orientation (1962–1980)
Korea changed its industrial policy to an export-oriented one and promoted labor-intensive exports such as textiles and plywood. During this period, which lasted until 1980,

---

[11] Saturo Okuda, "An Overview of Korea," in *Report on the Study of Private Economic Cooperation in Korea* (Tokyo: Institute of Developing Economies, 1993).

the policy was implemented according to the country's economic development plan to promote exports as follows:

- the first five-year plan (1962–1966): priority on exports
- the second five-year plan (1967–1971): exporting consumer goods and replacing intermediate-goods imports with domestically produced goods
- the third five-year plan (1972–1976): industrialization centered on heavy and chemical industries
- the fourth five-year plan (1977–1981): development of knowledge- and information-intensive industries

Priority industries were defined for each five-year economic plan. The first plan focused on exporting manmade fiber yarn, fertilizer, cement, and refined oil products. The second plan focused on exporting consumer goods, and on replacing intermediate-goods imports with domestic products, and it emphasized the petrochemical, medicine, and machinery industries; the Massan export-processing zone was established in 1970. The third plan was centered on the heavy and chemical industries, with emphasis on machinery, steel, shipbuilding, and other industries; but this policy of heavy industrialization was not implemented smoothly and had both positive and negative impacts. The fourth plan placed emphasis on industrial machinery, steel, and electric equipment/parts, as well as other related activities for developing them, such as knowledge- and information-intensive industries; during this process, annual per capita GDP in Korea rose from about $100 at the beginning of 1960 to more than $1,000 in 1977, and to $1,800 in 1981.

Toward maturity (1980–1984)
The Korean economy experienced negative growth in 1980, after many years of steady high growth. This downslide came as a result of a combination of events, including the political turmoil after the assassination of former President Park, the second oil shock of 1979, a bad rice harvest, and the increase in the country's outstanding foreign debts induced by overdependence on foreign loans. In order to improve Korea's external current-account balance, the government implemented a policy to cool down excessive consumption, by which the average annual growth rate of the country's economy in the 1980s ended up relatively "low" at 8.4 percent.

The "three-lows" economic boom (1984–1989)
The "three lows" refer to a depreciated won, low crude-oil prices, and low international interest rates. The depreciation of the won strengthened the competitiveness of exports, and the fall of crude oil-prices sharply reduced the value of imports by Korea. In addition, the low international interest rates reduced the burden of the nation's interest payment on foreign debts, which stood at $48.8 billion at the end of 1985.[12]

---

[12] Okuda.

Thus, Korea's external current-account balance, which had been $900 million in deficit in 1985, reversed to a $14.1 billion surplus in 1988. During this period, the Korean economy recorded an annual growth of more than 12 percent.

A major characteristic of Korean industrial policy is that there was little foreign investment, in part because several business groups (*chaebol*) already existed as entrepreneurs, while the country depended on foreign loans to provide capital for its industrial development (Japan depended mainly on domestic borrowing). Korea's openness to foreign technology was a different method of development from the methods used by the rest of East Asia. Therefore, the export-processing zone was not the sole decisive factor for the country's economic development.

Maturity (1990–present)

In the early 1990s, the Korean economy slowed down. Four factors explain this phenomenon. First, the Korean currency appreciated; the dollar was traded at 809 won at the end of 1985 and at 760 won at the end of 1991. Second, wages and prices increased. Third, trade friction arose as an economic issue; this friction was induced by competition between industrialized nations and Korea in household electronics, automobiles and other goods in which Korea increased its share because of the "three lows." The fourth factor was the issue of technology.

Although the Korean economy grew under strict regulation, deregulation has also become an important issue since 1993.[13] One characteristic of Korea is its group-centered economy. Therefore, the administration of President Kim Young-sam judged that *chaebol* domination would worsen if various deregulation measures were to be implemented under the current conditions and that such a situation would have a negative effect on narrowing the differential between the *chaebol* and the other companies. Thus the administration hammered out the requirement to spread out stock ownership of the *chaebol*, to open up corporate stocks, to limit inheritance and gift giving (via public-interest corporations), to mitigate the loan-dependency of corporations, to limit mutual financial guarantees, and to limit investment in affiliated companies (among other measures).[14]

Under such circumstances, various deregulation measures were implemented in 1993. Two examples are deregulation in the field of construction (where plant building had been previously banned), and liberalization of interest rates in the field of finance. In this way, Korea has recently been undergoing a dramatic change from regulation-centered industrial policy to deregulation.

---

[13] Nao Ishizaki, *Asia Trend Annual* (Tokyo: Institute of Developing Economies, 1994).

[14] Junko Mizuno, "The Barrier of Slower Growth Stands in the Face of Korea Which Tries to Become an Industrialized Economy," in *World Affairs Weekly* (August 10, 1993).

Taiwan: Toward a Sophisticated Industrial Structure[15]
Import substitution (1950s)

The policy adopted by the government of Taiwan to protect and develop industries in the infant stage consisted of high import tariff rates and trade regulation. Two industries in particular were the object of protection and promotion.

One was the spinning companies that had fled from Shanghai in mainland China (10 spinners, including Chung Shing Textile, Hua Nang Textile, and Taipei Textile, launched their operations in Taiwan from 1949 through 1952). The government of Taiwan enacted the spinning industry development encouragement law in 1949 and set up the Spinning Panel of the Taiwan District Production Operation Management Committee as a promotional organization in 1950. The preferential treatment granted to the spinners included rationing of the raw materials for spun cotton, advantageous exchange rates, an outsourcing system (the "contracting out" of spinning and textile production), and assistance with the procurement of operating funds and foreign currency.

The other protected industry consisted of various state-owned enterprises sold to the private sector under the farmland reform in 1952 (the main inheritors of these enterprises were former landowners). The firms included Taiwan Cement, Taiwan Tea, and Taiwan Pulp and Paper.

Export orientation (1960s)

In order to promote exports, the investment encouragement ordinance was put into effect in 1960, and preferential measures were introduced for exporters, including exemptions on income tax for a five-year period, permission to send back an unlimited sum of overseas profits to Taiwan, expansion of the scope of investment from manufacturing to other areas such as gas and water, and acquisition of public and farming lands. In 1965, U.S. foreign aid to Taiwan was discontinued, creating a need for promoting exports to balance Taiwan's external current account. Conditions to set up and manage export-processing zones were introduced in 1965 to achieve this goal.

These export-processing zones—a combined bonded processing system under the concept of an industrial park—became the first model to introduce foreign investment to Asian developing countries. The bonded processing system exempted firms from payment of import tariffs and other charges on the condition of exporting the resulting products. Other preferential treatment included permission to possess foreign currency in proportion to the value of the exports.

The method provided for outsourcing of production, enabling foreign investors to import capital and intermediate goods, to manufacture products by taking advantage of low-cost labor, and to then export them. Export-processing zones were set up in Kaohsiung, Taichung, and Nanzi. The foreign investors were predominantly Japanese and American, and the major industries in the export-processing zones were those manufac-

---

[15] The analysis here depends mostly on Takao Taniura, ed., *Taiwan's Industrialization*. (Tokyo: Institute of Developing Economies, 1988).

turing electronics equipment, primary metal products, and chemical products. Japan used the Kaohsiung export-processing zone as its substitute export base for third-country destinations, while the United States used the export-processing zones as its overseas base for production of products or parts for the U.S. parent companies. As a result, total value of exports by foreign-affiliated companies as a percentage of the total exports of Taiwan reached 23 percent, according to 1974 figures.[16]

Export-oriented import substitution (1970s)

Foreign investment in Taiwan in the early 1970s came mostly from three parties: overseas Chinese, Japan, and the United States. These parties' investment in 1973 was more than double that of the previous year. At that time, Taiwan's industry consisted mainly of small and medium-sized private enterprises. In the early 1970s, several small business groups based on family-style operations were set up. Consequently, by 1983 the following small business groups had successfully made it to the top: Taiwan Plastics, Cathay, Yulong, Taiwan Spinning Co., Tatung, Far Eastern, Taiwan Cement, and Shinkong Synthetic Fibers Corp. Among them, the only company with a size comparable to Taiwan's state-owned enterprises was Taiwan Plastics.

The worldwide recession induced by the 1973 oil crisis led the Taiwanese economy to its first zero annual growth in the post-World War II period. In order to put Taiwan on a track of stable economic growth, the government implemented a policy of heavy industrialization as an import substitution policy based on the first six-year plan in 1976. The government cut back on preferential measures for excessively labor-intensive industries and put emphasis on heavy and chemical industries: those included basic industries that required large-scale capital, industries that required high technology, and industries that were able either to boost exports or to develop new domestic markets.

Various important preferential measures were implemented by the 1977 amendments to the investment encouragement conditions. For instance, the starting date for the income tax exemption period (five years) that had been granted to capital-intensive and technology-intensive industries was delayed by a year to three years, rather than the launching date of product sales according to the original measure. Companies that went public received a 10 percent reduction in corporate income tax for three years from the date of the public offering. The limit on the ratio of the value of internal reserves to unpaid dividend was raised from the previous 50 percent to 100 percent. Payment of the import tariff on machines and equipment for research and testing purposes was eliminated, and research and experimental expenses were treated as a deduction for losses. Tax exemption was given on income from inventions and patent rights. Meanwhile, most heavy industrial and chemical firms in Taiwan were state owned, and some of them were closed down because of their inefficiency.

---

[16] Taniura.

Increasingly complex industrial structure (1980s)

Under such circumstances, the government decided that certain capital-intensive and technology-intensive industries should be boosted by the encouragement of foreign investment. The Taiwanese economy grew steadily in the 1980s to become a newly industrialized Asian economy with steadily increasing wages and a high-tech industrial base.

Taiwanese corporate structure includes several interesting features. The large private corporations tend to sell their output in the domestic market, while small and medium-sized enterprises are export oriented. The export-oriented small and medium-sized businesses play a major role in the economy. Taiwan's investment in foreign countries soared beginning in the late 1980s in part because of the surge in domestic wages, and a hollowing out of Taiwanese industries was apprehended. Investment in high-tech, heavy, and chemical industries is rising. The government is in the process of establishing free-trade/processing zones that will be provided with centralized facilities for research and development, financing, and transportation; Tainan Science Park City Special Zone is one successful example of such zones.

Singapore: Service and High-Tech Industries and Education

Import-substituting industrialization (late 1950s–1965)

In the process of implementing its industrial policy during this period, the government of Singapore formulated the national economic development plan (1961–1964) and enacted the industry creation law and the industry expansion law (1959) to provide the basis for an investment promotion policy in line with the plan. The Economic Development Board (EDB) was established as the main promoter of government's goals. But the island-state lost the opportunity to expand its trade with Malaysia because of its separation and independence from Malaysia in 1965. The badly damaged Singaporean economy transformed itself from one based on import substitution to one based on export-oriented industrialization, in order to rebuild its fortunes.

Export-oriented industrialization (1966–early 1970s)

This export-oriented industrialization was implemented with the help of foreign investment through the introduction of laws advantageous to foreign investment in Singapore, replacing the two 1959 laws enacted for the promotion of import-substituting industrialization. The new laws that favored foreign investment[17] included the economic-expansion encouragement law of 1967, designed to identify specific industries eligible to receive preferential tax treatment. In turn, the 1968 employment law unified, simplified, and cut back on different labor conditions. The amended labor-management relationship law of 1968 gave labor unions bargaining rights.

Another policy to stimulate exports was the development and expansion of the role of government through four organizations. The first such organization was Jurong Town

---

[17] Kayoko Kitamura, "Industrial Structure and Characteristics of Foreign Investments," in *Report of the Study on Private Economic Cooperation in Singapore* (Tokyo: Institute of Developing Economies, 1992).

Corporation, which was made independent from the Economic Development Board and became the exclusive development and overseeing organization for the industrial park; Jurong Industrial Park was successful in attracting foreign capital. The second such organization was the Development Bank of Singapore, which also became independent to form the core of industrial and development financing. The third was the International Trading Company, which was promoted and owned by the government and was set up to promote exports, imports, and third-country trading. The fourth was the state-owned enterprises in the heavy and chemical industries (such as shipbuilding, basic metals, chemicals, and textiles) and in the food and other industries; many of these state-owned enterprises became the local partners in joint ventures with foreign investors.

Capital-intensive and technology-intensive industrialization
(late 1970s–early 1980s)
This export-oriented industrialization stage improved the employment situation. The country's unemployment rate had been more than 7 percent in 1968, but declined to 4 percent in 1974. Subsequently, Singapore's unemployment rate approached zero, making the labor supply very tight. The government thus faced a new task: that of developing capital-intensive and technology-intensive industries. It implemented several policies to that end. First, the National Production Board and Skill Development Fund were set up to promote the development and training of the human resources required for corporations and industries in the new age. Second, the National Wage Committee—which had been established in 1972 and was composed of government officials, company managers, and representatives from labor unions—was given authority to issue recommendations on wage increases. Third, the National Wage Committee announced in 1979 a high-wage policy according to which the average annual rate of wage increase would be as high as 20 percent within a three-year period; this wage policy induced the withdrawal of labor-intensive foreign capital from Singapore (for instance, one Japanese company was forced to shift its production base to Sri Lanka and other countries), and all told, the policy produced negative effects for the Singaporean economy.

Increasingly complex industrial structure (1986–present)
The government of Singapore set up an economic committee to investigate the factors behind the country's recession and received the committee's final report in 1986. Based on this report, a policy was unveiled by the government to develop an industrial structure mainly in the services sector where Singapore enjoyed comparative advantages. This policy was based on the recognition of economic developments in neighboring countries, as well as an understanding of Singapore's limitations in providing labor and infrastructure. Specifically, two types of industry were designated for investment promotion: first, service industries that depend on foreign direct investment and that are expected to be the core for new growth promotion (business/professional services, medical services, agriculture-related technology services, computer services, and experiment/testing services) and second, high-tech industries that are inseparable from the aforementioned service industries (elec-

trical, telecommunications, information technology, bioengineering, pharmaceutical, optical, and other industries). Overall, Singapore's economic development has been successful, and its annual per capita income has come to exceed $10,000.

The Growth Mechanism in East Asia

Fact Finding on the Growth of the ASEAN and ANIES Economies

In 1993, the World Bank asserted in *The East Asian Miracle* that Malaysia, Thailand, and Indonesia should be models for other developing countries to follow and concluded that the common policy among these three model countries is an export-led strategy that utilizes foreign direct investment (FDI). But it cannot be said that the report sufficiently analyzed the processes by which those countries carried out the export-led strategy, and therefore the nature of the actual phasing from import substitution to export orientation did not become clear to readers.

One can classify the phases in which important policies were implemented by three ASEAN and three ANIES countries, based on the analysis just presented, according to the economic growth rates of each of these phases. This analysis enables us to identify four facts. First, the growth rates of Thailand and Indonesia were high during their first-phase import substitution periods. Second, the growth rates of Korea and Taiwan were high during their second-phase import substitution periods (heavy and chemical industrialization), but these two economies also concurrently implemented export-oriented policies during those periods. Third, all Asian economies implemented export-oriented policies in the 1990s. And fourth, the most important characteristic is that the ANIES economies (Korea, Taiwan, and Singapore) in the early stage of development and the ASEAN economies (Malaysia, Thailand, and Indonesia) in the latter half of the 1980s recorded historically high rates of economic growth.

As we have shown in the previous section, every ASEAN and ANIES economy has made use of industrial parks or export-processing zones. We shall expand on this policy tool in the following section.

The Asian EPZ Model

The East Asian model of economic growth is based on trade liberalization and on the principle of economic liberalization with respect to the introduction of foreign capital. At the same time, these governments have also employed preferential policies as a form of intervention (Table 3.32). We can find the optimal combination of these factors in the export-processing zone. The prototype of the Asian export-processing zone can be found in Kaohsiung, Taiwan. The typical success of EPZs in Asian economic growth during the late 1980s is reflected in the free-trade zone (FTZ) of Malaysia. Hereafter, we refer to the East Asian model as the EPZ model.

We shall explain this EPZ model according to five categories: companies that undertook their own foreign direct investment (FDI) in the late 1980s (Japan, Taiwan, and Korea); countries that received such FDI (Malaysia, Thailand, and Indonesia); economic effects; bottlenecks; and foreign direct investment in the 1990s.

TABLE 3.32. Preferential Policies in Malaysia, Thailand and Indonesia

	Malaysia	Thailand	Indonesia
Reduction of or exemption from import tariff	Import of machines that are not manufactured domestically is exempted from tariff and sales tax.	In the First District (six prefectures around Bangkok), for industries in which more than 80 percent of total sales amount is exported, import tariff on machinery is reduced by 50 percent.	Import tariff exemption for machines and parts. However, import tariff on supplementary equipment is reduced by only 50%.
Preferential measure based on corporate tax	Venture firms: 30% of the legally defined taxable income will be taxed for five years from the date of the start of production. Deduction of investment tax amount: 60% of capital spending within five years from the date when a permit is obtained will be deducted with the maximum of the equivalent of 70% of the legally defined taxable income.	The first District: Corporate tax will be exempted for three years if more than 80% of total sales amount is exported.	None.
Export finance	—	—	None.
Export insurance	—	—	None.
Export-processing zone (EPZ)	Conditions for tenants in free-trade zone: Export of all products (in some cases 80%): Penang (1971).	Conditions for tenants in export-processing zone: Export of all products: Lad Krabang (1979).	Conditions for tenants in export-processing zone: 75% of all products are exported: Jakarta (1986).
Permission for 100% foreign ownership of capital for FDI	Permission to set up full subsidiaries (if 50% of all products are exported) (1986); in FTZ, import tariff on raw material and others are exempted.	Permission to set up full subsidiaries (1983); in EPZ, import tariff on machine and raw materials are exempted.	Permission to set up full subsidiaries in EPTE (1993, amended in June 1994); in EPTE, import tariff on raw materials and capital assets are exempted
Support by export promotion agencies	Malaysian Industrial Development Authority	Board of Investment	Badan Koordinasi Penaman Modal (Investment Coordination Agency)

Source: Various publications by the Institute of Developing Economies (Tokyo).

FDI by multinational corporations in the late 1980s

A major incentive for FDI by Asian corporations—notably from Japan, Taiwan, and Korea—was the low wage level of the countries in which they invested. This incentive became even more attractive to Japanese companies after the yen appreciated (in part because of the 1985 Plaza Accord) and to Taiwanese and Korean companies after local wages started to rise sharply (because of labor shortages). What facilitated the corporate shift of production bases overseas was the standardization of technology. When a company invests in a foreign country, that company usually takes into account the host country's macroeconomic and political stability and its public security.

Countries that received FDI

In order to satisfy these requirements, recipient countries such as Malaysia and Thailand adopted positive industrialization policies, as well as a policy of economic liberalization. Such a liberalization policy typically consists of the following: first, the host country's authorization of the establishment of companies fully owned by foreign parents in export industries; second, preferential policies, especially in the area of taxes (deregulation in Indonesia began late and without the offer of such preferential measures to foreign investors, which helps explain why Indonesia's economic growth lagged behind that of Thailand and Malaysia); and third, development of the host country's infrastructure by the establishment of industrial parks.

Economic effects

When a recipient country gives sufficient incentives to foreign capital, capital is shifted to that country. The new capital creates employment and an increase in the host country's export of products. This change soon results in high economic growth, which in turn induces new domestic demand in the host country.

Tasks to be completed

Fast economic growth inevitably faces economic bottlenecks: insufficient infrastructure, a shortage of the needed human resources, and the emergence of economic enclaves. In particular, the economic-enclave phenomenon tends to hamper the smooth transfer of technology to the host country and to impede the development of supporting industries. This situation can then result in a lack of interlinkage between the EPZ firms and local industry.

Foreign direct investment in the 1990s

The major incentive for foreign direct investment in each Asian country has shifted from low wages (1980s) to the high demand by local markets (1990s). The increase in local income leads to an expansion of market size and then to a demand increase.

The recipient countries must resolve the issues that arise in the process of rapid economic growth. They must remove economic bottlenecks through the development of an adequate infrastructure and through the provision of the needed human resources (such as engineers). These countries also must actively invite foreign supporting industries prepared to transfer technology (including research and development operations), in order to avoid the problem of the creation of economic enclaves.

The governments in these countries have played a role by developing land with infrastructure, by setting up export-processing zones, and by offering preferential measures friendly to foreign investors. The features of this model include the following: zone-specific industrial policy (industrial parks); sector-specific industrial policy (multiple sectors); export-oriented policy; strategic use of foreign direct investment (FDI); and the market mechanism.

Concluding Remarks

Two Miracles and Industrial Policy

Professor Chalmers Johnson in his 1982 study considered MITI's industrial policy as the secret of the "Japanese Miracle." The World Bank revealed the "East Asian Miracle" in 1993. Although both studies paid attention to the high rate of economic growth, Johnson tended to emphasize the role of MITI from a historian's perspective, while the World Bank report was skeptical about the government's industrial-policy role from an economist's point of view. Opinions on Asian industrial policy have thus not reached consensus.

Characteristics of MITI's Industrial Policy

MITI's industrial policy has deployed different actions according to the stage of Japan's economic development and the changing international situation (see Appendix I and Table 3.31). MITI's share of Japan's total fiscal expenditure has historically been very small (Table 3.30). Instead, preferential fiscal loans and special tax treatment have played important roles, particularly in two areas: "infant" care and "terminal" care. An example of the former is the case of the burgeoning computer industry in 1961; an example of the latter is the assistance provided to weakening coal-mining and textile industries. "Infant" care and "terminal" care both involve the resolution of social and employment difficulties.

The typical administrative tools brought to bear are "papers, mice, and ears." The processes of formulating visions or drafting long-term perspectives (papers) and of noticing or persuading and making a consensus (mice) around these ideas are crucial to the government-business interface. This approach reduces uncertainty about the future and also promotes market activity and favorable competitive conditions. For this purpose, MITI must listen to a wide range of opinions and must gather information (ears).

The basic attitude behind Japanese industrial policy is support of the free-trade principle and respect for the market mechanism. The role of the government is to compensate for market failures: MITI's role is to make the market effective from the standpoint of dynamic efficiency.

Lessons from the Japanese Experience

First, compared with shock therapy, the transition to a market economy in postwar Japan can be called "gradualism." It consisted of macroeconomic stabilization, structural-adjustment programs, and industrial policies.

Second, macroeconomic stability is a precondition for industrialization.

Third, industrial policies comprised four steps and were not permanent but temporary.

Fourth, from among these four steps or stages of industrial policies, the two candidates that may apply to today's developing countries are the industrial-rationalization efforts (1950–1960) and the system of cooperation between government and business (1960–1970).

Fifth, the industrial-rationalization policy stands in contrast to the approach used in a controlled economy. It was aimed at promoting industries by policy measures (such as favorable financing and preferential taxation) through indirect control. In particular, financing or credit allocation was critical for developing domestic capital.

Sixth, the system of cooperation between government and business was intended to promote internationally competitive enterprises by coordinating prices, production, and investment in plant and equipment, as well as by coordinating mergers and reorganization efforts. The mergers played an important role from the standpoint of economies of scale.

The Asian EPZ Model

The experience of Asia in the 1980s is helpful for understanding export-oriented policy. ASEAN countries are trying to grow by introducing foreign direct investment. The export-processing zone system, or the Asian EPZ model, is not of the "flying-geese" type and has pump-priming effects on economic growth in Asia. Tax incentives and authorization for 100 percent capital ownership by foreign investors have both been critical for FDI. We can summarize the Asian EPZ model as follows:

First, the role of the government is to provide preferential conditions for desired industry, such as tax holidays, institutional financing by priority, and financing at a relatively low rate of interest.

Second, incentives for multinational corporations have included low labor costs (1980s) and the high level of local demand (1990s) that has now evolved from the host country's response to earlier FDI.

Third, pump-priming effects of EPZs include employment, export, technology transfer (with "enclave" problem), and growth.

Fourth, the EPZ model faces bottlenecks such as the shortage of human capital, the lack of supporting industries, and the insufficiency of infrastructure.

Fifth, preconditions for the EPZ model are political and macroeconomic stability and public security.

The dynamism of East Asia stems from the widespread use of the EPZ model. Export-processing zones have now been established throughout the region: in Guangdong Province in mainland China (as a special economic zone); in the north, the midlands, and the south of Vietnam; and at Subic Bay in the Philippines. Furthermore, the spread of EPZs can be seen not only in East Asia but also in South Asia: India and Bangladesh are about to introduce export-processing zones of their own.

Afterthoughts

The aim of the present paper has been to let our Latin American friends know the facts about the high rates of economic growth and the role of industrial policies in Japan and more recently in East Asia. The progress made by the modern world originated with the seventeenth-century Scientific Revolution in Europe led by René Descartes, Francis Bacon, Galileo, and Isaac Newton. This trend combined science and technology, and it led to the Industrial Revolution and to the present high-tech age. We are now materially and conceptually immersed in this mechanistically rational scientific paradigm. Neoclassical economic theory itself seems to have been mechanistically simplified and to apply only to some rigid set of idealistic conditions. The theory must be further developed in order for us to be able to apply it to the complex situation of the real world.

In addition to this effort, we must take into account the historical and cultural background of each particular country and region involved. For instance, Western observers recently pointed to Confucian thought when they saw the difference in the rates of growth over the last 25 years between Western advanced nations (2.5 percent yearly) and Asia (7 percent). "Confucius Rules" (*Financial Times*, January 1996) and "The Confucius Confusion" (*The Economist*, February 1996) were the headlines.

It might thus be fitting to close here with a few words spoken by that venerable fifth-century BC Chinese philosopher himself:

We learn and then practice. How enjoyable it is!

We have friends from far away. How wonderful it is!

If one learns from others but does not think, one is caught in a trap.

If one thinks but does not learn from others, one is in peril.

APPENDIX 1.

Changes in Priorities of MITI's Policy (1950–1997)

1950: Changeover from domestic-oriented economic policy to international-trade-oriented policy
- Promotion of trade
- Strengthening of productive forces
- Promotion of industrial rationalization
- Promotion of small and medium enterprises
- Promotion of industrial technology

1955: Promotion of self supporting development of economy
- Promotion of trade
  - —Exploration of overseas market
  - —Relaxation of import restrictions, etc.
- Strengthening of industrial foundation
  - —Industrial rationalization
  - —Expansion of the productive forces of bottleneck industries (steel, electric power, transportation, etc.)
  - —Promotion of new industries (electronics, petrochemical, synthetic rubber, etc.)
  - —Preparation of industry-related facilities
- Promotion of small and medium enterprises
- Promotion of industrial technology

1960: Cultivation of motive powers for economic development by means of trade liberalization and improvement of constitution of industries
- Promotion of liberalization of trade and foreign exchange
- Promotion of exports
- Strengthening of international competitiveness through industrial rationalization (heavy and chemical industries, in particular)
- Preparation of industry-related facilities
- Promotion of small and medium enterprises
- Measures against structural depression in the coal-mining industry
- Promotion of industrial technology
- Improvement of the distribution system and consumer policy

1965: Achievement of balanced growth under international cooperation
- Promotion of export and development assistance
- Epoch-making expansion of policies for small business
  - —Financing
  - —Mutual cooperation
  - —Guidance

—Proper adjustment of subcontract transactions
—Welfare
—Tax system
- Upgrade of industry quality for international competition
  —Strengthening of international competitiveness of industry
  —Promotion of technology and reinforcement of patent policy
  —Overall energy policy
  —Regional development and strengthening of industrial foundation
- Prevention of industrial pollution
- Extension of consumer policy
  —After-sale service for durable goods
  —Quality indication method and installment selling system

1970: Realization of prosperous way of living and the establishment of status in international society

- International development of economy
  —Structural improvement and strengthening of enterprise constitution
  —Promotion of economic cooperation
  —Promotion of trade, overseas direct investment, and financing
- Qualitative upgrading of national life
  —Prevention of environmental pollution
  —Protection of consumers' rights
- Assurance of basic conditions for economic development
  —Energy
  —Industrial sites
- Modernization of small business and distribution system
- Orientation toward creative development
  —Strengthening of technological-development power
  —Promotion of the information revolution
  —Promotion of new industries

1975: Improvement of national welfare and contribution to international society

- Stabilization of commodity prices and enrichment of consumers' lives
- Stable energy supply and consolidation of economic-security foundations
- Improvement of antipollution measures
- Upgrading and diversification of small-business policy
- Industrial-structure vision responding to national needs
- Positive development of external economic policy

1980: Perspective of the 1980s by visions
- Assurance of energy security
- Positive contribution to development of world economy
- Promotion of technological development and industrial policy to cultivate the future
- Promotion of active small and medium enterprises
- Balanced development of the national land and realization of national life

*1985: Establishment of foundation for long-term development
and international contribution*
- Construction of foundation for technological development
- Realization of a highly information-oriented society
- Foreign policy of international state "Japan"
- Energy policy from both of security side and economic side
- Small- and medium-enterprise policy responding to a changing period
- New industrial-site policy
- Diversified and high-quality national life

*1990: Global-scale mutual prosperity in coexistence
and economic society with comfort and vitality*
- Realization of internationally harmonized economic structure
  —Increase of imports
  —Promotion of industrial and cultural exchange
- International contribution in global scale
  —Measures against global environmental problems
  —Promotion of APEC, etc.
- Activation of local communities and rectification of the urban concentration in Tokyo
- Promotion of active small and medium enterprises
- National life with comfort and vitality
- Cultivation of new frontiers through technological development
- Resource and energy policy from medium-term and long-term viewpoint

*1995: Strengthening of market function and promotion
of industrial structure transformation*
- Economic reform and openness to international society
- Cultivation of new fields of economic activity
- Development of overall energy policy
- Realization of high-quality national life based on one's own responsibility
- Harmonized foreign economic relations and measures for global problems

1997: (under deliberation) Measures for reform of economic structure
- National investment in intellectual capital
  —Preparation of foundation for creative R and D
  —Preparation of foundation for information revolution
  —Education of creative human capital
- Creation of new business and development of programs for business innovation
  —Preparation of environment for cultivation of potential markets
  —Increase of value added by industry, utilizing integration, networking
- Creation of dynamic business environment with plenty of entrepreneurial spirit
- Formation of global economic network under the information revolution
- System formation toward construction of an environmentally friendly economic society
- Economic management to maintain vitality even in the aged community.

APPENDIX 2.

Chronological Keyword Table (1945–1996)

1945 The end of World War II. The dissolution of big business groups. Farmland reform.

1946 Living on sales of personal effects. Priority production system.

1947 The enactment of the Constitution. The enactment of the Basic Law of Education. Red ink among all government, business, and household finances. World record of 400m freestyle swimming by Furuhashi ("the Mt. Fuji Flying Fish").

1948 GHQ's announcement of the nine economic stabilization principles. The establishment of the Small and Medium Enterprise Agency. Cold War.

1949 The Dodge line. Fixed rate 360 yen=1 dollar. Hideki Yukawa awarded a Nobel Prize in physics.

1950 Special procurement boom (Korean War).

1951 Signing of the peace treaty and Japan–U.S. security treaty.

1952 Beginning motorbike production (Honda).

1953 TV watching on the street begins to boom.

1954 Three treasures emerge: the refrigerator, the washing machine, and the television.

1955 Two major political party systems (Liberal-Democratic Party and Socialist Party).

1956 "No longer termed postwar."

1957 Prime Minister Kishi visits nine Southeast Asian countries. "Carypso."

1958 Instant Chinese noodles on the market.

1959 Nissan Bluebird on sale ("my car age").

1960 Liberalization of trade and foreign exchange. Japan–U.S. security strike. Mitsui Miike coal-mining strike (282 days). National income-doubling plan. Consumption revolution.

1961 Start of the Industrial Structure Research Council.

1962 Tokyo metropolis reaches 10 million in population. The Cuban Missile Crisis.

1963 The Council reports the Industrial Structure Policy Vision for the 1960s (strengthening international competitiveness and practicing the system of cooperation between government and business). Farming by "mom, grandpa, and grandma."

1964 Acquiring the status of IMF Article 8 and joining the OECD. Start of New Tokaido Super Express Line. Tokyo Olympic games.

1965 Economic depression. Issuing deficit-covering national bonds (the first in postwar period).

1966 The 3Cs (color TV, car and cooler [air conditioner]).

The Beatles visit Japan.

MITI approves the export of steel to the U.S. cartel.

1967   Reaching of an agreement of the Kennedy Round (GATT).

Promulgation of the Basic Law for Environmental Pollution Control. "The bigger the better" at CM. ASEAN is founded.

1968   Promulgation of the Basic Law for Protecting Consumers.

1969   Spaceship Apollo XI goes to the Moon.

Opening of highway between Tokyo and Kobe.

1970   The Osaka Expo. Merger between Yawata Steel and Fuji Steel.

Japan–U.S. Textile conflict. The Special Diet for pollution control.

No. 2 position of GNP among OECD member countries.

1971   MITI's vision for the 1970s (knowledge-intensive industrial structure, from "seeking economic growth" to "practical use of growth").

Nixon shocks (announcement of his visit China, devaluation of U.S. dollar, etc.). 308 yen/U.S. dollar. The enactment of the industrialization promotion law for agricultural districts.

1972   Sapporo Winter Olympic games. The return of Okinawa to Japan.

Reform of Japan Islands Plan. Normalizing diplomatic relation between Japan and China.

1973   Tokyo Round. Seeking the welfare society without inflation.

The first oil crisis.

1974   Skyrocketing price hikes (compared to the previous year, wholesale price index up 31%, consumer price index up 23%).

The first negative rate of growth in postwar period (-0.6%).

1975   The end of the Vietnam War. The first Summit Meeting in France.

1976   The government announces 6% economic growth in the second half of the 1970s.

The law of business conversion of small and medium enterprises.

Limiting of defense budget to 1% of GNP.

1977   Effort toward reducing the surplus in the international balance of payment.

1978   Import promotion. 200 yen=1 US$. The opening of Narita International Airport. "The age of uncertainty."

1979   The second oil crisis. "Japan as number one" (Prof. Ezra Vogel). "A rabbit hutch" (Mr. Wilkinson—EC official).

1980   MITI's vision for the 1980s (economic security, technology- based nation, and vitalizing knowledge).

The law of the development and introduction of energy substitution.

1981   Reaganomics in the United States. Voluntary restraint of Japanese car exports to the United States.

1982   General principles of administrative reform. 280 yen=1 US$.

1983   "Oshin" boom (a symbolic character with industrious spirits in television drama).

Technopolis Act.

The first small business policy summit, Osaka.

Government indicated a 4 percent growth in the 1980s.

1984 Privatization of NTT (Nihon Telephone and Telegram).

The special meeting of the Education Council.

1985 Plaza consensus (G5 in New York)—correcting overvalued US$.

The Tsukuba Science Expo.

1986 Tax Reform (largest since 1950).

1987 Privatization of National Railway. Black Monday in New York Stock Exchange. 130 yen=1 US$.

1988 World's largest foreign-currency reserves.

1989 Passing of Emperor Showa.

BUBBLE boom. Fall of the Berlin Wall. Sales tax (3%) initiation.

Japan's FDI number one ($44 billion among world $198 billion).

1990 The Gulf Crisis.

1991 The end of the Cold War.

1992 Five-year plan for "super national life." Global Environment Summit in Brazil. "Restructuring." Emperor and Empress visit China.

1993 Akebono—the first foreign-born Sumo grand champion.

The end of LDP government (since 1955). 100 yen=1 US$.

The largest ODA among the DAC member countries.

1994 Start of NAFTA. Adoption of Uruguay Round (GATT). Opening of Kansai International Airport. Hottest summer in the postwar period. The single-member constituency system.

1995 Start of WTO. The Great Hanshin Earthquake. Terrorist acts in Tokyo subways by sarin (nerve gas)—Aum Religion Affair. 80 yen=1 US$. APEC Osaka summit meeting (leaders push liberalization).

1996 110 Yen=1 US$. Fiscal reform in discussion.

Merger of Mitsubishi Bank and the Bank of Tokyo.

Nancy Birdsall[1] on the Yamada/Kuchiki Paper
Lessons from Japan

Yamada and Kuchiki have provided a richly detailed story of economic policy in the "postwar developmental state," as they so aptly characterize Japan, and in Japan's East Asian neighbors. Their story is revealing both in its details and in its unstated assumptions. Here we shall combine their story with some of our own prejudices to extract six central themes and an extended metaphor of the economic-policy process as practiced in Japan and some countries of East Asia. Three of these themes have already acquired the status of near-truths among economists and policymakers in Latin America; we shall therefore not dwell much on those three. They are part of the so-called Washington consensus on the management of market-oriented economies, and they are also embodied in the East Asian Miracle study of the World Bank. Even Mr. Sakakibara would no doubt agree with them. The second three themes are either controversial or neglected and deserve some elaboration because of their salience today for policymakers in Latin America. Our comments will conclude with the extended metaphor. Let us begin now by examining the three near-truths or nostrums of economic growth.

A stable macroeconomic environment is necessary for effective functioning of the market mechanism and for growth.
The "Lessons from Japan" paper is about industrial policy and not about the conditions for growth, but the authors explicitly note that the framework for industrial policy (and thus for growth) is the market mechanism, and they implicitly note that this mechanism works well only when investors, producers, and creditors have confidence that fiscal discipline and sound monetary policy will ensure macroeconomic stability. The authors would probably concur that in Japan industrial policy was never a substitute for macroeconomic stability and that it was instead always a complement to such stability.

Education and other investments in human capital are necessary for economic growth.
Education is a critical form of capital accumulation. We shall be making more-general remarks about accumulation later but want to say now that accumulation as a concept nec-

---

[1] Executive Vice-President, Inter-American Development Bank.

essarily includes human as well as physical investment. On education's vital contribution to growth in East Asia, the authors would also probably concur.

Exposure to new technologies and to international competition is critical to competitiveness and productivity growth, and to ensuring that economic resources are efficiently allocated and used. This exposure can come via emphasis on exports, foreign direct investment, or aggressive acquisition of foreign licenses for new technologies, as in Taiwan. Note that we have used the term "exposure" rather than "openness." The latter could be associated with liberalization of the capital account, which in fact did not happen in East Asia. We have also avoided use of the term "exports" as being the *sine qua non* of economic growth. The critical element is exposure, by some mechanism, to the discipline of the global market.

The lessons in these three areas—macroeconomic stability, education, and exposure—have been fully absorbed and indeed are already reflected in Latin American policymaking today. Now let us turn to the three themes that are more contentious.

Sustainable growth from low initial levels of per capita income requires not only total productivity gains in the economy but high levels of capital accumulation.
A "high level of capital accumulation" means rates of public and private investment of 30 percent to 40 percent annually, as achieved in Japan and in the fast-growing East Asian economies over more than two decades. These rates contrast with rates in Latin America, which typically are closer to 20 percent (with the exception of fast-growing Chile in recent years). The East Asian levels of accumulation cannot be achieved in the public sector alone; they also require much higher rates of private savings (both corporate and household) and of private investment than have been typical in Latin America. Moreover, this private savings and investment must be largely domestic to avoid excessive reliance on volatile (and generally procyclical—most available when least needed) foreign-capital inflows.

The authors do not explicitly discuss savings and investment rates nor the controversial question of the economic-growth contribution by capital accumulation versus that by total factor productivity (TFP) growth in Japan and East Asia. They do not allude to the work of Alwyn Young on Singapore or to that of Krugman (who, relying mostly on Young's work, maintains that TFP growth in East Asia has been exaggerated and that the growth spurt of the "miracle" countries will collapse in the same way that the growth spurt of the Soviet economy collapsed once the limits of the extractive capacity of that totalitarian government were reached and savings and investment rates, at least in nonmilitary activities, fell).

Frankly, the interesting question here is not whether there has occurred low or high TFP growth. The interesting question is how Japan's and East Asia's extraordinary rates of investment were achieved. We need not be skeptical of investment-led growth. What if, in fact, the East Asian economies have been primarily "investment-led" economies with rather limited gains in productivity? Investment-led growth has been a success; after all, it has brought a quadrupling of per capita incomes in two to three decades! In fact, it may be that rapid accumulation, as in East Asia, is critical for generating productivity growth in low-income and middle-income economies.

In their paper, Yamada and Kuchiki are appropriately concerned with the issue that *is* relevant for Latin America today: What were the roots of the extraordinarily high rates of accumulation in postwar Japan and in East Asia? Implicitly, they attribute high rates of business investment to the strategic vision of an effective government in a developmental state. They refer explicitly to the "announcement effect," in the case of Japan embodied in MITI, of a well-formulated and well-communicated strategic vision. The vision—itself the outcome of intensive and continuous dialogue between government officials and the business community, by sector—produces information and coordination, countering the market failure Bardhan refers to, reducing investor uncertainty. The authors note that the "[MITI] vision is mightier than the [government] budget." Ajit Singh's paper suggests that there was more to it than vision and business-government dialogue—that the nature of government subsidies and taxes and the reliance on banks rather than on shareholders to raise credit both mattered a lot. We shall return to coordination and cooperation between government and business in our concluding metaphor. Meanwhile, there emerges an obvious lesson for Latin America—that no matter how efficiently markets are working, the present domestic investment and savings rates may simply be too low to generate, via accumulation, higher rates of growth while avoiding the volatility generated by such external shocks as sudden increases or declines in foreign-capital inflows or commodity prices.

A low level of income inequality is good for growth because growth must be generated from below (a theme that is both controversial and neglected).
Growth must in part be based on the savings and investment of poor households and on increasing the productivity of low-productivity sectors and workers. This outcome was easier to achieve in East Asia, where income inequality was low, than it has been in Latin America, where income inequality is high.

Here again, the authors are not explicit; given their emphasis on industrial policy, we should not be surprised that they do not discuss low initial income inequality, land reform, or educational opportunities as keys to rapid growth in Japan and elsewhere in East Asia. In any case, their emphasis is certainly not on trickle-down policies. On the contrary. They refer to government's explicit efforts to generate jobs—by promoting exports that were labor intensive and by making exportation and job creation conditions for foreign investment. They refer to government's intervention to bring about the breakup of Korea's *chaebol.* Noting that MITI saw failure to modernize the small business sector as a key potential bottleneck to Japanese growth, they refer to government support of small and medium-scale enterprises as one of the most long-standing and persistent aspects of Japan's industrial policy. All of these policies, programs, and interventions can be associated with the idea of growth from below.

Incidentally, growth from below—an outcome of good investment opportunities for small farmers and for small and medium-scale enterprises—may be necessary in order to achieve higher household savings and investment rates than are currently typical of

Latin America. In this sense, the connection between income equality and high household savings in East Asia deserves more attention.

This neglected theme of growth from below in East Asia may have an important lesson for Latin America—that growth rates in Latin America perhaps simply cannot exceed 3 percent to 4 percent until the bottom half of the population is participating and contributing. The issue is not so much that of growth with distribution; growth with distribution can be achieved by a few cooks preparing a pie and distributing the pieces to a larger group through transfers. It is a matter instead of the poor becoming cooks, too, and of more cooks preparing a bigger pie.

Role of government must include explicit strategic interventions (misleadingly called "industrial policy") if sustainable economic growth is to be achieved (the most controversial theme).
Comparing Latin America and East Asia, the question arises: Are strategic interventions—as Gert Rosenthal gently suggests at the micro level and as Ajit Singh explicitly suggests in the form of firmer government control of capital markets—necessary to lift growth rates in Latin America from the present range of 3 percent to 4 percent with considerable volatility to the steady range of 8 percent to 10 percent that East Asian economies have shown is achievable for sustained periods among countries of low and middle income levels? Gus Ranis has called the conclusions of the World Bank East Asia study "muddled." Having contributed to that study, the present writer must here note that the study is very clear on at least one point: industrial policy in the form of certain strategic interventions—managed well by effective governments and for the most part rather marginal in the magnitude of associated subsidies—did work in certain countries of East Asia. The modifiers in the foregoing sentence are important: managed *well* by *effective* governments and *marginal* in the magnitude of subsidies.

Yamada and Kuchiki mention several key elements of managed interventions by MITI. First, the interventions were the outcome of discussions and deliberations going on continuously in which the business sector, the scientific community, and academics all had an impact; the interventions were based upon a clear, broadly understood, and shared theory of dynamic comparative advantage—often associated with an "income elasticity standard" and a "productivity elasticity standard" that were understood and disseminated. Second, favors to industry were performance based and were linked to the business sector's use of the rents for investments, for export expansion, and for job creation. Third, favors were limited in time, typically a period of five years (the authors cite Malaysia, Thailand, and Indonesia as well as Japan on these sunset provisions). Fourth, favors and interventions were abandoned when they did not work—sometimes (as with the heavy and chemical industries program in Korea) with difficulty but sooner and with less political difficulty and lower accumulated economic costs than those with which (much bigger) favors have been abandoned in Latin America; in East Asia, in other words, governments were able to be flexible and pragmatic and to avoid capture by favored groups.

What does it mean to say that these government interventions worked? Our own suggested metric of success is simple: the interventions encouraged accumulation, meaning that they contributed to the countries' extraordinary rates of investment, especially the extraordinary rates of corporate savings. (This is a low standard, in that it allows for the possibility of efficiency losses in particular sectors at least in the short run; perhaps the standard needs to specify that strategic interventions "work" as long as they encourage accumulation without creating efficiency losses that undermine the growth process.) There were, incidentally, interventions for "terminal" industries (for instance, coal in Japan in the 1950s) as well as for infant industries. Terminal care helps illustrate how the announced strategic interventions were a mechanism by which the government of Japan reas-sured investors: if they supported the vision, they were not going to lose their shirts.

The question for Latin America then becomes, Could well-managed strategic interventions, embodying and reinforcing a strategic vision of dynamic comparative advantage, contribute to higher private investment rates and higher corporate savings (which would complement higher household savings created by better opportunities)? Our own conclusion is that, yes, growth rates could be increased—if there were well-managed, flexible, pragmatic interventions with credible deadlines and ties to performance. But all of that would require strong autonomous institutions; the real question is how to build such institutions in Latin America (when they barely seem to exist in Europe or in the United States). And as in Japan and elsewhere in East Asia, such strategic interventions would have to be built on a strong foundation of macroeconomic stability, with the interventions complementing, not substituting for, the fundamentals.

Now, let us turn to our extended metaphor for the reasons underlying the success of the economic-policy process as practiced in Japan and elsewhere in East Asia. This metaphor is not new. It is one we constructed a few years ago in the course of our World Bank research on the East Asian Miracle. The Kuchiki and Yamada paper, written by distinguished scholars immersed in developments in Japan and East Asia, brought the metaphor back to mind, and we cannot resist submitting it for those authors' scrutiny.

The metaphor is a list of the elements necessary for the success of a birthday party for young people, much like the parties that took place where the present commentator grew up, in suburban New Jersey. The elements necessary in order for a birthday party to work are the same elements needed in order for economic policy to ensure growth—namely, three *C*s and three *R*s:

Coordination (or Cooperation). The children at a birthday party must be organized, in order to ensure a productive afternoon. Without organization, unproductive and chaotic play results.

Competition. The interchange of play will produce more happiness if the children engage with each other and are not, for instance, distracted in unproductive efforts to plead for attention or favors from adults who may be present.

Contest. In order to combine coordination with competition, we need a contest. And the ingredients of a good contest are the following:

Rules. The children must know the rules.

Rewards. Each game has a winner or winners, who must receive a prize in recognition of their performance.

Referee. Parents are needed to enforce the rules and to distribute the rewards.

In East Asia, the governments, like the parents, organized a contest—with coordination, competition, rules, rewards, and effective referees. The question now for Latin America is: What is needed for a good, rewarding, productive *fiesta?*

Yung Chul Park[1] on the Yamada/Kuchiki Paper
Lessons from Japan

Yamada and Kuchiki have written a very informative and interesting paper on the evolution of Japanese industrial policy during the postwar period and on some East Asian countries' development experiences.

From the targeting of strategic industries in the 1950s to the formulating of visions since the mid-1960s, this paper tells the fascinating story of the evolution of MITI. Readers will learn a great deal from the way in which MITI develops visions for the future, reaches consensus on difficult policy issues, and then rallies Japanese industry and even secondary educational institutions to cooperate in pursuing these visions.

As the authors point out, MITI's current industrial policy is designed and implemented primarily to rectify market failures so that the free-trade principle is supported and the market mechanism is respected. Such a policy is completely befitting of an economic superpower such as Japan, and one cannot help but be greatly impressed by the tremendous foresight that the planners at MITI have brought to bear in formulating their visions. Perhaps it is because of this ability that MITI has been so readily able to guide Japanese industry in the right direction.

The authors put forward the argument that developing countries today can learn some meaningful lessons from Japan's experience in industrial policy from 1950 to about 1970. During the 1950–1960 period, industrial policy was geared toward restructuring such industries as shipping, synthetic fibers, and electric-power generation and toward subsidizing many other industries, including machinery, petrochemicals, and electronics, presumably for export promotion, by providing preferential credit and tax treatment. This kind of strategy is not unique to Japan, however. In fact, countries all over Asia have pursued similar strategies.

Once this period of industrial rationalization and promotion came to an end in Japan, the first phase of trade and financial liberalization began. This period lasted until 1970, and it saw the establishment of a system of cooperation and coordination between government and business that greatly facilitated the transition to a more mature and open phase by strengthening the competitiveness of Japanese firms. Investment, production, price setting, and mergers and restructuring in many industries were all coordinated by MITI. Again, this was nothing new. Any government, in fact, regardless of whether or

---

[1] Korea University and Korea Institute of Finance.

not it is seeking to intervene aggressively in the allocation of resources would find it necessary to coordinate these activities to some degree.

What then are the lessons that developing countries can learn from the Japanese experience? And how many developing countries are prepared, and will be allowed, to subsidize priority industries and firms in this age of globalization and trade liberalization? If permitted to do so, these countries would naturally be interested in learning how to choose and nurture the winning industries. As the paper deals with historical analysis, one might have expected the authors to engage in some discussion as to why such an industrial-development strategy was successful in Japan whereas similar policies have failed in many other countries.

It is common knowledge that coordination of investment and production in different industries is something that the market mechanism fails to do well and that because of this failure, some form of government intervention is often warranted. Japan's tremendous development record would therefore seem to indicate that MITI must have been very successful in handling coordination and cooperation. Because so many coordination efforts in different economies have at different times resulted in major failures, many readers would naturally have expected the authors to cite the reasons for Japan's success. The authors, however, do not take up this question at all.

Turning to their discussion of the industrialization policies of the ASEAN and ANIES countries, the authors whet the reader's appetite by claiming that the Asian export-processing zone (EPZ) model is the key to the East Asian miracle, but they fail to provide any kind of analysis to back up this claim. EPZs may indeed have been instrumental in developing some particular export industries, but considering their relatively small shares of total output and exports, it is difficult to believe that they were the key to development in East Asia, especially in South Korea and Taiwan.

Relying on a topological approach to economic development according to which the period under consideration is divided into clearly defined phases, the authors provide a detailed account of the different policy approaches that were pursued at different stages of development in the ASEAN and ANIES economies. A phase, as explained by the authors, seems to be a stage of development characterized by a certain pattern and mechanism of economic development. Unfortunately, they do not identify some of the criteria that would be necessary to break down the process of development in East Asia into phases and subphases (such as the import substitution and export orientation phases). It is therefore difficult to understand how and why import substitution was implemented at an early stage of development in East Asia and was followed by an export-oriented period. Which industries or which groups of people were leading the import substitution effort? How does an import substitution period come to an end? These are serious questions that would be of serious interest to the reader, but they have simply been left unanswered. Policymakers in developing countries would be interested in knowing the conditions under which import substitution policies should be introduced, as well as when the transition to the next subphase should be engineered. The only criterion the paper cites for identifying phases is changes in government policies. This criterion is inadequate, however. What is important is understanding the dynamic forces behind the transition of the economy from one subphase to another. Are the authors trying to suggest that East Asian governments have been so effective and foresighted that they have successfully shifted the economy from a primary to a secondary import substitution phase and then to an export-oriented phase through the implementation of industrial policy? If so, the authors will have to write another paper and elaborate at length.

Finally, after going through a most laborious analysis of phases, the authors give a blanket endorsement to the World Bank view that the economic growth of East Asia has been based on the market mechanism and achieved through market liberalization. It would therefore follow that they should attribute Japan's growth and industrialization to the same factors. Why then would developing countries have any interest in understanding the process of Japan's development in the 1950s and 1960s? It almost seems as if the authors are retreating from their initial assertions and suggesting that the economic transition from one phase to another in Japan and other countries has been driven by market forces.

PART IV

Latin America in the XXI Century

Albert Fishlow[1]

We are coming to the end of a century as well as to the beginning of a new conception of Latin American economic development. The ideas of import substitution, of rapid industrialization patterned after earlier U.S. and European development, and of powerful and positive state intervention in all aspects of economic life have yielded to the novel principles now in application. Whether these new principles will be described ultimately as neoconservative or neosocial is very much the issue in almost all of the larger economies of the region.

What is already clear is that there remain few adherents now to the older Latin American macroeconomic-policy staples like large public deficits, rapidly expanding monetary supply, negative real rates of interest, heavy reliance on foreign capital, and dependence upon substantial government policy direction. The past two decades—which saw an incredible and unyielding rise in average inflation rates to four-digit levels in a number of countries—have come to a decisive end. At root, countries have finally learned the importance of responsible fiscal and monetary policy as a central initial condition for economic development.

It has been a painful lesson. Put simply, Latin America—with the exceptions of Chile and Colombia—has not grown in per capita terms for some fifteen years, virtually since the beginning of the debt crisis. And much of the reason has been poor aggregate performance. Failed attempts at stabilization have alternated with temporary recoveries, until the secret of unwavering restraint has seemingly been absorbed.

Latin America has simultaneously made a new political commitment to democracy. It is largely the new civilian governments, rather than their military predecessors, that have taken the bold economic actions required. But the permanence of that transformation critically depends upon renewed and better-shared economic growth, growth that in the early 1970s seemed so easily attainable. To accomplish that objective, four particulars seem necessary.

These include in the first instance the creation of a different and widely held perception of what governments can reasonably be expected to accomplish in the economic realm. The state cannot be the do-all it has been converted into, managing investment, generating employment, controlling international trade, and absorbing seemingly un-

---

[1] Council of Foreign Relations, New York.

ending foreign resources. But on the other hand, the state must play a new, and critical, role of ensuring the continuity of macroeconomic stability. The finance minister, and the central bank become the critical players, in place of the ministers of planning, industry, and commerce.

A second requirement for growth is a substantial increase in domestic savings. Latin America cannot continuously expand on the basis of a level of savings equivalent to what it achieved some 35 years ago. Less than 20 percent of gross product is currently committed to the future. Achievement of a rate of expansion of the order of 6 percent a year on a continuous and sustainable basis requires investment of the magnitude of 25 percent. And unlike what happened under the apparently successful Salinas strategy, 5 percent of that total—or as in fact in 1994, some 8 percent—cannot reliably come from abroad. That hoped-for solution is inevitably of a short-term nature, incorrectly rationalized into long-term stability.

Third, Latin America must confront its extraordinarily unequal income distribution. This subject has generated interest for many years. Is improved equality consistent with increased growth? The fact is that the substantial deterioration of equality in the 1980s virtually throughout the region has made matters much worse. Whether (as Samuel Morley would sustain) the primary cause of such inequality is economic decline or (as Oscar Altimir would assert) the principal source is poor public policy, much needs to be done to ensure more satisfactory future performance.[2] Inequalities of the extreme Latin American magnitude must be confronted—and not merely by finding measures to assist the large numbers classified as poor. Inevitably, a central and immediate part of the answer is the improvement of education, in terms of quantity as well as quality.

And fourth, exports must be paid some mind, in order to ensure that development will occur in an open international setting. The World Bank has given considerable emphasis to this factor as a consequence of its study of the East Asian success, and a critical reaction has taken place.[3] Stated simply, export-led development is much less salutary in the case of Latin America than is export-adequate development. What is so striking in the case of Latin America is its history of a series of years of mixed export performance rather than of continuous expansion and changed structure. It is obviously difficult for the region to achieve the investment or commitment required for penetrating the developed-country markets. One will not see Latin American exports growing continuously at 15 percent a year; to propose such a strategy and then to fail to fulfill it is far more costly than to set as a goal a continuous increase in sales abroad on the order of 1 percent to 2 percent more than the growth of domestic product.

These then are the four central elements required in order for Latin America to enter

---

[2] See Samuel A. Morley, *Poverty and Inequality in Latin America* (Baltimore, MD: Johns Hopkins University Press, 1995) and Oscar Altimir, "Income Distribution and Poverty through Crisis and Adjustment," Working Paper 15 (Santiago: ECLAC).

[3] World Bank, *The East Asian Miracle: Economic Growth and Public Policy* (New York, 1993). Some further discussion may be found in Albert Fishlow *et al.*, "Miracle Design?" ODC Policy Essay 11 (1994), in a special issue of *World Development* 22, 4 (April 1994), 615–70, and elsewhere.

the next century confidently committed to high and sustained growth rates. Let us consider each issue now in more detail.

A Different Government Role

The extraordinarily high rates of inflation experienced in Latin America over the last decade and a half, and in some cases extending back longer, have greatly abated. Even Venezuela's Caldera has recently given up his populist rhetoric in favor of a more orthodox stance. And Colombian inflation rates—hovering at about 20 to 40 percent, which until recently had constituted a relative success—will soon be one of the highest in the region.

The earlier acceleration of inflation rates was clearly linked to the practice of indexing wages, interest rates, rents, and the like—a practice that became even more widespread as inflation rose. This backward-oriented adjustment process produced rates with a tendency to explode. Then, at four-digit and occasionally even higher levels, governments had to face up to the necessity for stabilization programs to cut their expenditures and raise their revenues.

It is no accident that privatization programs first really took hold as a consequence of the need for public resources. The sale of public enterprises offered a one-shot gain in revenues. At the same time, it frequently reduced ongoing deficits stemming from state control of prices and wages. What is key is that a temporary period of revenue enhancement such as this, although helpful to ensuring equilibrium, must pave the way for permanent increases in receipts. Otherwise, macroeconomic control will have a tendency to diminish over time. Argentina is illustrative of the importance such revenues have had in balancing the budget in the past, as well as of the need for additional policies to guarantee permanent improvement.

Responsible fiscal policy is clearly the prime target for the countries of the region. That commitment, after so many years of avoidance, is not readily believed. It has resulted in very high real rates of interest as citizens have to be persuaded of the continuity of such a stand. Only after a time does greater public confidence result in lower costs. The intermediate period is expensive as well as difficult to manage—in part because one of the consequences of these high interest rates is attraction of large capital inflows from the United States in search of extremely favorable returns. And an unfortunate and costly additional consequence, to which we shall later return, is overvaluation of the exchange rate as a consequence of large inflows of money from abroad.

On the other side, stabilization has real advantages for the lowest-income groups within society, those unable to take financial refuge in the continuous adjustments made in bank deposits and other holdings in response to rising prices. These low-income groups are the ones forced to accept the full effects of the continuing and rapid depreciation of the currency; they have no alternative form in which to hold their meager money stocks. Thus stabilization provides an important benefit to those at the bottom of the income distribution, but it is a once-only benefit and cannot be recurred to continuously.

Latin America (with the exception of Chile) is still in a trial period regarding its new framework of stability. The Mexican tragedy in 1994 greatly reinforced the sense of concern and unease within other countries. The much-feared "tequila effect" did not become permanent, thanks to timely response by national and international authorities. Quick resolution of the Mexican uncertainty (through cooperation by the United States and the IMF) and expanded World Bank and IDB lending to Argentina soon restored credibility to the region's stability efforts. Reserve levels went back up and in many cases even exceeded previous heights.

Success at stabilization and at subsequent growth will require not a zero governmental role but instead a modified one. Clearly this role has to involve a decrease in government's public responsibilities. Chile has been a leader in this regard. This new approach is one reason for the recent major efforts in some countries to change the way of providing pensions to the aged; a number of countries have followed the innovative Chilean pension model by encouraging private retirement accounts. The spread of private medical insurance goes in the same direction. And obviously, the decrease in the level of public ownership of the capital used in production has had similar effects. All of these are ways to help achieve a balanced budget.

Nor does government obligation have to be exercised solely at the central level. In a number of countries, federal revenues already are widely shared with states and municipalities. But still lacking is a similar division of specific obligations regarding the expenditure of these funds; as a consequence, one frequently finds expenditures that do not yield high rates of social return. Education, both primary and secondary, obviously cries out for greater local responsibility. Other public-sector obligations could similarly be decentralized. What is necessary is the efficient and responsible exercise of authority. Much can be done in a number of countries to promote and make effective such a reallocation. And some of the activities that local states and municipalities exercise can be productively handed off to the private sector. The success of these kinds of continuing changes will determine the real durability of fiscal responsibility.

Equally, government revenues can be expected to benefit from a period of demonstrated price stability. Some of the revenue shortfall in the region has stemmed from taxpayers' response to anticipated rates of high inflation; in such circumstances, individuals often prefer to try to evade taxes rather than to pay immediately. Economically rational response leads to significant evasion, as confirmed by the aggregate levels of revenue collection.[4] Even so, beyond this anticipated gain in tax receipts, public collection efforts will have to become more efficient. In many countries, the percentage of tax revenues captured relative to those legally required is woefully small. Thus there now exists an opportunity for nominal tax reduction (through price stabilization) and effective tax increase (through better collection), to meet continuing requirements for legitimate government expenditures.

Short-term policies designed to avoid pressure by deficits on price stability must be-

---

[4] See Albert Fishlow and Jorge Friedman, "Tax Evasion, Inflation and Stabilization," *Journal of Development Economics* (February 1994) for a discussion of the relation between expected inflation and tax collection.

come permanent. At the same time, some kinds of expenditure must be selectively pushed and others curtailed. Almost everywhere, capital expenditures by government have been severely cut. There exists legitimate concern that future outlays on public services will decline and that investment in human capital will therefore suffer as well. In fact, this area is exactly where the government role in Latin America has proven most deficient. If the pressure for immediate stability leads to failure to provide adequately for the future, then a great error will have been committed. There must be an adequate margin for necessary outlays not only in education but also in health (including adequate nutrition, housing, and the like)—areas of high social return relative to private gain.

A new and more positive government role requires resources. It also requires a keen sense of limits and the strict and effective structuring of priorities. Otherwise, high real interest rates will not be temporary, creating an atmosphere that will dampen growth prospects. Government outlays will consist of overly large interest payments and overly small social investment. Government payments for labor services will be inadequate and will attract an unsatisfactory work force. Price stability can be created under such conditions, but it will not yield adequate economic growth or productivity increases.

Many Latin American countries are still at an early stage of their stabilization processes. They are still or have been excessively dependent upon inflows of foreign funds responsive to the generous returns offered. They have not yet succeeded in dealing with high rates of unemployment and with their growing informal sectors. The conversion of policies away from their inflationary bias must not lead to a bias toward inadequate growth and increasingly skewed income distribution. The desired balance is difficult to achieve but the countries thus far appear to have made many of the right short-term choices. What now must be addressed is the need to ensure the right long-term basis for effective governance. An indispensable component of the latter is a more effective political process.

Domestic Savings Capacity

Unlike most other developing regions, Latin America faces the next century with a savings capacity totally inadequate for attaining the rate of investment required in order to achieve a rebirth of development. Most studies find an actual rate of less than 20 percent for virtually all countries except Chile.[5] At a minimum, an investment rate on the order of 25 percent of gross product will be needed in order to achieve a continuous expansion of around 6 percent a year. And that 6 percent annual growth will only slowly begin to absorb the currently unemployed and underemployed.

The single place that such a substantial increase in investment can occur in the short term is probably the public sector. This obligation turns former Latin American government priorities on their head. Here is another case in which effective official intervention involves important differences from the past. The key public-sector issue formerly was the

---

[5] For Western Hemisphere total savings rates, see IMF, *World Economic Outlook* (October 1996) 237, Table A44.

application of resources, even when one of the end results was a significant deficit. But now the key public-sector issue must be that of ensuring adequate sources of funds to enable the private sector to invest productively.

Two considerations speak to the priority argued here for the public sector to be the principal source of the added savings required. One is the region's extraordinary inequality in income distribution (which will be further discussed in the following section). To derive much larger savings exclusively from private sources almost inevitably would imply even more inequality of income in the future: savers would be the beneficiaries of positive rates of interest, and within a short while, even assuming reductions in rates, they would have claims to even larger shares of product.

A second consideration is the region's anticipated substantial preference for only limited foreign dependence, in response to the recent Mexican experience: to rely on foreign investment for more than 2 percent or 3 percent of product is to expose the economy to much greater dependence on external circumstance than is necessary. Throughout virtually the entire postwar period, Latin America has been substantially dependent on foreign investment. It is time to change that pattern.

The foregoing point still holds despite the fact that some of the countries of Southeast Asia have large current-account deficits that they seem able to manage. Malaysia and Thailand are now running at percentages comparable to those that brought Mexico down. South Korea has also increased its reliance on foreign investment. But what must be noted is that these Southeast Asian countries' domestic rates of savings are on the order of 30 percent rather than the 15 percent prevalent in Latin America; this rapid rise in domestic provision, rather than the access to foreign resources, has clearly been central to Southeast Asia's superior growth performance in recent years. And even the Southeast Asian countries are seeking to reduce their current-account imbalances rather than to justify these imbalances' continuation.

Furthermore, there seems to exist no evidence that high interest rates have had much, if any, positive influence on Latin American domestic savings rates. Although the IMF has found some positive influence of interest rates on savings in a broader international sample, these occur at much lower real rates and derive primarily from the Asian experience.[6] Latin America has maintained quite positive interest rates in recent years as part of the stabilization process, but they seem to have had no effect in inducing higher rates of private savings.

Much has been made of the successful Chilean case as evidence that conversion of pension funds to private management can induce much greater savings. But four observations are relevant here. The first is that despite the demonstration effect and the copying of the Chilean system in other countries, no similar result on savings is yet evident elsewhere. Second, the observed Chilean increase in domestic savings came long after the pension system went into effect; although some lag in effect might be assumed, proba-

---

[6] Jonathan Ostry and Carmen Reinhart, "Saving and the Real Interest Rate in Developing Countries," *Finance and Development* (December 1995).

bly much of the credit for the dramatic rise in Chilean savings should go to the success of the transition to civilian rule after Pinochet's departure. Third, the great bulk of increased savings in Chile seems to have emanated from the business rather than the private sector. And fourth, a recent econometric study conducted by an IMF economist finds a negative relationship between private savings in Chile and current increases in pension holdings.[7]

Further research on the savings question will doubtlessly yield a high return. But meanwhile, generating positive public accumulation is clearly a savings strategy that works. A casual look at the successful Asian experience confirms the importance of this factor—not only in Singapore, where it stands out in a savings rate of more than 40 percent, but also in many other cases.[8] This finding places even greater stress on the need for other economies to design current government expenditures to enable such surpluses to emerge. In the absence of such surpluses, Latin America seems destined to repeat the experiences of the 1970s and the early 1990s and to depend excessively on foreign-capital inflows. This is precisely what happened to Mexico. Such dependence is not a permanent solution for satisfying the investment requirements associated with more rapid growth but is instead potentially part of the problem.

Income Distribution

If there is to emerge greater reliance upon self-financed growth, then there also must occur a consistent move toward more-equal income distribution. Quantitative research on income distribution has increased rapidly in recent years, in part motivated by the continuing deterioration in performance. As noted earlier, Samuel Morley and Oscar Altimir have done substantial work (using data for the 1980s) in trying to assess the effect of the dramatic recession upon income inequality in Latin America. Their quantitative results and conclusions differ somewhat.

Morley argues that the level of per capita income is key and that recession was the principal factor responsible for the poor distributional performance during that tragic "lost" decade. Put another way, stabilization and increased integration into global markets raised interest rates and required competitive reductions in wages. But renewed growth can make a positive contribution.

Altimir emphasizes the regressive effects of stabilization policies that governments were forced to follow. He sees the need for much more vigorous policies requiring increased investment under state leadership. Precisely because of the region's continuing recession, however, it is difficult to make longer-term comparisons and to assess these alternative hypotheses.

What then should be done regarding income distribution? Virtually all economists now agree that policies to improve distribution must be compatible with the market sys-

---

[7] Robert Holzman, "Pension Reform, Financial Market Development, and Economic Growth: Preliminary Evidence from Chile," IMF Working Paper (August 1996).

[8] Sebastian Edwards, "Why Are Latin America's Savings Rates So Low? An International Comparative Analysis," *Journal of Development Economics* 51, 1 (October 1996), 5–44.

tem. There is much less belief in higher minimum wages or in price controls—or even in highly differentiated tax rates. Two important categories of possible interventions consist of those actions that seek to ensure the more equitable ownership of physical assets and those that seek to achieve the rapid accumulation of human capital.

Of the category of interventions pursuing the redistribution of wealth, land stands out as clearly the most potent target variable utilized in the past. Land reform, where actually used, has been a powerful factor in affecting income distribution. Korea and Taiwan stand out as the two most obvious cases in which an initial commitment to equalization played a major role; the implications of that experience are currently being closely studied in an attempt to find methods to generalize that approach. Beyond these two economies, the experiences of China and Vietnam, now showing signs of quite rapid and vigorous expansion, should not be overlooked. There, an imposed equality generated relatively little growth until it was combined with greater individual incentives and opportunities for productivity improvement. Strict communist doctrine did not work, but its initial redistributive measures served as a powerful equalizing device that those countries subsequently could draw upon to their advantage.

In economies with large rural populations, both productivity and equality are served by land reform efforts. The high rates of inequality found in contemporary Latin America most likely can be traced to the initially much higher inequality of land distribution in the region dating from the nineteenth century and even before; that inequality of land distribution significantly predated the later commitment to import substitution industrialization. And there can be little question, despite the lesser enthusiasm now found, that a fairer allocation of this basic asset can serve as an important stimulant to broad-based development.

For many reasons, there exists a seeming reluctance to act; significant land reform seems to await war or revolution for its imposition. Yet where land is poorly utilized and its productivity could be much enhanced, land redistribution, even with payment of current capital value, can be a very economically sound option.

What must be stressed in any case is that additional public inputs are required in order for any such distributive policy to be effective. Reallocation alone will not work. Only if viewed as a means toward the end of greater efficiency and larger output can reallocational efforts be successful. In addition, all too frequently, reform initiatives have encountered significant opposition from landholders reluctant to give up their command over resources, even when the latter have been poorly utilized. Such efforts also found themselves at one time caught up in the politics of the Cold War and were in favor during the Alliance for Progress and then out of favor as the region came under military dominance. Land reform does remain relevant and is perhaps now more practicable than it has been for a long time. In Central America and in Brazil, in fact, such efforts are currently proceeding more rapidly and effectively than ever before. But there is a fundamental reality: agricultural sectors are much less important today than 30 years ago. The population has moved. As a consequence, efforts at redistribution must go beyond land reform.

Human capital is the second major category of possible distributive interventions in which public actions can make a large difference. And it is an area in which developing countries have indeed made significant commitments over the last 40 years. One need only cite the record made available by the World Bank covering the years from 1960 to 1991. For lower-income countries, enrollment in primary school has increased from 54 percent to 101 percent of the relevant age group; for secondary school, from 14 percent to 41 percent; and for high levels, from 2 percent to 5 percent. For the other countries, it has gone from 81 percent to 104 percent; from 17 percent to 55 percent; and from 4 percent to 18 percent. Many countries have substantially increased their per-pupil expenditures—and for good reason.

All empirical studies on the matter reveal quite a high social return to educational investment. The World Bank finds rates in excess of 25 percent for primary education, 15 percent to 18 percent for secondary, and 13 percent to 16 percent for tertiary. There even exists a positive relationship with the number of years of schooling: East Asia, with an average of six years, yields a higher increase in GDP for additional investment than do other regions.[9] This finding reinforces the importance of achieving adequate *minimal* training levels, given that many students in rural areas, through grade repetition and lack of completion, wind up little better for their educational exposure. We should note as well that increases in female education regularly have an indirect downward feedback on fertility rates, as well as positive effects on family health and nutrition.

What is seen in this productivity sense tends to repeat in the realm of income distribution. For a large variety of countries in which some type of dismantling of the sources of inequality has been found, variation in education typically shows up as the principal explanatory variable. Its range of importance extends from 10 percent to more than 20 percent of observed inequality. Those who are better schooled regularly receive higher incomes (keeping age, sector, and other similar variables constant). Typically, at the bottom of the income distribution spectrum, increased education is more important: one recent study by Jere Behrman shows Latin Americans with no schooling having a 56 percent probability of being in the lowest-income 20 percent while those with university training had only a 4 percent chance.[10]

Undoubtedly, education here is partially serving as a proxy for other associated factors such as school quality and labor market and family characteristics. Even so, education's repeated relevance, even discounting some of the gross effect, gives it a crucial role as a policy target contributing to greater distributional equality. Moreover, investment in human capital involves not a transfer of resources but rather an overall increase in their supply.

More active participation by government is necessary, particularly at the local level, where efforts must be undertaken to promote attendance and to maintain school quali-

---

[9] George Psacharopoulos, "Returns to Investment in Education: A Global Update," *World Development* 22 (1994), 1325–43.

[10] Jere Behrman, "Investing in Human Resources," Inter-American Development Bank, *Economic and Social Progress in Latin America* (1993).

ty. Furthermore, curricular reform in many instances is urgently required; little good is accomplished by providing standard training that leads simply to grade repetition rather than to the acquisition of skills. Whatever their many deficiencies, the former communist countries stand out in terms of the speed with which they achieved universal education. It remains to be shown that the developing market-oriented economies can do so as well.

Beyond education itself lies a whole range of ancillary activities with similar effects in improving the quality of labor: these activities relate to improved nutrition, better health, and other social investments. Indeed, for very low-income countries the returns to such outlays may be greater than those received for investment in education, exactly because the latter is still insufficient in magnitude to have a direct impact. Countries that have made early and substantial commitments to universal access to such human-capital goods and services have been rewarded by lower inequality as growth proceeds. In turn, the social returns to expanded investment in education have permitted simultaneous gains in real product.

We are referring here to a generational phenomenon. Today's outlays will not have an immediate and observable impact on output, but rather an impact that is delayed. That lag obviously makes it easier for such outlays to be postponed when fiscal stringency is necessary. One of the great tragedies of the 1980s, besides the poor economic performance that occurred, was the simultaneous reductions in government expenditures that were necessarily imposed. In many ways it was much easier to cut back in areas that had initially failed to be universal in scope. This cutback meant shortfalls in reaching the very groups initially excluded from adequate coverage. In most cases, private outlays for education, health services, and the like continued, thus extending initial divisions between those who were better off and those who had enjoyed only a limited access initially.

These kinds of delayed response are still to be felt in future decades, even as growth recovers in the region. Not only has there occurred a "lost decade" of growth but also potentially a "lost generation" deprived of elementary skills and the capacity to acquire them.

Greater realism now exists in terms of understanding that major efforts to achieve better income distribution cannot rely on populist promises of higher wages or on extensive direct economic controls and regulations. Such tactics provide temporary relief at best. The evidence of failure, in Chile in the 1970s and Peru and Nicaragua in the 1980s, is quite marked. The initially improved distribution on such paths comes from arbitrary gains in income—gains that subsequently evaporate as the inevitable economic adjustment occurs. Even in less extreme cases, the adoption of policies relying heavily on subsidies, whether to agriculture or industry, frequently translates into efforts that distort incentives and benefit primarily certain well-placed groups; the multiplicity of interventions ironically cancels out any permanent real allocation effect that had been anticipated.

Indeed, the triumph of the market is now widely recognized, even where the market approach was at one time resisted. We no longer speak of economic planning in the same way we did two decades ago. But conversely, the recognition that markets should play a wider role in the development process is still consistent with the continued existence of important areas of public-sector responsibility. A danger is that the fear of excessive and inefficient government intervention might preclude productive official investment that could yield growth and could improve income distribution. That fear would thus cause a great tragedy in the midst of the present policy convergence. The commitment must be not merely to ensuring the current increases in product but also to guaranteeing such increases in the future through a strategy of continuing public investment and effective taxation to acquire the necessary resources.

Scope for achieving a progressive taxation structure is necessarily limited when government must also seek to advance private savings and investment. One cannot assess positive gains from redistribution without attention to its potential negative consequences. But equally, one cannot ignore possibilities for utilizing enhanced revenues productively. The real challenge for the future is to create an effective public-sector presence. Nowhere is such a presence more important than in the realm of income distribution.

Some of the gains achieved by economists in recent years in the analysis of growth have come from applying new models. Most prominent among such models has been the theory of endogenous growth—and that model's recent increasing attention to income distribution. The key result thus far obtained—characteristic of recent articles publishes by Persson and Tabellini as well as by Alesina and Rodrik—is that inequality is negatively related to growth.

In the Persson and Tabellini research, equality's effects on growth are not only statistically significant but also quantitatively important. Thus, an equality increase of one standard deviation, changing the income share of the middle quintile of the income distribution by about 3 percent, is capable of increasing growth by .5 of a percentage point. Moreover, and powerfully, this relationship seems to hold only for those countries that follow democratic policies; for those that do not (some 40 percent of the sample), inequality is not statistically different from zero.

In the Alesina and Rodrik article, the Gini coefficient for a larger number of countries is employed as a key variable and turns out to be statistically significant. A reduction of one standard deviation in the Gini coefficient increases growth by more than 1 percentage point. But these latter researchers also stress their result of no difference between democracies and nondemocracies.[11]

As of now, these findings—and newer ones in a similar vein—must still be regarded as tentative, even despite George Clarke's recent careful demonstration of the robustness of this result negatively relating inequality and growth. Even Clarke concludes that the negative relationship between inequality and growth, although statistically significant, is relatively small. And in Birdsall, Ross, and Sabot, one standard deviation in inequali-

[11] Torsten Persson and Guido Tabellini, "Is Inequality Harmful for Growth?" *American Economic Review* 84 (1994), 600–21; Alberto Alesina and Dani Rodrik, "Distributive Politics and Economic Growth," *Quarterly Journal of Economics* 106 (1994), 465–90.

ty has an even smaller growth effect: only .32 percentage point. Moreover, the income distribution data in all these studies relate to an early period, the 1950s through the early 1970s, and therefore are clearly doubtful; Alesina and Rodrik did experiment with a slightly later set of observations, without much difference in results.[12]

For a somewhat different sample of countries and a slightly different period, the present author has found evidence of there being no statistical significance for inequality, especially when a dummy is introduced for the Latin American observations. These results run counter to the aforementioned recent important contributions.[13]

Additional conceptual issues about this new approach can also be posed. The mechanisms through which the actual redistributive policies operated are not specified. The large place for developed countries in the sample, all located at one end, may make the findings for developing countries more dubious. A further nontrivial factor can also be cited: the implicit assumption of equilibrium can hardly be said to hold in an interval in which the debt crisis had already begun and growth was significantly affected. And finally, the model that was utilized for statistical testing is still not dynamic and is really only an imperfect model of reality.

In the end, the fundamental conclusion of this new research amounts to a recognition of the need for good policy sense more than for precise scientific demonstration of the growth effects of inequality. Let us cite the 1991 *World Development Report*: "…efforts to improve equity can sit comfortably within reform programs aimed at promoting growth. It is clear, however, that market-distorting and overzealous redistribution can quickly pose overwhelming financial problems…. Also, crude transfers through market-distorting interventions almost always end up worsening the distribution of income rather than improving it."[14] The difficulty always comes in the practical implementation of the advice.

Expansion of Export Capability

A main message of the World Bank's *East Asian Miracle* is that a key, and replicable, part of East Asia's success is reliance on rapid export growth: "Finally, we found that a successful export push…offers high economic gains. Of all the interventions we surveyed, those to promote exports were the most readily compatible with a wide diversity of economic circumstances."[15]

But in imagining all developing countries successfully pursuing an export-led strategy, the report exaggerates what is realistically possible. There exists an important difference between eliminating obstacles to the expansion of exports and acting aggressively to push exports as the mainstay of future progress. Indeed, in the case of Japan, the export

---

[12] George Clarke, "More Evidence on Income Distribution and Growth," *Journal of Development Economics* 47, 2 (1995), 403–27; Nancy Birdsall, David Ross, and Richard Sabot, "Inequality and Growth Reconsidered: Lessons from East Asia," *World Bank Economic Review* 9, 3 (1995), 477–508.

[13] Albert Fishlow, "Inequality, Poverty, and Growth: Where Do We Stand? Annual World Bank Conference on Development Economics (1995), 34 ff.

[14] World Bank, *World Development Report* (1991), 139.

[15] World Bank, *East Asian Miracle* (1993), 367.

push strategy was motivated by the need to increase foreign-exchange earnings, but trade has actually constituted only a relatively small share of Japan's GNP. The continuing expansion of Japan's domestic market via rising demand was far more important for growth—a point the study fails to analyze adequately.

Country size makes a difference here. Inevitably, smaller exporting countries will have to specialize more narrowly, while what may be more appropriate for larger developing countries is an *export-adequate* path plus openness to foreign investment. Regular annual export growth on the order of 1 or 2 percentage points above GDP expansion will ensure the following important advantages of sustained international engagement: the productivity advancement in the export sectors (and therefore in others as well) needed in order to compete with other suppliers; the establishment of an important objective measure of the gains from manufacturing specialization; the pressure to maintain a competitive exchange rate, or in other words an aversion to overvaluation and to its attendant consequences; the avoidance of excessive dependence on foreign investment; and the steady evolution of institutional rules (derived in part from participation in the larger international economy) important to the achievement of stable progress.

The issue of overvaluation requires additional comment. With reduction of inflation being so central an objective in recent years, and with recourse to cheaper imports being such a common route to ensuring market discipline, there has arisen a tendency for overvaluation to occur as part of the process of stabilization. Especially in view of the Mexican failure at the end of 1994, there now exists much greater sensitivity in other countries on this point. Two issues are in conflict: establishing low inflation levels (and credibility) and retaining international export competitiveness. What seems critical is that the overvaluation begin to decline after some initial period. The way to ensure that is through productivity advance and the development of competitive export capacity. Otherwise, there exists considerable danger of instability and of a growing lack of credibility.

In short, rapid export growth does not afford a simple or failproof mechanism for a rapid economic expansion in Latin America. But neither should we downgrade the importance of an adequate level of export expansion. Countries of the region have only in the last decade managed to attain a rate of expansion in excess of 5 percent a year. Balance-of-payments problems have had a tendency to recur regularly; one way to reduce these problems' weight is to establish consistent and regular export growth as a major policy target.

In many of the countries of the region, attention has recently focused on the possibility of expanded regional and hemispheric trade as a vehicle for future progress. Free trade from Alaska to Tierra del Fuego—pronounced by the Bush administration, implemented in the NAFTA agreement, and extended by the Clinton administration to the region more broadly through the Miami accords—has become more central. At the same time, the MERCOSUR initiative has thrived, increasing trade rapidly among the four member countries and leading to the partial incorporation of Chile and Bolivia. Indeed, there are even negotiations afoot between MERCOSUR and the EU.

Is such new-styled regionalism compatible with the simultaneous creation of the World Trade Organization and the continued expansion of overall international trade? That issue is increasingly pivotal and has divided economists into different camps of opinion. Some economists see such regionalism as simply a broader style of protectionism, as was the Latin American Free Trade Association of the 1960s. Other economists, including several within the current U.S. administration, are much more positive; they see an inherent consistency between regional advance toward expanded exchange and the subsequent achievement of globalism.

The latter position is much more compelling. Latin America has moved toward greater participation in trade in recent years, ending the previous tendency toward lesser and lesser participation. An important component of such liberalization was the latter's role in stabilization. Now comes the harder part: a commitment to using trade as an instrument of renewed growth. Achievement of that objective will require export competitiveness and continuing gains in productivity.

A Final Word

Our platform of four policy directions for the next century falls far short of the requisite ten established by the Washington consensus. Although no major inconsistency in context exists between the two approaches, there do exist certain subtle differences that must be delineated.

First, the group of priorities presented here clearly emerges from Latin American initiatives already adopted during the course of the last decade. It is not foreign in origin.

Second, heading our own list is a conversion of the very role of the state. That shift is central. Latin America has learned that stabilization and an open and competitive economy are essential to achieving steady progress, but it has also learned the importance of a more restricted but still-critical leadership role for the public sector.

Third, the resurgence in growth must occur alongside the granting of adequate attention to the question of income distribution. In the final analysis, for the new democratic processes finally to become permanent, all citizens of the region—and especially the poorest ones—must sense the gains associated with renewed expansion.

And fourth, we must not ignore the important reality of trade-offs among these objectives. Higher national savings may mean greater personal inequality. Stabilization implies greater attention to imports and thus lesser focus upon regular export growth. These questions become the central issues of economic policy. Here is where a rapidly maturing political process becomes essential to eventual success.

Andrés Solimano[1] on Albert Fishlow's Paper
Latin America in the XXI Century

Albert Fishlow highlights four policy directions to help Latin America get to the next century in good economic and social shape. I will first offer comments on each of these directions and then identify other issues that can be part of a broader "Agenda of the Twenty-First Century" in the region.

Stabilization
Latin America has made significant progress in fiscal adjustment over the last decade. In fact, many Latin American countries have today lower fiscal deficits than some OECD countries. The question is how sustainable this fiscal adjustment is, given the demand for resources in the social and infrastructure needs, and the limited taxation capacity of most governments of the region. Moreover, the problem of large internal public debt is serious in several countries. In spite of these obstacles, fiscal responsibility is the predominant stance in the region today and must be encouraged and preserved.

On stabilization, Fishlow correctly argues against excessively deflationary or restrictive anti-inflationary policies that can compromise output growth and employment creation. However, he does not define adequate anti-inflationary targets. Should we be satisfied with attaining inflation rates just below 10 percent per year, or should we rather strive for OECD-inflation levels, say for rates around 2-3 percent per year? We know that high and escalating inflation penalizes capital formation and growth, as evidenced by the experience of the 1980s. However, we are still uncertain concerning the negative welfare and growth effects of low inflation rates, say below 5 percent per year.

Domestic Savings Capacity
Fishlow argues for an increase in domestic savings to attain investment rates of around 25 percent of GDP, which he estimates are needed to support 6 percent annual GDP growth and reduce reliance on external savings. One reason to promote domestic savings is a volatility argument. A savings mix tilted toward national savings makes the economy less volatile than a mix that relies heavily on foreign savings, since international capital markets tend to be volatile.

Another reason to promote domestic savings is related to economic growth. This is consistent with the "active-savings school," or Marshall-Solow view, which sees an increase

---

[1] Executive Director for Chile and Ecuador, Inter-American Development Bank.

in savings as a precondition to accelerate output growth. In this view, the causality runs from savings to growth, or in other words, savings *lead* to growth.

An alternative view is the "passive-savings school," or Keynes-Schumpeter approach, in which savings are seen to *follow* growth. Here the causality goes from investment (Keynes) and/or innovation (Schumpeter) to growth, with savings adjusting endogenously to equalize investment to realize macro equilibrium.

Beyond causality issues, and assuming a need to boost national savings, the question is, of course, how? The experience of my country, Chile, is useful to address this question. In Chile, the national savings ratio was less than 7.5 percent of GDP in 1985. Today, 12 years later, the national savings rate has climbed to around 27 percent. If we decompose the sources of this important increase in national savings, we note that the more spectacular aspect is the increase in corporate rather than personal savings, with public savings remaining around 4 percent to 5 percent of GDP. In fact, corporate savings went up from 5.4 percent of in 1985 to 17 percent in 1995, while private savings increased from 2 percent to 4 percent.

A key factor to recognize in Chile is that as GDP growth has accelerated rapidly (around 7 percent per year in the last 10 to 12 years), the very process of fast growth has generated a virtuous circle of higher savings and investment that in turn reinforces the dynamism of growth. Other factors such as pension fund reform also support the level of national saving. However, they cannot alone explain the dramatic jump in total savings in Chile that took place in the last decade or so.

Inequality and Education

Fishlow considers education a crucial variable to reduce inequality. I agree, but think that looking at education only in quantitative terms can be deceiving. In many countries, including Chile and the United States, there is universal access to primary and secondary education, but there are substantial differences in the quality of education—measured by national score tests—between affluent and poor neighborhoods or between public and private schools. These differences perpetuate existing income inequalities. In this case, an education system of uneven quality across income levels fails as a mechanism for the equalization of opportunities in society.

An important factor in the delivery of education is the public/private sector mix. In this connection it is worth mentioning a little-noticed but highly relevant case put forward by Albert Hirschman long ago in his 1970 book *Exit, Voice and Loyalty*. Hirschman presents the paradox that more competition in social services, say from private or other nonpublic providers, can lead to deterioration rather than improvement in the quality of the services delivered by the public sector. This is because once the exit option is available (to withdraw from public schools), the voice mechanism in public schools is weakened. Families that can afford to send their children to private schools do not spend time and effort to improve the quality of public schools; they just withdraw their children. The weakening of this feedback mechanism can lead to a substantial deterioration in the quality of the public school system. The "Hirschman Paradox" is thus very relevant today, when new institutional mechanisms for the provision of education are discussed in Latin America. The lesson is, of course, not to suppress choice but to complement and regulate it in a way that individual choice and social equity can both be attained.

Export Expansion

Fishlow calls for a less grandiose approach to export promotion as an engine of growth: it is better to strive for a 1 percent or 2 percent increase in the exports-to-GDP ratio as a sustainable strategy of export expansion. This seems reasonable. The only caveat is that to maintain global consistency, some countries will need to increase their *import* share by an equivalent amount to realize the required demand for the additional exports.

A Twenty-First Century Development Agenda for Latin America

Beyond the factors already discussed, there is also a need for broadening the scope of the development strategy. One way to put it is to stress the need to go beyond "material" development toward what might be called "human" development. Human development is understood here as meaning a strategy that includes the attainment of high and sustained output growth as an important ingredient of the development process, but that also stresses the need for growth to be equitable (through poverty reduction and more egalitarian income distribution) and environmentally friendly. Issues of the quality of life and of distribution need to be emphasized more in the development agenda.

First, the quality of life is obviously declining in Latin American cities that are becoming too big, too polluted, unsafe and congested. Mexico City will have close to 20 million people in the year 2000; São Paulo and Buenos Aires more than 15 million; Santiago more than 5 million. In spite of rising per capita income, the quality of life of the average citizen living in large cities does not rise in the same proportion. This growth of megacities confirms, among other things, the persistency of strong centralist tendencies in Latin America, as Claudio Veliz put it some time ago in his book *The Centralist Tradition in Latin America.*

Second, the regional disparities of per capita income both within the region (say Central America versus the Southern Cone) or within countries (northeast vs. southern Brazil) are large and persistent. There are few signs of convergence in per capita income levels within and across countries of the region.

Third, there is evidence of rising violence and crime, particularly in urban centers of Latin America. The right of personal safety, which is ever more threatened, is fundamental to be able to enjoy the fruits of material development.

Fourth, the problem of ethnic and cultural diversity in Latin America cannot be ignored. Today, the indigenous population of the region stands at around 40 million people. This population speaks various languages, has different systems of economic organization, and, in general, is excluded or largely detached from the organization and benefits provided by the modern segments of the nation-state. Human development attaches high value to cultural diversity, and modern and integrated societies cannot afford to have large groups of their populations excluded or marginalized.

Mitsuhiro Kagami[1] on Albert Fishlow's Paper
Latin America in the XXI Century

I am impressed by Albert Fishlow's thoughtful paper and entirely agree with his four policy directions. I would like to summarize some important policy lessons from East Asian development experiences that seem to fit a new Latin American situation in the late 1990s and into the twenty-first century.

Development Stages of Markets

The World Bank and the International Monetary Fund have provided credits to debt-stricken, oil-shocked countries for the last 15 years with stabilization and structural-adjustment policies (SAPs). SAPs are backed by neoclassical thought which emphasizes the market mechanism. The World Bank has summarized the economic performance of these countries in *Adjustment Lending and Mobilization of Private and Public Resources for Growth* (World Bank, 1992). According to this report, the star adjustment performers were mostly from East Asia and included Korea, Thailand, and Indonesia. A second set of adjustment successes included Chile, Mexico, Morocco, and Venezuela. Low-income countries, however, showed weak or disastrous performances. The report recommended that these low-income countries adopt further reforms to reduce continuing distortions and to improve the environment for private-sector activities and public-sector resource management.

Shigeru Ishikawa (1994) argues that there are two types of price distortions: one from state intervention and the other from the market itself. Even if distortions from government intervention can be eliminated, there still remain intrinsic distortions from the market. The latter emerge in "underdeveloped" or "immature" markets. There are stages of development in markets that are affected by the condition of the traditional economy, the extent to which there is an informal economy, and institutional segmentation. The effectiveness of policies differs according to the stage of market development. Automatic application of SAPs in all countries, therefore, does not necessarily bring about satisfactory results, especially in low-income countries where markets are immature and can be nurtured or supplemented by government arrangements or coordination.

An example of development stages can be seen in financial markets. Exchanges of goods are the most primitive form of a market. Then money appears as a means of transaction. A productive business can save its profits for further production. At this stage,

---

[1] Director, Development Studies Department, Institute of Developing Economies, Tokyo.

savers and investors are one and the same. If monetization advances, the separation of savers from investors begins. Financial intermediaries gradually come into the transaction, and the banking system grows from the traditional or informal to the formal type. The central banking system is one of the most sophisticated hierarchical mechanisms. Stock and security markets also grow to supply funds directly to private firms.

The Role of the State

Are there any implications for Latin America and the Caribbean from the East Asian development experiences? During the 1980s, East Asian countries performed remarkably in terms of growth, inflation, debt management, and income distribution, while Latin America, with the exception of Chile, experienced a "lost decade." During the 1990s, however, the paradigm shifted: macroeconomic imbalances improved, and foreign capital came back to Latin America. Some suggestions and implications derived from the East Asian success story are useful in this new environment. In particular, the role of the state in every domain should be reconsidered.

High Savings

Investment is the key to establishing a sound economic base. High investment leads to high growth, as the East Asian economies have shown. Investment is usually channeled from domestic savings. If there are not domestic savings to cover investment, external funds are needed, thus causing or exacerbating external-debt problems. Basically, healthy internal savings were instrumental to achieving the good performance of Asian economies.

According to the Asian Development Bank, the average domestic saving ratio for East Asia in 1995 was 34 percent. (The lowest was 16 percent for the Philippines, and the highest was 45 percent for Singapore, while China was as high as 40 percent.) The corresponding figure for Latin America was around 20 percent, with the exception of Chile (26 percent). Growth that depends too much on external savings is an anomaly, as was proved during the 1980s.

Savings can be enhanced by positive real interest rates, frugal consumption patterns, efficient financial intermediaries, and good investment opportunities in the domestic market. Institutional arrangements such as the postal savings system in Japan and the privatization of social insurance in Chile also can provide long-term funds for development.

Utilization of Transnational Corporations (TNCs)

TNCs are often criticized for being footloose, exploitative, and insensitive to environmental concerns. However, recent experience has shown that competent TNCs do contribute to host country industrialization in terms of foreign currency earnings through exports. Other important roles of TNCs include job creation, tax contribution, technology transfer, and information sources of foreign markets. As business is increasingly linked worldwide, the horizontal division of labor of TNCs is useful for both developing and advanced countries. As Akifumi Kuchiki explained in his paper in the present volume, export processing zones (EPZs) are an example of the utilization of foreign power. A weak football team has to be reinforced by foreign star players until local team members can develop and be strong enough to be independent. (In the Olympic soccer games in Atlanta, Japan defeated Brazil using this method. I will call this a "football trick" or "soccer magic," as compared to Paul Streeten's "judo trick".) Governments can attract TNCs by providing good infrastructure, legal protection, and export-oriented policies.

With regard to technology transfer, the misunderstanding that technology is free and TNCs have to transfer their know-how to host countries should be corrected. Technology is not free of charge. Korea and Taiwan showed that technology is not free: they paid royalties for fundamental technologies and then gradually accumulated their technological base. Technology spillover is inevitable, but even more important is the absorptive capacity of management and labor in the host country. A learning process is necessary, but Schumpeterian entrepreneurs can find ways to establish their own businesses after a period of apprenticeship under TNCs.

Education Revisited

In Japan, it has been said since the samurai era that reading, writing and *soroban* (a traditional low-tech calculator for simple arithmetic) are basic necessities for all people. These abilities are developed by basic education. *Kaisen*, or continuous improvement, in factory level production does not require deep knowledge but rather general wisdom. Every single shop floor worker can participate sufficiently in this process if he or she has the three basic abilities that come from basic education.

Cost-efficient basic education systems are necessary and should be widely and easily available for all children. It is subsidized *university* education that should be changed and charged for in Latin America.

Institution Building

Every society has its own traditions, its own intrinsic social and economic arrangements. We should make use of these institutions. For instance, the subcontracting system in Japan, once criticized for being old-fashioned and exploitative, is now recognized as an efficient manufacturing production method when compared with vertically internalized production methods. Outsourcing and the formation of "supply chains" are desired by all contemporary "lean" producers.

Long-term contracts and close relationships between assemblers (prime firms) and subcontractors (small and medium-scale enterprises) can minimize risks and promote the sharing of long-term profits. The cooperation and coordination that come from the accumulation and sharing of knowledge between the prime firm and the subcontracting firms can save design time and improve production engineering.

Subcontracting is also widely used in Latin America (Kagami 1995), and a continuation of this kind of efficient networking is key to the region's competitive exports. This is an example of relational linkages among firms, but we can also find these linkages between banks and firms, between firms and distributors, and between firms and government. There is an urgent need to strengthen these relations and to build productive institutions efficiently.

On the other hand, there is a need to curb the excessive family ties and nepotism that are common in Latin American businesses. Transparency in management and the separation of ownership and management are essential. Otherwise, the monopolistic nature of Latin American bu. inesses will keep them from being able to compete with other modern companies, especially from Asia.

Reconsider ng the Role of the State

The *laissez-faire* principle is now predominant, and "small government" is a goal widely pursued. State intervention is criticized for distorting prices and hindering efficient resource allocation. This argument presupposes the existence of markets If markets do not exist or exist in an immature form, the price signal does not lead to efficient resource allocation. Moreover, the market sometimes fails in the case of externalities, scale economies, and public goods. On such occasions, the state needs to intervene in the market.

The government plays three important roles in this respect. It fosters markets if they are underdeveloped or immature. It supplements the market if the market mechanism does not function well. And it coordinates private agents with the market. Aoki *et al.* say that "government should be regarded as an endogenous player interacting with the economic system as a coherent cluster of institutions rather than a neutral omnipotent agent exogenously attached to the economic system with the mission of resolving its coordination failures." They introduce a "market-enhancing view" in which the government's role is to facilitate the development of private sector institutions that can solve coordination problems and overcome other market imperfections.

The Chinese example of liberalization is instructive. After the famous "Southern Province Instruction" of Deng Xiaoping in 1992, liberalization was encouraged along the coastal region of China. Rushed development with overly zealous liberalization policies brought about the devastation of agricultural land, a high level of income inequality, and heavy pollution. Reconsideration of excessive liberalization has now begun, with more weight given to central-government intervention or public guidance to private firms, foreign entities, and even local governments.

The time has come to return to the optimum mixture of economic policies—that is, a combination of *dirigisme* and neoclassical thought, or what I call the "flexible (and efficient) state" based on the market mechanism. Governments must intervene when markets are incomplete or immature according to the pertinent development stage.

REFERENCES

Aoki, Masahiko, Kevin Murdock, and Masahiro Okuno-Fujiwara. "Beyond the East Asian Miracle: Introducing the Market-Enhancing View." In *Role of Government in East Asian Economic Development.* Washington, D.C.: World Bank's Economic Development Institute, forthcoming.

Ishikawa, Shigeru. "Kouzou Chousei: Seginhousiki no Saikentou (Structural Adjustment: Reconsider the World Bank Method)." *Ajia Keizai* 11(35) Institute of Developing Economies, 1994.

Kagami, Mitsuhiro. *The Voice of East Asia: Development Implications for Latin America.* Institute of Developing Economies, 1995. Also see the Spanish version, *Voces del Asia Oriental: Posibilidades para el Desarrollo de América Latina.* Mexico, D.F.: Editorial Jus, S.A. de C.V., 1996.

World Bank. *Adjustment Lending and Mobilization of Private and Public Resources for Growth.* Washington, D.C.: World Bank Country Economics Department, 1992.

Francisco R. Sagasti[1] on Albert Fishlow's Paper

Beyond the Washington Consensus: Overcoming the Crisis of Governance in Latin America

By its title and the fact that it intends to offer "a new conception of Latin American development," Albert Fishlow's paper raises high expectations. To a certain extent, these expectations were satisfied, but I would have liked to be challenged even more.

Probably there is general agreement with his four suggested policy directions. Excepting a few minor clarifications and modifications, nobody could seriously quarrel with the need for "a different government," the call for a "substantial increase in domestic savings," the need "to confront the extraordinarily unequal income distribution," or the importance "of paying some mind to exports." One may quibble that there may be trade-offs between increasing domestic savings and reducing income inequality (at least for some time in some countries) or find fault with his emphasis on increasing government savings rather than private-enterprise savings or with the content of the policies to complement land reform. Nevertheless, I venture to say that there is nothing in his agenda of four points to motivate serious policy disagreement.

For this reason, I would like to focus my comments on a few complementary issues that may require further discussion. These comments arise from the perspective of someone concerned with global issues who, after spending many years at the World Bank and other international institutions, returned to his native country and spent three years traveling through it, conducting a highly participative exercise to prepare a diagnosis and an agenda to improve the prospects for democratic governance in Peru.[2]

Peru is a country where the worst and the best coexist in stark contrast. During the last decade and a half, we have experienced the terrorism of the Shining Path, a period of hyperinflation, the collapse of the state apparatus, a harsh stabilization program, policy reforms and economic recovery, messianic leadership, a self-inflicted presidential coup, and an enormously vital grassroots movement. It is a good antidote to the complacency that can gradually invade a person after years in the comfortable Washington offices of the international institutions.

---

[1] Director, Agenda: Peru.
[2] See F. Sagasti, P. Patron, N. Lynch, and M. Hernández, *Democracia y Buen Gobierno: Informe final del proyecto AGENDA: Perú* (Lima, Editorial Apoyo/Agenda: Peru, (2a. Edicion), September 1996).

The Washington Consensus in Practice: Local Interpretations

However we may define the content of the old or the new Washington consensus, in the final analysis the interpretations offered by senior policy makers in a specific country are the ones that matter. These local interpretations often tend to distort the meaning of the Washington consensus, transforming it into a definitive and imposed set of prescriptions—and even into a collection of slogans. Among other things, the Washington consensus has been used to justify rigid prescriptions for trade liberalization and financial deregulation, without regard for inconsistencies, second order effects or unintended consequences; inflexible schemes and timetables for hasty privatizations, which often involve large opportunity costs and by their nature make it impossible to learn from experience; and draconian public-expenditure cuts, frequently carried out without establishing sensible priorities and without public discussion. In this sense, we may say that the Washington consensus and John Williamson's name have been taken in vain on many occasions.

Furthermore, one of the heralded advantages of implementing the policy reforms listed in the Washington consensus—particularly those related to liberalization, privatization, reduction of government discretionary power, and the unleashing of market forces—was the reduction of opportunities for corruption. However, we have seen new forms of corruption emerge, linked to privileged access to information, to "revolving door" practices in which former government officials move to the private sector and benefit from the policies they implemented, and to the predatory behavior of privatized state enterprises (which in some cases have been bought by state enterprises from other countries). Similarly, the inviolability of the "market" is often invoked to ward off possible government interventions that would in fact help markets function properly, preventing collusion and abuses of market powers.

To a large extent, these problems emerge out of the fact that the transition toward the regulatory state, with all its associated institutions, has taken much longer than the liberalization process. As is pointed out by Eisuke Sakakibara elsewhere in the present volume, policy reforms have been put in practice assuming that all the institutions peculiar to the Anglo-Saxon variety of market economy were already in place—a rather costly mistake.

The Crisis of Governance

Such institutional failures, or the existence of what my teacher Eric Trist used to call "missing institutions," are symptoms of a broader set of problems that may be properly called a "crisis of democratic governance."

This crisis has been brewing for a long time, both in Peru and many other Latin American countries. It came into full view during the 1980s and early 1990s and can be defined as a situation in which *social, economic, and political demands grow tremendously and vastly exceed the capacity of the state, the private sector and civil society to process and respond adequately in a democratic manner.* In Latin America, demands grew in the quantitative sense because of the population explosion that began in the late 1950s and early

1960s and because of the migratory processes from rural to urban areas that followed. They also grew qualitatively because most of the excluded were no longer willing to tolerate the injustices that had characterized economic, social, and political structures for centuries.

The incapacity to process and respond adequately to the demands of a growing and increasingly restless population is associated with four different forms of exclusion: economic, social, political and those of future generations. Let us examine each of the four.

The inability of both the public and private productive sectors to generate employment opportunities has led to *economic exclusion*. The labor market appears actively to reject those who seek employment, particularly the poor whose only asset is their labor. Thus the market generates work only for a fraction of the economically active population. In the case of Peru, about two-thirds of the labor force is either unemployed or underemployed, while more than 200,000 young people enter the labor force every year. For those workers who are excluded from jobs in the formal labor market, the informal sector and various forms of self-employment are the only viable alternative to crime, drug trafficking, or subversion. But the informal sector is not a thriving hotbed of aspiring entrepreneurs, eager to move upward, as has been portrayed in some idealized accounts of their activities. For the most part, they are just poor people producing for and selling to the poor and making ends meet, with no capacity to save. They are often engaged in various forms of self-exploitation and the exploitation of their family members and dependents.

Social exclusion is associated with pervasive and persistent inequalities, which have reached unbearable levels in many countries of the region. Discrimination because of poverty, ethnic origin, gender, age and geographical location must be significantly reduced to overcome social exclusion. Two key questions must be confronted throughout Latin America. First, is there a "reasonable" level of inequality that could stimulate entrepreneurship, competition, and the desire for individual improvement without destroying social cohesion, solidarity, and the sense of common identity? And second, how does one define such a reasonable level of inequality in a democratic fashion and in a way that would generate support for the policies it would imply? There will be neither universal nor strictly technical answers to these questions. The region's heterogeneity, and the fact that determining such a sensible and tolerable level of inequality involves fundamental value choices preclude a universal technocratic solution to such highly charged and profoundly political issues.

Perhaps the most visible manifestation of the crisis of governance has been the fact that the state apparatus has become incapable of processing growing demands for basic social services, economic stability, and even personal security. This has led to widespread *political exclusion*, which implies that most people do not enjoy the benefits of full citizenship and do not feel represented by state institutions. The executive, the judiciary, and parliament are seen as remote entities difficult for most people to identify with and are considered inefficient, corrupt, and self-serving. Political systems, including parties and electoral procedures, often do not favor the full participation of citizens who have become increasingly alienated and find they do not even have a "voice" (in the Hirschman sense) to express their grievances. Overcoming political exclusion will require a fundamental reform of the state apparatus, which should go well beyond modernization and improvements in administrative efficiency. The state must become competent enough to represent the variety of interests of all citizens, define the common good, maintain an effective presence throughout the territory, and provide the range of public goods essential to the functioning of a modern society.

The *exclusion of future generations* is a dimension of the crisis of democratic governance closely associated with the prevalence of violence, deterioration of the physical environment, and failure to develop science and technology capabilities. Violence, drugs, and crime—which appear attractive to young people bereft of more sensible real options—destroy their future by leading them to prison and often cutting short their lives. Environmental degradation poses a slower but more pervasive and relentless threat to the possibilities of future generations to enjoy higher living standards. In the transition to the knowledge society that will dominate the next century, those countries that fail to develop local scientific and technological capabilities will be marginalized.

Overcoming the crisis of democratic governance and the various forms of exclusion associated with it will require major institutional changes in the state apparatus, the private sector and the organizations of civil society. However important, it is not enough to focus only on the reform of the state. Without significant changes to modernize and improve the efficiency of firms, the private sector will not be able to become the driving force of economic growth. Without repairing the social fabric and creating civil capital— a task for the institutions of civil society—it will not be possible to maintain social cohesion or construct a sense of common identity.

The intellectual and political elites in the region must articulate and put into practice development strategies that respond to the crisis of governance. These include promoting productive modernization and competitiveness, social integration and equity, the legitimation of state institutions, and measures to eliminate the exclusion of future generations. Above all, leaders are needed who can combine vision with practical imagination and who can persuade those who wield effective power that it is in their interest to support institutional reform, even if such reform implies a reduction in their privileges.

Latin America's Exits from the Liberal Transition

Alain Touraine[1]

The evolution of the Latin American economic and social situation is not necessarily unique. Like most parts of the world, the region has experienced the downfall and destruction of postwar national development policies that were intentionally designed and carried out by *desarrollista* country governments. Subsequently it entered into a liberal transition through a difficult adjustment process universally accepted and followed. There was limited resistance from the old economic policies and the social and political forces that supported them, partly because of dramatic inflation that swept through many countries. The world level triumph of the ideology of globalization, which involves not only the concrete internationalization of production and trade but also the dream of a self-regulated world economy free from all kinds of political and social controls, pushed many Latin American governments to believe the illusion that they were developing a liberal society in which a free market economy would foster the development of a free and pluralistic political system. From 1990 on, when the flow of foreign capital to Latin America again became positive, a new model of development not only became the official policy of most governments but also managed to convince international economic and financial operators that Mexico, by accepting the NAFTA agreement, had entered the developed world and that Chile, champion of free-trade policies, was already in.

Two years after the latest Mexican crisis, it is difficult to maintain such an optimistic analysis, even if Latin America's economic situation is far from being entirely negative. What must be challenged first is the assertion that economic success implies weakened political and social control and a growing autonomy of the economic subsystem. This conviction is deeply rooted in the Western pattern of modernization, particularly the British and American ones. For many historians and sociologists, following Max Weber himself, the growing differentiation of various subsystems, the separation between political and religious institutions or between kinship and political forms of organization, should be logically followed by a growing separation of economic from political institutions. Schumpeter, for example, condemned imperialism as a negative interference by political values and goals into economic activities. Nevertheless, the same Schumpeter announced the inevitable downfall of the capitalistic system because of its absence of public support and its inability to mobilize symbols and cultural or national identities.

---

[1] Ecole des Hautes Etudes en Sciences Sociales, Paris.

Karl Polanyi, in his review of the European modernization process, introduced an analysis still useful today. Economic modernization implies the breakdown or the serious limitation of former systems of cultural, social, and political control of economic activity. But a purely internally regulated economic system would be unable to create an integrated society. It would be a wild rather than a free economy. It is, therefore, indispensable to build a new system of political and social control completely different from the preceding one. Its main objective—after periods of growing concentration of resources, decisions, and representations—would be to promote major economic redistribution, better social integration, and more cultural creativity.

Is Latin America already engaged in such a process of social reconstruction, or is it unable to achieve or even to formulate it?

The heavy social price of British industrialization made a strong impression on Polanyi, who sympathized with efforts to create an industrial democracy. These efforts, in different forms, appeared during the last decades of the nineteenth century in Britain and Germany but began only during the 1930s in the United States and France.

It is no easy task to introduce new social actors and their political representation, to implement reform programs, and to organize the web of new relationships among various political, economic, social, and cultural institutions. Some groups—such as the Florence Club, many of whose member are high officials of the European Union—believe that the only future society to be built must be a world society. Following Jean Monet's inspiration, they are deeply reluctant to defend the positive role of national states. They insist on the growing capacity of intervention not only of international institutions, public and private, but of worldwide opinion forces, like Greenpeace, Amnesty International, or even CNN, all of which have already influenced transnational public opinion.

This view seems to be far removed from current reality, however. No international institution has ever reached the same level of representation that national parliaments, media, or even unions have achieved. It is useful to mention briefly the social and political forces and processes that play a major role today in the control of economic activities.

It is difficult to separate economic globalization entirely from American hegemony, just as it was difficult a century ago to separate imperialism from the British Empire. American domination is most noticeable in terms of mass culture and the information age. New and virtually unprecedented problems appear as American culture and identity begin to supplant the economic and social identities of other countries. Initiative is substituted by imitation.

At the same time, strong economic and political forces are pushing to transform a global economy into a trilateral (U.S., Japan, and European) world. The Japanese modernization has been achieved by a social and cultural system very different from the American one. In Europe, Jacques Delors's efforts to defend a European social model by creating an integrated political system have not been fully realized, his White Book forgotten; moreover, the Bosnian tragedy has also demonstrated the inability of the

European Union to act as a political decision maker, and a growing number of politicians and economists view the decisions of the Bundesbank as seeming to aim at building Germany instead of Europe as a major center of the international economic system. Apparently, the necessity of linking economic decisions with national interests is as widely accepted in Europe as it is in the United States and in Japan.

Countries that are farthest removed from the centers of economic and social transformation tend to view globalization as an attack on sovereignty. This attitude feeds "communalist" movements that in turn spawn parties and regimes with an authoritarian bent.

Is it possible under international circumstances such as these to maintain a self-regulating world economic system? Is it true that transnational production and trade increasingly are regulated by private instead of public institutions, by major international banks, by rating agencies or by New York or London based law firms? This growing autonomy of a global economy has, as its counterparts, political and cultural fragmentation and a growing impact of organized noneconomically oriented forces, ranging from ethnic to religious movements.

The notion of globalization lumps together phenomena that are largely independent from one another: worldwide extension of markets, rapid development of an information society, formation of new industrial states, extremely autonomous financial networks operating well beyond their traditional functions in international trade, and American political and cultural hegemony. In the same way, conservative thinkers from Auguste Comte to Raymond Aron introduced the concept of industrial society to include technological innovation, social relations of production, and even political institutions into an integrated societal model. We are summoned to globally accept or reject this new type of society, although rejection is actually impossible because any anti-liberal model reminds us of the mass repression and economic failure of the communist regimes. European leaders have imposed on their countries the idea not only that integration and free circulation of capital are the most important goals but also that national economic policies should be subordinated to the monetary unification of Europe. This idea is debatable, yet it has not led to any serious alternative program. Neither right- nor left-wing parties have been able to propose a viable compromise between an international open economy and an integrated national society. Will Latin Americans be more imaginative?

While some people view the present situation as a transition from state-oriented economies to free "market regulated" international economic systems, it seems more realistic to define it as a period of difficult reconstruction of political and a social control over economic activities. Total control of economic life by a political and ideological plan has proven to be dramatically destructive; equally dangerous is the opposite, a completely desocialized and depoliticized economy. Even in the best of cases, "market societies" often increase inequalities, social crisis, and violence; at worst, they can bring chaos and authoritarian revolution.

At the beginning of our century, the idea of globalization was widely accepted under a different name. Internationalized finance capital tended to prevail over national industrial capitalism, and the Austrian economist Hilferding called this predominance "imperialism". His book was published in 1910, and Lenin's pamphlet, which borrowed extensively from Hilferding's ideas, appeared in 1916. At the time, the Mexican revolution had already begun, Europe was involved in the bloodiest international war ever seen, Russia was on the verge of a total collapse, and China was dominated by warlords. Finally, a few years after the end of World War I, Germany, the United States, and, to a lesser degree, other countries began a period of intensive *Rationalisierung*, the revenge of industrial capitalism. Nothing was left of the illusory triumph of pure economic forces, and the world was much more visibly dominated by political than by economic forces; that is, by authoritarian and totalitarian regimes rather than by market economies. America after World War II seems an exception, but one must remember that, during the Cold War, the American economy and society were dominated by a huge mobilization of public resources to contain Soviet expansionism. It is not arbitrary to forecast that if countries continue to identify with the growing independence of the global economy from social and political controls, the world will again be dominated within a few decades by authoritarian nationalist regimes. Many countries could fall into a chaos already visible in Latin America in Mexico, Colombia, and Venezuela among the relatively advanced countries and in Haiti, and in Nicaragua and other Central American countries among the poorest. Simultaneously, in industrialized countries, marginalization, social exclusion, and the spread of ghettos will likely continue. In American and European cities, advanced technology and international networks will coexist side by side with isolated communities and ghettos.

As far as Latin America is concerned, one must consider to what extent the old nationalist-populist political system has been eliminated. Even more importantly, in which form and at what level of efficiency can free trade lead to economic growth and to more and better employment? Can the national product be more equally distributed and can structural heterogeneity be limited? Can new political forces and debates be created, and cultural creativity and "reflexivity" increased? Most of these questions call for mixed economic, social and political analysis, the latter two of which are the focus of the present article.

"Una Transición Malograda" or a Troubled Transition

The last quarter century in Latin America has been dominated by the downfall and disappearance of the predominant political and social organization: the nationalist-populist regime. Such regimes functioned through a process of distribution and investment of external resources by a national state that combined economic and social goals, was made up of national territory occupied by a heterogeneous population, and was loosely integrated by insufficient means of communication. There was no separation among political, economic, and social actors in such regimes. These two elements of definition—multidimensionality of political action and absence of differentiation among subsystems—have had important social and political consequences. The first explains the general absence of one-dimensional, class-conscious or nationalist political parties or unions.

The second makes wider the distance between insiders and outsiders—the world of participation and the world of exclusion—than that between upper and lower strata or classes (for example, employers and wage earners). Many studies have analyzed the decline of this political, social and economic system, which, despite its flaws, produced for most of the region a long period of economic growth, educational progress, and development of a middle class, but without overcoming the extreme social inequalities. The model fell into crisis because of excess protectionism, the priority given to consumption over investment, the absence or weakness of national entrepreneurs, corruption, and industrialization that tended to exacerbate the extremely unequal distribution of resources. This was especially true in populist countries such as Argentina or Venezuela, while more-nationalist regimes such as those in Brazil and Mexico were more able to resist this trend to *estancamiento*.

Social scientists such as Manuel Antonio Garretón have given central importance to the concept of transition. This concept emphasizes a certain continuity from the old nationalist-populist regime to the new market-oriented democracy. In the Chilean case, Garretón points to the role of the military regime, which cannot be limited to its repressive action, and the smooth transformation of the military dictatorship through the plebiscite into a democratic system that will be free from the political pressure of General Pinochet only in 1998. In Brazil, the continuity was even more visible and was well described by the expressions *distensão* and *abertura*, which were used in the 1970s. Everywhere, the Spanish process of modernization and democratization is referred to as a model.

Despite these cases, a different type of analysis seems more appropriate, not only because of the increased activity of urban guerrillas at the end of the nationalist-populist period and the violence of counterrevolutionary coups in the Southern Cone but more deeply because of the extreme ideological and political discontinuity in general between the old and the new situations. Most striking is the inability of the old system to imagine its own transformation. Its process of internal decomposition gave rise to the most radical initiatives. The crisis and decline of the nationalist-populist regimes was not even analyzed by its own leaders or ideologists. They generally considered the region's economic crisis of the 1980s to be a consequence of decisions made by external actors such as transnational companies or banks, the International Monetary Fund, and the American government. That attitude created a self-fulfilling prophecy: national actors disappeared, reform programs were abandoned, and economic and political ruptures and violence broke out. The road from one system to another was cut by violence, destruction of political institutions, and the inability of most intellectuals to interpret the ongoing changes. After a long period of debate, the region entered a period of intellectual silence, repression, and dependence on external decisions.

While some major intellectuals, especially *cepalinos*, from Celso Furtado to Aníbal Pinto and F.H. Cardoso, successfully incorporated dependency as one of the major elements of the analysis, the most radical exponents of the dependency theory were unable to understand the crisis. Years of guerrilla warfare, from the beginning of the 1960s to the very recent period in Central America, demonstrated the incapacity of radical middle-class intellectuals both to perceive the economic and international situation or to understand the problems of peasants and Indians. Even though the very nature of the Cuban regime was denied and the decomposition of the Sandinista revolution ignored, it took analysts a long time to accept the consequences of the fall of the Soviet empire. Moderate reformism lost influence, and during a long period change came only from the outside and was introduced by military or civilian leaders who destroyed or tried to destroy the former political system.

Because Latin America was the ideological continent *par excellence*, it seems appropriate to note the absence in most countries of an ability to understand and orient a process of transition.

In the Southern Cone, Peru, and Bolivia we have witnessed discontinuities and brutal ruptures rather than progressive transition. But we observe nevertheless, after the destruction of the nationalist-populist regimes, a process of reconstruction and differentiation of economic, political and cultural activities, which make these countries more similar to European countries.

Chile is the most interesting and successful case. From 1983 on, political opposition was reorganized, mass demonstrations were organized by unions and parties, and the possibilities of an open political conflict, loaded with violence on both sides, became real. Nevertheless, the 1989 plebiscite was won by democratic parties on a completely different platform: reconciliation rather than revenge. After the victory, President Aylwin's main achievements were to rebuild the political system and manage a difficult coexistence with General Pinochet. A vast majority of the population seemed to have simply left the past in the past. Even among those who deeply respect President Allende for having sacrificed his life, very few of his former supporters propose to return to the 1970 economic and social policy. Extreme right- and left-wing political forces have been marginalized. This does not mean that Chile has reached self-sustaining growth, but rather only that the country has successfully overcome a fundamental crisis—first economic, then political.

Such a transformation was especially difficult to achieve in Brazil because of the great successes of nationalist economic policy, especially at the time of the "Brazilian miracle". Longer than any other country, Brazil resisted the new international economic direction, in spite of many liberal official statements and initiatives. Only since President Cardoso has been in office has Brazil clearly admitted the necessity to accept the end of state control over the economy. This lag was aggravated by a fundamental weakness of the country's political system. There are no parties in Brazil, only changing electoral coalitions, so that the Congress is more a political market than a policymaking institution. Any president, from those who supported a traditional *política dos governadores* to those, like Cardoso, who have tried to get rid of it, must endlessly negotiate any decision with representatives of countless other political interests. In the end, presidents seem weaker than the sum total of private interests with which they had to bargain.

In contrast, the Bolivian case is a successful example of a dramatic change of orientation, following the episode of hyperinflation in 1985. Bolivia has very imaginatively rebuilt its political system by incorporating the Aymara authority system into national institutions, thus eliminating traditional *caudillismo* in the countryside.

Finally, Argentina reminds us that an autonomous and democratic political system, such as that organized by President Alfonsín, is powerless if the economic system is not competitive and oriented toward maintaining clientelism and speculation through state protection, rather than toward production.

Farther north in the region, especially in Mexico, Colombia, and Venezuela, the situation is very different because the process of differentiation between economic and political systems has not taken place. In Mexico, President De La Madrid reinforced the technocratic and administrative organization of the state in order to head off an increasingly independent PRI. President Salinas entered into a much more direct confrontation with the party-state. But instead of trying to democratize the political system, he instead moved to "presidentialize" the system, thanks largely to the neopopulist Pronasol. Salinas, like Berlusconi in Italy, was convinced that a liberal economic policy could not be sustained without some popular (but not necessarily democratic) support. He gained important political support while fighting for the NAFTA agreement with the United States and Canada, including support from formal leftists. His successor was then elected through a cleaner election than in the past. But the absence of an autonomous and representative political system, combined with the decline of the PRI, created a political vacuum that was a major element of the country's economic and financial crisis. The crisis could well have destroyed Mexico and the Latin American economy if the United States and the IMF had not extended massive support to Mexico.

It seems paradoxical to speak of the survival of the old political system in Colombia, one of the few countries in South America where populism never prevailed, at least since the death of Gaïtan and the Bogotazo in 1948. As in Mexico, the political system proved to be unable to control political violence or drug trafficking. Colombia today is an example of the almost complete destruction of "public life." Government, parties, and guerrillas are equally penetrated by private interests, and it is impossible to distinguish clean business from dirty money. Colombia has a high rate of growth, a relatively limited external debt, and a brilliant intelligentsia. Nevertheless, the country is in chaos. Only half of its territory—during the daytime—is under state control, and 30 thousand people are victims each year of political violence. Medellin's popular districts cannot be visited without the formal agreement of local bosses.

The political continuity of Venezuela is stronger, but the effects of huge oil resources are so negative that, in spite of a serious effort, the state is unable to maintain acceptable conditions of life for the poor. Military-populist coups and serious constitutional crises have demonstrated the fragility of the regime.

These quick summaries of various country situations are mentioned to support a general hypothesis. The capacity for Latin American countries to move from the nationalist-populist system to an internationally open economy depends first on the capacity to destroy the old political system, disentangle the political process from economic strategies, and build a new and more autonomous political system.

Yet social movements have been surprisingly weak during the 1980s. It must be recognized that no military dictatorship in the Southern Cone was eliminated by mass uprising. The same can be said of the Central European countries, Poland, Hungary, and even Czechoslovakia. In Romania, a semirevolutionary process was followed by an unsuccessful transition to a new economic and political system.

Latin America has been and still is faced with this transition, and there remains a major risk that the future of its societies will be determined solely by external forces. The region must get rid of this inefficient and unfair system of external control of its economic activities. It is not that this change will ensure the success of long-term economic development, but rather that if the rules of the nationalist-populist systems are not removed, countries will be unable to resist the shock of the liberal transition and will fall into major social, political, and economic crises.

The countries of the South eliminated in one way or another the old system of political management and now appear to be entering a new development process, while Northern countries have known no such rupture. The old confusion between economic and political power has been maintained, and countries are on the verge of collapse.

How can we explain the difference between these two categories of countries? Southern countries were more integrated, socially and ethnically, and have been more mobilized. Chile was an exception from the beginning because its political system has long been (at least since the Popular Front [1938] and the second Ibañez presidency) closer to European parliamentary democracies than other Latin American countries. A large part of its population participated actively in political life and the system was strongly autonomous—sometimes even too strongly, as demonstrated by the negative impact of *sectarismo* on the country's economic and social life. But whether peacefully, as in Uruguay, or through political violence, as in Bolivia, political life in the subregion was highly institutionalized. This judgment applies to Argentina, too, dating from the Cordoba reform movement and the Yrigoyen mass politics.

The situation in Mexico was, paradoxically, the opposite—this in a country that had been transformed by a long and violent revolution in which social mobilization by peasants and workers played a key role. Following political consolidation of the revolution, after Calles and up until Cárdenas, the country became politically apathetic. Its political life was limited to a monopolistic one-party system. For most Mexicans, especially the urban poor and the southern *campesinos*, political participation meant little, and *caciquismo* or *caudillismo* were more real than democracy.

Colombia was not an integrated country, and the control exerted by central power on the national territory was limited. Political life was even more limited in Venezuela, where parties and unions formed an isolated political class. The impact of guerrillas, urban and rural, demonstrated the narrow limits of political mobilization.

A large Indian population is linked everywhere in the region with internal colonialism. (Pablo González Casanova and Rodolfo Stavenhagen have acutely described the internal heterogeneity of Mexican society.) The same can be said of Peru but not of Bolivia, where the 1952 revolution and the action of the MNR were based on strong mobilization of peasants and tin miners and on tight links between social and political movements. The Bolivian case indicates that even in the transition period, active social and political participation and the formation and activation of social actors are essential components of development. We should not conclude from the previous analysis that political processes are independent from social phenomena. It is just that during the transition period, when the main problem is to eliminate the old political system, the key to success is having the capacity to build an autonomist political system as a countervailing force to an open economy.

This conclusion is supported by the double failure of both the new populist movements and liberal political programs.

After the end of dictatorships in the South and at the time of a ripening political crisis in Mexico, Venezuela, and other countries, leftist forces, linking neopopulist movements with parties or unions whose main following was in the modern economic sector, began to appear in many countries, including Mexico, Brazil, Argentina, and Uruguay. Some minor attempts appeared in Peru and Bolivia or in a noninstitutional form in Venezuela. None of these forces reached power, although some were able to win important local or regional elections. The most successful was the PT in Brazil, which combined militants of the old ideological left with free unions created by Lula from 1977 on. The PT was active in the modern industries of the São Paulo area and with a "party of the poor" best exemplified by Erundina, *nordestina,* who was elected mayor of São Paulo. But this coalition was too weak and the distance between moderates and radicals too wide for PT to become a government party. While modern unions become more conservative, adopting North American business unionism, the PT and the CUT identified themselves with the defense of the public sector (in the same way as the unions in France took action in November-December 1995). This transformed the political reform movement into a neoconservative corporatist force, whereas the major problem of the country is to rebuild a stronger state oriented more toward national integration rather than to the defense of middle-class vested interests.

In Mexico, the weakness of neo-Cardenismo has been even more visible. The distance between this neo-populism and the efforts of Muñoz Ledo, former president of the PRD, to revitalize the party-system, became so wide that the PRD lost the 1995 presidential election, and in so doing a large part of its previous popular support as well.

The inability of the neopopulist left to propose a convincing alternative is evidence that in the present situation, the reconstruction of the political system is a precondition for mass mobilization. This reconstruction appears to be even more strategically important than the implementation of a purely liberal policy. The Dominican Republic is one of the few examples of a successful liberal policy—not at the societal level but at a purely electoral level. But its relative success involved, essentially, incorporation into the American economy, which contradicts the general orientation of Latin American countries toward autonomous national economic systems. Is it not clear that in countries with such extreme inequalities, a purely liberal orientation, which can produce a still wider distance between rich and poor, leads to an enormous risk of social unrest?

A state busy managing the relationship between the country and the international market and institutions can no longer play its traditional double role of supporting both economic development and social integration. The latter, in particular, can no longer be carried out from the top down, through channels of political influence and clientele; it can be realized only through more-formal political processes, from elections to interactions among public authorities, interest groups, local leaders, and nongovernmental organizations. The reconstruction of the state—which is one of the major objectives of President Cardoso in Brazil and which has been an ongoing preoccupation in Argentina, Colombia, and Mexico—is the necessary counterpart to more-autonomous political institutions and the creation of a representative democracy. Here again, the Chilean situation is so different that it is tempting to consider it the main reason for Chile's positive economic achievement. The capacity both of right-wing parties and the *Concertación* to channel within the political system social or economic forces which could otherwise support political violence—especially on the extreme right, that could count on the support of Pinochet—has created a wide political spectrum favorable to economic initiatives, in the same way that the Moncloa agreement in Spain strongly enhances the chances of long-term economic modernization.

New Social Actors

What should be the main objective of a reconstructed political system? The answer finds a broad consensus. The pattern of Latin American development has been dominated by structural heterogeneity, dualization, and separation between informal and formal sectors. In some countries, such as Mexico, the contrast between the northern and southern portions of the country both in rural areas and in cities is constantly growing. Manufacturing industries increasingly are concentrated on the American border because of the advantages received by *maquiladoras*. So while poverty plagues Oaxaca, Guerrero, or Chiapas, frontier towns are booming. Both the public and the government are aware that national unity is threatened by such a situation. Occasional political violence has broken out from Vera Cruz to Chihuahua, and the two important guerrilla outbreaks that shook Guerrero in the early 1970s explain the country's more recent political violence.

Guatemala's extreme social inequalities and the decline of subsistence agriculture, especially in the Quiche area, as a consequence of the development of export crops on the coast are important factors behind the political violence that has devastated this country. In Peru, even if the Shining Path is by no means a poor-peasant movement, the "prolonged popular war" was made possible by the extreme poverty of *altiplano* peasants. The level of violence has been lower in Brazil, in spite of extreme social inequality and the boldness of large landowners in flouting the law. A large number of *posseiros* have been assassinated not only in the north but also in the northeast and even in São Paulo. Urban violence has spread, especially in Rio de Janeiro and nearby Baixada Fluminense. Uruguay is the only country that has successfully resisted this general trend toward wider inequality.

An autonomous political system is best understood if we recognize that the construction or strengthening of national integration is the most difficult, but the most important, goal to reach. Colombia is today an extreme example of disruption of national unity. Until recently, Guatemala was deeply divided by political violence which—especially during the 1978–1982 period, became a virtual ethnocide.

The situation is less dramatic in the South. In Brazil, the *Real Plan* has meant a relative improvement in the situation of the poor, who were directly hit by inflation while middle-class and rich people were protected by sliding scales. Here again, one must mention the strong plea made by PREALC and ECLAC economists for the repayment of the social debt and for development with equity. Even in Chile, where a high rate of economic growth has raised part of the population out of poverty, social inequality between the top two and bottom two population deciles has remained the same, and a large middle class rejects the poorest of the poor more and more openly, perceiving them as in nineteenth century Europe as "dangerous" classes.

This brings us again to the central argument of this analysis: priority must be given to building of a new autonomous political system, the main objective of which will be to limit the gap between rich and poor people and regions. Rich countries may be able to get away with temporarily increasing social inequality without risk of major crisis, even if there is some social violence. But Latin American countries, where economic and cultural integration is weaker, cannot exacerbate social inequality without major risks of social rupture, widespread violence, and political chaos.

In all countries, and especially in the institutionally weaker ones, reducing social inequity requires strong centralization because local authorities are influenced more by *caciques* or *caudillos* than by popular pressure groups. Here again, addressing political and institutional problems must be a priority. Chile gives strong decision-making capacity to the president, and the Mexican regime does so even more. But the situation is different in Argentina, especially now that the capital has the right to elect its mayor, whose power, as much as that of the governor of the Province of Buenos Aires, can limit the powers of the president. Brazil, which had a long discussion between presidentialists and parliamentarists during the constitutional debate, is suffering from a weak executive branch. Of course, a strong decision-making capacity in the hands of the president is not enough. There must also be complementarity between strong executive power and representative political institutions. From that point of view, the United States stands as the most replicable example.

The second "positive" priority needed for economic and social development is the creation or growth of an entrepreneurs class. Unfortunately, the present situation is more negative than positive in many countries. In Brazil in particular—where the most important *"núcleo endógeno de desarrollo,"* to use Fajnzylber's expression, had been created— the imperative to avoid any new inflationary trend creates problems for entrepreneurs handicapped by too high a rate of exchange. In Mexico, many small companies working for the domestic market have collapsed. The Barzón movement by small entrepreneurs protesting against the banks and government demonstrates their despair, a despair politically significant enough to have contributed to the signing of a political agreement with the Zapatista movement in Chiapas. Argentina is far from succeeding in building a strong national industrial base because speculation is still more attractive than investment, and corruption in government circles is still widespread. Even in Chile, primary exports and international financial operations are more significant than industrial development, technological innovation and social redistribution.

More generally, Latin America's political life has been influenced more by urban middle-class consumers than by entrepreneurs. The region's rate of internal savings has been generally insufficient. Nevertheless, there has been some progress: in universities, business-oriented programs have expanded, while traditional professions, more directly linked with the states, are losing ground.

That leads to an analysis of the formation of new "popular" actors. Until now, it has been maintained here that the role of such actors in the transition process has been limited because they were dependent on a nationalist-populist state. Examples are the *pelégos* unions in Brazil, the *charros* in Mexico, or even the Argentinian CGTs. But it would be misleading to conclude that the development process in Latin America should be limited to institutional reforms, free-trade policies, and a new inflow of foreign capital. It is difficult to conceive of transforming an outward-looking process into a policy that comes from within, without taking into consideration the organization and expression of internal demands. Here again, however, it is necessary to underline the deep differences between northern and southern Latin America.

In the southern countries, including Brazil, it seems that the political system itself will play the major role in developing the new social actors and that we are observing a "supply side" political system—that is, political influence determines to a large extent the formation of social demand. In Argentina, where the employment situation has seriously deteriorated, the CGT has come to life after a long period of ineffectiveness. In terms of reorganization of the political system, this is a favorable development, even though it could give new strength to the same radical ideologies that led from 1974 on to political violence. The dismissal of Domingo Cavallo by President Menem and the acute conflicts within presidential circles created an opening for the left. In Brazil, the PT channels popular protest, but in a more independent way, and the *Sem Terra* movement has become more influential. This pressure could be welcomed by a president who considers the intermediary bodies as his most dangerous opponents. Finally, there is a growing discontent in Chile, even within the majority parties, against the extreme liberal policy and the priority given by the government to join the NAFTA agreement. By signing an agreement with MERCOSUR, Chile seems to be giving new priority to a more regional pattern of development.

The situation is very different in northern countries where the political system is weak. In such a situation, several processes are likely to develop. The first is chaos, resulting from the inability to organize a national development model. In Colombia, lack of security prompts companies to work for foreign markets, while internal markets shrink and become fragmented as transportation difficulties worsen. Since the 1994 crisis, the Mexican situation is the most fragile. Serious efforts are being made to strengthen the political system: for example, the recent electoral law aims to eliminate fraud, and many Mexicans, including political observers, consider victory by PAN in next parliamentary elections a strong possibility. Others, however, foresee a quite different prospect in Mexico—that is, the possible militarization of a country where the army has traditionally been as subordinated to political power as it was in the Soviet Union. The unification of the two main military organizations, the subordination of the police in the Federal District to the army, and the militarization of Guerrero and part of Chiapas are arguments in favor of this thesis. A more positive scenario for Mexico, as well as for other countries with large indigenous populations, is that new Indian movements will fight both for the survival of their cultural identity and for more economic and political participation.

In the past, it was the guerrilla movements organized by middle-class radicals that tried to destroy the political system in the name of poor peasants and Indians, often either without their direct participation or with serious misunderstandings, as was the case in Guatemala. More recently, Indian movements have become active supporters of the democratization process. In the Mexican case after the 1994 insurrection, the Zapatista movement rapidly reoriented itself toward political negotiation. The group enjoyed the indirect support of many politicians and intellectuals, who saw in the San Andres negotiation, however briefly, an important element of political reconstruction, provided that negotiation covered the most general institutional or even constitutional problems. The importance of the message of Subcomandante Marcos, widely diffused by the media, is to substitute democratic action for armed protest, but at the same time to infuse social demands into a political system still almost entirely disconnected from those who are protesting. The weakness of Mexico's government makes it difficult to predict how it will react in the face of such a new challenge, which Jorge Castañeda has called "reformism in arms." But the Zapatista example is not isolated. In nearby Guatemala, Rigoberta Menchu, whose family participated in the guerrilla movement and was victim of the government's violence, launched the movement for democracy and peace, which is supported by women's organizations, NGOs, and elements of the Church. In Colombia, the guerrilla movement M19 was the first to lay down its arms and incorporate itself into institutional politics. More extreme is the transformation of the katharist movement in Bolivia, which, after a period of radical action, made an alliance with President Sanchez de Losada, who gave the Aymara leader, Victor Hugo Cárdenas, the honorific function of vice-President.

The main problem of postcommunist European countries is how to introduce a market economy and substitute it for the command economy. The problem of Latin American countries is now the opposite: how to transform an outward-looking economic policy into an integrated system of national or regional economic and social development. The fragility of the political system makes chaos a possibility. Several countries are far from being legal states; but, once the adjustment has broken traditional protections, the reconstruction of a development pattern must be based first on the relative autonomization of the economic and the political systems. Then, during the second phase of the process of societal change, the revitalization of the political system will require a more direct intervention of social actors directly interested in increasing society's self-control, particularly entrepreneurs and underprivileged urban and rural segments of the population. Rightly, many Mexicans speak of the growing activity of civil society in their country. It is possible that this informal political society will be limited to a subordinate role, like the informal sector in economic life. But the opposite hypothesis should be seriously considered. As in industrial countries, political life is being deeply transformed by NGOs, associations, and informal groups, which are often created or supported by intellectuals and by (a growing number of) politicians. This growing influence of the informal political sector and its transformation into a formal political role serve as important protection against political violence, which would likely increase if there were a prolonged crisis of political institutions.

Latin America has long been a region with a deficit of actors. In contrast with its superficial image as a continent of revolutions, Latin America has experienced more revolutionary situations than revolutionary movements, and frustrated hopes have been more common than organized radical action. Intellectuals have contributed to the weakness of radical politics by promoting ideologies that corresponded more to foreign theories than to national realities. Now that the region is emerging from a long and painful liberal transition, its main choice is between chaos, crime, and violence on one side and the formation of new social movements, serious political reforms, and a successful struggle against extreme inequality on the other.

Governability and Equity: Key Conditions for Sustained Development

Edgardo Boeninger[1]

Political stability, economic progress, and social peace are basic national goals shared by almost every country in the contemporary world. Democracy is clearly the only path that can lead to political stability in Latin America, fragile as in many cases it still is. Economic progress means growth. And social peace requires that people perceive that the development process is increasing social equity. These three are closely interrelated and interdependent. If any single one of them is absent for a significant period, the others cannot be sustained.

Whatever the differences on development issues and options among economists may be, they do appear to share a broad consensus on the policies required to produce or enhance growth. Most of the policies advocated in the Washington consensus have in fact become conventional wisdom. Yet economic performance in Latin America is uneven and on average rather poor despite the fact that well-trained economists increasingly hold key government positions throughout the region.

The only consistent regionwide progress in recent years has been in reducing inflation, and with some exceptions even there. These gains have been achieved through political determination, autonomous central banks, pressures by the IMF and the World Bank, and social consensus on the negative effect of inflation on real incomes of workers and lower-income groups. But sustained growth remains elusive for most of the region, unemployment soars, and income distribution worsens. Under these circumstances, full implementation of the orthodox policy menu will likely face strong opposition. It is therefore fair to say that the region faces problems of governability that must be dealt with if policies for stabilization and growth are to be sustained.

In the democratic framework of Latin America, governability requires an enduring political majority as well as social acquiescence. Only a solidly structured political system can provide such conditions. This is fundamentally a matter of political institutions such as party systems, parliaments, electoral systems, independent judiciaries and the rule of law, issues which are not usually part of the agendas of economic meetings.

Beyond the need for effective institutions, political majorities and social acceptance for economic policy cannot be sustained unless some highly sensitive sociopolitical issues

---

[1] Former Minister, President, Chilena del Pacífico Foundation.

are dealt with in ways perceived as contributing to fair outcomes. Economic processes are known to produce short-term losers, precisely identified as such, conscious of their fate and reluctant to bear the costs of change, in contrast with long-term winners widely spread throughout society and often unaware of future benefits during the early stages of policy implementation. Distributional issues are therefore at the heart of socio-political conflicts. Present trends suggest that environmental issues will also become increasingly contentious in the years ahead.

The political and economic (technical) dimensions of issues must be integrated into a cohesive whole if we are to deal simultaneously and consistently with social discomfort, the constraints of reality, the force of nostalgia, and the presumptuousness of new ideologies.

Consensus-weakening questions and concerns are on the rise. Is the Washington consensus a set of policies applicable to all countries and circumstances? Does macroeconomic policy translate by itself into a development strategy? If so, will Latin America have to face the high levels of structural unemployment that so many developed nations have had to live with in recent times? Even in fast-growing Chile, estimates indicate only a 1 percent increase in employment for 1996 (versus population growth of 1.3 percent), as compared to 7 percent growth in GDP.

There is no longer any room for planning in the conventional sense of the word, and success stories cannot simply be copied. For instance, in Southeast Asia and Japan, "industrial policy" involved export subsidies for prospective winners on a highly selective basis for limited periods of time, as well as a number of protectionist devices to shield domestic production from imports. In our age of economic internationalization, free-trade agreements, and worldwide liberalization, such policies are no longer feasible. Furthermore, in the political and cultural setting of Latin America, selective and supposedly temporary support for infant industries usually resulted in lasting across-the-board subsidies.

I do believe there is room for a contemporary governability-enhancing version of interventionism, perhaps best defined as a "strategic orientation." Conceived as a participatory process involving all relevant actors, it could lead to a long-term "national vision," a shared understanding of the most likely features and outcomes of the development process, and some insight into the kind of society that is actually being built over time. Job creation, equity concerns, and environmental issues should be built into such a vision.

Only if such a vision perceives the development process to be job-creating and equity-enhancing can we expect the political elite to exercise the leadership essential to achieve and sustain the political majority and social support required for governability.

Such politico-technical decisionmaking and policy implementation processes require a strong state. Certainly the bloated bureaucracies of former years do not fit into contemporary needs. On the other hand, in a democratic framework a strong state does not imply an isolated group of high-level technocrats dictating "good" policies. Instead, close and continuing interaction between technocrats and politicians is the only way to develop consistent policies integrating the political and technical dimensions of issues.

As stated earlier, substantial consensus on economic policy has been achieved, and options are on the whole precisely defined in areas where disagreements subsist. The basic ingredients for building institutions in the political system are well known. Unfortunately, in the field of social equity, no such common ground has as yet developed.

Conservative political forces and neoliberal economists attempt to restrict the equity issue to the task of achieving efficiency in fighting poverty, clearly an exercise in reductionism. On the other hand, progressives counter by emphasizing distribution of income and wealth above all other matters; demands in this regard escalate as the often spectacular increases in living standards of "social winners" become evident for all to see.

Available studies indicate that no important improvement in income distribution can be expected even in the relatively lengthy horizon of a decade. Furthermore, as we all know, most redistributive policies are not precisely growth friendly, and change is inherently gradual in a democratic framework. Its pace is slow and significant results require perseverance and continuity over lengthy periods of time. For these reasons, pro-equity policies focusing only on income redistribution risk coming to a "dead end."

Social equity must be understood as a multidimensional concept simultaneously involving state programs and policies to overcome poverty, reduce the disparities in the quality of life, achieve equality of opportunity, implement protection against uncertainty, discrimination and abuse of power, eliminate social segregation, and improve income distribution.

Antipoverty policies should include economic growth itself, focused and well-managed social programs, and policies for self-sustainment, self-improvement and self-esteem.

Attaining equity in the quality of life requires equalizing broad human development indicators (such as life expectancy, infant mortality rates, etc.) between social classes, and in terms of access to basic services, quality of housing and the surrounding environment, cultural and recreational opportunities, elimination of "social ghettos," and related issues.

Equality of opportunity between social classes, allowing for intergenerational mobility, requires achieving a reasonably even level of quality of education between schools in rich and poor neighborhoods, and in both urban and rural areas. It also means reaching out to ethnic minorities, and certainly addressing gender issues.

Protection against uncertainty means building safety nets such as unemployment insurance schemes (provided they are soundly financed). More broadly, it should be conceived as empowering the underdog, for instance by extending collective bargaining to a larger proportion of workers and transferring resources and decisionmaking power from the central to the local government and neighborhood levels, even though efficiency costs can hardly be avoided in the early stages of such processes. Protection also involves an effective regulatory framework to enhance competition and curb monopoly power.

The difficulty of improving income distribution is no excuse for not facing this most sensitive of issues. The quality of new jobs as well as training and retraining schemes are obvious areas of policy, as is the broader related issue of eventually extending economic modernization to small enterprises and the informal sector.

Tax systems and the rules governing labor relations are crucial elements for social equity. Though only growth-compatible policies are acceptable, there is significant scope for equity-enhancing change in both areas. Tax evasion must be sharply reduced, tax loopholes eliminated and tax credits carefully assessed. Enforcement is of course essential for tax compliance, but so is social attitude. Compliance will only improve significantly if evaders confront the disapproval of fellow citizens.

There is an obvious need for an increase in public resources. At the same time, the tax burden cannot be increased beyond certain levels that might have a negative impact on savings and investment. This leads to two key points:

First, the value-added tax is the single tax best suited to enhance fiscal revenue and fiscal balance. It may not be progressive in itself, but it will contribute to equity if translated into appropriate social expenditures. Second, the time has come for Latin America to produce regional disarmament agreements. No country can be expected to unilaterally reduce its defense expenditures, let alone disband its armed forces in Costa Rican fashion.

Economic and social policies must be both growth friendly and equity enhancing. Substantial progress can be achieved if equity is dealt with on a multidimensional basis. If at the same time Latin America succeeds in building or strengthening its fragile political institutions, the region could look more optimistically to the challenge of simultaneously achieving democratic stability, growth, and social equity.

Jobs and Solidarity: Challenges for Post-Adjustment in Latin America

Victor E. Tokman[1]

This paper examines the search for a new generation of employment policies that bring both jobs and solidarity. These two objectives were the foundation of the socioeconomic order prevailing in most Latin American countries up until the intensive adjustments that followed the debt crisis. What began as a traditional short-term stabilization adjustment in the early 1980s evolved into a full structural transformation that affected not only the foundation of the economic system but also the social order.

A brief review of the main employment and income trends is presented first in order to identify the issues emerging during the process of adjustment. In particular, it is necessary to determine whether jobs are being created fast enough and whether the quality and remuneration of the new jobs are socially acceptable. Poverty and equity outcomes are determined largely by developments in employment.

Establishing priorities and redesigning policies should take into account the transformation of the international economy and how it affects the functioning of the Latin American economies and labor markets. The main processes of change must be identified in order to set the scenario for the new generation of policies. Policy areas for employment creation are then identified, priorities assigned, and instruments redesigned. Some of the new measures are proven means for employment creation that need to be reconverted to fit the new scenario; others are innovations that respond to the emerging issues. As can be anticipated after several years of trial and error in policy innovation, there is increasing common ground that converts some of the new policies into already-accepted best practices. This, of course, leaves some policy areas still subject to controversy. This paper distinguishes between these two sets of policies in order to clarify a new conventional wisdom and to advance the discussion of still-controversial areas.

Finally, a comprehensive attempt is made to see the emerging system as a whole. Although it is recognized that the post-adjustment has only recently begun, the paper identifies the fundamental changes from the old socioeconomic order and offers hypotheses to advance efforts to reach new objectives. In particular, jobs and solidarity, which were the basis of social inclusion in the old system, are also guiding principles that need to be recovered in any emerging situation. The new generation of policies is then

[1] Assistant Director-General and Director for Latin America and the Caribbean, International Labor Office.

identified in a context in which economic progress must bring about social inclusion and increased equity.

Jobs and Incomes: Performance and Principal Emerging Issues

Economic performance and employment and income trends during the last decade and a half are well known. It will suffice here to review them in general terms in order to identify the main issues that must be addressed in the search for a new generation of development policies that relate to the dynamics of job creation and to poverty and equity outcomes during and after adjustment.

Table 4.1 presents the main social and economic trends for Latin America from 1980 to 1995. The decade of the 1980s was characterized by adjustment to the debt crisis and, more structurally, to the new economic environment. Adjustment and its effects were concentrated mainly in the first half of the decade, although country experiences differ. Total output was stagnant up to 1984 and then slowly recuperated. The recovery continued in the 1990s, although growth slowed in 1995 due to major adjustments in Mexico, Argentina, and Uruguay, among others. The sustainability of growth is then put in question. Slow or no growth was accompanied by rapid inflation in the 1980s, while the late 1980s and the 1990s showed continuous progress in reducing inflation in all countries. These trends took place in a context of accelerated reduction of fiscal deficits and an important opening up of economies, as expressed by the rapid expansion of exports and imports.

The supply of labor shows a double trend. On the one hand, and as a result of the advanced stage of demographic transition of most countries, population and labor force expansion began to slow down. On the other, the process of migration from rural to urban areas continued and by 1995 three-quarters of the labor force was in cities as compared to 67 percent in 1980. In spite of the lower supply pressure, the employment and income situation deteriorated. Three main changes can be observed in the employment evolution: insufficient job creation, lower quality of employment, and decreasing wages, particularly during the period of adjustment.

Low economic growth during the first half of the eighties was insufficient to absorb the newcomers to the labor market, resulting in an expansion of open unemployment, which reached its peak by 1985. Although unemployment levels reached are not high by international standards, this is partly explained by the accelerated expansion of low-quality employment, mostly in informal activities. Employment in the informal sector expanded as a percentage of nonagricultural employment from 40 percent to more than 50 percent between 1980 and the early 1990s. In fact, eight out of ten new jobs created were informal during the past 15 years. Public employment, particularly after 1985, reduced its contribution to employment creation as a result of adjustment and privatization. Finally, both minimum and manufacturing wages decreased during the 1980s, and in 1990 were below the 1980 level by 31 percent and 13 percent, respectively.

The poor economic performance of the 1980s resulted in an increase in poverty. The percentage of households below the poverty line increased from 35 percent to 39 percent,

TABLE 4.1. Latin America: Economic Activity, Employment, Wages and Poverty, 1980–95

(Annual rates of growth and index)

Indicator	1980	1985	1990	1995
Economic activity				
GNP[1]	—	0.6	1.9	2.9
GNP per capita[1]	—	-1.6	-0.1	1.0
Inflation[1]	—	134.8	487.5	279.4
Population and employment				
Population[1]	—	2.1	1.9	1.8
EAP total[1]	—	3.5	3.1	2.6
EAP urban (%)	66.9	70.0	72.8	75.3
Nonagricultural employment[1]	—	3.5	4.4	3.0
Rate of open unemployment	6.7	10.1	8.0	7.8
Informality (%)[2]	40.2	47.0	52.1	55.7
Public employment (%)[3]	15.7	16.6	15.5	13.6
Wages				
Real wages in manufacturing	100.0	93.1	86.8	96.3
Minimum real wages	100.0	86.4	68.9	70.1
Poverty				
Percentage of poor households	35.0	37.0	39.0	—
Urbanization of poverty[5]	—	91.3	82.9	n.a

Source: ILO on the basis of national statistics and ECLA.
[1] Annual change.
[2] Percentage of self-account workers, microenterprises, and domestic services of nonagricultural employment.
[3] Percentage of public employment on nonagricultural employment.
[4] Refers to 1994.
[5] Increase of urban poor in relation to the increase of all poor.

interrupting the declining trend shown prior to the crisis. Rural poverty, however, remained constant while urban poverty grew: 63 percent of poor households are now in cities. In addition, 88 percent of the 60 million new poor are urban. Poverty expansion has also concentrated in the nonindigent poor who account for 80 percent of the new poor. This is the result of the deterioration of middle-income groups because of changes in the employment situation and the reduction of social expenditure, combined with the processes of privatization and targeting. Middle-income groups, many of them public employees, were affected by job losses or reduction of wages, while at the same time they suffered from cuts in social expenditure or had to pay for public services previously free or subsidized.

The regional performance hides different performances by the various countries. Table 4.2 shows the performances of nine countries over three subperiods: adjustment, recovery, and post-adjustment. The years of each subperiod do not coincide in all countries, but clearly the bulk of adjustment is concentrated in the first half of the 1980s. The evolution of output, employment and poverty shows homogeneity during adjustment and more diversity in the successive periods.

TABLE 4.2. Adjustment and Post-Adjustment
(Indexes)

Countries	Period	Income per capita	Unemployment	Informality[1]	Real wages in manufacturing	Urban Poverty[2]	Income Concentration[2]
I) Adjustment period (compared to the precrisis level)							
Argentina	1980–83	86.1	180.8	102.0	103.9	144.4	100.0
Brazil	1979–83	91.7	104.7	130.3	81.9	127.3	109.3
Chile	1981–83	83.5	211.1	107.5	87.0	120.3	103.8
Colombia	1980–83	98.8	120.6	104.8	109.8	100.0	104.0
Costa Rica	1980–83	85.1	141.7	109.3	86.5	125.0	95.0
Mexico	1981–84	91.8	135.7	101.4	69.5	106.3	100.0
Peru	1982–84	90.2	134.8	100.0	69.9	110.2	114.7
Uruguay	1981–86	90.8	159.7	117.3	97.9	155.6	—
Venezuela	1981–86	86.7	177.9	130.2	93.7	138.9	108.0
II) Recovery period (compared to the level at the beginning of the recovery = 1985)							
Argentina	1991–95	115.0	269.2	108.0	104.0	111.7	—
Brazil	1993–95	106.5	88.9	101.5	105.4	—	—
Chile	1987–95	149.5	44.5	101.4	139.2	61.5	98.8
Colombia	1980–95	133.5	89.7	117.3	124.3	105.6	100.0
Costa Rica	1985–95	118.7	85.1	122.9	115.4	109.7	103.0
Mexico	1991–94	101.4	233.3	102.2	116.1	107.1	—
Peru	1992–95	121.9	75.5	102.8	111.6	92.5	—
Uruguay	1985–95	133.7	80.0	95.9	118.2	57.1	61.2
Venezuela	1989–95	106.7	97.9	115.5	70.9	122.2	101.0
III) Post-adjustment (compared to the precrisis level = 1980)							
Brazil	1987–95	106.5	75.0	167.4	102.9	130.0	104.0
Chile	1987–95	139.8	58.9	100.4	118.1	53.3	98.8
Colombia	1986–95	133.5	89.7	117.3	101.9	105.6	101.0
Costa Rica	1988–95	103.6	95.0	126.9	122.0	113.6	101.0
Uruguay	1989–95	112.8	161.2	117.2	108.2	88.9	79.0

Source: ILO on the basis of national statistics and ECLA.
1 The informality index of the last year of the recovery and post-adjustment refers to 1994.
2 The data for the post-adjustment period refers to 1992, with the exception of Chile (1994).

Adjustment meant a reduction of per capita income and a deterioration of the employment and income situation. Unemployment increased, the quality of jobs deteriorated, and wages fell. Poverty, as a result, expanded. By and large, this evolution was common to all countries, although the intensities were different. The adjustment in the labor market mostly affected unemployment in Argentina and Chile, where employment in the informal sector expanded only moderately. In Brazil, adjustment brought an expansion of low-quality jobs, contributing to keeping unemployment levels low. Real wages in manufacturing industry deteriorated in all the countries except Argentina and Colombia.

The recovery period (that is the period needed to recuperate to the level of output reached before the crisis) also shows some common behavior among countries, but less so than during adjustment. Output expansion allowed for a recovery of per capita income and a reduction of unemployment levels, except in Argentina and Mexico. The recovery was not strong enough to diminish the size of the informal sector, which continued to grow in all countries, while real wages recuperated in all countries except in Venezuela. The data show important reductions of unemployment, but mostly as a result of an expanded level of low-productivity employment. As a result, poverty has continued to grow, except in Chile and Uruguay.

The post-adjustment period is difficult to identify in most countries, since only Chile and Colombia have been able to maintain a high and sustained rate of growth for a significant number of years. The other countries registered growth during varying periods but were affected by successive macroeconomic adjustments of high intensity. The only countries able to recuperate the precrisis per capita output level (circa 1980), were Brazil, Chile, Colombia, Costa Rica, and Uruguay (see last panel of Table 4.2). All of those countries except Uruguay managed to reduce unemployment and increase real wages, but only in Chile did the share of informal jobs hold steady. The results in terms of poverty and equity are mixed. Chile and Uruguay were able to reduce poverty, while Brazil, Colombia, and Costa Rica did not. However, equity improved only in Uruguay.

While it is clear, then, that adjustment negatively affects employment performance and increases poverty and inequity, the effects during the post-adjustment are not as homogeneous. In particular, it is difficult to anticipate whether after adjustment a new policy behavior emerges. Several issues can, however, be identified for policy formulation. The first is that growth is a necessary condition for reducing unemployment, but its rhythm and stability also matter. The second is that wages are determined more by the degree of success in controlling inflation than by the evolution of the labor market. The third refers to the quality of the new jobs created. In spite of recovery, employment generation continues to be concentrated in the informal sector. The result is low-quality jobs and slow growth of productivity. This is a key aspect for competitiveness as well as for equity considerations. Finally, although strong recovery is associated with poverty reduction, improved equity does not necessarily follow. Only in Uruguay do we observe such a correlation, while in Chile, despite a significant reduction of poverty, income distribution remained highly unequal. The data suggest that an increase in the level of employment contributes to poverty reduction, reinforced in the cases of Chile and Uruguay by a significant increase in social expenditure targeted at the poor. But the majority of the new jobs for the poor were informal. Their incomes thus grow at a slower pace than average income and a much slower pace than those of high-income groups. Hence, income differentials tend to widen and consequently, inequality increases.

The New Structural Scenario

The emerging scenario is characterized by three main processes: globalization, privatization, and deregulation.

Globalization means that national economies are today more integrated into the international economy and that goods, capital, communications, and people are more closely linked than ever before in the past. This has been the result of opening up economies and of rapid technological change. Trade and financial liberalization has resulted from the reduction of tariff and nontariff barriers through multilateral agreements such as the GATT and the creation of its successor, the World Trade Organization (WTO); by new or reactivated integration schemes, such as NAFTA and MERCOSUR; by an explosion of bilateral trade agreements during recent years; and most importantly, by establishing unilateral tariff reduction as a key component of adjustment policy. The tariff for Latin America decreased from 35–100 percent on average for minimum and maximum levels in 1985, to 14–22 percent in the early 1990s. Diversification of the tariff structure was also greatly reduced, being limited in most countries to three or fewer tariff categories.

Globalization opens new opportunities for growth and job creation but at the same time affects the determinants of employment and wages and requires regulation to avoid spurious international competition. Given the differences in factor endowments, it is expected that trade from developing to developed countries will be concentrated in goods that are intensive in the use of unskilled labor.

The prevailing differences of remuneration and labor regulations among countries could generate trade expansion based on unfair labor practices or increased exploitation of workers. This has resulted in an international discussion about how to avoid this outcome and whether there is need for additional regulation. While there is no general agreement on how to proceed, it is clear that nobody postulates the equalization of wages among countries, since this would affect the competitive position of developing countries. Nor it is accepted that trade expansion should be based on labor exploitation. Trade sanctions for those who do not comply with minimum international standards have also been discussed.

Privatization is the second feature of the new scenario. This implies a decrease of size and functions of government and an increasing importance of the private sector and markets in the management and allocation of resources. Public-employment falls and public enterprises are transferred to national or international private capital. Privatization also meets the need to reduce fiscal deficits during adjustment. In addition, and this is a subject to which attention has not been sufficiently paid, the responsibility for investment is increasingly transferred to the private sector, limiting public investment to basic infrastructure and social sectors and even here with increasing participation of the private sector.

Deregulation, the third feature, has meant reducing protection and government intervention in trade, finance, and labor markets. Trade and financial liberalization are leading to increased globalization, while reducing protection in product and labor markets has been introduced to increase economic efficiency and to allow for a greater role for markets in the allocation of resources. The process of deregulation has also led to substantial legal reforms.

This triple process of globalization, privatization, and deregulation occurs in an international environment characterized by a universalization of economic and social problems and by an increased ideological homogeneity. The end of the Cold War broke ideological barriers, and present conflicts are led less by ideology than by local interests and reactions against the social cost of adjustment. Today, employment and social-exclusion problems are no longer concentrated solely in developing countries but constitute a major problem even in the more developed economies of the world. Unemployment in the OECD countries is high and has not decreased, affecting more than 30 million people. Another 10 million are no longer actively searching for jobs (OECD 1994a and ILO 1996). The average rate of unemployment exceeds 10 percent, and in some vulnerable groups, such as youth, one out of five is unemployed.

It is in this new scenario that the search for a new policy framework leading to more productive employment creation must be focused. The changes in societies and economies and increased universality require fundamental adaptations in instruments and strategies. Beyond that, a systemic change is needed that offers an alternative to the old socioeconomic order. In the following sections we shall review first the policy areas for employment creation where an emerging consensus exists and second, those in which different views and approaches still prevail.

Emerging Consensus on New Policies for Employment Creation

Growth

Job creation is determined mainly by what happens outside the labor market. This is an issue on which there is general agreement, and it highlights the dependency of job creation on economic growth, which in turn depends on investments and savings.

A clear lesson learned from the recent adjustment experience is that without economic growth there are no possibilities of creating productive employment.

Growth possibilities in a globalized world are increasingly associated with trade and international finance, since the opening up of economies means enlarged access to world markets and more-mobile capital. In addition, privatization transfers an increased responsibility for investments from government to the private sector. Public employment is no longer the main source (and in most cases, not even a source at all) of job creation as it was in the past in Latin America. This in turn has at least three important effects on the relationship between economic and social policies.

As private entrepreneurs assume increasing responsibility for the creation of new jobs, they will have to invest more. This requires adequate incentives and, in particular, sound macroeconomic policy, attractive returns to investment, and stability. Stability refers not only to low inflation but more comprehensively to the rules of the game. And that is closely related to the degree of social commitment to existing policies. Such commitment requires a perception of "fairness" by all social groups, in the sense that everybody receives a fair share of economic progress (Solow 1989). And this is difficult to achieve when there exist widespread poverty, very low wages, inadequate working conditions or unbalanced bargaining powers. On the other hand, labor policies can contribute to economic growth and, particularly, to savings and stability.

A more competitive international environment requires closer monitoring of the labor dimensions of trade. Trade expansion cannot be based on exploited labor, since this will increasingly affect not only the country where exploitation takes place but also its trading partners. That is the justification for the introduction of new regulatory mechanisms that can safeguard against labor abuses as an instrument for trade gains.

There is also agreement on the instruments that must be used to accelerate growth of the world economy: this refers in particular to better macroeconomic-policy coordination among major countries, a reduction of interest rates, and a better balance and sequencing between fiscal and monetary policies, as well as a reduction in exchange market fluctuations and in capital volatility.

A crucial aspect still under debate concerns the inadequacy of present macroeconomic-policy management to contribute to full employment. The required rate of growth generally exceeds that is allowed by sound macroeconomic management, particularly because of the post-adjustment features of financial and exchange markets. They mostly result in high interest rates and overvalued rates of exchange, both restricting economic growth. Thus, the employment creation responsibility is shifted to labor policies, which can have only a limited influence; but, in addition, overshooting in other markets transfers an exaggerated burden of adjustment to the labor market. Unless policy interventions ensure a more friendly financial environment for growth and employment creation, labor policy reforms alone will bear the principal burden of job creation, a policy doomed to failure.

The Return of "Industrial Policies"

After a period of relying mainly—and in some cases exclusively—on macroeconomic policies, the need to introduce additional dimensions to economic management is increasingly acknowledged. Three of these dimensions crucial for employment creation are sectoral policies, local policies, and size of enterprises.

Sectoral policies are needed, for example—particularly a specific policy for the rural sector, both in the traditional and the agribusiness segments. The traditional rural sector concentrates deep poverty and subsistence jobs, and in some countries, it is also the focus of a high concentration of vulnerable ethnic groups, particularly the indigenous population. The problems in this sector go beyond economic management and include the need for infrastructure to integrate the territory physically; land redistribution to alleviate land restriction; land ownership to avoid precariousness; and access to resources and markets. Special social investments are also needed, since social deficiencies in education, health, and nutrition reach their highest levels in these areas. Modernization of agriculture, which in many countries has meant the introduction of agribusinesses for export, is accompanied by new occupational problems that also require particular attention. The most pressing problems are the use of child labor, discrimination against women, occupational hazards, and lack of protection and of labor rights, particularly of collective bargaining for seasonal workers.

The second dimension is the local or regional aspect. Although related to sectoral issues, this dimension refers specifically to the concentrated impact of economic restructuring on local labor markets. Indeed, economic restructuring of major industries in mining, manufacturing, and basic services has affected big enterprises that were the main pillars of local labor markets. Restructuring has meant downsizing and privatizing. Increased unemployment at the local level is then accompanied by a lack of alternative opportunities for highly specialized workers in age cohorts of full activity. This requires policies for labor reconversion to adapt the affected workers to new opportunities; additional investment to generate such opportunities; and protection and indemnities to compensate for transitory costs, diminish vulnerability and stimulate mobility, both occupational and geographical.

A third dimension of utmost importance from an employment perspective is the size of establishments and, particularly, the need for policies to support small firms and microenterprises and the informal sector in general. More than half of nonagricultural employment in Latin America can be found in this sector, which also accounts for eight out of 10 new jobs created in the last 15 years (ILO 1995). Productivity levels are very low, and the gap with modern-sector enterprises is large and growing. This explains the concentration of underemployment and low incomes in these small enterprises. It follows that, given the constraints that exist for a sufficient expansion of employment in the modern sector, there is a need to improve the economic and social situation of people working in these small-scale and informal activities.

Policies for the informal sector are well known and widely applied, at least at pilot levels. They range from providing a friendly regulatory environment, to productive support and new forms of protection. The regulatory environment includes not only an adequate regulatory framework but also a more friendly administrative process to allow for compliance. Administrative simplification, automatic processing, and reduction of regulations constitute an urgently needed policy package. But the regulatory environment by itself will not solve structural deficiencies related to lack of access to resources and markets. This requires another set of policies to facilitate access to capital, skills, technology, and more dynamic markets. Finally, social and labor protection must be redesigned to incorporate those today excluded, since current forms of protection were conceived for those occupying jobs in modern activities (Tokman 1994).

There is also a need to pass from successful pilot projects to systemic results. General measures like providing a friendly regulatory environment or easing the access to credit have a great potential reach, but their effect will depend on the extent and sustainability of the response. To promote such a response, there is a need to combine general with selective interventions. This should be perhaps the main objective of programs supporting microenterprise development: to contribute during a limited period to creating an economic behavior that neither the market nor the characteristics of the informal units can automatically ensure.

Investing in People

A third area of consensus is on the need to invest in people, particularly in education and training. This is obviously not a new idea, but its priority and the way to approach it are affected by the changing world conditions.

The experience of recent decades shows that economic growth is increasingly knowledge intensive and that the more successful countries are those that have invested heavily in educating and training. It is also becoming clear that the illiterate and those who do not have access to adequate education are becoming the new marginalized segment in society. Investing in education and training, while always necessary, has now become an essential requirement for progress both of nations and individuals in a globalized world.

Changes in skill profile and job content associated with the new wave of technological change are creating a demand for competencies rather than for specialized skills. These competencies are associated with abilities mainly provided at primary level, and hence the reform has to go beyond the technical sphere. There is thus room for a new alliance between primary education and technical secondary-level training.

The emerging model presents several additional characteristics that differentiate it from the prevailing one, in particular a shift from supply to demand-driven education and training in order to respond better to labor market requirements. This requires closer links between training and the enterprises, as well as increased emphasis on the redesigning of secondary levels, since, as argued by Tillet (1995), those levels have proven to be important for those countries successfully experiencing productivity convergence. It is also clear that there are vulnerable groups that require special public attention, particularly youth from poor families, workers in need of labor reconversion (usually associated with privatization), and those already working in informal activities.

Two comments are in order regarding the new configuration of the system. The first refers to the priority allocated to secondary education, particularly at the technical level, since this can be read as contradictory to prevailing wisdom about giving preferential attention to the primary level. For the Latin American countries with almost universal coverage at the primary-education level, the challenge is one of increasing quality and leveling differences among schools attended by the children of the poor. Moreover, the technical capacities demanded by modern enterprises are closely linked to an adequate secondary-level education.

The second comment refers to institutional redesigning to increase the role of enterprises in the training system to ensure a closer link with demand. Not all training can be provided by enterprises, of course. Small and microenterprises are also unable to deliver training by themselves, and this will require other arrangements. But there is agreement to encourage the participation of the private sector in training delivery. All these changes challenge the existing training institutions developed in the framework of the earlier strategy. Should they be closed, or is there room for institutional adaptation? Some are already adapting to the new form of operating and trying to respond to the needs of vulnerable groups. In addition, although training policies should probably be decentralized in their execution, there will be a need for a centralized orientation and monitoring function, to ensure quality levels.

Increasing the Capacity for Employment Creation

In an open economic environment, productivity must be increased because it is the only way to compete internationally and, at the same time, to create adequately remunerated jobs. Labor productivity in Latin America is low. Recent studies show that in manufacturing branches such as food processing and steel, as well as in banking in the most advanced countries of the region (Argentina, Mexico, Brazil, Colombia, and Venezuela), labor productivity is around one-fourth to one-third the prevailing level in the United States. In telecommunications the differences are smaller, around 20 percent, because of the transnational characteristic of this sector (McKinsey Global Institute 1994). The same can be said when the region's labor productivity for the manufacturing sector as a whole is also low compared to that of more-developed countries or to Southeast Asia.

Moreover, productivity differences have increased during the last four and a half decades. Total factor productivity differentials have doubled with Japan, and have increased by 180 percent with the rest of OECD countries (Hoffman 1995). During the 1980s, productivity differentials among sectors and within sectors also tended to increase. Labor productivity of services decreased as a result of an expansion of low-productivity employment and was not offset by the fast expansion of modern services such as telecommunications and banking. A similar trend was observed in manufacturing, where the accelerated productivity growth during the 1990s is concentrated in medium-sized and large enterprises, while productivity increases in small enterprises have been lower or nonexistent.

Productivity is thus low by international standards, and differentials have expanded. At the same time, differences within countries have also tended to widen, creating an increasingly heterogeneous production structure.

There is clearly a need to increase productivity by investing and by adopting specific labor policies. Investment in human development is generally low, and little attention is paid to improving labor relations. There is need in Latin America to introduce a productivity culture not only among entrepreneurs but also among workers. Apart from investment in people, labor organization within enterprises must be improved. Little advance has been made in creating strategies geared toward value-added increases that both improve the situation of the enterprise and create jobs and benefit workers by higher wages.

Productivity strategies are related to changes in the organization of work within enterprises, such as group work, polyvalent functions, and task enrichment. Most big corporations at the international level have moved from cost-reducing strategies to productivity strategies designed to better use technology, which requires an improvement in the labor environment within enterprises. Fiat, for instance, fired 20 thousand workers in the 1980s, but in the 1990s was searching for strategic alliances with trade unions to introduce product innovation, which constituted its major constraint on competition. Increasingly, there is a strategic change from cost reduction to the search for higher quality.

The experience in OECD countries shows that although they have followed different adjustment strategies, there are at least four common features. First, there is a trend to increase the autonomy of the enterprise in adopting human-resources and collective-bargaining policies. Second, within enterprises, there has been more flexibility in terms of reorganizing the labor process, group work, total quality, job rotation and increased complementarity and coordination of tasks. Third, there are increases in training and higher remuneration for more skilled-work or for better performance. Finally, there is a fall in unionization rates (Locke 1995).

An important factor related to the introduction of a productivity culture is the widening of the collective-bargaining agenda to include other issues beyond wage adjustments. There has been too much concentration on wages and too little on how to increase productivity and share the eventual benefits.

It is equally important to promote a change in the entrepreneurial culture of the small entrepreneur. Productivity increases should result from the aforementioned policies, but small enterprises can also benefit from their comparative advantage in terms of flexibility and closeness to clients, which are key to modern productivity and competitiveness strategies. The market requires quality and dates of delivery, while expansion is accompanied by a formalization of labor relations. This exposes small entrepreneurs to a new world of social relations. They have to establish contact with the government to benefit from programs; with banks to gain access to credit; and with big enterprises to reach more-dynamic markets.

This is not an easy task, but recent experience has shown that it is possible. Economic liberalization in Latin America has demonstrated that there is entrepreneurial capacity to penetrate international markets and to compete at home. This has been the result of globalization and the change in macroeconomic management, but it has also been the outcome of public support through free-trade agreements and reciprocal investment guarantees at the international level and by fiscal and promotional instruments at the domestic level.

Targeting Vulnerable Groups

There remains a need for specific policies to assist vulnerable groups. A priority example is the support needed for youth from low-income families. Unemployment severely affects this group. Those who do work are often caught in a vicious circle of premature incorporation into the labor market, because of the family's need for additional income, but very little accumulated human capital. The ultimate result is either unemployment or access to dead-end jobs with scarce possibilities of learning or improving income.

As argued by Tendler on the basis of her analysis of direct programs for vulnerable groups, there is a good experience with government programs when the design follows the best practices applied in innovative enterprises. Decentralization is more effective not when central government disappears, as is usually thought, but when it plays an active role in improving local government and in empowering civil society (Tendler 1994).

Policy Areas under Discussion: Labor Policies for Employment Creation

Three policy areas will be covered here: flexibility, social protection, and the importance of labor costs in international competitiveness.

Increasing Flexibility and Strengthening Social Actors

Economic changes require that enterprises increase their capacity to adapt to demand fluctuations and to a more competitive situation. This has led to the search for flexibility in the production process and in labor organization. The main challenge is to achieve this flexibility without severely reducing workers' protection. Two ways to meet this challenge are to facilitate the process of firing and hiring labor and to decentralize collective bargaining. The first reduces costs and makes it easier to adapt the level of employment, while the latter tends to correlate better the economic conditions prevailing at the company level and wages.

Changes in labor contracts and the diversification of types of contracts have been the main objectives of the many labor legislation reforms introduced in recent years in Latin America. Contracts without time limits have been increasingly replaced by contracts with less stability and fewer commitments. The expected long-term result is an increased level of employment, but the usual short run impact is an expansion of unemployment and job instability. This affects incentives for investing in training both by entrepreneurs and by workers, and it diminishes workers' motivation to increase productivity.

A second major trend, although less important so far in Latin America, is the decentralization of collective bargaining at the company level. This allows enterprises to negotiate wages closer to productivity conditions and ensures wage flexibility according to economic possibilities. The process of decentralization has been universal. National negotiations have been replaced by negotiations by sectors and firms. In a few cases (United Kingdom, New Zealand, and Chile), the firm has been made the only level of wage bargaining (OECD 1994b).

Decentralization of collective bargaining to the company level can also affect the capacity of trade unions to influence national decisions, since their power base is partially derived from collective bargaining at sectoral or national levels. This is not an unavoidable outcome, provided that union strategies can be adapted to the new scenario of industrial relations. There is room in the new setting for national actors and collective action, since only at the national level can they contribute to ensuring solidarity and social incorporation into the economic system. Decentralization of collective bargaining should not be taken as synonymous for decentralization of collective action, nor should bargaining at the firm level be the only level of negotiation. There is a role to be played by federations and confederations of workers in supporting negotiations at different levels, and there are new areas that open possibilities for action at this level, such as training and social security.

The transformation of industrial relations goes further. The social dialogue, to be meaningful, requires incorporation of the "unrepresented." Unions and employer organizations are increasingly approaching the informals, while NGOs are becoming active participants and, on specific given issues, key actors. The agenda for discussion will go beyond wages into training, productivity, and organization of the labor process. Decentralization should not be restricted to the company level since the local community is also becoming a more important space for dialogue and policy implementation, particularly in the social field (Reilly 1996, Raczynski 1996, Hansenne 1996).

There are, then, new rules and new possibilities for collective action. It is clear that decentralization will contribute to responding more rapidly to economic challenges, but it is also recognized that collective action at the national level can contribute distinctive responses to economic stability with social progress. The challenge is to discover how to ensure consistency between negotiations and actions at the different levels.

Redesigning and Enlarging Social Protection

Another key issue in policy formulation is how to adapt social protection to the new situation and how to protect emerging job categories. Lifelong employment is increasingly questioned, and the trend is for permanent employability (Chirac 1996), which involves developing the capacity to adapt to new job requirements without affecting protection. Unemployment insurance combined with recurrent training are central tools in the new generation of protection policies.

A parallel problem that emerges is linked to new occupational forms, such as part-time, subcontracting, and seasonal employment. At present, social protection and labor rights are centered on full-time occupations. But workers in precarious jobs must also be able to exercise basic labor rights, such as freedom of association or collective bargaining, and have access to certain levels of protection related to their particular job situation. This means, for example, allowing such workers to form unions, to collectively negotiate wages and work conditions, and to be protected against work accidents.

To these new challenges for social protection must be added those that have not been covered by present systems of protection, particularly those in informal activities. To sum up, protection should be redesigned to cover a more mobile labor market and to include new categories of worker, while at the same time, the coverage of those traditionally excluded should be enlarged.

Labor Costs and International Competitiveness

It is usually argued that overpriced labor can affect access to international markets. Indeed, in a more competitive environment, costs are even more important. Overpriced labor can be the result of higher wages, high nonwage labor costs, or both.

Wages in most Latin American countries, in spite of the recent recovery, are still lower than in 1980. Minimum wages, on average, were 27 percent lower in 1995 than in 1980, and wages in manufacturing industry 8 percent lower. Nonwage labor costs vary according to countries between 40 percent to 60 percent of wages, higher than in Korea and the United States, but lower than those prevailing in European OECD countries. In addition, labor costs per hour in manufacturing industry are between $2 to $5, between one-fourth and one-eighth of the U.S. level and lower than the level of the Southeast

**TABLE 4.3. Evolution of Labor Costs and International Competitiveness
in Manufacturing, 1990–1995**
(Annual changes)

	Labor costs 1	Labor costs 2	Labor costs 3	Productivity	Competitiveness[4]		
					1	2	3
Argentina	-1.6	9.1	14.4	7.0	8.5	-1.9	-6.5
Brazil	2.9	12.5	8.5	7.5	4.5	-4.4	-0.9
Chile	4.3	6.9	9.4	3.2	-1.1	-3.5	-5.7
Mexico	1.2	4.3	1.5	5.2	4.0	0.9	3.6
Peru	5.1	17.2	11.6	6.6	1.4	-9.0	-4.5

Source: Martínez and Tokman (1996).
[1] Annual changes in real labor costs deflated by the consumer price index.
[2] Annual changes in real labor costs deflated by the producer price index.
[3] Annual changes in real labor costs in U.S. dollars.
[4] Defined as the difference between productivity changes and the respective changes in real labor costs, as defined in the first three notes.

Asian countries. Labor cost differences per unit of output are smaller because of higher productivity in competing countries. This points to the importance of productivity improvements rather than just cost reductions as a major priority to gain competitiveness (Martínez and Tokman, 1996).

Labor costs have not increased beyond productivity in such countries as Argentina, Brazil, Mexico, or Peru. Hence, labor costs in those countries were not constraints to increased access to international markets. But when expressed in foreign currency or observed in relation to producer prices, the situation shows in most cases a loss of competitiveness (see Table 4.3). This stems from the effects of macroeconomic policy during the period, which in most countries was based on overvalued national currencies, both as a result of the need for ensuring an anchor to reduce inflation and because of the liberalization of capital flows. Part of the loss is explained by the delay in adjusting rates of exchange. While labor costs expressed in consumer prices did not grow, they in fact grew rapidly when expressed in relation to producer prices.

Jobs and Solidarity Redefined:
The Basis for a New Generation of Policies

We have reviewed the main trends during and after adjustment, focusing on the identification of emerging labor and income problems. We have also identified the main features of the new structural context, which must be taken into account when designing policies to confront these problems. Globalization, privatization, and liberalization are the three main processes shaping a different economic and social order. Policy instruments cannot ignore these changes. Their adaptation constitutes a necessary condition for their effectiveness. At the same time there is need for new instruments, since the structural transformation has brought about new problems. Objectives remain unchanged, but they cannot be achieved by going back to the past and ignoring the substantial transformation that has taken place in recent years.

FIGURE 4.1. Latin America: Growth and Employment, 1990–1995
(index 1990 = 100)

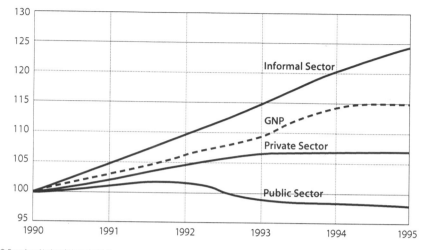

Source: ILO. Based on National Household Surveys.

We have identified policy areas for employment creation and their required specification for the new context. Some of these areas are increasingly accepted, while others are still subject to differing approaches. In fact, defining priorities and redesigning the policy instruments are important to developing a new generation of policies for employment creation.

A fundamental question regarding this new generation of policies is whether as a result of adjustment a new paradigm in terms of equity is emerging in the post-adjustment era. This is a crucial question that cannot yet be answered on the basis of available evidence but ultimately will have to be addressed in order to orient policy decisions in a strategic framework.

Labor and Income in the Post-Adjustment Era

The review of economic performances after adjustment shows that only five countries in Latin America (Brazil, Chile, Colombia, Costa Rica, and Uruguay) have per capita incomes above those prevailing prior to adjustment. Some countries are late reformers, and hence it is still too early to distinguish between short-run and long-term effects.

The available evidence suggests two key issues in the post-adjustment era. The first is that job quality constitutes an unsolved problem. In contrast to the case of the more developed countries, the post-adjustment era in Latin America has not been one of jobless growth, but rather of decreasing unemployment due to the rapid expansion of low-productivity employment. The data for the region as a whole after 1990 show that employment elasticity was 0.83. But this figure hides the fact that the bulk of jobs were of low quality, and employment in the informal sector (including microenterprises)

TABLE 4.4. Growth and Employment in the Post-Adjustment Era

	Elasticities				
	GNP growth (%) (annual rates)	Total urban employment	Employment large private enterprises	Share of informal employment in new employment (%)	Public employment growth (annual rates)
Latin America (1990–94)	3.6	0.83	0.47	84.1	-0.4
Early reformers					
Chile (1987–94)	6.7	0.7	0.9	39.0	3.3
Costa Rica (1988–94)	4.8	0.9	1.3	51.0	0.2
Colombia (1986–94)	4.1	1.0	0.8	75.0	0.1
Late reformers					
Argentina (1991–94)	7.4	0.2	0.2	142.0	-0.6
Brazil (1993–94)	5.8	0.4	-0.1	89.0	3.8
Peru (1992–94)	9.2	0.4	0.5	74.0	-7.0
Mexico (1992–94)	2.3	1.6	2.0	68.0	0.7

Source: ILO, on the basis of official data for each country.

accounted for more than eight of 10 new jobs (Figure 4.1). On the other hand, public employment continued to decrease due to efforts to balance fiscal accounts. Employment in large private enterprises resumed growth but its elasticity was lower than that for total employment (0.47). The situation varies according to countries as can be seen in Table 4.4.

The stage in which each country finds itself in the reform process also influences the employment outcome. If early reformers (Chile, Colombia, Costa Rica) are separated from late reformers (Argentina, Brazil, Peru), it is apparent that the latter group records a lower employment expansion (elasticities of 0.2 to 0.4 as compared to 07 to 1.0).[2]

The second issue is that poverty—and particularly inequity—has not improved. Only Chile and Uruguay show decreases in poverty levels. And even in Chile, which can be considered as the most successful case, the substantial decrease in poverty has not reduced significant income differences prevailing among social groups.

Successful Adjustment without Increased Equity: The Case of Chile

Chile is the only country in the region that has registered eight years of sustained growth in the post-adjustment era, and it has managed to reduce poverty from 38 percent to 24

---

[2] Mexico is also included in Table 4.4 and can be considered a late reformer. As these data are only up to 1994, the results are misleading, since they show a situation of low growth and high employment creation, both informal and in large private companies. The story of 1995 is well known and has resulted in doubling the rate of unemployment and a contraction of both output and employment in large enterprises.

TABLE 4.5. Evolution of Poverty and Income Distribution in Chile, Malaysia, and Indonesia

	Chile		Malaysia		Indonesia	
	1987	**1994**	**1970**	**1990**	**1980**	**1990**
Poverty[1]	38.1	24.1	49.3	17.3	39.1	15.8
Share in total income of						
bottom 20%	4.5	4.6	3.3	4.6	6.6	8.7
upper 20%	56.0	56.1	56.6	53.7	49.4	42.3
Income differentials[2]	12.4	12.2	17.0	12.0	7.5	5.0

Source: Malaysia and Indonesia: World Bank, World Development Report, several issues.
Chile: Ministerio de Planificación, *Encuestas Cassen, 1987 and 1992.* If the World Bank report were used as a source, as in the other countries, the income differential would have increased to 11.7 and 18.3 between 1988 and 1992, and the upper 20 percent would have increased from 51.4 percent to 60.4 percent between the two years.
[1] Percentage of poor households.
[2] Income differentials between the upper and bottom 20 percent.

percent. In addition to sustained and rapid growth there was also lower inflation, higher employment and higher real wages, and a substantial expansion of social expenditure. But income differentials between the top and the bottom 20 percent remain constant at around 4 percent to 5 percent for the bottom group and around 56 percent for the top group (Table 4.5). The question is, why is there no improvement in income distribution?

It is interesting to compare the Chilean evolution with that of other successful countries such as Malaysia and Indonesia, which also registered sustained growth and reduced poverty, yet managed to increase equity as well. Poverty decreased in Malaysia from 49 percent to 17 percent between 1970 and 1990, while income differentials between the top and the bottom 20 percent diminished from 17 to 12. A similar record is observed in Indonesia from 1980 to 1990 when poverty decreased from 39 percent to 16 percent and income differentials from 7.5 to 5.[3] Why?

The expectation is that inequality would decrease over time, as shown by Tinbergen in 1975 and in the pioneering studies of Kuznets, after a period of increased concentration in the early stages of development. In fact, the data available for developed countries show such a trend in the 1970s for countries other than the United States. Inequality fell in the United Kingdom in the first half of the 1970s and for the period up to 1981 in Sweden. In Finland, France, and Italy there was a fall in the Gini coefficient between 1970 and the mid-1980s of some 5 percentage points or more. But this trend has been interrupted, showing increases in inequality or at best no change. Inequality showed an upward trend in the United States from the end of the 1960s. In the United Kingdom there was a marked rise of income inequality from 1979 to 1989, and the same happened in Sweden between 1988 and 1991 (Atkinson 1996; Krugman 1995). In light of this empirical evidence, it could be argued that Chile is presently following a path similar to that

---

[3] As reported by Fukuchi (1996), there has also been a narrowing wage gap between higher and lower skill groups in Indonesia, while wage differentials in Chile have increased.

of developed countries as a result of the new and more universal orientation of economic policies, without having passed through the stage of increased equity registered in those countries.

Even in the case of Chile, where job quality is better than elsewhere in the region, it is important to note the differences among income groups in relation to access to education and employment. The first and second quintiles at the bottom register a decrease of formal employment and an expansion of more than 20 percent of informal employment between 1992 and 1994; for the upper quintile the reverse happened (13.5 percent and -2.7 percent respectively).[4] Access to new jobs is closely linked to differences in education. The expansion of employment in the two bottom quintiles is concentrated in jobs occupied by people without education, which grew by 30 percent between 1992 and 1994, and by those with secondary technical and professional training, which expanded by 11 percent. At the other extreme, the upper-quintile population had access to jobs requiring university education, which expanded by 13 percent. More than half the new jobs with higher educational content went to upper-income families. Low-quality employment concentrates on the poor, while the best jobs are occupied by the higher-income groups.

Jobs and Equity in the Emerging System

A crucial question that still needs to be answered is whether these features are inherent in the emerging model or whether they constitute a transitory stage. Here only preliminary comments can be offered. The first issue is to identify the pillars of the old system and determine how the new arrangements affect them. This will contribute to policy guidance in a broader sense.

The two pillars of the old system have been seriously questioned and in many cases abandoned. The first is the search for full employment, and the second is systemic solidarity. The first was the most important instrument for incorporating people into the economy and for moving them into channels of upward mobility, resulting in greater homogeneity of society. Systemic solidarity was geared to correcting social unbalances that could not be addressed through productive insertion, mainly through labor and welfare policies.

The objective of full employment has been progressively abandoned because of the overriding priority on stabilization has led to more-restrictive policies and because technological change makes economic growth possible through increases in productivity in the absence of job creation. This is labeled "jobless growth," an admission that the search for full employment is no longer a feasible strategy.

Systemic solidarity has also been affected by several factors and, particularly, by the predominance of economic over social objectives. Globalization and privatization are leading to adoption of more-flexible labor policies and to protection of entrepreneurs as

---

[4] In fact, the better jobs go to those from the third to the fifth quintile, but the rates of growth of the two upper quintiles are around 13 percent, while that of the third is 6.7 percent (Chacón 1995).

job creators. This affects the capacity to implement redistributive fiscal policies, since increasingly these are seen as antiproductive interventions. Social-policy changes also affect systemic solidarity, both because public transfers become easy targets in times of concerns about balancing the budget and because targeting, while justified on efficiency grounds, implies a redistribution from middle to bottom groups.

Changes in the economic environment have forced firms to become more competitive in order to survive, both internationally and at home. In addition, the expansion of informal activities also implies greater competition among individuals and family firms for survival. Similarly, social solutions are increasingly transferred to the individuals or the family, while collective action is concentrated on the very poor. Economic-efficiency considerations are important in order to make the system workable in the new environment, but unless compensatory mechanisms are introduced, social disintegration cannot be ruled out in the future.

Large income differences can coexist with successful policies for poverty reduction and with more-efficient social targeting, protecting the most vulnerable. How dysfunctional is equity, and how far can it be tolerated? These are difficult questions to answer, and we shall limit ourselves to making three comments.

First, contrary to prevailing economic wisdom that postulated that inequality was necessary in order to foster growth in the early stages of development, a recent and rapidly expanding literature suggests that inequality is negatively associated with growth (Perotti 1996; Alesina and Rodrik 1994; Clarke 1995; Bruno, Ravallion, and Squire 1996; Tokman 1996). While growth reduces poverty, its effects on equity are unclear. Greater equality generates faster growth because of enlarging markets, diminishing the costs of imperfections in capital markets, reducing needs for public transfers, decreasing political instability, and ensuring more-secure property rights. Hence, equality matters not only because of ethical considerations but on economic grounds: it facilitates growth.

Second, poverty and equity are not independent. The rhythm of progress in fighting poverty is linked to the capacity to change the distribution of income. If the rich cannot be taxed, there will be less resources to transfer to the poor. It is simple arithmetic.

Third, what kind of society is emerging before our eyes? O'Donnell (1996) suggests that polarization is already happening. There is a group that has access to better jobs, lives in nice urban areas, has special schools for their children and, increasingly, even have their own police force. This behavior is in part a reaction to increased violence in the city and to lower quality of public services, but to a great extent it also reflects an economic and social option. The other side of the coin is, of course, that the majority of the people stand still, at best. Thus, a two-track society arises. Children attending better schools will be better prepared for the future. This is increasingly the result not only of location and general environment, but also of quality differences between the public and private systems. The few evaluations available show higher quality levels in private schools, while at the same time the elites are not graduating from leading public schools, as in the past, when access was independent of socioeconomic background.

The policies suggested in the present paper are geared towards reintroducing the two key objectives of jobs and solidarity in the new economic and social context in Latin America. Job creation is a top priority if the region is to be able to compete in the new international environment. But job quality is a major issue as well. Full employment, while still valid as a guiding principle, must be adapted to a reality in which a substantial part of employment is no longer in stable and protected jobs. This, of course, does not mean acceptance of any kind of job, but rather the search for higher productivity and new forms of protection to ensure its social acceptability. Instruments to create or improve jobs include investing in people, changing entrepreneurial strategies from downsizing to productivity expansion, ensuring friendly industrial relations, and redesigning job protection. It will also be necessary to target low-productivity segments and, particularly, informal activities and microenterprises, since most of the jobs that need upgrading in terms of productivity, incomes and social protection are and will continue to be these types of activities. At the same time, these segments become a vehicle to decrease poverty and improve equity.

These measure themselves will not be sufficient, however, since the basis of systemic solidarity is also undergoing major change. There is a need to search for new instruments of collective solidarity in a labor field moving toward decentralization and individualism and a need to redesign social-protection policies to cover the vulnerable, the emerging precarious categories, and the structurally excluded. Redistributive measures, particularly tax reforms, must not be ruled out of the agenda.

The sum total of the measures proposed in the present article constitutes a basis for formulating a new generation of policies for jobs and solidarity. It is not a universal recipe, nor are the changes proposed marginal. Rather, these proposals are directed toward providing answers to fundamental questions that require innovative approaches in order to cope with old problems in a different economic environment.

REFERENCES

Alesina, A., and D. Rodrik. 1994. Distributive politics and economic growth. *Quarterly Journal of Economics* 109.

Atkinson, A.B. 1996. Income Distribution in Europe and the United States. *Oxford Review of Economic Policy* (12, 1).

Bronstein, A.S. 1995. Societal Change and Industrial Relations in Latin America: Trends and Prospects. *International Labor Review* (134, 2).

Bruno, M., M. Ravallion, and L. Squire. 1996. Equity and Growth in Developing Countries: Old and New Perspectives on the Policy Issues. Policy Research Working Paper 1563. (World Bank).

Chacón, B. 1995. Calidad de los empleos y su incidencia en los niveles de pobreza en Chile." ILO, Lima. Unpublished.

Chirac, J. 1996. Speech at the 83rd Session of the International Labor Conference, Geneva, June, 1996.

Clarke, G. 1995. More Evidence on Income Distribution and Growth. *Journal of Development Economics* 106.

Fukuchi, T. 1997. Comments on Victor Tokman's paper in this volume.

Gallart, M.A. 1996. Restructuring, Education and Training. Presentation at the Workshop on Poverty in Latin America, Issues and New Responses.

Hansenne, M. 1996. Address at the Forum on the Future of the European Society. Economic Social Committee of the European Union, Brussels, May 1996.

Hoffman, A. 1995. Economic Growth and Fluctuations in Latin America—The Long Run. North-South Center, University of Miami.

International Labor Organization. 1995. Labor Overview '95. *ILO News*, Regional Office, Lima.

_____. Employment Policies in a Global Context. Fifth Report of the 83rd Session of the International Labor Conference, Geneva, June 1996.

Krugman, P. 1995. *The Age of Diminished Expectations*. Cambridge: The MIT Press.

Locke, R., M. Pior, and T. Kotchan. 1995. Reconceptualizing Comparative Industrial Relations: Lessons from International Research. *International Labor Review* (2, 134).

Martínez, and V.E. Tokman. 1996. *Costo laboral en el sector manufacturero de América Latina: Incidencia sobre la competitividad en el sector y la protección de los trabajadores.* (Regional Office, Lima)

McKinsey Global Institute. 1994. Latin American Productivity. *Latin American Weekly Report* (June).

O'Donnell, G. Poverty and Inequality in Latin America: Some Political Reflections. Presentation at the workshop on Poverty in Latin America, Issues and New Responses.

Organization for Economic Cooperation and Development. 1994. Perspectivas del empleo. Madrid.

_____. 1994. *The OECD Jobs Study. Facts, Analysis, Strategies*. Paris: OECD.

Perotti, R. 1996. Growth, Income Distribution and Democracy: What the Data Say. *Journal of Economic Growth* (June).

Solow, R. 1989. *The Labor Market as a Social Institution.* The Royer Lectures, University of California, Berkeley. Basil Blackwell.

Raczynski, D. 1996. *The Crisis of Old Models of Social Protection and New Alternatives for Dealing with Poverty and Vulnerability.* Presentation at the workshop on Poverty in Latin America, Issues and New Responses.

Reilly, C. 1996. *Balancing Development: State, Markets, and Civil Society* in the workshop on Poverty in Latin America, Issues and New Responses.

Tendler, J., and S. Freedheim. 1994. Trust in a Rent-Seeking World: Health and Government Transformed in North East Brazil, in *World Development* (22, 12)

Tillet, A. 1995. Commentary on the paper Restructuring, Education and Training of María Antonia Gallart. IDRC, Montevideo.

Tinbergen, J. 1975. *Income Distribution.* Amsterdam: North Holland.

Tokman, M. 1996. *Inequality, Institutions and Growth.* University of California, Berkeley. Unpublished.

Tokman, V. E. 1994. "Informalidad y pobreza. Progreso y modernización productiva." *Trimestre Económico* 241. January–March, 1994.

Tokman, V. E. 1995. *Pobreza y equidad. Dos objetivos relacionados.* ILO Regional Office, Lima.

R. Ffrench-Davis[1] on Victor Tokman's Paper

Jobs and Solidarity: Challenges for Post-Adjustment in Latin America

During the last 15 years, Latin America has exhibited a poor record in economic growth, employment, and equity, as well as in terms of the interrelationship between people and policymaking.

Growth depends on capital formation, efficient investment, and increased productivity. Actual growth depends on the effective use of investment and potential productivity, which is something a macroeconomist should always try to achieve. Otherwise, these are idle resources. The relevant question that arises is how close to the production frontier is an economy usually working? That is, what is the utilization rate of available resources: human and physical capital? The record in Latin America has been poor, with low GDP growth of 1.2 percent during the 1980s and 3 percent from 1990-1995, compared with 5.5 percent from 1950 to 1980. Investment ratios have been about 30 percent lower than in those three previous decades, and actual use of capacity has remained persistently below its potential.

With regard to employment creation and poverty reduction, results have also been mediocre, as documented by Victor Tokman. Employment has grown slower than labor supply, the quality of employment has worsened, and wages have not kept up. In terms of sectorial composition, the result with respect to exports is rather good; employment has grown in many countries in the export sector. But in nonexports there has been limited or no growth. This has to do with systemic productivity, with favorable results in one segment and unsatisfactory ones in others. What is needed is for overall GDP to perform well, not just the 20 percent of it that is the share of exports.

Victor Tokman and Alain Touraine have emphasized the worrisome indifference of people to political parties, government, and the way economic policy is handled. The same indifference has been detected in polls as well. This distressing development is associated probably with jobs, wages, social industrial relations, and an increasingly mishandled interaction of policymakers and the political system with society.

---

[1] Principal Regional Advisor, ECLAC, Santiago.

Features of Labor Markets

Victor Tokman presents insightful data, diagnoses, and policy proposals in his search for more higher-quality jobs. The paper recalls some impressive data for Latin America:

- 80 percent of the increase in nonagricultural employment in the last 15 years has been in the informal sectors.
- 20 percent unemployment among youth means that newcomers to the labor force have more difficulty getting jobs; this situation is worse in formal markets than in informal ones.
- Average wages in manufacturing fell 13 percent between 1980 and 1990, and minimum wages dropped even more, with decreases in informal incomes the most significant. Even Chile, whose policies are among the most successful, reached the average formal real wage of 1970 only in 1992.
- There is also a disquieting decline in the position of middleincome groups, which is related to the sustainability of democracy. Tokman documents that significant middle-class groups have been falling into poverty.

The informalization of employment has hit middle income groups hard. Trade reforms, implemented in a way very different from those in East Asia, have generated a net drop in the production of tradables in many countries.[2] Also, public wages in education and health have worsened. Moreover, workers in the public sector have lost their jobs as the sector has lost significance as a provider of new jobs for the rising middle classes.

We also need more and better thinking in targeting. Targeting must be designed in such a way as to spread productivity through society; to charge polluters; and to encourage mobility of people.

Incomplete and Missing Markets

Tokman makes many interesting observations regarding labor training and small firms, which are crucial for employment and for spreading productivity and equity through the economic system. In this respect, the Latin American economies have several incomplete and missing markets. If we do not trust—as neoliberal or neoconservative approaches do—in our capacity to create and complete those markets (wherever there are missing technology, training, and long-term capital markets), we shall be doing only half of the task. Completing markets is an unavoidable requirement along the road leading to growth with equity. As our Asian colleagues have shown, a pragmatic policy must move in the direction of removing obstacles to development, thus upgrading the role of small firms.

With regard to education, it must be remembered that what we do today will hardly affect the labor market during the next 10 years. Right now the concern should be to improve the quality of education. Wages of teachers and their working conditions must

---

[2] See Agosin and Ffrench-Davis, "Trade Liberalization and Growth: Recent Experiences in Latin America." *Journal of Inter-American Studies* 37,3 (1995).

be improved, related to their performance. Not much is being done in labor training, where an intensive and urgent effort is required. This is an ideal area for collaboration among employer associations, labor unions, and government.

Macroeconomic Framework

Severe adjustments have been made in the last two decades in Latin America in terms of the macroeconomic-policy framework. Tokman recalls the ups and downs experienced by the region, particularly the decline of the 1980s and the crisis of 1995.

I would like to illustrate the issue with some country cases. Progress and modernization require permanent adjustment, but not on the scale of the adjustment suffered by Chile in 1982, with a 23 percent drop of domestic demand and a drop of 15 percent in GDP. In 1995, Mexico experienced a fall of 15 percent in aggregate demand, 26 percent in investment, and 7 percent of GDP.

During the adjustment of the 1980s there was underutilization of physical capital, thus discouraging new capital formation. There was widespread unemployment as well as the loss of income, discipline, and training that occurs when workers are forced from formal jobs to informal or temporary jobs. A repetition of these events took place in Argentina and Mexico in 1995, because of macro-policy approaches similar to those in the years prior to the 1982 debt crisis.

Reasons for this negative outcome are, first, that countries are tempted by capital surges in international markets, accepting large inflows, significant exchange rate appreciations, and growing deficits on the current account. Second, after the crisis emerges domestically, demand-reducing policies have been very effective. But the region has been weak in the implementation of switching policies, thus affecting the composition of demand and supply. Ideological barriers have discouraged selective policies that enhance factor reallocation and the volume of investment. East Asian countries offer numerous examples of notably more efficient processes of switching policies.

International capital markets need improvements. But given present trends, in the next few years they may become even more volatile, thus worsening conditions in many countries. With this in mind, domestic policies must be designed to absorb the pros and minimize the cons of those markets. This is what led Chile in 1991, and Colombia both in the 1970s and 1990s, to adopt active policies regarding the management of capital flows.

Ultimately, the intensity and quality of adjustment depend on what happens during adjustment and before it. What happened in the region during the 1980s had a direct connection with the expansive but unsustainable borrowing during the 1970s. What happened in 1995 in Mexico and Argentina on the one hand and in Chile and Colombia on the other was associated directly with policies applied during the 1991–1994 period.[3] Thus, we should always be planting the seeds of stability.

---

[3] See the overview paper in Ffrench-Davis and Griffith-Jones, eds., *Coping with Capital Surges,* Lynne Rienner, Boulder, Co., 1995.

We need to build sustainable balances in the fiscal, monetary, and external sectors. They must be managed in such a way that effective demand follows closely the evolution of the production frontier. This represents an obvious macroeconomic equilibrium, which paradoxically has been disregarded, as judged by the evidence. The typical situation in the last 20 years implied unsustainable gaps of aggregate demand/productive capacity, followed by sharp demand reductions leading to effective demand below capacity. The outcome was, among other things, a discouraged and insufficient capital formation,[4] inconsistent with the development of growth and equity. Consequently, we must take care that adjustment policies do not destroy the basis for equity and growth and that they do not weaken investment in people and physical capital.

---

[4] See Schmidt-Hebbel, Servén, and Solimano, "Savings and Investment: Paradigms, Puzzles, Policies," World Bank's *Research Observer,* World Bank, 2,1 (February 1996).

Takao Fukuchi[1] on Victor Tokman's Paper

Jobs and Solidarity: Challenges for Post-Adjustment in Latin America

How can a society eliminate unemployment and poverty and secure a sense of unity? From the point of view of a Japanese economist, human-resource development is the key. Japan achieved economic development based mainly on its human resources, including $33,000 per capita GDP, low unemployment, and a reasonably equitable income distribution. Having said that, it should also be acknowledged that Japan's current growth rate is modest and open unemployment is at a historical high of 3.5 percent.

Human resources also played an important role in the economic development of the high-performing Asian economies (HPAEs). On a foundation of human-resource development and strong investments, these countries more than doubled their per capita income from 1984 to 1992, catching up to the Latin American countries. Hong Kong and Singapore are already ranked as high-income countries. Korea ($6,721) caught up with Argentina ($6,921), and Malaysia ($3,087) with Mexico ($3,736), Uruguay ($3,523), and Chile ($3,030). Thailand ($1,967) is catching up with Brazil ($2,528) and Venezuela ($2,994).

My first comment regarding Mr. Tokman's paper is about the necessity of a comprehensive approach to the labor market, combining sectoral labor needs, technical capacity of workers, and the educational-production capacity. Every society has multistrata structures or two pyramids of labor (demand and supply) classified by different levels of skills. The mismatching of these pyramids creates quantitative and qualitative problems.

Let us look at human resources in Indonesia in comparison with Latin America. Indonesia grew rapidly after 1965. In thirty years its per capita income level increased from a mere $60 to nearly $900, and the ratio of the population under the absolute poverty line decreased from 40 percent to 13.7 percent in 1993 (Pangestu-Azis 1994, 33). The dissemination of primary education and rapid export growth based on unskilled labor-intensive goods greatly contributed to this remarkable growth.

Every country has a demand and supply pyramid of labor. We can summarize the trends of these two pyramids in Indonesia as follows: First, the employment growth rate is half of the economic growth rate but about 2 percent higher than the growth rate of the labor force. Labor demand grew more rapidly than labor supply.

---

[1] Nagoya City University, Japan.

Second, dissemination of primary education is completed. The enrollment for secondary education is comparable with Latin America, but the enrollment for higher education is lower. The labor supply pyramid is more bottom-thick and more top-thin than in Latin America.

Third, more than 85 percent of new employment is concentrated in the primary and tertiary sectors, and the secondary sector (industry, utility, construction) absorbs only 15 percent. Employment growth in the formal sector is very limited. The pyramid of labor demand has become more bottom-thick and top-thin.

Fourth, as a result (comparing the two pyramids), open unemployment is very low (1 percent) for primary school graduates or those without schooling. Unemployment is high for upper secondary graduates (13 percent) and university graduates (7 percent).

And fifth, the wage gap between higher and lower educational careers has decreased.

The general economic tendency differs between Latin America and Indonesia. Per capita income declined in Latin America, while it increased annually by 5 percent to 6 percent in Indonesia. But the characteristics of Latin American labor markets summarized in Tokman's five observations show many similarities with the corresponding five points in Indonesia.

While attempting further modernization, Indonesia is also trying to adjust its higher-education system in order to solve serious mismatches in the labor market, such as overpricing and a high unemployment rate for higher-education graduates, and to reform the industry into a more skilled-labor and technology-intensive structure. Through such efforts, Indonesia plans to quadruple its per capita income level in the second twenty-five year plan (1994–2019) and to reach the $3,600 level, which is comparable to the current level in Brazil.

How about human-resource development in Latin America? John Williamson, in his paper in the present volume, introduced improved education as the final item on his wish list. Gert Rosenthal said that skills keep pace with technical progress in Latin America. We hope that his "somewhat optimistic note" is realistic. Some comparative studies of human-resource development between HPAEs and Latin American countries would be quite useful for sketching out future strategies. The experience of Taiwan, which flexibly adjusted its educational system, could serve as a useful reference (Woo 1991).

Our second comment is about "the economic consequences of the size of nations." Chile is appraised in many places as a high-performing Latin American economy in terms of income growth, low unemployment, and real wage increases. The population of Chile is less than 20 million, roughly comparable to Malaysia. Both achieved rapid growth based on exports through successful introduction of foreign direct investments. HPAEs including South Korea, Singapore, Taiwan, and Hong Kong are not large countries. The population of Singapore (5 million) is only half of Jakarta, and that of Malaysia (18 million) is equal to the Jabotabek region (West Java industrial zone). A small country does not need a broad industrial base to provide job opportunities. Such a country can relatively easily improve education levels, quickly modernize some strategic industries (in the case of Chile, fishery, mining, wood, fruits, and agriculture) through foreign direct investment, and achieve rapid economic growth. In this sense, the Chilean miracle shares common features with the success of the HPAEs. The persistent inequality might come from the fact that the economic fruits of rapid growth concentrated in a narrow range of strategic sectors and the trickling down to the general population takes time.

A big country like Indonesia with 180 million people cannot solely rely upon a narrow range of strategic sectors and must cultivate a broad industrial base. Indonesia's industrialization is based on a wide range of labor-intensive sectors. This caused a quick decrease in poverty and gradual improvement of the inequality level. But a further jump to the status of a middle-income country needs deeper changes and more time. The economic development in Indonesia is concentrated mainly in Java, where 70 percent of the population and economic activities are concentrated. The per capita income level in the Jakarta or Jabotabek region is comparable to that of Malaysia, but the trickling down to other regions in the periphery takes time. The burden of big size, thus, can dominate the benefits: big interregional inequality, the financial cost of disseminating public services such as education and health to every region, big urban problems, enormous unemployment, and multiple ethnic issues. These big-size costs create additional problems for countries like Brazil and Mexico. The *maquiladoras* in northern Mexico could absorb the labor force and contribute greatly to the development of that region. If it were a small country, such an infusion could fuel up the whole economy to successful industrialization. On the other hand, the development of *maquiladoras* and the industrial triangle (Monterrey-Mexico-Guadalajara) has increased the interregional economic gap and the social frustration of local people in other regions. Thus, the export processing zone can be an effective development strategy for a small economy, but it can also create many side issues in a large country. The size of the economy and various geopolitical features add an additional dimension and require suitable treatment when jobs and solidarity are discussed.

REFERENCES

Bendesa, I Komang Gde. 1992. The Structural Change of Employment, and Education in Indonesia, *The Indonesian Quarterly* 20 (4): 447–60.

Fukuchi, Takao. 1989. Growth and the Subsectoral Pattern of the Manufacturing Sector in Indonesia—A Comparative Study of 16 Countries. *Asian Economic Journal* 8 (3): 239–59.

Greene, Anne. 1992. A Comparative Study of Education in Latin America and Indonesia. *The Indonesian Quarterly* 20 (4): 461–81.

Muta, Hiromitsu, and Budiono. 1987. Education and Manpower Training in Indonesia. *Asian Economic Journal* 1 (2): 94–146.

Pangestu, Mari, and Iwan Jaya Azis. 1994. Survey of Recent Development. *Bulletin of Indonesian Economic Studies* 30 (2): 3–47.

_____, and Mayling Oey-Gardiner. 1993. Human Resource Development and Management in Indonesia. *The Indonesian Quarterly* 21 (4): 461–82.

Tokman, Victor E. 1986. Adjustment and Employment in Latin America: The Current Challenges. *International Labour Review* 125 (5): 533–43.

Woo, Jennie Hay. 1991. Education and Economic Growth in Taiwan: A Case of Successful Planning. *World Development* 19 (8): 1020–44.

An Essay on the Macroeconomics of Social Development in Latin America

Martin Paldam[1]

During the first 30 years after World War II, economic development in Latin America took a particular path—a path we shall term the "old" ISI-path.[2] It turned out to be a *cul-de-sac* that led to economic stagnation and, often, to high inflation and very unequal income distribution. The last 10 to 20 years have seen many attempts to turn away from that path by an SA-package—where "SA" stands for structural adjustment.[3] The SA-package comes in many versions, but the core has always been deregulation and the twin policies of foreign trade liberalization and privatization. The idea of the package is to change the country from one path—the ISI-Path—to another path—the Washington-consensus-path, that is, the WC-path described by Williamson (1990 and 1995, and his article in this volume).

The new policies did in fact cause a reduction in the share of the (traditional) public sector by almost 15 percent in the average Latin American country. Later we shall discuss the reasons why this happened. It is obvious that the SA-package involves a large shift in the role of the public sector. It does not, however, necessarily mean that the public sector should be reduced; but rather that it should leave the production of private goods and concentrate on the production of public goods and the alleviation of poverty.[4]

The attempts to implement SA-packages have gradually succeeded in many countries, allowing them to break out from the cul-de-sac. The immediate result has been an

---

[1] Professor of Economics, University of Aarhus, Denmark. The essay is based on seven socio-economic country reports prepared by the Social Agenda Policy Group in the IDB listed in the references. I am grateful to Louis Emmerij for many discussions, as well as to Peter Skott and Helena Skyt for discussions, and Fernando Montenegro for research assistance. I have also taken advantage of the discussion of a preliminary version at a conference on Development Economics in Bergen, Norway. Given the author's background, ratios are termed small or large relative to the corresponding numbers in (West) European countries. Western Europe has about the same population as Latin America, and both continents are divided into many countries. As regards culture and history, much connects the two areas. I should finally mention that the word "model" is used in a broader way than in most economic texts, namely for an "ideal" economic system.

[2] The path of import substitution industrialization (ISI) is the one where money is squeezed out of agriculture to develop a protected modern sector. The ISI-path is no longer recommended by ECLAC, but it was strongly and successfully advocated till about one decade ago. The article by Rosenthal in this volume presents the new policies of ECLAC.

[3] Weaver (1995) and Fischer (1995) give a taxonomy of the many types of SA- packages attempted and discuss the way the IBRD-IMF assisted packages have evolved since 1980.

[4] The distinction between public and private goods in this essay follows national accounting practice, not the formal criteria of Samuelson, as found in the standard theory textbooks. "Our" public goods are the ones defined as general government consumption and investments.

aggravation of social problems. During the next decade the situation will probably improve by its own dynamics, but can one achieve quicker improvement and go even further, perhaps toward the alternative provided by the more successful NW European type welfare state? There are two main problems (both discussed later in some detail) for Latin America in following that model:

- the public sector inefficiency problem; and
- the tax constraint problem: effective marginal taxes are difficult to raise above some surprisingly low tax limit.

In our diagnosis the public sector's inefficiency problem has been aggravated during the ISI-period. We shall argue that the WC-path has its main advantage in being efficiency enhancing, but we are dealing with mechanisms with long lags. The tax constraint problem is both due to low tax rates and to low tax efforts; taxes are usually very difficult to collect.[5] The problems, consequently, hang together in a complex, dynamic way. Before we unravel this web, it is worth looking at the possible choices in the longer run.

A Stylized Transition from the ISI-path, via an SA-Package to the WC-Path

To discuss these economic strategy questions, we have traced the last 40 years of Latin American economic history in Figure 4.2. It is a simple drawing, and there are many variants; but the figure catches the strategy development in a nutshell.

The figure shows a country with an underlying constant steady- state growth path drawn as a straight line: the L1-line.[6] At time (A) the country adopts the ISI-package which gives some extra growth: the G1-area. Gradually, the growth tapers off and a loss emerges: the G2-area. Then an SA-package is implemented between times (B) and (C). After some transition trouble—the G3-area—the economy catches up at time (*). It might be before or after (C), where the SA-package is fully implemented. Sometimes all that happens is that the economy catches up with the old growth path, that is, it returns to the L1-line. In other cases the changes in the economy have been so strong that a new and steeper long-run growth path emerges as drawn in the form of the L2-line.

The stylized figure shows where disagreements lie. How large was G1? How should the responsibility for the restructuring-loss (G2+G3) be divided between the ISI-policies and the SA-package? Those who are most committed to the old ISI-policies tend to consider that very much of the (G2+G3)-sum should be classified as G3, that is, as problems caused by the SA-package. However, others note that countries only accept SA-packages

---

[5] That is, let income rise by z, then tz turns up in the treasury. Marginal tax rates are typically higher than t, but somehow it has proved difficult to collect more than tz. One should have a number like $t < 0.3$ in mind for the average Latin American country.

[6] Note that the vertical axis is logarithmic. When real GDP is drawn over half a century or more, an underlying straight line normally appears to dominate the picture—kinks occur, but rarely. In most of the developed OECD-countries there is just one kink during the last 50 years: it is a downward kink, by 1.5 percentage points in the growth rate 1974/75. This is often interpreted as showing that countries have natural growth rates, which are hard to change.

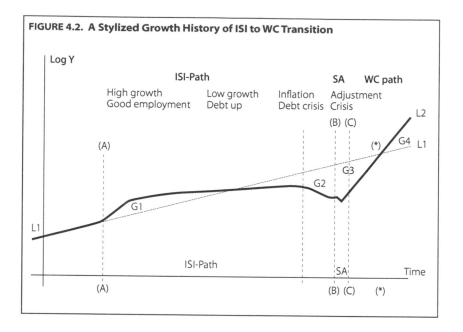

FIGURE 4.2. A Stylized Growth History of ISI to WC Transition

when the old policies have failed. Therefore, all (or most) of the loss (G2+G3) is caused by the old policies. Also, there are some examples of SA-packages causing a permanent upward kink, so that a G4-area emerges. There are yet other countries where such an area has not materialized, even after dramatic structural adjustments.

In this framework one may compare the G1-area and G2+G3-area and ask: has the sum of the ISI-policy been negative, positive or a zero-sum game? If the L2-high growth path (termed by some the NIC-path) does occur, one may ask whether it has always been available. If so, there has been a huge welfare loss from not having got onto the L2 path at (A), or even before.[7]

In the countries that did get on a new and higher growth path this was caused by an export boom generated by new exports such as table grapes from Chile and eco-tourism in Costa-Rica, that in both cases led to other exports, to make export-led growth continue. Unfortunately, there are other countries that did everything the doctor said, without experiencing an export boom. The medicine is thus stochastic in its effects, but this is the case for almost all macroeconomic cures. Perhaps it is only the lag that is stochastic? Assume that an export boom does occur: this is the import-liberalization puzzle. Trade liberalization is made to allow competition on the import side, and this generates an export boom! The explanation is not straightforward. We shall consequently return to this point.

---

[7] The reader will have noted that Figure 4.2 has managed to touch most of the important points within the macroeconomic development discussions of the last dozen years. One of the most heated has been whether the "Chilean type L2-path" is comparable to the NIC Asian Miracle L2-path?

Is There a Social Multiplier?

When one studies the seven socioeconomic country-reports, (see References) it is obvious that something important is missing in Figure 4.2. If similar graphs are drawn for equality, unemployment, and poverty, they show relatively large adjustment losses, and the catch-up point (*) comes later.

Everybody agrees that the adjustment was successful in Chile and, since the SA-package had been already adopted in 1974–75, it was the first such change in Latin America. It soon became an ideological testing ground, and Chile has many fine economists, so that the Chilean case has been intensely analyzed. The cul-de-sac property of the ISI-policies led to a gradual reduction in the growth rate during the 1960s. The adjustment loss was large, but the economy did get on a higher growth path (L2), that is, growth after 1980 is about 2 percent higher than growth before 1970. The catch-up point for the real product was about 7 years from the start of the adjustment. However, the catch-up point for the rate of unemployment was no less than about 14 years.[8] The reason for this will be discussed later in more detail.

One may speak of a social adjustment multiplier, in the sense that losses in the social sector are relatively higher than GDP-loss. If the economy gets on to a steeper growth path (L2), then the social losses also are compensated by later gains. If only the old path (L1) is reached, permanent problems may have emerged. It is, therefore, worth looking at the strategy choices in a broader perspective.

Capitalism/Socialism and the Welfare State: A 2x2 Classification

There are several methods for classifying economic systems. Table 4.6 presents the two main dimensions of classifications found in the literature. It is a crude way to look at the world, but it provides a start. The two dimensions are largely independent:

(i) The socialist/capitalist dimension considers the criteria of the classical economists, notably Karl Marx.[9] Who owns the means of production? We here look at property rights in the production of private goods. Closely related is the degree of liberalism in foreign trade.

(ii) The welfare dimension considers the size of the traditional public sector: What is the share of production of public goods, and how large a share of GDP is redistributed by the public sector?

The range along the vertical axis goes from 80–90 percent public ownership of the means of production in the old Communist Model of the Soviet Union and Eastern Europe, to public ownership of perhaps 12 percent in Hong Kong. In the typical OECD-country, the public sector owns mainly the means of production for producing

---

[8] See Meller (1992) for a description of social development during the structural adjustment phase and subsequent growth path. The whole Chilean case is covered in Bothworth *et al.* (1994).
[9] Modern economists speak of property rights, but it is the same concept as the classical one, even if a great deal of analytical rigor has been added.

TABLE 4.6. Main Economic Systems

		Socialism/Capitalism Dimension: Public ownership and trade control	
		Much: Socialism	Little: Capitalism
Welfare State Dimension	Much	Communist Model ↓→	Welfare Model (↓)
Public goods and transfers	Little	ISI Model →	Chicago Model

the public goods, that is, about 20 percent of all real capital, and in addition perhaps 2–4 percent of the remaining capital.

The "pure capitalism" of the Chicago Model has not been common in the last 50 years, and is now mainly found in the countries of the Chinese diaspora, notably the two small city-states of Hong Kong and Singapore. Something like this model is, however, emerging in the coastal zone of China.

The range along the horizontal axis goes from just above 50 percent (of GDP) in the Nordic countries—divided almost equally between public goods and redistribution—to about 10 percent in Hong Kong. In the larger West European countries, the share is around 40 percent and in the United States and Japan it is about 30 percent.

Comparing the Solutions of the ISI Model and the Welfare Model

According to the classical definition, the most extreme welfare states in Europe, such as Denmark, Norway, Sweden, and the Netherlands,[10] are also extremely capitalist states. They all have unusually liberal foreign trade regimes, with a freely convertible exchange rate and no taxes on international trade flows.[11]

The most puzzling observation is that the whole of the financial, trade, industry and agriculture sectors are privately owned. Parastatals exist for railways and air traffic, where efficiency is relatively low and rent seeking prevails. There is also a grey area in the field of utilities, with mixed public-private ownership, but that is as far as it goes. In Denmark, not even one industrial firm is publicly owned. In the financial sector only the Central Bank is public, though fairly independent. Municipalities are explicitly forbidden from getting into production of private goods or from subsidizing private firms.

Public expenditure is, however, much higher than in Latin America. There is a difference with respect to the production of traditional public goods, which amount to about 25 percent (of GDP) in most NW European countries, whereas it is about 15 percent on average in Latin America (see Table 4.9a). Defense, law and order, and administration take about 4 percent in both regions with defense accounting for one half.

---

[10] One may include Austria, Belgium, Iceland and Finland and perhaps Germany in this list, but the four countries considered in the text are slightly more extreme.

[11] Two of the countries—Sweden and Norway—have a tradition of protecting their small agricultural sectors while the other two—the Netherlands and Denmark—are net agricultural exporters fighting for agricultural trade liberalization. Also, during certain periods there was control over capital flows, but this is no longer the case.

However, the big difference is that almost 25 percent of GDP is redistributed via public sector social programs in NW Europe while the corresponding number in Latin America is only 5 percent.

To undertake large scale redistribution and collect the corresponding high taxes put a premium on public sector efficiency. It is interesting that public sectors have a reasonably high efficiency in the NW-European countries. It is, in fact, hard to tell if there is a difference between the efficiency of the tax administration and the national Coca-Cola company in the average NW-European country.

There is another important difference. It is easier and cheaper for a NW European firm to lay off workers than for a Latin American firm. The labor markets are typically more flexible in NW Europe.[12] This is possible precisely because social spending is at such a high level. People need some form of social security which they can obtain either through rules and regulations that make the labor market inflexible, or through social spending that alleviates structural change. If there is neither, people become desperate.

A final difference worth mentioning is that NW-European countries are less centralized politically and administratively. This is not, perhaps, as important when we look at the two models from a macroeconomic perspective; but when one considers the political basis for making the systems work, it might be an important factor.

Both models are a compromise between the socialist left wing and the liberal right wing.[13] Compromises are found along one or the other axis. Our main observation is that the welfare state solution has proved much more viable than the ISI compromise.

It is also interesting to note that the two compromise models emerged almost simultaneously (see Blomström and Meller, 1991). The welfare state and the protective trade regime were both founded in the 1920s and 1930s; but the starting up of both systems was slow and rather haphazard. After the Second World War, public expenditures differed little, when measured as a percentage of the GDP, in Latin America and NW-Europe. The strong rise in the share of public expenditure in NW-Europe (up to 25 percent of GDP) occurred only in the three decades after 1950, that is simultaneously with the great ISI-period.

The Time of Dénouement: The Feasibility-Axis of Capitalism

For more than a decade all these models appeared to converge toward the Chicago solution. The movement out of the Communist Model has been very strong—essentially because the system collapsed; and the movement out of the ISI Model has been strong (we shall discuss that movement in more detail later). The smallest movements have been from the Welfare Model—the arrow here is put in brackets (see Table 4.6).

---

[12] The casual observer may not discover this as economists and businessmen are constantly complaining that labor markets are inflexible in NW-European countries. However, if we compare regulations in the modern sectors in the Latin American and NW-European economies, the difference is as mentioned.

[13] The term "liberal" is used (in the European sense) for those preferring moves toward the Chicago Model, while "socialist" is used for those preferring to go toward the Communist Model. Moderate liberals do not want to go all the way. The same applies to moderate socialists.

In fact, we may say that the whole world is moving toward some compromise on the capitalist axis. One may perhaps go as far as to interpret the economic history of the last decade as a time of dénouement. It has become clear that the range of feasible models of society is much smaller than we all wanted to believe. This range is to be found on the capitalist axis at the right hand side of Table 4.6. However, that range is rather wide.[14] The underlying questions in the present essay are:

(1) Where, in the range from the Welfare to the Chicago solution, should countries aim? We shall argue that, to be viable in the long run, the socioeconomic system should be a compromise that is not too close to the Chicago solution.

(2) Which part of the axis is presently available as a realistic possibility? We shall argue that it is fairly close to the Chicago Model. This is unfortunate, but as time passes, more of the axis will surely become feasible.

The Welfare Model: Some Strong and Weak Points

Nearly all OECD countries have experienced a downward shift in the real growth rate—on average by 1.5 percentage points—in 1974–75. Viewed in a long-term perspective it is, however, the high growth rate of the preceding two decades that is exceptional, not the moderate growth of the last two decades (see Maddison's article in this volume). The United States did not experience this downward shift, nor did it have especially high growth rates from the mid-1950s to 1975. During the last two decades, labor force participation rates have risen sharply throughout the OECD area. Combined with moderate growth, this has caused unemployment to increase by no less than 8 percentage points during the late 1970s to about 11 percent.

This development has put the European welfare states under considerable stress, to such an extent that they have all had to stop the expansion of the share of public expenditures. However, the share of welfare expenditure has stabilized, not fallen in the main welfare states. In the process, it has become painfully clear that the Welfare Model lacks one essential mechanism. It is so effective in collecting taxes and in organizing transfers that it easily goes too far. For the model to work, it is essential that a proper long-term balance be struck between the public service sector and the private production sector. It has proved difficult to find a balance that can be stabilized.

High public expenditure generated high taxes and consequently high marginal taxes which have typically been well above 60 percent. Tax reforms have been undertaken to reduce these rates, but they are still high. It has often been argued that this is a big problem for efficiency. High unemployment benefits are also problematic in that they reduce efforts to find employment and generate an artificial labor supply of persons who do not really want to work. All these problems have been shown to exist, but their numerical magnitudes appear small (Atkinson and Mogensen, 1993, is a recent survey of the evidence from four countries. See also Paldam, 1997b). These problems are,

---

[14] Several alternative models—that need more dimensions than shown in Table 4.6—have all fared badly. The Yugoslav Model, the Israeli Model, and so forth, have all moved rapidly towards the capitalist axis.

moreover, smaller than those of the reverse mixture of the ISI Model, as will be discussed later.

For some time it seemed that Sweden had managed to escape the general downward shift by means of an important devaluation, but two years ago Sweden had to go the way of its neighbors and accept a 10 percent unemployment and lower economic growth. As the adjustment came so late it has been relatively strong. Some see the adjustment taking place in Sweden as pointing to a general crisis of the welfare state.[15]

In a later section we shall discuss why the Welfare Model has proved reasonably effective in the longer run. One set of reasons turns around the sociopolitical stability it seems to generate. Another is that part of social expenditures is, in fact, social investment. It has often been shown that the accumulation of human capital is as important for economic growth as physical capital. It can be shown that the distortions in the Welfare Model are smaller than they appear.

To summarize, the Welfare Model has proved efficient up to a point. There are no measurable efficiency losses up to tax pressures as high as 40 percent. Serious problems do not appear before well over 45 percent. The key point to note is that the condition allowing the Welfare Model to work is that efficiency is enforced by a fairly extreme form of capitalism when it comes to property rights and foreign competition.

Can the Welfare Model be Emulated?

It is not easy to change an economic system. Models are rarely deliberately chosen, but are rather the result of a complex historical process involving many decision makers. Much can go wrong on the way. However, economic models have strong inner dynamics, so that once a country gets on a certain path it is difficult to change. Many countries have tried to change from the ISI-path to the WC-path. Most countries had to try with one SA-package after the other before they succeeded, and others have not yet really succeeded, even after several attempts.

When we look at the movement among the four squares in Table 4.6, we note that the Latin American countries are moving from the ISI Model toward the Chicago Model. It would not be easy to move directly from the ISI Model to a Welfare Model, and the movement from an ISI Model to a Welfare Model via the Communist Model does not look promising. So, it would seem that the only way from the ISI Model to a Welfare Model is via Chicago.

The key point to note is that it is impossible to move in the direction of the Welfare Model without *higher taxes*. This is an essential ingredient of the Washington Consensus. Latin American countries have had bad experiences with financing public expenditures

---

[15] A committee of leading Nordic economists headed by Assar Lindbeck has recently concluded a major study of the Swedish welfare state, by saying that it has indeed gone too far and should be rolled back. A short version of the main thoughts and proposals of the study may be found in Lindbeck *et al.* (1993). But even if the most advanced NWE-country has to reduce the welfare state to the level in Germany, it is still only an adjustment in the level of transfer payments from 27 percent of GDP to about 22 percent. Compared to the Latin American level of 5 percent, it appears a marginal change only.

by means of the inflation tax and with foreign borrowing. This even applies to social investment. It thus appears that much hinges on the tax constraint.

Second, we note that efficiency problems in the public sector are likely to be a serious problem for the collection of more tax revenue. A later section argues that the inefficiency is (partly) a legacy of the ISI Model. However, the Chicago Model does lead to more efficiency in the public sector. As the SA-package begins to work better, the possibility for more welfare increases.

The author has often wondered why the Welfare Model has proved to be so efficient. Some, like Lindbeck (1995) who has given this much thought, believe that this is only a temporary situation. One can argue for an alternative explanation. The main theoretical objection against the Welfare Model is that it generates seemingly large distortions of the economy.[16] On the face of it, it seems that the distortions in the Welfare Model are larger than the distortions in the ISI Model. However, it can be demonstrated that the distortions are likely to be bigger in the ISI Model. The seemingly huge distortions in the Welfare Model are not, by far, as large as they seem, while the seemingly smaller distort in the ISI Model are much larger than they seem.

Economic Growth, Social Investment and Social Consumption

Social expenditures are partly an investment in economic growth and partly an attempt to change the income distribution. Inequality can be measured net or gross of taxes. One may thus make two conceptual distinctions:

(i) Social expenditures can be divided into social consumption and social investments. The latter includes most of education, some of health, and some minor items: in all, maybe half the social expenditures. (This distinction will be crucial for some of the upcoming discussion.)

(ii) People's income has a privately generated component, but there is also a social income that contains their share of public expenditures. (This distinction is also the basis for some of the upcoming discussions.)

The Growth-Equality Discussion: The Basic Stylized Fact of No Correlation

A large literature discusses the several relations between economic growth and equality. A broad, general pattern emerges when all countries are considered. This can be illustrated by two scatter-diagrams, with GDP per capita on the horizontal axis:

(1) The *distribution-diagram* has a measure of equality out of the vertical axis. A concave (U-shaped) average pattern emerges, known as the *Kuznets-curve*.

(2) The *growth-diagram* has an (average) growth rate out of the vertical axis. A convex (hat-shaped) average pattern emerges. One may term it a soft *Rostow-curve*.[17]

---

[16] A group of devout Chicago Economists—Gwartney, Lawson and Block (1996)—have recently tried to compare the "economic freedom" in a large sample of countries. They find that there are marginally fewer restrictions in the welfare states of the world than in typical ISI economies.

[17] The finding goes back to W.W. Rostow, who did, however, provide his "growth-pattern" with sharp kinks, that have proved elusive empirically. But the growth-pattern does have a convex form as demonstrated by Laursen and Paldam (1982) and Andersen (1994).

Given that (1) and (2) have a reverse form, one must find a weak negative correlation between growth and equality if all countries are considered. But, as the average curve in either (1) or (2) explains much of the variation, the correlation between the two is weak indeed. All of this is easily explained within the family of dual-growth models as already done in Chenery, Alhuwalia, Bell, *et al.* (1974) and Chenery and Syrquin (1975). However, once groups of countries at approximately the same level of development are considered, the correlation collapses. We conclude that the basic stylized fact is that the simple correlation between growth and equality is close to zero.

Sorting Out Two Causal Directions

Digging behind the simple stylized fact one first notes that both income distribution and economic growth are complex "end" variables. They are the result of everything else in the economy, and so there must be a whole network of causal links both ways. And, sure enough, many channels between the two have been proposed in the literature. The possible channels from growth to equality give the same result regarding sign. More channels have been proposed from equality to growth, and here no agreement exists on the sign.

(i) Causality from growth to equality: It is fairly clear that higher growth—at least in the short to medium term—does lead to inequality. If there is no reverse causality, we should expect a **negative** correlation between growth and equality.

(ii) Causality from equality to growth: Before we turn to the theories, we already know what we should find. Given the basic stylized fact, and the result under (i), we conclude that connection (ii) must have the reverse sign. Hence, a more equal distribution must—in the short to medium term—lead to higher growth. The **positive** correlation must dominate.[18]

The size of the two correlations is hard to determine. We only know they must be numerically similar. There is a typical identification problem that can only be solved by an identifying assumption. It must, of necessity, come from economic theory, and many theories are available. An uncertain guess is that the two causal links would prove to give correlations in the order of 0.2 to 0.3, if we had the true identifying assumptions.

The main reason why (i) must be true follows from basic general equilibrium theory. An upward kink in the growth curve must mean that some kind of innovation occurs in the economy. Some change makes a new activity profitable, or makes an old activity more profitable.[19] Those who get in first make a pile, then others gradually come in and profits are competed down again. Often some dynamics have been added, making the next breakthrough easier. Many examples can be given. Upward kinks in the growth curve generate inequality for periods up to 10 years. However, upward shifts in the

---

[18] This seems to be confirmed by the experiences of the NIC's as they have had both fairly equal income distributions and very high growth. But it is easy to provide counter examples: Chile first experienced a dramatic shift towards a skewed income distribution, and then growth took off. Also, the story of the high growth and very high inequality in Brazil warns against simplifying these issues.

[19] It might be a new product, a new technique, a new way of organizing production, a breakthrough in marketing, or whatever. The innovation is often imported, it might be induced by more education or by a macro-policy change, but there has to be some change. The key is that a new way to make money starts to spread in the country.

BOX 1. Main Theories of Causality from Distribution to Growth

(1) The social investment complex. Social expenditures are meant to make the distribution more equal. However, they contain social investments that contribute to economic growth. Optimal social investments occur if their marginal productivity is the same as that of private investments: MPIpublic = MPIprivate. If MPIpublic < MPIprivate, an increase in social investments increases growth even if private investments decrease correspondingly.

(2) The savings/entrepreneurship complex looks at the private sector. It exists in an old and a new version. The old assumes savings are invested and the generation of saving is the main constraint. The income distribution that generates most savings is best for growth. It is likely to be a skewed distribution. The new assumes entrepreneurship is the main constraint. Stiff traditional distributions restrict entrepreneurship of most of the population. The distribution should give a chance to all talent.

(3) The political stability complex. The causal chain has two parts: (a) Inequality is politically destabilizing; (b) Political instability generates economic volatility, and economic volatility is harmful to growth.

---

growth curve generate employment and hence also gradual changes in the lower half of the distribution. So, once the process gets under way, maybe after a decade, the distributional consequences become much more complex, but likely to make the distribution more equal.[20]

The Many Causal Channels from Equality to Growth

When we turn to (ii), things become difficult, as the number of channels proposed in the literature is almost endless.[21] Box 1 tries to introduce some order.

The logic behind the *social investment argument* (1) is clear and simple. A part of social expenditures is, in fact, social investment, and this should have its proper size relative to other investments. The liberalization-privatization development has squeezed these budget items with other items as will be shown in Tables 4.9a and b. All seven country case studies of the Social Agenda Policy Group argue that social investment needs to be increased and made more efficient. It is hard to come up with a number here, as countries differ and the rates of return are difficult to calculate; but we are probably speaking of 2 to 5 percent of GDP.

The largest and most controversial part of the literature deals with *the savings/entrepreneurship complex* (2). The old argument was, for long, taken to be self-evident. This is no longer the case for two reasons: first, it appears that saving patterns are quite complex in developing countries. Even while some rich people save a lot, many countries have had (some still have) wealthy traditional oligarchies with traditional lifestyles that allowed little saving. A fine description of the dynamics of such an oligarchy is found in Lampedusa (1958). Second, the main development constraint may not be saving, but something

---

[20] This is illustrated by the Chilean example. Here the income distribution deteriorated dramatically from 1974 to about 1980. Since then it has slowly improved. However, it is still much more skewed than it was in 1970.

[21] The literature up to 1970 is covered in Chenery *et al* (1974). Some of the latest literature is Alesina and Rodrik (1992a and b) and Persson and Tabellini (1994).

much less tangible, such as entrepreneurship. However, it is likely that there is always enough *latent* entrepreneurial talent. The key question then is whether the latent talent meets the right conditions to unfold. These conditions are perhaps susceptible to policies, but they are hard to identify.

Several names are in use trying to catch the endogeneity of this factor. The classical economists up to Schumpeter recognized this. However, this insight was crowded out of economic theory by the beautiful mechanics of the neoclassical growth model. Now it is coming back in many versions in the sprawling endogenous growth literature, where ways have been found to formalize—though not measure—the intangible.[22]

However, when we look at item (2), a great deal is essentially outside the realm of day to day policies, to the extent that it is not covered by (1) and (3). What is left deals with such large questions as property rights/land reform, law and order, patent laws, and various forms of minimum social support systems. These are large issues, but budgetwise they are not necessarily very expensive to reform.

The Political Stability Complex

The most intriguing item is no doubt (3). The two links in the chain are: (a) inequality is politically destabilizing; and (b) political instability generates economic volatility, and economic volatility is harmful to growth. There is no reason to go over (b). IDB (1995) covers much of the literature, and provides a great deal of evidence, forging that link. Another set of strong empirical evidence, coming to the same conclusion, has recently been provided by Borner *et al.* (1995).[23] It concludes that in a politically and economically volatile and unpredictable environment investment suffers and hence growth.

It is easy indeed to point out many instances where social and political unrest has been generated by inequality, so in some broad sense (a) must also be true. However, the notion of "fairness" enters into the causal connection as well. Inequalities that are broadly considered fair are no big political problem, while widely perceived unfair inequalities are destabilizing.[24] A skewed social income increases the feeling of unfairness. This is easy to see when countries with well defined ethnic groups are considered. If the groups have clearly different average incomes, this creates endless political instability. There might be trouble anyhow, but they are likely to be more peaceful, as the examples of Belgium and Canada illustrate.

---

[22] The neoclassical literature as started by R.M. Solow in the early 1950s dominated economics for a decade—here it was termed the "residual factor", and all authors deplored the fact that it explained 75% of growth. Several researchers, notably E.F. Denison, tried very hard to measure it; but somehow this literature went out of fashion. Now, a new class of models has been invented in an effort to explain the endogeneity of growth. Several of the main authors repeatedly warn that they are far from reaching good empirical measures allowing to catch the intangible. When empirical measures are put into the models, they often include factors that we have put under (1).

[23] Borner and his assistants reached their conclusions from a set of questionnaires posed to businessmen in 28 countries. The result is very "conservative" in the sense that businessmen will invest irrespective of the regime, as long as there is law and order, political stability, and predictable, transparent rules of the game.

[24] There might have existed an old system that proved stable over several centuries, and was accepted by people as the state of the world; but once modern economic growth starts, a new distribution game quickly emerges.

We are interested in the public policy component entering into the distribution and its effect on political stability.[25] There is a general welfare argument for social expenditures, as well as the argument that such expenditures might be socially stabilizing.

The relevant question is whether relatively small outlays—say a few percentage points of GDP—in strategically placed social expenditures can significantly decrease sociopolitical tensions. Several of the Social Agenda Policy Group reports consider this question. This applies in particular to the ones dealing with such divided countries as Guyana and Peru, where the ethnic divisions are strong economic division lines as well. Here serious attempts by the government to "do something" are a precondition for social stability. This means that social incomes should at the very least be seen as fairly distributed. However, it appears that cuts in these expenditures have often hit the groups least able to fight for themselves in the corridors of power. It follows that the political outsiders are the ones most likely to suffer if social expenditures are cut.

Should a Country Finance Social Investment with Loans?

It has been alleged above that even social *investments* should mostly be financed by taxes, not by loans. The point is often forgotten, so it is worth a short discussion. The key point here is that, while social investments improve the income of people, they do not correspondingly improve the income of government.

A simple example will show the orders of magnitude.[26] Imagine a country that has underinvested in education until it has a social rate of return of 15 percent. This is on the high side, but not unusual. The country now decides to expand its education system with a program estimated to cost X, or x a year. Simplifying, we set the discount rate $I = 0.1$, so that $10x = X$. The assumption that the social rate of return is 0.15 means that GDP increases with $y = 0.15X$ per year in future. The capitalized present value of that income flow is $Y = (0.15/0.1)X = 1.5X$. The benefit/cost-ratio here is $Y/X = 1.5$. This is a high ratio, and the expansion is decided.

Let us assume that the country decides to cover X by a loan. To make things simple, we further assume that the interest on the loan is $I = 0.1$, so that $L = X$. In future years the government has to collect X in taxes and repay the loan. The country is then left with a net gain of $0.5X$. In other words, welfare is improved by $0.5X$, as a result of the educational expansion. The reason for covering X by a loan is that the government finds it difficult to collect taxes now and thinks it will be easier in the future. This might be because of the time profiles of the x- and y-streams, so that a lot of the costs X comes early, while most of Y comes much later.

---

[25] Many attempts to sort out these complex issues have been made, and a large literature exists: some argue that the fairness of the process is what matters while others look at the fairness of the outcome. The key issue here is that it is easy to think of conditions where all kinds of unfairness pervade society—in such cases it is difficult to achieve political stability.

[26] The terminology used is that small letters, x, y,..., are flows, while the corresponding capitals, X, Y, ... are present values. The capitalization factor, i, is the opportunity cost of capital, set at 0.1, and taken to be the international borrowing rate.

However, the tax-difficulty can be translated into saying that the tax constraint binds, so that the effective marginal tax rate t is "stuck" at t. It might be higher according to tax laws; but the government has found that when GDP goes up with z, only tz "turns up" in the treasury. In Latin America it appears that t rarely reaches 0.3. That allows us to calculate that the government will receive at most a tax revenue of $T = 0.3Y = 0.3x1.5X = 0.45X$ as a result of educational expansion, 0.55X of the loan remains uncovered. If the tax constraint is binding, other public expenditures have to be cut by 0.55X. This is a simple crowding out effect. We now have a much less favorable welfare tradeoff: net gain from the education expansion is 0.5X, and net loss due to crowding out is 0.55X.

The argument for financing educational expansions by loans must, therefore, implicitly assume that the government can collect taxes more easily later, and will do so. This may or may not be the case. It could also be a typical example of government myopia, as is so often found in the political business cycle literature (see Paldam, 1997a, for a survey, dealing with this point). It is much better to solve the problem by financing the educational expansion through tax income right away.

To conclude, it is well known that the condition for countries financing *consumption* by loans is hard to meet. We have added that if countries have difficulties collecting tax revenue, they should think twice before financing social *investments* through loans.

The Lines Back: The Dead Hand of Path Dependency

We shall first look at the ISI-strategy and second at the results of the SA-package. The picture most people have in mind appears as presented in Figure 4.2. A main variation in the pattern is that the timing—notably the date of introducing the main SA-Package—differs by almost 20 years from the first to the last country. The first was Chile in 1974–80, that did it alone and in a hard way. It has gradually spread to the rest of Latin America, Africa, and the countries of the former Soviet block.

The Legacy of the ISI-Strategy

For many years the ISI-approach was the main policy in Latin America. The story has often been told, so we can be brief:

(1) The world market was seen as a problem, not as a solution, and most countries isolated themselves behind high tariff walls and often amazingly complex exchange regulations. The result was low trade shares and remarkably little interregional trade, as seen in Table 4.7. On the map, the border between Chile and Argentina resembles the one between Norway and Sweden. However, even when measured in percentages of GDP, trade across the latter border is about 10 times higher than across the former. The amount of paperwork and time it takes to cross the borders differ even more. The main crossing between Argentina and Chile has a great name: Los Libertadores; but it is surely not trade that has been liberated.

(2) The policies had a strong bias against agriculture and in favor of industry. Export taxes and especially unfavorable exchange rates and credit regulations were used to squeeze income and savings out of agriculture and into industry.

TABLE 4.7. Comparison of Trade Shares of Countries with Roughly the Same GDP (1993–94)
(Percentage)

LA-Country	Trade share	NWE-Country	Trade share
Brazil	13	Netherlands	55
Mexico	21	Sweden	32
Argentina	8	Denmark	35

Note: The trade share is the export of goods and services in percent of GDP.

(3) The parastatal became a major instrument of industrialization. Throughout the region the state came to own much of the modern sector: often the banks and insurance companies, utilities, sometimes even parts of the retail trade, and so forth. A large portion of public investment funds went into the creation of parastatals.

(4) Overstaffing in parastatals and other public agencies became the main social policy. As a result nearly all Latin American parastatals exhausted the rents generated by import protection, and, in addition, they developed deficits.

The Cul-de-Sac Property of the ISI-Strategy

It is important to remember that in the beginning ISI-policies did succeed impressively—the G1-area on Figure 4.2 did indeed appear.[27] Growth developed reasonably well and employment remarkably well. No wonder that this policy became the Latin American development strategy. However, it turned out to be a dead-end. This became increasingly clear during the 1970s, but it was difficult to change course immediately. Most countries only started the big turnaround during the 1980s, and some are, even today, in the middle of it. Such changes inevitably create huge problems. Only half of countries covered in the Social Agenda Policy Group reports have managed to complete the change and are feeling the positive effects of these changes. Privatization, in particular, has only run its course in some of the countries (see also IBRD, 1995), and only a few have managed to overcome the social problems as discussed.

Before we look at the policy changes, it is worth considering the three main reasons why the ISI-strategy turned out to be a dead-end. They follow from the fact that this strategy created an inefficient modern sector characterized by large-scale overstaffing, heavily protected by import regulation on the economic front and strong rent-seeking coalitions on the political front. The main political problem with rent-seeking coalitions is that they cut across political division lines. Management and workers here unite around the protection of dead-weight-losses. Large-scale overstaffing maintained by political power increases budget deficits that either generate debt and inflation, or crowd out other public programs.

The isolation from the world market, the rent-seeking coalitions, and the pressures

---

[27] The most concrete formal demonstration of the ISI-bubble, and the later stagnation, is probably by Rama (1993, 1994), working with (unique) data from Uruguay.

on the budget created decades of high inflation and growing debt in most Latin American countries. The inflation rates of the OECD countries are strongly correlated, constituting a world inflation rate.[28] The high inflation rates of Latin America have much less intercorrelation, and are largely independent of world inflation. High inflation and stagnating-to-falling real products have often resulted in decreasing real wages.

The inflation tax gradually became less efficient and debt burdens could grow no further. The result was a budget squeeze. When it started to bite, cuts had to be made since taxes could not be increased. What can easily be cut are "loose" expenditures, such as new investments, repairs and maintenance. Social expenditures are relatively easy to cut, as they are defended by politically weak groups. Inflation allowed cuts in real salaries of public sector employees. Falling real wages, overstaffing, and the general deterioration of the infrastructure have often been demoralizing throughout the public sector, as further discussed in a later section.

The SA-package: Liberalization and Privatization

The events sketched led to a widespread feeling of government failure, which got stronger from the mid-1980s. At the same time the wheels of history started to turn in Europe too, a turn that later became most dramatic: in spite of very high investment ratios the socialist countries lagged more and more behind the West. Finally, East European socialism collapsed altogether. The West European countries came to shine brighter in spite of the downward growth kink in the mid-1970s. The NIC's became the main success story. In Latin America, the example of Chile stood out as a demonstration that a change of development strategy could work.[29] From 1985 onward, changes became more common. They were often pursued halfheartedly, and were frequently defeated by the old strong rent-seeking coalitions. Nevertheless, the policy gradually changed in most countries.

There are serious problems involved in this type of policy change. With liberalization, the parastatals became subject to international competition. To cope with that, radical cost-cutting was necessary and overstaffing became impossible. This caused increases in unemployment.

The second serious problem is that privatization is difficult to carry out, both politically, as discussed, and economically. Privatization if done too quickly, will inevitably result in firms being sold at low prices. Groups with access to liquid funds score large profits and the income distribution deteriorates. If it is done slowly, however, time passes by, during which the ownership of the firm is blowing in the wind. That is very serious for the health of a firm.

---

[28] The author has calculated many correlation matrices between the inflation rates of OECD countries. They are typically in the range of 0.5 to 0.8. Similar correlations between the Latin American countries give numbers that are much more variable and small, often even negative.

[29] In connection with the Chilean example, it has often been argued that it shows that a tough dictator is necessary to keep the new policies in place long enough for them to work. The cure thus comes with a curse. However, there is also the example of Costa Rica which went through a serious debt crisis and a set of reforms in the mid-1980s, that turned the economy into a new growth and high employment path without an authoritarian regime.

These problems typically mean that a liberalization-privatization process gets many firms into serious difficulties, with the result that unemployment shoots up. The change of course is often undertaken as a reaction to some special shock to the political or economic system. It is often difficult to determine how much of the ensuing problems are due to the shock, to the old problems, and to the change of course. However, after some time the changes begin to work. This, is particularly the case when the change in economic regime has been helped externally by structural adjustment loans.

A Closer Look at Four Main Problems

The developments discussed so far brought many countries fairly closer to the Chicago Model. They may wish to move in the direction of the Welfare Model. Nevertheless, four main problems prevent movements in that direction, and they are likely to continue acting as brakes. They should be discussed simultaneously as they interact, but we have to present them one after another.

Overstaffing and Work Effort

Economic theory has increasingly discovered that work efforts matter. Next to the number of employees and the stock of physical and human capital, it also matters how much effort employees put into their work.[30] Effort is a tricky variable, but the following four factors are likely to impact upon it:

(i) *Real wages.* The efficiency wage theory looks at the firm's profits in terms of the wages it pays: it says that while too high wages are a waste of profits, too low wages reduce work effort so much that it is bad business too. Consequently, society has wage "norms," which everybody recognizes, and from which it is expensive for the firms to deviate.

(ii) *The amount of overstaffing.* It is often argued that it is better wel-fare-wise that two people share the work of one than that one person works and the other is unemployed. It has even been argued that this will cause competition among workers to do the work quickly and carefully. However, there is evidence that efficiency-wise this is not so. Overstaffing normally causes productivity to drop more than proportionally: if two men are employed to do the work of one, they tend to do only three-quarters of the work.

(iii) *Poor and politicized management* is demoralizing for work efforts. The management of a heavily protected parastatal knows that its success depends more on the relation to the political authorities than anything else. Politicians do not have profit maximization in the firms as their main goal, but rather employment, and so on.

In parastatals one has often seen that overemployment and pressures from the budget (see below) have led to inadequate deficit financing, causing serious cash-flow problems. Such problems cause serious disruption in production: suppliers and employees are

---

[30] This would seem a trivial point to the casual observer, but it was long disregarded by economists. It was something discussed in sociology and management science, but it was not thought to be relevant for macroeconomics. However, this is no longer true as one of the key models in modern labor market theory is "the efficiency wage model." See from a slightly different perspective, Congleton (1991).

TABLE 4.8. The Effort-Variable in the Four Squares of Table 4.6

Communist Model	Welfare Model
$e \downarrow$	$e \rightarrow e_m$ (slow)
ISI Model	Chicago Model
$e \rightarrow e_m/2$	$e \rightarrow e_m$ (fast)

Note: see Table 4.6

paid with long delays, spares are not available, and so forth.[31] In the Social Agenda Policy Group country reports underlying this essay, many such stories are told. One frequently meets an atmosphere of hopelessness in firms and administrations that are open only because they cannot go bankrupt.

(iv) *Poor maintenance and seemingly arbitrary production breaks* are demoralizing. The general feeling quickly emerges that nobody cares about such trifles as productivity.

These points explain the *import liberalization puzzle*, namely, the experience of many countries which, once they liberalize (that is, allow imports), see an upsurge of exports.

For many years the economist's case for free trade rested upon comparative advantage. However, those who have tried to calculate the size of the likely gains have found them negligible. The gain from raising trade shares from 10 percent to 20 percent is perhaps an upward shift of 1 percent of GDP. However, the gains from forcing the firms to be efficient and breaking up rent-seeking coalitions are substantial. We are probably speaking of differences in the growth rate of 1 to 2 percent.

The argument can be made using the 2x2-classification of Table 4.6. The Chicago Model forces the firms to compete so that much is done to keep efforts at a maximum: $e \rightarrow e_m$. In the Welfare Model firms are also forced to compete, but the interest of the individuals is smaller due to high marginal taxes. The ISI Model leads to severe overstaffing in the parastatal and protected sector. We have argued that overstaffing is by a factor two. We hence get efforts at $e_m/2$. It is a simple way to treat something very complex, but the basic logic seems to correspond to casual observation.

The main point we are making is that work effort is a variable that is affected by many things in society. It is important for any sector in the economy that there is efficiency in other sectors.

The Pressures on the Budget Balance—Some Orders of Magnitudes

To give quantitative "flesh" to the dry story of the budget balance pressure, we have constructed a stylized revenue-expenditure example, presented as Tables 4.9a and b. The

---

[31] In addition, there are the dramatic balance-of-payments crises caused by the debt burden (and before that, by fluctuations in export prices) leading to sudden restrictions on intermediate products and spare parts. If such (frequent) emergency restrictions hit a firm suffering from serious cash flow problems, the result is low capacity utilization, leading to spiralling problems.

TABLE 4.9a. The Tax-Constraint—Typical Public Sector Revenue and Expenditures, 1980

Public revenue/Gap filling		Share	Expenditures		Share
R1	Income tax and social security	9%	E1	Defense and administration	4%
R2	Indirect taxes incl. property tax	7%	E2	Education and health	7%
R3	Foreign trade and resource rent	4%	E3	Infrastructure and housing	3%
R4	Permanent seigniorage	1%	E4	Other expenditures	2%
R5	Permanent domestic borrowing	2%	E5	Social programs and pensions	6%
SR	Permanently financed	23%	SE	Traditional expenditures	22%
—	———	—	—	———	—
G1	Inflation tax	} 7%	E7	Support for parastatals	4%
G2	Foreign borrowing		E8	Debt service	4%

On the items: The numbers are averages for 16 Latin American countries, each showing a great deal of variation. R4 and R5 indicate that a country can live with a budget deficit of about 2 to 4 percent for a long time. G1 and G2 are the non-permanent sources of budget finance, they differ widely between the countries and over time, but the sum is more stable than the parts. E1 includes police and legal system. E2 includes investment, repair and maintenance. E4 includes support to agriculture, protection of the environment, church and culture, and so on. The division between E4, E5 and E7 is somewhat arbitrary.

items presented are an average for a typical country.[32] Let us first look at the old picture before the SA-policies (Table 4.9a). The tax-constraint means that the sum of total revenue is given (SR=23 percent).

It is difficult to provide a reasonable education and health system for less than 12 percent of GDP. In most developed countries the cost is about 15 percent, whereas in Latin America the public sector only provided around 7 percent. The users, therefore, have to pay something for this service, probably around 4 percent in 1980, rising to 5 percent in 1990. We thus know that users now pay almost half the total health expenditures in Latin America, and perhaps a third of the education expenditures. They paid a little less in 1980. The administration, defense, and legal systems take another 4 percent in most countries.[33] Given the expenditures on infrastructure and other services, there is about 8 percent left for social programs, investment subsidies, and deficit coverage in the parastatals plus debt service. Since the latter two items alone needed the 8 percent, the ends cannot meet. This creates very strong pressures on the budget balance.

During the 15 years preceding the debt crisis that started in August 1982, the budget was "balanced" in many Latin American countries by borrowing and the inflation tax. As the internal capital markets are thin in most of the countries, it was necessary to borrow abroad. The average budget-closure expenditures around 1980 amounted to about 10 percent of GDP.

Note the two "financial revenue items" in the table: R4 and R5. They suggest that countries can get away with a minor budget deficit in the longer run. It is hard to identify the exact limit, but the empirical evidence shows that countries can "live with" bud-

---

[32] The numbers published in the ECLAC yearbook and by IMF and IBRD are surprisingly hard to make comparable and put in the relevant categories, but we have tried.

[33] The military costs 2 percent of GDP in the average Latin American country. One may argue that it is too much, but it is not such a heavy burden as is often alleged.

TABLE 4.9b. The Tax-Constraint, 1990

Public revenue/Gap filling		Share	Expenditures		Share
R1	Income tax and social security	9%	E1	Defense and administration	4%
R2	Indirect taxes incl. property tax	7%	E2	Education and health	7%
R3	Foreign trade and resource rent	3%	E3	Infrastructure	2%
R4	Permanent seigniorage	1%	E4	Other necessary expenditures	2%
R5	Permanent domestic borrowing	2%	E5	Social programs and pensions	4%
SR	Permanently financed	22%	SE	Traditional expenditures	19%
—	——	—	—	——	—
G1	Inflation tax	} 4%	E7	Support for parastatals	3%
G2	Foreign borrowing		E8	Debt service	4%

get deficits of just below 3 percent of GNP without getting into serious problems.[34] Real seignorage is normally calculated to amount to just above 0.5 percent. There is some extra scope for non-inflationary deficits. The non-sustainable deficit was thus almost 5 percent.

Table 4.9b shows why budgets have been squeezed in most Latin American countries as a result of the SA-packages. The orders of magnitude are staggering to consider. Instead of net borrowing from abroad, many countries suddenly had to make net payments. By the mid-1980s the budget balance had worsened by 5–6 percent of GNP, making it extremely difficult to make ends meet. Here the inflation tax was used, but this is, like borrowing, only a temporary measure. By 1990, the inflation-tax gap had also been reduced, and the main expenditure items had been cut correspondingly. The net debt service is about the same as it was in 1980, which is about 2 percentage points lower than when it peaked in the mid-1980s.

As taxes were not raised, nearly all expenditure items had to be cut. The data tell that the share of education and health has remained at 7 percent. However, from the seven reports (of the Social Agenda Policy Group), and other information, we know that education and health have been squeezed. What has happened is probably that demand for these services has grown more than GDP and budgets, with the result that the situation has deteriorated. However, the big looser has been the social programs. Also, of course, support for the parastatal sector has decreased throughout Latin America; but as IBRD (1995) shows, the actual reduction in that sector has been slow.

In several countries privatization has been done via debt-equity swaps, or the proceeds of privatization have been used to reduce the debt burden. There have also been various debt reducing measures taken so that items E7 and E8 have fallen compared to their maximum sizes in the mid-1980s. However, it has been necessary to squeeze the remaining expenses as well. While privatization helps to close the budget, the other side of

---

[34] A large literature exists on this point. The crude rule of thumb is that a country can finance the sum of the growth rate and the rate of seigniorage. However, to this should be added the "deficit margin," that is the difference between the growth rate and the long-run real interest rate. The deficit margin has been negative for a decade now, before that it was positive for about three decades.

the SA-package is foreign trade liberalization. This works to reduce R3, the trade taxes, and hence makes it more difficult, once again, to balance the budget.

Why Are Taxes so Low in Latin America?

The typical tax pressure is around 45 percent of GDP in OECD countries while it is around 22 percent in Latin America. The difference is even bigger than it looks: foreign trade is marginally subsidized in OECD countries while it is taxed by 3 to 4 percent of GDP in Latin American countries.[35] The most dramatic difference is found in the field of income tax. Here, 20–30 percent of GDP is collected in the OECD countries, while less than 10 percent is the norm in Latin America. It has proved difficult to raise taxes above that limit even in the most advanced countries. There is no evidence that income taxes have been raised in Latin America in reaction to the budget squeeze discussed in the previous section.

It is a recurrent theme of all seven Social Agenda country reports that the public sector is seriously starved for funds. The nature of the short-run problem was discussed above. The long-run problem is that it has proved very difficult to raise taxes, both politically and, where the political will has been present, in practice. In the least developed countries this is part of a general pattern. These countries have a large subsistence sector, which is hard to tax. In the more advanced countries, where the subsistence sector is small, it is harder to understand.

Part of the problem is the low tax efforts made. As discussed earlier, it is difficult to *collect* taxes. A diligent and efficient administration is necessary. If work efforts are low, it becomes impossible to collect high taxes. In addition, high inflation makes tax collection particularly difficult. This is known as Tanzi's law. There are two such laws. Tanzi (1): Collection lags eat tax revenue. This is a problem for all taxes. Income taxes have an additional problem. Tanzi (2): Inflation makes income accounting harder, and hence income much more difficult to tax. With sufficiently high inflation, the administration of the income tax breaks down. Even when inflation is gone, it is difficult to revive an efficient tax collection system.

Alleviating Transition Costs

The preceding argument points to a dilemma: (a) the SA-package was necessary to break out of the ISI-cul-de-sac; (b) the package has large transition costs for a considerable period; and (c) it creates strong pressures on the budget. Hence, the package automatically reduces the public funds available to alleviate the medium-term social problems it creates.

Next to these obvious welfare problems are political problems: widespread discontent with the policies might cause social reactions that make them fail and, therefore, prolong

---

[35] The numbers vary widely, as some of the taxes are on resource rent (that is, the difference between production costs and the world market price), while others are a tax on farm incomes. The average foreign trade tax is just below 2 percent, as exports constitute about 10 percent of GDP and one-third is untaxed industrial exports, the tax rate takes about 30 to 40 percent of farm income from export.

the necessary adjustments. This is particularly clear when we look at the consumption support schemes in the oil countries. They are made to distribute wealth in times of high oil prices. When oil prices fall, they are hard to wind down.

In a broader perspective we see the ISI-package as creating something close to the oil consumption ratchet, though for smaller, easily focused, groups. What the ISI-policy does is to create pockets of *too high* salaries and employment. Those in the pockets know that they are the ones to bear the brunt of the adjustment. Everybody else stands to gain, but they will do so only gradually over time.

To put it another way, the whole idea of the SA-package is to *restructure the economy*. This means that a great deal of people must change jobs. This involves transition costs. There are two types of adjustment costs involved, one of which is income loss; and even when this mainly affects previously privileged groups, it does make things easier if they are given some help. The second is that the composition of human capital should be changed. This puts great stress upon the education sector, and it is therefore problematic that the most likely first outcome of the change is that social and education expenditures are cut.

Concluding Remarks

The reader will have noted that this is indeed an essay, drawing from many different sources and reaching tentative conclusions only. Most of the discussion has been heroic; but to discuss the macro-framework for social reform for a whole continent is heroic, so there was no way to keep both feet solidly on the ground.

On the level of choice of economic model, we presented a simple (2x2)-classification scheme, which allowed us to define a feasibility "capitalist" axis, with the Welfare Model of NW Europe at one end, and the Chicago Model at the other end. We earlier gave the two underlying questions of the essay as:

(1) Where on the feasible axis should the Latin American countries aim?

(2) What part of the axis is presently available as a realistic possibility?

Regarding (1), we argued that to be viable in the long run the socioeconomic system should be a compromise, that is, it should not be too close to the Chicago-end. Regarding (2), we argued that for a variety of historic reasons most Latin American countries were forced to move too close to the Chicago end of the axis. This is unfortunate, even when, as time passes more room for maneuvre will become available.

It was further argued that the key to moving upwards along the axis was an improvement in the collection of taxes. The idea that permanent public expenditure can be financed from anything but permanent taxes is dangerous, especially in view of the actual experiences of many Latin American countries. But Latin American taxes are notoriously low. It should be possible—without significant incentive effects—to increase taxation, and invest in education, health and some redistribution. This would create better, wealthier, and eventually more politically stable societies.

REFERENCES—SEVEN SOCIAL AGENDA POLICY GROUP COUNTRY REPORTS:

(From the Social Agenda Policy Group of the IDB, Washington DC. With joint subtitle: Report of the Pilot Mission on Socio-Economic Reform of the Inter-American Development Bank.)

IDB1: *Towards Effective Social Policy in* **Venezuela.** September 1993.

IDB2: *Building Consensus on Social Policy.* **Trinidad and Tobago.** October 1993.

IDB3: *Modernizar con todos. Hacia la integración de lo social y lo económico en* **Chile.** Enero de 1994.

IDB4: *A la búsqueda del Siglo XXI: nuevos caminos de desarrollo en* **Costa Rica.** Noviembre de 1994.

IDB5: *Building Consensus for Social and Economic Reconstruction.* The Cooperative Republic of **Guyana.** December 1994.

IDB6: **Bolivia.** *Desarrollo diferente para un país de cambios. Salir del círculo vicioso de la riqueza empobrecedora.* Febrero de 1995.

IDB7: *Challenges for Peace. Towards Sustainable Social Development in* **Peru.** April 1995.

OTHER REFERENCES

Alesina, A., and D. Rodrik. Distributive Policies and Economic Growth. *Quarterly Journal of Economics* CIX, (May) 465–490, 1992a.

_____. Distribution, Political Conflict and Economic Growth: A Simple Theory and Some Empirical Evidence. In Cukierman *et al.* 1992b.

Andersen, L.E. Convergence or Not? New Answers to Old Questions. Pt. Memo 1994–21. Økonomisk Institut, University of Aarhus, 1994.

Andersen, T.M., K.O. Moene, and A. Sandmo (eds.). 1995. The Future of the Welfare State. Special issue of *The Scandinavian Journal of Economics*, 97(2). Will appear also as book from Basil Blackwell, 1997.

Atkinson, T., and G.V. Mogensen (eds.). 1993. *Welfare and Work Incentives.* Oxford: Clarendon Press Oxford UP.

Bothworth, B.P., R. Dornbusch, and R. Labán (eds.). 1994. *The Chilean Economy. Policy Lessons and Challenges.* Washington D.C.: Brookings Institution.

Borner, S., A. Brunetti, and B. Weder. 1995. *Political Credibility and Economic Development.* London: MacMillan.

Blomström, M., and P. Mellor (eds.). 1991. *Diverging Paths. A Century of Scandinavian and Latin American Development.* Johns Hopkins University Press (for the IDB).

Chenery, H.B., and M. Syrquin. 1975. *Patterns of Development, 1950–70.* Oxford: Oxford U.P.

Chenery, H.B., M.S. Ahluwalia, C.L.G. Bell, *et al.* 1974. *Redistribution with Growth.* Oxford: Oxford UP.

Chenery, H.B., and T.N. Srinivasan (eds.). 1988. *Handbook of Development Economics*, Vol I. Amsterdam: North-Holland

Congleton, R.D. 1991. The Economic Role of Work Ethic. *Journal of Economic and Organization.* 15: 365–385.

Cukierman, A., Z. Hercovitz, and L. Leiderman (eds.). *Political Economy, Growth of Business Cycles.* MIT Press.

Fischer, S. 1995. Structural Adjustment Lessons from the 1980s. In Schydlowsky (1995).

Gwartney, J., R. Lawson, and W. Block. 1996. Economic Freedom of the World. Vancouver, B.C.: The Frazer Institute.

IBRD. 1995. *Bureaucrats in Business. The Economics and Politics of Government Ownership.* (A World Bank Policy Research Report) Oxford: Oxford UP.

IDB, 1995 Report: *Overcoming Volatility.* Washington, D.C.: IDB.

Krueger, A.O., M. Schiff, and A. Valdès. 1991, 1992. *The Political Economy of Agricultural Pricing Policy* (5 vols.) Baltimore, MD: John Hopkins University Press for the IBRD.

Laursen, K., and M. Paldam. 1982. The Dynamics of the World's Income Distribution 1955-2000. In *Economic Essays in Honour of Jørgen H. Gelting.* Special Issue of *Nationaløkonomisk tidsskrift.*

Lampedusa, G.T. di. 1958. *The Leopard.* (From Italian: Il Gattopardo).

Lindbeck, A., P. Molander, T. Persson, *et al.*, 1993. Options for Economic and Political Reform in Sweden. *Economic Policy* 17: 219–263.

Lindbeck, A. 1995. Welfare State Disincentives with Endogenous Habits and Norms. In Andersen, Moene and Sandmo (1995).

Meller, P. 1992. *Adjustment and Equality in Chile.* Paris: OECD Development Centre Studies.

Mueller, D.C. (ed.). 1997. *Issues in Public Choice.* New York: Cambridge UP. (Under printing).

Paldam, M. 1997a. Political Business Cycles. In Mueller (1997).

_____. 1997b. Behind the Vertical Supply Curve for Labor. *Nordic Journal for Political Economy,* 1997.

Perotti, R. 1992. Income Distribution, Politics and Growth. *American Economic Review, Papers and Proceedings:* 311–316.

Persson, T., and G. Tabellini. 1992. Growth, Distribution and Politics. *European Economic Review* 36: 593–602.

_____. 1994. Is Inequality Harmful for Growth? *American Economic Review* 84 (3): 600–621.

Pyle, H. 1883. *The Merry Adventures of Robin Hood.* Many editions.

Rama, M. 1993. Rent Seeking and Economic Growth. A Theoretical Model and Some Empirical Evidence. *Journal of Development Economics,* 42: 35–50.

_____. 1994. Endogenous Trade Policy: A Time-Series Approach. *Economics and Politics* 6: 215–232.

Schydlowsky, D.E. (ed.) 1995. *Structural Adjustment. Retrospect and Prospect.* Westport, Conn.: Praeger.

Syrquin, M. 1988. Pattern of Structural Change. In Chenery and Srinivasan (1988). Amsterdam: North Holland.

Weaver, J.E. 1995. What Is Structural Adjustment? In Schydlowsky (1995).

Williamson, J. 1990. What Washington Means by Policy Reform. In Williamson (1990).

Williamson, J. (ed.). 1990. *Latin American Adjustment: How Much Has Happened?* Washington, D.C.: Institute for International Economics.

Williamson, J. 1995. Policy Reform in Latin America in the 80s. In Schydlowsky (1995).

PART V

Development Thinking in the XXI Century

Is Development Economics Still Relevant?

H. W. Singer[1]

In one sense, our title's question as to the relevance of development economics actually answers itself. The development problem has certainly not disappeared. On the contrary, the economic gap dividing rich and poor countries has widened; there are more poor people in the world today than ever before; the problem of Africa's marginalization is becoming increasingly urgent; and many developing countries are racked by civil wars and tribal conflicts that are setting back the cause of development. The list goes on and on. Thus, an understanding of the difficulties of developing countries and the designing of policies that seek to provide a solution to the development problem are certainly still necessary—more necessary, in fact, than ever.

But those like Deepak Lal who speak of the "demise" of development economics mean something different. They do not contend that the development problem has been solved nor that it is on course to be solved, but rather that development economics—or at least the old style of development economics—is neither a necessary nor a suitable tool today for solving that problem. This contention holds that traditional development economics was misguided and that it thus misled developing countries into adopting harmful policies. It also holds that the rules of traditional development economics were supposedly identical to those of general economics (that is, that the "sound fundamentals" that supported growth in developed countries were seen as applicable and recommendable to developing countries ["monoeconomics"]). In the present paper we shall be considering both of these criticisms.

What are the specific accusations against the old-style development economics? In the first place, the old approach supposedly assigned an excessive role to government and placed excessive faith in government planning and in the wisdom of government intervention. There is certainly much truth in this contention insofar as it refers to the early development economists. But we must understand the historical context in which development economics emerged as a lively separate subdiscipline of economics some 50 years ago at the end of World War II. People like Rosenstein Rodan, Arthur Lewis, Gunnar Myrdal, Ragnar Nurkse, and Raúl Prebisch were strongly influenced by the successful U.K. economic planning experience during the war, by the war success of the centrally planned Soviet Union, by the Keynesian demonstration of the possibility of an

[1] Institute of Development Studies at the University of Sussex, England.

active interventionist macroeconomic full-employment policy, by the experiences of Roosevelt's New Deal, and by the creation of a social-welfare state in the United Kingdom along the lines of the Beveridge Report. In the optimistic spirit of 1945 it was assumed that such successes and precedents would be readily replicable throughout the world. As for market forces, it was partially a question of emphasizing market failures as stemming from externalities or from imperfect competition and partially (perhaps mainly) a matter of assuming that in developing countries, market forces simply did not exist and had first to be created by government action. Again, in the circumstances of the late 1940s and the early 1950s there existed more justification than today for both of these assumptions.

Where do we now stand on this issue? Very few—even among the most ardent advocates of the application of market principles to development—would deny that there exists an important role for the state in economic development. The government has to provide the following: the infrastructural investment that by definition is not normally profitable for private investors to undertake; the needed social expenditures on health services, education, sanitation, and the like (the importance of which is in fact increasingly emphasized today); the essential framework of law and order; and the macroeconomic conditions by means of which the economy is kept on a course of steady growth or expansion. All of these state obligations are undisputed. The only disputed function is the direct production process and the extent to which the state should involve itself in it. The early development economists would readily have agreed that the undisputed functions are vastly more important than this last disputed function. Thus, just as there can be no disputing that the development problem is as crucial as ever, there can be no question that the undisputed government functions are more important than ever, especially in the area of human development through health, education, and other social investments. Even the chief advocates for the application of market principles, such as the IMF and World Bank under the Washington consensus, not only deal with governments and operate through governments but also are themselves increasingly emphasizing the importance of the aforementioned undisputed governmental functions. They certainly would not speak of a demise of government, whatever they may think of the demise of development economics.

The criticism then has actually revolved not so much around whether the early development economics overrated the importance of governmental functions as around the actual ability of governments to carry out these assigned functions. The more extreme version of criticism would argue that governments are constitutionally incapable of carrying out such functions, that governments by their very nature are corrupt, incompetent, and too bureaucratic to understand the needs of the economy. These more extreme critics then subdivide into two smaller branches: the less extreme branch would conclude that government reform is the most important task of development economics, thereby drastically shifting the focus of development economics but not necessarily resulting in the latter's "demise;" the more extreme branch would despair of ever reforming governments and would "keep them out of development" altogether (which is not a common stance). In turn, the milder version of criticism would be to admit market failures but to argue that government failures are worse than market failures and that therefore keeping governments out of development amounts to choosing the lesser of two evils. Current economic-analysis techniques are unable to test this contention by means of comparable composite measurements of market failures and government failures, nor has the best technology for correcting market failures been sufficiently clarified, and thus, by and large, in development analysis applied to particular countries it remains a matter of judgment whether to put government reform or market reform first; an eclectic view would be that both have to be tackled and that there is no need to debate their relative importance.

The position of the early development economists on the question of state action versus market forces is closely related to their belief in the importance of "cumulative causation" (Myrdal's term). This term implies that development is largely a matter of the interaction of beneficial circles whereby an upward movement or improvement of sector A or factor A sets in motion an upward movement in sector B or factor B, which in turn continues to spread to other sectors or factors, with a positive backwash effect also on the original factor A. It will be readily seen that this view of "everything hanging together" in a system of cumulative causation or beneficial circles lies behind such ideas as the search for forward and backward linkages (emphasized by Albert Hirschman), input-output studies, and theories of balanced growth (associated with the name of Ragnar Nurkse). The belief in cumulative causation or beneficial circles also implies the possibility of its opposite—that is, the existence of vicious circles in which nothing moves because everything has to wait for action somewhere else. In assuming the possibility of such vicious circles, or "poverty traps," in developing countries, development economists were clearly influenced by the Keynesian demonstration of the possibility of "underemployment equilibrium" and by his view that some external force such as government intervention would be needed to break the vicious circle and to create a beneficial circle of expansion. Schumpeter, in his *Theory of Economic Development,* looked for such an external force to be provided through the innovator and the enterprising entrepreneur, while others looked to technology and research and development or to foreign aid or other external-capital inflows; but governmental intervention, even if limited to fiscal and monetary policy, remained the prime method, in the view of the early development economists, of breaking the vicious circle and escaping the poverty trap.

Another accusation leveled against the early development economists is that they concentrated too much on savings and physical-investment rates as the determinants of growth—on investing in concrete rather than in people—and that this emphasis led to the neglect of other factors that also determine growth (such as human-capital improvements, technological advances, rises in total factor productivity, increasing returns, and the like). They are also criticized for identifying development too much with economic growth and for ignoring key elements such as income distribution, poverty reduction, environmental protection, access to education, and so forth. How much truth was there in these accusations?

The mainstay of the old development economics was the Harrod-Domar formula (H-D). It is true that the H-D numerator does specifically mention the rate of physical investment, but attention should also be paid to its denominator (that is, to the capital-output ratio). The capital-output ratio (or investment productivity, in terms of streams of output) served as a catchall into which all the neglected factors could be thrown: improvements in human capital (a better-educated and healthier labor force) also increase the productivity of investment, as do technological progress and increasing returns. Thus, in formal terms the criticism is not really justified since all of the allegedly neglected factors could in fact be accommodated in the overall category of the capital-output ratio. But the fact that the rate of investment was the only factor specifically identified in H-D whereas all the other factors were broadly subsumed (and to some extent suppressed) in the capital-output ratio does give some substance to the criticism of such statements as Arthur Lewis's declaration that raising the savings and investment rate from 5 percent to 12 percent was "the central problem of economic development." Today we attribute much greater importance to all these other growth factors, and a modern version of H-D would make them explicit at the same level of emphasis as the rate of investment. Even so, the early development economists were by no means unaware of the importance of these other growth factors and in fact stressed them in their verbal expositions. This awareness on their part recasts the criticism into the assertion that the early development economics simply did not have the capacity to produce an adequate model for reflecting all the various factors in economic growth. In this respect much progress has been made, and there is no lack today of models that are more satisfactory.

The other accusation—that development was too much identified with economic growth—is much more justified. The H-D formula treats the rate of growth of per capita GNP as the independent variable. But increasingly, a clearer distinction is now drawn between means and ends. The final objective of development is surely more than just a growth in per capita GNP. In the current discussion the recognized end of development is defined in such terms as reduction of poverty, satisfaction of basic needs, creation of greater opportunities for human fulfillment through access to work opportunities or social services, and ultimately an increase in human opportunities or a wider range of choice. Thus, the UNDP's *Human Development Report* defines its objective of "sustainable human development" as "the process of enlarging people's capabilities and choices so as to enable them better to satisfy their own needs." The first approach of the early development economists was clearly too economistic, as is indeed indicated by the term itself: development *economics*. The new vistas opened up by John Keynes and Colin Clark in measuring and comparing national incomes proved too tempting for the early development economists not to base their discussions primarily on what happened to GNP. The backlash against this approach was not long in coming; the seminal articles were those by Dudley Seers on "The Meaning of Development" and "The Dethronement of GNP." With this backwash came also a shift from development economics to development studies—a recognition of ethical, social, and political elements in judging how to approach or measure the true objective of increasing the range of human opportunities.

Rather ironically, the more extreme backlash against the early development economics—in the form of the neoclassical monoeconomic counterrevolution—is in a way a throwback to the very early economistic stage of development economics. The IMF and World Bank stabilization and structural adjustment programs are criticized for putting too much emphasis on economic growth and for lacking a "human face." The neoclassical defense is that economic growth is essential for poverty reduction and other social improvements, that "a rising tide lifts all boats," and that the cake must first be produced before it can be distributed. Nobody doubts that, other things being equal, growth is better than no growth and that it provides (at least potentially) the resources to fulfill the true ends of development. Nevertheless, there exists considerable doubt in current development economics about the implied ease with which economic resources created by growth are being converted into human development. The *pattern* of growth is now considered to be as important as, (or more important) than the *rate* of growth, and certain patterns of growth are viewed as hostile to rather than contributory to human development. Under the impact of such criticism (which is similar to the criticism of the early economistic interpretation of H-D), the Bretton Woods Institutions and the followers of the Washington consensus have begun to pay greater attention to poverty alleviation, human indicators, and the like. In this way, the history of development economics can be treated as comprising two similar cycles: first, emphasis on GNP growth in the 1940s and 1950s followed by emphasis on distribution in the 1960s and 1970s and second, renewed emphasis on GNP growth in the neoclassical counterrevolution during the 1980s followed by renewed emphasis on human development and poverty alleviation in the 1990s.

Still remaining for discussion here is the criticism that development economists have given mistaken policy guidance to developing countries. This criticism centers on the strategy of import-substituting industrialization (ISI). Here again, however, it can be argued that the stand taken by the mainstream of the early development economists was correct for the circumstances of the day and that the lessons of development experience have been on their side. Certainly the successful tigers have industrialized, and they now produce domestically a vast range of previously imported manufactured products, while marginalized Africa is lagging both in industrialization and in the capacity to home-produce essential products that must continue to be imported. Where the early development economists may have gone wrong was in their placing too much emphasis on import substitution and not enough on industrialization. In other words, they did not foresee the scope for manufactured exports—but then, who really did, or could have, in 1945? Moreover, the present neoclassical demonization of the strategy of import-substituting industrialization, given the neoclassicists' approval of increasing domestic food production and the production of agricultural raw materials, is perhaps more a criticism of industrialization than of import substitution.

How Well Do Economists Serve Development Theory and Practice?

Emanuel de Kadt[1]

Practitioners of development have now lived for some fifteen years with the *de facto* dominance of one particular theory and one particular institution: neoclassical or neoliberal economics and the World Bank. There exists widespread agreement—well beyond the Washington consensus reexamined in the present volume by John Williamson—that the market-oriented perspective promoted by this combination did provide a salutary and necessary correction: earlier overreliance on the state in economic decision making and in resource allocation had indeed brought many economically disastrous results.

Yet neoliberal economics has had little to say about the social effects of economic policies: the social effects were supposed to sort themselves out all by themselves. Had it not been for UNICEF (Cornia, Jolly, and Stewart 1987), which convincingly showed the unnecessarily disastrous side effects of early structural-adjustment programs, the practitioners of neoliberal economics might have remained socially blind for many more years. That description fortunately no longer applies. A greater concern for the social effects of market-oriented policies has been clearly visible in structural-adjustment programs, even though social issues are almost inevitably "factored in" as "afterthoughts" to the "inevitable" economic decisions. In reaction to the latter phenomenon, one of the early aims of the Social Agenda Policy Group of the Inter-American Development Bank was to contribute to the integration of social and economic policies. The social should be as much a part of fundamental development policymaking as is the economic, and in no country should the conditionalities imposed by the Washington institutions or the priorities of the minister of finance totally determine the outlines of central-government policy and spending. It was, of course, understood that these issues were above all decided upon as part of a domestic political process and that therefore they were often beyond the influence of outsiders, even of economists.[2] There was less realization that such social and economic integration of policy, if it were to have a chance, also required the development of new analytical approaches that would provide the tools with which to give "equal space" to the economic and to the social.

---

[1] Institute of Development Studies at the University of Sussex, England.
[2] Especially in Africa, authoritarian personalistic heads of state kept such basic "development decisions" in their own hands, often with scant or no reference to professional policy advisers. See Healey and Robinson (1992, particularly part II).

Through much of the 1980s, real economies did not behave as the dominant model said they should. Those deviations often were related to the very assumptions built into the model, to the conditions assumed as given and unchanging, the economists' favored *ceteris paribus*. Such false assumptions—for that is what they are—usually refer to the noneconomic sphere and to factors that are often multiple and mutually interacting or reinforcing. Gradually it became obvious, even to many of its proponents, that the (dominant) theory had failed to explain various enduring, undesired, and unexpected realities. Policy problems were not resolved by "getting the prices right," "reducing public expenditure," or even "enhancing human resources." The international financial institutions (IFIs) have become alarmed by the fact that neoliberal economic policies have resulted in growing gaps between rich and poor, in terms of incomes as well as assets, and that this outcome has even put a damper on economic growth. In general, the IFIs, bilateral donors, and Southern-Hemisphere governments are becoming more preoccupied with issues hitherto not addressed by economic theory. Economists are increasingly colonizing some of the established domains of political science and sociology.

This broadening can also be seen in most of the papers presented in the present volume. Economists' "unfinished business" is said to concern issues that are social rather than economic, issues on which noneconomists have worked, published, and advised for decades but that have largely been ignored by the self-assured fraternity of economists. Gert Rosenthal, for example, writes in his paper that the single most important unfinished issue concerns equity, to which the economists have been alerted because of worsening income distribution and the failure to provide the poor with reasonable access to social services and benefits. He rightly links this lack of equity to the lack of sufficient job opportunities (the economy), to constraints on social spending because of budgetary discipline (part economics, part politics and ideology), and to the fact that "social-policy management has not progressed with the desired agility and effectiveness." The latter sounds remarkably like blaming the noneconomic sectors of government.

A more likely major cause of the problem is that macroeconomic policymaking remains "hegemonic" or dominant in government and that very little progress has been made toward integrating the management of macroeconomic and social policy in practice or even in theory in regard to the setup of government procedures, the organization of decision making, or the design of analytical approaches. Thus it does not sound very convincing when economists let it be known in passing that "the whole matter of participatory development…will no doubt be revisited" (Rosenthal), that land reform may again receive attention, or that decentralized democracy and NGOs provide hope for an improvement of the (economic) situation in the future. The considerable knowledge from other disciplines on matters such as these is largely ignored. Nor has the work done on these issues by the multidisciplinary Social Agenda Policy Group Missions had any apparent influence on development thinking (it is too early to judge whether that research has made more of a difference with respect to development practice). Only one of the authors in the present volume refers to the mission reports or to any other output produced by the group working with Louis Emmerij over the past four years or so.

Thus far we have briefly dealt with the resultant social impact of policies that are determined largely by economic considerations. But economists are becoming increasingly concerned of late about the underlying institutional preconditions for balanced economic development, about "key state institutions whose efficient functioning is important for rapid and equitable growth" (Williamson)—problems tackled also by the Social Agenda Policy Group Missions. These problems relate to what Rosenthal calls the "second generation of reforms," which followed those carried out in the 1980s under structural adjustment. The new reforms concern the area that has come to be referred to as governance.

Attention began to be focused on the governance area at the end of the 1980s, when governments and administrations came to be seen as potential obstacles to the efficient implementation of the recommended economic policies, notably in Sub-Saharan Africa and by the World Bank (World Bank 1989). Governance referred first of all to that conglomerate of issues around policy management—how governments and public administrations actually work—that had already been partially addressed in the first wave of structural adjustment, through policies such as civil-service reform (the latter only seldom effectively implemented). But governance also dealt with the relationship of citizens to the state: questions of accountability, democracy, participation, and "civil society." Good accountability mechanisms were seen as necessary in order to prevent the outcomes that the "new political economy" expected from rent seeking; such accountability mechanisms were viewed as unlikely to function well under autocratic regimes. It was thought that newly established formal democracy would not provide sufficiently robust structures of accountability at the grass roots level: hence the emphasis on participation and the importance of civil society and NGOs. These elements had earlier been given a boost—in a kind of sideshow to privatization—as providers of services no longer (properly) furnished by shrinking states.

We need to note, however, that governance came upon the scene as an issue of relevance to economics and economic development—as an issue that could and should be considered by the World Bank "in its strict sense of the good order required for a positive investment climate and the efficient use of resources" (Mr. Shihata, General Council of the World Bank, as quoted in von Benda-Beckman 1995). Michael Lipton suggests that this development represented the World Bank's "long-overdue recognition of the primacy of politics" (Lipton 1991, 22). The present writer is not convinced. Arguably, it was in fact the reverse: a move toward the incorporation of political, administrative, and other institutional elements into economics—even their subordination to it.[3]

Neoliberal economics had a decidedly one-sided approach to politics or to the institutions of government, the context in which economic policymaking takes place: neoliberal economists did apply themselves to this institutional context, but ultimately in order to reduce it to a market situation in which individuals pursue their private inter-

---

[3] Readers of Dutch will benefit from the perceptive analysis of these issues from a juridical perspective in von Benda-Beckman (1995).

ests and maximize their "rents."[4] On the other hand, "new institutional economics"—an economic approach quite different from neoliberalism—achieved a degree of respectability and acceptance among IFI economists. One of its prime exponents is Douglass North, who also has roots in the study of economic history.[5] North argues that institutions determine the performance of economies because institutions determine an economy's transaction costs (the "general" costs incurred in operating an economic system). Thus, the World Bank's booklet on *Governance and Development* (1992) underpinned its arguments by extensive reference to North (1990)—and not by direct reference to political science or to sociology, which have also been examining the same issues over a long period, in considerable depth, with much sensitivity to nuance and variance—and hence without forcing reality into modeled simplifications. Economics has indeed built up a body of rigorous (and mathematically formulated) theory, and its models have predictive value (no matter that many of the predictions have proved wrong). The more careful theories of the middle range in the other social sciences are viewed as simply too "soft" for most economists, so the latter feel the need to translate what we know about the functioning of institutions into the language of economics and to use economists as "translators" (and in the process, unfortunately, often distorters) of the findings of political science or sociology.

Let us look briefly at a couple of examples of how economists' simplified assumptions came to be corrected. Early in the 1990s, ideas about trust and reciprocity long established in sociology began to be fed into the governance debate, showing that the neoliberal emphasis on rent seeking and other egoistic motivations in public life was at the very least one sided and often even blatantly wrong, and hence misleading as a basis for policy prescription (Moore 1992, Tendler and Freedheim 1994). Another case refers to the vigorous promotion (by IFIs and bilateral donors) of NGOs and civil society in general as viable channels for donor-supported development programs, after it had become clear that "state" and "market" were not simple alternatives. A series of studies showed that rather than contrasting the potentials of "state" and "civil society," attention should be paid to the way they are complementary or even mutually entwined or "embedded" and to the resultant scope for "synergy" (Evans 1996). Desirable goods (housing, for example) and services (health services, but also civil protection) may be more effectively produced when public and private actors complement each other or actually work together on the same task.[6]

Economists today often recommend "participatory development" and the greater use of NGOs rather than state channels. Agricultural extension circles, health facilities that have been devolved to local authorities or controlled by local user associations, and urban NGO-driven improvement projects do indeed serve their purpose. Yet there is an additional side to this phenomenon, long stressed by the other social sciences. It arises from

---

[4] For a classical statement of this (neoliberal) approach to institutions, see Krueger (1974).

[5] A short and readable introduction to his ideas can be found in North (1992).

[6] The Social Agenda Policy Group also contributed to this debate. See de Kadt and Zuckerman (1997).

the view that institutions are "regulating and allocating mechanisms" that largely define the way state and society "include" or "exclude" their citizens and so affect the lives of the principal target groups of development programs: the rural poor, the urban working class (especially those in the informal sector), minority ethnic groups, poor women, and poor children (especially, in Latin America, street children). Many problems of exclusion or repression simply cannot be resolved at a local level, not least because local power configurations stand in the way of success.

Other work published in Evans (1996a) gives interesting theoretical clues on these problems. The paper on Mexican peasant communities shows how elites perceive threats to their position when local solidarities start to spill over regionally. State or elite actors have regularly used force to thwart the attempts of indigenous Mexican communities to form organizations of sufficient scale to defend their interests (Fox 1996, 1091). In contrast, in Kerala, India, the militancy of lower-class groups, organized upward from local communities over many years, eroded traditional structures of domination; pressure from below then made it possible for the state to provide social protection, which in turn further strengthened the urban and rural poor (Heller 1996, 1057). And actors from within the state (both politicians and officials) played an important role there. Such an involvement also occurred in Mexico (Fox 1996, 1090f). But while some parts of the Mexican state were working for reform, others wanted to suppress it[7] (Evans 1996b, 1125). There also occurred authoritarian backlashes, and semi-clientelist elites managed to capture, and thereby weaken, important parts of the programs.

Rather than bewailing the fact that the problem of equity has not been solved, donor-sponsored economics-based analysis and "reform" should begin to take notice of these other contributions to development thinking, including those ideas that rest on the tradition of a more radical and more class-based approach. This sort of approach has not been favored since the 1980s, not least because it had become identified with a sterile Marxist ideology incapable of seeing the errors (and horrors) of "real socialism." The Kerala case draws our attention to the still-unfashionable idea of building "instruments of class power" and of providing the disadvantaged with political leverage through "associational autonomy rather than the clientelistic exchange of material rewards for political subordination that characterizes authoritarian-corporatist regimes" (Heller 1996, 1058).

Of course, an alternative to political leverage and conflict is solidarity. Many countries in the thrall of the Washington consensus have lost sight of solidarity's importance. It has not been high on the agenda of policymakers; often it has been wholly displaced by the concern for the market. This orientation might change if the disadvantaged really begin to flex their muscles, perhaps through the aforementioned "instruments of class power," but more likely through the already widely visible signs of growing unrest, violence, and disregard of social norms. Historically, fear for the consequences of such situ-

---

[7] Kerala was the first case of a communist party reaching power through the ballot box (in the 1950s).

ations has led to a willingness to compromise on the part of elites: the labor legislation and institutions discussed in Victor Tokman's paper are one example, and John Toye reminds us of the role of elites in the emergence of the welfare state. It is impossible to say how much the needed change might result from pressure and fear and how much it might herald a recovery of a sense of social solidarity. Policymakers could have an influence here if only they took the issue seriously. Without solidarity, pressure from below—perhaps inchoate upheaval—becomes increasingly likely.

All of the foregoing suggests that we should reject the simplifications of state and society built into currently fashionable economic models. We should remember—with the eminent Argentine political scientist Guillermo O'Donnell (harking back to the work of Max Weber)—that the state is more than just the state apparatus, the bureaucracy, and the public sector. "The state is also…a set of social relations that establishes a certain order and ultimately backs it with a centralized coercive guarantee." He adds that this order "is not an equal, socially impartial order; …it backs, and helps to reproduce, systematically asymmetric power relationships" (O'Donnell 1993, 1356). He notes that in large parts of Latin America this unequal order is reproduced because the public authorities themselves operate without respect for the rule of law. They establish power circuits based on norms and rules inconsistent with, or even antagonistic to, the national ones; at worst, the official means of violence are routinely used for private ends. O'Donnell calls these regions "neofeudalized."

In such regions the formal conditions of representative democracy may be fulfilled when people can exercise their right to vote without being subject to overt pressure, and yet people may still have no equality in other areas constitutive of citizenship, such as access to the judicial system.[8] Where the rule of law extends very irregularly over the territory, "ineffective states coexist with autonomous, also territorially based, spheres of power" in outlying areas or even in inner cities. The consequences are well known: state-backed violence against landless peasants, unlawful police actions in poor neighborhoods, the denial of rights to women and minorities, and the abandonment of children to the streets, in addition to the general inequality in the operation of the legal system (O'Donnell 1993, 1358).

Again, in this respect the Social Agenda Policy Group Missions have made contributions that should not go unnoticed, even though these contributions were not expected to focus on "development thinking" *per se*. Like the earlier-mentioned analyses by researchers, these contributions challenge a number of frequently repeated and usually untested assumptions in the realm of governance and begin to give us a peek into what is still largely a "black box": the functioning of government institutions, especially away from the center.

In the limited space available we can touch on only a few examples and shall give

---

[8] O'Donnell calls these the "liberal component of democracy." Almost 50 years ago a similar approach was taken by T.H. Marshall in his lectures on "Citizenship and Social Class" (Marshall 1963).

these from the study on Fortaleza, Brazil (Social Agenda Policy Group 1996). The dynamics of power, which sustain inequity, function (as the sociological analysis of life chances has long known) in quite specific ways. Neither generalized calls for more and better education for the poor in order to improve their chances in the labor market nor even the supplying of extra funds from the center to decentralized authorities is likely to counteract those power dynamics unless targeting is wholly specific to the least-favored schools (not simply to those zones or municipalities with the most-unfavorable statistics). Similarly, the health status of the poor, even if improving over time, is unlikely to break through the pattern of inequity unless attention is paid to the need for specific and differentiated health service responses to localized poverty-induced ill health—a problem that will emphatically not be remedied by blanket decentralization. Also, some of the most burdensome health problems in large cities cannot be tackled by the health sector alone. Yet there is no indication that government at whatever level is ready to develop an intersectorial approach to ill health, even though there are tools available to promote such approach.

Then there is decentralization. The current "ideology" of governance suggests that decentralization is "a good thing" because it improves accountability by bringing decisions closer to the users and by preventing waste. Retention of functions at the center tends to be frowned upon regardless of the capacity lower down to fulfill tasks adequately, of the need to keep supervisory or compensatory responsibilities at the more central levels, or of the extent to which the mechanisms of accountability are at all effective. As the Fortaleza report stresses, there exist clear limits to the "subsidiarity principle" (the idea that responsibility should be kept at the lowest possible level of government), and these need to be assessed for each case separately. In the case of Brazil, spending has shifted significantly away from the center, giving the central government much less power to implement policies to which it is nationally committed. As a result, widespread use is made of special funds and of earmarking of transfers to the local states or municipalities, apparently contradicting the very rationale of decentralization. Economics as such has little to contribute to the analysis of these issues.

Our conclusion is as follows: it is time that powerful institutions like the IDB or the World Bank began to take seriously the need for a genuinely intersectorial approach to policymaking and the need for a genuinely interdisciplinary approach to development problems. These institutions do have to be concerned with finance and with financial accountability and probity, yet it really does not help to look at everything exclusively through economists' eyes. At the policy level, more-serious attention should be paid to the integration of economic (read: largely macroeconomic) and other policy areas, and instruments need to be developed that can be taken into account together with the minister of finance's macroeconomic indicators. Analytically, there should exist greater willingness to develop new ideas together with noneconomists, to work on truly interdisciplinary theories of the middle range. These theories should be rooted in reality, they should be able to cope with diversity, they should transcend the frankly often-spurious rigor of economic models and the latters' pretense of being all-encompassing and all-explanatory, and they should also transcend the frequently inward-looking, uncommunicative, and at times almost esoteric theories of other social scientists.

Hans Singer entitled his contribution "Is Development Economics Still Relevant?" Our answer is "Yes, provided development economics is willing to accept its limits and to reach out to others in a genuine effort at collaboration."

REFERENCES

Cornia, Giovanni Andrea, Richard Jolly, and Frances Stewart, eds. *Adjustment with a Human face*. Oxford: Clarendon Press, 1987.

de Kadt, Emanuel, and Elaine Zuckerman, eds. *The Public-Private Mix in Social Services: Health Care and Education in Chile, Costa Rica and Venezuela: Social Agenda Policy Group*. Washington, D.C.: IDB, 1997.

Evans, Peter, ed. "Special Section: Government Action, Social Capital and Development: Creating Synergy across the Public-Private Divide." *World Development* 24, 6 (June 1996).

_____. "Government Action, Social Capital and Development: Reviewing the Evidence on Synergy." In P. Evans 1996 (1119–30).

Fox, Jonathan. "How Does Civil Society Thicken? The Political Construction of Social Capital in Rural Mexico." In P. Evans 1996 (1089–1103) (see above).

Healy, John, and Mark Robinson. *Democracy, Governance and Economic Policy: Sub-Saharan Africa in Comparative Perspective*. London: ODI, 1992.

Heller, Patrick. "Social Capital as a Product of Class Mobilization and State Intervention: Industrial Workers in Kerala, India." In P. Evans 1996 (1055–71) (see above).

Krueger, Anne O. "The Political Economy of the Rent-Seeking Society." *American Economic Review* 14, 3 (1974).

Lipton, Michael. "The State-Market Dilemma, Civil Society, and Structural Adjustment. Any Cross-Commonwealth Lessons?" *The Round Table* 317 (1991): 21–31.

Marshall, T.H. *Sociology at the Crossroads and Other Essays*. London: Heinemann, 1963.

Moore, Mick. "Competition and Pluralism in Public Bureaucracies." IDS Bulletin 23, (1992): 65-77.

North, Douglass C., *Institutions, Institutional Change, and Economic Performance*. New York: Cambridge University Press, 1990.

_____. "Transaction Costs, Institutions, and Economic Performance." *Occasional Paper* 30. San Francisco, CA: International Center for Economic Growth, 1992.

O'Donnell, Guillermo. "On the State, Democratization and Some Conceptual Problems: A Latin American View with Glances at Some Postcommunist Countries." *World Development* 21, 8 (1993): 1355–69.

Social Agenda Policy Group. *Cities Divided against Themselves: The Case of Fortaleza, Social Reform in a Brazilian Metropolis*. Washington, D.C.: IDB, 1996.

Tendler, Judith, and Sara Freedheim. "Trust in Rent-Seeking World: Health and Government Transformed in North-East Brazil." *World Development* 22, 12 (1994): 1771–91.

van Cranenburgh, Oda, and Marijke Veldhuis, eds. *Good Governance, RAWOO Lunchlezingen 1993.* RAWOO, The Hague: RAWOO, 1995.

von Benda-Beckman, Franz. "Recht en Sociale Werkelijkheid: Problematische Verhoudingen." In O. Cranenburgh, and M. Veldhuis, 1995.

World Bank. *Sub-Saharan Africa: From Crisis to Sustainable Growth.* Washington, D.C.: World Bank, 1989.

_____. *Governance and Development.* Washington, D.C.: World Bank, 1992.

Nationalizing the Antipoverty Agenda

John Toye[1]

Contradictions of an International Antipoverty Agenda

The theme of the present paper is that research into poverty has to be multidisciplinary and, perhaps more controversially, that the dominant discipline should be political science. At present, to the extent that poverty research is multidisciplinary, the dominant discipline is economics. We are looking at a situation in which a small (but technically so phisticated) economics tail is trying to wag a very large political dog. We need to arrive at a position from which we understand much better how the politics of national antipoverty strategies works, so that the economists of poverty can play the role that Keynes once envisioned for them, similar to that of humble but competent dentists.

Our fundamental political assumption here will be the following: international agendas on poverty reduction, however sincerely espoused, can be effective only by influencing national political agendas. This point has been well put by the Indian political scientist Rajni Kothari: "History has shown very clearly that one cannot constructively transform a society from the outside. All genuine social transformations have been initiated from within the society, even though in many cases the genesis for such transformation lay in the cross-fertilization of ideas and experiences from different societies" (1993, 152). The problem is to move from the cross-fertilization of ideas on poverty reduction to internally driven political agendas.

But the 1990s revival in poverty studies is driven to a very significant extent by the policies of the international agencies, starting with UNICEF in the mid-1980s, joined by UNDP and then the World Bank with its 1990 *World Development Report.* There is nothing intrinsically wrong with this: it represents an achievement to have put poverty back onto the international organizations' agenda. Nevertheless, by the mid-1990s we can see that an antipoverty agenda that is driven largely by international agencies like these contains its own internal contradictions. The following ideas (by de Swaan, 1988) have been pointed out elsewhere by the present writer (Toye and Jackson 1996, 57):

> Any international effort, like that of the Bank, to promote poverty reduction in particular countries must face up to the implications of one very central difficulty. It is perhaps not fully appreciated that the poverty reduction agenda has received high political priority in the now developed countries only at particu-

[1] Institute of Development Studies at the University of Sussex, England.

lar historical moments and under well-defined conditions. Research shows that the attitudes of the elite were crucial. They took action on the poverty alleviation issue because they shared a consensus around three beliefs. They were that: (a) the welfare of the elite and the welfare of the poor were interdependent, and the elite was not able to insulate itself from the living conditions of the poor; (b) the poor did in fact have the means to affect the welfare of the elite, principally by three methods, namely crime, insurrection and epidemic disease; and (c) some actions by the state would be efficacious in reducing the threat to the welfare of the elite posed by the behavior of the poor.

If this historical interpretation is correct, then the Bank can only make progress by taking on, with the help of bilateral aid donors, a quasi-political role. The logic of the situation seems to dictate that the Bank and the members who subscribe its capital must initiate, and then carry forward as best they can, a participatory process aimed at changing elite perceptions in ways that raise the issue of poverty reduction to a much higher priority in the domestic political agenda. … [T]he task now is to push the policy dialogue forward to the point where governments that have not already done so recognize and internalize the three propositions (a, b, and c given above) which should trigger their own active engagement with the conditions of the poor.

The fact that the antipoverty agenda is being driven by these international organizations also results in the fact that the available diagnosis of the poverty problem is the diagnosis made by them. Because the international organizations have the resources to prepare poverty assessments for numerous poor countries over a fairly short time scale and because many of these countries have not tackled this task for themselves, the nature and scope of the poverty problem tend to get defined externally and in a particular highly economistic way. This definition in turn sets the parameters for the policies that count as solutions. The situation is not quite as simple as just stated; the international organizations have in fact sporadically tried to incorporate into their methods of poverty description and diagnosis certain more "bottom-up" anthropological and sociological methods consisting of an array of information-gathering techniques collectively called "participatory poverty appraisal." But the fit among the poverty descriptions, diagnoses, and prescriptions based on the (interestingly labeled) "objective" and "subjective" methods is frequently imperfect, when the latter are used at all.

The dominant conceptualization of poverty thus remains the narrow economistic one of private consumption (or income poverty), albeit now with the headcount indices for the traditional upper and lower poverty lines supplemented by the calculation of the poverty gap and the index of poverty severity on Foster-Greer-Thorbecke lines (Ravallion 1992, Blackwood and Lynch 1994). The "objectivity" of these numbers depends on prespecified standards of nutrition, the identification of discrete "households," the reliability of recall in a survey interview, knowledge of relevant local prices, and so on. The measures are *narrowly* economistic because they usually exclude even economic variables like the value of private assets, the use of common property resources, and the social dividend (public spending benefits minus taxes). They are *economistic* because they exclude social and political aspects of well-being such as leisure, personal security, cultural goods, social recognition, and political rights. All of these excluded variables are constituents of well-being in themselves but are also resources that vulnerable households and communities can use to try to cope when confronted by shocks.

The consumption poverty statistics are also highly aggregative. They can be broken down by region and the rural/urban split and by household descriptors. But these categories provide only very faint clues to the dynamics of impoverishment—the movements of those social groups that are moving in and out of poverty either temporarily or permanently. The descriptions that emerge from such measurement exercises tend to be banal. Typically, the majority of people in poor countries turn out to be poor, although given the data limitations it is difficult to know whether, say, 52 percent or 64 percent is the right number. Those in rural areas are found to be poorer than those in urban areas. Certain correlates of poverty are identified, such as the unemployed, women, households with a high dependency ratio, the disabled, the displaced, elderly single people, and so forth, and these vary from country to country. None of this can be the slightest surprise to anyone who has visited a poor country, however briefly.

But if the foregoing conceptualization is the appropriate description of the problem of poverty, then there really is only one possible solution—namely, the promotion of economic growth. The international antipoverty agenda reduces to that of more growth, and policies aimed at the direct reduction of poverty are sidelined or totally disappear. Once poverty, measured "objectively," has been revealed on such a vast scale, the antipoverty agenda must collapse back into the broad strategy for economic development. The wheel of the international organizations' antipoverty policy turns full circle, and their policy dialogue becomes the process of persuading countries of the inevitability of this perception and process.

An Alternative Perspective on the "Poverty Problem"

Does there exist another way to conceptualize the "poverty problem" in poor countries? There does once one breaks away from the universalistic definitions and criteria that are the stock-in-trade of international organizations in search of indicators of their own performance. Individual countries, or provinces within countries, from time to time arrive at their own formulations of their own particular poverty problem. Concepts of poverty can be geographically, historically, and culturally specific. Such concepts did emerge in countries that in economic or material terms were no better off than the poor countries of today.

Take as an example the perceptions of the poverty problem that led to the development of a national poor-law system in England by the early seventeenth century. At that time about half of the English population was poor in the sense of having no property beyond a few personal possessions. Economic conditions were deteriorating, and many of the poor had already become vagrants. State action was prompted by the following: the idea of society as a "commonwealth," the parts of which all had to function cooperatively to produce social order; the elite's fear of the social and political consequences of an increase in the number of the vagrant poor; and the humanist belief that idleness among the poor could be cured by education and training (Beier 1983, 16–18). Strict punishments for sturdy vagabonds were combined with state-regulated charity for the settled poor in both urban and rural areas.

What we see here is a specific state response to a perceived social and political threat (of rising crime, riot, and possibly rebellion) when the ranks of sturdy beggars, rogues, and vagabonds were swollen by impoverishment in a preindustrial society. Nobody did a poverty assessment first. The pioneer estimate of the number and income of vagrants in England, by Gregory King, relates to the year 1688. The state response was a mixed one, both punitive and reformative: there was to be harassment, not charity, for the dangerous poor.

The origin of the British welfare state lies in another time-specific episode, one that produced a quite different conceptualization of "the problem of poverty." In the late nineteenth century, the great depression was perceived as generating a process of urban impoverishment. In large cities, especially London, the bottom layers of the respectable working class were seen as threatened with descent into the ranks of the criminal and the destitute. The imminent absorption of part of the proletariat by the lumpen proletariat was the problem, not poverty in general. This was why the creation of new categories of universal benefits (old-age pensions, unemployment benefits), separate from means-tested poor relief, was eventually adopted as the solution. This time a poverty assessment was done first, by Charles Booth. But (unlike Rowntree's later estimate of primary poverty in York) Booth did not rely in his analysis of life and labor in London on a simple poverty line approach. Once again, the state response was selective: the respectable poor were to be protected, while the very poor were left to the mercies of the means test, once Booth's proposal for state labor colonies was dropped (Himmelfarb 1991, 123–28).

The current concern in France, and now in the European Union, with the problem of social exclusion has taken off from the social selectivity that remains in European welfare states. Contrasted with a French cultural and political ideal of social solidarity, the growth in numbers of the long-term unemployed, homeless, deviants, social misfits, and youth from broken families threatens violent disorder in poor suburbs, a threat that is expected to grow with structural economic change and the cutting back of the welfare state (Rodgers, Gore, and Figueiredo 1995, 1–3). The state response has therefore been to link targeting of income transfers to schemes of active reinsertion of beneficiaries into education and training, jobs, and community projects. But the social-inclusion agenda in France has its other face: the heightened fear of immigration and the raising of barriers to entry into the national territory.

These three examples underline the point made earlier that the way in which "the poverty problem" is defined differs according to time (England in the early seventeenth and late nineteenth centuries) and place (modern France and the United States—for the latter, see Patterson 1994). "The poor you have with you always," but poverty is always problematized differently. Also, the antipoverty policies that countries actually adopt depend on the specific way in which the problem of poverty is defined by the social and political processes of that place and date. Yet despite this specificity, there seem to be common conditions for catalyzing state action to reduce (some aspect of) poverty. They are the belief in the social interdependence of rich and poor; the existence of a credible threat from the poor, often in terms of increased social disorder; and the belief that state action can make a significant difference to the situation.

We must recognize, too, that in the real world, antipoverty policies are rarely an expression of pure humanitarian impulse. They tend to come in a package with policies like penalties for vagabondage, state labor colonies, and stricter immigration controls. Indeed, it may be that they become politically possible *because* they are packaged like this. This thought has evidently not occurred to those who are astonished to find that "sometimes a punitive piece of politics is presented as...welfare" or that "punitive and coercive forms of social policy [are] frequently deployed under the mantle of 'welfare'" (Schaffer and Lamb 1981, 61; Squires 1990, 1).

Alternative Approaches to Research and Policy

Elite Perceptions of Poverty

The alternative perspective emphasizes the importance of national elites and the specific way in which they formulate "their" problems of poverty. How do the elites of poor countries perceive the condition of their poor? Do they believe that there is, or ought to be, some kind of social compact that includes the poor? Do they distinguish between the deserving and the dangerous poor? Do they think that all or some aspects of poverty do or could constitute a threat to their own well-being? Do they have confidence that the state could act to defuse any threat? In what measure would that response be humanitarian and in what measure authoritarian? If the state lacks the capacity to act, are there other agencies that could substitute effectively for it?

It is too early to say what results might emerge from seeking the answers to such questions. But it is intriguing to speculate on possibilities. A possible result is to find that elites in poor countries do accept some notion of a social compact that includes the poor and do recognize that the poor can mount a threat to social order, but to find at the same time that these same elites have no confidence that the state or any substitute agency can do anything about poverty. If that were so and if genuine success stories in poverty alleviation could be identified, this would create an exciting opportunity. By feeding back the success stories to the representatives of the elites, it might even prove possible to shift elite perceptions in favor of pro-poor actions, and not merely to find out what they are. The cross-fertilization of ideas and experiences that Kothari referred to could then become more sharply focused and perhaps more effective.

Reframing the Problem of the Poor: The Dynamics of Impoverishment

The alternative perspective on the international antipoverty agenda has implications for economic, as well as social and political, research. As we have seen, the logic of poor countries' situation is that the consumption poverty of the masses can be significantly reduced only by broad-based economic growth. In saying that, the international organizations are quite right. But by the same logic, specific antipoverty interventions must be designed to affect particular problems of impoverishment and to assist particular groups of households and communities that are untouched by economic growth or even affected adversely by it. The design of antipoverty policies is then not helped at all by exercises that measure consumption poverty with the aid of one or two poverty lines and that at best permit point comparisons of the aggregate percentage in poverty over an interval of time. The point was well made by Amartya Sen: "as a category of causal analysis, 'the poor' is not a very helpful one, since different groups sharing the same predicament get there in widely different ways" (1981, 156).

So rather than taking undifferentiated mass poverty as "the problem" and looking for optimal solutions to it, it is necessary to try to reframe the problem. We need to find a new generative metaphor for antipoverty policy (Schon 1993, 137–9). We also need to stop thinking about poverty in terms of a *stock* of poor people, often seen as helpless victims who need some kind of treatment, and to start thinking about poverty in terms of *flows* of people whose powers of agency are impaired as they become poorer but can be enhanced sufficiently for them to escape from poverty. We need to know more about these flows. Some people, of course, are born into poverty and never escape: the congenitally disabled and the children of large families whose education cannot be afforded. Others enter and leave poverty within their life cycle: youthful unemployment may be followed by a more prosperous middle life, and then by the poverty caused by old age, infirmity, and the loss of relatives. There are other more contingent causes of poverty, like contracting AIDS or becoming a refugee from civil conflict. Then there are economic causes—bad husbandry or environmental disasters that lead to the loss of land and other assets, or technological change that outcompetes traditionally made products, or (dare one say it?) major price shifts that come from the removal of subsidies in an economic-reform process. There are so many ways to fall into poverty, and they are very different. And by the same token, the prospects for emerging from poverty are also many and different.

Distinguishing between Transitory and Chronic Poverty
In order to devise effective antipoverty policies, it is therefore necessary to understand better, in particular countries, the dynamics of impoverishment and the emergence from poverty. What could research do to make the task easier? A good beginning would be to do more work on the distinction between those experiencing transitory poverty and those experiencing chronic poverty. Can we learn more about which types of poor people are transiting and which are not? Can we show that the characteristics of the former are fundamentally different from those of the latter? Or are the "transitories" merely experiencing the same degree of fluctuation in their income/consumption as do the "chronics," but at a higher average level—that is just above and just below the poverty line?

Some Indian evidence suggests that even over a short period (3 years), three-eighths of households cross the poverty line, in one direction or the other. Even in a context of agricultural growth stemming from technical change, while one-fourth of all households escaped from poverty, a different one-eighth was becoming impoverished (Gaiha 1993, 43–58). These figures show a very dynamic situation, in which growth is impoverishing some groups while at the same time reducing the overall numbers of those in poverty. The same study also suggests that the chronically poor are not the poorest of the poor but are distributed through all strata of the poor. The main characteristics of the chronically poor were lack of land, little education, and large dependent families. At all levels of poverty, some households were flowing in, while others were flowing out.

Objectives of Antipoverty Policy

From the perspective of a flows model of poverty, the tasks of antipoverty policy are to prevent the fall into poverty of those who are not now poor but who face risks that make them vulnerable to poverty; to relieve the poor as far as this is possible; and to avoid forms of relief that will deter those that could escape from poverty by their own agency from doing so. Reconciling these three objectives of prevention, relief, and avoiding the creation of "poverty traps" has proved in practice to be extraordinarily difficult. Certainly, the recognition of the poor as agents and not patients reveals noteworthy complications in any attempt to reduce poverty through strict income-based targeting of state benefits (Sen 1995, 11–24).

In part these difficulties arise because some deep ethical dilemmas are involved. It is often taken as an article of faith that the best antipoverty policies are those that do most to improve the welfare of the poorest of the poor. Sen, for example, deplores "the distorting effects on policy matters" of the headcount measure of poverty, because "with (its) use... the best rewards to poverty removal policies are almost always obtained by concentrating on the people who are *just* below the poverty line rather than those suffering deep poverty" (Sen 1981, 157). Sen here takes it as axiomatic that resources should be concentrated on those whose suffering is greatest. This approach is characteristic of a rights-based ethics, which has a strong moral appeal, but not of a utilitarian ethics, which is willing to trade off increases in the welfare of the poorest and of better-off groups. One can either treat this as a pure choice of moral principles, or one can be more pragmatic and make a practical judgment after investigating what the trade-offs actually are.

These trade-offs have a time dimension. The problem cannot be reduced to one of maximizing collective welfare in a single time period. After all, the most venerable maxim of antipoverty policy is that it is good to give a poor man a fish but much better to teach him how to fish. The superiority of the skill transfer to the consumption dole arises precisely because of the multiperiod welfare consequences of the former. Once this investment feature of antipoverty policies is recognized, the rule of concentrating resources on the poorest of the poor becomes problematic if it happens that, because of their lack of assets or skills, they are the least able to make such investments fructify.

Parenthetically, it is hard not to speculate whether, if this is indeed the case, the perceived lack of realism of the policy agenda of the international agencies is not a factor (along with the perceived lack of capacity of national governments) in dissuading elites from embarking on antipoverty policies. In countries where resources for any kind of antipoverty programs are desperately short, recommendations to allocate them according to a moral principle that is unfamiliar to the culture and practically not credible may well undermine the elite's own will to action. On the field of battle, scarce medical resources should not be concentrated on the most severely wounded: there has to be some form of *triage*. In some respects, the current international antipoverty agenda resembles the Charge of the Light Brigade: *c'est magnifique, mais ce n'est pas la guerre.*

Vulnerability, Coping Strategies, and Safety Nets

If the poor are seen as agents and not as victims, we need to know more about how they act, what they do in the different situations of vulnerability and poverty. Presumably, individuals and households faced with high levels of uncertainty and that know they are vulnerable to sudden shocks will develop livelihood strategies that minimize their risks. In the complex, diverse, and risk-prone environments that prevail in many parts of poor countries, it is likely that livelihood strategies will be adopted that will involve the diversification of sources of income and the accumulation of assets that can be drawn down in an emergency (Davies 1996). When shocks do come they will be dealt with by a sequence of coping strategies: the progressive liquidation of assets, the drawing on support from available social networks, the search for new local income-earning activities, migration in search of employment, and ultimately movement to relief or refugee camps (Longhurst 1994). But if shocks are quickly repeated, the frequent use of these coping strategies will have the effect of eroding the ability to cope (for example, wage earning leading to the neglect of one's own fields), so that vulnerability is gradually further increased.

This account raises some interesting research hypotheses. What is the evidence that livelihood diversification is a response to covariate risk? Has the ability of social networks to provide satisfactory social security been weakened either by the spread of markets or by the development of alternative state-sponsored social security systems? Does the provision of state-sponsored social security have different effects on coping behavior according to its form, whether in terms of guaranteed employment, cash transfers, or food subsidies?

Evaluating Interventions

In the realm of antipoverty policy, we still need to do more research on the practical effects of different types of policy intervention. Building on the work by Singh and Hazell (1993) with a cross section of the ICRISAT dataset,[2] it should be possible to determine which types of antipoverty policies (asset redistribution, distributionally neutral growth, employment guarantee schemes, and so on) would have the greatest impact on different measures of poverty. Such policy simulation experiments could produce useful policy recommendations.

---

[2] For greater detail on the ICRISAT dataset, see Walker and Ryan (1990).

The choice is not merely among different types of intervention. Choices need to be made among different designs for the same basic type of intervention. For instance, an employment guarantee scheme can have limited coverage with relatively large benefits, or universal coverage with relatively small benefits. Evidence suggests that the cost-effectiveness of these alternative designs is sensitive to the amount of the total resources available for the scheme. When the budget is small, the former (limited coverage and large benefits) is more cost-effective because it will enable a subset of the poor to escape from poverty (Gaiha 1993, 127); this finding underlines the point that when resources are scarce, some form of *triage* is likely to be the best policy. But such a proposition needs testing over a wider range of interventions. The poverty-reducing effects of different schemes of land reform, different patterns of girls' education, and different types of credit unions for the poor (the Grameen Bank) could also be examined.

Successes in Poverty Reduction Policies

Experience from poor countries like Indonesia tells us that broad-based economic growth can, in the right conditions, make big inroads on overall poverty. But even with growth, some groups can be descending into poverty. We should be concerned to pinpoint specific additional state interventions that can be shown to have been beneficial, acting alongside general economic policy. If we can do this, we shall be vindicating a major theme, that intelligent state intervention can produce better outcomes than those produced by a combination of markets and a minimalist state.

We may also have a rare opportunity in front of us. If we produce these results and if we focus our dissemination well, we may even play our part in energizing national elites to formulate their own understandings of their poverty problems and to engage in better policymaking as a result. Surely we can now begin to advance beyond the present contradictions of an internationally driven antipoverty agenda.

REFERENCES

Beier, A. L. *The Problem of the Poor in Tudor and Early Stuart England.* London: Methuen, 1983.

Blackwood, D. L., and R. G. Lynch. "The Measurement of Inequality and Poverty: A Policymaker's Guide to the Literature." *World Development* 22, 4 (April 1994).

Davies, S. *Adaptable Livelihoods: Coping with Food Insecurity in the Malian Sahel.* New York: Macmillan, 1996.

De Swaan, A. *In Care of the State.* Oxford: Polity Press, 1988.

Gaiha, R. *Design of Poverty Alleviation Strategy in Rural Areas.* Rome: FAO, 1993.

Himmelfarb, G. *Poverty and Compassion: The Moral Imagination of the Late Victorians.* New York: Vintage Books, 1991.

Kothari, R. *Poverty: Human Consciousness and the Amnesia of Development.* London: Zed Books, 1993.

Longhurst, R. "Conceptual Frameworks for Linking Relief and Development," *IDS Bulletin* 25, 4 (October 1994) 17–23.

Moser, C. O. N. *Confronting Crisis: A Comparative Study of Household Responses to Poverty and Vulnerability in Four Poor Urban Communities.* Washington, D.C.: World Bank, 1996.

Patterson, J. T. *America's Struggle against Poverty, 1900–1994.* Cambridge, MA: Harvard University Press, 1994.

Ravallion, M. *Poverty Comparisons: A Guide to Concepts and Methods.* Washington, D.C.: World Bank, 1992.

Rodgers, G., C. Gore, and J. B. Figueiredo, eds. *Social Exclusion: Rhetoric, Reality, Responses.* Geneva: ILO Publications, 1995.

Schaffer, B., and G. Lamb. *Can Equity Be Organized?* Farnborough: Gower, 1981.

Schon, D. A. "Generative Metaphor: A Perspective on Problem-Setting in Social Policy." In A. Ortony, ed., *Metaphor and Thought* (second edition). Cambridge: Cambridge University Press, 1993.

Sen, A. K. *Poverty and Famines: An Essay on Entitlement and Deprivation.* Oxford: Clarendon Press, 1981.

_____. "The Political Economy of Targeting." In D. Van de Walle, D. Nead, eds. *Public Spending and the Poor: Theory and Evidence.* Baltimore, MD: Johns Hopkins University Press, 1995.

Singh, R. P., and P. Hazell. "Rural Poverty in the Semi-Arid Tropics of India: Identification, Determinants, and Policy Interventions." *Economic and Political Weekly,* 28, 12 and 13 (March 20–27, 1993).

Squires, P. *Anti-Social Policy: Welfare, Ideology, and the Disciplinary State.* New York: Harvester Wheatsheaf, 1990.

Toye, J., and C. Jackson. "Public Expenditure Policy and Poverty Reduction: Has the World Bank Got it Right?" In *IDS Bulletin* 27, 1 (1996).

Walker, T., and J. Ryan. *Village and Household Economies in India's Semi-Arid Tropics.* Baltimore, MD: Johns Hopkins University Press, 1990.

Development Thinking at the Beginning of the XXI Century

Amartya Sen[1]

Ideas do not move in units of centuries. Within the twentieth century itself, we have seen some radical shifts in development thinking. Nor need the centuries be defined in the way calendars bunch the years together—from 00 to 99. Henry Wallace, in his famous address on the 8th of May 1942, declared that the "century on which we are entering can be and must be the century of the common man," but he was talking neither about the twentieth century nor about the twenty-first. The much-heralded fact that these next few years are the ending years of the twentieth century need not, in itself, make this in any way a great time for reassessment; this applies equally to the proposed reexamination of our development thinking.

And yet, the present juncture does happen to be a reasonably good time to attempt such a scrutiny, and the topic that has been assigned for the present paper makes plausible sense. Much has happened in development experience as well as in development theory over the years since the new subject of "development" was born at the end of World War II. Some of the new events have given us reason to question, qualify, or revise our earlier understandings of the nature of economic and social development. The insights that have emerged call for fresh reflection. It is indeed as good a moment as any to ask where development thinking may be heading.

Experiences and Lessons

There have occurred many remarkable—and spectacularly diverse—"development experiences" in the postwar world, including the following:

- rapid reconstruction of war-destroyed Germany and Japan and their emergence as new economic leaders
- unprecedented economic growth in Europe and North America, followed by growth deceleration and persistently high unemployment (especially in Europe)
- birth of the welfare state, starting from Europe, with major impact on the quality of life but also with significant financial burden on the state
- advent of East Asia as a region of astonishing economic growth with remarkable social development and comparative equity

---

[1] Lamont University Professor and Professor of Economics and Philosophy at Harvard University.

- experience of fast economic expansion in parts of Latin America, without commensurate elimination of deprivation
- economic crises in the Soviet Union and East Europe and further decline immediately following their economic reform
- rapid transformation of the economy of China using trade and markets but without large-scale reform
- elimination of food dependency in many countries in the third world, including South Asia
- accentuation of famines in Sub-Saharan Africa but elimination of famines in other countries, including India and (since 1962) China
- astonishing increase in the volume of international trade and of capital movement across the world
- steady expansion of longevity in much of the world and that longevity's very speedy increase in some regions with fast economic growth (such as South Korea, Taiwan, and Hong Kong) and in others without much economic growth (such as Costa Rica, Sri Lanka, pre-reform China, and the Indian state of Kerala).

We shall not be able to comment here on each of these—and other—important happenings, but certainly there is no lack of variety of concrete experiences from which we can learn. Development theory itself has also moved along, sometimes on its own impetus and at other times in direct response to empirical observations. We certainly can claim to understand parts of the process of development much better now than we could half a century ago.

But along with better understanding, we also get some slanted and overly simple generalizations. There are much-repeated putative "lessons" that seem to be powered more by the use of selective information (and sometimes just by the force of enunciation) than by critical scrutiny.

A good example is the rather common generalization that the development experiences show the folly of state activism and the unconditional merits of the pure market economy and that all that is needed for development is to move "from planning to market." There certainly exists plenty of evidence from the experiences of many countries that shows that markets can be remarkably vigorous, that exchange within and between nations may be full of rewards, and that a predilection to shut out the markets tends to produce disasters rather than equity (in the name of which such shutting out is often carried out).[2] But to comprehend what the market can do so well need not involve either ignoring what the state can—and does—achieve or conversely, seeing the market mechanism as a freestanding success irrespective of state policy.[3]

Indeed, many countries in West Europe have successfully guaranteed broad social security, including public education and health care, in ways previously unknown in the

---

[2] Illuminating analyses of these issues can be found in Bauer (1972, 1991).
[3] On this general question, see Stiglitz (1988), Stern (1989), Suzumura (1995), and Malinvaud *et al.* (1996).

world; Japan and East Asia have had much government leadership in transforming their economies as well as their societies; the roles of public education and health care have been pivotal in bringing about social and economic change across the world (and quite spectacularly in East and Southeast Asia); and pragmatic policymaking has drawn both on the market and on the state—and also on nonstate, nonmarket institutions such as community organizations.[4]

Although governments can err by being overactive and too interventionist (examples of this are easy to find), they can also make the mistake of being underactive and too idle (evidences of costly inactivity are also plentiful). Indeed, sometimes examples of each can be found in the very same country. For instance, Indian economic planning, which the present writer has recently had the occasion to scrutinize (Drèze and Sen 1995), provides a good illustration of both failings: horrendous overactivity in controlling industries, thereby restraining gains from trade and blighting competitiveness; and soporific underactivity in the expansion of school education, health care, social security, gender equity, and land reform. India's ability to crash simultaneously into Scylla as well as Charybdis would have left Odysseus dumbfounded.

Much can be learned from seeing both what has actually happened around the world and what (although firmly expected) has not happened. An excellent case does exist for looking critically at possible generalizations that we can make, but it is not particularly helpful to try to see the lessons in terms of a "confrontation" between the market and the state.

Blood, Sweat and Tears?

In the present paper, we shall argue for a different type of contrast turning not on the notion of state-versus-market nor of planning-versus-profits nor on any other notion as "classical" as those but instead (roughly speaking) on the idea of how "hard-nosed" a view we take of development. There exist, on the one hand, approaches that see development as a "fierce" process, with a moral that invokes "blood, sweat and tears" (to use Winston Churchill's rousing phrase). Since we live in an age of acronyms, we shall take a little liberty and call this approach the BLAST view of development. We shall try to illustrate some of the interestingly distinct forms—very different from each other—that the BLAST view can take.

This characterization is to be contrasted with views that see development as essentially a "friendly" process, with a focus on people's helping each other and themselves, and with being able "to get by with a little help from their friends" (to apply a phrase from the Beatles). The aforementioned "little help" can come from interdependencies in the market (illustrated by Adam Smith's example of mutual gains in trades with the butcher, the brewer, and the baker) but also from public services that make people more capable of

---

[4] Albert Hirschman (1958, 1981) has persistently emphasized the breadth of the process of development and the very different influences that operate on it.

helping themselves and others well illustrated by Adam Smith's pointer to the advantages of public action in many fields: "For a very small expense the public can facilitate, can encourage, and can even impose upon almost the whole body of the people, the necessity of acquiring those most essential parts of education."[5] Taking the liberty of calling this view "getting by, with a little assistance," we shall employ the acronym GALA for it, to be contrasted with BLAST.

Before proceeding, let us briefly present a few qualifications and warnings. First, BLAST and GALA can each take quite diverse forms, invoking rather divergent economic theories (more on this later). Second, our twofold categorization is not in the strict sense a "partitioning": some developmental approaches may fit into neither group, and some can have particular features of both groups. Our categorization is rather a distinction between two major attitudes to development, each of which can occur in a pure or in a mixed form, and this basic contrast can be helpful without reflecting either attitude as existing in stark polarized isolation. Third, it need not be a secret that the present writer is more impressed with GALA than with BLAST, and indeed we shall argue that some of the more important development experiences can be better interpreted and explained in terms of GALA than of BLAST. But it is not our purpose to claim that there is no merit at all in BLAST. To some extent it is a question of balance. As we shall discuss in the next few sections, variants of the BLAST view, in different forms, have provided the underpinning of many of the traditional interpretations of the nature and requirements of development. If the present paper is somewhat "combative" against BLAST, it is in part because the latter's wisdom has been heavily oversold, but this fact does not require us to deny that there exist cases in which BLAST may provide some useful insight.

Hard Build-up and the Role of Accumulation

The rhetoric of BLAST is one of "needed sacrifice" in order to achieve a better future. For successful development, various contemporary ills may have to be tolerated. This general view can take various distinct forms focusing on different types of sacrifices related to low welfare, high inequality, intrusive authoritarianism, and so on. Blood, sweat and tears can be demanded in different ways, in line with the particular theory that invokes the general attitude of BLAST. Examples of each variety of "needed sacrifice" can be found plentifully in the literature; these particular theories may differ in their institutional preferences and in their politics, but they share a generally "hard" view of development and a common suspicion that "soft-hearted sympathy" could derail the long-run development process.

---

[5] The first example can be found in Smith (1776), I.ii (p. 27), and the second in V.i.f. (p. 785). Many readers of Smith seem to have an aversion (judging from their near-complete reliance on the butcher-brewer-baker example and market-based benefits) to venturing much beyond page 27 of the *Wealth of Nations*. In fact, Adam Smith's emphasis on the role of public cooperation and assistance can be seen plentifully not only in *The Wealth of Nations* (Smith 1776) but also in *Lectures on Jurisprudence* and *The Theory of Moral Sentiments* (Smith 1762–3, 1790).

One version of BLAST, focusing on the overwhelming need for high accumulation, was inspired to a great extent by the apparent success of the Soviet Union in achieving fast economic development through capital formation. Aside from the historical inspiration, such "accumulation blast" (as we may call it as a shorthand) drew much on "growth model" reasoning—emphasizing the need for keeping living standards down in the near future in order to attain rapid accumulation of capital and consequent economic growth, thereby "solving" the development problem.

The centrality of capital accumulation had, in fact, been an enduring characteristic of postwar development economics (going back at least to Nurkse [1953], Lewis [1955], and Baran [1957]). There was a comfortable "marriage" here with the literature on "optimum accumulation" (initiated by Ramsey [1928] and revived in the 1950s by Tinbergen [1956] and others). "Optimal growth paths" often suggested the need for a severe holding down of welfare in the short run in order to obtain much greater rewards in the future.[6] But in many versions of this approach, capital accumulation was interpreted mainly in terms of the formation of physical capital, thereby distracting attention from the importance of human resources (skill, education, and so forth). Nevertheless, the prominent role given to capital accumulation was not in itself misplaced, particularly when more note is taken of what soon came to be called "human capital."[7] Empirical studies of successful development experiences have given us no reason to reject the crucial importance that capital accumulation in the broadest sense has for economic development.

Even so, accumulation Blast, as an approach, suffers from various handicaps. They relate mostly to the comparative neglect of the well-being and quality of life in the present (and in the near future). One issue concerns the appropriate valuation to be placed on the terrible deprivations that exist right now (even when balanced against very large gains to the more prosperous future generations). The issues can be, in one type of presentation, put under the broad hat of "concavity" of the aggregative social objectives—corresponding to the extent of "equality preference" in the sense specified by Atkinson (1970). But these issues also call for closer scrutiny of the nature and reach of our social responsibilities to different generations (and to different groups within each generation),

---

[6] The dilemmas of such "intertemporal balancing" were very well discussed by Sukhamoy Chakravarty (1969). In my Ph.D. thesis (Sen 1960), I had tried to link the problem of intertemporal choice with the choice of techniques, because of the indirect impact of the latter on the rate of capital accumulation. While the compromise formulae of balancing present and future gains, which I argued for, put more weight on present welfare than happens in the "growth maximization strategy" (suggested by Galenson and Leibenstein [1955] and Dobb [1960], among others), my analysis still ended up (given the formulations) with a diagnosis of frequent "suboptimality" of savings and its influence on the shadow prices of capital and labor. These shadow prices and their implications for resource allocation were extensively investigated in Sen (1961, 1967), Marglin (1963a, 1963b, 1976), Little and Mirrlees (1969), and Dasgupta, Marglin, and Sen (1972), among other contributions.

[7] T.W. Schultz (1962, 1963, 1971, 1980) has been one of the pioneers in shifting attention toward the role of human resources. Robert Solow's (1956) pioneering analysis of economic growth did a lot to undermine the overwhelming interest in capital accumulation (compared particularly with technical change).

and we have to pay special attention to the priority of preventing deprivations that are known to be both definitely disastrous and definitely preventable.[8]

Second, the importance of human resources (and the role of "human capital") changes the nature of the problem of "intertemporal balancing" of welfare. When the modeling is based on the partitioning of national output into "consumption" and "investment," with the welfare function defined on consumption and the achievement of growth related to investment (as in Ramsey [1928] or Tinbergen [1955]), the conflict between present welfare and future welfare takes the classical form that has been so well investigated. But the problem requires reformulation when economic productivity is seen to depend also on education, health care, nutrition, and the like.[9] These factors, of course, immediately influence present well-being as well. As a result, the problem of "intertemporal balancing" has to depart from the dichotomous formulation of the "hard choices" on which the optimal-growth literature had so clearly focused.

Third, some of the effects of social consumption, including education and medical attention, go beyond both economic productivity and immediate welfare. For instance, the education and valued employment of females can make a big difference in reducing the gender inequalities that constitute a central feature of underdevelopment in many parts of the world.[10] School education (especially of women) and basic health care can also significantly influence fertility and mortality rates and can be important in the process of development for this reason as well, in addition to their substantial potential impact on the time profiles of welfare and freedoms that people enjoy.[11]

In this context, a GALA view of development provides a more natural way of seeing the interdependence between enhancing human welfare and expanding an economy's productive capacity and developmental potential. The need for intertemporal balancing and the powerful role of capital accumulation are not, of course, removed, but an understanding of the interdependence between quality of life and an economy's productive ability takes away some of the starkness of the dichotomy between living well and accumulating fast.

Hard Business and the Fear of "Bleeding Hearts"

The celebration of "blood, sweat and tears" in the process of development was not, of course, linked to the priority of separated accumulation. Nor was it always inspired by the toughness of Soviet industrialization. In fact, one "lesson" in hardness was derived directly from the ultimate success of classical capitalist expansion after a long and arduous slog.

---

[8] Public discussions on the claims of rationality in social choice may be particularly aimed in this direction, as exemplified by the priority given to famine prevention in working democracies (on this, see Sen 1984, 1995).

[9] See, for example, Bliss and Stern (1978), Bardhan (1984a), Sen (1984), Dasgupta and Ray (1987, 1988), Drèze and Sen (1989), Stern (1989), Osmani (1992), Birdsall (1993), Dasgupta (1993), and Malinvaud et al. (1996).

[10] I have tried to discuss these issues in Sen (1984, 1985, 1990, 1992). See also Bardhan (1984a), Drèze and Sen (1989), and Harriss (1990), among other contributors.

[11] On this, see Schultz (1981); Birdsall (1988); Caldwell et al. (1989); Dasgupta (1993), Cassen (1994); Sen, Germain, and Chen (1994); and Murthi, Ghio, and Drèze (1995). See also the collection of papers in Lindahl-Riessling and Landberg (1994).

Through the tough days of what William Blake had called "these dark Satanic mills" and the brutal history of inequity so forcefully reflected in Friedrich Engels's (1892) "the condition of the working class," modern capitalism—now equipped even with a "welfare state"—has firmly emerged.[12] Those who see in this a model to follow have continued to argue for giving priority to business interests so that the productive power of the nation can be radically expanded, and they warn against the spoiling of long-run benefits by the premature operation of sympathy; they are terrified of the harm that may result from the influence of "bleeding hearts."

Paying much attention to distributional concerns and to equity would seem, in this perspective, to be a mistake at early stages of development. The benefits will come to all in due course, through "trickle down"; deliberate attempts to hasten the sharing would only mess up the formation of the forceful stream from which the trickles would have to find their way down. Although this view is rarely stated formally, or even in very clear terms, its presence is not hard to detect in many pronouncements on economic development. The champions of this view are not confined to admirers of capitalism. Something of a general "lesson" on what is necessary for "the process of development" has been seen by many in the history of capitalism. For instance, Joan Robinson's remonstrance of Sri Lanka's attempt at welfare-related intervention at an early stage of development (and the related thesis that Sri Lanka was trying "to taste the fruit of the tree" before growing that tree) did not come from any admiration for the "hard way" but rather from a sad acceptance of the latter's necessity.

Sri Lanka has not really done very well in terms of economic growth; nor has the Indian state of Kerala, which also has gone early for widespread health care, education, social security, and egalitarian land reform. But there are other countries (such as South Korea or Taiwan) that have combined these helpful social moves with more freedom to use economic opportunities of trade and business, and they have been richly rewarded by rapid economic growth combined with more social equity and even relatively less unequal distributions of income. The fact that social development may not work on its own to generate economic growth is fully consistent with the possibility (for which there now exists a great deal of evidence) that social development does strongly facilitate fast and participatory economic growth if combined with market-friendly policies that encourage economic expansion.[13] The role of economic equity has also received attention in this context, in terms of the adverse effects both of income inequality and of unequal land distribution.[14]

---

[12] The United States seems under some political pressure right now to abandon the latter, and a step in that direction has recently been taken.

[13] For the interpretation of the "East Asian" experience in this light (both on its own and in comparative perspective), see World Bank (1993), Birdsall (1993), Birdsall and Sabot (1993a, 1993b), Fishlow et al. (1994), Rodrik (1994a, 1994b), and McGuire (1995). On other active roles of public policy in East Asia, see also Amsden (1989), Wade (1990), and Suzumura (1995).

[14] See the recent findings of Alesina and Perotti (1993), Alesina and Rodrik (1994), Persson and Tabellini (1994), Fishlow (1995), Bruno et al. (1996), and Deininger and Squire (1996), among others. On related issues, see also Fields (1980), Bardhan (1984a), Rakwani (1986), Stiglitz and Mathewson (1986), Drèze and Sen (1989), Stern (1989), Basu (1990), Sachs (1990), and Desai (1995).

Hard States and the Denial of Political Rights

The call for "hardness" of a different type is reflected in the view that development is helped by the suppression of human rights and that "sacrifices" are "necessary" in matters of democracy and of civil and political rights at early stages of development. There exists a much-repeated general belief that empirical studies of international comparisons "show" that political and civil rights hamper economic growth. Former Prime Minister Lee Ruan Yew of Singapore has articulated something of a "general theory" of the existence of such a conflict. The thesis itself is not new. Even the criticism of the "soft state" by Gunnar Myrdal in his *Asian Drama* (1964) had some ambiguities that did encourage such an interpretation.[15]

Is there really a conflict between economic development and civil and political rights? It is true that some relatively authoritarian states (such as South Korea, Lee's own Singapore, and post-reform China) have experienced faster rates of economic growth than have many less-authoritarian states (including India, Costa Rica, and Jamaica). Nevertheless, the "Lee hypothesis" is based on very selective and limited information (rather than on any general statistical testing over the wide-ranging data that are available). The high economic growth of China or South Korea in Asia cannot be taken as convincing proof that authoritarianism does better in promoting economic growth any more than we can convincingly draw the opposite conclusion from the fact that the fastest-growing African country (and one of the fastest-growing in the world)—namely, Botswana—has been a veritable oasis of democracy in that unhappy continent.

Systematic statistical studies give no real support to the claim that there exists a general conflict between political rights and economic performance.[16] The nature of that relationship seems to depend on many other circumstances, and although some note a weakly negative relation, others find a strongly positive one. On balance, it is hard to reject the hypothesis that not much relation exists between them in either direction. Since these rights have intrinsic importance of their own, the case for them stands, even without having to show that democracy actually encourages economic growth. Certainly, the case for a hard state, intolerant of civil and political rights, does not emerge from the international statistics of growth experience.

In fact, we must look not merely at statistical connections but must also examine and scrutinize the actual causal processes involved in economic growth and development. The policies and circumstances that led to the economic success of East Asian economies included openness to competition, the use of international markets, a high level of literacy and school education, successful land reforms, and the provision of incentives for

---

[15] In fact, Myrdal was not really asking for suppression of human rights but rather for robust public policies that would not be derailed by the machinations of vested interests that could bend public policies. Pranab Bardhan (1984b) has analyzed the barriers to economic development that arise from the influence of a multiplicity of powerful pressure groups in the particular case of India.

[16] See, among other studies, Barro and Lee (1993), Dasgupta (1993), Bhalla (1994), Helliwell (1994), and Przeworski and Limongi (1994).

investment, exporting, and industrialization. There is nothing whatsoever to indicate that any of these social policies is inconsistent with greater democracy or could be sustained only through the authoritarianism that happened to be present in South Korea or Singapore or China. The temptation of taking the *post hoc* to be also the *propter hoc* does not help causal scrutiny.

In this context, we must also look at the connection between political and civil rights, and the prevention of major social disasters and misfortunes. The incentive effects of political and civil rights would tend to link responsible governance with the exercise of these rights.[17] And there exists some real evidence in that direction.

A remarkable fact in the ghastly history of famines in the world is that no substantial famine has ever occurred in any country with a democratic form of government and a relatively free press. Major famines have occurred in colonial territories run by imperial rulers from abroad (for example, in pre-independence India or in Ireland), in modern military dictatorships controlled by authoritarian potentates (such as Ethiopia or Sudan), or in rigid one-party states intolerant of opposition (such as the Soviet Union in the 1930s or China at the time of the Great Leap Forward, in each of which tens of millions of people died: in China probably between 23 million and 30 million were killed by the 1958–1961 famine).[18] But no substantial famine has ever occurred in a country that is independent, that has systematic multiparty elections, that has opposition parties to voice criticisms, and that permits newspapers to report freely and to question without extensive censorship the wisdom of current government policies. This generalization applies not only to the affluent countries of Europe and America but also to countries that happen to be very poor, such as India, Botswana, or Zimbabwe.[19]

It is very hard for a government to weather elections successfully after a major social calamity, nor can it easily survive the criticism from the media and opposition parties that exist in a functioning democracy. It is precisely because the rulers in many countries can—given authoritarianism and censorship—"afford" to have famines, knowing that their leadership will not be challenged, that famines continue to arise in the modern

---

[17] The basic issue is not only the existence of political and civil rights in the official legal system but also their active use. Much depends, therefore, on the determination and dedication of opposition groups. In fact, even in deeply authoritarian states, sometimes the opposition groups have been able to make their presence felt through courageous political action, often at great personal sacrifice. It can be argued that persistent and intrepid opposition even in South Korea and Chile did succeed in making the ruling governments more conscious of popular concerns, thereby influencing social policies (if only to try to undermine the dissenters). On this general issue, see Drèze and Sen (1989). The need to take note of the actions of opposition groups as well as of the government in office can be quite critical in the political economy of development.

[18] The estimate by Ashton *et al.* (1984) is about 30 million extra deaths, whereas Peng (1987) comes to a figure closer to 23 million. See also Riskin (1990). A remarkable fact about the Chinese famine is that the disastrous economic policies that had led to it were not revised through three years of intense suffering and mortality during which the government lost none of its power and control—a situation that would be impossible in a multiparty democracy; on this, see Sen (1984), Essay 19.

[19] On this issue, see Sen (1984), Drèze and Sen (1989), Ram (1990), D'Souza *et al.* (1992), Human Rights Watch (1992), and Red Cross and Red Crescent Societies (1994).

world.[20] Even though democratic rulers themselves never actually have to starve, democracy does spread the penalty of famines to the ruling groups and political leaders.[21]

The incentive effect of civil and political rights can be very important indeed in the prevention of major disasters. There has been a good deal of discussion recently about economic incentives (in connection with the failure of overambitious state planning and overbureaucratized public enterprises), and the need for market incentives and other economic inducements has been extensively talked about and forcefully championed. But meanwhile, political (as opposed to economic) incentives have not received quite the attention they deserve. When things go smoothly, the incentive role of democracy may not be much noted. But when and if things do go wrong, the corrective function of democracy can make a world of difference.

Thus, not only do we have reason to question the "Lee hypothesis" of a generally negative relation between economic growth and political and civil rights but also there exist serious positive grounds for seeing these rights as being actually favorable to the process of development, through such benefits as the protection they offer against disasters and momentous policy mistakes. Once again, the alternative perspective of GALA provides a broader format for understanding the development process, in contrast to the viewpoint of celebrating "hard states" as being putative precursors to solid economic progress.

Capability Expansion: Human Capital and More

There has occurred a significant transformation in recent years in the analysis of economic growth and development, in that such analysis now gives greater recognition to the role of "human capital." This shift has involved a partial return to an approach to eco-

---

[20] This analysis is, of course, based on the presumption that if a government of even a poor country really makes an effort to prevent a famine, it can do so. That this is the case relates to the understanding of the nature and causes of famines and the means needed to prevent them, on which see Sen (1981) and Drèze and Sen (1989, 1990). See also Arrow (1982); Solow (1984); Ravallion (1987); Desai (1988, 1995); Harrison (1988); Basu (1990); Drèze (1990a, 1990b); Osmani (1990, 1995); Platteau (1990); Riskin (1990); Svedberg (1990, 1996); Drèze, Sen, and Hussain (1995); and Hussain (1995).

[21] Very closely related to the issue of political incentives is that of the information that decision takers can have and on which they can base their decisions. A free press and the practice of democracy contribute greatly to bringing out relevant information (e.g., information about the early effects of droughts and floods and about the nature and impact of unemployment). The news media are, in fact, the most elementary source of basic information about a threatening famine, especially when there are incentives (as are indeed provided by a democratic system) for bringing out facts that may be embarrassing to the government (facts that an authoritarian government would tend to censor out). Indeed, just as the Chinese famines following the failed Great Leap Forward were coming to a peak, Chinese central-government officials mistakenly believed that they had 100 million metric tons more of grain than they actually had. They were, in fact, relying on rosy reports from different localities competing for credit in Beijing in having been successful in greatly leaping forward. Even Chairman Mao himself identified the informational role of democracy, after the failure was belatedly acknowledged (on this, see Sen 1984, Essay 19). In 1962, just after the famine had killed so many millions, Mao addressed a gathering of seven thousand cadres thus: "Without democracy, you have no understanding of what is happening down below; the situation will be unclear; you will be unable to collect sufficient opinions from all sides; there can be no communication between top and bottom; top-level organs of leadership will depend on one-sided and incorrect material to decide issues;..." (Mao 1976, 277–8).

nomic development championed particularly by Adam Smith's (1776) *Wealth of Nations*, with distinctly Aristotelian roots. The development of human capability and the role experience and the of division of labor were quite central to Smith's analysis of "the wealth of nations."[22] This focus was very different from what was emphasized in the early models of postwar growth theory—for example, in the so-called Harrod-Domar model—and even in early neoclassical analysis.[23] More-recent works, however, tend to give much fuller recognition to the far-reaching role of human skill, and this "new" development has had the effect of reestablishing an old but neglected tradition.[24] There exists by now fairly abundant acknowledgment of the importance of human capital in economic development. The experiences of the more successful economies in East Asia and Southeast Asia are increasingly interpreted in this light.

The emphasis on human capital—especially on the development of skill and productive ability spread broadly across the population—contributes to shifting the focus of analysis from a "hard" view of development to a more "people-friendly" approach. We should, however, ask whether the recognition of the role of "human capital" is adequate for understanding the importance of human beings in the process of development. If development is seen, ultimately, as the expansion of the capability of people to do the things they have reason to value and choose, then the glorification of human beings as "instruments" of economic development cannot really be adequate.[25]

A crucial difference exists here between means and ends.[26] The acknowledgment of the role of human qualities in promoting and sustaining economic growth—momentous as that role is—tells us nothing about why economic growth is sought in the first place. If instead the focus is, ultimately, on the expansion of human freedom to live the kind of lives that people have reason to value, then the role of economic growth in expanding

---

[22] Adam Smith's belief in the power of education and learning was peculiarly strong. Regarding the debate that continues today on the respective role of "nature" and "nurture," Smith was an unreconstructed "nurturist," and this stance fit in with his confidence in the improvability of human capabilities:

> The difference of natural talents in different men is, in reality, much less than we are aware of; and the very different genius which appears to distinguish men of different professions, when grown up to maturity, is not upon many occasions so much the cause, as the effect of division of labor. The difference between the most dissimilar characters, between a philosopher and a common street porter, for example, seems to arise not so much from nature, as from habit, custom, and education. When they come into the world, and for the first six or eight years of their existence, they were, perhaps, very much alike, and neither their parents nor play-fellows could perceive any remarkable difference. (Smith 1776, I.ii, pp. 28–9.)

[23] But one of the most influential findings of neoclassical growth theory was Robert Solow's (1956) identification of how much remained to be explained, within the interpretative structure of that theory, after taking full note of the accumulation of capital and labor.

[24] Although much basic similarity exists between the "Smithian" approach and recent growth theory, there was of course a major need to work out the connections and to integrate them in fully articulated models; on this, see Romer (1987), Lucas (1988), Helpman and Krugman (1990), and related contributions. See also Jorgenson (1995).

[25] This issue is discussed in Sen (1973, 1984, 1985).

[26] On this, see Pigou (1952), Pan *et al.* (1962), Adelman and Morris (1973), Sen (1973, 1980, 1984), Bardhan (1974, 1984a), Haq (1976), Herrera *et al.* (1976), ILO (1976), Ghai *et al.* (1977), Grant (1978), Griffin (1978), Streeten and Burki (1978), Morris (1979), Chichilnisky (1980), Streeten (1981, 1984), Streeten *et al.* (1981), Osmani (1982), Ranis (1982), Rawls (1982), Stewart (1985), Behrman and Deolalikar (1988), Drèze and Sen (1989), Anand and Ranbur (1990), Griffin and Knight (1990), Dasgupta (1993), and Lipton and van der Gaag (1993), among other contributions.

these opportunities has to be integrated into that more foundational understanding of the process of development.

The expansion of human capabilities thus has both "direct" and "indirect" importance in the achievement of development. The indirect role works through the contribution of capability expansion in enhancing productivity, raising economic growth, broadening development priorities, and bringing demographic changes more within reasoned control. The direct importance of human-capability expansion lies in its intrinsic value and in its constitutive role in human freedom, well-being, and quality of life.[27]

The latter issue is not just a matter of the foundation of development thinking; it also has a significant practical bearing on public policy. Although economic prosperity and demographic respite help people to lead freer and more fulfilling lives, so do more education, health care, medical attention, and other factors that causally influence the effective freedoms that people actually enjoy.[28] These "social developments" must directly count as "developmental," since they help us to lead longer, freer, and more-fruitful lives, in addition to their role of helping to promote productivity or economic growth.

The traditional use of the concept of "human capital" tends to concentrate only on the second role played by human-capability expansion (particularly in income generation).[29] This particular aspect is important enough, but it needs supplementation by consideration of the "direct" or primary values and benefits. The broadening that is needed here is additional and cumulative in nature rather than being an alternative to the existing "human-capital" perspective. The process of development is not separable from the expansion of human capabilities because of such expansion's intrinsic as well as instrumental importance.

Weights, Values and Public Participation

Some critics have expressed great reservations about broadening the view of development from the growth of GNP per head to the expansion of human capabilities and freedom. It has been pointed out that the evaluation of different capabilities requires value judgments. T.N. Srinivasan (1994, 239) has also recently reminded us, quoting Robert Sugden (1993), that "the real-income framework includes an operational metric for weighing commodities—the metric of exchange value"—and that there exists no corresponding "operational metric" in judging capabilities and different aspects of the quali-

---

[27] This connection is scrutinized in Sen (1980, 1985a) and Nussbaum and Sen (1993). See also Sen (1985b), Roemer (1986), Nussbaum (1988), Arneson (1989), Cohen (1990), Griffin and Knight (1990), Anand and Ravallion (1993), Arrow (1995), Atkinson (1995), and Desai (1995), among other contributions.

[28] There is some evidence that the effectiveness of economic growth in expanding such basic achievements as longevity depends on particular aspects of the economic expansion, such as the increase in income going to the poorest sections and expansion of public-health services; on this see Drèze and Sen (1989) and Anand and Ravallion (1993).

[29] In the *World Development Report 1995* of the World Bank, there is plenty of emphasis on "the skills and capabilities of workers," which is an important part of what counts, but the discussion is almost entirely confined to their role in expanding commodity production and income earning.

ty of life.[30] But how much of an argument is this for sticking to the commodity and market valuation mode to make comparative judgments on personal advantages rather than using information on different features of the quality of life?

Although market prices certainly do exist for commodities and do not exist for human functionings, the evaluative significance of the market prices has to be established somehow. It is not obvious how, in making an evaluative judgment about progress, valuational decisions are to be avoided by simply "reading off" the market prices and the metric of exchange value. For one thing, the problems of externalities, missing markets, and other concerns will suggest that market prices be "adjusted," and we shall have to decide whether in fact such adjustments should be made and if so, how this should be done.[31] In the process, an evaluative exercise cannot really be escaped, even if it is our intention to make abundant use of market valuation. Even the blindness of the market to any difference between the millionaire's dollar and that of the pauper calls for some response, so that the "metric of exchange value" can scarcely be an automatic basis of evaluative comparison.[32]

No less importantly, "the metric of exchange value," although operational in its own context, cannot give us interpersonal comparisons of individual advantage or welfare. A basic confounding has occurred in this subject because of misuse of the tradition—a tradition sensible within its context—of taking utility to be simply the numerical representation of a person's choice. This is, of course, a most useful way of defining utility for the analysis of consumption behavior of each person taken separately, but it does not on its own offer any procedure whatever for substantive interpersonal comparison. Paul Samuelson's (1947) elementary remark that it was "not necessary to make interpersonal comparisons of utility in describing exchange" (page 205) is the other side of the very same coin: nothing about interpersonal comparison of utility is learned from observing market prices or exchange behavior, or "the metric of exchange value."

This is not just a matter of analytical purity. The tendency to use the metric of exchange value for interpersonal comparisons not only is unfounded in theory but also its practical use can make us overlook vital information that we have no reason to overlook. For instance, even if person A (who is disabled or ill) happened to have the same demand function as person B (who is not disadvantaged in these ways), it would be quite absurd to assume that A is having exactly the same utility or well-being from a given commodity bundle as B is having from it. Differences in age, gender, special talents, disability, proneness to illness, and the like can make two different persons have quite divergent substantive opportunities even when they have the very same commodity bundle. In going beyond simply "observing" market choices, which tell us little about interperson-

---

[30] Robert Sugden's own focus was more on questioning how the capabilities are to be valued than on rejecting the approach (as Srinivasan recommends), on this ground: "It remains to be seen whether analogous metrics can be developed for the capability approach" (Sugden 1993).

[31] See, for example, Nordhaus and Tobin (1972).

[32] On different ways of making distribution-corrected real income comparisons, see Sen (1976, 1979).

al comparisons, we have to use additional information, rather than just sticking to the good old "metric of exchange value."

Indeed, given the inescapable need for valuation in making judgments about progress and development, a strong case exists for making the values to be used as explicit as possible, so that they can be subjected to critical scrutiny and public discussion. The evaluation of quality of life and of diverse capabilities calls for public discussion as a part of a democratic "social-choice" procedure. In using any particular index—such as the human-development index (HDI), the gender-inequality-adjusted HDI proposed by UNDP, or any other such aggregative indicator—there exists a great need for explicit formulation and articulation, making the index open to public scrutiny, criticism, and correction. Trying to arrive at the measure in a concealed way (for example, by using market valuation, as if this comprised a predetermined set of values that can simply be "read off" for rapid evaluative use) is exactly the wrong move, especially for an approach to development that focuses on human freedom and reason.

It is important to bring the evaluative decisions within the people's own power of scrutiny.[33] Indeed, even the agreed merit of greater economic prosperity as a central part of the development process lies in the reasonable presumption that this is what the people involved would, *inter alia,* value. This focus on democratic social choice is a crucial part of moving away from the "blood, sweat and tears" view of development to one that celebrates people's cooperation and agency and the expansion of human freedom and capabilities. To reject the "hard state" that denies the importance of human rights (including political rights to the holding of open public discussion) is thus complementary to the rejection of other forms of "hardness" that view development as a terribly "fierce" process.

This shift in the understanding of the development process has many far-reaching implications. The arrival of the twenty-first century may be just incidental; this pivotal change involves something more than the simple passing of years.

---

[33] For different issues underlying this general recognition, *see Knight* (1947), Arrow (1951), Buchanan (1954), and Sen (1970, 1995).

REFERENCES

Adelman, Irma. Development Economics: A Reassessment of Goals. *American Economic Review* 65 (1975).

____, and Cynthia T. Morris. *Economic Growth and Social Equity in Developing Countries.* Stanford, CA: Stanford University Press, 1973.

Alesina, Alberto, and Roberto Perotti. "Income Distribution, Political Instability and Investment." National Bureau of Economic Research. Working Paper 4486 (1993).

____, and Dani Rodrik. "Distributive Politics and Economic Growth." *Quarterly Journal of Economics* 109 (1994).

Amsden, Alice H. *Asia's Next Giant: Late Industrialization in South Korea.* Oxford: Clarendon Press, 1989.

Anand, Sudhir, and S.M. Ravi Ranbur. "Public Policy and Basic Needs Provision: Intervention and Achievement in Sri Lanka." In Drèze and Sen (1990); reprinted in Drèze, Sen and Hussain (1995).

____, and Martin Ravallion. "Human Development in Poor Countries: On the Role of Private Incomes and Public Services." *Journal of Economic Perspectives* 7 (Winter 1993).

Aristotle. *The Nicomachean Ethics.* English translation, Ross (1980).

Arneson, R. "Equality and Equality of Opportunity for Welfare." *Philosophical Studies* 56 (1989).

Arrow, Kenneth J. *Social Choice and Individual Values.* New York: Wiley, 1963. (Second edition.)

____. "Why People Go Hungry." *New York Review of Books* 29 (1982).

____. "A Note on Freedom and Flexibility." In Basu, Pattanaik and Suzumura (1995).

Ashton, B., R. Hill, A. Piazza, and R. Zeitz. "Famine in China, 1958–61." *Population and Development Review* 10 (1984).

Atkinson, A.B. "On the Measurement of Inequality." *Journal of Economic Theory* 2 (1970).

____. "Capabilities, Exclusion and the Supply of Goods." In Basu, Pattanaik and Suzumura (1995).

Banerjee, Abhijit V., and Maitresh Ghatak. 1996.

Baran, Paul. *The Political Economy of Growth.* London, 1957.

Bardhan, Pranab. *Land, Labor and Rural Poverty.* New York: Columbia University Press, 1984a.

____. *The Political Economy of Development in India.* Oxford: Blackwell, 1984b.

Barro, Robert J., and Jong-Wha Lee. "Losers and Winners in Economic Growth." National Bureau of Economic Research. Working Paper 4341 (1993).

Basu, Kaushik. "The Elimination of Endemic Poverty in South Asia: Some Policy Options." In Drèze and Sen (1990); reprinted in Drèze, Sen and Hussain (1995).

____. *Agrarian Structure and Economic Underdevelopment.* Chichester: Hardwood, 1990.

____, Prasanta Pattanaik, and Rotaro Suzumura, eds. *Choice, Welfare and Development.* Oxford: Clarendon Press, 1995.

Bauer, Peter. *Dissent on Development.* London: Weidenfeld, 1972.

_____. *The Development Frontier.* Cambridge, MA: Harvard University Press, 1991.

Beneria, O., ed. *Women and Development: The Sexual Division of Labor in Rural Societies.* New York: Praeger, 1982.

Behrman, Jere R., and Anil B. Deolalikar. "Health and Nutrition." In Chenery and Srinivasan (1988).

_____, and T.N. Srinivasan, eds. *Handbook of Development Economics* III. Amsterdam: North-Holland, 1994.

Bhalla, Surjit. "Freedom and Economic Growth: A Vicious Circle?" Study presented at the 1994 Nobel Symposium in Uppsala on "Democracy's Victory and Crisis."

Birdsall, Nancy. "Economic Approaches to Population Growth." In Chenery and Srinivasan (1988).

_____. "Social Development Is Economic Development." World Bank Policy Research Working Paper 1123 (1993).

_____, and Richard H. Sabot. "Virtuous Circles: Human Capital, Growth and Equity in East Asia." Mimeographed. Washington, D.C.: World Bank, 1993a.

_____, eds. *Opportunity Foregone: Education, Growth and Inequality in Brazil.* Washington, D.C.: World Bank, 1993b.

Bliss, Christopher, and Nicholas Stern. "Productivity, Wages and Nutrition: Theory and Observations." *Journal of Development Economics* 5 (1978).

Boserup, E. *Women's Role in Economic Development.* London: Allen and Unwin, 1970.

Bruno, Michael, Martín Ravallion, and Lyn Squire. "Equity and Growth in Developing Countries." World Bank Policy Research Working Paper 1563 (1996).

Buchanan, James M. "Social Choice, Democracy, and Free Markets." *Journal of Political Economy* 62 (1954).

Caldwell, J.C., R.H. Reddy, and P. Caldwell. *The Causes of Demographic Change.* Madison: University of Wisconsin Press, 1989.

Cassen, Robert, with contributors. *Population and Development: Old Debates, New Conclusions.* Washington, D.C.: Transaction Books for Overseas Development Council, 1994.

Chakravarty, Sukhamoy. *Capital and Development Planning.* Cambridge, MA: MIT Press, 1969.

Chenery, Hollis, and T.N. Srinivasan, eds. *Handbook of Development Economics* I and II. Amsterdam: North-Holland, 1988.

Chichilnisky, Graciela. "Basic Needs and Global Models: Resources, Trade and Distribution." *Alternatives* 6 (1980).

Dasgupta, Partha. *An Inquiry into Well-Being and Destitution.* Oxford: Clarendon Press, 1993.

_____, Stephen Marglin, and Amartya Sen. *Guidelines for Project Evaluation.* New York: UNIDO, 1972.

_____, and Debraj Ray. "Inequality as a Determinant of Malnutrition and Unemployment: Theory." *Economic Journal* 96 (1986).

_____. "Inequality as a Determinant of Malnutrition and Unemployment: Policy." *Economic Journal* 97 (1987).

Deininger, Klaus, and Lyn Squire. "New Ways of Looking at Old Issues: Inequality and Growth." Mimeographed. Washington, D.C.: World Bank, 1996.

Desai, Meghnad. "The Economics of Famine." In Harrison (1988).

____. *Poverty, Famine and Economic Development.* Aldershot: Elgar, 1995.

Dobb, Maurice H. *An Essay on Economic Growth and Planning.* London: Routledge, 1960.

Drèze, Jean. "Famine Prevention in Africa: Some Experiences and Lessons." In Drèze and Sen (1990); reprinted in Drèze, Sen and Hussain (1995).

____. "Famine Prevention in India." In Drèze and Sen (1990); reprinted in Drèze, Sen and Hussain (1995).

Drèze, Jean, and Amartya Sen. *Hunger and Public Action.* Oxford: Clarendon Press, 1989.

____, eds. *The Political Economy of Hunger.* Oxford: Clarendon Press, 1990.

____. *India: Economic Development and Social Opportunity.* Oxford: Clarendon Press, 1995.

Drèze, Jean, Amartya Sen, and Athar Hussain. *The Political Economy of Hunger: Selected Essays.* Oxford: Clarendon Press, 1995.

D'Souza, Frances, Alex de Waal, and an anonymous Chinese scholar. *Starving in Silence: A Report on Famine and Censorship.* London. International Center on Censorship, 1990.

Engels, Friedrich. *The Condition of the Working Class in England in 1844.* London: Allen and Unwin, 1892.

Fields, Gary S. *Poverty, Inequality and Development.* Cambridge: Cambridge University Press, 1980.

Fishlow, Albert, C. Gwin, S. Haggard, D. Rodrik, and R. Wade. *Miracle or Design: Lessons from the East Asian Experience.* Washington, D.C.: Overseas Development Council, 1994.

Fishlow, Albert. "Inequality, Poverty and Growth: Where Do We Stand?" Paper presented at the World Bank's 1995 Annual Conference on Development Economics.

Galenson, Walter, and Harvey Leibernstein. "Investment Criteria, Productivity and Economic Development." *Quarterly Journal of Economics* 69 (1955).

Ghai, Dharam, Azuzur R. Rhan, E. Lee, and T.A. Alfthan. T.A. *The Basic Needs Approach to Development.* Geneva: ILO, 1977.

Griffin, R. *International Inequality and National Poverty.* London: Macmillan, 1978.

Griffin, Reith, and John Knight, eds. *Human Development and the International Development Strategy for the 1990s.* London: Macmillan, 1990.

Haq, Mahbub ul. *The Poverty Curtain.* New York: Columbia University Press, 1976.

Harrison, G.A., ed. *Famines.* Oxford: Clarendon Press, 1988.

Harriss, Barbara. "The Intrafamily Distribution of Hunger in South Asia." In Drèze and Sen (1990); reprinted in Drèze, Sen and Hussain (1990).

Helliwell, John. "Empirical Linkages between Democracy and Economic Growth." National Bureau of Economic Research. Working Paper 4066 (1994).

Helpman, Elhanan, and Paul R. Krugman. *Market Structure and Foreign Trade.* Cambridge, MA: MIT Press, 1990.

Herrera, A.O., *et al. Catastrophe or New Society? A Latin American World Model.* Ottawa: IDRC, 1976.

Hirschman, Albert. *The Strategy of Economic Development.* New Haven, CT: Yale University Press, 1958.

_____. *Essays in Trespassing.* Cambridge: Cambridge University Press, 1981.

Human Rights Watch. *Indivisible Human Rights: The Relationship between Political and Civil Rights to Survival. Subsistence and Poverty.* New York, 1992.

Hussain, Athar. "Introduction." In Drèze, Sen and Hussain (1995).

ILO. *Employment, Growth and Basic Needs: A One-World Problem.* Geneva, 1976.

Jorgenson, Dale. *Productivity.* Cambridge, MA: MIT Press, 1995.

Joshi, Vijay, and I.N.D. Little. *India's Economic Reforms 1991–2001.* Oxford: Clarendon Press, 1996.

Kakwani, Nanak. *Analyzing Redistributive Policies.* Cambridge: Cambridge University Press, 1986.

Kindleberger, Charles. *Economic Development.* New York, 1958.

Knight, Frank. *Freedom and Reform: Essays in Economic and Social Philosophy.* New York: Harper, 1947.

Leibenstein, Harvey. *Economic Backwardness and Economic Growth.* New York, 1957.

Lewis, W. Arthur. *The Theory of Economic Growth.* Homewood, IL: Irwin, 1955.

Lindahl-Kiessling, R., and H. Landberg, eds. *Population, Economic Development, and the Environment.* Oxford: Oxford University Press, 1994.

Lipton, Michael, and Jacques van der Gaag. *Including the Poor.* Washington, D.C.: World Bank, 1993.

Little, Ian, and James Mirrlees. *Manual of Industrial Product Analysis in Developing Countries.* Paris: OECD, 1968.

Lucas, Robert E. "On the Mechanics of Economic Development." *Journal of Monetary Economics* 22 (1988).

Malinvaud, Edmond, Jean-Claude Milleron, Amartya Sen, Arjun Sengupta, Nicholas Stern, Joseph Stiglitz, and Rotaro Suzumura. *Development Strategy and the Management of the Market Economy.* To be published by Clarendon Press (Oxford, 1996).

Mao Tse-tung (Zedong). *Mao-Tse-tung: Unrehearsed Talks and Letters: 1956–71.* Ed. By Schram. London: Penguin Books, 1976.

Marglin, Stephen A. "The Social Rate of Discount and the Optimal Rate of Investment." *Quarterly Journal of Economics* (1963a).

_____. "The Opportunity Cost of Investment." *Quarterly Journal of Economics* 77 (1963b).

_____. *Value and Price in the Labor-Surplus Economy.* Oxford: Clarendon Press, 1976.

McGuire, James W. "Development Policy and Its Determinants in East Asia and Latin America." *Journal of Public Policy* (1995).

Murthi, Mamta, Anne-Catherine Guto, and John Drèze. "Mortality, Fertility and Gender Bias in India: A District-Level Analysis." *Population and Development* 21 (1995).

Myrdal, Gunnar. *Asian Drama: An Enquiry into the Poverty of Nations.* London: Pelican, 1964.

Nordhaus, William, and James Tobin. "Is Growth Obsolete?" New York: National Bureau of Economic Research, 1972.

Nurkse, Ragnar. *Problems of Capital Formation in Underdeveloped Countries.* Oxford: Blackwell, 1953.

Nussbaum, Martha C. "Nature, Function, and Capability" Aristotle on Political Distribution." Oxford Studies in Ancient Philosophy (supplementary volume) (1988).

Nussbaum, Martha, and Amartya Sen, eds. *The Quality of Life.* Oxford: Clarendon Press, 1993.

Osmani, Siddiq R., ed. *Nutrition and Poverty.* Oxford: Clarendon Press, 1992.

____. "The Entitlement Approach to Famine: An Assessment." In Basu, Pattanaik and Suzumura (1995).

Pant, Pitambar, *et al. Perspectives of Development 1961–1976: Implications of Planning for a Minimal Level of Living.* New Delhi: Planning Commission of India, 1962.

Pasinetti, Luigi, and Robert Solow, eds. *Economic Growth and the Structure of Long-Term Development.* London: Macmillan, 1994.

Peng, X. "Demographic Consequences of the Great Leap Forward in China's Provinces." *Population and Development Review* 13 (1987).

Persson, Torsten, and Guido Tabellini. "Is Inequality Harmful for Growth?" *American Economic Review* 84 (1994).

Pigou, Arthur C. *The Economics of Welfare.* Fourth edition. London: Macmillan, 1952.

Platteau, Jean-Philippe. "The Food Crisis in Africa: A Comparative Structural Analysis." In Drèze and Sen (1990); reprinted in Drèze, Sen and Hussain (1995).

Przeworski, Adam, and Fernando Limongi. "Democracy and Development." Study presented at the 1994 Nobel Symposium in Uppsala on "Democracy's Victory and Crisis."

Ram, N. "An Independent Press and Anti-Hunger Strategies: The Indian Experience." In Drèze and Sen (1990); reprinted in Drèze, Sen and Hussain (1995).

Ramsey, Frank. "A Mathematical Theory of Savings." *Economic Journal* 38 (1928).

Ranis, Gustav. "Basic Needs, Distribution and Growth: The Beginnings of a Framework." In *Trade, Stability, Technology, and Equity in Latin America.* New York: Academic Press, 1982.

Ravallion, Martin. *Markets and Famines.* Oxford: Clarendon Press, 1987.

Rawls, John. *A Theory of Justice.* Cambridge, MA: Harvard University Press, 1971.

____. "Social Unity and Primary Goods." In Amartya Sen and Bernard Williams, eds. *Utilitarianism and Beyond.* Cambridge: Cambridge University Press, 1982.

Red Cross and Red Crescent Societies (International Federation of). *World Disaster Report 1994.* Geneva: Red Cross, 1994.

Riskin, Carl. "Feeding China: The Experience since 1949." In Drèze and Sen (1990); reprinted in Drèze, Sen and Hussain (1995).

Rodrik, Dani. "King Kong Meets Godzilla: The World Bank and *The East Asian Miracle.*" Center for Economic Policy Research. Discussion Paper 944 (London, 1994a).

____. "Trade and Industrial Policy Reform in Developing Countries: A Review of Recent Theory and Evidence." In Behrman and Srinivasan (1994b).

Roemer, John E. *A General Theory of Exploitation and Class.* Cambridge, MA: Harvard University Press, 1982.

_____. *Theories of Distributive Justice.* Cambridge, MA: Harvard University Press, 1996.

Romer, Paul M. "Growth Based on Increasing Returns Due to Specialization." *American Economic Review* 77 (1987).

Ross, D., ed. *Aristotle: The Noicomachean Ethics,* Oxford: Oxford University Press, 1980.

Sachs, I. "Growth and Poverty: Some Lessons from Brazil." In Drèze and Sen (1990).

Samuelson, Paul A. *Foundations of Economic Analysis.* Cambridge, MA: Harvard University Press, 1947.

Schultz, T.P. "Reflections on Investment in Man." *Journal of Political Economy* 70 (1962).

_____. *The Economic Value of Education.* New York: Columbia University Press, 1963.

_____. *Investment in Human Capital.* New York: Free Press, 1971.

_____. *Investing in People.* San Francisco: University of California Press, 1980.

_____. *Economies of Population.* New York: Addison-Wesley, 1981.

Sen, Amartya. *Choice of Techniques.* Oxford: Blackwell, 1960.

_____. "On Optimizing the Rate of Saving." *Economic Journal* 71 (1961). (Reprinted in Sen [1984].)

_____. "Isolation, Assurance and the Social Rate of Discount." *Quarterly Journal of Economics* 81 (1967). (Reprinted in Sen [1984].)

_____. Collective Choice and Social Welfare. *San Francisco: Holden-Day* 1970. (Republished in Amsterdam: North-Holland, 1979.)

_____. "On the Development of Basic Income Indicators to Supplement the GNP Measure." *United Nations Economic Bulletin for Asia and the Far East* 24 (1973).

_____. "Real National Income." *Review of Economic Studies* 43 (1976).

_____. "The Welfare Basis of Real Income Comparisons." *Journal of Economic Literature* 17 (1979).

_____. "Equality of What?" In S. McMurrin, ed. *Tanner Lectures on Human Values* I. Cambridge: Cambridge University Press, 1980.

_____. *Poverty and Famines: An Essay on Entitlement and Deprivation.* Oxford: Clarendon Press, 1981.

_____. *Resources, Values and Development.* Oxford: Blackwell, 1984. Cambridge, MA: Harvard University Press.

_____. "Well-Being, Agency and Freedom: The Dewey Lectures 1984." *Journal of Philosophy* 82 (1985a).

_____. *Commodities and Capabilities.* Amsterdam: North-Holland, 1985b.

_____. "Gender and Cooperative Conflict." In Irene Tinker, ed. *Persistent Inequalities.* New York: Oxford University Press, 1990.

_____. "Missing Women." *British Medical Journal* 304 (March 1992).

_____. "Rationality and Social Choice." *American Economic Review* 85 (1995).

Sen, Gita, Adrienne Germain, and Lincoln Chen, eds. *Population Policies Reconsidered: Health, Empowerment and Rights.* Cambridge, MA: Harvard University Press, 1994.

Smith, Adam. *Lectures on Jurisprudence.* Written in 1762–63 and later republished. R.K. Meek, D.D. Raphael, and P.G. Stein, eds. Oxford: Clarendon Press, 1978.

____. *An Inquiry into the Nature and Causes of the Wealth of Nations.* Written in 1796 and later republished. R.H. Campbell and A.S. Skinner, eds. Oxford: Clarendon Press, 1976.

____. *The Theory of Moral Sentiments.* (Revised edition.) Written in 1740 and later republished. D.D. Raphael and A.L. Macfie, eds. Oxford: Clarendon Press, 1975.

Solow, Robert M. "A Contribution to the Theory of Economic Growth." *Quarterly Journal of Economics* 70 (1956).

____. "Relative Deprivation?" *Partisan Review* 51 (1984).

Srinivasan, T.N. "Human Development: A New Paradigm or Reinvention of the Wheel?" *American Economic Review* 84 (1994).

Stern, Nicholas. "The Economics of Development: A Survey," *Economic Journal* 99 (1989).

Stewart, Frances. *Basic Needs in Developing Countries.* Baltimore, MD: Johns Hopkins University Press, 1985.

Stiglitz, Joseph. "Economic Organization, Information and Development." In Chenery and Srinivasan (1988).

Stiglitz, Joseph, and F. Mathewson, eds. *New Developments in the Analysis of Market Structure.* London: Macmillan, 1986.

Streeten, Paul. *Development Perspectives.* London: Macmillan, 1981.

____. "Basic Needs: Some Unsettled Questions." *World Development* 6 (1978).

Streeten, Paul, and S. Javed Burki. "Basic Needs: Some Issues." *World Development* 6 (1978).

Streeten, Paul, S. Javed Burki, Mahbub ul Haq, N. Hicks, and Frances Stewart. *First Things First: Meeting Basic Needs in Developing Countries.* New York: Oxford University Press, 1981.

Sugden, Robert. "Welfare, Resources and Capabilities: A Review of *Inequality Reexamined* by Amartya Sen." *Journal of Economic Literature* 31 (1993).

Suzumura, Kotaro. *Rational Choice, Collective Decisions and Social Welfare.* Cambridge: Cambridge University Press, 1983.

____. *Competition, Commitment and Welfare.* Oxford: Clarendon Press, 1995.

Svedberg, Peter. "Undernutrition in Sub-Saharan Africa: A Critical Assessment of the Evidence." In Drèze and Sen (1990).

____. 1996.

Tinbergen, Jan. "The Optimum Rate of Saving." *Economic Journal* 66 (1956).

____. *The Design of Development.* Baltimore, MD: Johns Hopkins University Press, 1958.

Tinker, Irene, ed. *Persistent Inequalities.* New York: Oxford University Press, 1990.

UNDP. *Human Development Report* 1990. New York: UNDP, 1990.

____. *Human Development Report* 1995. New York: UNDP, 1995.

Wade, Robert. *Governing the Market: Economic Theory and the Role of the Government in East Asian Industrialization.* Princeton: Princeton University Press, 1990.

World Bank. *The East Asian Miracle.* Oxford: Oxford University Press, 1993.

____. *World Development Report* 1995. New York: Oxford University Press, 1995.

Miguel Urrutia[1] on Amartya Sen's Paper

Development Thinking at the Beginning of the XXI Century

The main thrust of Professor Sen's paper addresses what is probably the most important issue in the social sciences: how to evaluate human progress. He convincingly shows that the way in which one evaluates or measures progress determines the development strategy that one would find preferable for society.

He summarizes relevant recent research in his discussion of the direct and indirect effects of the expansion of human capabilities. Obsessed with improving measured material welfare, many economists (the present commentator included) have overemphasized the indirect effects of the expansion of human capabilities; this indirect role works through the contribution that capability expansion makes to the enhancement of productivity, to the acceleration of economic growth, and to the deceleration of demographic growth. Professor Sen rightly emphasizes the intrinsic value of human-capability expansion itself and its constitutive role in human freedom, well-being, and quality of life.

To be able to make this direct effect of human-capability expansion more central to development thinking and policy, one must begin by improving the basic measurement of welfare; to do this, certain value judgments must be made. The development of these new indices of welfare owes much thus far to the theoretical and empirical work of Professor Sen and UNDP, and the continued improvement of these indices will be a prioriy task for development economics in the next decade.

In regard to political regimes and economic growth, Professor Sen suggests that political rights and democracy are favorable to development because they help protect against preventable disasters and momentous policy mistakes. This protection stems from the greater availability of information to decision makers in free societies. These conclusions are quite relevant to Latin America: the most momentous mistakes have indeed been made in periods of greater-than-average authoritarianism in the region. An interesting related question is how to use information constructively. There now exists the danger of information overload. There is also much talk of direct democracy and participation. Are institutions of direct democracy (such as referendums) the best way of using this increased information, or are there still advantages to be had from continuing to use the specialized skills of information processing in representative bodies?

---

[1] President, Banco de la República de Colombia.

There is an interesting group of institutions that may be very helpful in the processing of information for policy decisions—namely, universities and independent policy research institutes. Such institutions, if truly independent from government and from specific pressure groups, may be an important factor in the avoidance of momentous mistakes.

One of the features of Professor Sen's work is that it tempts one to explore further certain issues that are only hinted at in his exposition. For instance, his brief comments on the role of the state in development suggested to the present commentator that another insight of Adam Smith, the idea of the gains from specialization, could be used to understand the historical development of the role of government in Latin America.

It can be argued in the case of Latin America that when the state has specialized and has focused its attention and resources on specific priorities, it has not done too badly. For instance, when the Brazilian state specialized in creating and running certain strategic industries, these were fairly efficient and industrialization was quite rapid. When the government specialized in creating settlements and planning new cities in colonial times, the results in that regard were also admirable. But when development theory and popular demand generated the need for a more diversified state, the result was low efficiency in most of these multifarious governmental activities.

An additional problem has been that the state in Latin America traditionally has never specialized in education and health, the areas that have turned out to have the highest rates of return in terms of development. Until rather late in the nineteenth century, education and health were seen as private activities to be delegated to the church and charitable foundations. The first schools for women were started only at the end of that same century in Colombia (and most likely in other countries of the region as well).

Another feature of the Latin American state that has worked against specialization has been the centralization bias inherited from colonial times. To diversify its activities efficiently, the state should have built up specialized providers, particularly in service industries that have few economies of scale. Gustav Ranis alludes to this issue when he argues for the disaggregation not only of markets but also of government.[2]

Until recently, public education has been seen as a national responsibility in Colombia. The advantages of specialization would suggest a different management structure, with more specialized local units responsible for the service. It must be said that the resistance to this decentralization is often led by national teachers' unions, formed when education was centralized. In this area, as in others, past mistakes weigh heavily.

---

[2] See the paper by Gustav Ranis, "Successes and Failures of Development Practice since 1980," in the present volume.

Tetsuji Okazaki[1] on Amartya Sen's Paper

Development Thinking at the Beginning of the XXI Century

Professor Sen's paper is based on deep and serious thinking about economic development. He proposes a new contrast in development thinking, between the "blood, sweat, and tears" (BLAST) view and the "get by with a little assistance" (GALA) view. He defends the idea that we can interpret and explain development experiences largely in terms of the latter or GALA approach. In other words, he proposes "economic development without tears."

Professor Sen's paper is composed of two parts: one part deals with development economics, and the other with development philosophy. Although the highlight of his paper is the philosophical part, the present writer feels qualified to comment at length only on the former part, on development economics.

In that part, Professor Sen persuasively criticizes the BLAST view, also referring to recent theoretical and empirical research on economic development. His reasoning was quite impressive. Nevertheless, we shall pose several critical comments for purposes of further discussion.

In the last few decades, essential progress has been made in the theory of economic development and economic growth. First there is, as cited by Professor Sen, the so-called new growth theory elaborated by Romer (1986) and Lucas (1988), among others. This research stresses the role of human capital as a production factor with a large externality. Sen properly derives from this research strong evidence for the GALA view, a point on which he was most persuasive.

Nevertheless, recent theoretical work (for example, by Murphy Shreifer and Vishny [1989] and Matsuyama [1991]) stresses the significance of complementarity in the process of economic development. In this case, efforts within any given individual sector cannot make the economy take off. Therefore, each sector on its own does not have sufficient incentive to make an effort, and the economy stays at a low equilibrium. From this theory we can derive the implication that a big push is necessary for takeoff. Although it is not always the case, a big push is prone to be a BLAST policy, because a large amount of resources must be mobilized in order to move from the bad (low) equilibrium to the good (high) equilibrium.

---

[1] Faculty of Economics of the University of Tokyo.

Theoretical progress has also been made concerning the role of institutions, as discussed by North (1990). This research stresses that institutions substantially influence the behavior of agents and that it is very costly to modify institutions, because of fixed costs and institutional complementarity. For instance, let us consider the factory institution or system, meaning a system in which people work together in a disciplined fashion. Although the factory system is indispensable for economic development in the usual sense, it is not easy to introduce that system into a community-based agricultural society. In nineteenth-century Japan, there was a famous book entitled *Sad History of Female Workers* that contained many stories of the wretched experiences of female workers in the factories of that time and place. As Inoki (1996) explains, it is true that this situation resulted in part from the lack of appropriate government protection, but these stories can also be interpreted as describing a phenomenon similar to a "necessary evil" that is required in order to accustom people lacking the needed discipline to the modern factory system.

Our final point relates to the philosophical part of the paper. Professor Sen states that the quality of life depends a lot on the possibility of public discussion as part of a democratic "social-choice" procedure. Although it has not yet been theorized, economic development itself may bring about a change in people's preference and value system. For instance, if we compare subjective happiness between people of present-day Japan and people of eighteenth-century Japan, it is difficult to conclude that today's people are happier than those of eighteenth-century Japan. But most Japanese people today probably would prefer the state of present Japan to that of eighteenth-century Japan. This seems to suggest that economic development has changed people's preference itself. If so, we must seriously reexamine the role of democratic social choices in the process of economic development.

In conclusion, let us reiterate that Professor Sen's insightful paper was quite impressive and most instructive. It provides a solid philosophical basis for development thinking in the twenty-first century.

REFERENCES

Inoki, T. *Gakko to Kojo.* Tokyo: Yomiuri Shinbunsha, 1996.

Lucas, R. "On the Mechanics of Economic Development." *Journal of Monetary Economics* 22 (1998).

Matsuyama, K. "Increasing Returns, Industrialization, and Indeterminacy of Equilibria." *Quarterly Journal of Economics* 106 (1991).

Murphy, K., A. Shreifer, and R. Vishny. "Industrialization and the Big Push." *Journal of Political Economy* 97 (1989).

North, D. *Institutions, Institutional Change and Economic Performance.* Cambridge: Cambridge University Press, 1990.

Romer, P. "Increasing Returns and Long-Run Growth." *Journal of Political Economy* 94 (1986).

Index by Author
Index by Subject